PMP® Exam Success Series:
Certification Exam Manual

Crosswind
Project Management Training
An ISO 9001:2000 Certified Company

www.crosswindpm.com

Copyright Page

Published by Crosswind Project Management, Inc.
1930 Rosemeade Parkway, Suite 104
Carrollton, Texas 75007

PMP® Exam Success Series: Certification Exam Manual

Tony Johnson. – v.7.3

Second printing
p.cm.
ISBN Ten Digit: 0-9768660-5-6
ISBN Thirteen Digit: 978-0-9768660-5-3

Johnson, Tony 2. PMP 3. PMP Certification 4. Project Management I. Title

Disclaimer

Every attempt has been made by the publisher and author to have the contents of this book provide accurate information for the reader to pass the PMP (Project Management Professional) Examination. The publisher and author, however, accept no legal responsibility for the contents therein. The opinions of the author in this book do not necessarily reflect that of PMI (Project Management Institute).

Both the publisher and author of this book warn readers to use not just this book, but at the very least also the *PMBOK Guide (Project Management Body of Knowledge Third Edition)* in their attempts to pass the PMP (Project Management Professional) exam to become PMP-certified. The publisher and the author also acknowledge that the purchase of this book does not guarantee that the reader will pass the PMP (Project Management Professional) exam. Neither the author nor the publisher will be held liable for individuals who do not heed this warning.

"PMP" is a registered certification mark of the Project Management Institute, Inc.

PMI does not endorse or otherwise sponsor this publication and makes no warranty, guarantee, or representation, expressed or implied, as to its accuracy or content.

If you detect what you believe is an error in this book, please check our Web site for errata that have been discovered. If you don't see the item under a question listed, email the page, WBS #, and details to info@crosswindpm.com.

Trademarks and Copyrights

Throughout this manual, we reference and recognize the following trademarks, service marks, and copyrights of the Project Management Institute (PMI):

PMP®
PgMP®
PMI®
PMBOK®
CAPM®

Conventions

Throughout this manual, we post values and indicate special notations. Here are some of the conventions used in this manual:

All monetary values are U.S .dollars unless otherwise noted.

Special notes and points are indicated in bold text.

Supplemental and Errata Updates

Visit our Web site at www.crosswindpm.com and click "support" for updates on supplements and errata. This material includes content that supports the book as we keep you updated with the most current information to prepare for the PMP Examination. Errata (errors) updates are also included. If you feel you have discovered an errata item not listed in the updates, please forward the information to info@crosswindpm.com.

Dedication

The author would like to thank the following people for their influence, support, and belief in him and his dreams becoming reality.

Maria, my lovely wife: I waited what seemed like a lifetime to finally find you, now you are showing me daily what love and fun in life can be.

My daughter Nicole and son Jacob: let this PMP Exam Success Series serve as a prime example that planning and execution can make an idea become reality.

Duane and Patty Johnson, my parents: your love, support and belief in me over the years is unconditional and nonstop. You have been the role models of the century. Thank you!

Marjorie Siebert, my grandmother: she was like a third parent to me and helped show me as a child what things could be when you dream.

Norm Folger: for that first break as a PM and being a mentor to this day. Dave Hartwick, Barbara Sleeper, Dr. Toni McNutt, Dr. Andrew Schaffer, Mark Schottler, Barbara Fanshier, Ben Eckart, Dr. Jerry Strader, and the late John Richle; and teachers and professors from my past who have shown me their passion toward teaching and making a difference in the life of people through education. You are my role models.

To the students in the 40 countries to date around the world that use our products: I hope these materials provide a roadmap that will help you attain PMP Examination success.

PMP Exam Success Series: Certification Exam Manual
© 2007 Crosswind Project Management, Inc., www.crosswindpm.com

Thanks

Team is a very important piece of the Crosswind culture. From our alumni network of evangelists to the Crosswind staff, to the team of people who contributed in various ways to what you are about to read in this book.

The following played a key role with their contributions:

Sergio, Analaura, Ramya, Bill: Thank you for helping build the foundation to help us become the success we are today.

Jessica, Richard and Aaron: Focusing on product development and keeping things running each day as well. We aren't the same without you.

Kevin, Rachel, Boriana, Mythili, Tim, Venkat, Angie, Bob, Jessica, Soumya, and Joyce: The QC team of the decade…Your commitment to our products and our customers is unparalleled.

Brett, Beverly, Shelley, Chris & AJ: Thank you for your creativity and dedication to quality. Crosswind took it to the next level when you joined the team.

Michael, Gabe, Angela, Jeff, Craig, and Addison Road: You know the three words……You do it well!

The Dallas and Fort Worth PMI Chapters, Past Presidents John C. Baley, and Jonathan Overton; Current Presidents Dwaraka Iyengar and Dick Walz; and Fort Worth VP of Education Matthew Solodow, for your support!

Roger: For setting the example many years ago, to not quit as long as there is opportunity. It worked for the Cowboys then and our companies today as well.

The Crosswind Evangelist (Alumni) Network: For your never-ending desire to learn and keep me moving!

About Crosswind Project Management, Inc.

Crosswind Project Management, Inc. started in 1998 to serve the needs of various technical customers in the Dallas/Fort Worth, Texas area. As the company evolved, it stepped into the education and training arena in the local junior colleges and began to grow its curriculum while helping make a difference in people's lives and careers.

As the dotcom and telecom economies were at their peak, Crosswind was offering PMP Certification training to companies in the Dallas area, as well as the southern United States. All the while, the PMP Exam Success Series was being developed and fine-tuned.

Today, Crosswind Project Management's PMP Exam Success Series of products are some of the most integrated and efficient products on the market for PMP Certification. They are currently used in numerous industries and in various universities, colleges, and PMI chapters in at least 40 countries.

	PMP Exam Success Series Study pack includes the two books, two audio CDs, exam simulation CD, placemats, and flashcards listed below.
	Visit www.crosswindpm.com to see the new products we have available for your PMP Exam Success Series needs including PMTV™ online training and online testing. It includes any new products, corporate pricing, PMI Chapters, colleges, and other quantity purchasers.
	Our PMP Exam Success Series: Certification Exam Manual is the foundation of our series. This book was designed to allow the future PMP to create a solid foundation for understanding the PMI Processes and preparation for PMP Certification Examination success. The book includes matching and functional exercises, and over 500 test questions. It covers all nine Knowledge Areas, five Process Groups, Framework, Professional and Social Responsibility, exam preparation strategies and "must-knows," and a link for a PDF file on how to apply for the PMP Examination online, step by step.
	Our PMP Exam Success Series: Exam Simulation CD-ROM is unparalleled because it provides the ability to slice the questions by Knowledge Area, Process Group, perform integrated testing with all the questions together, as well as look at the output of your test by Knowledge Area or Process Group. With over 3500 questions, this CD is the perfect complement to the PMP Exam Success Series: Certification Exam Manual.

	The PMP Exam Success Series: Exam Questions Book is a manual full of PMP Examination questions different from our Certification Exam Manual. Each question has a full explanation to help reinforce learning.
	The PMP Exam Success Series: Placemat Volume 1, Volume 2, and Volume 3 provide a summary to the point of view of the information needed for the PMP Examination. Processes, Inputs, Tools and Techniques Outputs, Plans, Formulas, Mind Maps, and other key pieces are all there. A double-sided, laminated 11" X 17" card provides you the key to PMP for the exam and a long-term quick reference after you are a PMP.
	The PMP Exam Success Series: Understanding the Processes and PMP Exam Success Series: Terms and Definitions audio CDs are ideal for that late night listening or carpool study time. Designed to complement the rest of the PMP Success Series, this audio part of the process helps reinforce your development. Each CD contains 80 minutes of information professionally recorded to help get you ready for the PMP Examination.
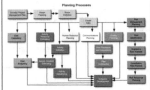	The PMP Exam Success Series: Certification Exam Flashcards are the key tool for working through lunch studying the 400+ terms, definitions, key inputs, key tools and key outputs, formulas, and variables. It helps reinforce the learning and understanding of all 44 processes and their associated pieces.

Also, please let us know of your success with becoming a PMP. Email info@crosswindpm.com to tell us what we did that worked for you. Your feedback helps us evolve our products to make them the most advanced, cutting edge products on the market today!

PMTV™ Online PMP Examination Review

PMTV's free online Tip of the Day and PMP Examination Review is available. Visit www.crosswindpm.com to sign up for automated Tip of the Day updates. You will receive updates plus information on the complementary trial account.

About the Author

Tony Johnson, MBA, PMP has over 18 years experience as a Project Manager in industries such as telecommunications, finance, consulting, hardware and software development, education, and manufacturing.

He has multiple years of experience in training and curriculum development plus training in areas such as technology, manufacturing, Internet, electronic commerce, and project management. He has delivered over 7500 hours of project management training in alignment with PMI Standards.

Former students come from companies such as:

AAFES	Accenture	ACS	Adea Solutions	Auto One
American Airlines	Anderson Consulting	AT&T	Avaya	Bank of America
Bank One	Bearing Point	Carreker	Ciber	Cisco
Cingular	Citi	CompUSA	Computer Associates	Crossmark
Dallas PMI Chapter Education Committee	Decision Consultants, Inc.	Department of Defense	Electronic Data Systems (EDS)	Excel Communications
Exe	Fujitsu	Harley-Davidson	Hewlett-Packard	Honeywell
IBM	Immedient	Intellimark-IT	Interstate Battery	JCPenney
Lucent	Genuity	KPMG	Macromedia	Match.com
MCI	Motorola	Nortel	Oracle	Perot Systems
PWC	Sabre	Source	Southwestern Bell Corporation	Technisource
Texas Instruments	Travelocity	Tyco	U.S. Air Force	Vartec
Verizon	U.S. Army	U.S. Navy	Wal-Mart	Worldcom

Mr. Johnson is also an award-winning member of the Dallas PMI chapter (one of the world's largest chapters with over 3000 members, 50% of whom are PMPs), as well as a past member of the chapter's education committee. He has also been a key presenter at the chapter's PMP Forum and chapter meetings.

Mr. Johnson has a bachelor's degree in Business Administration and Finance from Dallas Baptist University and an MBA in Operations and Strategic Management from Dallas Baptist University. He has taught at Southern Methodist University (SMU), as well as various colleges and universities in Dallas, Texas. He is the founder of Crosswind Project Management training (www.crosswindpm.com).

Table of Contents

SECTION I

INTRODUCTION AND INITIAL PREPARATION

1. **How to attain PMP Exam Success via the Certification Exam Manual**

2. **Registering with PMI for the Exam**

3. **Exam Environment**

4. **Pre and Post Test**

Chapter 1

How to Attain PMP Exam Success via the Certification Exam Manual

This book is for anyone seeking an unconventional yet solid presentation of PMI project management best practices, a book that maximizes learning and retention and leads to success at achieving PMP Certification. Its driving objective is to provide content that benefits readers the most as they study for PMP Certification.

Years ago, when I studied for the PMP Examination, I could not find many books on the topic. Also, there were not many PMPs to help me measure how prepared I was after months of study. I remember studying, not feeling I knew enough, and continuing to study. As time went on, either the Project Management Body of Knowledge (*PMBOK Guide*) didn't address an issue that I found in a preparation book, or the preparation book didn't have enough detail to help me truly understand why something was what it was. It seemed as though people were writing books to show how smart they appear to their readers or how much they could condense the information. Unfortunately, there wasn't a product providing a roadmap for success to let me know when I was ready and containing supporting detail behind that roadmap to help reinforce the material for the exam.

I remember thinking: why can't there be a book that has material broken out with what is needed for the exam, as well as the details behind it so I can feel comfortable with what is expected of me? I felt there should be a book with logical organization that was consistent from chapter to chapter. I felt that if (for example) formulas were not used in an area, there should be a note in the chapter stating: "no formulas in this area." I felt that if formulas were used, I should be able to locate them quickly in the chapter, and they would all be there. Also, I wondered: why can't a book explain the answers to the questions and present a complete 200-question test? Why isn't there a book that explains the items between the topics, such as how to decode the situational questions?

Well, that product is here. The PMP Exam Success Series: Certification Exam Manual provides the most comprehensive detailed product on the market today for PMP Examination success. In this part of the book, we discuss how to use its content to optimize your PMP Examination success.

1.1   Overhead and Exam Environment

This topic area describes the parts of exam environment you should begin preparing for. We also discuss the exam environment itself. Although this approach may sound elementary, you should understand and follow it. If you don't know to prepare for a particular content area, or you show up at a test center without the required material, it will not seem so elementary after all.

1.2   Terminology

In Terminology, we discuss how to synchronize your knowledge to align with PMI terminology. Some call this topic area brainwashing, but the sooner you start to do this while studying, the sooner you can experience PMP Examination success.

1.3   Questions

Here, you discover everything you wanted to know about the exam questions, what they look like, and how you can approach them to your advantage.

Question Format Analysis	Explains ways to look at exam questions so you can focus on what they are asking and ignore any disinformation (noise)
Question Formats	Breaks down the seven basic formats of exam questions
Question Translation and Breakdown	Shows how to translate situational questions and break them down to their basic elements
	People often encounter obscure or unfamiliar topics on the exam. Here, we show you how to eliminate noise and clutter in the questions.

1.4   Problem Solving on Situational Questions

We offer suggestions about how to address the challenging situational questions. There are certain rules that apply across all Knowledge Areas, rules not easily found in the *PMBOK Guide*. We list various "tests" and "rules" to steer you in the right direction on the situational challenges.

1.5   Pre and Post Test

This topic area contains a 200-question integrated test that attempts to emulate the actual PMP Examination. It covers all nine Knowledge Areas, plus Framework, as well as Professional and Social Responsibility. To emulate the exam, we randomize questions by Knowledge Area, as opposed to organizing questions according to each chapter.

1.6   Methodology and Position Descriptions

Here, we lay out the basic environment for the methodology by describing the following: Initiation, Planning, Executing, Monitoring and Controlling, and Closing. We also address various positions such as Project Manager, stakeholder, and sponsor, including how PMI views these roles in project management.

1.7   Chapters

The main topics for the chapters are the nine Knowledge Areas, as well as Framework and Professional and Social Responsibility. We also include information about the exam environment that can help prepare you for PMP Examination success.

Introduction	The introduction covers information you need to know before you proceed to the chapter contents.
Crosswind "Must Knows"	At the beginning of nearly all the chapters, you can find a Crosswind "Must Knows" list. Each list can serve as a checklist for each chapter and Knowledge Area. The items in these lists focus on what you need to know in preparation for the exam.
	Use the Check column ☑ to indicate that you know and understand the "Must Know" point.
	Throughout the chapter, we emphasize these points in boxes along the outside margin. Each point is flagged with an icon.

PMP Exam Success Series: Certification Exam Manual
© 2007 Crosswind Project Management, Inc., www.crosswindpm.com

	When you see [icon] -- make note of the point! We have given you plenty of white space where you can write your own notes relevant to the "Must Know" or for other content in the book. When gauging your knowledge for a chapter, use this "Must Know" list to see how thorough your knowledge is for the topic. When you find your knowledge lacking, you know right where to focus your study efforts.
Process Table	The exam addresses 44 processes from the *PMBOK Guide*. The process table summarizes the process concept, defining name and process plus key inputs, tools and techniques, and outputs. This information helps you understand what you must know to perform a process, what tools are used to create output, and what type of output you should expect when done. An example of a process table:

<table>
<tr><td colspan="3" align="center">Name (Process Area)</td></tr>
<tr><td>Key Inputs</td><td>Project Scope Statement</td><td>The Project Scope Statement helps define the project.</td></tr>
<tr><td>Key Tools & Techniques</td><td>WBS Templates</td><td>The WBS Templates can be derived from previous similar projects or industry standards.</td></tr>
<tr><td>Key Outputs</td><td>Work Breakdown Structure</td><td>The WBS provides a decomposition of the work of the project and can sometimes point out areas of the scope that were not sufficiently addressed in the project scope statement.</td></tr>
</table>

Description	Think of the description as a "primer" that leads you through the details of the process before we discuss inputs, tools and techniques, and outputs.
Key Inputs, Tools & Techniques, and Outputs	The *PMBOK Guide* has approximately 600 inputs, tools and techniques, and outputs. We list "key" inputs, tools and techniques, and outputs in the process table, and we include a narrative, where useful, to show you how they fit together.
Situational Question and Real World Application	The situational question and real world application element discusses what types of problems might arise if you ignore or only partially implement this process area. It also shows how a situational question could come from this area, plus where to apply this area in your daily project management.
Formulas and Variables	The topic on formulas and variables contains all the formulas for that Knowledge Area, as well as the variables that are part of the formulas. If the exam provides a variable, we list that variable so you know it doesn't need to be calculated. If there are no formulas for the section, we indicate that there are none, saving you the time and trouble of searching for them.

Terminology	Terminology lists words and terms the exam may ask and expect you to understand.
	We divide the terminology discussion by Knowledge Area, and if there is overlap -- such as earned value pieces that could be covered – we list the terms in the main area instead of in every area.
	Even though some terminology appears in this section but not in the chapter content, you should still know the information for the exam.
	One of our students once referred to this area of the exam as "brainwashing." That might not be the best description, but the sooner you adjust your thinking to PMI terminology, the sooner you will be on the road to PMP Examination success.
Mind Maps	Each Mind Map is a powerful graphic tool for visualizing the content.
Quick Test	At the end of each chapter's content, you can find a ten-question Quick Test that uses a non-simulation format. Instead of simply selecting the best answer in front of you, as the exam simulation format requires, this format requires you to fill in the answer, circle the correct answer, or use a variety of other options to see if you understand the contents and details of the chapter.
ITTO Matching Exercises	Each chapter has a key Inputs, Tools & Techniques, and Outputs (ITTO) matching exercise. Instead of patterning the exercises after the 600+ that are in the *PMBOK Guide*, we base these matching exercises on the KEY Inputs-Tools & Techniques-Outputs that we have listed in this book. This format makes it possible for you to test your understanding of how each of the 44 processes functions by selecting the key ITTOs, as well as a summary for each process.
Terminology Matching Exercises	Every chapter has a terminology-matching exercise that should help test your understanding of the PMI terminology you can expect to encounter on the exam.
Other Exercises	In some chapters, we provide exercises to help reinforce calculations and concepts and prepare you for the terminology and calculations parts of the exam.
Chapter Practice Test	This test lists 30 questions that give you a feel for the actual test format, as well as test your knowledge of material covered in the chapter or Knowledge Area.
	Unlike questions in some other books, these are not written to match the exact content of the chapter. Instead, they come from our database of over 2000 questions. Because they are based on terminology, calculations, concepts, and scenarios, they should test your knowledge, as well as your expertise on the different question formats.
Exercise Answers	These are the answers for the ITTO matching, terminology matching, and other exercises. For any calculations or other non-matching exercises, you can see how the answers were calculated along with the correct answers.
Chapter Practice Test Answers	These are the correct answers with explanations for the correct and incorrect answers. This is a key area of learning along with the chapter content. Use this area to "calibrate" your understanding or interpretation of a topic that the question covers. To help you grasp the logic behind the answer, we have inserted the relevant section number at the end of the answer.

1.8   Inconsistencies with PMBOK Guide

You will encounter what we consider inconsistencies with the *PMBOK Guide*. We have chosen to note these inconsistencies and point them out for purposes of reader clarity. We enclose them with braces {}. For example, an output of the Schedule Development process is Resource Requirements (Updates). If you search earlier in the *PMBOK Guide* to find where the Resource Requirements are created, the closest you will find are Activity Resource Requirements. Activity Resource Requirements (Updates) does then make sense; therefore, we have enclosed "activity" to create "{Activity} Resource Requirements (Updates)".

1.9   Exam Support CD-ROM

Your book comes with a CD-ROM that is full of additional material to help you prepare for PMI's certification exams. On the CD-ROM you will find the following:

- 200 question PMP Exam Simulation
- 150 question CAPM Exam Simulation
- 40 question pre-study exam
- 50 question post-study exam
- Terminology Crossword Puzzles in PDF format
- Matching Processes in PDF format (two different sizes)
- Matching ITTO exercises in PDF format
- Matching Terminology exercises in PDF format
- Excel workbook to breakdown your experience for the exam application
- Screen shots for the PMI exam application
- Sample files to our audio CDs and links and PMTV online training (Internet connection required)
- Various other tools to help with PMI's certification exams

To maximize the benefit of the CD-ROM, we suggest you click the READMEFIRST button on your CD-ROM; it will explain the details of the various items on the CD.

To install the PMP or CAPM exam simulation application, put the CD-ROM in your computer and follow the onscreen directions through product activation. If you have issues with activation, please email info@crosswindpm.com with your activation code and ask for activation support with CEM V7.3. **We STRONGLY suggest that you install this application as soon as you begin studying in case there are any technical issues which may delay your installation and impact your exam review strategies.**

If you do not receive a CD-ROM with this book, email info@crosswindpm.com. You may be asked to validate your purchase of the book before a copy is delivered via email.

If you wish to purchase more questions, you may do so by visiting www.crosswindpm.com and ordering our online testing, Exam Simulation CD-ROM, or questions book products. These products include even more questions and break them down into a number of formats including Knowledge Area, Process Group, Inputs/Tools & Techniques/Outputs, calculations, and more.

Using for a Study Group or Training Company

If you are using our products for your study group or training company, thank you for choosing us. There are a variety of approaches that work depending on your experience level, schedule, etc., but we suggest a few general principles. Use the table of contents as a roadmap for your studies.

- After covering materials, be sure to review questions in the chapter.
- In reviewing questions, focus on why the best answer is the best and why other answers aren't or don't fit the question. This review approach helps with double reinforcement.
- Follow the exercises in the book including matching, network diagram, and earned value.
- One principle about learning is that teaching a topic helps you learn more about it. If you don't know a topic, try teaching it to your group. You'll be surprised with what you learn.

Also, if you are a trainer, company, college, PMI Chapter, or other organization using our products, we welcome you to contact us about either group pricing or support material such as PowerPoint slides to help with your courses.

PMP Exam Success Series: Certification Exam Manual
© 2007 Crosswind Project Management, Inc., www.crosswindpm.com

Chapter 2

Registering with PMI for the Exam

To register for and take the exam, you must meet certain criteria. These criteria take into account your experience, formal education, and training hours. In this chapter, we explain what you will need. Plus, we hope to eliminate any confusion you may have about the process.

2.1 Qualifying for the Exam

The following table shows the requirements necessary to qualify for the PMP or CAPM exams. Following the table is a description of each field.

Exam Qualifications for PMP Certification Type

Minimum Education Requirements	Hours of Experience Needed	Time Frame for the Experience	Project Management Training Hours
Bachelor's Degree (or equal)	4500 hours	3 years within the last 6 of submitting application	35 hours
High School Diploma (or equal)	7500 hours	5 years within the last 8 of submitting application	35 hours

Exam Qualifications for CAPM Certification Type

High School Diploma (or equal) plus 1500 hours of work on a project	OR	23 hours of formal project management training

Certification Type	The PMP Project Management Professional or the CAPM Certified Associate in Project Management
Minimum Education Requirements	A completed bachelor's degree or high school diploma (or equivalent) If your bachelor's degree is not complete, you fit into the high school diploma criteria.
Hours of Experience Needed	Minimum hours of project-related experience required to qualify for the exam A rule of thumb: 2000 hours is equal to one year of experience. You cannot "double-dip" your hours. For example, if you worked as a Project Manager during a given year, and you also worked on a project for a charitable (or other type) group, you cannot claim both sets of hours as your experience.
Time Frame for the Experience	The years of project-related experience within the last number of years you must have to qualify for the exam For example, if you have four years of project-related experience over the last eight years of your career, you qualify as a bachelor's degree PMP candidate, assuming you meet the other criteria outlined above.

Project Management Training Hours	The actual hours of project management training you need to qualify Your successful completion of the Crosswind PMP Exam Review bootcamp course completes this requirement.

2.2   What Type of Experience Counts?

This question comes from people who have been involved in project management for a number of years but perhaps haven't held the title of Project Manager the entire time. I also see questions from people who have worked in project management but have performed other functions such as requirements gathering and scope verification.

2.2.1   How Much Does All My Experience Count Toward Hours Needed?

The answer lies in the type of work that generated this experience. A specific job title doesn't disqualify or qualify hours toward the experience needed, contrary to what many people think and even what some PMPs themselves have tried to explain.

Activities that you have led or directed are the revised standard for the exam. This revision means that you didn't necessarily need the title Project Manager, but if you helped figure out what needed to be done in an area on the project or helped lead a group of people to get the work done, this experience should be sufficient. For example, did you lead a group of people in creating a work breakdown structure (WBS) or schedule? How about leading a team to verify that the work of the project was completed as planned?

This is the type of experience that will work toward your hours and months of project management experience.

2.2.2   Must the Experience Hours Be Spread Across All Nine Knowledge Areas?

No. You might have all your experience in only a few of the Knowledge Areas, but if you qualify to sit for the exam, PMI assumes you are comfortable enough in all the Knowledge Areas to pass it.

2.2.3   How Do I Verify Experience?

Experience verification is often misunderstood. What PMI has released is that people applying will be notified instantly if they are receiving a pre-qualification audit of their applications. Each person must also submit manager or other appropriate person(s) contact information so you can contact the person in the event of a pre-qualification audit to complete appropriate documentation. If you don't have manager contact information, we advise you to evaluate the PDF listed in section 2.4, and if PMI hasn't provided information to address it in that document, contact PMI directly.

Description of Deliverables

In our classes, we are often asked about the deliverables description that the application requires. Remember -- this is the PMP Examination, so the focus is project management, not necessarily the product of the project. Therefore, PMI is interested in knowing more about project management deliverables that you were involved in. For example, did you lead or direct the creation of the WBS or schedule of the project, or were you leading the Scope Verification effort on the project?

Those are the type of deliverables PMI wants to know more about, not necessarily the coding that the software project accomplished, or the electrical work on a shopping mall.

2.3   PMP Certification Experience Hours (Included on CD)

Before you begin the experience section of the PMP application, map out your experience hours. If you have any questions about how to format your experience hours, please go to our Web site **http://www.crosswindpm.com/download/crosswindexphours.xls** and download the spreadsheet. You can use this to track your last seven projects and accumulate the hours in the format that PMI requires for the application. This spreadsheet is a good tool to document your hours for PMI application and your real world projects. In addition, it contains contact information you can use if you are audited by PMI.

2.4   PMP Online Application (Included on CD)

Effective August 29, 2005, PMI has a revised application process for the exam. Visit our Web site **http://www.crosswindpm.com/download/3rdpmbokguideexamprocess.pdf** and download the step-by-step process. The current link for the exam application is available at the support (then downloads) page of the Crosswind PM site www.crosswindpm.com.

Using the online application can significantly reduce the time it takes to complete the PMP application, compared to the paper application. It also lets you work on it at your convenience. Online registration does not require that you complete the application in a single session. You can save an incomplete application, log off, and return later to continue. If you plan to join the membership of PMI, we suggest that you complete your membership before you start the application. Having your membership will initiate the discount that you receive in the exam as a PMI member. Be aware that it is not a requirement to join the membership of PMI or any local chapter to take the PMP Examination.

2.5   Audit

As of this printing, PMI randomly audits 10% of online applications. There are no triggers for these audits; they are truly random.

If you are selected for audit, PMI sends you hyperlinks to experience validation documents to be completed for the audit. Print them and present them to individuals who can validate your work experience. These people are to complete the forms, seal them, and sign the seal as instructed. PMI also requests photocopies of any training certificates and diplomas or transcripts. Typically this process is completed within seven to ten days upon PMI's receipt of the requested documentation.

Chapter 3

Exam Environment

Here are general suggestions that can help you be more successful. The best plan for exam success is to know the content thoroughly, as well as the environment in which the test is given. We do not list short cuts or cheat sheet type concepts. Instead, we focus on getting you more comfortable with the exam environment and what it will demand of you.

We devote attention to the exam environment because you need to focus on the reason you are there – the PMP Examination – not on a room that is too cold, too warm, too noisy, or distracting in other ways. Also, we describe noise, which is disinformation that can confuse you on the exam.

3.1   Preparing for Exam Day

There are some special considerations you should address when preparing for your exam. When you go to the exam center, you must take a number of items. There are also some that we recommend.

Studying and Scheduling	Schedule your exam for a time when you are most alert. Try not to schedule your exam to follow a day's work. A good night's sleep the night before the exam and eating well a few days before will help greatly.
	Cramming the day before is not a bad idea. It can help you detect any final subject areas that need last minute study.
	The tables, charts, and other items that we suggest you memorize are "musts" for success. Know them cold and be able to recreate them in the test room.
Practicing	Practice tests help you become familiar with the environment, as well as the question layout and timing.
	When taking practice tests, focus on the speed at which you complete the questions. On average, you have 72 seconds per question. While there are no additional points for completing more quickly than anyone else, being practiced enough to set a good pace can give you an advantage, especially when you hit "the wall" on the exam. Your mind will be accustomed to processing questions at a pace that is above normal.
	Take the tutorial. It can help you better understand your options in the environment.
What to Take: Required	The following are required:
	• Your eligibility letter with the authorization number on it
	• A photo ID and two other forms of ID (credit card, etc.) Verify that the names on the IDs and the letter are identical. For example, Anthony and Tony could cause problems.
What to Take: Recommended	Dress in layers so you can be comfortable in the room environment whether it be cold, warm, or unstable. A t-shirt with a sweater is a good combination.
	Earphones are usually provided, but consider taking some in case they aren't. They will shut out the noise around you.
	Although you may take food and drink, you must leave them in the provided locker.
	You may take the locker key plus the provided calculator, pencils, and paper into the test room.

3.2   About the Exam

3.2.1   PMP Examination and Success Manual Alignment

The following table shows how the exam is broken down (in percentages) and how this book aligns to those areas of the examination.

PROCESS AREA	EXAM OBJECTIVE	CHAPTER
Initiating the Project	Conduct Project Selection Methods	6, 9
(11.59%)	Define Scope	6,7
	Document Project Risks, Assumptions, and Constraints	5,6,7,13
	Identify and Perform Stakeholder Analysis	5,6,7,12,13
	Develop Project Charter	6,9
	Obtain Project Charter Approval	6,9,12
Planning the Project	Define and Record Requirements, Constraints and Assumptions	5,6,7
(22.7%)	Identify Project Team and Define Roles and Responsibilities	6,7,11
	Create the WBS	6,7
	Develop Change Management Plan	7,8,9,10,11,12,13,14
	Identify Risks and Define Risk Strategies	7,10,13
	Obtain Plan Approval	6,7,12
	Conduct Kick-off Meeting	5,7
Executing the Project	Execute Tasks Defined in Project Management Plan	6,7,8,10,11,12
(27.5%)	Ensure Common Understanding and Set Expectations	6,12
	Implement the Procurement of Project Resources	6,14
	Manage Resource Allocation	6,8,11
	Implement Quality Management Plan	7,10
	Implement Approved Changes	7,8,9,10,11,12,13,14
	Implement Approved Actions and Workarounds	7,8,9,10,11,12,13,14
	Improve Team Performance	11,12
Monitoring and Controlling the Project	Measure Project Performance	6,7,8,9,10,12
(21.03%)	Verify and Manage Changes to the Project	7,8,9,10,11,12,13,14
	Ensure Project Deliverables Conform to Quality Standards	6,7,10,12
	Monitor All Risks	6,7,10,12,13
Closing the Project	Obtain Final Acceptance for the Project	6,7,10,12
(8.57%)	Obtain Financial, Legal, and Administrative Closure	6,7,9,10,12
	Release Project Resources	6,11
	Identify, Document and Communicate Lessons Learned	6,7,11,12
	Create and Distribute Final Project Report	6,12
	Archive and Retain Project Records	6,12
	Measure Customer Satisfaction	6,7,10,12
Professional and Social Responsibility	Ensure Individual Integrity	15
(8.61%)	Contribute to the Project Management Knowledge Base	15
	Enhance Personal Professional Competence	15
	Promote Interaction Among Stakeholders	12,15

PMP Exam Success Series: Certification Exam Manual
© 2007 Crosswind Project Management, Inc., www.crosswindpm.com

3.2.2   In and Out of Scope

Too many Project Managers think that 12 to 20 years of experience and reading the *PMBOK Guide* a few times will give them what they need to pass the exam. That is rarely (if ever) the case.

The exam tests your understanding of the *PMBOK Guide* and PMI processes (across all Knowledge Areas, regardless of the ones you use and how you use them at work), as well as the ability to know how to deal with these processes in situational questions.

Know the formulas that we have listed in the formulas section of each chapter. You need to know the terms and definitions we have listed in each chapter as well. You should be familiar with how to recognize the definition of a given term, as well as recognize it in a situation.

Be familiar with the documents such as the project charter, WBS, schedule that PMI uses in the methodology, especially if these are used differently in your work place. These are the types of instances for which your experience can hurt you if you don't recognize the difference.

The exam is not an IQ test. Nor is it used to validate your project management experience, college degree applicability, or project scheduling software. It's used to test your understanding of how to apply the PMI processes in the workplace and in situations.

3.2.3   PMI "Theory Pills"™

A number of basic assumptions and givens factor into how PMI addresses project management as opposed to how you perform it within your company. We suggest that you be familiar with the PMI "Theory Pills" listed below because they are underlying factors in how most questions are presented.

- Historical information about existing projects can contribute to the corporate knowledge base, future estimating, and organizational process assets.
- Assume that documentation exists to detail the project so that it could be recreated if necessary.
- Conduct meetings following the meeting rules listed in this book.
- Consider risk when estimating time and cost.
- Put changes through an official change control process with appropriate parties reviewing for impact and approval.
- Use the *PMBOK Guide* processes as PMI describes them in the *PMBOK Guide*, regardless of what you use in the workplace or past projects.
- Do not underemphasize the value of the WBS. Literally all planning stems from it.
- As the Project Manager, be responsible for delivering the project results in scope, on schedule, and on budget.
- If one parameter of the triple constraint is modified, the others will likely change. For example, if a schedule must be shortened, consider revising or updating the scope of the project if the sponsor decides to do so.
- The PMI approach generally calls for a great deal of planning before actual execution of work, contrary to how your industry might address projects.
- Assume that the company performing the work is fairly mature in project management regarding their methodology, processes, etc.
- The work of the project is built from the project management plan, which is what the team follows to complete the work of the project.
- The Project Manager should follow the company's project management processes.
- Fix the problem as soon as possible; do not let it linger.
- Ideally, influential stakeholders should be defined before the project starts to ensure that they have had an opportunity to provide input to the project management plan.
- Do not assume that the project or work is complete just because the team believes it is complete. Until the customer/sponsor gives formal acceptance, there may still be work to do.

- Understand the roles and responsibilities as defined in the *PMBOK Guide*, regardless of how they are defined within your company.
- "Analysis" is always a technique.
- Reality is not often addressed in the questions. Therefore, if you need time or money, time or money should be no object. Ask for it; it should be provided via the project sponsor(s). [We saved the biggest "Theory Pill" for last.]

3.2.4   Brain Dump List

The brain dump is a key piece of preparation for PMP Examination success. Let's clarify what a brain dump is. A brain dump is important information that you write down as you begin your PMP Examination. We recommend that you write down your brain dump during the tutorial of the exam. This tutorial happens in the first fifteen minutes before your four hours actually start. Ensure that you can do this cold in fifteen minutes or less before you take the test.

Some people take the approach that using a brain dump means you don't know what is needed to pass the test. The reality is that the exam has a lot of information you are expected to understand and know how to address in situational and other formats of questions. This brain dump can also help you ensure that you don't get key information twisted in your mind as you go through the test. One of our staff said that when she took the test, she knew the information, but she preferred to write it out just to ensure she could quickly reference it and not get it confused.

Every brain dump is personal and relates to key items people feel they need to have presented in the brain dump, but the following table lists items that are ideal to provide in most cases:

Content		Location
EV formulas including our table • Cost Performance Index (CPI) • Cost Variance (CV) • Schedule Performance Index (SPI) • Schedule Variance (SV) • Estimate at Completion (EAC)	• Estimate to Complete (ETC) Variance at Completion (VAC) • Earned Value (EV) • Planned Value (PV) • Budget at Completion (BAC) • To Complete Performance Index (TCPI)	Cost Chapter
Percentages for 1, 2, 3, and 6 Sigma		Quality Chapter
Present and Future Value Formulas		Cost Chapter
Cost Estimate Range Table		Cost Chapter
Forward and Backward Pass Formulas		Time Chapter
Slack Formulas		Time Chapter
Organizational Structure Characteristics		Framework Chapter
Risk Response Strategies		Risk Chapter
Types of Power for the Project Manager		Human Resource Chapter
Conflict Resolution Types		Human Resource Chapter
Levels of Maslow's Hierarchy of Needs		Human Resource Chapter
Point of Total Assumption Formula and Variables		Procurement Chapter
Process Table Map -- This is the table that lists the 44 processes and the five Process Groups horizontally across the top and the nine Knowledge Areas vertically on the side.		*PMBOK Guide*

PMP Exam Success Series: Certification Exam Manual
© 2007 Crosswind Project Management, Inc., www.crosswindpm.com

Planning Diagram	*PMBOK Guide* or PMP Exam Success Series: Volume 1 Placemat
List of Management Plans and Change Control Systems	From Various Chapters

3.2.5   Black and White vs. Gray

When some people start studying for this exam, they find themselves frustrated, especially if they come from a technical environment. In a technical environment, for example, you could be asked for a technical certification on what makes something work. The answer can be black and white or ABSOLUTE. The PMP Examination often uses gray words that are not extreme, such as GENERALLY, but can relate to "shades" of the condition. These "gray" words can take a bit of getting used to with sample questions.

The PMP Examination can include questions with absolute words such as ALWAYS, NEVER, COMPLETELY, and gray words as SOMETIMES, SHOULD, COULD, GENERAL, and MAY.

Be very sensitive to these words because absolute words compared to gray words can significantly change the meaning of a question.

3.2.6   "The Wall"

"The wall" is the point where you find it more difficult to think through the questions and material. Everyone who takes the exam eventually hits "the wall." Some won't hit it until after leaving the test environment, but most hit it sometime during the exam.

To minimize the impact of "the wall," we recommend that you mentally break the exam into percentages. When you have completed the first 50 questions, you are 25% done. When you have completed 100 questions, consider yourself 50% done. From that point on, you are on your way to completion. Setting milestones gives you a sense that the exam is not so big.

3.2.7   Time Management

Time Management is a key area many people glance over or overlook entirely. It's important to remember the time you will have per question on average, regardless of your knowledge of the information. If you can't make it through the information in time, you may come up short on the exam.

As you take practice exams, pay attention to how quickly you go through the questions instead of simply how many you answer correctly. Make sure you provide answers to questions that you mark in case you run out of time on the exam. Be sure to allocate enough time to go back and check your marked answers. We recommend that you get through all questions in about two and a half hours before you review marked questions. By following this recommendation, you should have enough time to address marked questions plus a little risk reserve if you run longer on questions than in your practice tests.

3.2.8   Marking Questions

The exam lets you mark questions and return later to review them. Studies show that your initial response to a question is usually the right answer. Many times, you can second-guess yourself out of the best answer if you are not careful. While we suggest marking questions you are unsure about, and perhaps math questions (if you simply want to go back and double check the math), we recommend that you don't mark too many questions. You may run out of time on the exam. Typically, our classroom students who score well on the exam mark about ten to fifteen questions. Those who mark more than that usually don't score as well.

3.2.9   Scoring

106 correct of 175 is a PMP Examination passing score. It translates to 61% of 175 of the 200 questions. There are 25 pretest questions included as well, for a total of 200 questions on the exam. The pretest questions aren't scored; they are reviewed by PMI to see how people perform on them. You will not know which questions are pretest or regular test questions. If, after reading this book or taking our

course, you score in the mid 160s or above, email the author (info@crosswindpm.com). You might be a record-setter. As of this printing, we are not aware of anyone ever scoring perfect on the exam.

3.3   Exam Questions

3.3.1   Question Characteristics and Components

There are different characteristics and components you must recognize when interpreting questions, especially the situational ones. They include noise, common terminology, too much information, and others. If you recognize them in the questions, you may determine more easily what the question is actually asking.

Noise	We use this word to reference information that has no value or bearing in a question. We call it "noise" because it is content that has been inserted to distract you in the exam environment. We also call such content "disinformation."
Common Terminology	The exam typically uses PMI terminology. A question could have one possible answer commonly connected with the question but not PMI terminology. Another possible answer uses the PMI terminology for the common description (e.g., budget at completion vs. budget). In this example, if you answered "budget" because you weren't familiar with the true definition of "budget at completion," you are technically wrong because "budget at completion" is the better answer.
Too Much Information (TMI)	The exam could present questions that contain a great deal of information. For example, you might encounter a situational question in which a number of variables are thrown at you, such as time, cost, scope, and quality. Look at each variable and see how it relates to what the question is asking. For example, if you are given variables associated with time, quality, and scope, and they are all good or not enough information, and the cost variable listed shows that you are over budget, then that variable is likely the one you are concerned about.
Wrong Area, or Wrong Point in Time	The exam could present questions that have an answer or answers that are from a wrong Knowledge Area or from the correct Knowledge Area but the answer is too early or late in the process to be acceptable. Questions could have references to "what would you do (first, last, before, after) this." In this case, more than one answer is in the general range, but only one is correct.

3.3.2   Question Formats

The exam uses a number of question formats. Some of the questions use multiple formats. Understanding the formats helps you dissect the question and the available answers. Here are some formats:

- Select
- Select NOT/EXCEPT
- All (or a combination of) the answers
- None of the answers

- Chicken or the egg (sequence)
- Situational
- Calculation

Question Format	Description	Example
Select	This is likely the most straight-forward question format on the exam. It simply asks you to select the best answer. Be aware, however, because it can also include other question formats, including the Chicken or the Egg format questions.	A milestone has what duration? A. 1 day B. 0 (no duration) (Correct) C. 1 hour D. 8 hours
Select NOT/EXCEPT	For this the type of question, you must select the answer that does not apply. Generally, this question type is not a big deal unless you have already hit "the wall" that we discussed in the exam environment part of this book. The key to handling this type of question is to determine which three answer selections have something in common. The fourth answer selection is the exception and the answer to choose.	All the following are areas of communications management except… A. Manage Stakeholders B. Performance Reporting C. Quantitative Risk Analysis (Correct) D. Information Distribution
All (or a Combination of) the Answers	With this question format, all -- or a combination -- of the answers are acceptable. The main thing to consider is that there isn't a bad choice. The odds are that if two of the answers (other than "All the answers") look good, so will the third.	Which of the following are areas of risk management? A. Risk Identification B. Quantitative Risk Analysis C. Risk Response Planning D. All the answers (Correct)
None of the Answers	With this format, every available answer (other than "none of the above") fails to apply to the question. You must evaluate each answer to determine its relevant Knowledge Area. If the relevant Knowledge Area for each answer lies outside the scope of the question, then none of the answers applies.	What Knowledge Area is part of the triple constraint? A. Communications B. Procurement C. Professional and Social Responsibility D. None of the answers (Correct)
Chicken or the Egg	With this format, more than one answer is acceptable. The key is to understand their order -- what comes first (last, before, or after something depending on what the question is asking). In this case, look at what the question is asking and determine the best answer based on the timeline of the answers.	What comes before Activity Duration Estimating? A. Activity Sequencing B. Cost Estimating C. Activity Definition (Correct) D. Project Plan Development
Situational	This question format is probably the most challenging, and the exam will include at least 75 questions using this format, some in combination with other formats. This question format expects you to leverage your PM experience and understanding of the *PMBOK Guide* and the PMI way of thinking. Typically, you will see a Chicken or the Egg (what comes first) -- with whom do you communicate regarding a project, or what is your next action on the project. Keys to success in this area are to understand the chart in the Framework area of this book, plus the key role players in the methodology.	You've taken over an existing project and discover that it has suffered major scope creep because the former Project Manager couldn't say "no" to the sponsor, and it lacked enough supporting documentation. What document do you first want to see (or create if it doesn't exist) about the project foundation? A. Risk List B. Project Charter (Correct) C. Communications Plan D. Budget

Calculation	This question format typically falls under the Select or the None of the Above (sometimes "not enough information") formats. If you know the formulas for the exam, you shouldn't have a problem with calculation questions. In some, you could encounter possible answers that "add up" correctly if you don't know the formula, but attempt to reverse-engineer the question. An example: you are to calculate CPI (divide EV by AC). You have incorrect answers that total other calculations as well (SP, SPI, CV, or others). It is not uncommon for the exam to have questions that do not give you enough data, such as future value or present value. Therefore, it is important that you know all the components of a formula.	What is the CPI for the following data? AC=$200, PV=$400, EV=$200, BAC=$1,000 A. $200 B. -$200 C. 1.0 (Correct) D. 0.5

3.4   Question Translation and Breakdown

The PMP Examination is known for its long rambling situational questions, so if you were like the author and hated word problems in school, you likely will appreciate any method that helps minimize the headache associated with questions such as those below. Numerous times in my public classes, I have heard students make assumptions based on what they think are key items in the question. They have fallen into the trap of incorrect translation and have listened to the noise. One approach that many people believe makes them successful is to focus on the final sentence of a question and answer just that. We don't recommend this approach. Instead, we recommend that you look at the last part of the question to see what you are being asked to do, analyze, etc., before you read the complete question.

Next, eliminate the two worst answers. Remember, you are trying to find the best answer, not always the correct answer. After you have narrowed your selection to two answers, determine the best answer. If you see something that appears important in the question but there is no supporting evidence around it, it likely is noise. For example: "The hard-to-secure resource is on the critical path" tells you nothing about the state of the work that person is doing. To contrast, a CPI of 0.81 has measurable absolute value as not being on the good side of the measurement.

Let's analyze some questions and convert them to "plain" English.

Question #1

You are a Project Manager on an environmental excavating project. As you monitor progress, you determine that the activities are taking longer than estimated on the schedule because of holidays you hadn't planned for in the schedule. What is the best solution to fix this problem?

Breaking down the question	The first sentence establishes that you are the Project Manager. Unless something specific about the type of project comes up, that should be sufficient (environmental excavating wasn't covered in my version of the *PMBOK Guide*!). The second statement has two items of value in it. The first is that activities are taking longer than estimated, and the cause is from not planning in holidays into your schedule. The final sentence simply asks the best way to fix this problem.
Translation (Plain English version)	You are a Project Manager. Your project is behind schedule because you didn't factor holidays into the schedule. What is the best solution to fix this problem?
Answer	Implement a schedule change control and re-baseline the schedule with the holidays factored in.

Question #2

You have taken over a project from another Project Manager who wasn't having success according to the sponsor. The project is a new type of work at your company. The cost is $50,000 over budget, and the former Project Manager did not view the schedule as a useful tool. What should you focus on first?

Breaking down the question	The first sentence establishes that you are replacing an existing Project Manager. The sponsor issue is possible noise. The second sentence is primarily noise but can help reinforce a later sentence. The fact that cost is $50K over budget is not helpful because you don't know if it's a $100K project or a $10M project. In the case of a $10M project, $50K is a drop in the bucket. The fact that the former Project Manager failed to use the schedule is definitely an issue with PMI's processes. The final sentence is simply asking you to identify the most urgent area needing focus.
Translation (Plain English version)	You are a new Project Manager on a project for which you are replacing someone. The project is a new type of work at your company. You don't have a total budget value to tell you if the $50K is a big or small amount over, so assume that is noise. There is either no schedule or not much of a schedule if there is one. What should you focus on first?
Answer	You first focus on seeing what was available for a schedule, and if needed, readjust/modify or create one.

Question #3

You are halfway through an Internet upgrade project. Presently, you know the following: Activity F has an early start of day 7 and a late start of day 12. The cost performance index (CPI) is 0.92, and the schedule performance index is 0.87. The project has 18 stakeholders. Activity G requires a very experienced resource. What should you focus on first?

Breaking down the question	Try your hand at translating this question to see if you are starting to translate PMI fluently.
Translation (Plain English version)	You are 50% done on a project. Because there is not enough information about the network diagram and Activity F, it appears to be noise. The spending efficiency is only getting $0.92 value for every dollar spent. The productivity is 87% of what is planned. The number of stakeholders is insignificant in this question, as is the resource issue on Activity G. What do you focus on first?
Answer	The first area of focus is the schedule because the SPI is 0.87. After that, you focus on the budget because the CPI is 0.92.

Question #4

You have been involved in a project as a Project Manager. After much analysis, arguing, and debate with the 17 stakeholders, the sponsor has made the decision to outsource a key piece of work on the project because of the risk associated with it. This is an example of what?

Breaking down the question	Try your hand at translating this question to see if you are starting to translate PMI fluently.
Translation (Plain English version)	You are the Project Manager. It has been decided that a piece of the work will be outsourced. This is an example of what?
Answer	This is a situational terminology question. They describe a make-or-buy analysis.

3.5   Problem Solving on Situational Questions

The challenge of how to address problems on situational questions is one of the most complicated you will face on the exam. Here, we explain some basic logic you can use to help you determine the person you need to contact for problem resolution, or what you must do before you go to certain parties. Look at the following rules for situational questions.

Situational Question #1

When a problem arises and it doesn't violate the triple constraint, the Project Manager has the authority to approve a solution.

> Example: You are the Project Manager on a project. It has been discovered that testing will begin a week late. Which is the best solution?
>
> A. (Correct) Perform analysis about the delay and if it indeed will not impact the scope, time, or cost of the project, approve it and keep the project running.
> B. Ask senior management for a choice in a solution.
> C. Ignore the testing issue because that part of the project hasn't come up yet.
> D. Ask the sponsor for an opinion about converging system testing and user acceptance testing.

Situational Question #2

When a problem arises and it does violate the triple constraint, senior management or the sponsor must approve the solution. Typically, the Project Manager would not go to senior management or the sponsor for problem resolution without first having potential solutions to present.

> Example: You are the Project Manager on a project. It has been discovered that testing will begin a week late, thereby causing the project finish date to slip a week. Which is the best solution?
>
> A. Perform analysis about the week delay and if it will not impact the scope, time, or cost of the project, approve it and keep the project running.
> B. (Correct) After analyzing the problem and potential solutions, alert senior management to the problem and potential solutions, and implement the solution they recommend.
> C. Ignore the testing issue; that part of the project hasn't come up yet.
> D. Ask the sponsor for an opinion about converging system testing and user acceptance testing.

Situational Question #3

When the customer won't sign off or a similar situation arises, the key solution is to involve senior management. Your role is to inform the client that they must approve something. If they don't approve, you do not pursue the issue; instead, you involve senior management.

> Example: You are a Project Manager on a project awaiting some new positions to be filled. The schedule is already set to include the work of these new resources. The start date of these resources has passed without hearing back from the client on signing approval for these new resources. Who can best resolve this problem?
>
> A. (Correct) Senior management
> B. Project Manager
> C. Sales Executive
> D. Program Manager

Situational Question #4

Generally, the Project Manager does not go to senior management with a problem without first having potential solutions. (The previous rule was an exception.) Going to senior management without a solution is like screaming that the sky is falling. Remember, they hired you to get the work of the project complete, and you are to work through issues instead of running to senior management all the time.

> Example: The project is not progressing well. It is behind schedule and over budget. The Project Manager has determined that the schedule was created without adequate team input and needs to be recreated. Reworking the schedule could effect the overall project finish date. Who can best fix this problem?
>
> A. (Correct) The Project Manager (because the Project Manager needs to put together a new schedule for approval by senior management).
> B. Senior management because senior management needs to approve a violation of the triple constraint
> C. Functional Manager because the Functional Manager is in control of the resources on the schedule
> D. Team member(s) because team members have input to the schedule

Situational Question #5

When asked what would fix a problem, examine the problem and select the answer that will resolve it.

> Example: The project is behind schedule because the key estimator wasn't available when the schedule was created. Senior management is aware of this and has allowed the Project Manager to re-baseline the schedule. What process will fix this problem?
>
> A. Schedule Development
> B. Activity Sequencing
> C. Work Breakdown Structure
> D. (Correct) Schedule Control

Situational Question #6

When asked what would have eliminated the problem, examine the answers and select the answer that indicates the point where the problem had been created.

> Example: The project is behind schedule as the key estimator wasn't available when the schedule was created. Senior management is aware of this and has allowed the Project Manager to re-baseline the schedule. In what process did this problem get created?
>
> A. (Correct) Schedule Development
> B. Activity Sequencing
> C. Work breakdown structure
> D. Schedule Control

Chapter 4

Pre and Post Test

We recommend that you take this test before you start your studies and again after you have gone through this book at least twice. This test lets you see how you respond to 200 questions over four hours. It also serves as an integrated test in which the questions come from a variety of Knowledge Areas similar to the actual exam instead of simply one Knowledge Area (as is the case in each chapter).

4.1 Practice Test Answer Sheets

We recommend that you print answer sheets from the CD or make multiple photocopies of them from this book so you can practice the test as many times as you like.

Chapter Answer Sheet

Topic Name:	Date:
1.	16.
2.	17.
3.	18.
4.	19.
5.	20.
6.	21.
7.	22.
8.	23.
9.	24.
10.	25.
11.	26.
12.	27.
13.	28.
14.	29.
15.	30.

200 Question Practice Test Answer Sheet

Date:		Start Time:		
		Stop Time:		
1.	41.	81.	121.	161.
2.	42.	82.	122.	162.
3.	43.	83.	123.	163.
4.	44.	84.	124.	164.
5.	45.	85.	125.	165.
6.	46.	86.	126.	166.
7.	47.	87.	127.	167.
8.	48.	88.	128.	168.
9.	49.	89.	129.	169.
10.	50.	90.	130.	170.
11.	51.	91.	131.	171.
12.	52.	92.	132.	172.
13.	53.	93.	133.	173.
14.	54.	94.	134.	174.
15.	55.	95.	135.	175.
16.	56.	96.	136.	176.
17.	57.	97.	137.	177.
18.	58.	98.	138.	178.
19.	59.	99.	139.	179.
20.	60.	100.	140.	180.
21.	61.	101.	141.	181.
22.	62.	102.	142.	182.
23.	63.	103.	143.	183.
24.	64.	104.	144.	184.
25.	65.	105.	145.	185.
26.	66.	106.	146.	186.
27.	67.	107.	147.	187.
28.	68.	108.	148.	188.
29.	69.	109.	149.	189.
30.	70.	110.	150.	190.
31.	71.	111.	151.	191.
32.	72.	112.	152.	192.
33.	73.	113.	153.	193.
34.	74.	114.	154.	194.
35.	75.	115.	155.	195.
36.	76.	116.	156.	196.
37.	77.	117.	157.	197.
38.	78.	118.	158.	198.
39.	79.	119.	159.	199.
40.	80.	120.	160.	200.

PMP Exam Success Series: Certification Exam Manual
© 2007 Crosswind Project Management, Inc., www.crosswindpm.com

4.2   200 Question Practice Test

Answers are in section 4.3.

1. You have been the Project Manager on a new project for a foreign company, and the engagement has been successful. In the foreign country, it is customary to show appreciation by presenting a gift, so the company wants to award the Project Manager a new Rolex watch. It will be presented to you at the next meeting. What is the professional and social responsibility for the Project Manager?

   (A) To accept the watch and not offend the company
   (B) To decline the watch because it is against your company policies
   (C) To decline the watch and give it to the president of your company
   (D) To accept the watch and donate it to your favorite charity

2. Retailer USA Company is putting a policy in place to use Just-in-Time (JIT) inventory because its inventory costs are greater than the industry average. The company feels this policy helps minimize excess inventory costs and increase efficiency. What is the amount of inventory needed for this type of process?

   (A) Warehouse capacity
   (B) 25%
   (C) Zero
   (D) Minimal

3. The project charter is used to formally authorize a project. It also provides the following except...

   (A) Gives the project existence
   (B) Defines the project scope statement
   (C) Contains or makes reference to the product description
   (D) Outlines the Project Manager's authority

4. A Project Manager has decided to outsource the installation of router hardware. The buyer has given specific details to the vendor on the schedule and cost of each site. The contract will be a fixed-price contract. What type of scope of work is being provided to the sellers?

   (A) Time and materials
   (B) Functionality
   (C) Design
   (D) Project scope statement

5. Crosswind Custom Homes is building a customer's dream house. However, rain has delayed the finish by two weeks. The Project Manager evaluates the schedule and determines that by crashing, the project could be placed back on schedule. After discussing this with senior management, the Project Manager has decided to crash the project. By doing so, the Project Manager is adding what to the project?

    (A) Time change
    (B) Responsibility
    (C) Cost change
    (D) Scope change

6. The Project Manager is creating an estimate for raised flooring in a data center. The project has four different bids from four vendors. Two of the bids are $1.00/sq. ft higher than the Project Manager wants to pay. The other two bids are $0.05 higher, but fall within the project's cost range of plus or minus 5%. Which of the following types of estimates is the Project Manager using?

    (A) Parametric
    (B) Analogous
    (C) Gut Feel
    (D) Bottom-up

7. You are a Project Manager trying to estimate the duration of a project. You want to use an activity-on-arrow diagram as your network diagram. You decide to use an estimating method with three activities: optimistic, pessimistic, and idealistic. What estimating method do you use?

    (A) PERT
    (B) CPM
    (C) GERT
    (D) None of the above

8. Which of the following best relates to unknown unknowns?

    (A) Schedule reserves
    (B) Risk management
    (C) Contingency reserves
    (D) Management reserves

9. The project management team has just completed the process of creating risk categories for the risks on the project, displaying the risks in a graphical format to help team members have a better understanding of what could happen on the project. What have they created?

    (A) Risk management plan
    (B) Risk breakdown structure
    (C) Risk register
    (D) Prioritized list of quantified risks

10. A new tape backup server has just been purchased for backing up the company's development and release software. The tape backup server costs $85,000, and it was necessary to upgrade the local area network with an Ethernet switch at a cost of $15,000. The Project Manager is told that she needs to set up a depreciation schedule for the tape backup server over a five-year period with a value of $0 at the end of this period. She will use standard depreciation in the calculation. What is the amount per year the server will depreciate?

(A) $14,000
(B) Not enough information
(C) $20,000
(D) $17,000

11. You are a Project Manager assigned to a project that has spent $3,000,000. The original budget was $2,000,000. Senior management is considering stopping this project. What term describes the $1,000,000 that is over budget?

(A) Expected monetary value
(B) The budgeted cost of work performed
(C) Sunk cost
(D) Opportunity cost

12. You are defining the quality standards for the project. You have defined the variables to measure and determined what attributes are important to you. Which of the following is not an attribute?

(A) Inches
(B) Depth
(C) Pounds
(D) Kilometers

13. The Project Manager has completed the project scope on time, but over budget, and is getting signoff from the customer. What is this activity called?

(A) Formal acceptance
(B) Scope Verification
(C) Project archives
(D) Contract closeout

14. As a Project Manager, you are managing a project that is starting to fall behind schedule. By your calculations, the project is one week behind. After meeting with the project team, the team believes that it can make up the one week in the next four weeks and bring the project back on schedule. You are scheduled to report your status to management this week. Which of the following should you do?

(A) Report that the project is behind schedule.
(B) Report that the project is on schedule with no major problems.
(C) Report that the project is behind schedule, but the team has a solution to bring the project back on schedule in the next four weeks.
(D) Report that the project is behind schedule, but will finish on schedule.

15. The project planning is progressing on schedule. The Project Manager and the team meet regularly and are ready to estimate cost. It is important that an accurate estimate be created. What estimating method should the team use?

   (A) Cost estimating
   (B) Bottom-up estimating
   (C) Analogous estimating
   (D) Parametric estimating

16. A Project Manager has completed the Scope Planning and Scope Definition processes. The Project Manager and the project team have spent the last week working on the work breakdown structure. All the following are benefits of using a WBS except...

   (A) Identifies special work packages that can be created outside the WBS, but within the project
   (B) Describes the deliverables of the project
   (C) Provides the justification for staff, cost, and time
   (D) Helps the project team members understand their roles and buy-in on the project

17. The project team has established the anticipated risks for the project, assigned probabilities, impact, and risk owners to them. As the project management plan evolves, where will this information end up?

   (A) Risk list
   (B) Risk trigger
   (C) Risk register
   (D) Risk response

18. The PMO is conducting a meeting and a fellow Project Manager is reporting that the project is behind schedule by two weeks and under budget by $40K. You discover from the project's team members that the project is behind schedule by six weeks and is on budget. What should you do?

   (A) Notify senior management
   (B) Report the Project Manager to PMI
   (C) Ask the PMO to investigate the project status
   (D) Review with the Project Manager how this status was produced

19. You are the Project Manager on a defense project. The buyer wants to get an idea on how much they will pay on cost overruns. With the following variables, calculate the point of total assumption (PTA): Expected Cost=$100,000; Expected Profit=$20,000; Target Price=$120,000; Buyer/Share Ratio=70/30%; Ceiling Price=$140,000; Maximum Overrun=140%.

   (A) $128,571.43
   (B) $122,142.86
   (C) $135,000.00
   (D) $115,714.29

PMP Exam Success Series: Certification Exam Manual
© 2007 Crosswind Project Management, Inc., www.crosswindpm.com

20.   You are a Project Manager at Dewey, Cheatum, and Howe and have been assigned to a major construction project. The project is on schedule and under budget, but you are constantly in conflict with a member of your project team. This conflict is apparent to the team members. According to the PMI Code of Ethics and Professional Conduct, what is the best solution?

(A) Treat the team member as a professional with respect.
(B) Hold a team meeting to vote if the team member should be removed.
(C) Remove the team member from the project.
(D) Avoid the team member as much as possible.

21.   Which of the following roles controls resources and manages a business unit?

(A) Functional management
(B) Senior management
(C) Sponsor
(D) Project management

22.   The Project Manager is creating an estimate for building a company WAN (wide area network). It is something that is new to the Project Manager and his team, and they want to make sure all the work of the project is covered. They decide to create a bottom-up estimate. All the following are advantages of this type of estimate except...

(A) It provides supporting detail of the estimate.
(B) It provides team buy-in when they help create it.
(C) It takes a great amount of time to create.
(D) It has a greater degree of accuracy because of the detail at which it was created.

23.   A Project Manager is assigned to a project that is in the construction phase of a video computer board. The Project Manager is reviewing deliverables and work results to gain formal acceptance. This activity is known as what?

(A) Quality Assurance
(B) Quality Control
(C) Scope Verification
(D) Scope Control

24.   What are the five phases of a project management life cycle?

(A) Initiating, Planning, Executing, Testing, Signoff
(B) Initiating, Planning, Executing, Monitoring and Controlling, Closing
(C) Initiating, Planning, Executing, Testing, Closure
(D) Requirements, System Development, Testing, UAT

25.   What does a responsibility assignment matrix do for the Project Manager?

(A) Shows who is on the project
(B) Shows who is to perform the work and how long it will take
(C) Shows what order the activities come in
(D) Shows who is to perform work in certain areas of the project

26. The consulting company has been awarded a $60M, 10-year contract to provide consulting and support services to an automobile manufacturer. The company realizes that this work is going to require a specific skill set for 500 people. Their current workforce has only 100 people with this skill set. This skill set is somewhat rare and specialized. They have chosen to buy a company much smaller than they are, but this company's core focus is this type of skill set. The company employs 600 people with this skill set. This is an example of what type of risk response strategy?

    (A) Exploit
    (B) Share
    (C) Mitigate
    (D) Accept

27. Which of the following is used to control cost-related items on a project?

    (A) Cost control
    (B) Budget management plan
    (C) Cost management plan
    (D) Work breakdown structure

28. The team has just completed the process of evaluating how the project went. The team members analyzed what worked well and what didn't. They evaluated the Planning and Executing. They documented how the sponsor and senior management supported the project. What have they just completed?

    (A) Lessons learned
    (B) Project closure
    (C) Procurement audit
    (D) Administrative closure

29. All the following are typically part of the project management plan except…

    (A) Work breakdown structure (WBS)
    (B) Responsibility assignment matrix (RAM)
    (C) Organizational breakdown structure (OBS)
    (D) Time management plan

30. Which of the following formulas calculates float?

    (A) Late finish-early start (LF-ES)
    (B) Late finish-early finish (LF-EF)
    (C) Early finish-late start (EF-LS)
    (D) Late finish-late start (LF-LS)

PMP Exam Success Series: Certification Exam Manual
© 2007 Crosswind Project Management, Inc., www.crosswindpm.com

31. Crosswind Custom Homes is building a customer's dream house. However, the city inspector for building permits has been in training for the last two weeks, and he has no backup. His absence causes a delay in the completion of the house. This is an example of what?

(A) Mandatory dependencies
(B) Crashing
(C) Lag
(D) External dependencies

32. The Project Manager is creating an estimate for raised flooring in an IT computer room that is being built. The customer is now creating his budget for the next calendar year and needs this estimate as soon as possible. A senior Project Manager has managed many projects that required raised floors and is considered an expert. You solicit his help on the estimate. Which of the following types of estimates is the Project Manager using?

(A) Parametric
(B) Analogous
(C) Delphi Technique
(D) Bottom-up

33. You are the Project Manager on a defense project. The buyer wants to get an idea on how much they will pay on cost overruns. With the following variables, calculate the point of total assumption: Expected Cost=$500,500; Expected Profit=$150,150; Target Price=$650,650; Buyer/Share Ratio=50/50%; Ceiling Price=$750,750; Maximum Overrun=150%.

(A) $700,700
(B) $650,650
(C) $735,735
(D) $630,630

34. The project selection committee is reviewing two different projects for approval. It has determined that the company has enough resources to do only one project. Project A is worth $500,500 and Project B is worth $510,000. What is the opportunity cost of selecting Project B?

(A) $510,000
(B) $500,500
(C) $550,000
(D) Not enough information

35. The information technology system for the national power grid has been working well. Today, the main control processor crashed, disabling the west coast delivery of power to four states. Implementation of the risk response plan didn't fix the problem. Which of the following steps do they perform first?

(A) Determine why the risk response plan failed.
(B) Fix the problem.
(C) Determine why the problem happened.
(D) Adjust the risk response plan.

36. The software development project is going through Planning. In evaluating the triple constraint, which of the following has the highest priority?

(A) Scope
(B) Time
(C) Cost
(D) They are all equal unless otherwise stated in the project charter.

37. The consulting company has been awarded a $60M contract to provide consulting and support services to a battery company. The consulting company is relatively small, and this contract is bigger than anything they have been awarded to date. To ensure that they can effectively complete the contract and not jeopardize their other work, they have chosen to partner with another company to do the work. This is an example of what type of risk response strategy?

(A) Exploit
(B) Share
(C) Mitigate
(D) Accept

38. Fixed-price contracts are also known as which of the following?

(A) Cost-plus
(B) Lump-sum
(C) Purchase order
(D) Time and materials

39. The client has requested a four-week delay on the project while the company retools its machine lab. This delay was not planned, but the equipment had to be replaced. The company has limited resources. What is the best way to make up the four-week slip?

(A) Fast tracking
(B) Integrated Change Control
(C) Put more resources on the project
(D) Crashing

40. The project team is involved in defining what is needed to ensure quality for the project and is trying to determine what the cost of quality would be for the project. Cost of quality is based on what?

(A) Conformance versus Nonconformance
(B) TQM versus Kaizen
(C) Gold Plating versus Approved Changes
(D) Zero Defects versus Defects

PMP Exam Success Series: Certification Exam Manual
© 2007 Crosswind Project Management, Inc., www.crosswindpm.com

41. You are the Project Manager of an infrastructure project for a wide area network with a one-year schedule as defined by the project management plan. You need a LAN analyzer. During the procurement process, you have decided to rent this equipment. The rental cost is $142 per month. What type of cost is this?

  (A) Indirect
  (B) Direct
  (C) Fixed
  (D) Variable

42. The Project Manager has scheduled weekly status meetings with the team. The meetings have been unorganized with multiple people addressing their own needs and taking longer than planned with no discipline. Which of the following would improve the meetings?

  (A) Create and publish an agenda.
  (B) Create and publish an agenda, and establish the leader of the meeting.
  (C) Send the team to communication training.
  (D) Determine who is in charge of the meeting.

43. The team is involved in defining what is needed to ensure that the quality process will capture the intended results of the testing. This activity is known as what?

  (A) Quality Planning
  (B) Quality Assurance
  (C) Measuring the output of the project
  (D) Quality Control

44. A Project Manager was assigned to manage a project to develop pink widgets for the Project Manager's company. The project will cost the company $650,000 over the next 12 months. It is projected that the widgets will earn the company $20,500 per month. How much time will it take to recover the cost for this project?

  (A) 28 months
  (B) 32 months
  (C) 36 months
  (D) Not enough information

45. A Project Manager has completed the Scope Definition process. The customer and sponsor have shortened the schedule by four weeks and decided to exclude the work breakdown structure. The Project Manager informs the customer and sponsor that, by excluding the WBS, the project could be subjected to many problems. Which of the following is not considered a problem of bypassing the work breakdown structure?

  (A) There are constant changes to the project.
  (B) Planning areas may lack supporting details.
  (C) Budget is not well defined.
  (D) Project may be subject to unforeseen delays.

46. You are doing quality control on a project, trying to determine if a project is producing a low quality or low-grade product. Which statement best describes the differences?

    (A) Low quality is always a problem, but low grade may not be.
    (B) Low quality may not be a problem, but low grade is always a problem.
    (C) Products can have high quality but low grade.
    (D) Products can have low quality but high grade.

47. You are the owner of a construction company. As you begin work on a large building that covers 20,000 square feet, you need to rent a backhoe tractor to clear the property. This is the third time you have needed the backhoe, and you want to know if you should buy or rent it. A new backhoe sells for $19,000 and costs $30 a day to maintain. You can rent one for $125 a day with the maintenance included. How many days would you need to use this tool before it makes sense to buy instead of rent?

    (A) 100 days
    (B) 150 days
    (C) 200 days
    (D) 250 days

48. Which of the following is an example of a lag?

    (A) The latest a telephone system can be ordered from the manufacturer without delaying the project
    (B) The earliest a new Ethernet switch can be ordered from the manufacturer
    (C) The critical path
    (D) The need for concrete to cure an additional day because of the weather before painting the parking lines

49. Activity A is worth $300, is 100% complete, and actually cost $350. Activity B is worth $100, is 95% complete, and actually cost $85 so far. Activity C is worth $200, is 75% complete, and has cost $175 so far. The total budget is $1,500. What is the estimate to complete for the activities listed?

    (A) $1,100.04
    (B) $1,500
    (C) $1,685.39
    (D) $1,075.39

50. The project team is working together on the tollway repaving project. The Project Manager has delivered a report that describes how much work should have been accomplished, how much work is actually accomplished, and the actual cost to complete the work. What type of report is this?

    (A) Earned value report
    (B) Status report
    (C) Variance report
    (D) Progress report

PMP Exam Success Series: Certification Exam Manual
© 2007 Crosswind Project Management, Inc., www.crosswindpm.com

51. Activity A is worth $300, is 100% complete, and actually cost $350. Activity B is worth $100, is 95% complete, and actually cost $85 so far. Activity C is worth $200, is 75% complete, and has cost $175 so far. The total budget is $1,500. What is the cost variance for the activities listed?

    (A) $0.84
    (B) $65.00
    (C) -$65.00
    (D) -$57.50

52. The project Planning is progressing on schedule. The Project Manager and the team meet regularly and are ready to estimate cost. The customer needs an estimate as soon as possible. What estimating method should the team use?

    (A) Cost estimating
    (B) Parametric estimating
    (C) Bottom-up estimating
    (D) Analogous estimating

53. The engineer is considering quitting his engineering job to develop a new memory upgrade project for the new Kiwi computer, an idea he created outside his job. If it sells well, he plans to start his own company and sell them full time. What characteristic is he showing toward risk?

    (A) Risk-averse
    (B) Risk seeker
    (C) Risk-neutral
    (D) To be meeting stockholder expectations

54. You are the Project Manager on a TV transmission tower project. Due to the rough terrain, the scope of the project had to be modified to compensate for the required foundation changes. You need to verify that these changes have been put in place. What best helps you determine this?

    (A) Scope control system
    (B) Project scope statement updates
    (C) Scope management plan
    (D) Scope changes

55. The Project Manager is closing the project and wants to discuss with the project team the success and failures of the project and document this information. This activity is known as what?

    (A) Project archives
    (B) Lessons learned
    (C) Performance Reporting
    (D) Project reports

56. Your project needs some database software but the budget on the project doesn't include this software. You are at the gym after work with a friend from your old job. He has a lot of different types of software and suggests that he can make you a copy of this software that you need. What is the best way to acquire the software?

    (A) Take his copy and use it on your project.
    (B) Order a copy from the company or an authorized reseller.
    (C) Download a copy from a file sharing system.
    (D) Use a demo copy.

57. The engineering team is building a new product. This is a new product type at the company, and the market for the product is new and changes every six months. According to the Product Manager, a key to success is the ability to evolve the Planning as more information about the market is discovered. Which type of scheduling approach best fits this need?

    (A) Rolling wave planning
    (B) Crashing
    (C) Fast tracking
    (D) Precedence diagramming

58. The company is in the testing phase of its project, tracking defects that come in from beta customers who are testing the project. Given the nature of a new project, a variety of defects is being discovered over time. Which chart or diagram helps display these?

    (A) Flowchart
    (B) Pareto chart
    (C) Fishbone diagram
    (D) Run chart

59. The architect has recently been promoted from senior architect to department manager. In this new position, he will be responsible for managing projects and project resources. Over the seven years he has been with the company, he was always ranked as one of the top employees but lacks formal project management training. Which of the following best describes this situation?

    (A) Problem solving
    (B) Equal opportunity employment
    (C) Halo Theory
    (D) Reward power

60. Senior management has asked a Project Manager to set milestones on the current project. What are the characteristics of a milestone?

    (A) The completion of a major event in the project
    (B) The completion of major deliverables
    (C) A duration of zero (0)
    (D) All the answers

PMP Exam Success Series: Certification Exam Manual
© 2007 Crosswind Project Management, Inc., www.crosswindpm.com

61. As a Project Manager, you are managing a multi-story building project for a customer who has requested that you have special marble flooring installed in the entryway. Your father-in-law has been doing floor covering for 20 years and is an expert. You decide to give him the work. This is an example of what?

    (A) Appearance of impropriety
    (B) Conflict of solicitation
    (C) Giving him the work because he is an expert is OK.
    (D) Sole sourcing

62. The Project Manager is creating an estimate for building a company WAN (wide area network). As the Project Manager, you have undertaken the make-or-buy decision and determined that the WAN implementation should be outsourced because your company does not have the expertise. After receiving all the vendor proposals, you find that two of the proposals specify cost-plus-fixed-fee, two other of the vendors specify fixed-price, another two specify cost-plus-incentive-fee, and the last two specify time and materials. Which of the proposals present the least probability of loss for the company?

    (A) Proposals that use fixed-price
    (B) Proposals that use cost-plus-fixed-fee
    (C) Proposals that use time and materials
    (D) Proposals that use cost-plus-incentive-fee

63. Which of the following best shows reporting relationships on a project?

    (A) Staffing management plan
    (B) Resource histogram
    (C) Responsibility assignment matrix
    (D) Organizational breakdown structure (OBS)

64. Activity A is worth $300, is 100% complete, and actually cost $350. Activity B is worth $100, is 95% complete, and actually cost $85 so far. Activity C is worth $200, is 75% complete, and has cost $175 so far. Total budget is $1,500. What is the schedule variance for the activities listed?

    (A) $55.00
    (B) $0.84
    (C) -$55.00
    (D) $0.89

65. You are the Project Manager on a defense project. The buyer wants to get an idea on how much they will pay on cost overruns. With the following variables, calculate the point of total assumption: Expected Cost=$275,000; Expected Profit=$78,750; Target Price=$343,750; Buyer/Share Ratio=65/35%; Ceiling Price=$412,500; Maximum Overrun=150%.

    (A) $380,769.23
    (B) $361,730.77
    (C) $399,807.69
    (D) $342,692.31

66. Calculate the PERT estimate for the following: Pessimistic=20, Optimistic=10, Realistic=17.

(A) 16.67
(B) Not enough information
(C) 15
(D) 16.33

67. Which of the following is not a regulation?

(A) The building code for a city
(B) The documented way to dispose of old paint
(C) The average speed on a highway in a week
(D) The zoning for an industrial area

68. Which of the following is an output of Initiating?

(A) Work results
(B) A signed contract
(C) Corrective action
(D) Assignment of the Project Manager

69. The sponsor on the e-commerce project has just told the Project Manager about a change he wants. He says that the change will cost 20% less and should not cause any problems to the existing environment. Which of the following should concern the Project Manager the most?

(A) Scope impact
(B) Schedule impact
(C) Quality impact
(D) Scope and schedule impact

70. A Project Manager is beginning the solicitation process to find companies that can potentially provide the needed services. The buyer wants to consider only sellers of the services that have met rigid predefined qualifications. What screening mechanism is this?

(A) Advertising
(B) Bidders conference
(C) Weighting system
(D) Qualified sellers list

71. In what Knowledge Area does Activity Resource Estimating occur?

(A) Scope
(B) Human Resource
(C) Time
(D) Procurement

PMP Exam Success Series: Certification Exam Manual
© 2007 Crosswind Project Management, Inc., www.crosswindpm.com

72. The Project Manager is involved in acquiring the project team on a highway expansion project. She is presently discussing salary, working hours, travel, and benefits. What is the key tool she is utilizing?

   (A) Staffing management plan
   (B) Organizational chart
   (C) Project team directory
   (D) Negotiations

73. A project will be using a vendor to purchase infrastructure equipment for a national network upgrade venture for the U.S. government. The government has requested a proposal from prospective sellers of the equipment. What type of document is being provided to the sellers?

   (A) Request for information (RFI)
   (B) Request for proposals (RFP)
   (C) Invitation for bid (IFB)
   (D) Request for quote (RFQ)

74. Calculate the variance for the following: Pessimistic=20, Optimistic=10, Realistic=17.

   (A) 2.78
   (B) 5
   (C) Not enough information
   (D) 5.67

75. Crosswind Custom Homes is building a customer's dream house. However, rain has delayed the finish by two weeks. The schedule shows that the next activity is to install the roof followed by the shingles. This is an example of what?

   (A) Crashing
   (B) Mandatory dependencies
   (C) Discretionary dependencies
   (D) Lag

76. You are beginning a new project and a portion of the development will be created by a foreign company. You are not sure how to do business with this company because it is offshore. What document is best to guide you in this business?

   (A) Company's policies and procedures
   (B) PMI Code of Ethics and Professional Conduct
   (C) Local laws of the offshore company
   (D) Historical information from past projects

77. What is an organization that defines standards, audits projects, and helps mentor Project Managers called?

   (A) Projectized organization
   (B) Balanced matrix organization
   (C) Tight matrix organization
   (D) Project Management Office

78. You are a Project Manager who will be using GERT as an estimating method. By definition, GERT has loops and conditional branches. Which of the following is not a function of GERT analysis?

    (A) Some activities may be performed only in part.
    (B) Some activities may be fast tracked.
    (C) Some activities may be performed more than once.
    (D) Some activities may not be performed.

79. The sponsor plays a key role in project success. Which of the following is the best description of the sponsor?

    (A) Senior management
    (B) Customer
    (C) Product manager
    (D) CIO

80. To develop a call center application for your company, a project requires some new test equipment and a voice over IP system. The finance department explains that this is a capital purchase to be depreciated using the sum of the years digits. This is an example of what?

    (A) Accelerated depreciation
    (B) Standard depreciation
    (C) Straight-line depreciation
    (D) Fixed direct cost

81. Crosswind Custom Homes is building a customer's dream house. However, rain has delayed the finish by two weeks. The Project Manager evaluates the schedule and determines that the electrical and plumbing could occur at the same time instead of right after each other as laid out in the schedule. After discussing this with senior management, the Project Manager has decided to fast track the project. By doing so, the Project Manager adds what to the project?

    (A) Risk
    (B) Scope change
    (C) Responsibility
    (D) Time change

82. The Project Manager and the team have just completed determining what will be done if risk events happen, and who will be responsible for executing those actions. Which of the following roles will be responsible for acting if the risk events happen?

    (A) Risk seeker
    (B) Team lead
    (C) Project Manager
    (D) Risk owner

83.   The finance department is building a call center for its new auto finance division. Given that this is its first venture utilizing a call center, a number of new processes have been created. Which of the following help verify that these processes are being accomplished?

      (A) Process flow
      (B) Checklist
      (C) Quality audit
      (D) Control chart

84.   Your wireless access project is almost complete. You have outsourced the network fine-tuning to an out-of-state company to complete. As the project closes down, what will be completed last?

      (A) Closing the project
      (B) Release of resources
      (C) Assignment of contracts for the next phase
      (D) Contract Closure

85.   The project is going through quality control. Which of the following are used to validate that the output is in compliance with the specifications of the work?

      (A) Inspection
      (B) Checklists
      (C) Rework
      (D) Acceptance decisions

86.   The team is involved in Risk Management Planning. The team members have been meeting to determine their risk approach to the project, as well as identify risks and triggers. The most recent activities they completed created an overall project risk ranking for the project. What process did they just complete?

      (A) Qualitative Risk Analysis
      (B) Risk Identification
      (C) Risk Monitoring and Control
      (D) Risk Mitigation

87.   A Project Manager studying different motivation theories is impressed with one theory which states that people are not motivated by money but by appreciation and working on challenging projects. What theory is the Project Manager referring to?

      (A) McGregor's Theory of X and Y
      (B) Maslow's Hierarchy
      (C) Herzberg's Theory
      (D) None of the answers

88.   What is the main purpose of utilizing a work authorization system?

      (A) To serve as a time-tracking system
      (B) To help ensure that work is done in the appropriate sequence
      (C) To show who is responsible for what work
      (D) To show what work is to be done in the project

89. The project team is planning an upgrade to a client's Web site and infrastructure. During Planning, the team members discover that the lab where the staging server is to reside does not have sufficient space, forcing the client to lease another building. This building will also be shared with another department. What type of cost is this?

(A) Indirect
(B) Direct
(C) Indirect fixed
(D) Variable

90. The project is in a projectized environment. There are significant challenges with the scope of the project. Project personnel have been complaining to senior management about the environment. In this type of environment, who controls the resources?

(A) Project Manager
(B) Functional Manager
(C) Senior management
(D) Project Coordinator

91. You are in the initiation phase of a project and are doing an estimate for a project that requires a major software package for a healthcare system. What is the estimate range to use for this project?

(A) -10% to +25%
(B) -25% to +75%
(C) -5% to +10%
(D) -25% to +85%

92. Activity A is worth $300, is 100% complete, and actually cost $350. Activity B is worth $100, is 95% complete, and actually cost $85 so far. Activity C is worth $200, is 75% complete, and has cost $175 so far. Total budget is $1,500. What is the total earned value for the activities listed?

(A) $550.00
(B) $545.00
(C) $610.00
(D) $600.00

93. The following are forms of contracts except...

(A) Agreement
(B) Purchase order
(C) Memorandum of understanding
(D) Proposal

PMP Exam Success Series: Certification Exam Manual
© 2007 Crosswind Project Management, Inc., www.crosswindpm.com

94. The Project Manager is working with the customer to gain formal acceptance on the project deliverables. The customer is saying that three of the deliverables are not meeting project goals and are unusable in their present form. Upon reviewing documentation, the customer tells the Project Manager that the requirements are not accurate, to meet the needs for which the project was undertaken. Which of the following will help fix this problem?

(A) Create WBS
(B) Scope Control
(C) Scope Definition
(D) Scope Verification

95. You are managing a project and senior management has removed the two previous Project Managers on the project because they could not keep the project on schedule. According to your current project schedule, this project is behind schedule two weeks. As the current Project Manager, you are afraid you will also be removed if you report this status. What is the best response you can tell senior management?

(A) Report the delay to senior management and the reasons.
(B) Tell senior management the project is two weeks behind with a contingency plan.
(C) The schedule is only two weeks behind so you don't report the delay.
(D) Don't report the delay and begin looking for a new job.

96. The client has requested a six-week delay on the project while the company calibrates its test equipment. This delay wasn't planned, but the equipment had to be calibrated. The company has limited resources. This delay is best shown in what?

(A) Responsibility assignment matrix (RAM)
(B) Network diagram
(C) Budget
(D) Work breakdown structure (WBS)

97. In the Communication Model, who is responsible for ensuring that the message is in a clear, understandable format?

(A) Receiver
(B) Both the sender and receiver
(C) Project Manager
(D) Sender

98. Calculate expected monetary value of the following: 0.4 probability of $2,500, 0.3 probability of -$1,200, 0.2 probability of $1,000, 0.1 probability of $3,000.

(A) $2,700
(B) $10,500
(C) $2,500
(D) $1,140

99. The Crosswind multimedia development has recently been awarded a large contract to create a new science fiction series for a well known producer. This requires the company to move into a new office complete with production facilities 500% larger than what it presently has. The schedule is tight for this new project, and there can be no delay. The new facility is behind schedule with the cubicles and network wiring on pace to finish two months late. The company is trying to use an incentive fee to motivate the provider of these services to complete the work as quickly as possible even if it results in a smaller delay. This is an example of what type of risk response?

(A) Avoid
(B) Accept
(C) Transfer
(D) Mitigate

100. All the following are advantages of using a bidders conference except...

(A) Opportunity for vendors to inquire about the procurement
(B) Assurance that vendors have a clear, common understanding of the procurement
(C) Opportunity for vendors to inquire about the bids of other sellers
(D) Opportunity for vendors to respond to questions that have been incorporated into the procurement document

101. The project Planning is progressing on schedule. The Project Manager and the team meet regularly and are ready to estimate cost. In this estimation, what input into the Cost Estimating process will help the team the most?

(A) WBS
(B) Project management plan
(C) Risk list
(D) Network diagram

102. The project has six people on it. Three more are added. What is the total number of communication channels added to the project?

(A) 28 channels
(B) 10 channels
(C) 15 channels
(D) 21 channels

103. The team is involved in defining what is needed to ensure quality for the project, evaluating different tools to use in Quality Planning. All the following tools are used in Quality Planning except...

(A) Cost-benefit analysis
(B) Quality control data
(C) Flowcharts
(D) Design of experiments

104. You are the Project Manager for a highway construction project. You have just finished putting together all the various plans into an integrated complete document. What step have you just completed?

    (A) Developing the project management plan
    (B) Executing the project management plan
    (C) Developing the schedule
    (D) Signing off the project charter

105. Which of the following formulas shows the remaining amount to be spent on the project based on current spending efficiency?

    (A) SV = EV - PV
    (B) EAC = BAC / CPI
    (C) CV = EV - AC
    (D) ETC = EAC - AC

106. In reporting variance on the project, the Project Manager needs which of the following?

    (A) Status reports
    (B) Baseline measurements
    (C) Project archives
    (D) Change request

107. Market conditions, time limitations, budget amounts, and number of people available for the project are examples of what?

    (A) Assumptions
    (B) Constraints
    (C) Economic consumption
    (D) Strategic planning

108. The project team is involved in decomposition of the work of the project. What two things will they create as a result of decomposition on the project?

    (A) Activity lists and activity duration estimates
    (B) Work packages and activity lists
    (C) Work packages and activity sequences
    (D) Activity resource estimates and activity sequences

109. You are managing an IT project and senior management has come to you with a high priority project that could make the company significant revenue. According to your current project schedule, the IT project is scheduled to be completed in four weeks. Senior management has also provided you with a schedule and the scope of the project they described. According to professional and social responsibility, how should you respond to senior management?

    (A) Inform senior management you can work on the project once you have completed your current project.
    (B) Begin execution of this project.
    (C) Begin implementation of project as soon as possible.
    (D) Decline the project because, as a Project Manager, you have not created the schedule and budget, and your current project is still in execution.

110. The team implemented a risk response plan when a vendor was unable to fulfill a contract commitment. The response was to choose another vendor. However, in this industry, it's hard to find a good company, and the one selected isn't that much better. The new company is somewhat better at meeting the terms of the contract, but still has some issues from time to time. What best describes these issues?

    (A) Secondary risk
    (B) Workaround
    (C) Residual risk
    (D) Risk response plan

111. Which process involves user cost estimates and the schedule to determine when these costs are expected to occur during the project?

    (A) Cost Baseline
    (B) Cost Budgeting
    (C) Cost Control
    (D) Cost Estimating

112. In what Process Group does Contract Administration occur?

    (A) Monitoring and Controlling
    (B) Closing
    (C) Executing
    (D) Planning

PMP Exam Success Series: Certification Exam Manual
© 2007 Crosswind Project Management, Inc., www.crosswindpm.com

113. The Crosswind multimedia development has recently been awarded a large contract to create a new science fiction series for a well known producer. This requires the company to move into a new office complete with production facilities 500% larger than what it presently has. The schedule is tight for this new project, and there can be no delay. The new facility is behind schedule with the cubicles and network wiring is on pace to finish two months late. The company is attempting to validate data. If this delay proves imminent, it plans to move to a new building temporarily with the infrastructure that will meet its needs until the building is complete. This is an example of what type of risk response?

     (A) Accept
     (B) Avoid
     (C) Mitigate
     (D) Transfer

114. A call center is being built to support a new product at a national telephone company. The company doesn't have data on how long it will take to sign up customers via the call center. This data is important because it will help drive the number of employees needed in the call center. The Project Manager remembers that a similar call center project was completed last year and begins to review data from the previous year. This is a best example of what?

     (A) Historical information
     (B) Lessons learned
     (C) Constraints
     (D) Assumptions

115. Activity A is worth $300, is 100% complete, and actually cost $350. Activity B is worth $100, is 95% complete, and actually cost $85 so far. Activity C is worth $200, is 75% complete, and has cost $175 so far. Total budget is $1,500. What is the estimate at completion for the activities listed?

     (A) $1,704.55
     (B) $0.88
     (C) $1,685.39
     (D) $185.39

116. Activity A is worth $300, is 100% complete, and actually cost $350. Activity B is worth $100, is 95% complete, and actually cost $85 so far. Activity C is worth $200, is 75% complete, and has cost $175 so far. Total budget is $1,500. What is the cost performance index for the activities listed?

     (A) 1.16
     (B) 1.12
     (C) 0.84
     (D) 0.89

117. A Project Manager has completed the Scope Definition process. The customer and sponsor have shortened the schedule by four weeks and decided to exclude the work breakdown structure. The Project Manager informs the customer and sponsor that this process creates the work breakdown structure for their project. Which answer best explains why the WBS is so important to a project?

(A) It provides a hierarchical diagram of the project.
(B) It is the foundation of planning for the project.
(C) It provides templates that can be reused on other projects.
(D) It helps in team commitment to the project.

118. What is used to define the accounts that the WBS and organizational structures align to for project cost tracking?

(A) Work packages
(B) Chart of accounts
(C) Cost estimates
(D) Cost baseline

119. A contract is a legal agreement between a buyer and a seller. There are five components of a contract. Capacity and consideration are two of five components. Which of the following is not a component of a contract?

(A) Negotiation
(B) Legal purpose
(C) Acceptance
(D) Offer

120. You are doing some analysis associated with project selection. There is a lot of debate concerning which projects to select. You have the following to choose from: Project A with an IRR of 10.5%, Project B with an IRR of 17%, Project C with an IRR of 14%, and Project D with an IRR of 12%. If you can select only one project, which do you choose?

(A) Project A
(B) Project B
(C) Project C
(D) Project D

121. Which of the following roles helps support the project and resolves resource conflicts?

(A) Functional management
(B) Senior management
(C) Sponsor
(D) Project management

122. Activity-on-arrow diagramming uses which of the following (What is the best answer)?

(A) Finish-to-start
(B) Start-to-finish
(C) PERT
(D) Finish-to-start and PERT

PMP Exam Success Series: Certification Exam Manual
© 2007 Crosswind Project Management, Inc., www.crosswindpm.com

123. The company is implementing a new project management approach. In the past, its projects have been disorganized, not in alignment with business goals, and not focused on interactivity between the projects where applicable. It wants to have a better focus on grouping-related projects together by business unit and product lines. Which of the following best describe what it is trying to accomplish?

(A) Project management
(B) Operations management
(C) Management by objectives
(D) Portfolio management

124. A Project Manager is-progressively elaborating and documenting the project work. With help for the project charter and product description, the Project Manager has defined the scope of the project. The Project Manager is performing what process?

(A) Scope Verification
(B) Scope Control
(C) Scope Planning
(D) Scope Definition

125. The project management plan contains all the following except…

(A) The schedule
(B) Team development
(C) The change control system
(D) Staffing management plan

126. Your company is evaluating two projects for consideration. Project A has a 40% probability of a $25,000 loss and a 60% probability of a $650,000 gain. Project B has a 30% probability of a $15,000 loss and a 70% probability of a $570,000 gain. Which of the projects do you select based on the greatest expected monetary value?

(A) Project A and B are of even value
(B) Project A
(C) The expected monetary value is not high enough on either to make a selection
(D) Project B

127. The manufacturing company has added a new line for its electronic assembly business. It involves new technology to build printed circuit boards more quickly and with fewer errors. The company anticipates that this new technology will allow it to make a greater type of products and improve the efficiency of its output. The company is also increasing the amount of insurance it has on its main facility because there has been flooding in the area in recent years from excessive rain. Adding this insurance is an example of what?

(A) Business risk
(B) Insurable risk
(C) ISO 9000
(D) Conformance to quality

128. A close friend of yours is being investigated by PMI for the number of experience hours given on the certification application. You know he reported invalid hours on the application. PMI has been trying to contact you in this investigation. Which of the following best describes what you should do?

(A) Tell PMI that you have no knowledge of the allegation.
(B) Explain to PMI that he is your close friend and that you would rather not testify against him.
(C) Contact PMI and cooperate with the investigation.
(D) Avoid any contact by PMI so you do not have to testify against your close friend.

129. The team has an approved project charter and has started planning, determining potential risks that could occur on the project. Which of the following best describe project risk?

(A) It can be a negative event only.
(B) It can be a positive event only.
(C) It can be either a negative or positive event.
(D) It can be something that has already happened.

130. You are the Project Manager working with the customer on a call center implementation. You are required to purchase and integrate a workflow software product into the call center. As the Project Manager, you want one price from the vendors for the purchase and implementation of this product. What type of document should be used?

(A) Invitation for bid
(B) Request for quote
(C) Request for proposal
(D) Request for information

131. The Crosswind multimedia development has recently been awarded a large contract to create a new science fiction series for a well known producer. This requires the company to move into a new office complete with production facilities 500% larger than what it presently has. The schedule is tight for this new project, and there can be no delay. The new facility is behind schedule with the cubicles and network wiring on pace to finish two months late. If this can't be done on time and slips two months, the company has decided there is nothing it can do, and it will simply deal with the consequences. This is an example of what type of risk response?

(A) Accept
(B) Avoid
(C) Mitigate
(D) Transfer

PMP Exam Success Series: Certification Exam Manual
© 2007 Crosswind Project Management, Inc., www.crosswindpm.com

132. You are the Project Manager working with the customer on a call center implementation. You are required to purchase and integrate a workflow software product into the center. A contract is signed with a vendor and work has begun. Halfway through the project, the customer decides to add features to the workflow software. This addition of features will require changes to the signed contract. Who has the authority to change the contract?

(A) Sponsor
(B) Project Manager
(C) Customer
(D) Contract administrator

133. The project team has begun development on a very important project in a new evolving technology market. Because the market is so volatile, the product they are creating doesn't necessarily have all the details defined before Planning begins. The team chooses to take an approach to plan as much as they can and begin to create work based on that effort, while continuing the Planning as they learn more about the project. Which of the following best describes the approach?

(A) Extreme programming
(B) Progressive elaboration
(C) Project management
(D) Total Quality Management

134. You are the Project Manager on a DOD project, and you are creating a network diagram. Activity A (four days) and Activity B (six days) can start immediately. Activity C (five days) can start after Activity A is complete. Activity D (four days) and Activity F (two days) can start after Activity B is complete. Activity E (four days) can start after Activity C and Activity D are complete. Activity G (five days) can start after Activity D and Activity F are complete. When Activity E and Activity G are complete, the project is done. What is the critical path?

(A) ACE
(B) BDE
(C) BDG
(D) BFG

135. Using the original network diagram question, select the slack of Activity E.

(A) Two days
(B) Zero
(C) Four days
(D) One day

136. In the original network diagram question, if Activity G decreases from five days to one, what is the critical path, and what is the length?

(A) ACE, 14 days
(B) BDG, 12 days
(C) BDE, 14 days
(D) BFG, 13 days

137. A Project Manager has completed the Scope Definition process. The customer and sponsor have shortened the schedule by four weeks and decided to exclude the work breakdown structure. What is the best action the Project Manager should take?

(A) Begin execution of the project.
(B) Provide the customer and sponsor an updated schedule and budget.
(C) Call a meeting and notify the team of the change in schedule.
(D) Discuss with the customer and sponsor the ramifications of excluding the WBS.

138. Which of the following breakdown structures are used in project scope management?

(A) Bill of materials
(B) Risk breakdown structure
(C) Work breakdown structure
(D) Resource breakdown structure

139. All the following are needed for Scope Planning except...

(A) Work breakdown structure
(B) Project charter
(C) Preliminary project scope statement
(D) Project management plan

140. The construction project is almost finished. The team is involved in many different activities to close the project. The team members are-creating project archives. All the following are examples of project archives except...

(A) Contracts
(B) Financial records
(C) Government clearance applications
(D) Internal project documentation

141. The professional and social responsibility of a Project Manager is described in the PMI Code of Ethics and Professional Conduct. A PMP has responsibilities to the profession, to customers, and to the public. Which is not a professional and social responsibility of the Project Manager?

(A) Adhering to time, cost, and scope as specified by senior management
(B) Following the company's project management processes
(C) Reporting a violation
(D) Balancing stakeholders' interest

142. A project will be using a vendor to install fire-extinguishing equipment in a large twenty-floor building. The buyer is requesting how the different vendors will do this work and how much will it cost. What type of document will be used to solicit this information?

(A) Request for information (RFI)
(B) Request for proposals (RFP)
(C) Invitation for bid (IFB)
(D) Request for quote (RFQ)

PMP Exam Success Series: Certification Exam Manual
© 2007 Crosswind Project Management, Inc., www.crosswindpm.com

143. The project management team is working in the Executing phase of the project. There are two sponsors and 14 stakeholders on the project. Which of the following is the most likely to focus on communication at this point in the project to ensure the project achieves the quality standards established in Planning?

(A) At key interface points where the various work packages come together
(B) During revision planning
(C) When the change control board (CCB) meets
(D) In negotiating the Project Manager assignment

144. A Project Manager is creating a network diagram and needs to show a dependency between activities with no work or time. All the following network diagram techniques display this dependency except...

(A) Activity-on-line (AOL)
(B) Arrow diagramming method (ADM)
(C) Activity-on-arrow (AOA)
(D) Activity-on-node (AON)

145. A Project Manager has been assigned to manage a project that requires two development teams. One team will create the server software and is local, and the other team will create the client software and resides in a foreign country. For the most recent 10 conference calls with the foreign country, the foreign team is consistently 15 minutes late to the meeting. How should the Project Manager handle this problem?

(A) Report this to senior management.
(B) Review the customs and traditions of the foreign country.
(C) Call the development manager of the foreign country.
(D) Ignore the problem.

146. Project Planning is ongoing as the team analyzes how long it will take to process a customer through the new call center. This analysis will help them determine how many employees to have in the call center based on their sales projections. This is an example of what?

(A) Constraints
(B) Assumptions
(C) Strategic planning
(D) Operations management

147. You are the Project Manager on the development of a 4-way fully redundant computer system for the government. The government has been very concerned about the correctness and acceptance of the work results. You are not sure what the government is saying so you review your *PMBOK Guide*. What areas below will likely be involved in attaining what the government is concerned about?

(A) Scope Control and Scope Verification
(B) Administrative closure and Quality Assurance
(C) Quality Planning and Quality Control
(D) Scope Verification and Quality Control

148. A risk rating matrix is used in which of the following processes?

    (A) Workarounds
    (B) Risk triggers
    (C) Qualitative risk analysis
    (D) Expected monetary value (EMV)

149. Calculate the standard deviation for the following: Pessimistic=20, Optimistic=10, Realistic=17.

    (A) 6
    (B) Not enough information
    (C) 5.67
    (D) 1.67

150. The project has had some challenges with team ownership of work on the project. The Project Manager has been challenged with continually having to tell the team what to do, and management feels that the team is unmotivated. This is an example of what?

    (A) Theory X environment
    (B) Theory Y environment
    (C) Theory Z environment
    (D) Bad performance

151. As a Project Manager, you are managing a project that has many deliverables from outside vendors. One vendor has been in negotiations with a union that could cause the vendor to stop production on one of your deliverables. A rumor is out that the vendor's plant will be shutting down because of a strike. What is the best course of action you should take?

    (A) Contact the vendor and discuss this problem.
    (B) Start contacting other vendors as a backup plan.
    (C) Change vendors as soon as one is found.
    (D) Initiate the risk response plan created for this vendor.

152. Activity A is worth $300, is 100% complete, and actually cost $350. Activity B is worth $100, is 95% complete, and actually cost $85 so far. Activity C is worth $200, is 75% complete, and has cost $175 so far. Total budget is $1,500. What is the variance at completion for the activities listed?

    (A) $1,000
    (B) -$185.39
    (C) $1,185.39
    (D) $690.39

153. You are a Project Manager of a home remodeling project. The budget at completion for this project is $56,000. By looking at your schedule, you should be 55% complete, but you are only 40% done. What is your earned value?

    (A) $22,400
    (B) $22,000
    (C) $30,800
    (D) $30,400

154. You are doing Quality Planning on a project. The sponsor puts into the project charter that the quality standard wanted on the project is +/- 3 Sigma. This value translates to what percentage?

    (A) 68.26%
    (B) 95.46%
    (C) 50%
    (D) 99.73%

155. A large part of a Project Manager's time is spent communicating. What is the main benefit of this activity to the project?

    (A) A detailed project file
    (B) A greater emphasis on successful integration of the various pieces of the project
    (C) A Theory Y management style
    (D) An accurate communications management plan

156. As a Project Manager, you are managing a project that has many deliverables from outside contractors. One contractor forgot to acquire a building permit for plumbing work to be done on the project. The city building inspector is now requesting to see the building permit. Who is ultimately responsible for acquiring the building permit?

    (A) Contractor
    (B) Project Manager
    (C) Plumber
    (D) City inspector

157. Which of the following is an advantage of a functional organization?

    (A) Business unit competency
    (B) Optimization for a single focus on the project
    (C) Having to obtain approval from project management
    (D) Having a place to go when the project starts

158. A Project Manager has completed the Scope Definition process and is now-creating the work breakdown structure. The Project Manager and the project team have spent the last week working on the work breakdown structure. They have broken down the WBS to an appropriate level of decomposition. Which of the following best describes this?

    (A) Breaking down work where it's completely and clearly defined
    (B) Breaking down work where it's budgeted and scheduled
    (C) Breaking down work where it's budgeted, scheduled, and completely and clearly defined
    (D) Breaking down work where the bottom levels of the WBS represent work packages

159. The project is going well until a stakeholder requests a significant change based on a modification in the stakeholder's business process. The change could totally alter the work of the project. The change request and its impact analysis are going before the change control board for review and potential approval. What is the purpose of the change control board?

    (A) To work with the change control manager for analyzing changes
    (B) To analyze changes that are requested for the project
    (C) To eliminate as many changes as possible on the project
    (D) To control change by approval of needed changes and rejection of unneeded changes to the project

160. You are the Project Manager on a software game project and are in the initiation phase. During a team meeting, a Functional Manager arrives to see if the project meets company goals. The Functional Manager will report this finding back to senior management to determine if the project should continue or be cancelled. What is this process called?

    (A) Delphi technique
    (B) Management by objectives
    (C) Return on investment
    (D) Management product analysis

161. A Project Manager has been assigned to manage a project to develop digital signal processor for a company that does not have this expertise. The project is two weeks ahead of schedule and under budget. After calculating the estimate at completion, the Project Manager finds that the project will be $124,403 under budget. What should the Project Manager do?

    (A) Implement gold plating to make up for the difference.
    (B) Bill the customer for the total approved contracted amount.
    (C) Report the current baseline project status and budget to the customer.
    (D) Report the project status and budget to the customer.

162. The Project Manager is reviewing testing output. Generally, the data looks good. He does observe seven consecutive data points on one side of the mean in a couple of areas on the control chart. What is this called?

    (A) A violation of the Seven Run Rule
    (B) Lucky Seven Gets Eleven
    (C) Acceptable measurements
    (D) Too loose of specification limits

PMP Exam Success Series: Certification Exam Manual
© 2007 Crosswind Project Management, Inc., www.crosswindpm.com

163. As a Project Manager you are managing a project that has many requirements. The project is for one of your high profile customers, one who spends more than $5,000,000 a year with your company. To attain customer satisfaction, what must be met?

    (A) Completing the project with the product having inherent characteristics that fulfill the requirements that it was to be built around
    (B) Completing products requirements
    (C) Completing the project on schedule and on budget
    (D) Completing the project's scope

164. You own a construction company. As you begin work on a large building that covers 20,000 square feet, you need to rent a backhoe tractor to clear the property. This is the third time you have needed the backhoe, and you want to know if you should buy or rent it. A new backhoe sells for $19,000 and costs $30 a day to maintain. You can rent one for $125 a day with the maintenance included. Which type of contract would be used to purchase the backhoe?

    (A) Purchase order
    (B) Fixed-price-economic-price-adjust
    (C) Fixed-price
    (D) Time and materials

165. The Project Manager has asked the software developer to report on what is keeping him from completing his project activities. The developer keeps delaying his answer to the Project Manager. Finally, the Project Manager tells him to stop anything else and do just what is needed on the project. This is an example of what type of conflict resolution technique?

    (A) Penalty
    (B) Smoothing
    (C) Forcing
    (D) Formal

166. A Project Manager has been assigned to manage a project to develop a digital signal processor in a foreign country. The Project Manager must be on-site for six months and is having problems adjusting to this job. What could cause this problem?

    (A) Cost differences
    (B) Time difference
    (C) Language differences
    (D) Culture differences

167. You are managing a database warehouse project and senior management has come to you with a high priority project that could make the company significant revenue. According to your current project schedule, the database warehouse project is scheduled to be completed in four weeks. What is the best response you can tell senior management?

    (A) Managing both projects as requested by senior management
    (B) Telling senior management that you will consider the project once it has a project charter
    (C) Assigning the Functional Manager on the project to finish the current project
    (D) Implementing crashing and fast tracking to complete your current project ahead of schedule so you can start immediately on this project

168. Float on a network diagram is also known as what?

    (A) Slack
    (B) GERT
    (C) Lag
    (D) PERT

169. A $6B company is implementing formal project management in its organization. It has decided to implement a Project Management Office (PMO). In the creation of this structure, which of the following is the best option to have in place to help ensure success of the organization?

    (A) A solid time-reporting system for all the team members
    (B) Competent Project Managers
    (C) A detailed set of templates
    (D) Clearly defined goals and objectives for the PMO

170. A retail expansion project is going relatively well, but the people doing work on the project are complaining that it seems as though they answer to two bosses on the project, each with conflicting agendas. This is an example of what type of project environment?

    (A) Functional
    (B) Matrix
    (C) Tight matrix
    (D) Projectized

171. You are a Project Manager starting negotiations with a vendor. In the negotiations, you are aware that the vendor has used a number of negotiation strategies. You remember these from your PMP class and ask the vendor to be fair and reasonable. All the following are negotiation strategies except…

    (A) Deadline
    (B) Withdrawal
    (C) Force majeure
    (D) Lying

172. You are doing Quality Planning on a project, discussing with the sponsor the probabilities of finishing the project on schedule. There is some confusion about the sum of all probabilities and probabilities and impact. What must the sum of all probabilities equal?

    (A) 99.9997%
    (B) 100%
    (C) 99.73%
    (D) 68.26%

173. Which of the following best describes a unilateral contract?

    (A) Statement of work
    (B) Purchase order
    (C) Time and materials
    (D) Cost-plus

PMP Exam Success Series: Certification Exam Manual
© 2007 Crosswind Project Management, Inc., www.crosswindpm.com

174. The civil engineering project has been relatively smooth. The cost performance index is presently 0.93 and the schedule performance index is 0.89. Risk could have been managed better from the start of this project. 75% through the execution of the project management plan, the Project Manager assigned three people to do nothing but monitor for risks and work with the people who will implement the risk response plans. What are these people called?

(A) Risk-averse
(B) Sponsor
(C) Risk owners
(D) Project Manager

175. The Project Manager and team are planning a banking software project. They are discussing what could go differently than planned on the project. They are also trying to identify warning signs which show that these events could be on the verge of occurring. What are these warning signs called?

(A) Risk analysis
(B) Triggers
(C) Problem solving
(D) Risks

176. The database project is approximately 85% complete. The project has had its challenges. As of the last status report, the project appears to be on track regarding cost, schedule, and scope. Senior management lets you know that the sponsor has some very serious concerns about the project. You don't understand why, based on the last status report. What is the best action to take first?

(A) Ignore senior management because the project is in good shape.
(B) Meet with the sponsor to determine the sponsor's concerns.
(C) Tell senior management that the project is in good shape.
(D) Evaluate the schedule and budget to verify the triple constraint health of the project.

177. The quality team is having problems getting the product to test per the requirements and test plan. The results are very uncharacteristic. The team suspects that there are a couple of pieces of the project not interacting as planned with each other. Which of the following could show if this is the case?

(A) Pareto diagram
(B) Run chart
(C) Scatter diagram
(D) Control chart

178. The project is in the phase of doing procurement audits. It is important to identify successes and failures of the procurement process. This identification is important for formal acceptance and closure. What process is the project in?

(A) Quality Assurance
(B) Closing
(C) Close Project
(D) Contract Closure

179. The IT initiative project is on schedule and under budget. The customer is pleased but wants a scope change. As a result, a new team is brought in to help the existing team implement this scope change. Before the team arrives, senior management wants to see where the project stands. Which of the following do you show them?

    (A) Milestone chart
    (B) Gantt chart
    (C) Work breakdown structure
    (D) Network diagram

180. A new call center is being built to support a new product at a national telephone company. The company doesn't have any data on how long it will take to sign up customers via the call center. This data is important because it will help drive the number of employees needed in the call center. The company performs some tests to determine how long it will take to sign up customers. These tests must be completed and the data analyzed three weeks before the call center comes online. This is an example of what?

    (A) Historical information
    (B) Product analysis
    (C) Constraints
    (D) Assumptions

181. The team is determining what is needed on the project, focusing on developing a product based on the customer-defined requirements. What is this activity called?

    (A) Meeting the customers needs
    (B) Scope verification
    (C) Definition of quality
    (D) Qualitative analysis

182. Which of the following are examples of non-competitive forms of procurement?

    (A) Sole source
    (B) Open source
    (C) Source selection
    (D) Qualified sellers list

183. As a Project Manager, you are managing a project that has many requirements. The project is for a high profile customer that spends more that $5,000,000 a year with your company. You have completed this project on schedule and on budget. The customer is not pleased with the product that was built. What should you do?

    (A) Review the scope and determine why it did not satisfy the customer.
    (B) Refund 10% of the cost of the project back to the customer.
    (C) Hold a project risk meeting to determine why the project does not satisfy the customer.
    (D) Hold a project quality meeting to determine why the project does not satisfy the customer.

PMP Exam Success Series: Certification Exam Manual
© 2007 Crosswind Project Management, Inc., www.crosswindpm.com

184. All the following are correct regarding risk triggers except...

   (A) A trigger does not mean a risk will occur.
   (B) A trigger comes before a risk.
   (C) A trigger is an indicator that a risk event could occur.
   (D) A trigger is an indicator that a risk event will occur.

185. You are a Project Manager at Dewey, Cheatum, and Howe and assigned to a major construction project. The project is on schedule and under budget, but you are constantly in conflict with a member of your project team. This team member is sabotaging the project. What is the best solution to resolve this problem?

   (A) Firing the team member from the project as soon as possible
   (B) Reporting this problem to senior management
   (C) Reporting this problem to senior management with a solution of replacing this team member
   (D) Holding a team meeting to vote if the team member should be removed

186. A project will be using a company to provide technicians for a national network upgrade project. Presently, the Project Manager is in contract negotiation with a vendor and the negotiations have been very difficult. In what process is the Project Manager involved?

   (A) Plan Contracting
   (B) Plan Purchases and Acquisitions
   (C) Select Sellers
   (D) Request Seller Responses

187. On a retail construction project, the team is sizeable, and controlling communication has been a challenge. The Project Coordinator has been used to help with this problem. What is one of the main differences between the Project Coordinator and the Project Expeditor?

   (A) The Project Expeditor is another title for the Project Manager.
   (B) The Project Coordinator has decision-making ability.
   (C) The Project Expeditor is another title for Project Coordinator.
   (D) The Project Expeditor has decision-making ability.

188. A contract has been signed and is expected to cost $750K over a one-year engagement. At project completion, the actual cost is $700K, but the project is behind schedule due to a delay in shipping. There is a 60/40% share for any cost savings. What is the total value of the contract?

   (A) $730K
   (B) $750K
   (C) $700K because the project was behind schedule
   (D) $720K

189. A change control document on a project is viewed as what type of communication?

    (A) Formal written
    (B) Formal
    (C) Verbal
    (D) Contract

190. You are a Project Manager trying to decide what quality approach to implement at your company. You have decided that it is in the best interest of the company to do testing while in the developing phase to get immediate feedback. This philosophy is known as what?

    (A) Quality Assurance
    (B) Quality Management Plan
    (C) Total Quality Management
    (D) ISO 9000 quality system

191. Crosswind Custom Homes is building a customer's dream house. However, rain has delayed the finish by two weeks. The Project Manager evaluates the schedule and determines that the electrical and plumbing could occur at the same time instead of right after each other, as laid out in the schedule. This is an example of what?

    (A) Mandatory dependencies
    (B) Crashing
    (C) Lag
    (D) Discretionary dependencies

192. What type of contract provides the buyer with the most risk and the seller with the least risk?

    (A) Fixed-price
    (B) Time and materials
    (C) Cost-plus-fixed-fee
    (D) Cost-plus-percentage of cost

193. Which of the following is an output of a change control system?

    (A) Change requests
    (B) Approved changes
    (C) Impact analysis
    (D) Signoff

194. The professional and social responsibility of a Project Manager has many responsibilities to the profession. A PMP has responsibilities to the profession, to customers, and to the public. Which is not a professional and social responsibility of the Project Manager?

    (A) Complying with laws, regulations, and ethical standards
    (B) Reporting accurate, truthful information
    (C) Disclosing conflict of interest to clients, customers, owners, or contractors.
    (D) Creating a project charter that has a win-win situation for your company and your customer

PMP Exam Success Series: Certification Exam Manual
© 2007 Crosswind Project Management, Inc., www.crosswindpm.com

195. You are the finance controller with your company. Your job is to analyze projects when they close. This could be the result of when a project is complete or by any other means. When do you expect to close a project?

(A) When a project is cancelled
(B) When a project runs out of money
(C) When a project completes Scope Verification
(D) All the answers

196. You are the Project Manager for a project that has many deliverables. One deliverable is a new version of an Ethernet switch. You have completed the project on time and on budget. A vendor is now starting the rollout of the new Ethernet switch to your customers. The vendor has scheduled you to help with the rollout. What is your response to the vendor?

(A) Ask for a schedule to see what the timelines are for each installation.
(B) Contact the vendor to discuss the financial cost for your help.
(C) Consult your manager on your schedule.
(D) Tell the vendor that the scope of the project has been fulfilled, the project is closed, and you are no longer available.

197. Project Scope Management is characterized by processes in the Planning, as well as the Monitoring and Controlling phases. Which group of processes defines project scope management?

(A) Initiation, Scope Planning, Scope Definition, Scope Verification, Scope Management
(B) Scope Forecasting, Scope Definition, Scope Verification, Scope Control
(C) Scope Planning, Scope Definition, Create WBS, Scope Verification, Scope Control
(D) Scope Planning, Scope Description, Scope Verification, Integrated Change Control

198. The team is involved in defining what is needed to ensure quality for its project. One team member says, "Do it right the first time." Another team member says, "Let's incorporate a method that reduces errors and helps the company make money." What best describes this process?

(A) Kaizen
(B) TQM
(C) Fitness for Use
(D) Zero Defects

199. The Project Manager has been negotiating with a vendor for the last two months. The vendor received the statement of work and has responded with a proposal using cost-plus-fixed-fee. The Project Manager answers back with a letter of intent. Why did the Project Manager send this letter?

(A) The Project Manager plans to request a bid from the vendor.
(B) The Project Manager plans to buy from the vendor.
(C) The Project Manager plans to sue the vendor.
(D) The Project Manager plans to buy the vendor.

200. You are the Project Manager on a project. You have the work breakdown structure and have begun subdividing the project work packages into smaller, more manageable components. The output from this process is critical for creating the network diagram and duration estimates. What process are you executing and what is the output?

(A) Activity Sequencing and network diagram
(B) Activity Definition and activity list
(C) Activity Duration Estimating and duration estimates
(D) Schedule Development and project schedule

PMP Exam Success Series: Certification Exam Manual
© 2007 Crosswind Project Management, Inc., www.crosswindpm.com

4.3   200 Question Practice Test Key

1.   You have been the Project Manager on a new project for a foreign company, and the engagement has been successful. In the foreign country, it is customary to show appreciation by presenting a gift, so the company wants to award the Project Manager a new Rolex watch. It will be presented to you at the next meeting. What is the professional and social responsibility for the Project Manager?

Correct Answer: (B) To decline the watch because it is against your company policies
Explanation: Professional and Social Responsibility dictates that a PMP is not to be put into a position where there may be a conflict of interest. All other answers describe actions that conflict with the company's policies on accepting gifts. [section 15.2.1]

2.   Retailer USA Company is putting a policy in place to use Just-in-Time (JIT) inventory because its inventory costs are greater than the industry average. The company feels this policy helps minimize excess inventory costs and increase efficiency. What is the amount of inventory needed for this type of process?

Correct Answer: (C) Zero
Explanation: The amount of inventory needed for Just-in-Time (JIT) inventory is optimally zero days, implying that inventory arrives when needed. [section 10.8.7]

3.   The project charter is used to formally authorize a project. It also provides the following except...

Correct Answer: (B) Defines the project scope statement
Explanation: The project scope statement is an output from the Scope Definition process. The other answers are included in the project charter. [section 6.3.1, section 7.2]

4.   A Project Manager has decided to outsource the installation of router hardware. The buyer has given specific details to the vendor on the schedule and cost of each site. The contract will be a fixed-price contract. What type of scope of work is being provided to the sellers?

Correct Answer: (C) Design
Explanation: A design scope of work shows specifically what is to be created. The functionality scope of work shows the general functional specifications that the outcome of the project needs to have when complete. A time and materials (T&M) is a contract used for smaller projects or staff augmentation. A project scope statement defines exactly what it is being created or accomplished by the procurement initiatives. [section 14.1.6]

5.   Crosswind Custom Homes is building a customer's dream house. However, rain has delayed the finish by two weeks. The Project Manager evaluates the schedule and determines that by crashing, the project could be placed back on schedule. After discussing this with senior management, the Project Manager has decided to crash the project. By doing so, the Project Manager is adding what to the project?

Correct Answer: (C) Cost change
Explanation: By adding more resources to the project, cost increases. Time change is not valid because the Project Manager is trying to recover the time due to the rain delay. Scope change is not valid because the scope never changed. "Responsibility" is noise because the Project Manager is still responsible for this project. [section 8.5.8]

6.   The Project Manager is creating an estimate for raised flooring in a data center. The project has four different bids from four vendors. Two of the bids are $1.00/sq. ft higher than the

Project Manager wants to pay. The other two bids are $0.05 higher, but fall within the project's cost range of plus or minus 5%. Which of the following types of estimates is the Project Manager using?

Correct Answer: (A) Parametric
Explanation: Parametric is an estimating technique that uses parameters, such as so much cost per unit ($/sq. ft). The analogous estimate is considered a top-down estimate. It can be quickly created because it is based on expert knowledge of an area from previous projects. A bottom-up estimate is created by the team and can take time to create because of the details. "Gut feel" is noise. [section 9.11, section 8.3.2]

7. You are a Project Manager trying to estimate the duration of a project. You want to use an activity-on-arrow diagram as your network diagram. You decide to use an estimating method with three estimates: Optimistic, Pessimistic, and Idealistic. What estimating method do you use?

Correct Answer: (D) None of the above
Explanation: You have only two estimates here: Optimistic and Pessimistic. "Idealistic" is noise. CPM uses a one-time estimate per activity. GERT uses a feedback loop. PERT uses Optimistic, Pessimistic, and Most Likely estimates per activity. [section 8.5.1, section 8.2.3, section 8.3.2]

8. Which of the following best relates to unknown unknowns?

Correct Answer: (D) Management reserves
Explanation: Management reserves are created to address unknown unknowns. These are factors that aren't expected to happen. Contingency reserves are created for known unknowns. These are events that we know will happen; we just don't know how much of it will happen. Schedule reserves and risk management are noise. [section 13.6]

9. The project management team has just completed the process of creating risk categories for the risks on the project, displaying the risks in a graphical format to help team members have a better understanding of what could happen on the project. What have they created?

Correct Answer: (B) Risk breakdown structure
Explanation: The risk breakdown structure (RBS) is a graphical representation of the risk categorization and risks within those categories of the project. The risk management plan is the management approach to project risk. The risk register contains risk lists, analysis, responses, and risk owners for the project. Prioritized list of quantified risks comes in the risk register and involves risk ranking, not identification categorization. [section 13.2.2]

10. A new tape backup server has just been purchased for backing up the company's development and release software. The tape backup server costs $85,000, and it was necessary to upgrade the local area network with an Ethernet switch at a cost of $15,000. The Project Manager is told that she needs to set up a depreciation schedule for the tape backup server over a five-year period with a value of $0 at the end of this period. She will use standard depreciation in the calculation. What is the amount per year the server will depreciate?

Correct Answer: (D) $17,000
Explanation: To calculate depreciation, you must determine a few facts. What is the value of the asset at the end of the schedule? What is the amount of the asset to begin with? What is the number of years of the depreciation schedule? First, subtract the ending value of the asset from the beginning value of the asset ($85K-$0=$85K). Then divide the $85K by the years (5) of the depreciation schedule. This calculation results in $17K per year of depreciation. The question asked for only the depreciation of the tape backup server. [section 9.7.1]

11. You are a Project Manager assigned to a project that has spent $3,000,000. The original budget was $2,000,000. Senior management is considering stopping this project. What term describes the $1,000,000 that is over budget?

Correct Answer: (C) Sunk cost

Explanation: Sunk cost is cost that has already been spent on the project. It should not be taken into consideration when determining whether to continue the project. Expected monetary value is the product of probability and impact in risk management. *The budgeted cost of work performed* is the earned value (EV). Opportunity cost does not apply here. [section 9.6]

12. You are defining the quality standards for the project. You have defined the variables to measure and determined what attributes are important to you. Which of the following is not an attribute?

Correct Answer: (B) Depth

Explanation: Depth is a variable. A variable is something that you want to measure. An attribute is the specific characteristic being evaluated. The other answers are attributes. [section 10.10.3, section 10.10.4]

13. The Project Manager has completed the project scope on time, but over budget, and is getting signoff from the customer. What is this activity called?

Correct Answer: (A) Formal acceptance

Explanation: Scope Verification helps lead to formal acceptance. Contract closeout (correctly called Contract Closure) occurs when closing a contract with a vendor. Project archives are created when a project is closed. [section 7.4]

14. As a Project Manager, you are managing a project that is starting to fall behind schedule. By your calculations, the project is one week behind. After meeting with the project team, the team believes that it can make up the one week in the next four weeks and bring the project back on schedule. You are scheduled to report your status to management this week. Which of the following should you do?

Correct Answer: (C) Report that the project is behind schedule, but the team has a solution to bring the project back on schedule in the next four weeks.

Explanation: Professional and Social Responsibility requires that you report honestly and truthfully the status of projects and provide solutions to correct the problems. Reporting that the project is behind schedule but will finish on schedule does not provide a solution to the problem. Reporting that the project is on schedule with no major problems violates professional and social responsibility. [section 15.5.1]

15. The project Planning is progressing on schedule. The Project Manager and the team meet regularly and are ready to estimate cost. It is important that an accurate estimate be created. What estimating method should the team use?

Correct Answer: (B) Bottom-up estimating

Explanation: In bottom-up estimating, the Project Manager and the project team work together to create a complete estimate from the bottom up. Cost Estimating is the process the Project Manager and team are executing. Analogous estimating creates a high estimate with no significant detail. [section 9.11, section 8.3.2]

16. A Project Manager has completed the Scope Planning and Scope Definition processes. The Project Manager and the project team have spent the last week working on the work breakdown structure. All the following are benefits of using a WBS except...

Correct Answer: (A) Identifies special work packages that can be created outside the WBS, but within the project

Explanation: If the work is not in the WBS, it is not part of the project. All other answers represent benefits of using a WBS. [section 7.3.1]

17.   The project team has established the anticipated risks for the project, assigned probabilities, impact, and risk owners to them. As the project management plan evolves, where will this information end up?

Correct Answer: (C) Risk register
Explanation: The risk list and risk triggers are being created in this situation. The risk list and triggers end up in the risk register. Risk responses end up in the risk register after they are created in Risk Response Planning. [section 13.3.1]

18.   The PMO is conducting a meeting and a fellow Project Manager is reporting that the project is behind schedule by two weeks and under budget by $40K. You discover from the project's team members that the project is behind schedule by six weeks and is on budget. What should you do?

Correct Answer: (D) Review with the Project Manager how this status was produced
Explanation: As a Project Manager, you should review this information with the original Project Manager with regard to accuracy. Asking the PMO to investigate the project status is the next step, followed by notifying senior management. The final step is to report the Project Manager to PMI. [section 15.5.1]

19.   You are the Project Manager on a defense project. The buyer wants to get an idea on how much they will pay on cost overruns. With the following variables, calculate the point of total assumption: Expected Cost=$100,000; Expected Profit=$20,000; Target Price=$120,000; Buyer/Share Ratio=70/30%; Ceiling Price=$140,000; Maximum Overrun=140%.

Correct Answer: (A) $128,571.43
Explanation: The formula for point of total assumption (PTA) is as follows:
((Ceiling Price-Target Price)/Buyer Share)+Target Cost.
$128,571.43 = ($140,000 - $120,000)/0.7 + $100,000
[section 14.1.8]

20.   You are a Project Manager at Dewey, Cheatum, and Howe and have been assigned to a major construction project. The project is on schedule and under budget, but you are constantly in conflict with a member of your project team. This conflict is apparent to the team members. According to the PMI Code of Ethics and Professional Conduct, what is the best solution?

Correct Answer: (A) Treat the team member as a professional with respect.
Explanation: Treating the team member as a professional with respect increases the advancement of the project management profession. Removing the team member from the project may not be possible because of limited resources. Avoiding the team member as much as possible does not resolve the problem. Holding a team meeting to vote if the team member should be removed only increases the conflict. [section 15.3]

21.   Which of the following roles controls resources and manages a business unit?

Correct Answer: (A) Functional management
Explanation: Functional Managers control resources and run business units. Senior management is responsible for a number of areas on a project. The main responsibility is to help support the project and resolve resource conflicts as they occur. For situational questions, assume that you are in a balanced matrix environment, unless otherwise stated. The Project Manager's responsibility is to drive the project work to completion. Typically, the sponsor's responsibility is to pay for the project and own it when it is complete. [section 5.4.4, section 5.6.1]

22.   The Project Manager is creating an estimate for building a company WAN (wide area network). It is something that is new to the Project Manager and his team, and they want to make sure all the work of the project is covered. They decide to create a bottom-up estimate. All the following are advantages of this type of estimate except...

Correct Answer: (C) It takes a great amount of time to create.
Explanation: Taking a great amount of time to create is not an advantage of the estimating. All the other answers are advantages characteristic of the bottom-up estimate. [section 8.3.2]

23. A Project Manager is assigned to a project that is in the construction phase of a video computer board. The Project Manager is reviewing deliverables and work results to gain formal acceptance. This activity is known as what?

Correct Answer: (C) Scope Verification
Explanation: Scope Verification is the process of obtaining formal acceptance of the project scope by the stakeholders. Scope Control ensures that changes are agreed upon, determines if the scope change has occurred, and manages the actual changes. Quality Assurance and Quality Control are concerned with the correctness of the work results, not necessarily the acceptance of the work results. [section 7.4]

24. What are the five phases of a project management life cycle?

Correct Answer: (B) Initiating, Planning, Executing, Monitoring and Controlling, Closing
Explanation: Per the *PMBOK Guide Third Edition*, the Process Groups that make up the PMI methodology or "project management life cycle" are Initiating, Planning, Executing, Monitoring and Controlling, and Closing. It is not uncommon for these Process Groups to be considered phases of a project, although technically inaccurate per the *PMBOK Guide Third Edition*. [section 5.4.1]

25. What does a responsibility assignment matrix do for the Project Manager?

Correct Answer: (D) Shows who is to perform work in certain areas of the project
Explanation: The responsibility assignment matrix (RAM) shows who is to perform certain work on the project. It could show who has signoff authority, has primary responsibility, or is on the team in that area. The resource list or organization chart shows who is on the project. The network diagram shows the order of the activities. The other answer is noise. [section 11.1.2]

26. The consulting company has been awarded a $60M, 10-year contract to provide consulting and support services to an automobile manufacturer. The company realizes that this work is going to require a specific skill set for 500 people. Their current workforce has only 100 people with this skill set. This skill set is somewhat rare and specialized. They have chosen to buy a company much smaller than they are, but this company's core focus is this type of skill set. The company employs 600 people with this skill set. This is an example of what type of risk response strategy?

Correct Answer: (A) Exploit
Explanation: Exploiting the risk is to carry out activities to grow or expand the positive aspects of the risk. Sharing the risk is to work with someone else to maximize the risk. Mitigate attempts to minimize the bad impact of the risk. Accepting the risk is to tolerate whatever happened. [section 13.6.5]

27. Which of the following is used to control cost-related items on a project?

Correct Answer: (A) Cost Control
Explanation: Cost Control is the process used to control cost on a project. The cost management plan helps establish the cost rules for the project. The work breakdown structure helps decompose the work of the project. "Budget management plan" is noise. [section 9.14]

28. The team has just completed the process of evaluating how the project went. The team members analyzed what worked well and what didn't. They evaluated the Planning and Executing. They documented how the sponsor and senior management supported the project. What have they just completed?

Correct Answer: (A) Lessons learned
Explanation: The lessons learned is an analysis of how the project went. It includes Initiating to Closing activities. It documents what worked on the project and what didn't so that lessons can be learned and good methods repeated and bad ones eliminated. Administrative closure is the activity in which lessons learned occurs. "Procurement audit" is noise. "Project closure" is noise. [section 6.9.3]

29. All the following are typically part of the project management plan except…

Correct Answer: (D) Time management plan
Explanation: "Time management plan" is noise. The real item associated with the schedule is the schedule management plan. The other items are typically part of the project management plan. [section 6.5.1]

30. Which of the following formulas calculates float?

Correct Answer: (B) Late finish-early finish (LF-EF)
Explanation: Float is calculated by subtracting either the early finish (EF) from the late finish (LF) or the early start (ES) from the late start (LS). [section 8.5.7, section 8.7]

31. Crosswind Custom Homes is building a customer's dream house. However, the city inspector for building permits has been in training for the last two weeks, and he has no backup. His absence causes a delay in the completion of the house. This is an example of what?

Correct Answer: (D) External dependencies
Explanation: The external dependency is a dependency that is outside the control of the internal organization. Mandatory is required but internal to the organization. Crashing and lag are noise. [section 8.2.1]

32. The Project Manager is creating an estimate for raised flooring in an IT computer room that is being built. The customer is now creating his budget for the next calendar year and needs this estimate as soon as possible. A senior Project Manager has managed many projects that required raised floors and is considered an expert. You solicit his help on the estimate. Which of the following types of estimates is the Project Manager using?

Correct Answer: (B) Analogous
Explanation: The analogous estimate is also considered a top-down estimate. It can be quickly created because it is based on expert knowledge of an area from previous projects. Parametric is an estimating technique that uses parameters, such as a given cost per unit ($/sq. ft). A bottom-up estimate is created by the team and can take time to create because of the details. Delphi Technique is a method to obtain expert opinions; it is not an estimate tool. [section 8.3.2, section 9.11]

33. You are the Project Manager on a defense project. The buyer wants to get an idea on how much they will pay on cost overruns. With the following variables, calculate the point of total assumption: Expected Cost=$500,500; Expected Profit=$150,150; Target Price=$650,650; Buyer/Share Ratio=50/50%; Ceiling Price=$750,750; Maximum Overrun=150%.

Correct Answer: (A) $700,700
Explanation: The formula for point of total assumption (PTA) is as follows:
((Ceiling Price-Target Price)/Buyer Share)+Target Cost.
$700,700 = ($750,750 - $650,650)/0.5 + $500,500
[section 14.1.8]

34. The project selection committee is reviewing two different projects for approval. It has determined that the company has enough resources to do only one project. Project A is worth $500,500 and Project B is worth $510,000. What is the opportunity cost of selecting Project B?

Correct Answer: (B) $500,500
Explanation: The opportunity cost of selecting Project B is the value of what is not selected. This is the value of Project A ($500,500). [section 6.3.3, section 9.2]

35. The information technology system for the national power grid has been working well. Today, the main control processor crashed, disabling the west coast delivery of power to four states. Implementation of the risk response plan didn't fix the problem. Which of the following steps do they perform first?

Correct Answer: (B) Fix the problem.
Explanation: This is a chicken or the egg question in that you more than likely will do all the answers, but which comes first? The sequence for the other answers is: Fix the problem then determine why the risk response plan failed, and why the problem happened then adjust the risk response plan. [section 13.6]

36. The software development project is going through Planning. In evaluating the triple constraint, which of the following has the highest priority?

Correct Answer: (D) They are all equal unless otherwise stated in the project charter.
Explanation: The triple constraint implies that all three components (scope, time, and cost) are equal unless otherwise defined in the project charter or determined by the sponsor or senior management. [section 5.2]

37. The consulting company has been awarded a $60M contract to provide consulting and support services to a battery company. The consulting company is relatively small, and this contract is bigger than anything they have been awarded to date. To ensure that they can effectively complete the contract and not jeopardize their other work, they have chosen to partner with another company to do the work. This is an example of what type of risk response strategy?

Correct Answer: (B) Share
Explanation: Sharing the risk with another company is what is happening here. Exploiting the risk is to carryout activities to grow or expand the positive aspects of the risk. Mitigate attempts to minimize the bad impact of the risk. Accepting the risk is to tolerate whatever happens. [section 13.6.5]

38. Fixed-price contracts are also known as which of the following?

Correct Answer: (B) Lump-sum
Explanation: A fixed-price contract is also known as a lump-sum contract. It involves the seller providing services for a set price. The cost-plus contract pays the seller for expenses and a negotiated fee. A purchase order is a unilateral purchasing mechanism to purchase commodity type items. Time and materials contracts are typically for smaller durations or staff augmentation. [section 14.1.6]

39. The client has requested a four-week delay on the project while the company retools its machine lab. This delay was not planned, but the equipment had to be replaced. The company has limited resources. What is the best way to make up the four-week slip?

Correct Answer: (A) Fast tracking
Explanation: Fast tracking is the best option listed because it re-sequences activities to attain compression of the schedule. Crashing adds resources which isn't an option based on the question. "Integrated Change Control" is noise. [section 8.5.8]

40. The project team is involved in defining what is needed to ensure quality for the project and is trying to determine what the cost of quality would be for the project. Cost of quality is based on what?

Correct Answer: (A) Conformance versus Nonconformance

Explanation: With the cost of conformance, a company pays for quality in a proactive way in the planning of a project. With the cost of nonconformance, a company pays for quality by reacting to an issue and waits for problems to come up. The other answers are noise. [section 10.8.5]

41. You are the Project Manager of an infrastructure project for a wide area network with a one-year schedule as defined by the project management plan. You need a LAN analyzer. During the procurement process, you have decided to rent this equipment. The rental cost is $142 per month. What type of cost is this?

Correct Answer: (D) Variable

Explanation: Variable cost fluctuates with what is produced or the amount of time something is used. Fixed cost is cost that is consistent on a project. Indirect cost is cost incurred for the benefit of one or more projects or departments. Direct cost is directly attributable to the project and spent only on the project work. [section 9.1]

42. The Project Manager has scheduled weekly status meetings with the team. The meetings have been unorganized with multiple people addressing their own needs and taking longer than planned with no discipline. Which of the following would improve the meetings?

Correct Answer: (B) Create and publish an agenda, and establish the leader of the meeting.

Explanation: Creating and publishing an agenda, and knowing who is in charge of a meeting are two ways to have a highly organized effective meeting. [section 12.4.4]

43. The team is involved in defining what is needed to ensure that the quality process will capture the intended results of the testing. This activity is known as what?

Correct Answer: (B) Quality Assurance

Explanation: Quality Assurance ensures that the quality plan will achieve the desired results of the project. Defining the quality rules as they relate to the project is done in Quality Planning. Measuring the output of the project is Quality Control. [section 10.9]

44. A Project Manager was assigned to manage a project to develop pink widgets for the Project Manager's company. The project will cost the company $650,000 over the next 12 months. It is projected that the widgets will earn the company $20,500 per month. How much time will it take to recover the cost for this project?

Correct Answer: (B) 32 months

Explanation: The return on investment is $20,500 per month and the cost of the project is $650,000. The amount of time to recover this investment is ($650,000 / $20,500 = 31.70 months or 32 months). [section 9.8]

45. A Project Manager has completed the Scope Definition process. The customer and sponsor have shortened the schedule by four weeks and decided to exclude the work breakdown structure. The Project Manager informs the customer and sponsor that, by excluding the WBS, the project could be subjected to many problems. Which of the following is not considered a problem of bypassing the work breakdown structure?

Correct Answer: (B) Planning areas may lack supporting details.

Explanation: Planning areas may lack supporting details. Without a defined WBS, constant changes to the project, unforeseen project delays, and a poorly defined budget can be present because the work has not been broken down into work packages. All answers are correct, but the Planning areas may lack supporting details is the best answer as the other answers could occur as a result of that answer. [section 7.2]

46. You are doing quality control on a project, trying to determine if a project is producing a low quality or low-grade product. Which statement best describes the differences?

Correct Answer: (A) Low quality is always a problem, but low grade may not be.
Explanation: Low quality is always a problem on a project, and low grade may be acceptable to the customer. Products can have high quality but low grade in which a product does not have bugs but has low grade because of the limited features. Products can have low quality, but high grade in which a product can have many bugs with numerous features. *Low quality may not be a problem, but low grade is always a problem* is inaccurate. In this case, low quality is always a problem. [section 10.8.2]

47. You are the owner of a construction company. As you begin work on a large building that covers 20,000 square feet, you need to rent a backhoe tractor to clear the property. This is the third time you have needed the backhoe, and you want to know if you should buy or rent it. A new backhoe sells for $19,000 and costs $30 a day to maintain. You can rent one for $125 a day with the maintenance included. How many days would you need to use this tool before it makes sense to buy instead of rent?

Correct Answer: (C) 200 days
Explanation: To complete this question, solve for the number of days. The number of days is the variable D in the formula: $19,000+$30D=$125D. First, move D to one side of the equation. Subtracting $30D from both sides gives $19,000=$95D ($19,000=$125D-$30D). Next, divide both sides by 95, isolating D. That equals 200, which means you must use the tool for 200 full days before it makes sense to buy it. [section 14.1.2, section 14.7]

48. Which of the following is an example of a lag?

Correct Answer: (D) The need for concrete to cure an additional day because of the weather before painting the parking lines
Explanation: The need for concrete to cure an additional day because of the weather before painting the parking line is an example of a lag. The other answers are noise. [section 8.2.5]

49. Activity A is worth $300, is 100% complete, and actually cost $350. Activity B is worth $100, is 95% complete, and actually cost $85 so far. Activity C is worth $200, is 75% complete, and has cost $175 so far. The total budget is $1,500. What is the estimate to complete for the activities listed?

Correct Answer: (D) $1,075.39
Explanation: Earned value (EV) and actual cost (AC) must be calculated first. To determine the EV for each activity, multiply the percent complete of each activity by its planned value (PV). To determine the total actual cost, sum the actual cost of each activity. To determine the total earned value, sum the earned value of each activity. Then divide the earned value of $545 by the actual cost of $610, deriving a CPI of 0.89. Finally, divide the BAC of $1,500 by the CPI to produce an estimated at completion of $1,685.39. Determine the estimate to complete by subtracting the actual cost (AC) of $610 from the estimate at completion (EAC) of $1,685.39. The difference is $1,075.39. [section 9.14.5, section 9.15]

50. The project team is working together on the tollway repaving project. The Project Manager has delivered a report that describes how much work should have been accomplished, how much work is actually accomplished, and the actual cost to complete the work. What type of report is this?

Correct Answer: (A) Earned value report
Explanation: The earned value report focuses on earned value measurement. It focuses on actual cost (AC), earned value (EV), planned value (PV), and a number of measurements that can come from that. The progress report shows what has been done in a certain time period on the project. The status report shows what has been completed to date on the project. The variance report shows the difference between what is happening on the project and what should have happened. [section 12.5.1]

51. Activity A is worth $300, is 100% complete, and actually cost $350. Activity B is worth $100, is 95% complete, and actually cost $85 so far. Activity C is worth $200, is 75%

complete, and has cost \$175 so far. The total budget is \$1,500. What is the cost variance for the activities listed?

Correct Answer: (C) -\$65.00

Explanation: Earned value (EV) and actual cost (AC) must be calculated first. To determine the EV for each activity, multiply the percent complete of each activity by its planned value (PV). To determine the total actual cost, sum the actual cost of each activity. To determine the total earned value, sum the earned value of each activity. Then subtract the actual cost of \$610 from the earned value of \$545, deriving a CV of -\$65. This value means that the project is \$65 over budget. [section 9.14.3, section 9.15]

52. The project Planning is progressing on schedule. The Project Manager and the team meet regularly and are ready to estimate cost. The customer needs an estimate as soon as possible. What estimating method should the team use?

Correct Answer: (D) Analogous estimating

Explanation: Analogous estimating creates a high estimate with no significant detail. The main advantage of this estimate is that you can create it quickly. In bottom-up estimating, the Project Manager and the project team work together to create a complete estimate from the bottom up. Cost Estimating is the process the Project Manager and team are executing. [section 9.11, section 8.3.2]

53. The engineer is considering quitting his engineering job to develop a new memory upgrade project for the new Kiwi computer, an idea he created outside his job. If it sells well, he plans to start his own company and sell them full time. What characteristic is he showing toward risk?

Correct Answer: (B) Risk seeker

Explanation: A risk seeker mentality is that of looking for the big reward and being prepared to pay significantly if it's missed. The risk-averse mentality is a very conservative approach to risk. A risk-neutral mentality is somewhere between that of a risk seeker and risk-averse mentality. The other answer is noise. [section 13.2.7]

54. You are the Project Manager on a TV transmission tower project. Due to the rough terrain, the scope of the project had to be modified to compensate for the required foundation changes. You need to verify that these changes have been put in place. What best helps you determine this?

Correct Answer: (B) Project scope statement updates

Explanation: Project scope statement updates help provide validation that updates to the project scope had been added to the plan and into execution if they should have been acted upon by that point in time. Scope control system defines the procedures by which the project scope may be changed. Scope management plan describes how project scope will be managed and how scope changes will be integrated into the project. Scope changes are any modifications to the agreed-upon project scope as defined by the approved WBS. [section 7.3]

55. The Project Manager is closing the project and wants to discuss with the project team the success and failures of the project and document this information. This activity is known as what?

Correct Answer: (B) Lessons learned

Explanation: Lessons learned is the process of discussing and documenting what went good and bad on a project so those lessons learned can help projects in the future run more efficiently. [section 6.9.3]

56. Your project needs some database software but the budget on the project doesn't include this software. You are at the gym after work with a friend from your old job. He has a lot of different types of software and suggests that he can make you a copy of this software that you need. What is the best way to acquire the software?

PMP Exam Success Series: Certification Exam Manual
© 2007 Crosswind Project Management, Inc., www.crosswindpm.com

Correct Answer: (B) Order a copy from the company or an authorized reseller.
Explanation: Software created by someone else should be purchased and the license terms and conditions followed. That often includes defining how copies, demo copies, and file sharing systems are to be used with the software. [section 15.2.2]

57. The engineering team is building a new product. This is a new product type at the company, and the market for the product is new and changes every six months. According to the Product Manager, a key to success is the ability to evolve the Planning as more information about the market is discovered. Which type of scheduling approach best fits this need?

Correct Answer: (A) Rolling wave planning
Explanation: In an environment where there is a great degree of flexibility or instability, it's good to use a rolling wave planning approach. This approach allows team members to plan as much as possible. While executing that part of the plan, they continue to plan future work as they learn more about it. Crashing puts more resources on the critical path activities. Fast tracking re-sequences already defined activities to compress the overall duration of the schedule. Precedence diagramming is a network diagramming technique. [section 8.1]

58. The company is in the testing phase of its project, tracking defects that come in from beta customers who are testing the project. Given the nature of a new project, a variety of defects is being discovered over time. Which chart or diagram helps display these?

Correct Answer: (D) Run chart
Explanation: A run chart gives a picture of the process output over time. The Pareto diagram shows frequency of defects in a graphical format. The flowchart shows process flow. Fishbone diagram shows what problems could happen or might be happening. [section 10.10.9]

59. The architect has recently been promoted from senior architect to department manager. In this new position, he will be responsible for managing projects and project resources. Over the seven years he has been with the company, he was always ranked as one of the top employees but lacks formal project management training. Which of the following best describes this situation?

Correct Answer: (C) Halo Theory
Explanation: The Halo Theory implies that because people are good at their current jobs, they would be good at project management regardless of their background or training. The other answers are noise. [section 11.2.3]

60. Senior management has asked a Project Manager to set milestones on the current project. What are the characteristics of a milestone?

(A) The completion of a major event in the project
(B) The completion of major deliverables
(C) A duration of zero (0)

Correct Answer: (D) All the answers
Explanation: A milestone is the completion of major deliverables, the completion of a major event, and has duration of zero (0). These are all characteristics of a milestone. [section 7.7, section 8.2, section 8.5.12, section 8.8]

61. As a Project Manager, you are managing a multi-story building project for a customer who has requested that you have special marble flooring installed in the entryway. Your father-in-law has been doing floor covering for 20 years and is an expert. You decide to give him the work. This is an example of what?

Correct Answer: (A) Appearance of impropriety
Explanation: Appearance of impropriety is the correct answer. To others, awarding your father-in-law the job may appear as an impropriety, regardless if it actually is or not. Conflict in solicitation is invalid because no other vendor was requested to bid. The fact that he is an expert does not address the appearance of impropriety. "Sole sourcing" is noise because there are other vendors that can also do the job. [section 15.4.1]

62. The Project Manager is creating an estimate for building a company WAN (wide area network). As the Project Manager, you have undertaken the make-or-buy decision and determined that the WAN implementation should be outsourced because your company does not have the expertise. After receiving all the vendor proposals, you find that two of the proposals specify cost-plus-fixed-fee, two other of the vendors specify fixed-price, another two specify cost-plus-incentive-fee, and the last two specify time and materials. Which of the proposals present the least probability of loss for the company?

Correct Answer: (A) Proposals that use fixed-price
Explanation: Proposals that use fixed-price contain the least amount of risk for the buyer; the seller assumes all the risk. In cost-plus-fixed-fee, the buyer pays all the cost, but the fee is fixed at a specific amount. In cost-plus-incentive-fee, the buyer pays all the cost, but the fee is paid if the incentive was met. For time and materials, the buyer pays the cost on a per hour basis plus any material. [section 14.1.6]

63. Which of the following best shows reporting relationships on a project?

Correct Answer: (D) Organizational breakdown structure (OBS)
Explanation: The organizational breakdown structure (OBS) is also known as an organizational chart. It shows what reporting relationships are on the project. The staffing management plan defines the staffing rules as they relate to the project. The responsibility assignment matrix shows who is responsible for what on the project. The resource histogram shows what quantities of resources are utilized over time. [section 11.1.3]

64. Activity A is worth $300, is 100% complete, and actually cost $350. Activity B is worth $100, is 95% complete, and actually cost $85 so far. Activity C is worth $200, is 75% complete, and has cost $175 so far. Total budget is $1,500. What is the schedule variance for the activities listed?

Correct Answer: (C) -$55.00
Explanation: Earned value (EV) and planned value (PV) must be calculated first. To determine the EV for each activity, multiply the percent complete of each activity by its planned value (PV). To determine the total planned value, sum the planned value of each activity. To determine the total earned value, sum the earned value of each activity. Then subtract the planned value of $600 from earned value of $545, deriving a SV of -$55. This value means that the project is $55 behind schedule. [section 9.14.3, section 9.15]

65. You are the Project Manager on a defense project. The buyer wants to get an idea on how much they will pay on cost overruns. With the following variables, calculate the point of total assumption: Expected Cost=$275,000; Expected Profit=$78,750; Target Price=$343,750; Buyer/Share Ratio=65/35%; Ceiling Price=$412,500; Maximum Overrun=150%.

Correct Answer: (A) $380,769.23
Explanation: The formula for point of total assumption (PTA) is as follows:
((Ceiling Price-Target Price)/Buyer Share)+Target Cost.
$380,769.23 = ($412,500 - $343,750)/0.65 + $275,000
[section 14.1.8]

66. Calculate the PERT estimate for the following: Pessimistic=20, Optimistic=10, Realistic=17.

Correct Answer: (D) 16.33
Explanation: The PERT formula is Pessimistic + Optimistic+ (4*Realistic) divided by 6. The answer is (20+10+(4*17))/6 = 16.33. [section 8.3.2, section 8.7]

67. Which of the following is not a regulation?

Correct Answer: (C) The average speed on a highway in a week
Explanation: The average speed on a highway in a week is simply a value. It's not a regulation; the other answers are. The other answers have defined criteria that they must meet to be acceptable. [section 5.3]

68. Which of the following is an output of Initiating?

Correct Answer: (D) Assignment of the Project Manager
Explanation: As a result of the project charter's creation, the Project Manager is assigned to the project. Work results come from Executing. Corrective action comes from Monitoring and Controlling. "A signed contract" is noise. [section 5.4.1, section 6.3, section 6.3.1]

69. The sponsor on the e-commerce project has just told the Project Manager about a change he wants. He says that the change will cost 20% less and should not cause any problems to the existing environment. Which of the following should concern the Project Manager the most?

Correct Answer: (D) Scope and schedule impact
Explanation: Scope and schedule impact should be the most concerning, assuming the cost impact is true. "Quality" is noise. [section 7.5]

70. A Project Manager is beginning the solicitation process to find companies that can potentially provide the needed services. The buyer wants to consider only sellers of the services that have met rigid predefined qualifications. What screening mechanism is this?

Correct Answer: (D) Qualified sellers list
Explanation: A qualified sellers list has information on relevant past experience and other characteristics of prospective sellers. Advertising lets prospective vendors know what about the company's potential needs. Weighting System is a tool used in source selection. A bidders conference lets companies ask a buyer questions and get clarification on any potential issues. [section 14.3.1]

71. In what Knowledge Area does Activity Resource Estimating occur?

Correct Answer: (C) Time
Explanation: Activity Resource Estimating is a major process of time management. It determines what resources and what quantities of each should be used. [section 8.3]

72. The Project Manager is involved in acquiring the project team on a highway expansion project. She is presently discussing salary, working hours, travel, and benefits. What is the key tool she is utilizing?

Correct Answer: (D) Negotiations
Explanation: Negotiation is key in acquiring staff for a project. It can include salary, benefits, and job responsibilities. A staffing management plan defines the staffing rules for the project. The project team directory shows who is on the team. The organizational chart shows reporting structures on the project. [section 11.2, section 14.4.3]

73. A project will be using a vendor to purchase infrastructure equipment for a national network upgrade venture for the U.S. government. The government has requested a proposal from prospective sellers of the equipment. What type of document is being provided to the sellers?

Correct Answer: (C) Invitation for bid (IFB)

Explanation: An invitation for bid (IFB) is similar to the RFP but is typically used in government contracting. A request for quotes (RFQ) deals with obtaining prices from a company for goods or services. A request for proposals (RFP) deals with a very detailed and specific approach to a customized solution. A request for information (RFI) deals with finding potential vendors for consideration for proposals or quotes. [section 14.2.1]

74. Calculate the variance for the following: Pessimistic=20, Optimistic=10, Realistic=17.

Correct Answer: (A) 2.78

Explanation: The formula for variance is Pessimistic-Optimistic divided by 6, squared. The answer is ((20-10)/6)^2 = 2.78. [section 8.7]

75. Crosswind Custom Homes is building a customer's dream house. However, rain has delayed the finish by two weeks. The schedule shows that the next activity is to install the roof followed by the shingles. This is an example of what?

Correct Answer: (B) Mandatory dependencies

Explanation: A mandatory dependency is required and internal to the organization. The external dependency is a dependency that is out of control of the internal organization. Crashing and lag are noise. [section 8.2.1]

76. You are beginning a new project and a portion of the development will be created by a foreign company. You are not sure how to do business with this company because it is offshore. What document is best to guide you in this business?

Correct Answer: (A) Company's policies and procedures

Explanation: A company's policies and procedures define how it does business with local and global businesses. The PMI Code of Ethics and Professional Conduct gives you a general overview. Historical information may not contain any information about doing offshore development. The local laws of the offshore company may not play a part in the business. [section 15.2.1]

77. What is an organization that defines standards, audits projects, and helps mentor Project Managers called?

Correct Answer: (D) Project Management Office

Explanation: The Project Management Office (PMO) can define standards, audit projects, and help mentor Project Managers or perform any other activity needed, within reason, for the management of projects within an organization. [section 5.1]

78. You are a Project Manager who will be using GERT as an estimating method. By definition, GERT has loops and conditional branches. Which of the following is not a function of GERT analysis?

Correct Answer: (B) Some activities may be fast tracked.

Explanation: Fast tracking is a tool of Schedule Development and is used in duration compression. Fast tracking is not a function of GERT. [section 8.2.3, section 8.5.8]

79. The sponsor plays a key role in project success. Which of the following is the best description of the sponsor?

Correct Answer: (B) Customer

Explanation: The customer is the best description of the sponsor because sponsors pay for the work of the project and can own it when it is complete. Senior management, Product Manager, and CIO are all names of what could be the sponsor, but not necessarily on every project. [section 5.4.4]

80. To develop a call center application for your company, a project requires some new test equipment and a voice over IP system. The finance department explains that this is a capital purchase to be depreciated using the sum of the years digits. This is an example of what?

Correct Answer: (A) Accelerated depreciation
Explanation: Sum of the digits and double declining balance are examples of accelerated depreciation. Standard and straight-line depreciation are the same. "Fixed direct cost" is noise. [section 9.7.2]

81. Crosswind Custom Homes is building a customer's dream house. However, rain has delayed the finish by two weeks. The Project Manager evaluates the schedule and determines that the electrical and plumbing could occur at the same time instead of right after each other as laid out in the schedule. After discussing this with senior management, the Project Manager has decided to fast track the project. By doing so, the Project Manager adds what to the project?

Correct Answer: (A) Risk
Explanation: By executing two or more activities at once, the Project Manager introduces more risk into the project. Time change is not valid because the Project Manager is trying to recover the rain delay. Scope change is not valid because the scope never changed. "Responsibility" is noise because the Project Manager is still responsible for this project. [section 8.5.8]

82. The Project Manager and the team have just completed determining what will be done if risk events happen, and who will be responsible for executing those actions. Which of the following roles will be responsible for acting if the risk events happen?

Correct Answer: (D) Risk owner
Explanation: Risk owners are responsible for implementing risk response plans if the risk they are responsible for occurs. The risk seeker is an aggressive personality toward risk. The Project Manager and team lead don't act unless they are the risk owners. [section 13.6.4]

83. The finance department is building a new call center for its new auto finance division. Given that this is its first venture utilizing a call center, a number of new processes have been created. Which of the following help verify that these processes are being accomplished?

Correct Answer: (B) Checklist
Explanation: A checklist helps verify that a set of required steps has been performed. The process flow helps define how the company employees on the phone with customers manage the customer. A control chart shows output over time. A quality audit ensures that the quality standards of the project are met. [section 10.8.15]

84. Your wireless access project is almost complete. You have outsourced the network fine-tuning to an out-of-state company to complete. As the project closes down, what will be completed last?

Correct Answer: (B) Release of resources
Explanation: Closing the project occurs before Contract Closure, based on the simple order of the processes per the *PMBOK Guide Third Edition*. In the detail, release of resources is part of closing the project and is done after everything else on the project is completed. The other answer is noise. [section 6.9.5]

85. The project is going through quality control. Which of the following are used to validate that the output is in compliance with the specifications of the work?

Correct Answer: (A) Inspection
Explanation: Inspection is a key tool in Quality Control. It provides validating that the product was built as intended. Checklists help establish process repeatability. Rework comes when products are not built correctly. Acceptance decisions deal with defining what is and isn't acceptable. [section 10.10]

86. The team is involved in Risk Management Planning. Team members have been meeting to determine their risk approach to the project, as well as identify risks and triggers. The most recent activities they completed created an overall project risk ranking for the project. What process did they just complete?

Correct Answer: (A) Qualitative Risk Analysis
Explanation: Qualitative Risk Analysis helps establish the overall risk of the project. [section 13.4]

87. A Project Manager studying different motivation theories is impressed with one theory which states that people are not motivated by money but by appreciation and working on challenging projects. What theory is the Project Manager referring to?

Correct Answer: (C) Herzberg's Theory
Explanation: Herzberg's Theory deals with hygiene factors and motivating elements. The motivating elements can include appreciation, safety, working on challenging opportunity and other variables that do not necessarily relate to money. Maslow's Hierarchy states that there are various motivation strategies that motivate people. McGregor's Theory of X and Y classifies workers into one of two groups. Theory X states that management is in charge and that labor does not want to work. Theory Y states that labor wants to work and requires little supervision. [section 11.1.4]

88. What is the main purpose of utilizing a work authorization system?

Correct Answer: (B) To help ensure that work is done in the appropriate sequence
Explanation: A work authorization system helps ensure that certain work is done at a certain time in a certain order. It helps minimize the opportunity for gold plating on a project. The work breakdown structure (WBS) shows what work is to be done on the project. The responsibility assignment matrix (RAM) shows who is responsible for what work. "To serve as a time-tracking system" is noise. [section 6.6.1]

89. The project team is planning an upgrade to a client's Web site and infrastructure. During Planning, the team members discover that the lab where the staging server is to reside does not have sufficient space, forcing the client to lease another building. This building will also be shared with another department. What type of cost is this?

Correct Answer: (A) Indirect
Explanation: Indirect cost is cost incurred for the benefit of one or more projects or departments. Direct cost is directly attributable to the project and spent only on the project work. Variable cost fluctuates with what is produced. "Indirect fixed" is noise. [section 9.1]

90. The project is in a projectized environment. There are significant challenges with the scope of the project. Project personnel have been complaining to senior management about the environment. In this type of environment, who controls the resources?

Correct Answer: (A) Project Manager
Explanation: In a projectized environment, the Project Manager traditionally controls the resources. The Project Manager has those resources available for project work as necessary. Senior management helps resolve resource conflicts. "Project Coordinator" is noise. [section 5.6.3]

91. You are in the initiation phase of a project and are doing an estimate for a project that requires a major software package for a healthcare system. What is the estimate range to use for this project?

Correct Answer: (B) -25% to +75%

Explanation: The range of an order of magnitude (OOM) estimate is -25% to +75% and is used during the initiation phase of a project. The budget estimate has a range of -10% to +25%. The definitive estimate has a range of -5% to +10%. The "-25% to +85%" is noise. [section 9.12]

92. Activity A is worth $300, is 100% complete, and actually cost $350. Activity B is worth $100, is 95% complete, and actually cost $85 so far. Activity C is worth $200, is 75% complete, and has cost $175 so far. Total budget is $1,500. What is the total earned value for the activities listed?

Correct Answer: (B) $545.00

Explanation: To calculate earned value (EV), multiply the percent complete of each activity by its planned value (PV), deriving the EV for each activity. To determine the total earned value for the project, add the earned value for each activity. The sum is $545.00. [section 9.14.4, section 9.15]

93. The following are forms of contracts except...

Correct Answer: (D) Proposal

Explanation: Proposals are seller-prepared documents that describe the seller's ability and willingness to provide the requested product. It is not a contract. [section 14.1.4, section 14.4]

94. The Project Manager is working with the customer to gain formal acceptance on the project deliverables. The customer is saying that three of the deliverables are not meeting project goals and are unusable in their present form. Upon reviewing documentation, the customer tells the Project Manager that the requirements are not accurate, to meet the needs for which the project was undertaken. Which of the following will help fix this problem?

Correct Answer: (B) Scope Control

Explanation: Scope Control is used to review and create change requests related to the scope of the project. Such review and change request activity help fix the problem by directing the Project Manager to adjust the project scope statement, scope baseline, or work breakdown structure. Creating the work breakdown structure produces a graphical breakdown structure of the project work. Scope Verification helps validate that the project created what it was to create. It is the process that discovered the problem of the difference in scope planned and created. [section 7.5]

95. You are managing a project and senior management has removed the two previous Project Managers on the project because they could not keep the project on schedule. According to your current project schedule, this project is behind schedule two weeks. As the current Project Manager, you are afraid you will also be removed if you report this status. What is the best response you can tell senior management?

Correct Answer: (B) Tell senior management the project is two weeks behind with a contingency plan.

Explanation: Tell senior management that the project is two weeks behind and present a contingency plan to bring it back on schedule. You are required to report timely and accurate status and facts about the project. A contingency plan provides senior management with an alternate plan. Report the delay to senior management, and the reasons will justify the delay, but as a Project Manager, you are required to be proactive with a solution. The other answers do not follow the PMI Code of Ethics and Professional Conduct. [section 15.5.1]

96. The client has requested a six-week delay on the project while the company calibrates its test equipment. This delay wasn't planned, but the equipment had to be calibrated. The company has limited resources. This delay is best shown in what?

Correct Answer: (B) Network diagram

Explanation: The network diagram shows the sequencing and length of the project. The responsibility assignment matrix shows who is responsible for what and does not include time. The WBS shows what work is in the project but doesn't focus on how long it should take. The budget deals with the cost of the project, not time. [section 8.2.2]

97.   In the Communication Model, who is responsible for ensuring that the message is in a clear, understandable format?

Correct Answer: (D) Sender

Explanation: The sender is responsible for verifying that the message is clear. The receiver acknowledges that it was received and interpreted correctly. This acknowledgement typically comes from feedback provided by the receiver. [section 12.4.1]

98.   Calculate expected monetary value of the following: 0.4 probability of $2,500, 0.3 probability of -$1,200, 0.2 probability of $1,000, 0.1 probability of $3,000.

Correct Answer: (D) $1,140

Explanation: To calculate the expected monetary value (EMV), multiply each probability by its dollar amount and add the products of the multiplications. The result is a value of $1,140. [section 13.5.3, section 13.8]

99.   The Crosswind multimedia development has recently been awarded a large contract to create a new science fiction series for a well known producer. This requires the company to move into a new office complete with production facilities 500% larger than what it presently has. The schedule is tight for this new project, and there can be no delay. The new facility is behind schedule with the cubicles and network wiring on pace to finish two months late. The company is trying to use an incentive fee to motivate the provider of these services to complete the work as quickly as possible even if it results in a smaller delay. This is an example of what type of risk response?

Correct Answer: (D) Mitigate

Explanation: Risk mitigation attempts to minimize the bad risk or maximize the good risk. In this case, management is attempting to minimize the impact of a schedule delay. Risk acceptance simply deals with the risk if it happens. Risk avoidance involves doing what can be done to eliminate the risk. Transference assigns or transfers the risk to someone else. [section 13.6.5]

100.   All the following are advantages of using a bidders conference except...

Correct Answer: (C) Opportunity for vendors to inquire about the bids of other sellers

Explanation: Giving any vendor an opportunity to inquire about the bids of other sellers gives an unfair advantage to that vendor. [section 14.3.2]

101.   The project Planning is progressing on schedule. The Project Manager and the team meet regularly and are ready to estimate cost. In this estimation, what input into the Cost Estimating process will help the team the most?

Correct Answer: (A) WBS

Explanation: The WBS identifies work that requires a cost. The network diagram shows the project's activities and logical relationships. "Project management plan" is noise because cost is part of the project management plan. [section 9.11, section 7.3.1]

102.   The project has six people on it. Three more are added. What is the total number of communication channels added to the project?

PMP Exam Success Series: Certification Exam Manual
© 2007 Crosswind Project Management, Inc., www.crosswindpm.com

Correct Answer: (D) 21 Channels
Explanation: To calculate this value, calculate the number of communication channels with six people. The formula is N*(N-1)/2. This means that, with six people, there are 15 channels of communication. Next, add the three additional people for a total of nine people and use the communication channel formula. This shows that there are 36 communication channels with nine people on the project. Subtract 15 from 36 for a difference, the answer of 21 communication channels. [section 12.3.3, section 12.7]

103. The team is involved in defining what is needed to ensure quality for the project, evaluating different tools to use in Quality Planning. All the following tools are used in Quality Planning except...

Correct Answer: (B) Quality control data
Explanation: Cost-benefit analysis, flowcharts, and design of experiments are tools used in the Quality Planning process according to the *PMBOK Guide Third Edition*. Quality control data is an output of Quality Control. [section 10.8, section 10.10]

104. You are the Project Manager for a highway construction project. You have just finished putting together all the various plans into an integrated complete document. What step have you just completed?

Correct Answer: (A) Developing the project management plan
Explanation: The project management plan is the cumulative document that contains all the project management plans including the budget, schedule, project scope statement, WBS, risk, staffing, and other plans. Developing the schedule and executing the project management plan do not fit here. Signing off the project charter occurred before the project Planning began. [section 6.5]

105. Which of the following formulas shows the remaining amount to be spent on the project based on current spending efficiency?

Correct Answer: (D) ETC = EAC - AC
Explanation: Estimate to complete (ETC) shows how much money remains to be spent to complete the project based on the current efficiency of the spending. The current efficiency of the spending is based on the CPI (cost performance index). The cost variance (CV = EV – AC) shows the difference between what the project has created and what is paid to make the work. The schedule variance (SV = EV – PC) shows the difference between work completed and what should have been accomplished. Estimate at completion (EAC = BAC / CPI) is the overall revised cost estimate based on the current spending efficiency of the project. The budget remaining answer is noise. [section 9.14.5]

106. In reporting variance on the project, the Project Manager needs which of the following?

Correct Answer: (B) Baseline measurements
Explanation: Baseline measurements set the groundwork that the Project Manager can use to report performance by comparing work results to what had been planned on the project. Status reports are generally an output of this area. Status reports can lead to change requests. Status reports typically end up in the project archives. [section 12.5.1, 6.5.4]

107. Market conditions, time limitations, budget amounts, and number of people available for the project are examples of what?

Correct Answer: (B) Constraints
Explanation: Constraints are variables that can limit the options available for the project. Constraints typically deal with resources, time, or money. Assumptions are educated guesses made on the project about items that are not known. The other answers are noise. [section 6.5.3]

108. The project team is involved in decomposition of the work of the project. What two things will they create as a result of decomposition on the project?

Correct Answer: (B) Work packages and activity lists
Explanation: Work packages and activity lists are created as a result of decomposition in the Create WBS and Activity Definition processes. The other answers involve other pieces of the scheduling processes. [section 7.3.1]

109. You are managing an IT project and senior management has come to you with a high priority project that could make the company significant revenue. According to your current project schedule, the IT project is scheduled to be completed in four weeks. Senior management has also provided you with a schedule and the scope of the project they described. According to professional and social responsibility, how should you respond to senior management?

Correct Answer: (D) Decline the project because, as a Project Manager, you have not created the schedule and budget, and your current project is still in execution.
Explanation: Because you have not worked on the scope, schedule, and budget, you do not know how accurate these values are. You could be working on a project with an unrealistic schedule. Informing senior management that you can work on the project once you have completed your current project is the next best answer, but you do not know if the schedule is unrealistic. Beginning implementation of project as soon as possible is unfeasible; you cannot do two jobs at once. "Begin execution of this project" is noise because a project management plan has not been created. [section 15.5.1]

110. The team implemented a risk response plan when a vendor was unable to fulfill a contract commitment. The response was to choose another vendor. However, in this industry, it's hard to find a good company, and the one selected isn't that much better. The new company is somewhat better at meeting the terms of the contract, but still has some issues from time to time. What best describes these issues?

Correct Answer: (C) Residual risk
Explanation: Residual risk is potential risk exposure that can remain after a risk event has occurred. Secondary risk involves the creation of new risk from implementing a risk response. The risk response plan shows what is done and who is responsible for doing it if a risk event occurs. The workaround is done when risk responses do not work. [section 13.6.1]

111. Which process involves user cost estimates and the schedule to determine when these costs are expected to occur during the project?

Correct Answer: (B) Cost Budgeting
Explanation: Cost Budgeting applies costs to the individual work packages or activities, along with the schedule, to establish a cost baseline for measuring project performance. Cost Estimating generates a high level cost estimate for the overall project. Cost Control manages the cost of the project. Cost baseline is the output of Cost Budgeting. [section 9.13]

112. In what Process Group does Contract Administration occur?

Correct Answer: (A) Monitoring and Controlling
Explanation: Contract Administration occurs in the Monitoring and Controlling Process Group. [section 14.5]

113. The Crosswind multimedia development has recently been awarded a large contract to create a new science fiction series for a well known producer. This requires the company to move into a new office complete with production facilities 500% larger than what it presently has. The schedule is tight for this new project, and there can be no delay. The new facility is behind schedule with the cubicles and network wiring is on pace to finish two months late. The company is attempting to validate data. If this delay proves imminent, it plans to move

to a new building temporarily with the infrastructure that will meet its needs until the building is complete. This is an example of what type of risk response?

Correct Answer: (B) Avoid
Explanation: Risk avoidance involves doing what can be done to eliminate the risk. In this case, moving to a building that meets the company's needs avoids the risk. Risk acceptance simply deals with the risk if it happens. Mitigation attempts to minimize the bad risk. Transferring assigns or transfers the risk to someone else. [section 13.6.5]

114. A call center is being built to support a new product at a national telephone company. The company doesn't have data on how long it will take to sign up customers via the call center. This data is important because it will help drive the number of employees needed in the call center. The Project Manager remembers that a similar call center project was completed last year and begins to review data from the previous year. This is a best example of what?

Correct Answer: (A) Historical information
Explanation: Historical information contains the results of previous projects and performance. Lessons learned is the reason behind the corrective action chosen and becomes historical information. Constraints are factors that limit the options available on the project. Assumptions come into play when something on the project is not known. [section 3.2.3, section 6.1, section 5.8]

115. Activity A is worth $300, is 100% complete, and actually cost $350. Activity B is worth $100, is 95% complete, and actually cost $85 so far. Activity C is worth $200, is 75% complete, and has cost $175 so far. Total budget is $1,500. What is the estimate at completion for the activities listed?

Correct Answer: (C) $1,685.39
Explanation: Earned value (EV) and actual cost (AC) must be calculated first. To determine the EV for each activity, multiply the percent complete of each activity by its planned value (PV). To determine the total actual cost, sum the actual cost of each activity. To determine the total earned value, sum the earned value of each activity. Then divide the earned value of $545 by the actual cost of $610, deriving a CPI of 0.89. Finally, divide the BAC of $1,500 by the CPI to produce an estimated at completion of $1,685.39. [section 9.14.5, section 9.15]

116. Activity A is worth $300, is 100% complete, and actually cost $350. Activity B is worth $100, is 95% complete, and actually cost $85 so far. Activity C is worth $200, is 75% complete, and has cost $175 so far. Total budget is $1,500. What is the cost performance index for the activities listed?

Correct Answer: (D) 0.89
Explanation: Earned value (EV) and actual cost (AC) must be calculated first. To determine the EV for each activity, multiply the percent complete of each activity by its planned value (PV). To determine the total actual cost, sum the actual cost of each activity. To determine the total earned value, sum the earned value of each activity. Then divide the earned value of $545 by the actual cost of $610.00. This result provides a CPI of 0.89, indicating that the project gets $0.89 for every dollar it spends. [section 9.14.3, section 9.15]

117. A Project Manager has completed the Scope Definition process. The customer and sponsor have shortened the schedule by four weeks and decided to exclude the work breakdown structure. The Project Manager informs the customer and sponsor that this process creates the work breakdown structure for their project. Which answer best explains why the WBS is so important to a project?

Correct Answer: (B) It is the foundation of planning for the project.
Explanation: The WBS is the foundation of planning for the project. The WBS is used for planning, as well as for monitoring and controlling on the project. Budgets, staffing, and schedules are derived from the WBS, along with the deliverables. All other answers describe benefits of using a WBS. [section 7.3.1]

118. What is used to define the accounts that the WBS and organizational structures align to for project cost tracking?

Correct Answer: (B) Chart of accounts

Explanation: Chart of accounts helps align project cost with the WBS and organizational structure on the project. Work packages are the lowest level of decomposition of the work breakdown structure. [section 9.13.1]

119. A contract is a legal agreement between a buyer and a seller. There are five components of a contract. Capacity and consideration are two of five components. Which of the following is not a component of a contract?

Correct Answer: (A) Negotiation

Explanation: Negotiation undertakes clarifications and mutual agreement on the requirements of the contract prior to the signing of the contract. [section 14.1.4, section 14.4.3]

120. You are doing some analysis associated with project selection. There is a lot of debate concerning which projects to select. You have the following to choose from: Project A with an IRR of 10.5%, Project B with an IRR of 17%, Project C with an IRR of 14%, and Project D with an IRR of 12%. If you can select only one project, which do you choose?

Correct Answer: (B) Project B

Explanation: With internal rate of return for a project selection technique you select the biggest percentage. In this case, Project B has the IRR of 17%. [section 6.3.3]

121. Which of the following roles helps support the project and resolves resource conflicts?

Correct Answer: (B) Senior management

Explanation: Senior management is responsible for a number of areas on a project. The main responsibility is to help support the project and resolve resource conflicts as they occur. For situational questions, assume that you are in a balanced matrix environment, unless otherwise stated. This environment has Functional Managers controlling resources. The Project Manager's responsibility is to drive the completion of project work. Typically, the sponsor's responsibility is to pay for the project and own it when it is complete. [section 5.4.4]

122. Activity-on-Arrow diagramming uses which of the following (What is the best answer)?

Correct Answer: (A) Finish-to-start

Explanation: The activity-on-arrow (AOA) diagramming type calculates estimates and the finish-to-start relationship between activities. The start-to-finish answer is used in the activity-on-node (AON) diagramming type. [section 8.2.3]

123. The company is implementing a new project management approach. In the past, its projects have been disorganized, not in alignment with business goals, and not focused on interactivity between the projects where applicable. It wants to have a better focus on grouping-related projects together by business unit and product lines. Which of the following best describe what it is trying to accomplish?

Correct Answer: (D) Portfolio management

Explanation: Portfolio management focuses on aligning project by business unit or product line where there is some common overlap and subject matter expertise in the area of the projects. Project management creates products via projects. Operations management focuses on the day-to-day repetitive activities of a business. Management by objectives is a goal-setting technique. [section 5.1]

124. A Project Manager is progressively elaborating and documenting the project work. With help for the project charter and product description, the Project Manager has defined the scope of the project. The Project Manager is performing what process?

Correct Answer: (D) Scope Definition
Explanation: Scope Definition is the process of progressively elaborating and documenting the project work. Scope Control ensures that changes are agreed upon, determines if the scope change has occurred, and manages the actual changes. Scope Verification is the process of obtaining the stakeholder's formal acceptance of the project work and deliverables. Scope Planning creates the scope management plan for the project. [section 7.2]

125. The project management plan contains all the following except...

Correct Answer: (B) Team development
Explanation: Team development occurs throughout the project. The schedule is required to complete the project management plan. The staffing management plan is used to develop the staffing needs of the project. The change control system is usually defined in the plan. [section 6.5.1, section 11.3]

126. Your company is evaluating two projects for consideration. Project A has a 40% probability of a $25,000 loss and a 60% probability of a $650,000 gain. Project B has a 30% probability of a $15,000 loss and a 70% probability of a $570,000 gain. Which of the projects do you select based on the greatest expected monetary value?

Correct Answer: (D) Project B
Explanation: To calculate the expected monetary value (EMV), multiply each probability by its dollar amount and add the products of the multiplications. The results are a value of $380,000 for Project A and $394,500 for Project B. With the highest expected monetary value (EMV), Project B is the one to select. [section 13.5.3, section 13.8]

127. The manufacturing company has added a new line for its electronic assembly business. It involves new technology to build printed circuit boards more quickly and with fewer errors. The company anticipates that this new technology will allow it to make a greater type of products and improve the efficiency of its output. The company is also increasing the amount of insurance it has on its main facility because there has been flooding in the area in recent years from excessive rain. Adding this insurance is an example of what?

Correct Answer: (B) Insurable risk
Explanation: Pure risk is also known as insurable risk. This is something that you can buy insurance for such as to protect a building. Business risk is the risk associated with being in business for a profit or loss. Conformance to quality is part of the definition of quality. ISO 9000 is a quality standard. [section 13.2.5]

128. A close friend of yours is being investigated by PMI for the number of experience hours given on the certification application. You know he reported invalid hours on the application. PMI has been trying to contact you in this investigation. Which of the following best describes what you should do?

Correct Answer: (C) Contact PMI and cooperate with the investigation.
Explanation: The PMI Code of Ethics and Professional Conduct requires that Project Managers cooperate with PMI during investigations. [section 15.2.3]

129. The team has an approved project charter and has started planning, determining potential risks that could occur on the project. Which of the following best describe project risk?

Correct Answer: (C) It can be either a negative or a positive event.

Explanation: Risk can be of negative or positive consequence on a project. It is something that can happen but hasn't yet. Because it involves uncertainty, it deals with what could happen, not what has happened. [section 13.1]

130. You are the Project Manager working with the customer on a call center implementation. You are required to purchase and integrate a workflow software product into the call center. As the Project Manager, you want one price from the vendors for the purchase and implementation of this product. What type of document should be used?

Correct Answer: (C) Request for proposal

Explanation: A request for proposal (RFP) deals with a detailed, very specific approach to a customized solution and a total price. An invitation for bid is a sealed bidding process that lists the seller's firm price to complete the detail work. This type is typically used in government bidding. A request for information (RFI) deals with finding potential vendors for consideration for proposals or quotes. A request for quotes (RFQ) obtains prices from a company for goods or services. [section 14.2.1]

131. The Crosswind multimedia development has recently been awarded a large contract to create a new science fiction series for a well known producer. This requires the company to move into a new office complete with production facilities 500% larger than what it presently has. The schedule is tight for this new project, and there can be no delay. The new facility is behind schedule with the cubicles and network wiring on pace to finish two months late. If this can't be done on time and slips two months, the company has decided there is nothing it can do, and it will simply deal with the consequences. This is an example of what type of risk response?

Correct Answer: (A) Accept

Explanation: Risk acceptance simply deals with the risk if it happens. In this case, the project could fall through if the failure of the project to start on time impacts the schedule causing delays. Risk avoidance involves doing what can be done to eliminate the risk. Mitigation attempts to minimize the bad risk. Transferring assigns or transfers the risk to someone else. [section 13.6.5]

132. You are the Project Manager working with the customer on a call center implementation. You are required to purchase and integrate a workflow software product into the center. A contract is signed with a vendor and work has begun. Halfway through the project, the customer decides to add features to the workflow software. This addition of features will require changes to the signed contract. Who has the authority to change the contract?

Correct Answer: (D) Contract Administrator

Explanation: A Contract Administrator's main responsibility is to protect the integrity and purpose of the contract. The Contract Administrator has the authority to change the contract. The sponsor provides the financial resources for the project. The Project Manager helps to ensure that the contract is executed successfully. The customer can request changes, but the Contract Administrator must integrate them into the contract. [section 14.5.1]

133. The project team has begun development on a very important project in a new evolving technology market. Because the market is so volatile the product they are creating doesn't necessarily have all the details defined before Planning begins. The team chooses to take an approach to plan as much as they can, and begin to create work based on that effort, while continuing the Planning as they learn more about the project. Which of the following best describes the approach?

Correct Answer: (B) Progressive elaboration

Explanation: Progressive elaboration is used when not all the details are known about the project. The team begins Planning and Executing while continuing to plan as they learn more about the project. Extreme programming is a form of progressive elaboration, but not covered on the exam. Project management is doing projects to create products. Total Quality Management is a proactive approach to quality on the project. [section 5.1.2]

134. You are the Project Manager on a DOD project, and you are creating a network diagram. Activity A (four days) and Activity B (six days) can start immediately. Activity C (five days) can start after Activity A is complete. Activity D (four days) and Activity F (two days) can start after Activity B is complete. Activity E (four days) can start after Activity C and Activity D are complete. Activity G (five days) can start after Activity D and Activity F are complete. When Activity E and Activity G are complete, the project is done. What is the critical path?

Correct Answer: (C) BDG
Explanation: The critical path is the longest path in the diagram. Of the four paths, BDG is the longest at 15 days. ACE is 13 days long. BDE is 14 days. BFG is 13 days. [section 8.5.4, section 8.5.5]

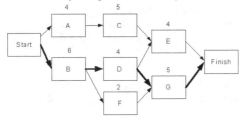

135. Using the original network diagram question, select the slack of Activity E.

Correct Answer: (D) One day
Explanation: The longest path with Activity E on it is path BDE with a duration of 14 days. The critical path of BDG is 15 days. Subtracting the length of BDE from the critical path (15-14) shows a difference of one day. This value is the slack of Activity E. [section 8.5.6, section 8.7]

136. In the original network diagram question, if Activity G decreases from five days to one, what is the critical path, and what is the length?

Correct Answer: (C) BDE, 14 days
Explanation: By decreasing Activity G from five days to one day, the path BDE becomes the critical path. This path is the longest of all paths on the network diagram. [section 8.5.4]

137. A Project Manager has completed the Scope Definition process. The customer and sponsor have shortened the schedule by four weeks and decided to exclude the work breakdown structure. What is the best action the Project Manager should take?

Correct Answer: (D) Discuss with the customer and sponsor the ramifications of excluding the WBS.
Explanation: The Project Manager should discuss the value of the WBS with the customer, explaining that the WBS is the foundation of planning for the project. Providing the customer and sponsor an updated schedule and budget is not a true estimate because the WBS has not been defined. Beginning the execution of the project is a possible answer, but without the WBS, the Project Manager does not have the work packages. Calling a meeting to notify the team of the schedule change is de-motivating because the schedule has been shortened and the team does not know what to develop. [section 7.3.1, section 7.3.4]

138. Which of the following breakdown structures are used in project scope management?

Correct Answer: (C) Work breakdown structure
Explanation: The work breakdown structure is used in scope management to break down the work of the project into work packages. Bill of materials (BOM) is used in procurement. Risk breakdown structure is used in Risk. Resource breakdown structure is used in Activity Resource Planning. [section 7.3.1]

139. All the following are needed for Scope Planning except...

    Correct Answer: (A) Work breakdown structure
    Explanation: The work breakdown structure is created in the Create WBS process, which follows Scope Planning and Scope Definition. The other answers are inputs to the Scope Planning process. [section 7.1]

140. The construction project is almost finished. The team is involved in many different activities to close the project. The team members are creating project archives. All the following are examples of project archives except...

    Correct Answer: (C) Government clearance applications
    Explanation: Archives are created as a result of the project. They include financial records, contracts, and internal project documentation. Completed government clearance applications could be part of archives. Government clearance applications are not part of the archives. [section 6.9]

141. The professional and social responsibility of a Project Manager is described in the PMI Code of Ethics and Professional Conduct. A PMP has responsibilities to the profession, to customers, and to the public. Which is not a professional and social responsibility of the Project Manager?

    Correct Answer: (A) Adhering to time, cost, and scope as specified by senior management
    Explanation: Adherence to time, cost, and scope as specified by senior management does not follow PMI's project management philosophy. A Project Manager is responsible for determining the time, cost, and scope of a project and reporting these back to senior management. [section 15.5.1, section 5.4.4]

142. A project will be using a vendor to install fire-extinguishing equipment in a large twenty-floor building. The buyer is requesting how the different vendors will do this work and how much will it cost. What type of document will be used to solicit this information?

    Correct Answer: (B) Request for proposals (RFP)
    Explanation: A request for proposals (RFP) deals with a detailed, very specific approach to a customized solution and cost. A request for quote (RFQ) obtains prices from a company for goods or services. A request for information (RFI) deals with finding potential vendors for consideration for proposals or quotes. An invitation for bid (IFB) is similar to the RFP but is typically used in government contracting. [section 14.2.1]

143. The project management team is working in the Executing phase of the project. There are two sponsors and 14 stakeholders on the project. Which of the following is the most likely to focus on communication at this point in the project to ensure the project achieves the quality standards established in Planning?

    Correct Answer: (A) At key interface points where the various work packages come together
    Explanation: The key interface points are where pieces of the project come together in Executing. If the Project Manager fails to ensure that they come together as needed, there will be problems completing the project work as intended. Revision planning happens in Planning as a result of change control. The other answers are noise. [section 6.6.2]

144. A Project Manager is creating a network diagram and needs to show a dependency between activities with no work or time. All the following network diagram techniques display this dependency except...

    Correct Answer: (D) Activity-on-node (AON)
    Explanation: Activity-on-node (AON) doesn't use dummies in its network diagram. A dummy is a dependency between activities with no work or time. AOA, AOL, and ADM do display this dependency [section 8.2.3]

145. A Project Manager has been assigned to manage a project that requires two development teams. One team will create the server software and is local, and the other team will create the client software and resides in a foreign country. For the most recent 10 conference calls with the foreign country, the foreign team is consistently 15 minutes late to the meeting. How should the Project Manager handle this problem?

    Correct Answer: (B) Review the customs and traditions of the foreign country.
    Explanation: The customs and traditions of the foreign country may show that meetings do not start on time, but around 15 minutes late. By understanding this cultural difference, you can adjust your schedule accordingly. Ignoring the problem is a possible solution, but it does not help understand the problem. You could have senior management contact the company's senior management to correct the problem, but the foreign country's senior management may not see the tardiness as a problem. Calling the development manager of the foreign country has the same effect as reporting this to senior management. [section 15.3.1]

146. Project planning is ongoing as the team analyzes how long it will take to process a customer through the new call center. This analysis will help them determine how many employees to have in the call center based on their sales projections. This is an example of what?

    Correct Answer: (B) Assumptions
    Explanation: Assumptions are educated guesses made on the project about items that are not known. Constraints are variables that can limit the options available for the project and typically deal with resources, time, or money. The other answers are noise. [section 6.5.2]

147. You are the Project Manager on the development of a 4-way fully redundant computer system for the government. The government has been very concerned about the correctness and acceptance of the work results. You are not sure what the government is saying so you review your *PMBOK Guide*. What areas below will likely be involved in attaining what the government is concerned about?

    Correct Answer: (D) Scope Verification and Quality Control
    Explanation: Scope Verification seeks to obtain formal acceptance of the work, and Quality Control focuses on the correctness of the work. Scope Control ensures that changes are agreed upon, determines if the scope change has occurred, and manages the actual changes. Quality Assurance evaluates overall project performance. Quality Planning identifies which quality standards are relevant to the project. Administrative closure documents project results to formalize acceptance of the product of the project. [section 7.4, section 10.10]

148. A risk rating matrix is used in which of the following processes?

    Correct Answer: (C) Qualitative risk analysis
    Explanation: Qualitative Risk Analysis is a process that uses a risk rating matrix to rank risks and create an overall risk rating for the project. Expected monetary value (EMV) is used in Quantitative Risk Analysis. Workarounds are done when risk responses fail. Risk triggers are indicators that a risk event could happen. [section 13.4.1]

149. Calculate the standard deviation for the following: Pessimistic=20, Optimistic=10, Realistic=17.

Correct Answer: (D) 1.67
Explanation: The formula for standard deviation is Pessimistic-Optimistic divided by 6. The answer is (20-10)/6 = 1.67. [section 8.7, section 10.8.9, section 10.11]

150. The project has had some challenges with team ownership of work on the project. The Project Manager has been challenged with continually having to tell the team what to do, and management feels that the team is unmotivated. This is an example of what?

Correct Answer: (A) Theory X environment
Explanation: In a Theory X environment, employees typically are told what to do, distrust management, and lack motivation. Theory Y is the opposite. The other answers are noise. [section 11.1.4]

151. As a Project Manager, you are managing a project that has many deliverables from outside vendors. One vendor has been in negotiations with a union that could cause the vendor to stop production on one of your deliverables. A rumor is out that the vendor's plant will be shutting down because of a strike. What is the best course of action you should take?

Correct Answer: (A) Contact the vendor and discuss this problem.
Explanation: Contacting the vendor and discussing this problem is the best course of action. At this point, the news is a rumor and the vendor can give you more information about the negotiations. The risk response plan created for this vendor should not be initiated because the risk has not triggered. As a backup plan, contact with other vendors could be undertaken, but may not be necessary. Changing vendors as soon as one is found violates the current contract. [section 15.2.2]

152. Activity A is worth $300, is 100% complete, and actually cost $350. Activity B is worth $100, is 95% complete, and actually cost $85 so far. Activity C is worth $200, is 75% complete, and has cost $175 so far. Total budget is $1,500. What is the variance at completion for the activities listed?

Correct Answer: (B) -$185.39
Explanation: The variance at completion is the difference between the budget at completion and the estimate at completion. To calculate this value, subtract EAC ($1,685.39) from BAC ($1,500) for a difference of -$185.39. [section 9.14.3, section 9.15]

153. You are a Project Manager of a home remodeling project. The budget at completion for this project is $56,000. By looking at your schedule, you should be 55% complete, but you are only 40% done. What is your earned value?

Correct Answer: (A) $22,400
Explanation: Earned value (EV) is calculated by multiplying the percent complete of each activity by its planned value (PV) EV = $56,000 * 40%, EV = $22,400. [section 9.14.4, section 9.15]

154. You are doing Quality Planning on a project. The sponsor puts into the project charter that the quality standard wanted on the project is +/- 3 Sigma. This value translates to what percentage?

Correct Answer: (D) 99.73%
Explanation: 3 Sigma is 99.73%. The percentage for 1 Sigma is 68.26% and for 2 Sigma is 95.46%. "50%" is noise. [section 10.8.9]

155. A large part of a Project Manager's time is spent communicating. What is the main benefit of this activity to the project?

Correct Answer: (B) A greater emphasis on successful integration of the various pieces of the project
Explanation: When the Project Manager ensures successful communication among the various pieces of the project, there is a greater likelihood for the successful integration of those pieces. A detailed project file is a byproduct of successful communication. An accurate communications management plan helps ensure communication with the right people. "A Theory Y management style" is noise. [section 12.3.2]

156. As a Project Manager, you are managing a project that has many deliverables from outside contractors. One contractor forgot to acquire a building permit for plumbing work to be done on the project. The city building inspector is now requesting to see the building permit. Who is ultimately responsible for acquiring the building permit?

Correct Answer: (B) Project Manager
Explanation: The Project Manager is ultimately responsible for everything in the project. If anything goes wrong on a project, it is the Project Manager's responsibility. The contractor and the plumber were delegated by the Project Manager, but it is still the Project Manager's responsibility. "City inspector" is noise. [section 5.4.4]

157. Which of the following is an advantage of a functional organization?

Correct Answer: (A) Business unit competency
Explanation: Business unit competency comes from a functional organization. For example, accounting expertise resides in an accounting department. The other answers are characteristic of a project management environment. [section 5.6.1]

158. A Project Manager has completed the Scope Definition process and is creating the work breakdown structure. The Project Manager and the project team have spent the last week working on the work breakdown structure. They have broken down the WBS to an appropriate level of decomposition. Which of the following best describes this?

Correct Answer: (D) Breaking down work where the bottom levels of the WBS represent work packages
Explanation: Breaking down work where it is a work package or 4 to 80 hour activity is the heuristics for WBS and activity decomposition. The other answers verify the correctness of the decomposition. [section 7.3.1]

159. The project is going well until a stakeholder requests a significant change based on a modification in the stakeholder's business process. The change could totally alter the work of the project. The change request and its impact analysis are going before the change control board for review and potential approval. What is the purpose of the change control board?

Correct Answer: (D) To control change by approval of needed changes and rejection of unneeded changes to the project
Explanation: The purpose of a change control board (CCB) is to control change via approval of only the needed changes and rejection of those changes not vital to the success of the project. [section 6.8.3]

160. You are the Project Manager on a software game project and are in the initiation phase. During a team meeting, a Functional Manager arrives to see if the project meets company goals. The Functional Manager will report this finding back to senior management to determine if the project should continue or be cancelled. What is this process called?

Correct Answer: (B) Management by objectives
Explanation: Management by objectives determines if a project fits in the "big picture" of the Planning at the company. If a project does not support the company's objectives, it is likely to be de-prioritized or cancelled. Delphi Technique is used to obtain expert options on the development of a project. Return on investment

compares the net benefits of a project versus its total cost. "Management product analysis" is noise. [section 7.1.2]

161. A Project Manager has been assigned to manage a project to develop digital signal processing processor for a company that does not have this expertise. The project is two weeks ahead of schedule and under budget. After calculating the estimate at completion, the Project Manager finds that the project will be $124,403 under budget. What should the Project Manager do?

Correct Answer: (D) Report the project status and budget to the customer.
Explanation: Professional and Social Responsibility requires that a Project Manager report accurate and truthful information for services provided. "Bill the customer for the total approved contracted amount" and "Report the current baseline project status and budget to the customer" do not relay honest information about the project. "Implementing gold plating to make up for the difference" is not part of the scope and should not be added. [section 15.5.1]

162. The Project Manager is reviewing testing output. Generally, the data looks good. He does observe seven consecutive data points on one side of the mean in a couple of areas on the control chart. What is this called?

Correct Answer: (A) A violation of the Seven Run Rule
Explanation: The Seven Run Rule is a situation in which there are at least seven consecutive data points on one side of the mean, implying that the process could have some type of problem. The other answers are noise. [section 10.10.11]

163. As a Project Manager, you are managing a project that has many requirements. The project is for one of your high profile customers, one who spends more than $5,000,000 a year with your company. To attain customer satisfaction, what must be met?

Correct Answer: (B) Completing products requirements
Explanation: Completing products requirements addresses what the customer has requested from the overall project. Completing the project with conformance to requirements addresses only quality. Completing the project's scope does not address schedule and budget. Completing the project on schedule and on budget does not address scope. [section 10.1, section 10.2, section 7.4]

164. You own a construction company. As you begin work on a large building that covers 20,000 square feet, you need to rent a backhoe tractor to clear the property. This is the third time you have needed the backhoe, and you want to know if you should buy or rent it. A new backhoe sells for $19,000 and costs $30 a day to maintain. You can rent one for $125 a day with the maintenance included. Which type of contract would be used to purchase the backhoe?

Correct Answer: (A) Purchase order
Explanation: Purchase order is used for commodity items such as those that can be mass-produced. The fixed-price-economic-price-adjust contract deals with offering a contract that generally has a fixed price, but because of the length of the contract, will adjust year by year as a neutral economic indicator moves upward or downward. Under a fixed-price contract, the seller performs work for a set price. Time and materials (T&M) is a contract used for smaller projects or staff augmentation. [section 14.1.6]

165. The Project Manager has asked the software developer to report on what is keeping him from completing his project activities. The developer keeps delaying his answer to the Project Manager. Finally, the Project Manager tells him to stop anything else and do just what is needed on the project. This is an example of what type of conflict resolution technique?

Correct Answer: (C) Forcing

Explanation: Forcing people to do something they don't want to do will have the worst long-term impact on the team. Smoothing is not as bad as forcing. Formal and penalty are types of power that the Project Manager has. [section 11.4.2]

166. A Project Manager has been assigned to manage a project to develop a digital signal processor in a foreign country. The Project Manager must be on-site for six months and is having problems adjusting to this job. What could cause this problem?

Correct Answer: (D) Culture differences

Explanation: Culture differences cause anxiety in a person visiting a different country. Cost differences are the responsibility of the company and not a problem. The time difference is a temporary problem. Language differences are managed by the on-site company. [section 15.3, section 15.3.1]

167. You are managing a database warehouse project and senior management has come to you with a high priority project that could make the company significant revenue. According to your current project schedule, the database warehouse project is scheduled to be completed in four weeks. What is the best response you can tell senior management?

Correct Answer: (B) Telling senior management that you will consider the project once it has a project charter

Explanation: As a Project Manager, you are responsible for maintaining the scope and objectives of your project. A project without a project charter is not a project. You could implement crashing and fast tracking to complete your current project ahead of schedule, but you are increasing risk and cost on the project. You could assign the Functional Manager on the project to finish the current project, but the Functional Manager has not been involved in the managing of the project, and such an assignment could result in a disaster. [section 15.2.2, section 15.5.1]

168. Float on a network diagram is also known as what?

Correct Answer: (A) Slack

Explanation: Slack and float are interchangeable terminology. Lag is a delay between activities on a network diagram. GERT and PERT are noise. [section 8.5.2]

169. A $6B company is implementing formal project management in its organization. It has decided to implement a Project Management Office (PMO). In the creation of this structure, which of the following is the best option to have in place to help ensure success of the organization?

Correct Answer: (D) Clearly defined goals and objectives for the PMO

Explanation: All the answers can contribute to the success of a PMO, but without clearly defined goals, they will not make a difference. [section 5.1]

170. A retail expansion project is going relatively well, but the people doing work on the project are complaining that it seems as though they answer to two bosses on the project, each with conflicting agendas. This is an example of what type of project environment?

Correct Answer: (B) Matrix

Explanation: In a matrix organization, there is a functional supervisor for the employee and a Project Manager/Coordinator. The functional supervisor has daily operational activities that the employee needs to perform. The Project Manager has project activities that are expected of the employee. Here is the point where the conflict occurs. The functional organization is organized by "silos" of departments such as accounting and marketing. A projectized environment is project-focused. "Tight matrix" is noise. [section 5.6.2]

171. You are a Project Manager starting negotiations with a vendor. In the negotiations, you are aware that the vendor has used a number of negotiation strategies. You remember these from your PMP class and ask the vendor to be fair and reasonable. All the following are negotiation strategies except...

Correct Answer: (C) Force majeure
Explanation: Force majeure is an act of God such as a flood or a tornado. Deadline implies that the negotiations must finish before a given time or the deal is off. Withdrawal implies that you are beginning to lose interest. Lying is not telling the truth. [section 14.4.3]

172. You are doing Quality Planning on a project, discussing with the sponsor the probabilities of finishing the project on schedule. There is some confusion about the sum of all probabilities and probabilities and impact. What must the sum of all probabilities equal?

Correct Answer: (B) 100%
Explanation: The sum of all probabilities must equal 100% or 1.0. The percentage for 1 Sigma is 68.26%, 2 Sigma is 95.46%, and 3 Sigma is 99.73%. [section 10.8.10]

173. Which of the following best describes a unilateral contract?

Correct Answer: (B) Purchase order
Explanation: In a unilateral contract, with *uni* meaning one-sided negotiations, a purchase order is the answer. The other answers are noise. [section 14.1.6]

174. The civil engineering project has been relatively smooth. The cost performance index is presently 0.93 and the schedule performance index is 0.89. Risk could have been managed better from the start of this project. 75% through the execution of the project management plan, the Project Manager assigned three people to do nothing but monitor for risks and work with the people who will implement the risk response plans. What are these people called?

Correct Answer: (C) Risk owners
Explanation: The Risk owners are the people responsible for implementing the risk response plans if the risk events occur. The Project Manager and sponsor aren't risk owners unless the risk response plan defined them as owners. Risk-averse is a conservative mentality toward risk. [section 13.6.4]

175. The Project Manager and team are planning a banking software project. They are discussing what could go differently than planned on the project. They are also trying to identify warning signs which show that these events could be on the verge of occurring. What are these warning signs called?

Correct Answer: (B) Triggers
Explanation: A trigger is an indicator that a risk event could be getting ready to happen. There is no assurance that, after a trigger happens, a risk event is imminent or could happen soon. Risks are factors that happen on a project and have some degree of uncertainty about them. Risk analysis and Problem solving are noise. [section 13.3.3]

176. The database project is approximately 85% complete. The project has had its challenges. As of the last status report, the project appears to be on track regarding cost, schedule, and scope. Senior management lets you know that the sponsor has some very serious concerns about the project. You don't understand why, based on the last status report. What is the best action to take first?

PMP Exam Success Series: Certification Exam Manual
© 2007 Crosswind Project Management, Inc., www.crosswindpm.com

Correct Answer: (B) Meet with the sponsor to determine the sponsor's concerns.
Explanation: Meeting with the sponsor to determine the sponsor's concerns is the best solution because it is the most proactive action and can provide either an immediate fix or the clearest information you can use to identify a concern or problem. The answers involving senior management are noise because they don't deal with addressing the problem. The triple constraint answer is also noise. [section 5.5, section 12.6]

177. The quality team is having problems getting the product to test per the requirements and test plan. The results are very uncharacteristic. The team suspects that there are a couple of pieces of the project not interacting as planned with each other. Which of the following could show if this is the case?

Correct Answer: (C) Scatter diagram
Explanation: The scatter diagram shows a potential relationship between multiple variables. The run chart and the control chart are generally the same thing. They show output over time. The Pareto diagram shows defect by count. [section 10.10.8]

178. The project is in the phase of doing procurement audits. It is important to identify successes and failures of the procurement process. This identification is important for formal acceptance and closure. What process is the project in?

Correct Answer: (D) Contract Closure
Explanation: Contract Closure uses procurement audits to determine the successes and failures of the procurement process. Closing the project is done in the Closing process and is performed when the project or phase stops. Quality Assurance validates the quality standards defined for the project. In Closing, the project finishes. [section 6.9.4, section 14.6]

179. The IT initiative project is on schedule and under budget. The customer is pleased but wants a scope change. As a result, a new team is brought in to help the existing team implement this scope change. Before the team arrives, senior management wants to see where the project stands. Which of the following do you show them?

Correct Answer: (A) Milestone chart
Explanation: The milestone chart is used for executive reporting. It shows the target dates and status of the high level milestones. The Gantt chart shows the people doing the work where the project is working to the plan. The network diagram shows the sequencing of activities on the project. The work breakdown structure (WBS) shows the work that is in the project. [section 8.5.12]

180. A new call center is being built to support a new product at a national telephone company. The company doesn't have any data on how long it will take to sign up customers via the call center. This data is important because it will help drive the number of employees needed in the call center. The company performs some tests to determine how long it will take to sign up customers. These tests must be completed and the data analyzed three weeks before the call center comes online. This is an example of what?

Correct Answer: (C) Constraints
Explanation: Constraints are factors that limit the options available on the project. Because the data must be collected and analyzed three weeks before the call center can come online, a time constraint is part of the project. Product analysis is a technique used in Scope Planning. Historical information contains the results of previous projects and performance. Assumptions come into play when something on the project is unknown. [section 6.5.3]

181. The team is determining what is needed on the project, focusing on developing a product based on the customer-defined requirements. What is this called?

Correct Answer: (C) Definition of quality
Explanation: The PMI definition of quality is the degree to which a set of inherent characteristics fulfill requirements. It implies that you build what the requirements say should be built, and that the product built will perform and function as defined and needed. [section 10.1]

182. Which of the following are examples of non-competitive forms of procurement?

Correct Answer: (A) Sole source
Explanation: One type of non-competitive forms of procurement is sole source, in which there is only one source available. The other form is single source, in which a single company is chosen even though others are available. This type of procurement is usually undertaken when the provider possesses a patent or some other type of ownership associated with intellectual property. The other answers are noise. [section 14.3.3]

183. As a Project Manager, you are managing a project that has many requirements. The project is for a high profile customer that spends more that $5,000,000 a year with your company. You have completed this project on schedule and on budget. The customer is not pleased with the product that was built. What should you do?

Correct Answer: (A) Review the scope and determine why it did not satisfy the customer.
Explanation: If the product created from the scope did not satisfy the customer, you should conduct a review to find out what was not included or if what was built was what the customer requested. "Refunding 10% of the cost of the project back to the customer" is noise. The other answers are not valid because the project has closed and resources have been released. [section 10.2]

184. All the following are correct regarding risk triggers except...

Correct Answer: (D) A trigger is an indicator that a risk event will occur.
Explanation: A trigger is a factor which indicates that a risk event is possible. Just because a trigger occurs doesn't automatically mean that a risk event is imminent. A trigger normally won't become a risk. [section 13.3.3]

185. You are a Project Manager at Dewey, Cheatum, and Howe and assigned to a major construction project. The project is on schedule and under budget, but you are constantly in conflict with a member of your project team. This team member is sabotaging the project. What is the best solution to resolve this problem?

Correct Answer: (C) Reporting this problem to senior management with a solution of replacing this team member
Explanation: Reporting this problem to senior management with a solution of replacing this team member resolves the problem and is a proactive solution. Reporting this problem to senior management is a solution but doesn't go far enough. A Project Manager should be proactive and provide options to senior management. Firing the team member as soon as possible is not a solution because a Project Manager does not have the authority. Holding a team meeting to vote if the team member should be removed increases the conflict. [section 15.5.1, section 15.3]

186. A project will be using a company to provide technicians for a national network upgrade project. Presently, the Project Manager is in contract negotiation with a vendor and the negotiations have been very difficult. In what process is the Project Manager involved?

Correct Answer: (C) Select Sellers

Explanation: Select Sellers involves negotiating with more than one vendor and ultimately selecting the vendor for the contract. Plan Contracting determines the approach to find a company that can do the work for you. Plan Purchases and Acquisitions involves a make-or-buy analysis to determine if your company will do the work itself or outsource it. Request Seller Responses handles the receipt and review of proposals from companies being considered for the work. [section 14.4]

187. On a retail construction project, the team is sizeable, and controlling communication has been a challenge. The Project Coordinator has been used to help with this problem. What is one of the main differences between the Project Coordinator and the Project Expeditor?

Correct Answer: (B) The Project Coordinator has decision-making ability.

Explanation: The Project Coordinator and Project Expeditor are similar in responsibility except that the Project Coordinator also has decision-making ability. [section 5.4.4]

188. A contract has been signed and is expected to cost $750K over a one-year engagement. At project completion, the actual cost is $700K, but the project is behind schedule due to a delay in shipping. There is a 60/40% share for any cost savings. What is the total value of the contract?

Correct Answer: (D) $720K

Explanation: This is a calculation question. $750K is the expected value of the contract. Actual cost of the contract is $700K, meaning that there is a $50K savings. The 60/40% share means that $20K of the savings goes to the seller. The actual cost of $700K and $20K savings share make the total value of the contract worth $720K. "$700K because the project was behind schedule" is not correct because the contract did not specify any penalties for being behind schedule. [section 14.1.7]

189. A change control document on a project is viewed as what type of communication?

Correct Answer: (A) Formal written

Explanation: Any documentation associated with the contract or project management documentation is considered formal written. [section 12.2]

190. You are a Project Manager trying to decide what quality approach to implement at your company. You have decided that it is in the best interest of the company to do testing while in the developing phase to get immediate feedback. This philosophy is known as what?

Correct Answer: (C) Total Quality Management

Explanation: Total Quality Management uses continuous improvement as employees find ways to improve quality. Quality Assurance ensures that the quality plan will achieve the desired results of the project. The quality management plan describes how the project management team will implement its quality policy. ISO 9000 is a Quality System Management Standard. [section 10.3]

191. Crosswind Custom Homes is building a customer's dream house. However, rain has delayed the finish by two weeks. The Project Manager evaluates the schedule and determines that the electrical and plumbing could occur at the same time instead of right after each other, as laid out in the schedule. This is an example of what?

Correct Answer: (D) Discretionary dependencies

Explanation: A discretionary dependency can be determined by the Project Manager. A mandatory dependency is required and internal to the organization. Crashing and lag are noise. [section 8.2.1]

192. What type of contract provides the buyer with the most risk and the seller with the least risk?

Correct Answer: (D) Cost-plus-percentage of cost
Explanation: Cost-plus-percentage of cost covers the cost of the seller to build something and pays that seller a percentage of the total cost as a fee. The more that seller spends, the greater the fee. The fixed-price contract provides the seller with the most risk because the contract limits the amount that the buyer will pay for the project. Time and materials contracts are typically used for smaller amounts of work and staff augmentation and provide minimal risk for both the seller and buyer. Cost-plus-fixed-fee covers the cost of the seller and also includes a fee for the work, medium risk for the buyer, and minimal risk for the seller. [section 14.1.6]

193. Which of the following is an output of a change control system?

Correct Answer: (B) Approved changes
Explanation: Approved changes are the output of a change control system. These are change requests that have gone into the system and have been approved. Change requests involve a desired change that hasn't been approved yet. Impact analysis identifies what impact the change might have on the project or environment. Signoff involves receiving approval. In this case, "signoff" is noise. [section 6.8.1, section 6.8.2]

194. The professional and social responsibility of a Project Manager has many responsibilities to the profession. A PMP has responsibilities to the profession, to customers, and to the public. Which is not a professional and social responsibility of the Project Manager?

Correct Answer: (D) Creating a project charter that has a win-win situation for your company and your customer
Explanation: The Project Manager does not create a project charter. That is the job of the sponsor. [section 5.4.4, section 15.2]

195. You are the finance controller with your company. Your job is to analyze projects when they close. This could be the result of when a project is complete or by any other means. When do you expect to close a project?

(A) When a project is cancelled
(B) When a project runs out of money
(C) When a project completes Scope Verification

Correct Answer: (D) All the answers
Explanation: Whenever a project ends, closing the project should be completed. A project ending lets the team and organization learn from what worked on the project and what did not, and formally closes out the initiative. [section 6.9]

196. You are the Project Manager for a project that has many deliverables. One deliverable is a new version of an Ethernet switch. You have completed the project on time and on budget. A vendor is now starting the rollout of the new Ethernet switch to your customers. The vendor has scheduled you to help with the rollout. What is your response to the vendor?

Correct Answer: (D) Tell the vendor that the scope of the project has been fulfilled, the project is closed, and you are no longer available.
Explanation: Once the scope of a project is completed, the project is completed, and the resources are released and reassigned. Consulting your manager on your schedule notifies your manager that the vendor is requesting your help, but you are no longer on the project. Asking for a schedule to see what the timelines are for each installation and contacting the vendor to discuss the financial cost for your help are not valid because you are not officially assigned to the project. [section 15.5.1]

197. Project Scope Management is characterized by processes in the Planning, as well as the Monitoring and Controlling phases. Which group of processes defines Project Scope Management?

Correct Answer: (C) Scope Planning, Scope Definition, Create WBS, Scope Verification, Scope Control
Explanation: Scope Planning, Scope Definition, Create WBS, Scope Verification, and Scope Control are the processes that define Project Scope Management. The other answers are noise. [chapter 7]

198. The team is involved in defining what is needed to ensure quality for its project. One team member says, "Do it right the first time." Another team member says, "Let's incorporate a method that reduces errors and helps the company make money." What best describes this process?

Correct Answer: (D) Zero Defects
Explanation: The Zero Defects practice aims to reduce defects as a way to directly increase profits. The concept of Zero Defects led to the development of Six Sigma in the 1980s. Total Quality Management uses continuous improvement where employees find ways to improve quality. Kaizen is the continuous, incremental improvement of an activity to create more value with less waste. Fitness for Use is a concept that focuses on meeting the customer and stakeholder needs. [section 10.4]

199. The Project Manager has been negotiating with a vendor for the last two months. The vendor received the statement of work and has responded with a proposal using cost-plus-fixed-fee. The Project Manager answers back with a letter of intent. Why did the Project Manager send this letter?

Correct Answer: (B) The Project Manager plans to buy from the vendor.
Explanation: A letter of intent is a document which declares that the buyer intends to hire or buy from the seller for a specific project. The other answers are noise. [section 14.1.6]

200. You are the Project Manager on a project. You have the work breakdown structure and have begun subdividing the project work packages into smaller, more manageable components. The output from this process is critical for creating the network diagram and duration estimates. What process are you executing and what is the output?

Correct Answer: (B) Activity Definition and activity list
Explanation: The Activity Definition process takes the WBS and uses decomposition to create an activity list. Activity Sequencing uses the activity list as input to create the network diagram. Activity Duration Estimating uses the activity list as input to create duration estimates. Schedule Development and project schedule use the network diagram and duration estimates as inputs. [section 8.1]

PMP Exam Success Series: Certification Exam Manual
© 2007 Crosswind Project Management, Inc., www.crosswindpm.com

Section 2

SUPPORT AND KNOWLEDGE AREAS

5.   Framework

6.   Integration

7.   Scope

8.   Time

9.   Cost

10.   Quality

11.   Human Resource

12.   Communications

13.   Risk

14.   Procurement

15.   Professional and Social Responsibility

Chapter 5

Framework

Framework is a distinctive subject in PMP studies. Although straightforward with regard to general concepts and terminology, it presents challenges in the details. Even people with extensive workplace experience can have difficulty conceptualizing material such as a project, a program, or a particular type of organizational structure, as PMI defines them. Regardless of your experience, if your working knowledge doesn't concur with PMI standards, it won't earn you credit on the PMP Examination. However, if you approach the Framework chapter (and the other chapters as well) with the goal of understanding the details as PMI defines them, your road to PMP Examination success will be much smoother.

In this chapter, we discuss the following:

Disciplines

The Triple Constraint

Organizational Structures

✓	**Crosswind "Must Knows" For Framework**
	Organizational structure in Figure 2-6 on page 28 of the *PMBOK Guide* Third Edition
	Project management life cycle, project life cycle, and product life cycle
	Characteristics of programs and program management
	Characteristics of portfolios and portfolio management
	How to align plan-do-check-act with project management life cycle
	Triple constraint and how it functions
	Characteristics of a functional organization
	Characteristics of a weak matrix organization
	Characteristics of a balanced matrix organization
	Characteristics of a strong matrix organization
	Characteristics of a projectized organization
	Characteristics of a composite organization
	Role of the stakeholder and management of that position (how to identify their needs)
	Responsibilities of and differences between a Project Coordinator and Project Expeditor
	Responsibilities and characteristics of the various personnel involved in project management
	Characteristics of a project, a subproject, a program, and a portfolio
	Characteristics and purpose of strategic planning
	Characteristics and benefits of a PMO (Project Management Office)
	How to balance stakeholder interests

Although helpful, this list is not all-inclusive for information needed from this area for the exam. It is only suggested material that, if understood and memorized, can increase your exam score.

5.1   Overlap of Disciplines

Whenever project management is used, there is an overlap of the *PMBOK Guide*, technical knowledge, knowledge of the project atmosphere, general management ability, and interpersonal (soft) skills.

The project atmosphere can consist of things such as **cultural, social, political, and international** variables.

General management can include areas such as finance, purchasing (procurement), sales, law, manufacturing and logistics, planning, organizational characteristics, health (safety), and information technology.

Interpersonal skills can include communication, **influence**, leadership, motivation, **negotiation**, and problem solving.

Project Management	Project management is the **application of information, skills, tools, and techniques to activities involved with a project in order to meet project needs**. It can include developing requirements, determining realistic goals, managing the triple constraint, and adapting the various plans as needed to achieve the goals of the project and stakeholders. Project management can start with selection of the suitable processes associated with completing the work of the project. In addition, it can involve using an established methodology to align project and product requirements with the product specifications.
Project Management System	The project management system is a **set of procedures, tools and techniques, processes, and methodologies that an individual Project Manager, PMO, or company can use to manage projects**. This system can be formal or informal in nature. Typically, it is supported by the project management plan as the project work is executed.

Project Management Life Cycle (PMLC)	Project management life cycle includes five process groups: Initiating, Planning, Executing, Monitoring and Controlling, and Closing. These processes **can be performed throughout the entire project, or they may be applied phase-by-phase.**	Know the project management life cycle.
Project Life Cycle	Project life cycle is the **process of completing work on the project.** It is not the project management of the work, but rather the work process such as the building process of creating a house, or that of developing a computer program. This life cycle typically coexists with the project management life cycle. The project life cycle can describe what work is done (and who does the work) in each phase of the project, what the deliverables are, and approval for each phase.	Know the project life cycle.
Product Life Cycle	The product life cycle **involves the product or service from concept to divestment (closure).** This cycle can begin with a business plan, project, transition to operations, and finally the exit or finish of the product or service.	Know the product life cycle.

PMP Exam Success Series: Certification Exam Manual
© 2007 Crosswind Project Management, Inc., www.crosswindpm.com

Figure 5-1: Life Cycle Interaction demonstrates how the three life cycles interrelate. Understand their characteristics, why you would focus on one more than another, and the purpose of each.

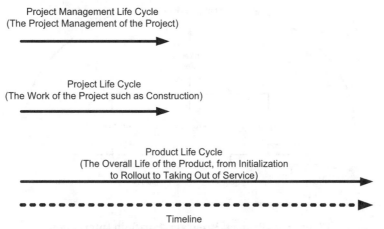

Project Management Life Cycle
(The Project Management of the Project)

Project Life Cycle
(The Work of the Project such as Construction)

Product Life Cycle
(The Overall Life of the Product, from Initialization
to Rollout to Taking Out of Service)

Timeline

Figure 5-1: Life Cycle Interaction

Project

The project is an initiative that has the following characteristics:

- Has a specific purpose
- Creates specific results
- Has definite start and finish dates
- Is temporary
- Could be progressively elaborated as more is learned about the project details

A project could occur as a result of a business opportunity or market need, which could have a limited time window. Examples of project efforts could be product or artifact, service, or a result such as new documents or outcomes.

Know the characteristics of a project and a subproject.

Subproject

Subprojects are created when there is a need to break something down into smaller pieces that are easier to manage. Various criteria could apply to the creation of a subproject. Some common examples are types of technology, types of labor used (skill set), or a phase-by-phase approach to a project.

Program and Program Management

A program encompasses projects of similar work or correlated activities **managed in a coordinated way to attain benefits that could not be achieved separately**. This could also involve the program interacting with operations as a result of the integration of a program (and its project) into operations. An example of program management could be the creation of a computer as a result of a number of projects designing the pieces (such as the motherboard, disc drives, and other assemblies), with the computer finally being built on the assembly line.

Know the characteristics of a program and program management.

Portfolio and Portfolio Management

Portfolio management involves a group of projects (and/or) programs that have some degree of interactivity related to an overall strategic business goal. The interactivity could be related to funding, performing organization, or type of project.

Know the characteristics of a portfolio and portfolio management.

Figure 5-2: Project, Program, Portfolio Interaction demonstrates how projects, programs, and portfolios interrelate with the strategic planning of a company.

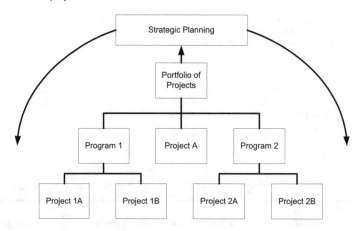

Figure 5-2: Project, Program, Portfolio Interaction

Strategic Planning	Strategic planning is a practice by which a company looks into the future for products or services it must have, typically **three to five years** in the future. Projects are the tools that the company will use to implement these strategic goals, because the operations of the company typically encompass the day-to-day (repeatable) activities. Thus, when the strategic goals are complete, they roll into the operations of the company. Projects can be created as a result of market demand, legal needs, technology updates, and customer or organizational needs. PMI has a tool and methodology approach called OPM3 (Organizational Project Management Maturity Model) for aligning a company's goals and strategic planning to project management.	Know the characteristics and purpose of strategic planning.

Project Management Office (PMO)	The Project Management Office (PMO) concept became popular in the late 1990s and can take a number of configurations, with the main being as follows: • A centralized area for all project management personnel to work and be assigned to projects as they arise • A centralized area for documentation and process support for project management throughout the organization • A centralized area for project management support and auditing of projects in the organization For a PMO to be successful, project goals must be clearly defined and backed by strong executive support.	Know the characteristics and benefits of a PMO (Project Management Office).

5.1.1   Project Management vs. Operations Management

Know the difference between project and operations management. While both involve running a business, project management deals with the creation of temporary specific initiatives, whereas operation management deals with the ongoing repetitive day-to-day activities of running the business. There are common characteristics such as Planning, Executing, Monitoring and Controlling, people doing the work, and resource constraints.

PMP Exam Success Series: Certification Exam Manual
© 2007 Crosswind Project Management, Inc., www.crosswindpm.com

5.1.2   Progressive Elaboration

The term "Progressive Elaboration" often confuses people when they first read the *PMBOK Guide*.

It means to work on a project for which you might not know all the details. You plan based on what you know. You begin the work while learning about (and planning) the future details of the unknown work. As you learn more about the work of the project, the plan progresses, becoming more elaborate. Typically, you start out in small steps and make multiple increments in the Planning and Executing of the project as work is completed.

5.2   Triple Constraint

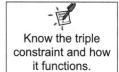

Know the triple constraint and how it functions.

One of the most basic foundations of project management is the triple constraint, defined by the following:

- Scope (could be referenced as quality)
- Time
- Cost

Every project can have these constraints, and all of them are connected. If one is impacted, there will very likely be an impact on the others.

You need to define scope before you can determine how much time something will take to create. You need to know how long something will take to create before you can determine cost. Note that a change in one can impact the others.

Unless otherwise stated, all three constraints are of equal importance. If the scope, time, and cost goals are attained, then you have achieved quality, and thus (more than likely) satisfied the customer. If you had a situation in which the sponsor said: "Money is no object. Just get this scope done as soon as possible," scope is your main priority.

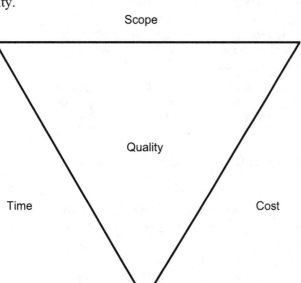

Figure 5-3: Triple Constraint

A more modern approach to the triple constraint is shown in Figure 5-4:

Enhanced Triple Constraint. Note that it includes more than three items. Because the additional components of risk and customer satisfaction can have significant influence on a project, the graphic has been enhanced to include them. Be aware that customer satisfaction needs and risk tolerances (of key stakeholders) can influence the scope, time, cost, and quality goals of the project.

Figure 5-4: Enhanced Triple Constraint

5.3   Standards and Regulations

It is important to understand the difference between a standard and a regulation.

Standard	A standard is a **specification in place** for an item or process that is suggested **and typically common.** It is optional. An example of a specification is the storage capacity of a CD-ROM.
Regulation	A regulation is **more like a law, in that compliance is required.** It is mandatory. Examples of regulations are city building codes or how to dispose of old computers.

5.4   Process Groups and Position Descriptions

5.4.1   Process Groups

The general approach to this group of processes can even be applied to everyday life. **There are five main Process Groups: Initiating, Planning, Executing, Monitoring and Controlling, and Closing.** One philosophy to take into consideration is that this approach is not necessarily a methodology meant to be used consistently on all projects. The Project Manager should work with the team to determine what processes are appropriate to use (and to what extent) on each project to achieve the project goals.

Another concept to understand is that, as you go through the Process Groups (Initiating, Planning, Executing, Monitoring and Controlling, and Closing), **if you have to go from Executing or Monitoring and Controlling back to adjust the**

plan, you are indeed going back to a Planning process. That said, it is acceptable to go back to an earlier Process Group and revisit it if needed for the project.

Finally, it's fair to say that not all processes (and interactions of them) occur on every project, nor are they needed on every project. The processes and the interactions should be defined as needed for the specific project. **For the exam, it's good to understand all the processes and generally how they interact as described in this book and the third edition of the** *PMBOK Guide*.

Initiating	In the Initiating stage, the **initial work is put into place** on a project. A project can continue or it can be killed at this point. Typically, when a project moves beyond initiation, a Project Manager is assigned, a sponsor is defined, and a high level project scope statement, among other things, is put into place. These items should make it possible for the project to move forward to Planning. This Initiating stage can also be applied to the beginning of every phase of a project. Typically, a **project charter and a preliminary project scope statement** are created here.
Planning	Planning is perhaps the **most important** of all the stages. If you plan badly, your project likely will never be better than the plan. Therefore, you need to spend as much time planning as allowed by the sponsor, your company, or anyone else involved. In this stage, the Project Manager makes a management plan for each of the Knowledge Areas (Scope, Time [schedule], Cost, Human Resource [staffing], Communications, Quality, Risk, Procurement, and Integration) and integrates them. The Project Manager also makes a plan for adjusting (controlling) each stage as changes occur. The team should be involved in a great deal of this planning. After all, they will be doing the work; they should have input with regard to their efforts. The Planning processes develop the overall **project management plan**.
Executing	It is in the execution stage that the **project scope is built**. In Planning, you "planned the work." Now, you "work the plan." Throughout the process of executing the plan, the project team will discover things they hadn't planned for or forecasted. As a result, the Monitoring and Controlling process stage comes into play, the point at which the team experiences variance from the plan. The Executing processes **create work results**.
Monitoring and Controlling	In Monitoring and Controlling, the team **maintains what it has planned**. By putting a plan (Planning) in place, the team executes the plan, and when the team encounters variance (as usually happens), the Controlling stage comes into play as a means to adjust the plan to compensate for new discoveries (dates, resources, cost, scope, etc.). A key perspective to have in this process area is adherence to the official change control process so that only formally approved changes are implemented. Monitoring and Controlling results in **corrective actions**.
Closing	In Closing, the **project ends**. Assuming that the project has been executed and worked to the point of nearing completion, the bulk of what will be happening in this process stage is closing the project and Contract Closure. In the case of

	Contract Closure, the main goal is to verify that what should have been done in the contract was done, including payment and signoff. Closing the project involves Contract Closure, as well as archiving any project records, documents, etc. Closing the project **results in the product, service, or result** of the project.

Project Management Process Groups in the Plan-Do-Check-Act Format

The American Society for Quality (ASQ) defines the Plan-Do-Check-Act cycle as an approach to process development. The Project Management Process Groups are more complicated than the basic Plan-Do-Check-Act format, but Figure 5-5: Comparison of Plan-Do-Check-Act to PMLC shows a view of how they can overlap or co-exist. Note that Monitoring and Controlling actually works around the other four Process Groups.

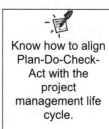

Know how to align Plan-Do-Check-Act with the project management life cycle.

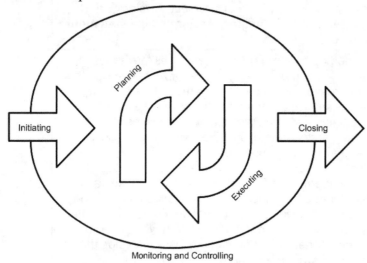

Figure 5-5: Comparison of Plan-Do-Check-Act to PMLC

5.4.2   Phases vs. Process Groups

It's not uncommon for people to confuse the Initiating, Planning, Executing, Monitoring and Controlling, and Closing Process Groups of a project with project phases. Upon studying the *PMBOK Guide*, you should see the Process Group approach that PMI has established for these five items. Think of it this way: if a project has multiple pieces, or phases, as they are commonly called, you could easily do Initiating, Planning, Executing, Monitoring and Controlling, and Closing for each phase.

PMI situational questions assume that the organization has a project management methodology in place with this group of processes working together. Be prepared for situational questions that use the terms Process Groups or phases representing Initiating, Planning, Executing, Monitoring and Controlling, and Closing. Also, understand that **going through the five Process Groups is not always a "start-to-finish" approach. The Process Groups can overlap and have various iterations as needed to complete the goals of the project.** For example, if you are in execution and have to revise (or learn more about) the plan, you return to the Planning Process Group to do so. This is the case even if a change request was approved in Monitoring and Controlling that sent you back to Planning.

5.4.3   Phase Gate

A phase gate is a review process undertaken to determine if a project is likely to succeed. At the end of a program or project phase, an authorized group (such as a steering committee or independent party) reviews the work of the phase and either approves to continue the project or makes the decision to stop future work on the initiative. As a result of this activity, projects that are not likely to succeed are "killed" early. A phase gate could also be considered a "**kill point**."

5.4.4   Position Descriptions

There are about half a dozen key players in PMI's perspective on project management and the test environment. Here, we generally describe their responsibilities roles, as well as a little about their interactions with other players in the methodology.

Project Manager	The role of Project Manager is the primary role of our discussion. Everything we consider revolves around it. The general viewpoint is that **this role involves communication with all others and the integration of activities with all others**, as needed. Project Managers **describe to the team members what activities need to be done per the plan**; they **maintain Scope Control of the project**; and they **communicate project status** as it evolves. They are the bus drivers in this scenario. An example is someone in charge of executing the project charter goals. The Project Manager has the ultimate responsibility to deliver the project.	Know the differences and characteristics of the various personnel involved in project management.
Project Management Team	A project management team member is **anyone on the team** who is working on project management-related items. Activities can include scheduling, cost budgeting, and change management.	
Project Coordinator	A Project Coordinator is put into place when the organization structure doesn't support a full-scale project management environment, or it is used to support the Project Manager. A Project Coordinator **acts as a communications link to senior management** and has some **limited decision-making abilities**.	Know the responsibilities and differences between a Project Coordinator and a Project Expeditor.
Project Expeditor	Like a Project Coordinator, a Project Expeditor is put into place when the organization structure doesn't support a full-scale project management environment, or is used to support the Project Manager. Project Expeditors act as communications links. They perform activities such as **verifying that some assignment is complete, checking on the status of some undertaking,** and communicating to senior management. Typically, they **do not have decision-making abilities**.	
Customer/User	A Customer or User is the **person or group that makes use of the work of the project**. It could include two descriptions in which the customer can be the **owner of the project work** and the user can be the **end person/group using the work**.	

Sponsor (sometimes referred to as Senior Management)	The sponsor is the **key person (or group) who has secured financing for the project, creates the project charter, and signs off upon project completion.** The Project Manager manages the sponsor's expectations and secures the acceptance signature(s) so the project team can move on to other projects.
	Typically, the Project Manager consults the sponsor for approval on changes that could impact the project charter.
	The sponsor could also be referred to as senior management, but typically, senior management works for the sponsor and helps accomplish company goals.
Senior Management (sometimes referred to as the sponsor)	Senior management usually refers to management that **supports the sponsor, the project charter, and ultimately the project.** Some of the activities that senior management undertakes include helping **to prioritize items associated with other projects** and helping to coordinate with other groups or activities that can interfere with the project.
	Do not confuse senior management with the Functional Manager (or functional management). An example of senior management is a director of an e-commerce-related project.
	The assumption is that senior management could also be referred to as the sponsor, but typically senior management is the management that works for the sponsor and helps accomplish company goals.

	Figure 5-6: Senior Management Focus
Functional Manager	This Functional Manager position doesn't play much of a role in the process other than **dealing with people and controlling resources.** Typically, you see this role **conflicting with the Project Manager and direction of the project.** This potential conflict stems from the fact that the Functional Manager has a primary interest in running some business division or department and only a secondary – if any – interest in a project that often pulls people away from their regular jobs in that division or department. An example is a manager in the accounting department.

Project Team Members (Also called Project Staff)	Team members are **those who actually do the work** that goes toward meeting the scope of the project. They can be analysts, programmers, technical writers, construction personnel, testers, etc. These people perform activities delegated by the Project Manager, who assumes that they know enough to manage their own workload without the need for micromanagement. If team members are unclear about their workload, they can contact the Project Manager for direction. One main difference between a team member and a stakeholder is that a team member typically bills (is a cost) to the project.
Performing Organization	The performing organization is the **company or division** of a company that is **doing the work** of the project.
Influencer	The influencer is a **person or group indirectly related** to a project; they can have a **negative or positive influence** on that project.
PMO (Project Management Office)	The PMO (if one is associated with the project) could have **responsibility associated with the completion of the project**. See the PMO description earlier in this chapter.
Stakeholders	**Stakeholders can be any of the roles listed above**, anyone actively involved in, or anyone impacted (negatively or positively) by the project. They are not just people associated with project creation and completion, but upon project completion, they may be impacted by its result and functionality. An example is a consumer who depends on the project or someone who is employed as a result of the project completion and deployment.

5.5   Stakeholder Management

Stakeholder management is a complex topic because of the people involved and the situations a Project Manager can encounter. Some project management training discusses "negotiations" instead of stakeholder management. It is fair to say that stakeholder management is not always negotiation, but if you encounter problems on the project, stakeholder management can often be resolved by negotiation.

Understand the role of the stakeholder and management of that position.

A key characteristic of stakeholder management to remember is that early in the project, the stakeholder can have a great degree of influence, but the level of that influence decreases as the project evolves. This influence is indirectly proportional to the cost characteristic associated with changes. Early in the project, changes typically cost less to implement. Later, as more of the project work is done, changes typically increase in cost.

Some key areas of stakeholder management that need to be considered include the **identification and analysis of the stakeholders and their goals or agendas for the project.** It is also important that you include the key stakeholders on the project as needed so they have appropriate input and contribution as the project evolves.

Finally, when events are complete, the appropriate stakeholders sign off and approve the project work so project participants can move on to the next project.

5.5.1 Balancing Stakeholder Interests

Situational questions in this area can be very challenging. The really challenging questions could go to the point of determining if the project actually continues or is radically altered. In these cases, refer to the following rules in this order:

> Understand how to balance stakeholder interests.

1. Why is the project being done? What is the market condition or business need? Why is it a priority compared to other projects?
2. What does the project charter and foundation of the project describe to do?
3. What does the project management plan say?

An example is: Two stakeholders have conflicting needs. You look to rule number 1 overriding rules 2 and 3. If one stakeholder wants to use an older reporting application to develop reports because that stakeholder is familiar with it, you could argue that rule 3 provides flexibility to go either way. However, if market conditions driving the project and how it was defined in the project charter state that it is imperative to use this new software to gain entry into a new market, that necessity takes precedence over the desire to use the old reporting application.

With regard to addressing project-specific changes, the following order should help ensure success:

1. Do not tell customers "no" when asked about a request. Remember, you are there to do what they have documented that they want. If they are willing to encounter a delay or pay more to get the change created, the decision to do so is theirs, not yours as the Project Manager.
2. Listen to the wishes of the stakeholders. Figure out what they want and what the existing timeframes and cost parameters or constraints might be.
3. Communicate the impact and options associated with the request after (if needed) involving team members to determine those options.
4. Let the customer (sponsor) make the call on what they want and don't want based on the options you have provided them.

5.6 Organizational Structures

Key to the foundation of project success is the type of organizational structure in which a project exists. Most project environments have some common components such as values, norms, expectations, policies, procedures, established authority relationships, and work hours. For the PMP Examination, there are six key types of organizations, and you must learn the characteristics of each. They are:

- Functional
- Weak matrix
- Balanced matrix
- Strong matrix
- Projectized
- Composite

5.6.1   Functional Organization

The functional organization structure is the established, more common structure used in business today. It works more in an **operations mindset, where projects typically aren't a high priority, and people of a similar skill set are grouped together and managed by someone with that same skill set**. This structure is sometimes called a silo organizational structure because the people in the individual groups (or silos) typically work among themselves more than with the other groups.

This structure makes managing resources in relation to project management activities rather difficult because there is little, if any, reason for the resources to listen to the project management role instead of their functional supervisor.

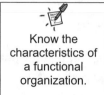

Know the characteristics of a functional organization.

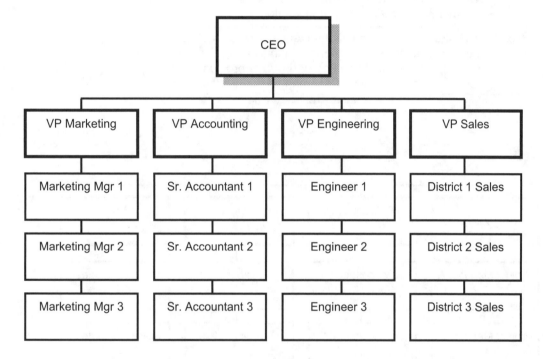

Figure 5-7: Functional Organization Chart

	Project Manager Authority	Resources Available for Project Work	Who Controls Project Spending	Person's Role as a PM	PM Support Staff
Functional	Little, if any	Almost none	Functional Manager	Part time	Part time

Functional characteristics include the following:
- Primary focus on operations and daily repetitive activities
- Lack of focus on projects
- Lack of focus for full-time project personnel

5.6.2   Matrix Organization

Many companies use the matrix organization to accommodate established functional organization structures while being flexible enough to implement projects. A company can retain its functional foundation and use cross-functional teams, letting people from various silos work together on a project. However, under the matrix organization, a team member may report to **multiple bosses** and work under multiple (usually conflicting) sets of priorities.

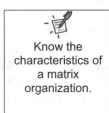

Know the characteristics of a matrix organization.

Matrix Organization Types

Weak Matrix	A weak matrix organization does tend to a functional organization with a few extra benefits toward the project.
Balanced Matrix	The balanced matrix organization is simply that, somewhere in the middle between strong and weak.
Strong Matrix	The strong matrix organization tends to be almost "projectized," but the roots are still functional. In this case, there is usually a project management function or group to provide a solid foundation for project management in the organization.

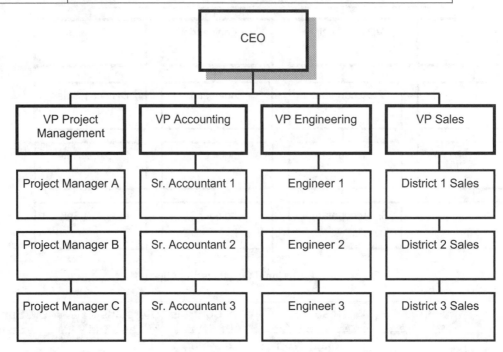

Figure 5-8: Matrix Organization Chart

Matrix	Project Manager Authority	Resources Available for Project Work	Who Controls Project Spending	Person's Role as a PM	PM Support Staff
Weak	Limited	Limited	Functional Manager	Part time	Part time
Balanced	Low to medium	Low to medium	Mixed	Full time	Part time
Strong	Medium to high	Medium to high	Project Manager	Full time	Full time

PMP Exam Success Series: Certification Exam Manual
© 2007 Crosswind Project Management, Inc., www.crosswindpm.com

Matrix characteristics include the following:
- Dual focus on operations and projects (as transition from weak to strong, the project focus increases)
- Dual bosses (Functional and Project Manager) for employees
- In a balanced matrix, Functional Manager controls resources and Project Manager runs the projects
- People focus on dual priorities (projects and operations)

5.6.3   Projectized Organization

Know the characteristics of a projectized organization.

The projectized organization is a modern structure that has eliminated the silos of specialization seen in the functional organization. Although this structure has silos, they focus on the project (or operations by project) instead of on the specialization of the individual. **This focus greatly increases the team's ability to optimize focus and performance because the project is the main focus.**

One key consideration is that, upon project completion, there might not be positions (jobs) for all team members. In a matrix or functional environment, team members simply return to their former departments or project duties.

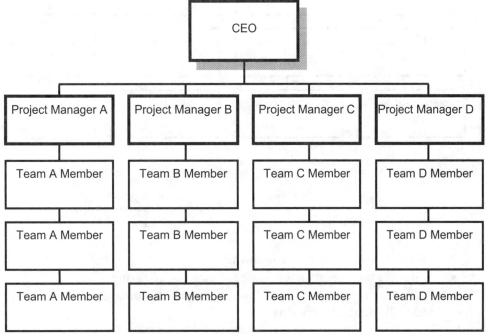

Figure 5-9: Projectized Organization Chart

	Project Manager Authority	Resources available for Project Work	Who Controls Project Spending	Person's Role as a PM	Project Management Support Staff
Projectized	High to total	High to total	Project Manager	Full time	Full time

Projectized characteristics include the following:
- A team focus on the project work
- Teams consisting of mixed skills because of a project focus (instead of departmental)

5.6.4   Composite Organization

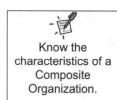

A composite organization is a **hybrid** type of structure that can have characteristics of a matrix and projectized and functional environment. It could have a silo for project management that has people from that branch managing projects, plus people from other silos managing projects as well.

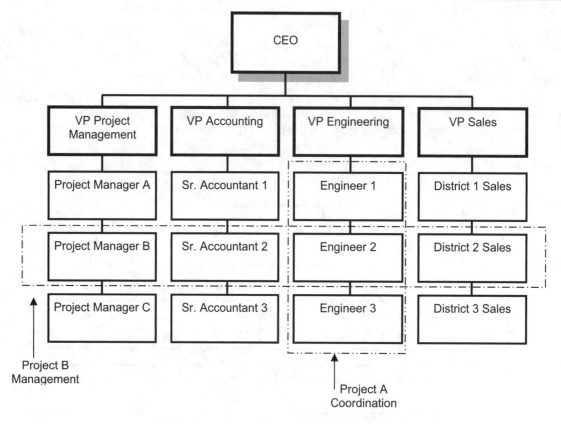

Figure 5-10: Composite Organization Chart

Composite characteristics include the following:
- A flexible configuration for doing projects in a company
- Project management or leadership vary depending on originator and skills/people on projects

5.7   Framework Formulas and Variables

No formulas for Framework

5.8   Framework Terminology

Term	Description
Authority	The agreement to be able to assign project resources, make project decisions, and spend project funding
Closing Processes	Activities during which formal acceptance and completion procedures are attained from either a phase or the project itself
Co-location	A team-building technique in which team members are located together or as close to each other as possible
Criteria	Standards to which project variables are compared for acceptability
Customer	The individual, group, or company that will own the work of the project when it is complete
Deliverable	A finished work product that results from completion of a series of activities
Enterprise	A company, business, or other formal structure that encompasses a business function
Enterprise Environmental Factors (Output/Input)	Any internal or external organization variables that can influence the project success Examples: company culture, the business market, technology, and personnel
Executing Processes	The coordination of personnel and additional resources to implement the project management plan and create the deliverables of the project
Functional Organizational Structure	A structure within a company where people are grouped by similar skill set (e.g., accounting, marketing, engineering)
Goods	Products that have been created and are available for purchase
Historical Information	Information from previous projects that can be used to learn from success and failure
Influencer	A person or organization that is not necessarily directly related to the project but can influence the project in either a good or bad way
Initiating Processes	The beginning processes in a project, which happen prior to Planning In this process, it is common to assign a Project Manager, create a high level scope definition, and give the project life to move on to the Planning process.
Initiator	An organization or individual authorized and capable of starting a project
Management by Projects	Performing day-to-day operations by a project management approach
Matrix Organizational Structure	A structure within a company where people are organized by (and report to) a combination of Project and Functional Managers
Monitoring and Controlling Processes	Actions to make sure the project objectives are completed successfully
Operations	The day-to-day repeatable activities that a company performs
Organization	A group of people formed for the purpose of performing work within a company or enterprise
Organizational Process Assets (Output/Input)	The various process-related assets from the organizations involved in the project work; can include templates, documentation, methods and procedures, and policies
Planning Processes	The development of an approach (and estimates) to successfully meet project objectives
Portfolio	A group of programs or projects related and managed in a coordinated way to achieve specific strategic business goals
Portfolio Management (Technique)	Managing various portfolios that include the projects and programs of which they consist; can include prioritization, authorization, and management
Program Management	The management of projects in a coordinated way to achieve better results than if managed separately
Progressive Elaboration (Technique)	The process of beginning a project and, as more information is discovered, adjusting the plan to reflect the information and progress
Project Life Cycle	The process of completing work on the project It is not the project management of the work, but rather the work process such as the building process of creating a house, or that of developing a computer program. This life cycle typically coexists with the project management life cycle.

Project Management Office	The central group of project management at a company; can be a centralized group of Project Managers or the office that standardizes policy or procedures
Project Management Process Groups	The group of processes that complete a project (Initiating, Planning, Executing, Monitoring and Controlling, and Closing)
Project Phase	A group of project activities making up a piece of the project that interrelates with other pieces to make up the project
Regulation	A requirement developed by a government organization
Service	Work performed without resulting in a physical product
Skill	The capability to execute project-related activities based on individual subject matter expertise and abilities
Subphase	A division of a phase of a project
Subproject	A smaller piece of the project, as a result of decomposition; is usually created as a result of creating the work breakdown structure
Technique	A procedure executed by a resource to complete activities on the project
Template	A partially filled-out document that can serve as a shell for completion of project documents
Tight Matrix	A phrase that describes a war room or close environment for the team; can also be used as a noise answer on organizational-related questions
Variance Analysis (Technique)	An approach for measuring the variance associated with the scope, time, or cost of the project
Virtual Team	A group of people with similar goals who form a team but spend little (if any) time together
Voice of the Customer (VOC)	A Planning process that considers the requirements the customer really needs when technical requirements are created
War Room	A room shared by project personnel that can be used for planning and meetings, and display charts, graphs, and various other project information

5.9 Framework Practice Tests and Exercises

5.9.1 Matching Exercise

This exercise can help with memorization of the Process Groups, Knowledge Areas, and the 44 processes that the *PMBOK Guide* references. Use the Process Groups and Knowledge Areas table to fill the white cells in the top row and left column of the table. Use the Processes table to fill the remainder of the table. The exercise also includes noise answers that do not fit in the exercise. The main table of the exercise contains empty cells because there are not enough processes to fill every cell. Answers are in section 5.10.1.

Process Groups and Knowledge Areas

Monitoring	Verification	Quality	Monitoring and Controlling	Time
Closing	Procurement	Scope	Integration	Communications
Executing	Implementing	Completion	Cost	Human Resource
Change Control	Risk	Planning	Initiating	Selection

Processes

Contract Administration	Project Plan Execution	Scope Control	Human Resource Planning	Scope Planning
Communications Planning	Select Sellers	Schedule Control	Acquire Project Team	Risk Response Planning
Risk Monitoring and Control	Perform Quality Assurance	Develop Project Management Plan	Project Plan Change Control	Plan Purchases and Acquisitions
Cost Estimating	Scope Implementation	Activity Definition	Risk Analysis	Cost Planning
Activity Duration	Information Distribution	Schedule Development	Risk Management	Qualitative Risk

PMP Exam Success Series: Certification Exam Manual
© 2007 Crosswind Project Management, Inc., www.crosswindpm.com

Estimating			Planning	Analysis
Cost Control	Resource Planning	Integrated Change Control	Contract Management	Quantitative Risk Analysis
Activity Sequencing	Scope Verification	Cost Budgeting	Quality Analysis	Request Seller Responses
Perform Quality Control	Quality Planning	Scope Definition	Develop Project Charter	Close Project
Develop Project Team	Plan Contracting	Performance Reporting	Contract Closure	Risk Identification
Organizational Behavior	Direct and Manage Project Execution	Monitor and Control Project Work	Legal Compliance	Manage Stakeholders
Activity Resource Estimating	Develop Preliminary Project Scope Statement	Process Improvement Planning	Manage Project Team	Create WBS

Process Groups						
Knowledge Areas						

5.9.2   Framework Quick Test

In this quiz, answer the question in a short essay of only a sentence or two or circle all correct answers for the question. Note that some questions may have more than one answer. Answers are in section 5.10.2.

1.   What type of organization structure utilizes full-time project support staff?

   Functional   Weak Matrix   Balanced   Strong Matrix   Projectized
                                            Matrix

2.   What are the three components of the triple constraint?

3.   Which of the following uses Initiating, Planning, Executing, Monitoring and Controlling, and Closing?

   Product life cycle
   Project management life cycle

4.   Which of the following is the most correct statement?

   Projects can be parts of programs.
   Programs can be part of projects.

5.   What are the nine Knowledge Areas?

6.   Circle all the following that a PMO can do.

   Provide documentation for Project Managers
   Provide Project Managers for projects
   Audit projects
   Report to executives

7.   What organization gives a Project Manager the least authority?

   Functional   Weak Matrix   Balanced   Strong Matrix   Projectized
                                            Matrix

8.   A milestone has what duration?

9.   What type of organization has greater than 50% of the company doing full-time project work?

   Functional   Projectized

10.   Which life cycle represents the product from inception to shutdown?

5.9.3   Framework Terminology Matching Exercise

Match the correct term in the left column to the correct definition in the right column. See the exercise answer section of this chapter for the correct answer. Answers are in section 5.10.3.

Matching Exercise #1

	Term	Answer	Definition
1	Closing Process		A. The beginning processes in a project, which happen prior to Planning In this process, it is common to assign a Project Manager, create a high level scope definition, and give the project life to move on to the Planning process.
2	Deliverable		B. A requirement developed by a government organization
3	Executing Processes		C. An approach for measuring the variance associated with the scope, time, or cost of the project
4	Functional Organizational Structure		D. Activities during which formal acceptance and completion procedures are attained from either a phase or the project itself
5	Initiating Processes		E. A Planning process that considers the requirements the customer really needs when technical requirements are created
6	Management by Projects		F. A structure within a company where people are grouped by similar skill set (e.g., accounting, marketing, engineering)
7	Organizational Process Assets (Output/Input)		G. A room shared by project personnel that can be used for planning and meetings, and display charts, graphs, and various other project information
8	Planning Processes		H. The development of an approach (and estimates) to successfully meet project objectives
9	Program Management		I. A finished work product that results from completion of a series of activities
10	Project Life Cycle		J. A smaller piece of the project, as a result of decomposition; is usually created as a result of creating the work breakdown structure
11	Project Phase		K. The process of completing work on the project It is not the project management of the work, but rather the work process such as the building process of creating a house, or that of developing a computer program. This life cycle typically coexists with the project management life cycle.
12	Regulation		L. A partially filled-out document that can serve as a shell for completion of project documents
13	Subproject		M. The management of projects in a coordinated way to achieve better results than if managed separately
14	Technique		N. The coordination of personnel and additional resources to implement the project management plan and create the deliverables of the project
15	Template		O. Performing day-to-day operations by a project management approach
16	Variance Analysis (Technique)		P. A group of project activities making up a piece of the project that interrelates with other pieces to make up the project
17	Virtual Team		Q. The various process-related assets from the organizations involved in the project work; can include templates, documentation, methods and procedures, and policies
18	Voice of the Customer (VOC)		R. A procedure executed by a resource to complete activities on the project
19	War Room		S. A group of people with similar goals who form a team but spend little (if any) time together

Matching Exercise #2

	Term	Answer	Definition
1	Authority		A. Standards to which project variables are compared for acceptability
2	Co-location		B. A company, business, or other formal structure that encompasses a business function
3	Criteria		C. A group of people formed for the purpose of performing work within a company or enterprise
4	Enterprise		D. A person or organization that is not necessarily directly related to the project, but can influence the project in either a good or bad way
5	Enterprise Environmental Factors (Output/Input)		E. The group of phases or processes that complete a project (Initiating, Planning, Executing, Monitoring and Controlling, and Closing)
6	Goods		F. The agreement to be able to assign project resources, make project decisions and spend project funding
7	Historical Information		G. The capability to execute project-related activities based on individual subject matter expertise and abilities
8	Influencer		H. The process of beginning a project and, as more information is discovered, adjusting the plan to reflect the information and progress
9	Initiator		I. Products that have been created and are available for purchase
10	Matrix Organizational Structure		J. Work performed without resulting in a physical product
11	Organization		K. A group of programs or projects related and managed in a coordinated way to achieve specific strategic business goals
12	Portfolio		L. A structure within a company where people are organized by (and report to) a combination of Project and Functional Managers
13	Progressive Elaboration (Technique)		M. A team-building technique in which team members are located together or as close to each other as possible
14	Portfolio Management (Technique)		N. An organization or individual authorized and capable of starting a project
15	Project Management Office		O. The central group of project management at a company; can be a centralized group of Project Managers or the office that standardizes policy or procedures
16	Project Management Process Groups		P. A phrase that describes a war room or close environment for the team; can also be used as a noise answer on organizational-related questions
17	Service		Q. Managing various portfolios that include the projects and programs of which they consist; can include prioritization, authorization, and management
18	Skill		R. Any internal or external organization variables that can influence the project success Examples: company culture, the business market, technology, and personnel
19	Tight Matrix		S. Information from previous projects that can be used to learn from success and failure
20	Controlling Processes		T. The day-to-day repeatable activities that a company performs
21	Customer		U. The individual, group, or company that will own the work of the project when it is complete
22	Operations		V. Actions to make sure project objectives are completed successfully
23	Subphase		W. A division of a phase of a project

PMP Exam Success Series: Certification Exam Manual
© 2007 Crosswind Project Management, Inc., www.crosswindpm.com

5.9.4   Framework Practice Test
Answers are in section 5.10.4.

1.   What is an organization that controls Project Managers, documentation, and policies called?

    (A) Project Management Office
    (B) Tight matrix
    (C) Functional
    (D) Projectized

2   You are brought into a planning meeting by senior management at your company. They inform you that you have been selected to be the Project Manager for a new project that will help the company create a new product line to be introduced about four years from now. This project is the result of what type of Planning?

    (A) Portfolio planning
    (B) Program planning
    (C) Strategic planning
    (D) Product life cycle

3.   All the following are part of the project management plan except…

    (A) Budget
    (B) Risk management plan
    (C) Schedule
    (D) Information distribution plan

4.   What is the main output of Monitoring and Controlling?

    (A) Project charter
    (B) Controlling stakeholders
    (C) Corrective action
    (D) Project product

5.   Which of the following is the most important component of the triple constraint?

    (A) Time then scope then cost
    (B) Quality then time then cost
    (C) Scope
    (D) They are all of equal importance unless stated otherwise

6.   Which of the following is an example of a standard?

    (A) 640K capacity for a floppy disk
    (B) The number of slides in your last presentation
    (C) The shade of paint selected to paint your office
    (D) The average speed that someone drives to work

7.   On a large medical billing system project, the team is large and communication has been quite a challenge to control. The Project Expeditor has been used to help with this problem. What is one of the main differences between the Project Expeditor and Project Coordinator?

(A) The Project Expeditor is another title for the Project Manager.
(B) The Project Expeditor is another title for Project Coordinator.
(C) The Project Expeditor has limited or no decision-making ability.
(D) The Project Expeditor has decision-making ability.

8.   What is the main role of the Functional Manager?

(A) To control resources
(B) To manage the project when the Project Manager isn't available
(C) To define business processes
(D) To manage the Project Managers

9.   What is the main output of Closing?

(A) Project product
(B) A signed contract
(C) Project charter
(D) Work results

10. Which of the following is used to control schedule-related items on a project?

(A) Schedule Control
(B) Schedule management plan
(C) Work breakdown structure
(D) Time management plan

11. Which of the following uses cross-functional work teams?

(A) A data warehouse practice
(B) An offshore company
(C) A project that utilizes all groups across a company
(D) Union-approved workplaces

12. Which of the following is the more important job for the Project Manager?

(A) Controlling stakeholders
(B) Controlling unnecessary change
(C) Creating the project management plan
(D) Exceeding customer expectations

13. What is the typical role of senior management on a project?

(A) Support the project
(B) Pay for it
(C) Support the project and resolve resource and other conflicts
(D) Resolve resource and other conflicts

PMP Exam Success Series: Certification Exam Manual
© 2007 Crosswind Project Management, Inc., www.crosswindpm.com

14. A new project has just completed the initiation process. Planning is getting ready to begin. Which of the following have just been accomplished, and which are getting ready to start?

    (A) The project management plan and project Executing
    (B) The project charter and project Planning
    (C) The project execution and Monitoring and Controlling
    (D) The project charter and project Executing

15. Which of the following people pays for the project and/or typically "owns" the work of the project when the project is complete?

    (A) The stockholders
    (B) The Project Manager
    (C) The department manager
    (D) The sponsor

16. What is the difference between a project management life cycle and a project life cycle?

    (A) They are the same.
    (B) The project management life cycle is the project management piece of the project and the project life cycle is the process of completing the work of the project.
    (C) The project management life cycle is done in the project and the project life cycle is done after the project is complete.
    (D) The project management life cycle is the process of completing the work of the project and the project life cycle is the project management piece of the project.

17. The Functional Manager is planning the billing system replacement project with the newest Project Manager at the company. In discussing this project, the Functional Manager focuses on the cost associated with running the system after it is created and the number of years the system will last before it must be replaced. What best describes what the Functional Manager is focusing on?

    (A) Project life cycle
    (B) Product life cycle
    (C) Project management life cycle
    (D) Program management life cycle

18. What is the ideal Project Manager function regarding project changes?

    (A) To delay changes so the project can be completed
    (B) To control unnecessary change
    (C) To prevent the change control board from seeing any more change than it needs to see
    (D) To expedite all change requests to the change control board

19. What is in the Initiating Process Group?

    (A) Project charter
    (B) Work results
    (C) Corrective action
    (D) Project charter and preliminary project scope statement

20. A business analyst has a career path that has been very important to her throughout the 10 years of her career. She is put on a project with a strong matrix organizational structure. Which of the following is likely viewed as a negative of being on the project?

   (A) Being away from the group and on a project that might make it more difficult to get promoted
   (B) Working with people who have similar skills
   (C) Working long hours because the project is a high priority
   (D) Not being able to take the BAP Certification test because she will be so busy

21. Which of the following is the definition of program management?

   (A) Managing related or similar projects in a coordinated way
   (B) The process of computer program management
   (C) Managing a television program
   (D) Done for a purpose

22. Who is responsible for creating and executing the project management plan?

   (A) The team
   (B) The company that was awarded the outsourcing contract
   (C) The Project Manager and the team
   (D) The Project Manager

23. What are the five processes used in the PMI methodology?

   (A) Initiating, Planning, Executing, Monitoring and Controlling, Closing
   (B) Initiating, Planning, Executing, Testing, Signoff
   (C) Requirements, System Development, Testing, UAT, Signoff
   (D) Initiating, Planning, Executing, Testing, Closure

24. Which of the following is an advantage of a projectized organization?

   (A) Business unit competency
   (B) Optimization for a single focus on the project
   (C) Having to get approval from Functional Management
   (D) A place to go when the project is complete

25. What is the main output of Planning?

   (A) Project charter
   (B) Work results
   (C) Project management plan
   (D) A signed contract

26. Which of the following best describes a stakeholder on a project?

   (A) A team member
   (B) The Project Manager
   (C) Someone who works in an area impacted by the work of the project
   (D) All the answers

27. The data warehouse project is about halfway complete at a major retail client. Your company is doing the implementation and has twelve team members in various locations across three different buildings. Communication and team-building has been a real challenge. Which of the following would fix or improve this problem?

    (A) Changing the organization to a functional structure
    (B) Co-location
    (C) Replacing the Project Manager
    (D) Hiring Project Coordinators

28. The project management life cycle is similar to which of the following?

    (A) Project life cycle
    (B) SDLC
    (C) Plan-Do-Check-Act
    (D) Use case analysis

29. Which of the following is not a regulation?

    (A) The building code for a city
    (B) The documented way to dispose of old computers
    (C) The average speed on a street in a day
    (D) The zoning for an area

30. Which of the following is an advantage of a functional organization?

    (A) Having a home to go to when the project is complete
    (B) Not having a home when the project is complete
    (C) Having more than one project to work on
    (D) Having more than one boss

5.10   Framework Tests and Exercises Answers

5.10.1   Matching Exercise Answers

Process Groups					
	Initiating	**Planning**	**Executing**	**Monitoring and Controlling**	**Closing**
Integration	Develop Project Charter	Develop Project Management Plan	Direct and Manage Project Execution	Monitor and Control Project Work	Close Project
	Develop Preliminary Project Scope Statement			Integrated Change Control	
Scope		Scope Planning		Scope Verification	
		Scope Definition		Scope Control	
		Create WBS			
Time		Activity Definition		Schedule Control	
		Activity Sequencing			
		Activity Resource Estimating			
		Activity Duration Estimating			
		Schedule Development			
Cost		Cost Estimating		Cost Control	
		Cost Budgeting			
Quality		Quality Planning	Perform Quality Assurance	Perform Quality Control	
Human Resource		Human Resource Planning	Acquire Project Team	Manage Project Team	
			Develop Project Team		
Communications		Communications Planning	Information Distribution	Performance Reporting	
				Manage Stakeholders	
Risk		Risk Management Planning		Risk Monitoring and Control	
		Risk Identification			
		Qualitative Risk Analysis			
		Quantitative Risk Analysis			
		Risk Response Planning			
Procurement		Plan Purchases and Acquisitions	Request Seller Responses	Contract Administration	Contract Closure
		Plan Contracting	Select Sellers		

Knowledge Areas (row label, left side)

PMP Exam Success Series: Certification Exam Manual
© 2007 Crosswind Project Management, Inc., www.crosswindpm.com

5.10.2   Framework Quick Test Answers

1.   What type of organization structure utilizes full-time project support staff?

Functional   Weak Matrix   Balanced Matrix   **Strong Matrix**   **Projectized**

[section 5.6.2, section 5.6.3]

2.   What are the three components of the triple constraint?
Scope, time, cost [section 5.2]

3.   Which of the following uses Initiating, Planning, Executing, Monitoring and Controlling, and Closing?
Product life cycle   **Project management life cycle**
[section 5.1, section 5.4.1, section 5.8]

4.   Which of the following is the most correct statement?
Projects can be parts of programs.

Programs can be part of projects.
[section 5.1, section 5.8]

5.   What are the nine Knowledge Areas?
Integration, Scope, Time, Cost, Quality, Human Resource, Communications, Risk, Procurement [page 143]

6.   Circle all the following that a PMO can do.
Provide documentation for Project Managers
Provide Project Managers for projects
Audit projects
Report to executives

[section 5.1, section 5.4.4, section 5.8]

7.   What organization gives a Project Manager the least authority?
Functional   Weak Matrix   Balanced Matrix   Strong Matrix   Projectized

[section 5.6.1]

8.   A milestone has what duration?
Zero (0)
[section 7.7, section 8.8, section 8.5.12]

9.   What type of organization has greater than 50% of the company doing full-time project work?
Functional   **Projectized**
[section 5.6.3]

10.   Which life cycle represents the product from inception to shutdown?
The product life cycle
[section 5.1]

5.10.3   Framework Terminology Matching Exercise Answers

Matching Exercise #1 Answers

Term		Definition
1	Closing Process	D. Activities during which formal acceptance and completion procedures are attained from either a phase or the project itself
2	Deliverable	I. A finished work product that results from completion of a series of activities
3	Executing Processes	N. The coordination of personnel and additional resources to implement the project management plan and create the deliverables of the project
4	Functional Organizational Structure	F. A structure within a company where people are grouped by similar skill set (e.g., accounting, marketing, engineering)
5	Initiating Processes	A. The beginning processes in a project, which happen prior to Planning In this process, it is common to assign a Project Manager, create a high level scope definition, and give the project life to move on to the Planning process.
6	Management by Projects	O. Performing day-to-day operations by a project management approach
7	Organizational Process Assets (Output/Input)	Q. The various process-related assets from the organizations involved in the project work; can include templates, documentation, methods and procedures, and policies
8	Planning Processes	H. The development of an approach (and estimates) to successfully meet project objectives
9	Program Management	M. The management of projects in a coordinated way to achieve better results than if managed separately
10	Project Life Cycle	K. The process of completing work on the project It is not the project management of the work, but rather the work process such as the building process of creating a house, or that of developing a computer program. This life cycle typically coexists with the project management life cycle.
11	Project Phase	P. A group of project activities making up a piece of the project that interrelates with other pieces to make up the project
12	Regulation	B. A requirement developed by a government organization
13	Subproject	J. A smaller piece of the project, as a result of decomposition; is usually created as a result of creating the work breakdown structure
14	Technique	R. A procedure executed by a resource to complete activities on the project
15	Template	L. A partially filled-out document that can serve as a shell for completion of project documents
16	Variance Analysis (Technique)	C. An approach for measuring the variance associated with the scope, time, or cost of the project
17	Virtual Team	S. A group of people with similar goals who form a team but spend little (if any) time together
18	Voice of the Customer (VOC)	E. A Planning process that considers the requirements the customer really needs when technical requirements are created
19	War Room	G. A room shared by project personnel that can be used for planning and meetings, and display charts, graphs, and various other project information

PMP Exam Success Series: Certification Exam Manual
 © 2007 Crosswind Project Management, Inc., www.crosswindpm.com

Matching Exercise #2 Answers

	Term	Definition
1	Authority	F. The agreement to be able to assign project resources, make project decisions and spend project funding
2	Co-location	M. A team-building technique in which team members are located together or as close to each other as possible
3	Criteria	A. Standards to which project variables are compared for acceptability
4	Enterprise	B. A company, business, or other formal structure that encompasses a business function
5	Enterprise Environmental Factors (Output/Input)	R. Any internal or external organization variables that can influence the project success. Examples: company culture, the business market, technology, and personnel
6	Goods	I. Products that have been created and are available for purchase
7	Historical Information	S. Information from previous projects that can be used to learn from success and failure
8	Influencer	D. A person or organization that is not necessarily directly related to the project, but can influence the project in either a good or bad way
9	Initiator	N. An organization or individual authorized and capable of starting a project
10	Matrix Organizational Structure	L. A structure within a company where people are organized by (and report to) a combination of Project and Functional Managers
11	Organization	C. A group of people formed for the purpose of performing work within a company or enterprise
12	Portfolio	K. A group of programs or projects related and managed in a coordinated way to achieve specific strategic business goals
13	Progressive Elaboration (Technique)	H. The process of beginning a project and, as more information is discovered, adjusting the plan to reflect the information and progress
14	Portfolio Management (Technique)	Q. Managing various portfolios that include the projects and programs of which they consist; can include prioritization, authorization, and management
15	Project Management Office	O. The central group of project management at a company; can be a centralized group of Project Managers or the office that standardizes policy or procedures
16	Project Management Process Groups	E. The group of phases or processes that complete a project (Initiating, Planning, Executing, Monitoring and Controlling, and Closing)
17	Service	J. Work performed without resulting in a physical product
18	Skill	G. The capability to execute project-related activities based on individual subject matter expertise and abilities
19	Tight Matrix	P. A phrase that describes a war room or close environment for the team; can also be used as a noise answer on organizational-related questions
20	Controlling Processes	V. Actions to make sure project objectives are completed successfully
21	Customer	U. The individual, group, or company that will own the work of the project when it is complete
22	Operations	T. The day-to-day repeatable activities that a company performs
23	Subphase	W. A division of a phase of a project

5.10.4   Framework Practice Test Answers

1.   What is an organization that controls Project Managers, documentation, and policies called?

   Correct Answer: (A) Project Management Office
   Explanation: The Project Management Office (PMO) can control Project Managers, documentation and policies or anything else needed within reason for the management of projects within an organization. [section 5.1, section 5.8]

2.   You are brought into a planning meeting by senior management at your company. They inform you that you have been selected to be the Project Manager for a new project that will help the company create a new product line to be introduced about four years from now. This project is the result of what type of Planning?

   Correct Answer: (C) Strategic planning
   Explanation: Strategic planning is typically done three to five years in advance. It is very common for projects to be driven by strategic initiatives at a company. Product life cycle involves the entire life cycle from "cradle to grave" for a product. The other answers are noise. [section 5.1]

3.   All the following are part of the project management plan except…

   Correct Answer: (D) Information distribution plan
   Explanation: The budget, schedule, and risk management plan are parts of the project management plan as they deal with the time, money, and risk parts of the project. "Information distribution plan" is noise. [section 6.5.1]

4.   What is the main output of Monitoring and Controlling?

   Correct Answer: (C) Corrective action
   Explanation: Corrective action is the main output of Monitoring and Controlling. The project charter comes from Initiating. The project product comes from Closing. "Controlling stakeholders" is noise. [section 5.4.1]

5.   Which of the following is the most important component of the triple constraint?

   Correct Answer: (D) They are all of equal importance unless otherwise stated.
   Explanation: The triple constraint of project management states that scope, time, and cost are all equal unless otherwise defined as such. Quality is often confused in place of scope with the triple constraint. Quality is actually achieved when scope, time, and cost goals have been met. [section 5.2]

6.   Which of the following is an example of a standard?

   Correct Answer: (A) 640K capacity for a floppy disk
   Explanation: A standard is a measurement for something that is consistent and generally accepted. In this case, the capacity of a floppy disk is the only "standard" listed in the answers. [section 5.3]

7.   On a large medical billing system project, the team is large and communication has been quite a challenge to control. The Project Expeditor has been used to help with this problem. What is one of the main differences between the Project Expeditor and Project Coordinator?

   Correct Answer: (C) The Project Expeditor has limited or no decision-making ability.
   Explanation: The Project Expeditor and Project Coordinator have similar responsibilities with the difference being that the Project Coordinator has some decision-making ability. [section 5.4.4]

8.   What is the main role of the Functional Manager?

       Correct Answer: (A) To control resources
       Explanation: The Functional Manager runs the day-to-day business and is responsible for resources. Project Managers do not always report to Functional Managers. The Functional Manager runs a department or area of business, not the Project Manager. "Defining business processes" is noise. [section 5.4.4]

9.   What is the main output of Closing?

       Correct Answer: (A) Project product
       Explanation: The project product is the main output of Closing. It is what the project has created. The project charter comes from Initiating. Work results come from the project execution. "A signed contract" is noise. [section 5.4.1]

10.   Which of the following is used to control schedule-related items on a project?

       Correct Answer: (A) Schedule Control
       Explanation: The Schedule Control process is used to control schedule-related items. The schedule management plan establishes the rules as they relate to the schedule for the project. The work breakdown structure is the graphical decomposition of the work of the project. "Time management plan" is noise. [section 8.6]

11.   Which of the following uses cross-functional work teams?

       Correct Answer: (C) A project that utilizes all groups across a company
       Explanation: A project that utilizes all groups across a company utilizes cross-functional teams to take advantage of the knowledge and skills available. A data warehouse practice is likely a projectized organization. An offshore company is too vague an answer. "Union-approved workplaces" is noise. [section 5.6.2]

12.   Which of the following is the more important job for the Project Manager?

       Correct Answer: (B) Controlling unnecessary change
       Explanation: Controlling unnecessary change is one of the biggest challenges for Project Managers. If they don't do this well, the project can go out of control. Creating the project management plan is a good answer, but if changes are out of control, the best plan won't do any good. Exceeding customer expectations is unnecessary and could likely result in gold plating, which isn't good. "Controlling stakeholders" is noise. The expectations of stakeholders are to be managed, not controlled. [section 5.4.4]

13.   What is the typical role of senior management on a project?

       Correct Answer: (C) Support the project and resolve resource and other conflicts
       Explanation: Senior management outranks the Project Manager. They support the project by helping resolve resource issues and other conflicts. The sponsor pays for the project. [section 5.4.4]

14.   A new project has just completed the initiation process. Planning is getting ready to begin. Which of the following have just been accomplished, and which are getting ready to start?

       Correct Answer: (B) The project charter and project Planning
       Explanation: The project management life cycle is Initiating, Planning, Executing, Monitoring and Controlling, and Closing. The main output of Initiating is the creation of a project charter. Once this project charter is done, the creation of the project management plan can start. The other answers are either out of sync with the life cycle or are noise. [section 5.1, section 5.4.1, section 6.3]

15.   Which of the following people pays for the project and/or typically "owns" the work of the project when the project is complete?

Correct Answer: (D) The sponsor
Explanation: The sponsor typically pays for the work of the project and owns the work of the project when it is complete. [section 5.4.4]

16. What is the difference between a project management life cycle and a project life cycle?

Correct Answer: (B) The project management life cycle is the project management piece of the project and the project life cycle is the process of completing the work of the project.
Explanation: The project management life cycle (PMLC) is the project management methodology used on a project. The project life cycle applies to whatever is being built. It can be the software approach for a software project or a building approach for construction. [section 5.1]

17. The Functional Manager is planning the billing system replacement project with the newest Project Manager at the company. In discussing this project, the Functional Manager focuses on the cost associated with running the system after it is created and the number of years the system will last before it must be replaced. What best describes what the Functional Manager is focusing on?

Correct Answer: (B) Product life cycle
Explanation: The product life cycle focuses on the overall ownership cost of the product of the project, not just the project cost to create the product. The project life cycle involves the processes used to create the product of the project such as the steps to build a house or a computer system. The project management life cycle is the project management approach to the project. "Program management life cycle" is noise. [section 5.1]

18. What is the ideal Project Manager function regarding project changes?

Correct Answer: (B) To control unnecessary change
Explanation: The main job of a Project Manager, other than managing the project itself, is to control unnecessary changes that can derail the project. Delaying changes and protecting the change control board from changes are both unprofessional. Expediting changes to the CCB is not a bad answer but not the best because it doesn't help in controlling unnecessary change. [section 5.4.4]

19. What is created in the Initiating Process Group?

Correct Answer: (D) Project charter and preliminary project scope statement
Explanation: The main outputs of the Initiating Process Group are the project charter and preliminary project scope statement. Work results come from project execution. Corrective action comes from Monitoring and Controlling. [section 5.4.1, section 6.3, section 6.4]

20. A business analyst has a career path that has been very important to her throughout the 10 years of her career. She is put on a project with a strong matrix organizational structure. Which of the following is likely viewed as a negative of being on the project?

Correct Answer: (A) Being away from the group and on a project that might make it more difficult to get promoted
Explanation: Being away from the normal group and not being able to be as easily promoted is the best answer. Being in a strong matrix environment feels fairly similar to being in a projectized organization where skill set specialty in groups does not have as high a priority. The other answers are noise. [section 5.6.2]

21. Which of the following is the definition of program management?

Correct Answer: (A) Managing related or similar projects in a coordinated way
Explanation: Program management utilizes a coordinated management of related projects. Done for a purpose is a characteristic of a project. The other answers are noise. [section 5.1, section 5.8]

22. Who is responsible for creating and executing the project management plan?

Correct Answer: (D) The Project Manager
Explanation: The Project Manager is responsible for creating the project management plan. This creation typically comes with the help of the team. The Project Manager is responsible for execution of the plan and the team members are responsible for the plan's activities. The outsourcing answer is noise. [section 5.4.4]

23. What are the five processes used in the PMI methodology?

Correct Answer: (A) Initiating, Planning, Executing, Monitoring and Controlling, Closing
Explanation: Per the *PMBOK Guide Third Edition*, the Process Groups that make up the PMI methodology or "project management life cycle" are Initiating, Planning, Executing, Monitoring and Controlling, and Closing. [section 5.4.1]

24. Which of the following is an advantage of a projectized organization?

Correct Answer: (B) Optimization for a single focus on the project
Explanation: Optimization for a single focus on the project means that the team can focus on what the work of the project is and usually only that. The other answers are associated with functional organizations. [section 5.6.3]

25. What is the main output of Planning?

Correct Answer: (C) Project management plan
Explanation: The main output of Planning is the project management plan. The project charter comes from Initiation. Work results come from project execution. "A signed contract" is noise. [section 5.4.1]

26. Which of the following best describes a stakeholder on a project?

(A) A team member
(B) The Project Manager
(C) Someone who works in an area impacted by the work of the project

Correct Answer: (D) All the answers
Explanation: The stakeholder can be anyone impacted by the project. The stakeholder could be the sponsor, senior management, Project Manager, Functional Manager, team member, or end user. [section 5.4.4]

27. The data warehouse project is about halfway complete at a major retail client. Your company is doing the implementation and has twelve team members in various locations across three different buildings. Communication and team-building has been a real challenge. Which of the following would fix or improve this problem?

Correct Answer: (B) Co-location
Explanation: Co-location is the process of putting personnel closer together or in the same room to help with team-building and project communication. [section 5.8, section 11.3]

28. The project management life cycle is similar to which of the following?

Correct Answer: (C) Plan-Do-Check-Act
Explanation: The Plan-Do-Check-Act is defined by the American Society for Quality as an approach to process development. It can show how the project management life cycle components co-exist or overlap. The project life cycle builds the work of the project. SDLC and use case analysis are software development approaches. [section 5.4.1]

29.   Which of the following is not a regulation?

Correct Answer: (C) The average speed on a street in a day
Explanation: The average speed on a street in a day is simply a value. It's not a regulation, which the other answers are. The other answers have defined criteria that they must meet to be acceptable. [section 5.3, section 5.8]

30.   Which of the following is an advantage of a functional organization?

Correct Answer: (A) Having a home to go to when the project is complete
Explanation: Having a home when the project is complete is a key advantage of a functional organization. Having more than one boss and more than one project could be characteristics of a matrix organization. [section 5.6.1]

Chapter 6

Integration

The Integration Knowledge Area can be misleading. It includes a lot of activities associated with pulling together the various Knowledge Areas from project conception to closure. Integration is the glue that connects all the Knowledge Areas together. There can also be a lot of "between the lines" activities that occur that should be taken into consideration. If there is a change in scope, the integration aspect could impact time, cost and risk, for example. If this area seems a bit more challenging or confusing compared to others, don't get frustrated. We recommend that you have a solid grasp on time, cost, and risk especially before getting into this too deeply; it could get a little confusing without the foundation from other Knowledge Areas. We definitely recommend that you are very comfortable with this area before you take the exam.

Integration is the Knowledge Area that ties together the other eight Knowledge Areas: Scope, Time, Cost, Quality, Human Resource, Communications, Risk, and Procurement.

In this chapter, we discuss the following:

Process Group	Process Name		Main Outputs
Initiating	Develop Project Charter	→	Project Charter
	Develop Preliminary Project Scope Statement	→	Preliminary Project Scope Statement
Planning	Develop Project Management Plan	→	Project Management Plan
Executing	Direct and Manage Project Execution	→	Deliverables
			Work Performance Information
Monitoring and Controlling	Monitor and Control Project Work	→	Forecasts
			Requested Changes
	Integrated Change Control	→	Deliverables
			Project Management Plan (Updates)
			Approved Change Requests
Closing	Close Project	→	Final Product, Service, or Result

☑	**Crosswind "Must Knows" For Integration**
☐	Key Inputs, Tools & Techniques, and Outputs for Develop Project Charter
☐	Key Inputs, Tools & Techniques, and Outputs for Develop Preliminary Project Scope Statement
☐	Key Inputs, Tools & Techniques, and Outputs for Develop Project Management Plan
☐	Key Inputs, Tools & Techniques, and Outputs for Direct and Manage Project Execution
☐	Key Inputs, Tools & Techniques, and Outputs for Integrated Change Control
☐	Key Inputs, Tools & Techniques, and Outputs for Monitor and Control Project Work
☐	Key Inputs, Tools & Techniques, and Outputs for Close Project
☐	General attributes of organizational process assets and enterprise environmental factors
☐	Characteristics of the project charter
☐	Characteristics of a project scope statement
☐	Characteristics and components of a project management plan
☐	Characteristics of a preliminary project scope statement
☐	Characteristics of a Project Management Information System
☐	Characteristics of a work authorization system
☐	What a change control system is and how it works
☐	Characteristics and importance of a baseline
☐	Characteristics of a configuration management system
☐	What constraints and assumptions are as they relate to a project
☐	How to close a project and the documentation associated with it
☐	What lessons learned is and why it is important
☐	How to correctly interpret stakeholder requests for project changes
☐	Project selection techniques and their importance
☐	Differences between requested changes and approved changes

Although helpful, this list is not all-inclusive for information needed from this area for the exam. It is only suggested material that, if understood and memorized, may increase your exam score.

6.1   Organizational Process Assets

> Know the general attributes of organizational process assets.

Organizational process assets can be inputs to many processes because they deal with variables external to the project, such as information systems and company policies and procedures. They can include process definitions, templates, criteria to complete (close) projects, organization communication needs, issue management, financial infrastructure, change control processes, risk management, and work authorization.

A corporate knowledge base can also be expanded by adding the following to organizational process assets: process data, project files and records, lessons learned, historical information, configuration management data, databases, and financial data.

PMP Exam Success Series: Certification Exam Manual
© 2007 Crosswind Project Management, Inc., www.crosswindpm.com

6.2   Enterprise Environmental Factors

Enterprise environmental factors can be inputs to many processes because they deal with variables external to the project, such as information systems and company policies and procedures. **These factors potentially influence project success; thus, they should be known and taken into consideration during project Planning.** Examples are organizational structure and culture, business infrastructure systems, government standards, personnel policies, the business market, stakeholder tolerance for risk, and PMIS (Project Management Information Systems).

Know the general attributes of enterprise environmental factors.

6.3   Develop Project Charter (Initiating Process Group)

Develop Project Charter is the process by which the project or project phase is authorized. When this area is complete, a project or phase exists as a result of the development and signoff of the project charter.

Know the Key Inputs, Tools & Techniques, and Outputs for Develop Project Charter.

Develop Project Charter (Initiating)		
Key Inputs	Contract (when applicable)	If work is done for an outside party, a contract is needed **between buyer and seller**. This contract can lead to a project because of potential opportunity
	Project Statement of Work	The project statement of work (SOW) provides a **description of the services or products that the project is to accomplish**. It could also include a business need, product scope description, and strategic plan associated with the work.
Key Tools & Techniques	Project Selection Methods	Tools include project selection methods, such as net present value (NPV), Internal rate of return (IRR), opportunity cost, etc.
	Project Management Methodology	The project management methodology is the project **management approach currently used** on the project.
	Project Management Information System (PMIS)	The project management information system (PMIS) can define **how project information is stored and distributed**.
	Expert Judgment	Expert judgment is of great value. Often more significant and accurate than the best modeling tools available, it can come from other parts of the company, stakeholders, professional organizations or groups, and consultants.
Key Outputs	Project Charter	The project charter is a document that **gives the project existence**. At this point, the project is alive, a Project Manager is assigned, and any assumptions and constraints are defined. At this point, an assumption can be any unknown with a "best guess" applied to it. Constraints are factors such as project completion deadline, budget threshold, and a limit on the number of employees to bring to the project.

Situational Question and Real World Application
If you fail to address the Develop Project Charter process thoroughly, you may not have a project.

6.3.1   Project Charter

According to PMI, if there is no project charter, there is no project.
Therefore, an initiative typically goes through some degree of preliminary planning
or feasibility study before a project charter is completed. When signed off, the
project charter gives the project life. It is the document which states the main details
of the project.

Typically, the project charter includes the following:

- Scope (requirements) of the project
- Any constraints and assumptions
- Time and cost goals
- Project justification
- Authority level of the Project Manager
- Stakeholder definition and level of influence
- Organizational information

Know what a
project charter is,
how it is used in a
project, who
creates it, and how
a Project Manager
uses it.

This document is usually created and signed by senior management or the
sponsor. Think of it as the laws of the project and the Project Manager as law
enforcement. Thus, it's a good idea to have the Project Manager assigned as early in
the process as possible.

If the project charter is not entirely complete, confusion may arise with
regard to constraints, assumptions, or who is actually the Project Manager. For
clarification, the project charter should be a physical document. Verbal project
charters can expose you to the same issues that the lack of a project charter does.

6.3.2   Kickoff Meeting

Projects generally include a kickoff meeting to officially start the project.
This meeting can be held at the beginning of Planning or Executing, depending on
priority and approach.

As you start Planning, the meeting helps set expectations of what the project
Planning will include and create when complete.

As you start Executing, it can include setting expectations on the project and
communicating details of the project management plan to the team members so they
know what is expected of them and what should have been created when the work of
the project is complete.

6.3.3   Project Selection

A company can decide in a number of ways which projects to pursue.
Typically, benefit and cost are examined in a variety of ways, such as by a steering
committee review, project ranking and prioritization, or financial performance.

Basic needs for a project could be created from problems, opportunities, or
business requirements. More specific factors that can result in the creation of a
project could include a business need, market demand, technological advance,
customer request, or legal requirement.

Be familiar with
project selection
techniques and
their importance.

PMP Exam Success Series: Certification Exam Manual
© 2007 Crosswind Project Management, Inc., www.crosswindpm.com

Mathematical Models	There are various mathematical models that can be used for project selection. They include the following: • Constrained Optimization • Linear • Non-linear • Dynamic • Integer • Complex calculation • Algorithms (multi-objective programming) This approach ultimately comes down to trying to forecast as many variables as possible and predict the outcome via mathematical analysis.
Benefit Measurement Model	This could also be considered a Scoring Model. This model takes the following into consideration: • Comparative approach • Scoring models • Benefit contribution • Economic model

Typically, selected projects relate to the strategic "big picture" goals of the company and corresponding financial performance. Don't worry about calculations. PMI doesn't expect you to be an accountant to pass the exam. Use the following table as a shortcut for financial metrics. Details are in the Cost chapter.

Financial Metrics Table

Project Selection Tool	Also Known As	Option to Select	Example
Return on Investment	ROI	The Biggest Number or Percentage	$50,000 or 7%
Internal Rate of Return	IRR	The Biggest Percentage	15.50%
Net Present Value	NPV	The Biggest Number (Years are already factored in.)	$47,500
Benefit Cost Ratio	BCR	The Biggest Ratio	3.5:1
Opportunity Cost	--	The Amounts That Are Not Selected	Project A ($7,000) over Project B ($5,000)
Payback Period	--	The Shortest Duration	7 months

6.4   Develop Preliminary Project Scope Statement (Initiating Process Group)

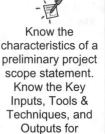

Know the characteristics of a preliminary project scope statement. Know the Key Inputs, Tools & Techniques, and Outputs for Develop Preliminary Project Scope Statement.

Preliminary project scope statement development includes creating a **high level statement of the project scope in a narrative format to facilitate a greater understanding of the scope of the work.** This information is typically provided by the sponsor(s) and can include the following:

- Project goals
- Criteria for formal acceptance
- Deliverables definition
- Requirements
- Constraints
- Assumptions

- Known risks
- Preliminary project scope
- Preliminary WBS
- Preliminary organizational structure
- Preliminary estimates for time and cost

Develop Preliminary Project Scope Statement (Initiating)		
Key Inputs	Project Charter	The project charter is a document that **gives the project existence**. At this point, the project is alive, the Project Manager is assigned, and any assumptions and constraints are defined. Assumptions can be anything unknown at this point but with a "best guess" applied to it. Constraints can be factors such as project completion deadline, budget threshold, and a limit on number of employees to bring to the project. At this point, we elaborate on the project charter to obtain additional details for project planning.
	Project Statement of Work	The project statement of work (SOW) provides a **description of the services or products that the project is to accomplish**. This SOW could also include a business need, product scope description, and strategic plan associated with the work.
Key Tools & Techniques	Project Management Methodology	The project management methodology is the project **management approach currently used on the project**.
	Project Management Information System	The project management information system (PMIS) can define **how project information is stored and distributed**.
	Expert Judgment	Expert judgment is of great value. It can be more significant and accurate than the best modeling tools available.
Key Outputs	Preliminary Project Scope Statement	The preliminary project scope statement includes the product scope description and provides an **initial description of the project scope** and supporting details.

Situational Question and Real World Application
Problems in this area generally start when the customer thought he knew what he wanted but didn't have (or take) the time to provide an initial high level project scope statement. This preliminary project scope statement is more than the project charter generally provides, but not as much as a project scope statement referenced later in the project life cycle or the work breakdown structure (WBS).

6.5   Develop Project Management Plan (Planning Process Group)

Know the Key Inputs, Tools & Techniques, and Outputs for Develop Project Management Plan.

Project management plan development is the process of creating an integrated project management plan. Many activities and documents come together to create this plan, which is the integration of various management plans. **These plans can include (but are not limited to) the scope, schedule, cost, quality, staffing, communication, risk, and procurement management plans.**

Ultimately, this integrated document becomes the overall document that the project references as its plan. It becomes the baseline to measure any performance against. As things change on a project (and they always do), various updates could be added to the project management plan as a result of change control procedures.

This Knowledge Area pulls many factors together. Falling short in one area can greatly impact other areas.

Develop Project Management Plan (Planning)		
Key Inputs	Preliminary Project Scope Statement	The preliminary project scope statement includes the product scope description and provides an **initial description of the project scope** and supporting details.
	Project Management Processes	Project management processes are used to **create the project management plan** in accordance with the project management methodology in the organization.
Key Tools & Techniques	Project Management Methodology	The project management methodology is the project **management approach currently used on the project**.
	Project Management Information System	The project management information system (PMIS) can define **how project information is stored and distributed**.
	Expert Judgment	Expert judgment is of great value. It can be more significant and accurate than the best modeling tools available.
Key Outputs	Project Management Plan	A project management plan (not a schedule!) **integrates plans representing various Knowledge Areas** in the PMI approach to project management. Supporting detail is also included to help validate the information in the project management plan.

Situational Question and Real World Application
In most cases of project management reality, the "plan" lacks a number of the Knowledge Areas.   **Scope Management:** If you fail to address scope management, your client may start requesting additional items that could impact project goals. There is no control loop for scope.   **Time Management:** In the case of time management, the schedule could slip rapidly or the Project Manager can't tell if the project is on track or not (or how much on or off track it is).   **Cost Management:** Cost issues can put the Project Manager in a position of not knowing how much the project should cost or, if there were a cost baseline, not knowing or having a way to track how much was spent and how much remained to finish the project.   **Quality Management:** When quality issues arise, it may not be possible to get signoff on completed work products because there weren't clearly defined standards of acceptable completion criteria, possibly resulting in cost and time overruns.   **Human Resource Management:** Human resource shortfalls could result in the placement of the wrong people (skill sets or experience level) on the project at the wrong time.

> **Communications Management:** Communication management issues could result in strained stakeholder expectations or activity completion issues from a lack of communication to the appropriate parties.
>
> **Risk Management:** If you fail to address risk, the project could encounter unforeseen (and thus, unplanned) risk events that could damage or potentially destroy the project.
>
> **Procurement Management:** If procurement with an outside vendor is involved, there may be communication, scope, and completion issues.

6.5.1 Project Management Plan

The project management plan (previously called the project plan) is a cumulative document that **contains all the documents** used in the project management approach on the project. **It describes steps associated with Executing, Monitoring and Controlling, and Closing** of the project. It can be at a summary or detailed level depending on the need for the project. Generally, this document includes the processes associated with definition, integration, and coordination of the various documents in the following table. As Integrated Change Control occurs, the document should be updated to reflect the changes discovered on the project.

Know characteristics and components for a project management plan.

The documents contained can differ from project to project as needed. Generally speaking, consider including the following management plans and documents in the project management plan.

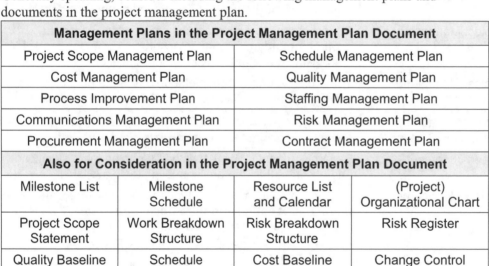

Management Plans in the Project Management Plan Document	
Project Scope Management Plan	Schedule Management Plan
Cost Management Plan	Quality Management Plan
Process Improvement Plan	Staffing Management Plan
Communications Management Plan	Risk Management Plan
Procurement Management Plan	Contract Management Plan

Also for Consideration in the Project Management Plan Document			
Milestone List	Milestone Schedule	Resource List and Calendar	(Project) Organizational Chart
Project Scope Statement	Work Breakdown Structure	Risk Breakdown Structure	Risk Register
Quality Baseline	Schedule Baseline	Cost Baseline	Change Control Systems

6.5.2 Assumptions

When you perform project management, part of the concept of Planning is to deal with items that you do not know the characteristics of yet. Here, you make assumptions for scheduling, budgeting, or any other "unknown" area of the project. Lessons learned is valuable in helping to create valid assumptions. In most cases, as the project evolves and you learn more about it, assumptions become fewer.

Know constraints and assumptions as they relate to a project.

6.5.3 Constraints

Every project has constraints. Constraints are factors that limit project options, such as the number of people available, amount of time or money available to finish the job, or other resource or asset issues.

Know constraints and assumptions as they relate to a project.

6.5.4   Baseline

The baseline is the original estimate plus any approved changes. The baseline value is the value against which the work results (sometimes called actuals) are compared. There is a baseline value for any item on the project to be measured, including **scope, time, cost, and quality** at a minimum.

Know the characteristics and importance of a baseline.

6.5.5   Project Management Information System (PMIS)

The Project Management Information System is used for communication and information distribution on the project. It is not necessarily a high tech system, but whatever is used for project communication on the project. Normally, it is a mixture of technology and non-technology tools used by various people on the project.

Know the characteristics of a PMIS.

6.6   Direct and Manage Project Execution (Executing Process Group)

You have planned the work; now it is time to **work the plan**. There is a little more to it than that, but working the plan is definitely a good start. The Project Manager and team initiate plan activity and move forward. These two undertakings are key to this area. The short, sweet, and simple of it is: creating work products.

In **Direct and Manage Project Execution**, we focus on creating tangible deliverables such as houses, bridges, computer applications, etc. Intangibles, such as training and process definitions, can also be created. As the project team toils to complete activities that create the work described in the project scope statement, they could work toward project goals, staff personnel, train and manage personnel, get quotes and work on other procurement needs, validate that work was accomplished as planned, adapt the plan as needed to accomplish the project goals, and collect project documentation and data associated with historical information and lessons learned. The effort can also include corrective action, preventive action, and approved defect repair as needs on the project warrant.

Know the Key Inputs, Tools & Techniques, and Outputs for Direct and Manage Project Execution.

Direct and Manage Project Execution (Executing)		
Key Inputs	Project Management Plan	The project management plan **allows the team to know what work to do and when**. Supporting detail helps with any questions or clarifications needed regarding data in the plan. Organizational policies help define the structure in which the project will function. Preventive action helps maintain a proactive (instead of reactive) approach to completion of the plan. Corrective action comes into the process when you must adjust the plan to meet the necessary outputs.
	Administrative Closure Procedure	The administrative closure procedure **closes a project whenever the project ends**. It could occur when the work is complete, when funding is consumed, when the project is cancelled, or when other terminating events take place.
Key Tools & Techniques	Project Management Methodology	The project management methodology is the project **management approach currently used on the project**.
	Project Management Information System	The project management information system (PMIS) can define **how project information is stored and distributed**.

Key Outputs	Deliverables	Deliverables represent the **completion of predefined project work pieces**.
	Requested Changes	Requested changes are **changes requested but not yet formally approved** by the official change control process on the project.

Situational Question and Real World Application
As stated in the previous section, there are numerous Knowledge Areas of impact with integration. Generally from an Executing perspective, if you fail to address Planning area(s) appropriately, work results may fail to reach completion. An example might be a situation in which there are Executing issues due to unplanned risk events. Thus, the risk events impact other Knowledge Areas of the project because they were not taken into account in the original (or revised) Planning.

6.6.1 Work Authorization System

A work authorization system is a formal or informal system used in project management to ensure that work is done as planned. It ensures that the right work is done in the right order at the right time by the right people. It can help control cost.

If work is not done in the sequence as planned, sequence deviation can potentially cause issues that result in rework. These issues can be anything from checking with the Project Manager when something is done, to a detailed check-in and sequencing system.

A work authorization system can also be used to minimize or eliminate gold plating. Discussed in the Quality chapter, gold plating involves providing more than was promised or committed.

> Know the characteristics of a work authorization system.

6.6.2 The Project Manager's Role in Integration

Project Managers start with Planning because they are responsible for pulling together the people for Planning and completion of the project management plan. This effort results in the integration of all documents into the project management plan. They are also responsible for project integration while various project pieces come together for plan completion. Project Managers must be sensitive to the project's needs, especially at **key interface points** on the project.

6.7 Monitor and Control Project Work (Monitoring and Controlling Process Group)

This process involves managing and controlling the Initiating, Planning, Executing, and Closing pieces of a project to attain the goals described in the project management plan. It can include **collecting, measuring and interpreting performance information** on the project. Monitoring the project provides details on the project status so the team can respond, based on project health.

Monitoring can include comparing actual data to baseline estimates, determining if corrective or preventive action needs to be applied, monitoring risk, keeping project data current and timely, forecasting project progress, and tracking status of approved changes as they are implemented.

> Know the Key Inputs, Tools & Techniques, and Outputs for Monitor and Control Project Work.

Monitor and Control Project Work (Monitoring and Controlling)		
Key Inputs	Project Management Plan	A project management plan (not a schedule!) **integrates plans representing the various Knowledge Areas** in the PMI approach to project management. Supporting detail is also included to help validate information in the project management plan.
	Work Performance Information	Work performance information **provides a status on what has been completed (or not completed)** on the project.
Key Tools & Techniques	Project Management Methodology	The project management methodology is the project **management approach currently used on the project**.
	Project Management Information System (PMIS)	The project management information system (PMIS) can define **how project information is stored and distributed**.
	Earned Value Technique	An earned value technique (EVT) system is necessary to **allow performance to be measured and variances analyzed**.
	Expert Judgment	Expert judgment is of great value. It can be more significant and accurate than the best modeling tools available.
Key Outputs	Recommended Corrective Action	Recommended corrective actions are **modifications to the plan** that adjust the activities to achieve a desired result that wasn't (typically) planned or expected.
	Forecasts	Forecasts provide information about **what is expected to happen** on the project.
	Requested Changes	Requested changes are **changes that have been requested but not yet formally approved** by the official change control process on the project.

Situational Question and Real World Application
The biggest problem that could arise from this area is project surprise. This surprise arises if the Project Manager or team has failed to monitor what was happening on the project, forcing them to react so they can compensate for having missed something in this process.

6.8   Integrated Change Control (Monitoring and Controlling Process Group)

Know the Key Inputs, Tools & Techniques, and Outputs for Integrated Change Control.

Integrated Change Control can affect a variety of the Knowledge Areas and their management plans within the overall project management plan. This process deals with the analysis of other Knowledge Areas that are impacted when one Knowledge Area encounters a change request. Integrated Change Control can happen from project conception to closure.

An example might be: Due to a scope change, there are cost and time (and possibly risk) impacts that could require change control in those areas, as well as in the original scope area.

Integrated Change Control can include any of the following, as appropriate:
- Determining that changes have occurred or need to occur
- Influencing change requests so that only needed changes occur
- Reviewing and approving change requests
- Monitoring and adjusting baselines as needed
- Implementing needed corrective action and preventive action
- Communicating status on the project regarding implemented changes

Integrated Change Control (Monitoring and Controlling)		
Key Inputs	Project Management Plan	The project management plan serves as a **baseline** to measure against regarding changes.
	Requested Changes	Requested changes are **changes that have been requested but not yet formally approved** by the official change control process on the project.
	Work Performance Information	Work performance information provides a **status on what has been completed (or not completed)** on the project.
	Deliverables	Deliverables represent the **completion of project work pieces** defined in Planning.
Key Tools & Techniques	Project Management Methodology	The project management methodology is the project **management approach currently used on the project**.
	Project Management Information System	The project management information system (PMIS) can define **how project information is stored and distributed**.
	Expert Judgment	Expert judgment is of great value. It can be more significant and accurate than the best modeling tools available.
Key Outputs	Approved Change Requests	Approved change requests are **changes that have been formally approved** by the official change control process on the project.
	Rejected Change Requests	Rejected change requests are those **change requests that have been rejected** by the change control process on the project.
	Project Scope Statement (Updates)	The project scope statement (Updates) **helps define the project**. Supporting detail provides the in-depth research and planning that the project scope statement rolls into.
	Project Management Plan (Updates)	Project management plan (Updates) can result **from approved changes** to a project.
	Deliverables	Deliverables represent the **completion of project work pieces** defined in Planning or modified from a change control process.

Situational Question and Real World Application
As stated previously, there are a number of Knowledge Areas impacted here. Problems in this area could result in undocumented or unapproved changes on the project that still need to achieve the needed project objectives. Problems could also come from one area being impacted and addressed, and other impacted areas not discovered and addressed appropriately.

PMP Exam Success Series: Certification Exam Manual
© 2007 Crosswind Project Management, Inc., www.crosswindpm.com

6.8.1   Requested Changes vs. Approved Changes

One key item you can expect on the challenging situational exam questions is the subtle difference between requested changes and approved changes as described in the questions. Know the difference between the two.

Requested changes are simply that -- requests made by someone on a project. **In situational questions, a requested change typically isn't considered approved unless stated so. It's important to explain the impact of requested changes to the authorized requestor or sponsor and let that person make the call on approving the changes based on the impact.** Unless it's a situation like that, a requested change is simply a wish list, not likely to impact the outcome of the situation.

Approved changes are those that have been through the change control system and approved; they are now part of the project, with any potential impact now affecting the project.

Know how to correctly interpret stakeholder requests for project changes.

Know the difference between requested changes and approved changes.

6.8.2   Change Control System

A change control system is used to assess the impact and consequences of requested changes on the project. A change is requested, analyzed for impact and consequences, then typically either approved or rejected.

An overall change control system can address a variety of areas on the project. If the change control system is for a specific Knowledge Area such as scope or cost, it addresses only that area and usually no others. In this case, there are various change control systems working together from the various Knowledge Areas on the project, with Integrated Change Control being the process that typically connects them. For example, a scope change is likely to impact both schedule (schedule management plan) and cost (cost management plan).

Know the characteristics of a change control system.

6.8.3   Change Control Board (CCB)

A change control board is typically used on larger projects. Generally, these projects involve various areas of a company; thus, the board is a representative of the areas of the company. **The function of the board is to review (and approve or reject) changes on the project as they relate to the various areas of the represented business.** Every change control board can have different rules with the key being that these rules meet the needs of the company and the project.

6.8.4   Configuration Management

Configuration management is a process used to control product features and details through change control. It could be a rigorous change control system that helps standardize the change process associated with the project baseline. Such management helps define and lock down details associated with the project scope, thereby ensuring that the project creates only what was intended so the stakeholders have Conformance to Requirements and Fitness for Use.

Know the characteristics of a configuration management system.

The three main goals of a configuration management system are as follows:
- To develop a consistent process to evaluate changes
- To create an environment in which you can review and approve appropriate changes to modify the project for the better
- To establish communication standards so project management team can communicate those changes to the appropriate stakeholders

Integrated Change Control can involve activities related to configuration management. It can include configuration identification which helps establish the baseline and validate (verify) status accounting which deals with documentation, storage, and access to project product data, and verification/auditing which deals with verification of the product of the project.

6.9   Close Project (Closing Process Group)

Know the Key Inputs, Tools & Techniques, and Outputs for Close Project.

Close Project involves completing activities across Process Groups to close a project or phase. When it is complete, a phase or project is closed. It is important to remember that when a project stops (regardless of reason), the project must be closed. This process deals with executing the Close Project part of the project management plan. If the project is scoped out over multiple phases, this process closes out each project phase as the activities being completed warrant it. In this process, there are two documentation-related outputs to be concerned about: the administrative closure procedure and the contract closure procedure.

The administrative closure procedure deals with the collection of project records, validation of project success or failure, lessons learned, and the archival of project information for historical information.

The contract closure procedure deals with closing out any contract-related activities on the project. These can include activities such as the following:

- Product verification that all work on the project (as related to the contract) was done as defined (correct and to satisfaction)
- Administrative closure, which includes updating archived and historical contract documentation on the project for future use

Close Project (Closing)		
Key Inputs	Project Management Plan	A project management plan (not a schedule!) **integrates plans representing the various Knowledge Areas** in the PMI approach to project management. Supporting detail is also included to help validate the information in the project management plan. This detail helps validate that the project is ready for completion.
	Contract Documentation	Contract documentation **validates that all the terms and conditions of the contract have been met** before the project is closed, then to communicate that status between the buyer and seller.
	Work Performance Information	Work performance information provides a **status on what has been completed (or not completed)** on the project.
	Deliverables	Deliverables represent the **completion of project work pieces** defined in Planning.
Key Tools & Techniques	Project Management Methodology	The project management methodology is the project **management approach currently used on the project**.
	Project Management Information System	The project management information system (PMIS) can define **how project information is stored and distributed**.
	Expert Judgment	Expert judgment is of great value. It can be more significant and accurate than the best modeling tools available.

Key Outputs	Administrative Closure Procedure	The administrative closure procedure **closes a project whenever the project ends**. It could occur when the work is complete, when funding is consumed, when the project is cancelled, or when other terminating events take place.
	Contract Closure Procedure	A contract closure procedure **begins the process of formally closing out a contract** when the work is complete or other circumstances occur that warrant stopping the work associated with the contract. This procedure is completed in the Contract Closure process in procurement.
	Final Product, Service, or Result	The final product, service, or result of the project is delivered to the customer or sponsor. This is the **main work of the project**.

Situational Question and Real World Application
There are a number of symptoms that could arise when closing the project fails to have appropriate support. They involve inappropriate closing of the project and potentially lack lessons learned, project archives, complete records, and correct storage. Those items will not necessarily stop the project in its tracks, but they will keep it from being completed correctly. Bigger items could include failure to attain signoff (formal acceptance) for the product or extensive rework associated to attain the signoff.

6.9.1   Project Files and Contract File

Project files and a contract file are created in the closing of a project. Project files are created in the Close Project process; the contract file is created in the Contract Closure process.

Project files are any project documents that record what happened, what decisions were made, and what changes were approved. **Financial records, legal documents,** etc. are part of these files.

The **contract file** created in the procurement process (if procurement is done) contains documentation associated with the **contract, approved changes, and formal acceptance.**

Understand that closing a project includes product verification, lessons learned, updating of records, reporting, archiving, and formal acceptance of components.

6.9.2   Closing the Project

Close Project is a sticky process. It is the point at which the customer agrees to accept the product of the project. The customer or sponsor is basically signing off, indicating satisfaction with the work and other activities of the project. This closure basically says that the work (product) of the project and the project are complete. After the project is closed, any additional work is warranty work or new work.

6.9.3   Lessons Learned

Lessons can come along before the end of a project, as an opportunity that allows the team to learn from past experience and improve on the project as they complete it. If lessons come at the end of the project, the administrative closure procedures come into play. If they come before the end of the project, the closing procedures are not a factor.

Know what lessons learned (post mortem) is and why it is important.

Lessons Learned at the end of the phase or project

After formal acceptance, the execution and work of the project are done. At this point, it is time for lessons learned, which can happen a number of ways.

Normally, it is a process by which the team gets together and meets to discuss what worked and didn't work on the project, and what could have been done to maximize the good and minimize or eliminate the bad. There could also be a questionnaire used to collect detailed feedback. This survey could be anonymous to help get true opinions expressed without fear or negative consequences for speaking openly. There could also be a combination of both, thereby allowing greater discovery and quantitative details. This combination makes it possible to take the lessons learned of the project and apply them to other projects so project participants can learn from the past instead of repeating it.

When the archiving of project files is complete, when formal acceptance has been approved, and when the lessons learned is complete, it is time to return resources to the resource pool, transfer them to other projects, or end their work in the environment.

Lessons learned can also occur at the end of each project phase. Similar principles apply, but it could be more difficult to extract the true feelings from project participants who may fear repercussions on future phases of the project.

6.9.4   Close Project and Contract Closure

From a process standpoint, the Close Project process precedes Contract Closure. In other words, from a high level overall perspective, you close the project then you close the contract. However, the view is much more granular with regard to the outputs of concurrent activities in both the closing of the project and the closing of the contract. Timing and resource usage can impact the activities. Therefore, at a high level, closing the project precedes closing the contract. The details, however, can be like a finish/finish situation where the outputs intertwine as needed. The sequence in section 6.9.5 "Sequence for Closure" shows the ideal sequence.

Notice that under "Sequence for Closure," files are archived and resources released after contracts are closed. PMI states that not all process interactions are shown in the *PMBOK Guide Third Edition*.

> Know how to close a project and the documentation associated with it.

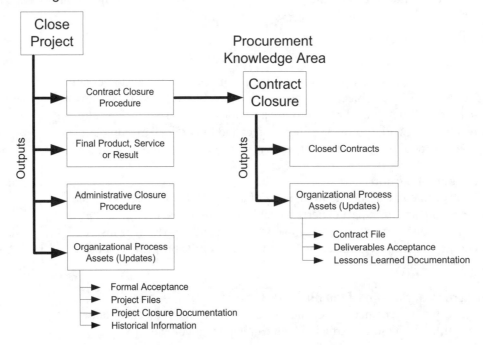

Figure 6-1: Close Project and Contract Closure Interaction

6.9.5   Sequence for Closure

Be prepared to understand the Closing sequence of items for a project. While this sequence can be somewhat vague in the *PMBOK Guide*, it can also vary in reality from company to company, depending on the needs.

The general order is as follows:

1. Complete any Close Project activities.
2. Deliver any required reports associated with closure (Organizational Process Assets updates).
3. Close out any contracts with outside vendors.
4. Perform Lessons Learned.
5. Complete the archives of any project files (Organizational Process Assets updates).
6. Release resources for other projects.

6.10   Integration Formulas and Variables

There are no formulas for Integration only. See the Cost chapter for earned value management formulas.

6.11   Integration Terminology

Term	Description
Administrative Closure	The process of accumulating, finishing, and interpreting information to achieve completion of a phase or project
Approved Change Request (Output/Input)	A request for a change on a project that has been approved via formal or informal change request
Assumption	An educated, logical guess about a variable when its details are unknown on a project
Change Control	The formal or informal process of reviewing changes associated with a project; will result in approval or rejection of changes
Change Control Board (CCB)	A group of people formally recognized to approve or reject requested changes on a project
Change Control System	A documented, formal process that manages change associated with the project
Change Request	A request to change something on the project
Configuration Management	A process which verifies that the products of the project are complete and accurate
Corrective Actions	Actions on a project that will correct a component of the project that is out of alignment with the baseline
Formal Acceptance	Attaining signature for a piece of the project or the complete project, where the signature represents completion or closure of the project or that piece of the project
Initiation	Commitment from the sponsor and organization to start a project or to continue it to the next phase
Integrated Change Control	The change control process as it relates to all project Knowledge Areas
Lessons Learned	A process, meeting, or questionnaire (possibly all) to discuss what worked and didn't work on the project, with the purpose of not repeating what didn't work and maximizing what did work correctly
Log	A document which tracks items that occur during a project (Ex: change, issue, and defect)
Net Present Value (NPV)	A process to calculate the anticipated net monetary gain (or loss) from a project by discounting future cash inflows and outflows to the current point in time
Payback Period	The amount of time needed to recover the investment in the project
Project Archives	A set of records that correctly describe and document the history of the project

Project Charter (Output/Input)	The foundational document which states the main details of the project; typically includes the following: * Scope of the project * Any constraints and assumptions, including time and cost goals * Why the project is being done * Description of Project Manager authority
Project Integration Management	The processes used to manage all Knowledge Areas across the project life cycle; can include plan creation, execution, and change control
Project Management Plan (Output/Input)	(Formerly called the project plan) A formal comprehensive document that describes how the plan of the project will be implemented and monitored; can include various management plans (from the Knowledge Areas) and documents such as the work breakdown structure, project scope statement, and organizational chart
Return on Investment (ROI)	The amount of income from an investment; income divided by the investment
Stakeholder Analysis	The process of discovering key needs, names, position, focus, and influences on the project of all stakeholders
Statement of Work (SOW)	A description of services, products, and work results to be accomplished on a project or other initiative
Strategic Planning	Long-term planning by a company (usually three to five years in the future)
System	An integrated set of pieces used to achieve a specific project goal; could be an actual process or management process, or some mix of both approaches
Technical Performance Measurement (Technique)	A measurement approach that compares what was technically created in the project compared to what the project management plan shows should have been created
Tool	An item such as the template of a computer application used in a project to help complete project work
Trend Analysis (Technique)	An approach that attempts to forecast future results based on historical information
Weighted Scoring Model	A project-selection technique in which criteria are defined and a weight given to it Each project is then measured on the sum of each of those components and selections made from that result.
Work Authorization (Technique)	A technique which ensures that the right work is done at the right time in the right order
Work Authorization System	A system in the project management approach that allows the right work to begin at the right time (or sequence) by the right people; can be something as informal as Project Manager approval to something as formal as documented predecessors and signoff before work can begin

PMP Exam Success Series: Certification Exam Manual
© 2007 Crosswind Project Management, Inc., www.crosswindpm.com

6.12   Integration Mind Map

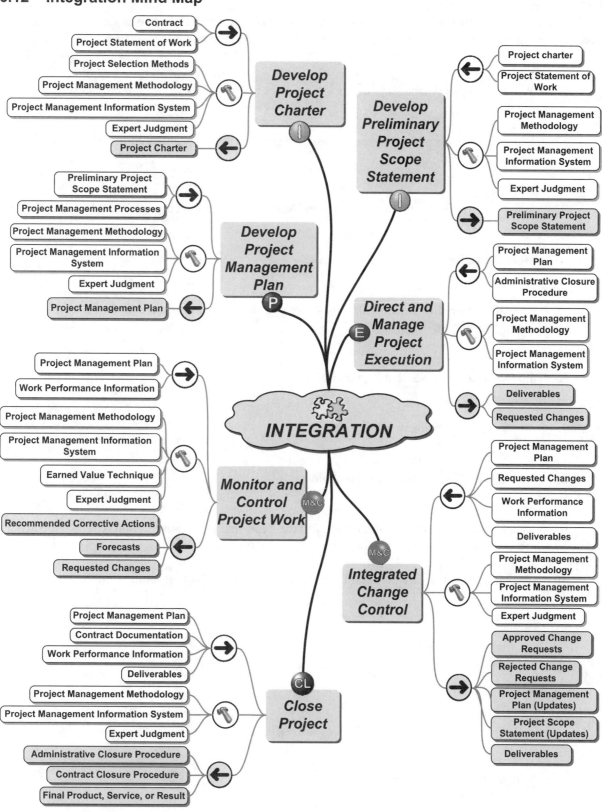

6.13   Integration Tests and Exercises

6.13.1   Integration Quick Test

In this quiz, answer the question in a short essay of only a sentence or two or circle all correct answers for the question. Note that some questions may have more than one answer. Answers are in section 6.14.1.

1.   What is a project management plan? How does it differ, if at all, from a project schedule?

2.   What is the name of the change process that accommodates changes across all Knowledge Areas in Integration?

3.   What is the main output of the Direct and Manage Project Execution process?

4.   How does a baseline differ from actuals?

5.   How do constraints and assumptions factor into the definition and creation of the project management plan?

6.   List the risk processes that happen in Planning.

7.   What is configuration management?

8.   List at least four examples of stakeholders.

9.   What is name of the multi-dimensional status reporting system used in project management?

10.   What are the three variables that the system in the previous question measures?

6.13.2   Integration ITTO Matching Exercise

Match the correct ITTO term at the bottom of the page with the blanks to the right of the process. When a term is used multiple times, it is flagged by a parenthetical value indicating the number of times used. Also, match summary sentences with the process name that fits. Answers are in section 6.14.2.

	Inputs	Tools &Techniques	Outputs
Develop Project Charter	1) 2)	1) 2) 3) 4)	1) Project Charter
Summary:			
Develop Preliminary Project Scope Statement	1) Project Chart 2)	1) 2) 3)	1)
Summary:			
Develop Project Management Plan	1) 2)	1) 2) 3)	1) Proj Mgmt Plan
Summary:			
Direct and Manage Project Execution	1) Proj Mgmt Plan 2)	1) 2)	1) 2)
Summary:			
Monitor and Control Project Work	1) Proj Mgmt Plan 2)	1) 2) 3) 4)	1) 2) 3)
Summary:			
Integrated Change Control	1) Project Mgmt Plan 2) 3) 4)	1) 2) 3)	1) 2) 3) 4) 5)
Summary:			
Close Project	1) Proj Mgmt Plan 2) 3) 4)	1) 2) 3)	1) Final Product Service or result 2) 3)
Summary:			

Creating a project charter and formalizing existence of a project
To create a high-level narrative of the project scope
The steps to formally close the project
Activities associated with overall change control

Executing a project management plan to complete project work
To integrate all the management plans and supporting documents into the overall plan
Observing the activities on the project for compliance to the plan

Administrative Closure Procedure (2)	Final Product, Services, or Result	Project Management Plan (Updates)
Approved Change Requests	Preliminary Project Scope Statement (2)	Project Management Processes
Contract (when applicable)	Project Charter (2) ✓✓	Project Scope Statement (Updates)
Contract Closure Procedure	Project Management Information System (7)	Project Selection Methods
Contract Documentation	Project Management Methodology (7)	Project Statement of Work (2)
Deliverables (4)	Project Management Plan (5) ✓✓	Recommended Corrective Actions
Earned Value Technique		Rejected Change Requests
Expert Judgment (6)		Requested Changes (3)
Forecasts		Work Performance Information (3)

6.13.3   Integration Terminology Matching Exercise

Match the correct term in the left column to the correct definition in the right column. See the exercise answer section of this chapter for the correct answer. Answers are in section 6.14.3.

Matching Exercise #1

	Term	Answer	Definition
1	Administrative Closure	N	A. A project-selection technique in which criteria are defined and weight given to it Each project is then measured on the sum of each of those components and selections made from that result.
2	Approved Change Request (Output/Input)	B	B. A request for a change on a project that has been approved via formal or informal change request
3	Change Control Board (CCB)	B	C. Attaining signature for a piece of the project or the complete project, where the signature represents completion or closure of the project or that piece of the project
4	Configuration Management	L	D. The foundational document which states the main details of the project; typically includes the following: * Scope of the project * Any constraints and assumptions, including time and cost goals * Why the project is being done * Description of Project Manager authority
5	Formal Acceptance	C	E. A measurement approach that compares what was technically created in the project compared to what the project management plan shows should have been created
6	Integrated Change Control	M	F. The process of discovering key needs, names, position, focus, and influences on the project of all stakeholders
7	Log	O	G. A group of people formally recognized to approve or reject requested changes on a project
8	Payback Period	K	H. An integrated set of pieces used to achieve a specific project goal; could be an actual process or management process, or some mix of both approaches
9	Project Charter (Output/Input)	D	I. An approach that attempts to forecast future results based on historical information
10	Stakeholder Analysis	F	J. A system in the project management approach that allows the right work to begin at the right time (or sequence) by the right people; can be something as informal as Project Manager approval to something as formal as documented predecessors and signoff before work can begin
11	System	H	K. The amount of time needed to recover the investment in the project
12	Technical Performance Measurement (Technique)	E	L. A process which verifies that the products of the project are complete and accurate
13	Trend Analysis (Technique)	I	M. The change control process as it relates to all project Knowledge Areas
14	Weighted Scoring Model	A	N. The process of accumulating, finishing, and interpreting information to achieve completion of a phase or project
15	Work Authorization System	J	O. A document which tracks items that occur during a project (Ex: change, issue, and defect)

Matching Exercise #2

	Term	Answer	Definition
1	Assumption	C	A. The processes used to manage all Knowledge Areas across the project life cycle; can include plan creation, execution, and change control
2	Change Control	M	B. A technique which ensures that the right work is done at the right time in the right order
3	Change Control System	W	C. An educated, logical guess about a variable when its details are unknown on a project
4	Change Request	E	D. A description of services, products, and work results to be accomplished on a project or other initiative
5	Corrective Actions	I	E. A request to change something on the project
6	Initiation	L	F. A set of records that correctly describe and document the history of the project
7	Lessons Learned	J	G. Long-term planning by a company (usually three to five years in the future)
8	Net Present Value (NPV)	K	H. The formal or informal process of reviewing changes associated with a project; will result in approval or rejection of changes
9	Project Archives	F	I. Actions on a project that will correct a component of the project that is out of alignment with the baseline
10	Project Integration Management	A	J. A process, meeting, or questionnaire (possibly all) to discuss what worked and didn't work on the project, with the purpose of not repeating what didn't work and maximizing what did work correctly
11	Project Management Plan (Output/Input)	N	K. A process to calculate the anticipated net monetary gain (or loss) from a project by discounting future cash inflows and outflows to the current point in time
12	Return on Investment (ROI)	O	L. Commitment from the sponsor and organization to start a project or to continue it to the next phase
13	Statement of Work (SOW)	D	M. A documented, formal process that manages change associated with the project
14	Strategic Planning	G	N. A formal comprehensive document that describes how the plan of the project will be implemented and monitored; can include various management plans (from the Knowledge Areas) and documents such as the work breakdown structure, project scope statement, and organizational chart
15	Work Authorization (Technique)	B	O. The amount of income from an investment; income divided by the investment

6.13.4   Integration Practice Test

Answers are in section 6.14.4.

1.   In defining a milestone, which of the following is correct?

(A) It has a duration of no more than one day.
(B) It has value in the project charter but not in the plan.
(C) It has a duration of zero (0).
(D) It is used to define the phase of a project.

2.   The project charter has just been signed off. There were items in the project charter that described market conditions which could affect the project and also resource limitations on the project. These are examples of what?

(A) Assumptions
(B) Constraints
(C) Economic consumption
(D) Authority level of the Project Manager

3.   When does a project close?

(A) When a project completes Scope Verification
(B) When a project is cancelled
(C) When a project runs out of money
(D) All the answers

4.   Which of the following is the best description of tools used for communication on a project?

(A) Communication system
(B) Instant messaging system
(C) Information distribution planning
(D) Project Management Information System (PMIS)

5.   You are assigned to a new data warehouse project and notice on the project charter that there are four business units listed as sponsors. The data warehouse system has been discussed at your organization for some time, but it's everyone's first exposure to implementing one. Which of the following could present the biggest challenge on the project?

(A) Conflicting goals of the sponsors
(B) The implementation team
(C) The work breakdown structure (WBS)
(D) Integrated Change Control

6.   Which of the following is the best description of configuration management?

(A) A thorough change control system to ensure the project produces the desired results
(B) A system used to store versions of software code
(C) A system used to store versions of documentation on a project
(D) A piece of an automated project management system used to set up project variables

PMP Exam Success Series: Certification Exam Manual
© 2007 Crosswind Project Management, Inc., www.crosswindpm.com

7. The team has completed project Planning and received approval from the sponsor and senior management to move to execution. To which of the following will they compare their work?

    (A) The actuals
    (B) The baseline
    (C) The order of magnitude estimate
    (D) The variance

8. The team has just completed the process of evaluating how the project went. The team members analyzed what worked well and what didn't. They evaluated the Planning and Executing. They documented how the sponsor and senior management supported the project. What phase of the project are they in?

    (A) Lessons learned
    (B) Closure
    (C) Executing
    (D) Controlling

9. What is the main purpose of utilizing a work authorization system?

    (A) To show what work is to be done in the project
    (B) To show who is responsible for what work
    (C) To control gold plating
    (D) To serve as a time-tracking system

10. You and your supervisor are having a disagreement about some terminology with project management documentation. He is asking you where the project management plan is, and when you provide it to him, he says, "I don't need a book." You don't understand why he is saying this. Which answer below best describes the confusion?

    (A) He is incorrectly calling a schedule a project management plan.
    (B) He lacks project management training.
    (C) You have a really big schedule on the project.
    (D) You are having a communication breakdown with him.

11. Which of the following roles pays for the project and could own the work of the project when it is complete?

    (A) Senior management
    (B) Project management
    (C) Functional management
    (D) Sponsor

12. The e-commerce project has gone well, other than the fact that the sponsor changed two different times. The project is approaching closure. Which of the following are not expected to come from closing a project?

   (A) Lessons learned
   (B) Release of resources
   (C) Procurement audit
   (D) Project archives

13. Given the complex nature of projects, which area of change generally has the highest priority?

   (A) A change in the company that is creating the project
   (B) A change in the market where the work of the project will operate
   (C) A change in the team on the project
   (D) A change in the project

14. When creating a project management plan, which of the following is the best to create it?

   (A) Project Manager
   (B) Project Manager and team
   (C) Team
   (D) Sponsor

15. You are the Project Manager on a Restaurant POS System project for Hamburger Prince Restaurants. You are fortunate in having the top technical architect in the company on your project. The corporate headquarters is implementing an enterprise reporting system. At the last minute, the CEO pulls your key resource for the new enterprise project. After unsuccessfully lobbying to keep the resource on your project, you concede. What is the best action to take next?

   (A) Evaluate the impact of the person's absence on the project and communicate to senior management.
   (B) Continue to lobby for the person to be back on your project.
   (C) Change the scope of the project to accommodate for the loss of the resource.
   (D) Continue as the original plan, but without the resource.

16. The project will be starting the Executing phase next week. The project sponsor and Project Manager have a meeting scheduled with the team and the business units that are impacted by the project. They explain what is expected to happen on the project and how each of the people can help contribute to the success of the project. What is this event called?

   (A) Kickoff meeting
   (B) Initiation
   (C) A verbal project charter
   (D) Project management plan development

PMP Exam Success Series: Certification Exam Manual
© 2007 Crosswind Project Management, Inc., www.crosswindpm.com

17. The Project Manager is meeting with various people impacted by his new project. He is attempting to find out their needs for the project, as well as any constraints and assumptions that they might be aware of. At the same time, the Project Manager is beginning to set expectations for the project. What is the best description for this activity?

    (A) Stakeholder management
    (B) Change control board
    (C) Team member analysis
    (D) Stakeholder identification

18. At the end of the project, project team members have assembled to review what happened on the project, discussing what went well and what didn't. They undertake this discussion for the sake of future projects so that they can repeat the things that worked on the project and eliminate repeating the things that didn't work so well. This activity is known as what?

    (A) Contract Closure
    (B) Lessons learned
    (C) Closing the project
    (D) Procurement audit

19. The Project Manager has worked diligently to complete the project scope on time and budget. The team has completed the work of the project and is getting signoff from the customer. When they've achieved this, what will they have accomplished?

    (A) Formal acceptance
    (B) Scope Verification
    (C) Project archives
    (D) Contract Closure

20. The team has just completed the work on the project. It has been a long project with a churn rate of 18% on project personnel. Which of the following is the best step to complete next?

    (A) Release of resources
    (B) Lessons learned
    (C) Formal acceptance
    (D) Procurement audit

21. The Internet project is about 65% complete and has had its challenges. As of the last status report, it appears to be on track regarding cost, schedule, and scope. Senior management tells you that the sponsor has some serious concerns about the project. You don't understand why, based on the last status report. What is the best thing to do first?

    (A) Evaluate the schedule and budget to verify the triple constraint health of the project.
    (B) Ignore senior management because the project is in good shape.
    (C) Tell senior management that the project is in good shape.
    (D) Meet with the sponsor and find out what their concerns are.

22. The client has requested a three-week delay on the project while they calibrate their test equipment. This delay wasn't planned, but the equipment had to be calibrated. The company is limited on available resources. This delay will be best shown in what?

    (A) Responsibility assignment matrix
    (B) Network diagram
    (C) Budget
    (D) Work breakdown structure (WBS)

23. The healthcare project is going through Planning. In evaluating the triple constraint, which of the following is of the greatest importance?

    (A) Quality
    (B) Time
    (C) Cost
    (D) They are all equal unless otherwise stated in the project charter.

24. The project is nearing completion. The team is involved in a lot of different activities to close the project. They are grouping together various documents associated with financial records, contracts, internal project documentation, and client-related documentation. What are they creating?

    (A) Project closure
    (B) Contract file
    (C) Lessons learned
    (D) Archives

25. Your network upgrade project is almost complete. You have outsourced the remote upgrades to three different companies for completion. As the project closes down, what comes first?

    (A) Contract Closure
    (B) Assignment of contracts for the next phase
    (C) Release of resources
    (D) Closing the project

26. Which of the following is an input to a change control system?

    (A) Approved changes
    (B) Change requests
    (C) Signoff
    (D) Impact analysis

27. The company is implementing an enterprise reporting system across the entire company. This system will integrate a number of business units. As a result, it will be very resource-consuming and could cause reprioritization of other projects that it will replace. Which of the following concerns you most?

    (A) How many resources you can keep
    (B) How your raise or promotion might be impacted by not being on the project
    (C) What impact the new project is expected to have on your biggest project
    (D) How many resources you might lose to the new project

PMP Exam Success Series: Certification Exam Manual
© 2007 Crosswind Project Management, Inc., www.crosswindpm.com

28. You are the Project Manager for a highway construction project. You have just finished putting together all the various plans into an integrated complete document. What step will you perform next?

    (A) Develop Project Management Plan
    (B) Integrated Change Control
    (C) Direct and Manage Project Execution
    (D) Project charter signoff

29. All the following are typically part of the project management plan except...

    (A) Schedule management plan
    (B) Budget management plan
    (C) Risk management plan
    (D) Scope management plan

30. The customer has just attended the weekly staff meeting for the infrastructure project and has stated that the market is changing for the product being created. As a result of this change, the customer has requested a significant change to the project. The project is 85% complete. What does the Project Manager do?

    (A) Tell the customer the project is too close to being complete to integrate the change.
    (B) Evaluate the impact to the project and let the customer know the options and impact of the change.
    (C) Ignore the customer hoping the change will disappear.
    (D) Make the new work a new project and release the project as-is to the market.

6.14   Integration Tests and Exercise Answers

6.14.1   Integration Quick Test Answers

1.   What is a project management plan? How does it differ, if at all, from a project schedule?
The project management plan is the cumulative document that contains plans from all the Knowledge Areas to create an overall comprehensive plan that addresses scope, schedule, cost, quality, staffing, communication, risk, and procurement. The schedule is a piece of the plan. [section 6.5, section 6.5.1, section 6.11]

2.   What is the name of the change process that accommodates changes across all Knowledge Areas in Integration?
Integrated Change Control [section 6.8, section 6.11]

3.   What is the main output of the Direct and Manage Project Execution process?
Work results [section 6.6]

4.   How does a baseline differ from actuals?
A baseline is the estimated or planned value that you are going to try to attain on the project. Actuals are what has been done. Ideally, the two are the same but not always. [section 6.5.4]

5.   How do constraints and assumptions factor into the definition and creation of the project management plan?
Constraints are factors that limit the project. They are found typically in the areas of scope, time, or cost. Assumptions are educated guesses or speculations on unknown Planning Area items that typically have more information known about them as the project evolves. [section 6.5.2, section 6.5.3]

6.   List the risk processes that happen in Planning.
Risk Management Planning, Risk Identification, Qualitative Risk Analysis, Quantitative Risk Analysis, Risk Response Planning
[section 13.2, section 13.3, section 13.5, section 13.6, section 13.10]

7.   What is configuration management?
A process that helps ensure that the results of the project will meet the defined needs of the project [section 6.84]

8.   List at least four examples of stakeholders.
Team members, Project Manager, Functional Manager, sponsor, senior management
[section 5.4.4]

9.   What is name of the multi-dimensional status reporting system used in project management?
Earned value management [section 6.7, section 9.14.1, section 9.16]

10.   What are the three variables that the system in the previous question measures?
Scope, time, and cost [section 6.7, section 9.14.1, section 9.16]

PMP Exam Success Series: Certification Exam Manual
© 2007 Crosswind Project Management, Inc., www.crosswindpm.com

6.14.2   Integration ITTO Matching Exercise Answers

	Inputs	Tools &Techniques	Outputs
Develop Project Charter	1) Contract (when applicable) 2) Project Statement of Work	1) Project Selection Methods 2) Project Management Methodology 3) Project Management Information System 4) Expert Judgment	1) Project Charter
Summary:	Creating a project charter and formalizing existence of a project		
Develop Preliminary Project Scope Statement	1) Project Charter 2) Project Statement of Work	1) Project Management Methodology 2) Project Management Information System 3) Expert Judgment	1) Preliminary Project Scope Statement
Summary:	To create a high-level narrative of the project scope		
Develop Project Management Plan	1) Preliminary Project Scope Statement 2) Project Management Processes	1) Project Management Methodology 2) Project Management Information System 3) Expert Judgment	1) Project Management Plan
Summary:	To integrate all the management plans and supporting documents into the overall plan		
Direct and Manage Project Execution	1) Project Management Plan 2) Administrative Closure Procedure	1) Project Management Methodology 2) Project Management Information System	1) Deliverables 2) Requested Changes
Summary:	Executing a project management plan to complete project work		
Monitor and Control Project Work	1) Project Management Plan 2) Work Performance Information	1) Project Management Methodology 2) Project Management Information System 3) Earned Value Technique 4) Expert Judgment	1) Recommended Corrective Actions 2) Forecasts 3) Requested Changes
Summary:	Observing the activities on the project for compliance to the plan		
Integrated Change Control	1) Project Management Plan 2) Requested Changes 3) Work Performance Information 4) Deliverables	1) Project Management Methodology 2) Project Management Information System 3) Expert Judgment	1) Approved Change Requests 2) Rejected Change Requests 3) Project Scope Statement (Updates) 4) Project Management Plan (Updates) 5) Deliverables
Summary:	Activities associated with overall change control		
Close Project	1) Project Management Plan 2) Contract Documentation 3) Work Performance Information 4) Deliverables	1) Project Management Methodology 2) Project Management Information System 3) Expert Judgment	1) Administrative Closure Procedure 2) Contract Closure Procedure 3) Final Product, Service, or Result
Summary:	The steps to formally close the project		

6.14.3   Integration Terminology Matching Exercise Answers

Matching Exercise #1 Answers

	Term	Definition
1	Administrative Closure	N. The process of accumulating, finishing, and interpreting information to achieve completion of a phase or project
2	Approved Change Request (Output/Input)	B. A request for a change on a project that has been approved via formal or informal change request
3	Change Control Board (CCB)	G. A group of people formally recognized to approve or reject requested changes on a project
4	Configuration Management	L. A process which verifies that the products of the project are complete and accurate
5	Formal Acceptance	C. Attaining signature for a piece of the project or the complete project, where the signature represents completion or closure of the project or that piece of the project
6	Integrated Change Control	M. The change control process as it relates to all project Knowledge Areas
7	Log	O. A document which tracks items that occur during a project. (Ex: change, issue, and defect)
8	Payback Period	K. The amount of time needed to recover the investment in the project
9	Project Charter (Output/Input)	D. The foundational document which states the main details of the project; typically includes the following: * Scope of the project * Any constraints and assumptions, including time and cost goals * Why the project is being done * Description of Project Manager authority
10	Stakeholder Analysis	F. The process of discovering key needs, names, position, focus, and influences on the project of all stakeholders
11	System	H. An integrated set of pieces used to achieve a specific project goal; could be an actual process or management process, or some mix of both approaches
12	Technical Performance Measurement (Technique)	E. A measurement approach that compares what was technically created in the project compared to what the project management plan shows should have been created
13	Trend Analysis (Technique)	I. An approach that attempts to forecast future results based on historical information
14	Weighted Scoring Model	A. A project-selection technique in which criteria are defined and weight given to it Each project is then measured on the sum of each of those components and selections made from that result
15	Work Authorization System	J. A system in the project management approach that allows the right work to begin at the right time (or sequence) by the right people; can be something as informal as Project Manager approval to something as formal as documented predecessors and signoff before work can begin

PMP Exam Success Series: Certification Exam Manual
 © 2007 Crosswind Project Management, Inc., www.crosswindpm.com

Matching Exercise #2 Answers

	Term	Definition
1	Assumption	C. An educated, logical guess about a variable when its details are unknown on a project
2	Change Control	H. The formal or informal process of reviewing changes associated with a project; will result in approval or rejection of changes
3	Change Control System	M. A documented, formal process that manages change associated with the project
4	Change Request	E. A request to change something on the project
5	Corrective Actions	I. Actions on a project that will correct a component of the project that is out of alignment with the baseline
6	Initiation	L. Commitment from the sponsor and organization to start a project or to continue it to the next phase
7	Lessons Learned	J. A process, meeting, or questionnaire (possibly all) to discuss what worked and didn't work on the project, with the purpose of not repeating what didn't work and maximizing what did work correctly
8	Net Present Value (NPV)	K. A process to calculate the anticipated net monetary gain (or loss) from a project by discounting future cash inflows and outflows to the current point in time
9	Project Archives	F. A set of records that correctly describe and document the history of the project
10	Project Integration Management	A. The processes used to manage all Knowledge Areas across the project life cycle; can include plan creation, execution, and change control
11	Project Management Plan (Output/Input)	N. A formal comprehensive document that describes how the plan of the project will be implemented and monitored; can include various management plans (from the Knowledge Areas) and documents such as the work breakdown structure, project scope statement, and organizational chart
12	Return on Investment (ROI)	O. The amount of income from an investment; income divided by the investment
13	Statement of Work (SOW)	D. A description of services, products, and work results to be accomplished on a project or other initiative
14	Strategic Planning	G. Long-term planning by a company (usually three to five years in the future)
15	Work Authorization (Technique)	B. A technique which ensures that the right work is done at the right time in the right order

6.14.4   Integration Practice Test Answers

1.   In defining a milestone which of the following is correct?

Correct Answer: (C) It has a duration of zero (0).
Explanation: The milestone has a duration of zero. The milestone is typically used to define the completion of a series of activities. The other answers are noise. [section 8.5.12, section 8.8]

2.   The project charter has just been signed off. There were items in the project charter that described market conditions which could affect the project and also resource limitations on the project. These are examples of what?

Correct Answer: (B) Constraints
Explanation: Constraints are variables that can limit the options the project has. They typically deal with resources, time, or money. Assumptions are educated guesses made on the project about items that are not known. The other answers are noise. [section 6.5.3]

3.   When does a project close?

(A) When a project completes Scope Verification
(B) When a project is cancelled
(C) When a project runs out of money

Correct Answer: (D) All the answers
Explanation: Whenever a project ends, it should be formally closed. This closure allows the team and organization to learn from what worked and didn't on the project and to formally close out the initiative. When a project completes scope verification, the deliverables of the project are formally accepted and thus, the project complete. When a project is cancelled or when it runs out of money the closure activities to close the project would be done to complete the administrative activities associated with closure of the project. [section 6.9]

4.   Which of the following is the best description of tools used for communication on a project?

Correct Answer: (D) Project Management Information System (PMIS)
Explanation: The Project Management Information System (PMIS) is a system that stores and distributes project information. It can be a low tech or high tech system. The other answers are noise. [section 6.5.5]

5.   You are assigned to a new data warehouse project and notice on the project charter that there are four business units listed as sponsors. The data warehouse system has been discussed at your organization for some time, but it's everyone's first exposure to implementing one. Which of the following could present the biggest challenge on the project?

Correct Answer: (A) Conflicting goals of the sponsors
Explanation: Conflicting sponsor goals can significantly impact the project because any attempt to build what works for all involved could radically alter the plan. The creation of the WBS is a challenge as well, but not as big as the best answer. The other answers are noise. [section 5.5.1]

PMP Exam Success Series: Certification Exam Manual
© 2007 Crosswind Project Management, Inc., www.crosswindpm.com

6. Which of the following is the best description of configuration management?

Correct Answer: (A) A thorough change control system to ensure the project produces the desired results
Explanation: Configuration management ensures that the project is building what it should build. It utilizes a very thorough and detailed change control process to ensure that project results conform to requirements and have Fitness for Use. [section 6.8.4]

7. The team has completed project Planning and received approval from the sponsor and senior management to move to execution. To which of the following will they compare their work?

Correct Answer: (B) The baseline
Explanation: The baseline is the estimate for the project. It can be for the scope, time, and cost of the project. The actuals are the real data on what the project has done regarding scope, time, and cost. The variance is the difference between the baseline and actual. "The order of magnitude estimate" is noise. [section 6.5.4]

8. The team has just completed the process of evaluating how the project went. The team members analyzed what worked well and what didn't. They evaluated the Planning and the Executing. They documented how the sponsor and senior management supported the project. What phase of the project are they in?

Correct Answer: (B) Closure
Explanation: They are in the Closing phase. The activities described in the question are lessons learned. Controlling has already happened on the project. So has Executing. [section 6.9]

9. What is the main purpose of utilizing a work authorization system?

Correct Answer: (C) To control gold plating
Explanation: A work authorization system helps ensure that certain work is done at a certain time in a certain order. It helps minimize the opportunity for gold plating on a project. The work breakdown structure (WBS) shows what work is to be done on the project. The responsibility assignment matrix (RAM) shows who is responsible for what work. "To serve as a time-tracking system" is noise. [section 6.6.1]

10. You and your supervisor are having a disagreement about some terminology with project management documentation. He is asking you where the project management plan is, and when you provide it to him, he says, "I don't need a book." You don't understand why he is saying this. Which answer below best describes the confusion?

Correct Answer: (A) He is incorrectly calling a schedule a project management plan.
Explanation: Many Project Managers incorrectly call a schedule a project management plan. The schedule is actually a part of the project management plan. The project management plan is a cumulative document that contains items such as the schedule, budget, project scope statement, work breakdown structure, change control procedures, and more. [section 6.5, section 6.5.1]

11. Which of the following roles pays for the project and could own the work of the project when it is complete?

Correct Answer: (D) Sponsor
Explanation: Typically, the sponsor's responsibility is to pay for the project and own it when it is complete. Senior management is responsible for a number of areas on a project. The main responsibility is to help support the project and resolve resource conflicts as they occur. Remember, unless otherwise stated, for situational questions assume that you are in a balanced matrix environment. This environment has Functional Managers controlling resources. The Project Manager's responsibility is to drive the completion of the work of the project. [section 5.4.4]

12.   The e-commerce project has gone well, other than the fact that the sponsor changed two
      different times. The project is approaching closure. Which of the following are not expected
      to come from closing a project?

   Correct Answer: (C) Procurement audit
   Explanation: Procurement audits come from the Contract Closure process. The other answers are expected from
   closing the project. [section 14.6]

13.   Given the complex nature of projects, which area of change generally has the highest
      priority?

   Correct Answer: (B) A change in the market where the work of the project will operate
   Explanation: The highest priority in these options goes to the change in the market that could impact the project.
   This is the case because it has the biggest impact of all four options. In a bad situation, the market could be
   radically altered or eliminated. In a good situation, the change could totally reinvent the market and the products
   that work in that market. [section 6.3.3, section 5.5.1]

14.   When creating a project management plan, which of the following is the best to create it?

   Correct Answer: (B) Project Manager and team
   Explanation: The Project Manager and team are the best to create the project management plan and the estimates
   that feed into it. They are the people doing the work, so they should have the opportunity to estimate and plan it,
   as well as possible. The sponsor pays for the project. The Project Manager or the team only isn't a good choice
   because both are needed for a realistic plan. [section 5.4.1, section 6.5]

15.   You are the Project Manager on a Restaurant POS System project for Hamburger Prince
      Restaurants. You are fortunate in having the top technical architect in the company on your
      project. The corporate headquarters is implementing an enterprise reporting system. At the
      last minute, the CEO pulls your key resource for the new enterprise project. After
      unsuccessfully lobbying to keep the resource on your project, you concede. What is the best
      action to take next?

   **Correct Answer: (A) Evaluate the impact of the person's absence on the project and
   communicate to senior management.**
   Explanation: Letting senior management know the impact of not having the resource on the project is the best
   action to take next. You don't change the scope of the project because that isn't the call of the Project Manager. If
   you encountered a significant change such as the loss of a resource, you are expected to revise the plan to
   accommodate the change. [section 5.2, section 5.5, section 12.6]

16.   The project will be starting the Executing phase next week. The project sponsor and Project
      Manager have a meeting scheduled with the team and the business units that are impacted by
      the project. They explain what is expected to happen on the project and how each of the
      people can help contribute to the success of the project. What is this event called?

   Correct Answer: (A) Kickoff meeting
   Explanation: The kickoff meeting is what is commonly used on a project to formally start the project. It allows
   the sponsor to set expectations, and the team to learn about details of the plan. Initiating produces a project charter
   and a preliminary project scope statement. Project management plan development produces a project management
   plan. "A verbal project charter" is noise. [section 6.3.2]

17. The Project Manager is meeting with various people impacted by his new project. He is attempting to find out their needs for the project, as well as any constraints and assumptions that they might be aware of. At the same time, the Project Manager is beginning to set expectations for the project. What is the best description for this activity?

Correct Answer: (A) Stakeholder management
Explanation: Stakeholder management determines the needs and expectations of the stakeholders and managing those needs and expectations. Stakeholder identification determines the impacted stakeholders. The other answers are noise. [section 5.5, section 12.6]

18. At the end of the project, project team members have assembled to review what happened on the project, discussing what went well and what didn't. They undertake this discussion for the sake of future projects so that they can repeat the things that worked on the project and eliminate repeating the things that didn't work so well. This activity is known as what?

Correct Answer: (B) Lessons learned
Explanation: Lessons learned is a valuable tool to learn from success and failure on a project. It can technically happen anywhere on the project, but traditionally happens at the end of a phase or project. The other answers are all part of the Close Project process. [section 6.9.3]

19. The Project Manager has worked diligently to complete the project scope on time and budget. The team has completed the work of the project and is getting signoff from the customer. When they've achieved this, what will they have accomplished?

Correct Answer: (A) Formal acceptance
Explanation: They will have accomplished formal acceptance. Scope Verification helps lead to this acceptance. Contract Closure occurs when closing out a contract with a vendor. Project archives are created when a project is closed out. [section 6.9.2, section 6.11]

20. The team has just completed the work on the project. It has been a long project with a churn rate of 18% on project personnel. Which of the following is the best step to complete next?

Correct Answer: (C) Formal acceptance
Explanation: Formal acceptance is the next step to complete. Scope Verification reveals that the team is done with the work, and that formal acceptance is a good next step. Lessons learned and release of resources follow the formal acceptance. Procurement audit follows as well if there were an outside party working with the company. [section 6.9.2, section 7.4, section 6.11]

21. The Internet project is about 65% complete and has had its challenges. As of the last status report, it appears to be on track regarding cost, schedule, and scope. Senior management tells you that the sponsor has some serious concerns about the project. You don't understand why, based on the last status report. What is the best thing to do first?

Correct Answer: (D) Meet with the sponsor and find out what their concerns are.
Explanation: Meeting with the sponsor to figure out their concerns is the best solution; it is the most proactive and can provide either an immediate fix or clearest information you can use to identify a concern or problem. The answers involving senior management are noise; they don't help resolve the problem. The triple constraint answer is noise as well. [section 5.5, section 12.6]

22.   The client has requested a three-week delay on the project while they calibrate their test equipment. This delay wasn't planned, but the equipment had to be calibrated. The company is limited on available resources. This delay will be best shown in what?

Correct Answer: (B) Network diagram
Explanation: The network diagram shows the sequencing and length of the diagram. The responsibility assignment matrix shows who is responsible for what and does not include time. The WBS shows what work is in the project but does not focus on how long it should take. The budget deals with the cost of the project, not time. [section 8.2.2, section 8.8]

23.   The healthcare project is going through Planning. In evaluating the triple constraint, which of the following is of the greatest importance?

Correct Answer: (D) They are all equal unless otherwise stated in the project charter
Explanation: The triple constraint is scope, time, and cost. Scope is sometimes replaced with quality. This view is an older view of the triple constraint, assuming that quality is associated with what is being built and ignoring the time and cost goals. Quality actually looks at the scope, time, and cost parameters of the project. If you see a question like this on the exam, the correct interpretation is that quality is similar to scope. The triple constraint implies that all three components (scope, time, and cost) are equal unless otherwise defined in the project charter. [section 5.2]

24.   The project is nearing completion. The team is involved in a lot of different activities to close the project. They are grouping together various documents associated with financial records, contracts, internal project documentation, and client-related documentation. What are they creating?

Correct Answer: (D) Archives
Explanation: Archives are the documents that are created as a result of the project. They can later serve as verification of the details of the project. They are finalized in closing the project. Lessons learned happen in closing the project. The contract file is created in the procurement process. [section 6.9.4, section 6.9.5, section 6.11]

25.   Your network upgrade project is almost complete. You have outsourced the remote upgrades to three different companies for completion. As the project closes down, what comes first?

Correct Answer: (D) Closing the project
Explanation: Closing the project happens before Contract Closure. Release of resources is part of closing the project. The other answer is noise. [section 6.9.4, section 6.9.5]

26.   Which of the following is an input to a change control system?

Correct Answer: (B) Change requests
Explanation: Change requests involve a desired change that hasn't been approved yet. Approved changes are the output of a change control system. These are change requests that have gone into the system and been approved. Impact analysis identifies what impact the change might have on the project or environment. Signoff involves receiving approval. In this case, "signoff" is noise. [section 6.8, section 6.8.2]

Crosswind
Project Management Inc.
An ISO 9001: 2000 Certified Company

PMP® Exam Success Series:
Quick Reference for Third Edition PMBOK® Guide

For PMP® Exam Products, Courses and PMTV Online Training go to
www.crosswindpm.com
www.pmtvnetwork.com

If used as a Brain Dump for the PMP® Exam, we suggest you memorize the content to fit your study needs.

Conflict Resolution Types (HR)

Problem Solving / Confrontational – (Best)
Compromise
Forcing – (Worst)
Smoothing
Withdrawal

Types of Power for the Project Manager (HR)

Formal – (Given By Charter)
Expert – (Earned on Your Own)
Reward – (Best)
Penalty – (Worst)
Referent – (Presence Based)

Contract Types

Purchase Order
Time & Materials
FP, FPIF, FPEPA (Focus on Scope Design) – Seller Risk
CPFF, CPIF, CPPC (Focus on Scope Function) – Buyer Risk

Planning Processes

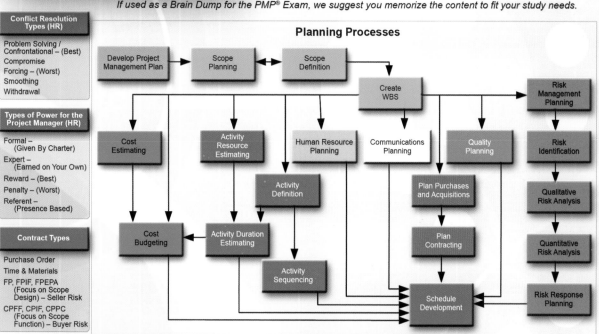

Maslow's Hierarchy of Needs (HR)

Self-Actualization
Esteem
Belonging
Safety
Physiological

EV Formulas (Cost)

Earned Value (EV) = Percent Complete x Planned Value (PV)
Cost Performance Index (CPI) = EV/AC
Cost Variance (CV) = EV-AC
Schedule Performance Index (SPI) = EV/PV
Schedule Variance (SV) = EV-PV
Estimate at Completion (EAC) = BAC/CPI
Estimate to Complete (ETC) = EAC-AC
Variance at Completion (VAC) = BAC-EAC
To Complete Performance Index (TCPI) = (BAC-EV)/(BAC-AC) or $\frac{\text{Remaining Work}}{\text{Remaining Budget}}$
Sum of PV=BAC

Organizational Structure Characteristics (Framework)

	PM Authority	Resource Availability	Who Controls $	Role of PM	Support Staff
Functional	Little or None	Little or None	Functional Mgr	Part-time	Part-time
Weak Matrix	Limited	Limited	Functional Mgr	Part-time	Part-time
Balanced Matrix	Low-Med	Low-Med	Mixed	Full-time	Part-time
Strong Matrix	Strong	Strong	Project Mgr	Full-time	Full-time
Projectized	High - 100%	High - 100%	Project Mgr	Full-time	Full-time

Slack, Forward and Backward Pass Formulas (Time)

Forward: Duration = EF-ES+1   Early Finish: EF=ES+Duration-1

Slack = LS-ES (-)   Slack = LF-EF

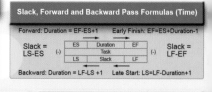

Backward: Duration = LF-LS +1   Late Start: LS=LF-Duration+1

Risk Response Strategies for Positive Risks

Share	Joining with someone to Maximize the Impact
Exploit	To Maximize the Impact of the Risk
Enhance	Taking Steps to Improve the Opportunity

Risk Response Strategies for Negative Risks

Avoid	To Eliminate the Risk
Transfer	To Pass the Risk to Someone Else
Mitigate	To Minimize the Negative Impact

Communication Model

Sender → Message → Receiver
Sender ← Feedback ← Receiver

Various Formulas

PERT = (P+O+(4*R))/6   Variance = $((P-O)/6)^2$
Stand Dev = (P-O)/6   3 Point Est. = (P+O+R)/3

Cost Estimate Range Table (Old)

Est. Name	Process	Range
Order of Mag	Initiation	-25 to +75%
Budget	Planning	-10 to +25%
Definitive	Planning	-5 to +10%

Cost Estimate Range Table (New)

Est. Name	Range
Rough Order of Mag (Rom)	-50 to +100%
Definitive (or Control)	-10 to +15%

% for sigma (Quality)

+/- 1 = 68.26%   +/- 3 = 99.73%
+/- 2 = 95.46%   +/- 6 = 99.9997%

Present-Future Value Formulas

n= # of periods $PV = FV/(1+r)^n$
r= interest rate $FV= PV*(1+r)^n$

Point of Total Assumption (PTA)

$\frac{(\text{Ceiling Price} - \text{Target Price})}{\text{Buyer Share}}$ + Target Cost

Earned Value Management Table 1

	Cost				Time		
	AC (ACWP)		EV (BCWP)			PV (BCWS)	
CPI	=	/		/		=	SPI
$ CV	=	-		-		=	SV $

Earned Value Management Table 2

EAC	= BAC	/CPI
ETC	= EAC	– AC
VAC	= BAC	- EAC

Expected Monetary Value (EMV) = Probability (P) * Impact (I)

Quality Processes: Q-PAC (Planning, Assurance, Control)

Communication Channels = (N*(N-1))/2 *(N = Number of People)*

PTA Variables

Ceiling Price = Percentage of Target Cost (TC)
Target Price = Target Cost + Target Profit
Target Cost = Expected Cost of the Work

PMP® Exam Success Series:
Quick Reference for Third Edition PMBOK® Guide

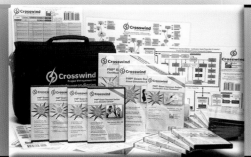

For PMP® Exam Products, Courses and Online Training go to

www.crosswindpm.com
www.pmtvnetwork.com

	Process Groups				
	Initiating	Planning	Executing	Monitoring & Controlling	Closing
Integration	Develop Project Charter	Develop Project Management Plan	Direct and Manage Project Execution	Monitor and Control Project Work	Close Project
	Develop Preliminary Project Scope Statement			Integrated Change Control	
Scope		Scope Planning		Scope Verification	
		Scope Definition		Scope Control	
		Create WBS			
Time		Activity Definition		Schedule Control	
		Activity Sequencing			
		Activity Resource Estimating			
		Activity Duration Estimating			
		Schedule Development			
Cost		Cost Estimating		Cost Control	
		Cost Budgeting			
Quality		Quality Planning	Perform Quality Assurance	Perform Quality Control	
Human Resource		Human Resource Planning	Acquire Project Team	Manage Project Team	
			Develop Project Team		
Communications		Communications Planning	Information Distribution	Performance Reporting	
				Manage Stakeholders	
Risk		Risk Management Planning		Risk Monitoring and Controlling	
		Risk Identification			
		Qualitative Risk Analysis			
		Quantitative Risk Analysis			
		Risk Response Planning			
Procurement		Plan Purchases and Acquisitions	Request Seller Responses	Contract Administration	Contract Closure
		Plan Contracting	Select Sellers		

(Left axis label: Knowledge Areas)

Have Crosswind On Location at Your Company

PMI® Project Management Institute

Registered Education Provider

"PMP" and "PMBOK" are registered marks of the Project Management Institute, Inc.

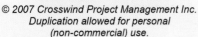

27.   The company is implementing an enterprise reporting system across the entire company. This system will integrate a number of business units. As a result, it will be very resource-consuming and could cause reprioritization of other projects that it will replace. Which of the following concerns you most?

Correct Answer: (C) What impact the new project is expected to have on your biggest project

Explanation: How the new initiative impacts your biggest project is a valid concern because it could cause your project not to be needed any more. The two options dealing with resources follow in priority. Your raise or promotion follows after that. [section 5.2]

28.   You are the Project Manager for a highway construction project. You have just finished putting together all the various plans into an integrated complete document. What step will you perform next?

Correct Answer: (C) Direct and Manage Project Execution

Explanation: After completing the development of the project management plan, the next step listed in the answers is to execute the plan or do the work of the project. Project management plan development is what the question is describing so that isn't an answer. Integrated Change Control comes as a result of project management plan execution. Project charter signoff was completed before the project Planning started. [section 6.6]

29.   All the following are typically part of the project management plan except...

Correct Answer: (B) Budget management plan

Explanation: "Budget management plan" is noise. The real item associated with cost is the cost management plan. The other items are typically in the project management plan. [section 6.5.1]

30.   The customer has just attended the weekly staff meeting for the infrastructure project and has stated that the market is changing for the product being created. As a result of this change, the customer has requested a significant change to the project. The project is 85% complete. What does the Project Manager do?

Correct Answer: (B) Evaluate the impact to the project and let the customer know the options and impact of the change

Explanation: The Project Manager needs to evaluate the impact to the project and let the customer know the options. The Project Manager is there to do what the customer needs according to the plan or modified plan. Telling the customer the project is too close to being complete to integrate the change isn't the Project Manager's decision to make; neither is defining the work as a new project. Ignoring the customer and hoping things disappear is professionally irresponsible. [section 6.8.1, section 5.5]

Chapter 7

Scope

The Scope Knowledge Area can seem as though it's not as complex as some of the other Knowledge Areas, such as time, cost, and procurement, but failing to give it the needed attention can cause problems on a project and even the exam. The more detail you give to the defining and decomposition of the scope and the creation of the work breakdown structure (**WBS**), the more successful your project is likely to be. If you fail to pay attention to scope, problems will definitely show up in the Scope Verification process where work results are compared to what should have been built. Remember that the **project scope statement and WBS are key outputs** you need when planning your project.

In this chapter, we discuss the following:

Process Group	Process Name		Main Outputs
Planning	Scope Planning	→	Project Scope Management Plan
	Scope Definition	→	Project Scope Statement
	Create WBS	→	Work Breakdown Structure
Monitoring and Controlling	Scope Verification	→	Accepted Deliverables
	Scope Control	→	Project Scope Statement (Updates)
			Scope Baseline (Updates)
			WBS (Updates)

☑	**Crosswind "Must Knows" For Scope**
	Key Inputs, Tools & Techniques, and Outputs for Scope Planning
	Key Inputs, Tools & Techniques, and Outputs for Scope Definition
	Key Inputs, Tools & Techniques, and Outputs for Create WBS
	Key Inputs, Tools & Techniques, and Outputs for Scope Verification
	Key Inputs, Tools & Techniques, and Outputs for Scope Control
	Principles, characteristics and importance of a work breakdown structure (WBS) in graphical and tabular formats
	Various types of breakdown structures available
	Delphi concept
	How to define, decompose, and verify scope
	Importance and characteristics of a project scope statement
	What management by objectives (MBO) is and where it fits in project management

Although helpful, this list is not all-inclusive for information needed from this area for the exam. It is only suggested material that, if understood and memorized, can increase your exam score.

7.1   Scope Planning (Planning Process Group)

In Scope Planning, the emphasis is on creating the project scope management plan, which helps to define and manage the scope of the project. The project scope management plan helps define how the scope of the project will be managed, including the creation of the project scope statement, work breakdown structure (WBS), verification, and controlling the scope of the project.

Know the Key Inputs, Tools & Techniques, and Outputs for Scope Planning.

Scope Planning (Planning)		
Key Inputs	Project Charter	The project charter provides the **foundation for the project**. Any constraints or assumptions are factored into the decision-making processes as well.
	Preliminary Project Scope Statement	The preliminary project scope statement includes the **product scope description and provides an initial description of the scope of the project**.
	Project Management Plan	A project management plan (not a schedule!) **integrates plans representing the various Knowledge Areas** in the PMI approach to project management. Supporting detail is included to help validate the information in the project management plan.
Key Tools & Techniques	Expert Judgment	Expert judgment provides the subject matter expertise for the product.
	Templates, Forms, Standards	Templates and forms are used to **help ensure the project follows a consistent approach** to the project management methodology. Standards are defined within the project management methodology.
Key Outputs	Project Scope Management Plan	The project scope management plan is the **basic rulebook for addressing scope management issues** on the project.

Situational Question and Real World Application
The biggest issue that arises from inadequate Scope Planning is scope creep. When scope is not adequately defined and locked down, the client or group receiving the product has carte blanche to request changes, regardless of impact to the schedule, budget, or people on the project; therefore, a scope management plan is a key document to help contain scope.

7.1.1   Project Scope Management Plan

The project scope management plan helps the Project Manager and team do the following:

- Establish a scope statement and requirements
- Create the WBS (Work Breakdown Structure)
- Validate that the deliverables and work (scope) of the project were built correctly
- Address scope-related changes to the project

PMP Exam Success Series: Certification Exam Manual
© 2007 Crosswind Project Management, Inc., www.crosswindpm.com

7.1.2   Management by Objectives (MBO)

Management by objectives helps determine where a project fits in the "big picture" of planning at the company. If your project fails to align with where the company is headed, you could find it de-prioritized or even cancelled.

Management by objectives also could be used to address a goal-setting technique, which emphasizes establishing attainable goals and monitoring for variance then adjusting as needed.

7.1.3   Delphi Technique

The Delphi Technique is the process of using expert opinion, which could come from people already on the project or those outside the project or even the organization. Typically, this technique involves trying to gain a consensus of the experts by keeping their identities protected and working in iterations.

7.2   Scope Definition (Planning Process Group)

In Scope Definition, the emphasis is on creating a written project scope statement to be used in future project decision-making. It should include the following:

- What the project consists of
- What is involved to create the project
- What it is expected to do when complete (To eliminate any confusion later, the project scope statement can also state what is not in the project.)

Understand what Management by Objectives (MBO) is and where it fits in project management.

Know and understand the Delphi concept.

Know how to define and decompose scope. Know the Key Inputs, Tools & Techniques, and Outputs for Scope Definition.

Scope Definition (Planning)		
Key Inputs	Project Charter	The project charter provides the **foundation for the project**. Any constraints or assumptions are factored into the decision-making processes as well.
	Preliminary Project Scope Statement	The preliminary project scope statement includes the **product or service scope description and provides an initial description of the scope of the project**.
	Project Scope Management Plan	The project scope management plan is the **basic rulebook for addressing scope management issues** on the project.
	Approved Change Requests	Approved change requests are **changes that have been formally approved** by the official change control process on the project.
Key Tools & Techniques	Product Analysis	Product analysis **translates project goals into realistic deliverables** so the service or product of the project can be created per the project management plan.
	Alternatives Identification	Alternatives identification **looks at different techniques to achieve the goals** of the project. It can include brainstorming and lateral thinking.
	Expert Judgment	Expert judgment is of great value. It can be more significant and accurate than the best modeling tools available.
	Stakeholder Analysis	Stakeholder analysis is a key tool in that it **helps define the needs of the stakeholders** in the process of defining the scope of the project.

Key Outputs	Project Scope Statement	The project scope statement **helps define the project**. Supporting detail provides the in-depth research and planning that the project scope statement rolls into. This detail can include information associated with project deliverables and any constraints or assumptions considered for project Planning. The statement should provide all stakeholders with a common interpretation of the scope of the project. Also associated with the statement could be documentation describing project goals, requirements, deliverables, acceptance criteria, constraints, assumptions, and cost estimates.
	Requested Changes	Requested changes are **changes that have been requested but not yet formally approved** by the official change control process on the project.
	Project Scope Management Plan (Updates)	The project scope management plan (Updates) **helps manage scope-related items or project changes**.

Situational Question and Real World Application
The primary potential problem in Scope Definition is the later discovery of needed items that were not mentioned (or known) in Planning and therefore have not been accounted for. This problem can cause variance with scope, schedule, or cost.

7.2.1   Project Scope Statement

The project scope statement is a document that develops and helps attain buy-in on a common interpretation of the project scope. It can describe **what is, as well as what is not, in the project**.

Know the importance and characteristics of a project scope statement.

7.3   Create WBS (Planning Process Group)

In Create WBS, the major deliverables are divided into smaller components that can be easily estimated (time and cost), managed, and controlled. Here is the point at which the overall project is broken down into pieces that are easier to track and ultimately roll into the work breakdown structure (WBS).

Rolling wave planning can be used when information about the project is sparse, thereby resulting in a failure to appropriately decompose for a deliverable or subproject until future project information is known later in the project. **The lowest level of the WBS is the work package. Any subsequent decomposition generally results in creating activity lists.**

Know the Key Inputs, Tools & Techniques, and Outputs for Create WBS.

PMP Exam Success Series: Certification Exam Manual
© 2007 Crosswind Project Management, Inc., www.crosswindpm.com

Create WBS (Planning)		
Key Inputs	Project Scope Statement	The project scope statement **helps define the project**. Supporting detail provides the in-depth research and planning that the project scope statement rolls into.
	Project Scope Management Plan	The project scope management plan **helps manage scope-related changes**.
Key Tools & Techniques	Work Breakdown Structure Templates	The WBS templates can be **derived from previous similar projects** or industry standards then modified or adjusted, as appropriate, to fit the needs of the project.
	Decomposition	Scope decomposition **breaks down major work pieces into smaller pieces** where they ultimately end up in the work breakdown structure (WBS).
Key Outputs	Project Scope Statement (Updates)	The project scope statement (updates) **helps define the project**. Supporting detail gives the in-depth research and planning that the project scope statement rolls into.
	Work Breakdown Structure	The WBS provides **a decomposition of the work of the project** and can sometimes point out areas of the scope that were not sufficiently addressed in the project scope statement, thereby resulting in project scope statement updates. The WBS can be decomposed in a variety of formats including by major deliverables, subproject, or phase.
	WBS Dictionary	The WBS dictionary is a result of the Create WBS process. It **complements the WBS** by documenting the work packages, control accounts, and listing the organizations responsible for completion of the work among other things.
	Scope Baseline	The scope baseline provides **details of the planned scope for the project**. It likely includes what is and what is not in the scope of the project. Also included could be the work breakdown structure and the WBS dictionary.

Situational Question and Real World Application
The primary potential problem in Create WBS is the later discovery of needed items that were not mentioned (or known) in initial Planning and therefore have not been accounted for or addressed in the work breakdown structure (WBS). This problem can cause variance with scope, schedule, or cost. Remember, decomposition is meant to (among other things) bring out all the necessary details of the work to be done.

7.3.1   Work Breakdown Structure

The work breakdown structure (WBS) is one of the most important pieces of the project management Planning process. The main output of Create WBS is decomposition of the project scope statement and the project scope. Generally **created by the Project Manager and the team** doing the work, the WBS describes the work breakdown and restricts its content to listing only the project work. It also helps the team buy into the project by allowing input to the details of the work.

Know the principles, characteristics, and importance of a work breakdown structure (WBS) in graphical format.

To create the WBS, define the main pieces of the project work then decompose each to encompass all the work on the project, down to an appropriate level of detail where each activity is definable, trackable, and manageable. Generally, a heuristic (rule of thumb) is used to determine how the **work is broken**

down into pieces and the level of decomposition for the work packages. These packages could also be loosely considered deliverables.

These are pieces of work that, when completed, should complete the work of the project. Once the WBS is created, you can start a number of key items. (These are not finished yet because there will be remaining items needed to complete them.) They include the network diagram, the schedule, the budget, any resources to be assigned, and risk planning. If you fail to devote time and attention on WBS, you may set your project up for failure or challenges.

You can expect a fair number of exam questions associated with the WBS. Occasionally, Crosswind has a student who encounters challenges with the decomposition of the WBS. If this is the case with you, try to look at the WBS as if it were a skeleton or nervous system. The skeleton or nervous system basically goes through every area of the body, and the WBS is no different. If this still isn't clicking, take something you know and try to create a WBS around it.

In the following example, note the main pieces of the WBS, which can include **planning packages, control accounts, and work packages (the lowest level of the WBS)**. Dashed lines define the WBS boundary of decomposition with the most detailed output being the work package. The **Activity Definition** process follows the Create WBS process. It creates the activity and milestone lists.

In short, a **control account** is a point placed in the WBS above the work package and planning package to help with estimating when all the details are not immediately available at the work package level. A **planning package** is a piece of the WBS between the control account and the work package. It is used to plan work that has been scoped but lacks sufficient work level details. For more information on these two, refer to the Time chapter.

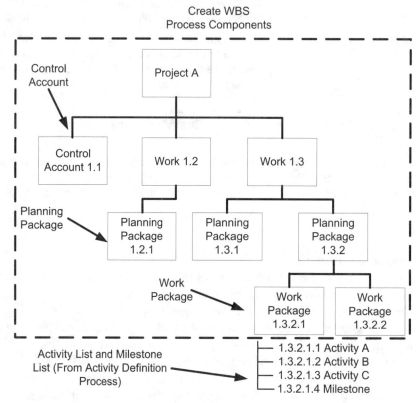

Figure 7-1: WBS Process Components

7.3.2   WBS Numbering

Work breakdown structure numbering lets project team members know where work fits in the project. Look inside the *PMBOK Guide* and notice the WBS numbering system. For example, 9.0 is the Cost chapter; 9.1 is Resource Planning; 9.2, Cost Estimating, and so on, to make up the major pieces of 9.0. In addition, each major component has sub-elements that are numbered. Inside 7.1 Resource Planning, you find 7.1.1, 7.1.2, etc., that make up the pieces of 7.1. (You get the picture.) Ultimately, all these pieces roll up to make the scope of the project.

7.3.3   WBS Dictionary

The WBS dictionary provides supporting detail that is typically not practical to apply to the graphical format of the WBS (work breakdown structure). It can include items such as the following:

- Description of the work package
- Overall time and cost characteristics of the work package
- Billing/Charging account for the work package
- Department or individuals responsible for completing the work package

7.3.4   Value of the Work Breakdown Structure

A common mistake many Project Managers make is failing to conduct appropriate decomposition of the project. This mistake typically leads to scope creep and estimating inaccuracies and could ultimately jeopardize project delivery. Figure 7-2: Planning Processes Interaction demonstrates how the *PMBOK Guide* shows nine Planning processes connected to the creation of the WBS. If the WBS is not appropriately defined, those nine areas are directly and adversely impacted. A project management plan is no better than its WBS decomposition.

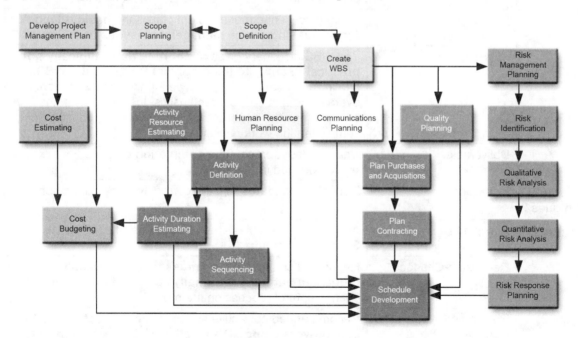

Figure 7-2: Planning Processes Interaction

7.3.5   Various Breakdown Structures

There are numerous breakdown structures in project management. Know the differences so you don't confuse them on the PMP Examination. They are as follows:

Know the various types of breakdown structures that are available.

- **Organizational breakdown structure (OBS)** - The OBS is also known as an organizational chart. It shows how the project organization is structured to accomplish project activities. See the Human Resource chapter.
- **Risk breakdown structure (RBS)** – The RBS shows the risks that can potentially occur on a project, broken down by risk category. See the Risk chapter.
- **Resource breakdown structure (RBS)** – The RBS shows the type of resources used on a project. See the Time Chapter.
- **Bill of materials (BOM)** – The BOM includes components, sub-assemblies, and assemblies used to build a product or service.

7.4   Scope Verification (Monitoring and Controlling Process Group)

Know how to verify scope. Know the Key Inputs, Tools & Techniques, and Outputs for Scope Verification.

The main goal of Scope Verification is to secure signoff (formal acceptance) of the project scope as each milestone or the entire work of the project is completed.

Scope Verification (Monitoring and Controlling)		
Key Inputs	Project Scope Statement	The project scope statement **helps define the project**. Supporting detail provides the in-depth research and planning that the project scope statement rolls into.
	Project Scope Management Plan	The project scope management plan is the **basic rulebook for addressing scope management issues** on the project.
	WBS Dictionary	The WBS dictionary gives **supporting detail typically not practical to apply to the graphical format of the WBS**. It can include items such as the work package description, the overall time and cost characteristics, the billing/charging account, and the department or individuals responsible for completing the work package.
	Deliverables	Deliverables represent the **completion of project work pieces** defined in Planning.
Key Tools & Techniques	Inspection	Inspection **validates** that the correct work has been done.
Key Outputs	Accepted Deliverables	Accepted deliverables are the **outcome of acceptable Scope Verification**.
	Requested Changes	Requested changes are **changes that have been requested but not yet formally approved** by the official change control process on the project.
	Recommended Corrective Actions	Recommended corrective actions are **modifications to the plan or work being completed** that will alter the output to achieve a desired result that wasn't (typically) planned.

7.5 Scope Control (Monitoring and Controlling Process Group)

Scope Control is the process for handling scope change requests.

Know the Key Inputs, Tools & Techniques, and Outputs for Scope Control.

Scope Control (Monitoring and Controlling)		
Key Inputs	Project Scope Statement	The project scope statement **helps define the project.** Supporting detail provides the in-depth research and planning that the project scope statement rolls into.
	Work Breakdown Structure (WBS)	The WBS **details what work is being done** as broken down into work packages.
	WBS Dictionary	The WBS dictionary gives **supporting detail typically not practical to apply to the graphical format of the WBS**. It can include items such as the work package description, the overall time and cost characteristics, the billing/charging account, and the department or individuals responsible for completing the work package.
	Project Scope Management Plan	The project scope management plan is the **basic rulebook for addressing scope management issues** on the project.
	Performance Reports	Performance reports **help show variance**.
	Approved Change Requests	Approved change requests can be issued as a **result of variance** on the project.
Key Tools & Techniques	Change Control System	The change control system **manages changes** that occur to the scope of the project. It is likely to be integrated with other change control systems into the Project Management Information System (PMIS) for the project.
	Variance Analysis	Variance analysis **determines if any variance or required change exists** between the work to be done and that completed.
	Configuration Management System	A configuration management system **ensures that project work is being completed as planned**.
Key Outputs	Project Scope Statement (Updates)	The project scope statement (Updates) **helps define the project**. Supporting detail provides the in-depth research and planning that the project scope statement rolls into.
	Work Breakdown Structure (Updates)	The updated WBS provides a **revision of the decomposition** of the project work and can sometimes point out areas of the scope that were not sufficiently addressed in the project scope statement, thereby resulting in project scope statement updates.

| Key Outputs (cont.) | Scope Baseline (Updates) | Updates to the Scope Baseline **provide the details of the planned scope** for the project. This information likely includes what is in and what is not in the scope of the project. Also included could be the work breakdown structure and the WBS dictionary. |
| | Requested Changes | Requested changes are **changes that have been requested but not yet formally approved** by the official change control process on the project. |

Situational Question and Real World Application
Scope Control is one of the more common project problems. Scope changes happen (or should happen or sometimes shouldn't happen yet still do) and the team completes work relative to some type of change that hasn't officially occurred. Until the change officially occurs, it's simply a request for a change, so the team should continue to work to the latest version of the scope (original or most recently approved revision) until any new approvals happen.

7.6 Scope Formulas and Variables

No formulas for scope

7.7 Scope Terminology

Term	Description
Acceptance	The process of formally receiving the work of the project. The work should be complete and fulfill the needs for which it was created.
Acceptance Criteria	Requirements that are defined to be completed before the work can be accepted
Analogy Approach	An approach in which a previous project of similar characteristic is used to obtain the values (duration, resources, budget, etc.) for the current project being planned
Bottom-Up Approach	An approach in which the team or at least the Project Manager is involved in deciding on and estimating the individual pieces of the project to create the summary estimate
Decomposition (Technique)	The process of breaking down the work of the project into smaller more controllable pieces
Deliverable (Output/Input)	A key piece of work for the project; can be physical work, a process, a document, or other measurable result of work
Delphi Technique	A technique to attain consensus within a group of experts; typically used to gain vision about future direction or development
Milestone	A major point in the project; typically involves beginning or completing a major piece of the work of the project
Product	The measurable, definable work of the project
Project Scope Management	Processes associated with determining and controlling what a project includes or does not include
Project Scope Management Plan	Document that explains how to establish a scope statement and requirements, create the WBS, validate that deliverables were built correctly, and address scope-related changes to the project
Project Scope Statement	Document that develops and helps attain buy-in on a common interpretation of project scope
Requirement	A need that must be completed to attain project goals; could be business or technical
Scope	The desired outcome of the project; the work that will be encompassed in the project and the final product or service
Scope Baseline	Original (or approved revised) definition of the scope the project should create; can include project scope statement, work breakdown structure (WBS), and WBS dictionary

PMP Exam Success Series: Certification Exam Manual
© 2007 Crosswind Project Management, Inc., www.crosswindpm.com

Scope Change	An approved change to the scope of the project
Scope Control	The process of controlling the scope of the project
Scope Creep	Unauthorized request for change that usually occurs in a project as time evolves
Scope Definition	The process of developing a project scope statement
Scope Planning	Determining documentation needs associated with how the scope of the project will be managed; can include approaches for project decomposition and verification
Scope Verification	Gaining approval of the project scope
Top-Down Approach	The point at which a WBS is created with the major (or bigger) pieces, then they are broken down into the smaller pieces
User	The person, division, or company that will be the user or owner of the product when the project is complete
Validation (Technique)	The process of evaluating something that was created in the project to ensure that it meets the needed requirements for formal acceptance
Verification (Technique)	The process of evaluating something that was created in the project to ensure that it meets the specified conditions
WBS Dictionary	A tool that works with the WBS to ensure that the right work happens in the right order by the correct resources; helps improve the quality of work by verifying that the needed conditions have been met before future work begins
Work Breakdown Structure	An organized breakdown of the total work scope of the project Each level of descent provides a greater level of detail with the deliverable being a key focus.
Work Package	A deliverable at the smallest level of the WBS; represents the completed piece of the project from the culmination of a series of activities being complete

7.8   Scope Mind Map

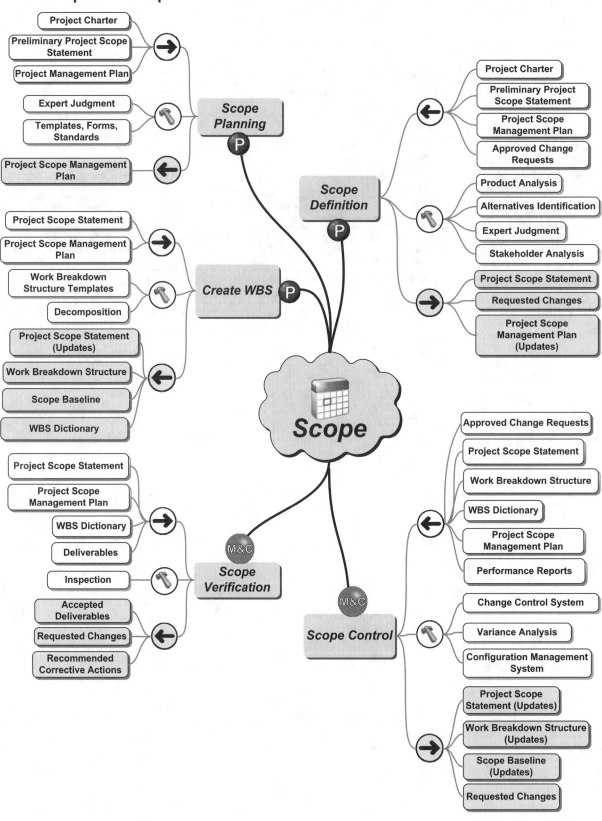

PMP Exam Success Series: Certification Exam Manual
© 2007 Crosswind Project Management, Inc., www.crosswindpm.com

7.9   Scope Practice Tests and Exercises

7.9.1   Scope Quick Test

In this quiz, answer the question in a short essay of only a sentence or two or circle all correct answers for the question. Note that some questions may have more than one answer. Answers are in section 7.10.1.

1.   What is the lowest level of decomposition called in a WBS?

2.   What is the process which validates that the project created what was to be built?

3.   What shows the work that is in the project, and if it is not there, it is not in the project?

4.   Variance analysis generally compares what two things?

5.   What is created from the lowest level of the WBS?

6.   What is prepared first: a project scope statement or a work breakdown structure (WBS)?

7.   What type of estimate looks at the overall price or timeline of the project, instead of the details?

8.   In Scope Verification, the work created in the project is potentially compared to what three documents?

9.   Why is it a good idea for the project scope statement to describe what is not included in the project?

10.   Which of the following is correct about the project scope management plan?

      It includes how to address scope changes on the project.
      It does NOT include how to address scope changes on the project.

7.9.2   Scope ITTO Matching Exercise

Match the correct ITTO term at the bottom of the page with the blanks to the right of the process. When a term is used multiple times, it is flagged by a parenthetical value indicating the number of times used. Also, match summary sentences with the process name that fits. Answers are in section 7.10.2.

	Inputs	Tools &Techniques	Outputs
Scope Planning	1) _____ 2) _____ 3) _____	1) _____ 2) _____	1) _____

Summary: _____

	Inputs	Tools &Techniques	Outputs
Scope Definition	1) _____ 2) _____ 3) _____ 4) _____	1) _____ 2) _____ 3) _____ 4) _____	1) _____ 2) _____ 3) _____

Summary: _____

	Inputs	Tools &Techniques	Outputs
Create WBS	1) _____ 2) _____	1) _____ 2) _____	1) _____ 2) _____ 3) _____ 4) _____

Summary: _____

	Inputs	Tools &Techniques	Outputs
Scope Verification	1) _____ 2) _____ 3) _____ 4) _____	1) _____	1) _____ 2) _____ 3) _____

Summary: _____

	Inputs	Tools &Techniques	Outputs
Scope Control	1) _____ 2) _____ 3) _____ 4) _____ 5) _____ 6) _____	1) _____ 2) _____ 3) _____	1) _____ 2) _____ 3) _____ 4) _____

Summary: _____

Activities associated with controlling project scope
Establishing the detailed project scope statement
Creation of the scope management plan

Validating that the work of the project was successfully created
Establishing the work breakdown structure for the project

Accepted Deliverables	Project Charter (2)	Recommended Corrective Actions
Alternatives Identification	Project Management Plan	Requested Changes (3)
Approved Change Requests (2)	Project Scope Management Plan (5)	Scope Baseline
Change Control System	Project Scope Management Plan (Updates)	Scope Baseline (Updates)
Configuration Management System	Project Scope Statement (4)	Stakeholder Analysis
Decomposition	Project Scope Statement (Updates) (2)	Templates, Forms, Standards
Deliverables		Variance Analysis
Expert Judgment (2)		WBS Dictionary (3)
Inspection		Work Breakdown Structure (2)
Performance Reports		Work Breakdown Structure (Updates)
Preliminary Project Scope Statement (2)		Work Breakdown Structure Templates
Product Analysis		

7.9.3   Scope Terminology Matching Exercise

Match the correct term in the left column to the correct definition in the right column. See the exercise answer section of this chapter for the correct answer. Answers are in section 7.10.3.

Matching Exercise #1

	Term	Answer	Definition
1	Acceptance Criteria	O	A. Processes associated with determining and controlling what a project includes or does not include
2	Decomposition (Technique)	I	B. The point at which a WBS is created with the major (or bigger) pieces, then they are broken down into the smaller pieces
3	Milestone	N	C. A need that must be completed to attain project goals; could be business or technical
4	Product	L	D. Requirements that are defined to be completed before the work can be accepted
5	Project Scope Management	M	E. Document that develops and helps attain buy-in on a common interpretation of project scope
6	Project Scope Statement	E	F. The measurable, definable work of the project
7	Requirement	C	G. An organized breakdown of the total work scope of the project. Each level of descent provides a greater level of detail with the deliverable being a key focus.
8	Scope		H. Original (or approved revised) definition of the scope the project should create; can include project scope statement, work breakdown structure (WBS), and WBS dictionary
9	Scope Baseline	H	I. The process of breaking down the work of the project into smaller more controllable pieces
10	Scope Control	A	J. A tool that works with the WBS to ensure that the right work happens in the right order by the correct resources; helps improve the quality of work by verifying that the needed conditions have been met before future work begins
11	Scope Definition	D	K. The process of developing a project scope statement
12	Top-Down Approach	J	L. A deliverable at the smallest level of the WBS; represents the completed piece of the project from the culmination of a series of activities being complete
13	WBS Dictionary		M. The process of controlling the scope of the project
14	Work Breakdown Structure	B	N. A major point in the project; typically involves beginning or completing a major piece of the work of the project
15	Work Package	K	O. The desired outcome of the project; the work that will be encompassed in the project and the final product or service

Matching Exercise #2

	Term	Answer	Definition
1	Acceptance	E	A. A key piece of work for the project; can be physical work, a process, a document, or other measurable result of work
2	Analogy Approach	C	B. An approved change to the scope of the project
3	Bottom-Up Approach	K	C. An approach in which a previous project of similar characteristic is used to obtain the values (duration, resources, budget, etc.) for the current project being planned
4	Deliverable (Output/Input)	A	D. Gaining approval of the project scope
5	Delphi Technique	H	E. The process of formally receiving the work of the project. The work should be complete and fulfill the needs for which it was created.
6	Scope Change	B	F. The process of evaluating something that was created in the project to ensure that it meets the specified conditions
7	Scope Creep	G	G. Unauthorized request for change that usually occurs in a project as time evolves
8	Scope Planning	J	H. A technique to attain consensus within a group of experts; typically used to gain vision about future direction or development
9	Scope Verification	D	I. The person, division, or company that will be the user or owner of the product when the project is complete
10	User	I	J. Determining documentation needs associated with how the scope of the project will be managed; can include approaches for project decomposition and verification
11	Validation (Technique)	L	K. An approach in which the team or at least the Project Manager is involved in deciding on and estimating the individual pieces of the project to create the summary
12	Verification (Technique)	F	L. The process of evaluating something that was created in the project to ensure that it meets the needed requirements for formal acceptance

PMP Exam Success Series: Certification Exam Manual
© 2007 Crosswind Project Management, Inc., www.crosswindpm.com

7.9.4   Scope Practice Test

Answers are in section 7.10.4.

1.   What is the best reason to create a work breakdown structure?

(A) It provides authority for the Project Manager.
(B) It allows the project budget to be determined.
(C) It helps attain buy-in from the team doing the work.
(D) It allows the project completion date to be determined.

2.   There has been a great delay in waiting to get the project charter approved. It's finally complete and you are assigned as the Project Manager. Senior management wants you to begin Planning as soon as possible. If you are in the process of planning the project, what is the best way to schedule Scope Verification?

(A) At the end of every phase on the project
(B) After the sponsor defines what they want the project to create
(C) When the project management plan is awaiting signoff
(D) When the work of the project is done

3.   When is work decomposition performed?

(A) Creating the WBS and Activity Definition
(B) Cost Control
(C) Schedule Control
(D) Scope Planning and Scope Control

4.   A new call center is being built to support a new product at a national telephone company. The company doesn't have any data on how long it will take to sign up customers via the call center. This data is important because it will help determine the number of employees needed in the call center. The company performs some tests to try to determine how long it will take to sign up customers. This test data is then incorporated into the projections and Planning. What has the company just created?

(A) Team development
(B) Staff acquisition
(C) Assumptions
(D) Constraints

5.   Which of the following best describes a milestone?

(A) It has slack of zero.
(B) It is only used in the project scope statement.
(C) It can represent the beginning or completion of a deliverable, work package, phase, or project.
(D) It is only used with the project charter.

6.   The project team has just begun breaking down the components of the project into smaller pieces that are easier to maintain and manage. This is known as what?

(A) Scope Verification
(B) Scope Definition
(C) Scope Planning
(D) Create WBS

7.   The road construction project has been going on for over a year with a great deal of change and issues involved. The Project Manager is getting ready for the project to be completed. Which of the following will help close the project?

(A) Team development
(B) Scope Verification
(C) Planning for the next project
(D) Release of resources

8.   The medical billing system project has entered closure. As the Project Manager and the team prepare for closure, they are told that Scope Verification will be very important to the success of the project. Why is this?

(A) Scope Verification should have been done earlier in the project and since it wasn't done then, it's important to complete it before the project is complete.
(B) Scope Verification validates that the sponsor signed the project scope statement at the beginning of Planning.
(C) Scope Verification is the process of comparing what the project created to the project scope statement, product description, and anything else that helps ensure that the results of the project will function as intended.
(D) Scope Verification is used to confirm that the project team understands the scope of the project.

9.   The Project Manager is working with the customer to gain formal acceptance on the project deliverables. The customer is saying that three of the deliverables are not meeting project goals and are unusable in their present form. Which of the following will be used to correct the problem?

(A) Scope analysis
(B) Team-building
(C) Scope Control
(D) Scope Verification

10. All the following are breakdown structures used in project management except...

(A) Bill of materials
(B) Communication breakdown structure
(C) Risk breakdown structure
(D) Resource breakdown structure

PMP Exam Success Series: Certification Exam Manual
© 2007 Crosswind Project Management, Inc., www.crosswindpm.com

11.   _____ is an input of Scope Planning.

   (A) Project charter
   (B) Work breakdown structure
   (C) Scope control system
   (D) Change request

12.   Which of the following best describes a work breakdown structure (WBS)?

   (A) The work should be decomposed to a realistic level of detail.
   (B) If the work is not listed in the WBS, it is not in the project.
   (C) The accumulation of the work in the WBS should be equal to the work of the project.
   (D) All the answers

13.   Which of the following will likely result in the greatest customer satisfaction?

   (A) Work breakdown structure (WBS)
   (B) Scope Verification
   (C) A signed contract
   (D) Gold plating

14.   Which of the following is a heuristic for WBS decomposition?

   (A) Breaking down work until it is done by a single resource
   (B) Using an organizational structure appearance
   (C) Creating a WBS in which the summary activities are equal to the detail underneath
   (D) Breaking work down to realistic level where work packages are the lowest level

15.   During project Planning, the work breakdown structure (WBS) is a key to successful Planning. Which of the following can begin as a result of work breakdown structure (WBS) completion?

   (A) Cost Estimating
   (B) Schedule Development
   (C) Activity Duration Estimating
   (D) All the answers

16.   Project A is two months long, has three stakeholders, and has completed Planning. Project B is 12 months long, has 10 stakeholders, and is in execution. Project C is 12 months long, has three stakeholders, and is in Planning. Which project is most likely to experience scope creep?

   (A) Project A
   (B) Project B
   (C) Project C
   (D) Not enough information

17. What can a WBS dictionary do for the project?

    (A) Control gold plating
    (B) Provide activity definitions
    (C) Verify the scope of the project
    (D) Define the work of the project

18. The Project Manager is working with the customer to establish a clear understanding of what the customer needs the new project to create. They discuss what the project is to include and what it is not to include. What is the Project Manager creating?

    (A) Project scope statement
    (B) Work breakdown structure
    (C) Scope change request
    (D) Scope Verification

19. All the following are true about a work breakdown structure (WBS) except...

    (A) The team and the Project Manager should be involved in creating it.
    (B) It will resemble an organizational chart in appearance when complete.
    (C) Activity Sequencing of the WBS can be done only in parallel.
    (D) It is a decomposition of the work of the project.

20. The Project Manager and team are involved in project Planning. They are breaking the work down into the smallest level of the WBS. What are they creating?

    (A) To-do list
    (B) Activity list
    (C) Work package
    (D) Activity definitions

21. The work breakdown structure represents what?

    (A) The decomposition of the work of the project
    (B) The activity list of the project
    (C) The schedule
    (D) The decomposition of the activity list

22. The project to create a new database system is approximately halfway complete when a senior manager says that a major change needs to occur with the scope of the project or the system will not function in his department when it's rolled out. He further explains this change is going to delay the anticipated finish date of the project. After he explains the details of the proposed change in scope, what do you do first?

    (A) Let him know what the delay to the project will be.
    (B) Implement change control to incorporate the new work.
    (C) Tell him "no" because it will change the finish date of the project.
    (D) Meet with the team to determine the impact.

PMP Exam Success Series: Certification Exam Manual
© 2007 Crosswind Project Management, Inc., www.crosswindpm.com

23. The project team has just begun defining what is involved and not involved in the project. This is known as what?

     (A) Scope Planning
     (B) Scope Control
     (C) Scope Definition
     (D) Scope Verification

24. A Project Manager is involved in Scope Definition. What is the most important item below to perform?

     (A) Create a list of preferred vendors for outsourcing.
     (B) Create the work breakdown structure (WBS).
     (C) Create it as quickly as possible to continue Planning.
     (D) Verify that all key stakeholders have provided their input.

25. Scope Verification has been started at the end of phase 3 of the project. The main deliverable was sent to the customer. Three weeks have passed and the customer acts as if the deliverable was never received. Which of the following is the best action to take?

     (A) Stop work on the project until the customer acknowledges and approves the deliverable.
     (B) Communicate to senior management for assistance.
     (C) Document the issue in the issue log.
     (D) Ask the customer's supervisor why the deliverable has not been acknowledged.

26. The project team has just started breaking down the components of the project into smaller pieces that are easier to maintain and manage. After doing this, at what level of decomposition will they ultimately stop?

     (A) Scope Definition
     (B) Scope Verification
     (C) Create WBS
     (D) Activity Definition

27. A new call center is being built for a national telephone company. The project to create it is nearing completion and will soon begin project Scope Verification. This activity will involve a number of people, but who will ultimately approve it?

     (A) Project Manager
     (B) The customer
     (C) Senior management
     (D) Stakeholders

28. In defining a milestone, which of the following is most correct?

     (A) It is used to define the phase of a project.
     (B) It has a duration of no more than one day.
     (C) It has a duration of zero (0).
     (D) It has value in the project charter but not in the plan.

29. The Project Manager is working with the customer to gain formal acceptance on the project deliverables. The customer is saying that three of the deliverables do not meet project goals and are unusable in their present form. Upon reviewing documentation, the customer tells the Project Manager that the requirements are not accurate to meet the needs for which the project was undertaken. In what part of the Planning process did this problem occur?

    (A) Create WBS
    (B) Scope Control
    (C) Scope Definition
    (D) Scope Verification

30. A new highway project is being planned. This project involves creating four new lanes within an existing highway. Because of where the new highway is being built, it is impossible to shut down lanes of traffic during the weekdays. The lanes can be shut down only during the evenings after midnight or on weekends. This is an example of what?

    (A) Successful buyer negotiations
    (B) Constraints
    (C) Assumptions
    (D) Negotiation points

PMP Exam Success Series: Certification Exam Manual
© 2007 Crosswind Project Management, Inc., www.crosswindpm.com

7.10 Scope Tests and Exercise Answers

7.10.1 Scope Quick Test Answers

1. What is the lowest level of decomposition called in a WBS?
    A work package is the lowest level of decomposition in a WBS. [section 7.3.1, section 7.7]

2. What is the process which validates that the project created what was to be built?
    Scope Verification [section 7.4, section 7.7]

3. What shows the work that is in the project, and if it is not there, it is not in the project?
    The WBS (work breakdown structure) shows only the work that is in the project. The project scope statement could actually define what is and IS NOT in the project for clarification. [section 7.3.1]

4. Variance analysis generally compares what two things?
    The plan or baseline to actuals. This analysis could be for the scope, schedule, budget, quality, or other property characteristic. [section 7.5]

5. What is created from the lowest level of the WBS?
    Activity lists are created from the work packages listed in the WBS. [section 8.1]

6. What is prepared first: a project scope statement or a work breakdown structure (WBS)?
    A project scope statement is prepared before a WBS. [section 7.2.1, section 7.3]

7. What type of estimate looks at the overall price or timeline of the project, instead of the details?
    Analogous or top-down estimating [section 8.3.2]

8. In Scope Verification, the work created in the project is potentially compared to what three documents?
    The work created in the project is compared to what the project management plan, the project scope statement, and the WBS dictionary documented should have been built. [section 7.4]

9. Why is it a good idea for the project scope statement to describe what is not included in the project?
    Describing what is AND is not in the scope of the project helps eliminate any area for misinterpretation of the scope of the project. [section 7.2]

10. Which of the following is correct about the project scope management plan?
    It includes how to address scope changes on the project.
    It does NOT include how to address scope changes on the project.
    [section 7.1.1]

7.10.2   Scope ITTO Matching Exercise Answers

	Inputs	Tools &Techniques	Outputs
Scope Planning	1) Project Charter 2) Preliminary Project Scope Statement 3) Project Management Plan	1) Expert Judgment 2) Templates, Forms, Standards	1) Project Scope Management Plan
Summary:	Creation of the scope management plan		
Scope Definition	1) Project Charter 2) Preliminary Project Scope Statement 3) Project Scope Management Plan 4) Approved Change Requests	1) Product Analysis 2) Alternatives Identification 3) Expert Judgment 4) Stakeholder Analysis	1) Project Scope Statement 2) Requested Changes 3) Project Scope Management Plan (Updates)
Summary:	Establishing the detailed project scope statement		
Create WBS	1) Project Scope Statement 2) Project Scope Management Plan	1) Work Breakdown Structure Templates 2) Decomposition	1) Project Scope Statement (Updates) 2) Work Breakdown Structure 3) WBS Dictionary 4) Scope Baseline
Summary:	Establishing the work breakdown structure for the project		
Scope Verification	1) Project Scope Statement 2) Project Scope Management Plan 3) Deliverables 4) WBS Dictionary	1) Inspection	1) Accepted Deliverables 2) Requested Changes 3) Recommended Corrective Actions
Summary:	Validating that the work of the project was successfully created		
Scope Control	1) Project Scope Statement 2) Work Breakdown Structure 3) Project Scope Management Plan 4) Performance Reports 5) Approved Change Requests 6) WBS Dictionary	1) Change Control System 2) Variance Analysis 3) Configuration Management System	1) Project Scope Statement (Updates) 2) Work Breakdown Structure (Updates) 3) Scope Baseline (Updates) 4) Requested Changes
Summary:	Activities associated with controlling project scope		

7.10.3   Scope Terminology Matching Exercise Answers

Matching Exercise #1 Answers

#	Term	Definition
1	Acceptance Criteria	D. Requirements that are defined to be completed before the work can be accepted
2	Decomposition (Technique)	I. The process of breaking down the work of the project into smaller more controllable pieces
3	Milestone	N. A major point in the project; typically involves beginning or completing a major piece of the work of the project
4	Product	F. The measurable, definable work of the project
5	Project Scope Management	A. Processes associated with determining and controlling what a project includes or does not include
6	Project Scope Statement	E. Document that develops and helps attain buy-in on a common interpretation of project scope
7	Requirement	C. A need that must be completed to attain project goals; could be business or technical
8	Scope	O. The desired outcome of the project; the work that will be encompassed in the project and the final product
9	Scope Baseline	H. Original (or approved revised) definition of the scope the project should create; can include project scope statement, work breakdown structure (WBS), and WBS dictionary
10	Scope Control	M. The process of controlling the scope of the project
11	Scope Definition	K. The process of developing a project scope statement
12	Top-Down Approach	B. The point at which a WBS is created with the major (or bigger) pieces, then they are broken down into the smaller pieces
13	WBS Dictionary	J. A tool that works with the WBS to ensure that the right work happens in the right order by the correct resources; helps improve the quality of work by verifying that the needed conditions have been met before future work begins
14	Work Breakdown Structure	G. An organized breakdown of the total work scope of the project. Each level of descent provides a greater level of detail with the deliverable being a key focus.
15	Work Package	L. A deliverable at the smallest level of the WBS; represents the completed piece of the project from the culmination of a series of activities being complete

Matching Exercise #2 Answers

Term		Definition
1	Acceptance	E. The process of formally receiving the work of the project The work should be complete and fulfill the needs for which it was created.
2	Analogy Approach	C. An approach in which a previous project of similar characteristic is used to obtain the values (duration, resources, budget, etc.) for the current project being planned
3	Bottom-Up Approach	K. An approach in which the team or at least the Project Manager is involved in deciding on and estimating the individual pieces of the project to create the summary
4	Deliverable (Output/Input)	A. A key piece of work for the project; can be physical work, a process, a document, or other measurable result of work
5	Delphi Technique	H. A technique to attain consensus within a group of experts; typically used to gain vision about future direction or development
6	Scope Change	B. An approved change to the scope of the project
7	Scope Creep	G. Unauthorized request for change that usually occurs in a project as time evolves
8	Scope Planning	J. Determining documentation needs associated with how the scope of the project will be managed; can include approaches for project decomposition and verification
9	Scope Verification	D. Gaining approval of the project scope
10	User	I. The person, division, or company that will be the user or owner of the product when the project is complete
11	Validation (Technique)	L. The process of evaluating something that was created in the project to ensure that it meets the needed requirements for formal acceptance
12	Verification (Technique)	F. The process of evaluating something that was created in the project to ensure that it meets the specified conditions

PMP Exam Success Series: Certification Exam Manual
© 2007 Crosswind Project Management, Inc., www.crosswindpm.com

7.10.4   Scope Practice Test Answers

1. What is the best reason to create a work breakdown structure?

    Correct Answer: (C) It helps attain buy-in from the team doing the work.
    Explanation: The WBS has a number of positives. The best one of the options in the question is to help get buy-in from the people doing the work. If they aren't involved in the creation of the plan, it's not as easy to get buy-in, and the planning likely won't be as accurate as it could be when the people doing the work are involved. The WBS focuses on the WHAT of the project, so the completion date doesn't come from the WBS. Authority comes from the project charter. Cost Estimating and Cost Budgeting deal with the project budget. [section 7.3.1]

2. There has been a great delay in waiting to get the project charter approved. It's finally complete and you are assigned as the Project Manager. Senior management wants you to begin Planning as soon as possible. If you are in the process of planning the project, what is the best way to schedule Scope Verification?

    Correct Answer: (A) At the end of every phase on the project
    Explanation: It is better to do Scope Verification more frequently on a project instead of simply waiting until the end. Such verification makes it possible to detect issues early in the project, facilitating adjustment of work as the project evolves. Scheduling it after the sponsors define what they want the project to create is too early in the project to do Scope Verification. [section 7.4]

3. When is work decomposition performed?

    Correct Answer: (A) Creating the WBS and Activity Definition
    Explanation: The work of the project is decomposed in the Create WBS process to establish work packages and in the Activity Definition process to create activity lists. Schedule Control and Cost Control deal with maintaining control of the schedule and cost, not decomposition. Scope Planning and Scope Control are noise. [section 7.3, section 8.1]

4. A new call center is being built to support a new product at a national telephone company. The company doesn't have any data on how long it will take to sign up customers via the call center. This data is important because it will help decide the number of employees needed in the call center. The company performs some tests to try to determine how long it will take to sign up customers. This test data is then incorporated into the projections and Planning. What has the company just created?

    Correct Answer: (C) Assumptions
    Explanation: Assumptions are created when there is an absence of certain information on a project. It's an educated guess. As the project evolves, the assumptions should be fewer. Constraints are items that limit a project environment. Team development and staff acquisition are noise. [section 6.5.2]

5. Which of the following best describes a milestone?

    Correct Answer: (C) It can represent the beginning or completion of a deliverable, work package, phase, or project.
    Explanation: A milestone can be used to represent the beginning or completion of something significant on the project. It could also include a phase or project. A milestone always has a duration of zero. It has a slack of zero only if it were on the critical path of the schedule. Milestones are used throughout the project management plan, not just in the project scope statement or the project charter. [section 7.7, section 8.5.12, section 8.8]

6. The project team has just begun breaking down the components of the project into smaller pieces that are easier to maintain and manage. This is known as what?

Correct Answer: (D) Create WBS
Explanation: The Create WBS process takes the scope of the project and breaks it down into smaller pieces that are easier to define, estimate, and manage. Scope Verification compares the project scope to work results. Scope Planning determines the project scope statement and scope management approach for the project. Scope Definition establishes the project scope statement. [section 7.3]

7. The road construction project has been going on for over a year with a great deal of change and issues involved. The Project Manager is getting ready for the project to be completed. Which of the following will help close the project?

Correct Answer: (B) Scope Verification
Explanation: Scope Verification validates that the project created what was described to be created. Team development goes on throughout the project. Planning for the next project is not appropriate while the project is still ongoing. Release of resources happens around this point in the project, but it does not help close the project. [section 7.4, section 7.7]

8. The medical billing system project has entered closure. As the Project Manager and the team prepare for closure, they are told that Scope Verification will be very important to the success of the project. Why is this?

Correct Answer: (C) Scope Verification is the process of comparing what the project created to the project scope statement, product description, and anything else that helps ensure that the results of the project will function as intended.
Explanation: Scope Verification is used to compare the work the project created to that which was planned to build. It can include using the project scope statement, work breakdown structure (WBS), or product description. If the verification process is satisfactory, the work of the project is typically viewed as acceptable. [section 7.4, section 7.7]

9. The Project Manager is working with the customer to gain formal acceptance on the project deliverables. The customer is saying that three of the deliverables are not meeting project goals and are unusable in their present form. Which of the following will be used to correct the problem?

Correct Answer: (C) Scope Control
Explanation: Scope Control is used to review and approve or reject scope change requests to the project. "Scope analysis" is noise. Team-building helps the group of people on the project become more productive and is not applicable in this situation. Scope Verification helps validate that the project created what it was to create. It is the process that discovered the problem of the difference between scope, planned and created. [section 7.5, section 7.7]

10. All the following are breakdown structures used in project management except...

Correct Answer: (B) Communication breakdown structure
Explanation: The communication breakdown structure is a noise answer. It doesn't exist. The bill of materials shows all the pieces of an assembly. The risk breakdown structure decomposes the risks on a project. The resource breakdown structure shows resource being utilized on a project, regardless of what functional organization they are associated with. [section 7.3.5]

PMP Exam Success Series: Certification Exam Manual
© 2007 Crosswind Project Management, Inc., www.crosswindpm.com

11. _____ is an input of Scope Planning

Correct Answer: (A) Project charter
Explanation: The project charter is an input into Scope Planning, because it provides the foundation of the project and allows the Scope Planning to begin. The WBS is an output of Scope Definition. Change-related items don't show up in the process yet; Scope Planning is still in the Planning process. [section 7.1, section 7.8]

12. Which of the following best describes a work breakdown structure (WBS)?

(A) The work should be decomposed to a realistic level of detail.
(B) If the work is not listed in the WBS, it is not in the project.
(C) The accumulation of the work in the WBS should be equal to the work of the project.

Correct Answer: (D) All the answers
Explanation: A WBS includes all the work in the project. If it is not listed in the WBS, it's not part of the project. A WBS should be decomposed to a realistic level of detail. Not breaking it down far enough opens the way for work to slip through the cracks. Breaking it down into too much detail can turn the project into micro-management. Adding up the work in the WBS should equal the work that is in the project. [section 7.3.1]

13. Which of the following will likely result in the greatest customer satisfaction?

Correct Answer: (B) Scope Verification
Explanation: In Scope Verification, the work of the project has been verified to meet the needs of the project. If it is successful, the customer should be satisfied. A WBS is simply part of the Planning process. Gold plating is providing the customers something they didn't ask for. "A signed contract" is noise. [section 7.4, section 7.7]

14. Which of the following is a heuristic for WBS decomposition?

Correct Answer: (D) Breaking work down to a realistic level where work packages are the lowest level
Explanation: A general rule of thumb is to break down the work of the project into work packages. Breaking work packages or activities down to a single resource assigned is not always practical. Creating a WBS where the summary activities are equal to the detail underneath is a characteristic of a WBS. "Using an organizational structure appearance" is noise. [section 7.3.1, section 10.10.10]

15. During project Planning, the work breakdown structure (WBS) is a key to successful Planning. Which of the following can begin as a result of work breakdown structure (WBS) completion?

(A) Cost Estimating
(B) Schedule Development
(C) Activity Duration Estimating

Correct Answer: (D) All the answers
Explanation: The WBS serves as a primary input for determining what types of resources and their durations are needed on the project, what the high level costs should be for the project, and what shape the schedule will take when complete. [section 7.3.4]

16.   Project A is two months long, has three stakeholders, and has completed Planning. Project B
       is 12 months long, has 10 stakeholders, and is in execution. Project C is 12 months long, has
       three stakeholders, and is in Planning. Which project is most likely to experience scope
       creep?

       Correct Answer: (B) Project B
       Explanation: Project B is tied for the longest project but has the most stakeholders. The longer the project and the
       greater the number of stakeholders involved, the more an environment is prone to scope creep. [section 5.5,
       section 12.6]

17.   What can a WBS dictionary do for the project?

       Correct Answer: (A) Control gold plating
       Explanation: The WBS dictionary focuses on defining what work should happen in what order. Thus, it helps
       create a structure for only the work of the project to be done in the right sequence and can help eliminate gold
       plating. Defining the work of the project is done in the Initiating process and in Scope Planning. Verifying the
       scope of the project is done after the work of the project is complete. "Provide activity definitions" is noise.
       [section 7.3.3, section 10.7]

18.   The Project Manager is working with the customer to establish a clear understanding of what
       the customer needs the new project to create. They discuss what the project is to include and
       what it is not to include. What is the Project Manager creating?

       Correct Answer: (A) Project scope statement
       Explanation: The project scope statement defines what is in the scope of the project, and possibly what is not in
       the scope of the project, to help provide clarification. The work breakdown structure shows only what work is in
       the project. A scope change request involves modifying the scope of the project to reflect different work. Scope
       Verification validates that what was created is in alignment with the defined scope of the project. [section 7.2.1]

19.   All the following are true about a work breakdown structure (WBS) except...

       Correct Answer: (C) Activity Sequencing of the WBS can be done only in parallel.
       Explanation: Activity Sequencing of the WBS can be done only in parallel is a noise answer because it makes no
       logical sense. The other answers are characteristic of a work breakdown structure (WBS). [section 7.3.1,
       section 8.2]

20.   The Project Manager and team are involved in project Planning. They are breaking the work
       down into the smallest level of the WBS. What are they creating?

       Correct Answer: (C) Work package
       Explanation: The work package is the smallest level that the WBS is broken into. The next level of decomposition
       is to create activity definitions, which are sometimes known as activity lists. "To-do list" is noise. [section 7.3.1,
       section 7.7]

21.   The work breakdown structure represents what?

       Correct Answer: (A) The decomposition of the work of the project
       Explanation: The WBS represents the decomposition of the work of the project. If the work is shown in the WBS,
       it is in the project; if it's not shown in the WBS, it's not in the project. Activity lists are sometimes called activity
       definitions, and the schedule is created after the WBS is created. [section 7.3.1, section 7.7]

22. The project to create a new database system is approximately halfway complete when a senior manager says that a major change needs to occur with the scope of the project or the system will not function in his department when it's rolled out. He further explains this change is going to delay the anticipated finish date of the project. After he explains the details of the proposed change in scope, what do you do first?

Correct Answer: (D) Meet with the team to determine the impact.

Explanation: Meet with the team to determine the impact to the project plus solutions and any violation of the finish date that was defined in the project charter then pass solution options to senior management and the sponsor so they can select the best one. It's key in the situational questions not to tell a senior manager or sponsor "no," but instead let them know the options and impact associated with the request. You cannot explain a project delay until the team helps determine what the project impacts are. Change control of this size is not likely to be implemented by a Project Manager, but more likely by the senior management or sponsor. [section 6.8.1]

23. The project team has just begun defining what is involved and not involved in the project. This is known as what?

Correct Answer: (C) Scope Definition

Explanation: Scope Definition determines the project scope statement for the project. The project scope statement generally defines what is and is not in the project. Scope Planning determines the scope management approach for the project. Scope Verification compares the scope of the project to work results. Scope Control comes into the process after the plan has been signed off and is in project plan execution. [section 7.2, section 7.7]

24. A Project Manager is involved in Scope Definition. What is the most important item below to perform?

Correct Answer: (D) Verify that all key stakeholders have provided their input.

Explanation: Verifying that all key stakeholders have provided their input is the most important item. If this doesn't happen, the project could be delayed or derailed. The WBS isn't addressed in Scope Planning. The other answers are noise. [section 7.2, section 5.5.1, section 12.6]

25. Scope Verification has been started at the end of phase 3 of the project. The main deliverable was sent to the customer. Three weeks have passed and the customer acts as if the deliverable was never received. Which of the following is the best action to take?

Correct Answer: (B) Communicate to senior management for assistance.

Explanation: If the customer is not fulfilling his expectations of the project and the Project Manager has communicated to the customer already, then senior management is the role that provides assistance. Stopping work and asking the customer's supervisor is unprofessional. Documenting the issue and doing nothing else is inappropriate because a Project Manager should be proactive in addressing problems. [section 5.4.4]

26. The project team has just started breaking down the components of the project into smaller pieces that are easier to maintain and manage. After doing this, at what level of decomposition will they ultimately stop?

Correct Answer: (D) Activity Definition

Explanation: Create WBS takes the scope of the project and breaks it down into smaller pieces that are easier to define, estimate, and manage. Scope Verification compares the scope of the project to work results. After that, the team continues decomposing the project work packages, stopping at Activity Definition when they have created activity lists. Scope Definition creates the project scope statement. [section 7.3.1]

27.   A new call center is being built for a national telephone company. The project to create it is nearing completion and will soon begin project Scope Verification. This activity will involve a number of people, but who will ultimately approve it?

Correct Answer: (B) The customer

Explanation: The customer ultimately approves (or verifies) the scope of the project. The Project Manager will likely perform an initial verification before showing the customer, but the customer has the ultimate signoff. The stakeholder is too vague an answer. Senior management is not as good an answer as the customer. [section 7.4]

28.   In defining a milestone, which of the following is correct?

Correct Answer: (C) It has a duration of zero (0)

Explanation: The milestone has a duration of zero. The milestone is typically used to define the completion of a series of activities. The other answers are noise. [section 8.5.12, section 7.7]

29.   The Project Manager is working with the customer to gain formal acceptance on the project deliverables. The customer is saying that three of the deliverables do not meet project goals and are unusable in their present form. Upon reviewing documentation, the customer tells the Project Manager that the requirements are not accurate to meet the needs for which the project was undertaken. In what part of the Planning process did this problem occur?

Correct Answer: (C) Scope Definition

Explanation: Scope Definition creates the project scope statement. Scope Verification attains formal acceptance of the work of the project. Create WBS generates the WBS and the decomposition of the project, resulting in work packages at the lowest level of decomposition. Scope Control is used to review and approve or reject scope change requests to the project. [section 7.2, section 7.7]

30.   A new highway project is being planned. This project involves creating four new lanes in with an existing highway. Because of where the new highway is being built, it is impossible to shut down lanes of traffic during the weekdays. The lanes can be shut down only during the evenings after midnight or on weekends. This is an example of what?

Correct Answer: (B) Constraints

Explanation: Constraints are elements that limit the options available on the project. Negotiation points could fit here but is not the best answer. Assumptions come into play when we don't know something on a project. "Successful buyer negotiations" is noise. [section 6.5.3]

PMP Exam Success Series: Certification Exam Manual
© 2007 Crosswind Project Management, Inc., www.crosswindpm.com

Chapter 8

Time

Anyone familiar with project scheduling software might consider Time Management an easy topic. However, it is probably the most difficult Knowledge Area for understanding concepts, performing calculations, and memorizing characteristics of tools, processes, and other items. We recommend that you examine each process piece and its characteristics, tools, and outputs. After completing your study of the first one, examine the key outputs to see how they work toward subsequent processes. Understand each, memorize it, and continue through the processes; you will have a schedule and a Schedule Control process with many creation and analysis tools used along the journey. Figure 8-1: Overview of Time Processes shows how processes and pieces of time work together.

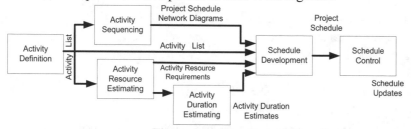

Figure 8-1: Overview of Time Processes

It is good to note that **on smaller projects, Activity Definition, Activity Sequencing, Activity Resource Estimating, and Schedule Development may occur as a single overall process.**

In this chapter, we discuss the following:

Process Group	Process Name		Main Outputs
Planning	Activity Definition	→	Activity List
			Milestone List
	Activity Sequencing	→	Project Schedule Network Diagrams
	Activity Resource Estimating	→	Activity Resource Requirements
	Activity Duration Estimating	→	Activity Duration Estimates
	Schedule Development	→	Schedule
			Schedule Management Plan (Updates)
Monitoring and Controlling	Schedule Control	→	Schedule Baseline (Updates)
			Performance Measurements

Crosswind "Must Knows" For Time

☑	
	Key Inputs, Tools & Techniques, and Outputs for Activity Definition
	Key Inputs, Tools & Techniques, and Outputs for Activity Sequencing
	Key Inputs, Tools & Techniques, and Outputs for Activity Resource Estimating
	Key Inputs, Tools & Techniques, and Outputs for Activity Duration Estimating
	Key Inputs, Tools & Techniques, and Outputs for Schedule Development
	Key Inputs, Tools & Techniques, and Outputs for Schedule Control
	Schedule Development concepts
	Rolling wave planning, control accounts, and planning package details
	Characteristics of a resource breakdown structure
	Characteristics of critical chain scheduling method
	Characteristics and benefits of "fast tracking" and "crashing"
	Principles of a network diagram, plus how to draw one from a word problem, analyze from a pop-up screen in either precedence diagramming method (PDM) or arrow diagramming method (ADM)
	Differences of the precedence diagramming method (PDM) and arrow diagramming method (ADM) and GERT network diagramming methods
	Concepts of PERT and CPM estimating methods
	How to recognize a critical path and why it is important
	How to do a forward pass and a backward pass on a network diagram
	Four predecessor types finish-to-start, start-to-start, finish-to-finish, and start-to-finish
	Characteristics of free slack (free float), total slack (total float), project slack (project float)
	Definition of lag and lead
	Characteristics of the three dependencies (mandatory, discretionary, external)
	Characteristics of a Logic Bar chart (Gantt chart), summary schedule, and milestone schedule
	Key characteristics and differences of the estimating methods (analogous, bottom-up, parametric, computerized)

Although helpful, this list is not all-inclusive for information needed from this area for the exam. It is only suggested material that, if understood and memorized, can increase your exam score.

8.1   Activity Definition (Planning Process Group)

For Activity Definition, focus on the activities required to create the deliverables of the project. In creating this "activity list," you **focus on what is being done**, not who is doing it, how long it will take, or when it is being done.

> Know the Key Inputs, Tools & Techniques, and Outputs for Activity Definition.

Activity Definition (Planning)		
Key Inputs	Project Scope Statement	The Project Scope Statement helps you **determine what the project is going to create**. Constraints and assumptions come into play when you determine what the needed activities for the project will be. Also helpful is expert judgment, which can guide you in any estimation associated with the project.
	Work Breakdown Structure	The Work Breakdown Structure (WBS) is a graphical depiction of the project work and it is broken out to work packages that are broken down even further to create activity and milestone lists.

PMP Exam Success Series: Certification Exam Manual
© 2007 Crosswind Project Management, Inc., www.crosswindpm.com

Key Inputs (cont.)	Project Management Plan	A Project Management Plan (not a schedule!) **integrates plans representing various Knowledge Areas** in the PMI approach to project management. Supporting detail is also included to help validate the information in the project management plan.
Key Tools & Techniques	Decomposition	Helpful tools include **decomposing the work** to be done. and any **templates** that provide standards of success from past projects or industry standards.
	Templates	Templates provide **standards of success** from past projects or industry standards.
	Expert Judgment	Expert Judgment is of great value. It can be more significant and accurate than the best modeling tools available.
Key Outputs	Activity List	The Activity List describes **what needs to be done**. It can be considered a list that ties to a work package from the work breakdown structure. Be sure to remember that the activity list is a **component of the schedule, but NOT of the WBS**. A rule of thumb is to break down the activity list to the point where the activities are 4-80 hours in duration. Project Managers commonly call activities "tasks," but according to PMI standards, the term "activities" is generally appropriate.
	Milestone List	A Milestone List **defines the milestones** to be achieved on the project. It can help with the verification that work is accomplished as planned.

Situational Question and Real World Application
Issues you might expect include work products taking longer than expected, or not having an idea of how long activities should take to complete. The introduction of out-of-scope items into the project could pose problems, depending upon how much discovery was done in Planning. Time and cost estimates could be out of line also if there were a great number of items not discovered originally but needed to be completed to make the product of the project complete.

Rolling Wave Planning	Rolling wave planning is a **concept that utilizes the progressive elaboration concept in Planning**. It defines a low level of detail on the WBS for the immediate work being accomplished while the work to be done in the future is only at a high level of decomposition in the WBS until it is soon to be started.	Know the concepts of rolling wave planning, control account, and planning package.
Control Account	Control account is a point placed in a WBS above the work package level to **help with estimating** when all the details aren't immediately available at the work package level. Any associated activities are defined in a control account plan. See Figure 7-1: WBS Process Components.	
Planning Package	The planning package is a **piece of the WBS between the control account and the work package.** It is used to plan work that has been scoped but lacks sufficient work package level details. See Figure 7-1: WBS Process Components.	

8.1.1   Schedule Management Plan

The schedule management plan helps the Project Manager and team do the following:

- Decompose work packages (deliverables) into activities and milestones
- Establish the network diagram
- Determine what resources are needed for the project
- Determine the durations for the activities
- Integrate all activity components into a schedule
- Deal with schedule changes and updates

8.2   Activity Sequencing (Planning Process Group)

In Activity Sequencing, focus on the order of the activities. What is being done has already been defined; now **the focus is to arrange the activities in the most efficient and effective order.**

Know the Key Inputs, Tools & Techniques, and Outputs for Activity Sequencing.

Activity Sequencing (Planning)		
Key Inputs	Project Scope Statement	The project scope statement **helps define the project**. Supporting detail provides the in-depth research and planning that the project scope statement rolls into.
	Activity List	The activity list is the basis for **what is being done**. The product description helps provide a big picture view to ensure that the sequencing produces the desired results.
	Milestone List	Milestones close things out in **defining major steps** of the project.
Key Tools & Techniques	Precedence Diagramming Method (PDM)	The precedence diagramming methods (PDM) is the technique most used by modern project scheduling software. It **shows the activities on the blocks or boxes with arrows connecting them**.
	Arrow Diagramming Method (ADM)	The arrow diagramming method (ADM) is an older more restrictive technique that **uses the arrow for the activities and dots to connect them**. Conditional networking techniques, such as Graphical Evaluation Review Technique (GERT), are used for activities like testing, for which a feedback loop is needed.
	Schedule Network Templates	Schedule network templates are used when templates are available for the type of work the project is doing.
	Dependency Determination	Dependency determination is a key tool because it **defines the mandatory (hard logic), discretionary (soft logic), and external dependencies** that exist on the project.
	Applying Leads and Lags	Applying leads and lags is done to **show a true duration of the various paths in the network diagram**.
Key Outputs	Project Schedule Network Diagrams	Project schedule network diagrams are completed to **show the sequencing of the activities** on the project.
	Activity List (Updates)	Activity list (Updates) can **occur as you learn more** about the activity sequence.

PMP Exam Success Series: Certification Exam Manual
© 2007 Crosswind Project Management, Inc., www.crosswindpm.com

---

Situational Question and Real World Application

Sequencing issues could cause problems, such as being ready to start work but not having the necessary work before it is completed, or performing work that doesn't make logical sense in relation to the overall output of the project.

8.2.1   Dependencies

When you create a project schedule, you must consider dependencies for the sequencing. Dependencies may be flexible, causing no real impact on you and your team. They also may be inflexible, giving you no option other than to work around them.

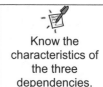

Know the characteristics of the three dependencies.

Type	Definition	Example
Mandatory (Hard Logic)	A constraint that **must** be completed before subsequent items can start	You must have the roof on before you can begin to apply shingles to it.
Discretionary (Soft Logic)	A constraint that **should** be completed but is not absolutely required to be completed before subsequent items can start	You prefer but do not absolutely have to finish system testing before beginning user acceptance testing.
External	A constraint put in place by something **external** to the project team or organization	The city inspector must approve any construction before issuing a certificate of occupancy so the tenant can move in.

8.2.2   Network Diagram

This network diagram is a schematic of project activities. It shows how the various activities are connected as a result of Activity Sequencing. This diagram gives you a picture of how the work of the project will flow. It is also the **tool used to evaluate schedule compression techniques** such as **crashing** and **fast tracking.**

Know the principles of a network diagram, as well as how to draw one from a word problem, or analyze from a pop-up screen as either precedence diagramming method (PDM) or arrow diagramming method (ADM).

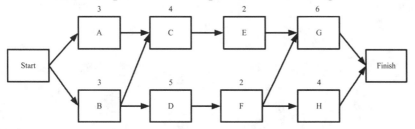

Figure 8-2: Network Diagram Sample

8.2.3   Diagramming Types

If you have used scheduling software without doing very much manual network diagram drawing, this area can be a little confusing. It doesn't need to be. The main difference is what the box and the arrow represent in each.

We describe both precedence diagramming method (PDM) and arrow diagramming method (ADM) so you can learn more about the differences in the table that follows, a must for memorizing for the exam. **NOTE: Both diagrams** (Figure 8-3: Precedence Diagramming Method Sample and Figure 8-4: Arrow Diagramming Method Sample) **represent the same data set in different formats.**

Sometimes called activity-on-node (AON), the precedence diagramming method (PDM) diagramming method is what most people use when they use modern project management scheduling software. In this method, the activity is in the box (sometimes called the node) and the arrow connects the activities.

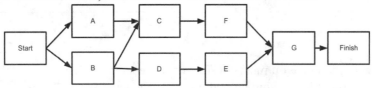

Figure 8-3: Precedence Diagramming Method Sample

Know the differences between the precedence diagramming method (PDM) and arrow diagramming method (ADM).

The arrow diagramming method (ADM), sometimes called activity-on-arrow (AOA), is older. In this method, the activity is on the arrow or line, and the circle or box connects the activities. A dummy is also used in this diagramming type, where needed. A dummy is a dashed line that connects two activities where a relationship is needed, but the diagram doesn't otherwise connect the relationship. **The dummy is not an activity and has a zero duration.** The dummy "H" has been added in Figure 8-4: Arrow Diagramming Method Sample to show the dependency between activity B and C.

The ADM drawing can display activities in another format as well. This is the point where the appearance is more like the PDM diagram, and the activities are represented in the format of "Start-A," "A-C," and "H-Finish." The exercises later in this chapter give you an opportunity to use that format.

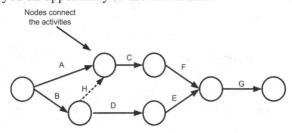

Figure 8-4: Arrow Diagramming Method Sample

Full Name	Abbreviated Name	Predecessor Types	Maximum Number of Predecessor Types	Special Diagram Types and Characteristics	Application	Graphic Appearance
Precedence Diagramming Method Activity-on-Node	PDM AON	Finish-to-Start Start-to-Start Finish-to-Finish Start-to-Finish	4	No Dummies allowed	Most modern project scheduling software	Figure 8-3: Precedence Diagramming Method Sample
Arrow Diagramming Method Activity-on-Arrow Activity-on-Line	ADM AOA AOL	Finish-to-Start	1	Dummies allowed	Outdated manually drawn mostly	Figure 8-4: Arrow Diagramming Method Sample

GERT (Graphical Evaluation Review Technique)

GERT is a diagramming technique that uses feedback *loops* or multiple passes through a diagram as iterations are completed. It can be a "noise" answer on questions from this area. Unless asked about a technique with a **feedback loop**, when GERT is listed as an answer, it is usually noise. Be sure not to bite on GERT just because it sounds familiar.

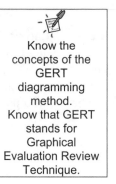

Know the concepts of the GERT diagramming method. Know that GERT stands for Graphical Evaluation Review Technique.

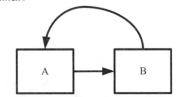

Figure 8-5: GERT Diagramming Sample

A practical example is software testing. When you start, you assume that you will make it through the routine on the first pass. But reality is that you will probably have to make multiple passes through the routine until testing is complete.

8.2.4   Predecessors

When you create a project schedule, use predecessors to establish the sequencing needed to accomplish the work. Later in this chapter is a table showing the characteristics of and differences between these diagramming techniques.

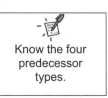

Know the four predecessor types.

Predecessor	Diagram
Finish-to-Start With the finish-to-start predecessor, Activity A must be completed before Activity B begins. This predecessor is usually the default type for most modern project scheduling software and is usable in the activity-on-arrow (AOA) and activity-on-node (AON) diagramming techniques. The other types (start-to-start, finish-to-finish, and start-to-finish) are used only on the activity-on-node (AON) diagram.	
Finish-to-Finish With the finish- to-finish predecessor, Activity B must finish by the time Activity A is finished. Use this predecessor when two or more teams are developing something, and all activity must finish at the same time to be converged into the total system.	
Start-to-Start Under the start-to-start predecessor, when Activity A starts, Activity B can start. Use this predecessor when multiple activities can start simultaneously.	
Start-to-Finish Under the start-to-finish predecessor, Activity A starts before Activity B finishes. You use the start-to-finish predecessor in situations where the new system must start before you could finish (shut down) the old system. Start-to-finish is the orphan of the predecessors. Think about it: how many of you have used this compared to any of the other predecessors when you create a schedule? One example that seems to be ideal for this type of predecessor is a project in which you create a new system to replace an existing one.	

8.2.5   Lag and Lead

A lag is a delay between activities. You use it when there is some type of constraint in which something must wait before it can continue. An example is: you are building the interior of a house, so you wait a day for the texturing on the walls to dry before you paint the walls.

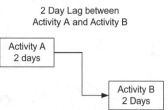

A lead is an accelerant of an activity. You use a lead when something can begin before its predecessor is totally complete. An example is: to begin user testing software if the system testing was significantly complete.

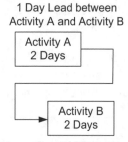

Be sure not to confuse **lag** or **lead** with **slack** and **float** on the exam.

If you are looking at lag or a lead in a network diagram, refer to Figure 8-6: Lead and Lag Displayed in Network Diagram to see how they are represented from one day to the next. Later in this chapter, you will read about how to apply the early start (ES) and early finish (EF) dates to the activities.

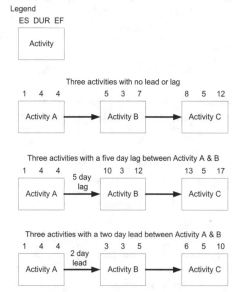

Figure 8-6: Lead and Lag Displayed in Network Diagram

Know the definition of a lag.

Know the definition of a lead.

PMP Exam Success Series: Certification Exam Manual
© 2007 Crosswind Project Management, Inc., www.crosswindpm.com

8.3   Activity Resource Estimating (Planning Process Group)

Know the Key Inputs, Tools & Techniques, and Outputs for Activity Resource Estimating.

In Activity Resource Estimating, **determine all the resources required for the project, not just the most obvious.** Examine your needs in terms of **personnel, material, and equipment,** and how much of each you require. Your concerns are what you need and how much of it, as well as when you need it.

Activity Resource Estimating (Planning)		
Key Inputs	Activity List	The activity list **describes what needs to be done**. View it as an activity list that ties to a work package from the work breakdown structure.
	Resource Availability	Resource availability is used **to determine what types of resources are utilized**. It could also include time or duration and geographical availability.
	Project Management Plan	A project management plan (not a schedule!) **integrates plans representing various Knowledge Areas** in the PMI approach to project management. Supporting detail is also included to help validate the information in the project management plan.
Key Tools & Techniques	Expert Judgment	Expert judgment can be helpful in determining resource specifics and quantities.
	Project Management Software	Project management software such as scheduling, cost, or estimating software **can be helpful in organizing all the pieces that make up the schedule** and other pieces of the PMI processes.
	Bottom-Up Estimating	In bottom-up estimating, the team and Project Manager **create an estimate from the activity level and roll the estimates up to create a total project estimate**.
Key Outputs	Activity Resource Requirements	Activity resource requirements **defines the resources needed** for the project. It can include non-people resources such as infrastructure and conference rooms or personnel such as programmers and architects. It can also include quantity, start and finish dates, needed skill sets and experience levels of the needed resources.
	Resource Breakdown Structure	The resource breakdown structure (RBS) is similar to a work breakdown structure for the work of the project, but the RBS **shows what type of resources are on the project and how they are structured or organized**.
	Resource Calendars (Updates)	Resource calendar updates are **done when changes to resource availability should be reflected in the calendar**. The resource type can be personnel or material.

Situational Question and Real World Application
If you fail to consider and complete your Activity Resource Estimating, your project could suffer serious schedule slippage for a variety of resource reasons, such as not having enough personnel or enough personnel with the appropriate skills sets and not having access to material or equipment in the quantities and qualities you need.

8.3.1   Resource Breakdown Structure

The resource breakdown structure displays a breakdown by resource type across an organization. This breakdown makes it possible to view where resources are being used regardless of organizational group or division they are in. Because this information can include non-HR resources, as well as personnel, there is the potential to track project cost especially if the RBS aligns to the company accounting system. The example in Figure 8-7: Resource Breakdown Structure Sample shows classrooms and teachers with fall semester being the common criteria.

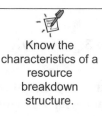
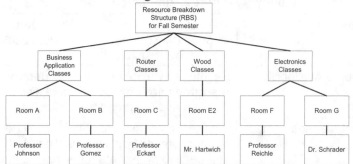

Figure 8-7: Resource Breakdown Structure Sample

8.3.2   Estimating Methods

Method	Description	Example
Analogous (Sometimes called Top-Down)	This estimate is usually a total time or cost estimate that has no significant detail. The main advantage of this estimate is that you can create it **quickly**; the disadvantage is that it **lacks detail** or individual piece estimates.	An executive or someone who is a subject matter expert (SME) creates a high level estimate based on experience or past project history with the company.
Bottom-Up	Compared to the analogous estimate, the main advantage is **detail and accuracy.** The disadvantage is that it **can take significant time to create,** and the team can pad the estimates to compensate for unknowns.	The Project Manager and the team work together to create a complete estimate from the bottom (activity level) up and roll it up to the total estimate.
Parametric	Based on an **existing parameter**, this method is usually created by industry standards or experience. The advantage is that it **can be done quickly** and is usually **accurate.**	A house builder quotes a house at $75.00 per square foot. A carpet installer quotes $2 per square yard for installation.
Computerized/ Monte Carlo	Monte Carlo is a **computerized tool that simulates project outcome** to determine factors such as **time** or **cost** outcomes or number of needed **resources**. The main advantages are the accuracy of estimates and the "what-if" analysis that can be performed. The main disadvantages are the ramp-up time and cost associated with the setup of the tool.	Variables simulated could include the overall time and cost estimates, as well as the confidence levels of the estimates. Variables could also include the number of people needed to achieve project goals.

PMP Exam Success Series: Certification Exam Manual
© 2007 Crosswind Project Management, Inc., www.crosswindpm.com

*PERT (*Program Evaluation Review Technique*)*

The Program Evaluation Review Technique (PERT) uses three estimates per activity. It performs a weighted average of the pessimistic, optimistic, and realistic (most likely) estimates. The theory is that having three estimates provides a more accurate PERT estimate. The goal is consistency on time and flexibility on Cost. You can use the PERT formula to calculate time or cost. The formula for PERT is:

$$\frac{(O + P + (4 * R))}{6}$$

O is Optimistic, P is Pessimistic, and R is Realistic or could be substituted for M as Most Likely. See the formula section of this chapter for the PERT formula or more information on PERT.

Know the concepts of the PERT estimating method. Know that PERT stands for Program Evaluation Review Technique.

8.4   Activity Duration Estimating (Planning Process Group)

In this process, the key is to estimate the number of work days (or hours) to complete each activity. That estimation then rolls up to create summary (high level) estimates.

Know the Key Inputs, Tools & Techniques, and Outputs for Activity Duration Estimating.

Activity Duration Estimating (Planning)		
Key Inputs	Project Scope Statement	The project scope statement helps define the project. Supporting detail provides the in-depth research and planning that the project scope statement rolls into.
	Activity List	The activity list helps you determine what activities need their durations estimated.
	Activity Resource Requirements	Activity resource requirements provide resources needed for the project. They can include non-people resources such as infrastructure and conference rooms or personnel such as programmers and architects. They can also include quantity, start and finish dates, needed skill sets, and experience levels of the needed resources.
	Resource Calendars	Resource calendars show availability of the resources being used on the project.
	Project Management Plan • Risk Register • Activity Cost Estimates	The risk register (from the project management plan) is a piece of the project management plan that **contains information associated with what risks could occur** on a project, **potential responses** for them, their **root causes**, and **categorization**. It expands as risk management processes are further implemented.
		Activity cost estimates (from the project management plan) can be used **to create estimates for the resource quantities** for the activities on the schedule.

Key Tools & Techniques	Expert Judgment	Expert judgment is of great value. It can be more significant and accurate than the best modeling tools available.
	Analogous Estimating (Top-Down)	Analogous estimating requires expert judgment (or historical information) and is created by an expert or group of experts, not just an executive pulling a number from the air. It is a **high level estimate**, not a detailed estimate.
	Parametric Estimating	Parametric estimation is an estimating technique that **uses a quantitative approach** based on the quantity of work and the productivity rate per unit of work.
	Three-Point Estimates	Three point estimates is a mathematical function that **uses an average in calculating an estimate** based on the pessimistic, optimistic, and realistic (most likely) estimates. This estimate differs from a PERT estimate in that the realistic estimate doesn't receive additional emphasis of a weighted average.
	Reserve Analysis	Reserve analysis is used when a team wants to plan for known unknowns (contingency reserves). This analysis **adds extra time to the estimates from a work units or percentage estimate**
Key Outputs	Activity Duration Estimates	Activity duration estimates **reveal how long the tasks will take**, along with the supporting evidence of those estimates and any updates to the activity list. This estimate could differ from a typical format of so many days; for example, 4 weeks +/-3 days, which could be 17 to 23 days (based on five business days in a week).

Situational Question and Real World Application
The main problems to arise from this area are schedule and cost overruns resulting from inaccurate duration estimates. Bad estimates can cause time slippage, which then factors into the cost component of the triple constraint.

8.4.1   Parkinson's Law

According to Parkinson's Law, work expands to consume the time scheduled for its completion. It's a comical observation of economics made by C. Northcote Parkinson, based on his experience in the British Civil Service. He noted that as the British empire shrank in both size and significance, the colonial office staff actually increased.

You could generalize Parkinson's Law as: "The demand upon a resource expands to match the supply of the resource." In computer terms, it works out to: "Data expands to fill the space available for storage." In financial terms, it reads as: "Expenses rise to meet income."

PMP Exam Success Series: Certification Exam Manual
© 2007 Crosswind Project Management, Inc., www.crosswindpm.com

8.5   Schedule Development (Planning Process Group)

Schedule Development is the process during which you review resource needs, Activity Sequencing, and Activity Duration Estimates to develop the project schedule. At this point, the "what" (activity list and work breakdown structure), "when" (start and finish dates), "who" (resources), and "what order" (Activity Sequencing) come together and the schedule is born.

Know the Schedule Development concepts. Know the Key Inputs, Tools & Techniques, and Outputs for Schedule Development.

Schedule Development (Planning)		
Key Inputs	Project Scope Statement	The project scope statement **helps define the project**. Supporting detail provides the in-depth research and planning that the project scope statement rolls into.
	Activity List	The activity list helps you **determine what activities need their durations estimated**.
	Project Schedule Network Diagrams	Project schedule network diagrams are completed to **show the sequencing of the activities** on the project.
	Activity Resource Requirements	Activity resource requirements **provide the resources needed for the project**. They can include non-people resources such as infrastructure and conference rooms or personnel such as programmers and architects. They can also include quantity, start and finish dates, needed skill sets and experience levels of the needed resources.
	Resource Calendars	Resource calendars **show the availability of the resources** that are being utilized on the project.
	Project Management Plan • Risk Register	The risk register (from the project management plan) **contains information associated with what risks could occur** on a project, **potential responses** for those risks, **root causes** of the risks and risk **categorization**. It expands as risk management processes are further implemented.
	Activity Duration Estimates	Activity duration estimates reveal **how long the activities will take**, along with the supporting evidence of those estimates and any updates to the activity list.
Key Tools & Techniques	Schedule Network Analysis	Schedule network analysis is a technique that **creates the schedule.** It takes into account techniques such as critical path analysis, critical chain analysis, and resource leveling.
	Critical Path Method	Critical path method is a schedule network analysis technique that **uses forward and backward pass approaches to calculate the early start, late start, and finish dates of each activity.** This approach provides the amount of flexibility (slack) for each activity.
	Schedule Compression	Schedule compression techniques such as **crashing** and **fast tracking** are used for optimization.
	Resource Leveling	Resource leveling **helps you attain a consistent level of hours (usually either daily or weekly) for the resources** on the project.

Key Tools & Techniques (cont.)	Project Management Software	Project management software such as scheduling, cost, or estimating software can be **helpful in organizing all the pieces that make up the schedule** and other pieces of the PMI processes.
	Applying Calendars	Applying calendars to the schedule **shows when work can be accomplished**. The two main types of calendars are the project calendar and the resource calendar.
	Adjusting Leads and Lags	Adjusting leads and lags are done to **fine tune the schedule** for adding the delays (lags) and accelerants (leads) that sometimes come between activities.
Key Outputs	Project Schedule	Key outputs include the project schedule with the **activities, start and finish dates, resources, and sequencing** (at a minimum) integrated into it. Supporting detail helps provide the logic behind the decisions that created the schedule.
	Schedule Baseline	The schedule baseline is the **planned timeline** for the project to be executed around. This is the timeline the project team will execute the plan against.
	{Activity} Resource Requirements (Updates)	{Activity} resource requirements are **updated if resource leveling changes the characteristics of the resources** and their amount of time needed on the project.
	Project Calendar (Updates)	Project calendar is **updated if there are changes in the calendar** from which the project works.
	Project Management Plan (Updates)	The project management plan is **updated to address any changes related to schedule management.**
	• Schedule Management Plan (Updates)	Schedule management plan is updated **when approved change requests impact how the schedule is managed.**

Situational Question and Real World Application
Trying to complete a project without a schedule generally results in not knowing how far into the project the activities truly are. If resources are not addressed appropriately, issues focus on not knowing who should do what. If duration estimates are significantly out of alignment, problems are associated with schedule slippage. Inaccurate Activity Sequencing causes work to be done in the wrong order, or causes stoppage because certain activities aren't complete; thus, others dependent on those cannot continue.

8.5.1   Critical Path Method (CPM)

The critical path method is used with scheduling environments in which a **forward pass** establishes the **earliest the activities can start (ES) and finish (EF)**, and a **backward pass** establishes the **latest the activities can start (LS) and finish (LF).** Looking at this information for each path and activity allows the calculation of the critical path and the amount of slack on each activity as well. **Any activity that is on the critical path typically has zero slack. There can be negative slack if the project is behind schedule.** In most cases, the activities on the critical path are the ones that should receive the most focus and attention from the Project Manager.

Know the concepts of the CPM estimating methods.

8.5.2   Slack (Also Known as Float)

Slack is the amount of time that an activity can slip or be delayed without delaying the finish date of the project (or activity or published project completion date). Typically, you calculate slack using a forward and backward pass.

If an activity has no slack, it is on the critical path; therefore, if it slips, it pushes out the finish date. **Negative or positive float can also exist. This float is a scenario in which the project's actual finish date extends past a targeted finish date, or the project's actual finish date comes before the targeted finish date.**

If a project is scheduled to be done by the end of May and it finishes two weeks early, there are two weeks of positive float. In the same example, if it were to run two weeks over (without approval of a new date), the project has two weeks of negative float.

Know the characteristics of free slack (free float), total slack (total float), and project slack (project float).

Free Slack	Free slack involves determining the latest that an activity can start without delaying the activities that follow it.
Total Slack	Total slack is described above. It is the latest an activity can start without delaying the project finish date.
Project Slack	Project slack is the amount of time something can be delayed without delaying the published finish date. Note that it could be different from what the project is privately anticipating. Most scheduling software will calculate these dates for you.

The concepts needed for the exam are in the following pages; they focus on the total slack.

8.5.3   Critical Path

Critical path is the **longest path on the project network diagram.** It typically has no slack yet the duration can change as the project evolves.

A project can have **multiple critical paths.**

A project can have **negative slack if it were behind schedule.** For example: a project was to take 20 weeks to complete. After 24 weeks, it is still not complete. With the assumption that management had not approved a new date yet, the slack is negative four weeks because the project should have been done four weeks earlier.

The greatest project risk normally occurs on the critical path. The project end date can be delayed if an activity on the critical path has a problem. The increase or slippage of an activity on the critical path can cause the overall finish date to slip.

Know how to recognize a critical path and why it is important.

8.5.4   How to Calculate the Critical Path

Examine the following word problem or data table for the data to create a network diagram then determine the critical path.

When the project starts, Activity A (4 days) and B (5 days) can begin. When Activity A is done, Activity C (4 days) can begin. When Activity B is done, Activity D (2 days) can begin. Activities C and D must finish before Activity E (6 days) can begin. Activity F (1 day) can begin when Activity D is complete. Activity G can begin when Activities E and F are complete. When Activity G (5 days) is complete, the project is complete. The durations are in the following table.

Activity	Preceding Activities	Duration in days
A	Start	4
B	Start	5
C	A	4
D	B	2
E	C, D	6
F	D	1
G	E, F	5

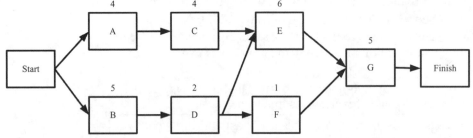

Figure 8-8: Network Diagram for Critical Path Analysis (A)

Paths: A,C,E,G = 19   B,D,E,G =18   B,D,F,G =13

The critical path is the path that is the longest. That is path A,C,E,G with a total of 19 days. Some rules to remember are as follows:

1. If given a word problem, draw the network diagram and double check that you have connected everything correctly and have labeled the activities and durations correctly.
2. List out all paths on the network diagram (example B,E,D,J, etc.) then add up the durations path by path so you can see the overall duration of each path. We recommend that you use a top to bottom approach when listing out the paths, meaning that you list the paths as they start at the top of the diagram and work toward those on the bottom. With the diagram in this example, you list the paths in the following order: Paths ACEG, BDEG, BDFG -- the paths of the network diagram. By working from the top to the bottom, you ensure that you don't accidentally miss a path. Be sure to use the letters of the path, not the durations, because that can get confusing during exam questions. For example, use ACEG instead of 4,4,6,5 when listing the paths.
3. Determine the longest (duration) path of all that are listed. That is the critical path.

8.5.5   Forward and Backward Pass Calculation

A forward and backward pass calculation is a standard calculation used to determine the critical path of the network diagram. It also shows how much slack (or float) there is for an activity, which is the amount of time an activity can slip before delaying the next activity. It also shows how much total slack there is, which is how much time an activity can slip before it delays the project finish date. A memory tool to help you remember the forward backward pass steps is **FIB and opposite**. FIB means when performing the **Forward** (pass), **Increment** (one day to another between activities) **Bigger** (choose the bigger of all Early Finish (EF)) feeding into an Early Start (ES) for the next activity. For the **backward pass, do the opposite of FIB**, that is BDS, or when performing the **Backward** (pass), **Decrement** (one day to another between activities) and **Smaller** (choose the smaller of all Late Starts (LS)) feeding into the Late Finish (LF) of the next activity. Remember the Forward pass starts at the start (left) of the network diagram and works through to the finish establishing the Early Start (ES) and Early Finish (EF) of the activities. The Backward pass starts at the finish and works backward to the left of the diagram establishing the Late Finish (LF) and Late Start (LS) of the network diagram.

Forward Pass Purpose	Provides the early start (ES) and early finish (EF) dates of each activity on the network diagram
Forward Pass Formula	ES+Duration-1=EF
Variables	**Early Start (ES)** - The earliest an activity can start based on network diagram logic **Early Finish (EF)** - The earliest an activity can finish based on network diagram logic **Duration** - The length of an activity **Convergence** - Where the output of more than one activity is a predecessor to an activity on the network diagram
Assumptions	A day starts at 8:00 a.m. and finishes at 5:00 p.m.
Starting Point	At the left of the network diagram, typically the start activity

Use Figure 8-9: Network Diagram for Critical Path Analysis to start your calculation.

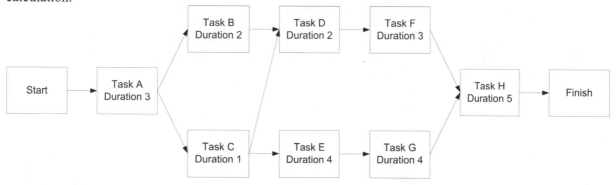

Figure 8-9: Network Diagram for Critical Path Analysis

How to Perform a Forward Pass

We recommend that you read the section below at least once then try to work the steps on the diagram above.

1. Set the early start (ES) of Activity A to 1 because that is the first day of the project.
2. Apply the forward pass formula (EF=ES+Duration-1) to the network diagram activity-by-activity from start to finish. If you encounter a convergence (see in step 3), return to the beginning of the diagram and continue this step for all activities leading into the convergence. As you move from one activity to another, increment the early finish

(EF) of the current activity by one to give you the early start (ES) of the next activity. For example, Activity A has an early finish (EF) of 3; the early start (ES) of the following activity is 4.

3. Wherever you encounter a convergence, select the larger of the early finish (EF) values and continue applying the forward pass formula from start to finish on the network diagram.

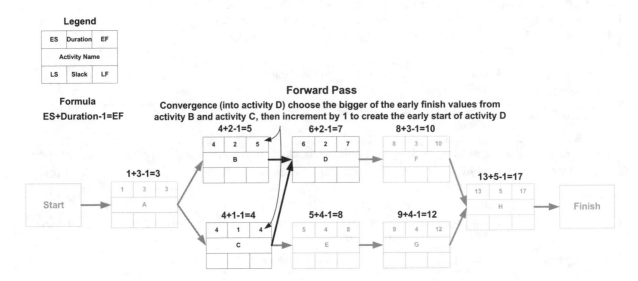

Figure 8-10: Forward Pass Calculation Description

4. Perform steps 2 and 3 until you have applied the forward pass formula to all activities. The forward pass is complete at this point.

At this point, the network diagram should have the following completed on it. The calculations are not part of a typical diagram but are shown for clarification.

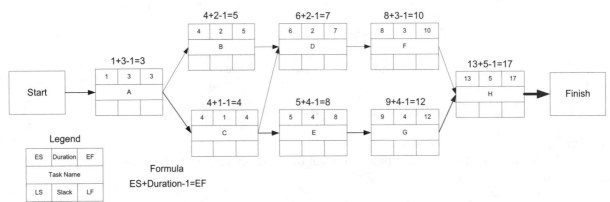

Figure 8-11: Forward Pass

PMP Exam Success Series: Certification Exam Manual
© 2007 Crosswind Project Management, Inc., www.crosswindpm.com

How to Perform a Backward Pass

Backward Pass Purpose	Provides the late start (LS) and late finish (LF) dates of each of the activities on the network diagram
Backward Pass Formula	LF-Duration+1=LS
Variables	**Late start (LS)** - The latest an activity can start based on the network diagram logic **Late finish (LF)** - The latest an activity can finish based on the network diagram logic **Duration** - The length of an activity **Burst** – Where an activity has multiple outputs that are Predecessors to more than one activity
Assumptions	A day starts at 8:00 a.m. and finishes at 5:00 p.m.
Starting Point	At the right of the network diagram, typically the finish or end activity

1. The late finish (LF) becomes the same as the early finish (EF) on the last activity (also, the duration of the critical path). If the network diagram ends with multiple activities, the Late Finish (LF) for all is the greatest Early Finish (EF).

2. Apply the backward pass formula (LF-Duration+1=LS) from the finish (right) to the start (left) of the network diagram. If you encounter a burst (see Figure 8-12: Backward Pass Calculation Description in this step), return to the finish (right) of the diagram and continue this step for all activities leading (from the right to the left) into the burst. As you move from one activity to another, decrease the late start (LS) by one to give you the late finish (LF) of the next activity. For example, Activity H has a late start (LS) of 13; the activity that precedes it has a late finish (LF) of 12.

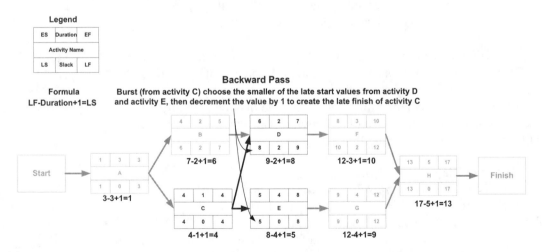

Figure 8-12: Backward Pass Calculation Description

3. At any burst on the network diagram, select the smaller of the late start (LS) values.
4. Perform steps 2 and 3 until all activities are done. At this point, the network diagram should look like the following.

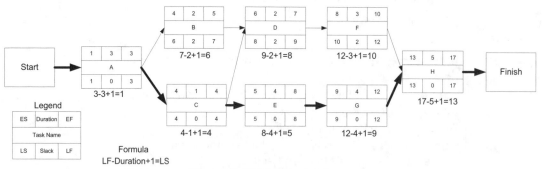

Figure 8-13: Backward Pass

Critical Path: The critical path is the longest path in the network diagram. Any activities on the critical path have an early start and late start that are the same value, as well as an early finish and late finish that are the same value. They have zero slack, meaning that if any of those activities slips, the overall network diagram slips as well.

8.5.6   Forward and Backward Pass Substitute Technique
To calculate the slack (float) of a path (or activity):

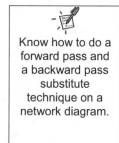
Know how to do a forward pass and a backward pass substitute technique on a network diagram.

1. Calculate the critical path of the network diagram.
2. Determine which paths have the activity you are calculating slack for. (Ex: All the paths that have Activity B in them, if they are the activities you are calculating the slack for.)
3. Determine which path is the longest. (If it is the critical path, you have zero slack.)
4. Subtract the total duration of the longest path (with the activity for which you are determining slack) from the critical path; the difference is the slack for that path or activity.

(You will not be quizzed on the slack for multiple activities on one path.)
If the path under review is not at the end of the path, you can still use this method. Other methods show subtracting all the activities one by one until you have the slack value you are calculating for. You need to do that method only if you must calculate an early start or early finish of an activity. The next paragraph covers calculation of the early/late start and finishes.

8.5.7   Network Diagram Analysis
Occasionally on the exam, you may see a question requiring you to calculate duration or slack from Figure 8-14: Network Diagram Analysis. The arrows and formulas below show what you need to calculate the duration or slack. The arrows point in the direction that you start the formula from (late start or finish with slack, for example). The formulas you can memorize are also listed. Remember, if the activity is on the critical path, the slack is zero.

PMP Exam Success Series: Certification Exam Manual
© 2007 Crosswind Project Management, Inc., www.crosswindpm.com

Alternative method to calculate the slack or float of an activity:

Use the formula LF-EF (late finish-early finish) or LS-ES (late start-early start) to calculate the slack of an activity by using the date provided in the exercise. If the difference is zero, the activity is on the critical path. If the value is negative, the activity has negative float and could be on the critical path or another activity, depending upon the health of the project.

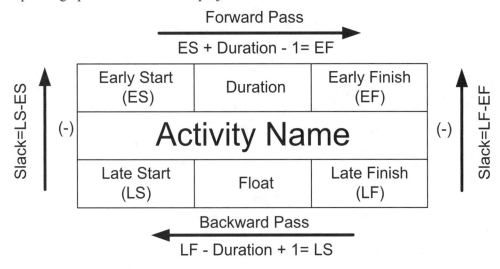

Figure 8-14: Network Diagram Analysis

8.5.8   Schedule Compression Techniques

After the initial schedule has been put together or after the project is in execution, you may have to compress the schedule to achieve a more aggressive time goal. The two main techniques are **crashing** and **fast tracking**. To achieve an earlier completion date, you could apply either technique or both to a schedule.

Crashing mainly puts more people on the critical path items, excluding any re-sequencing activities.

Fast tracking analyzes the network diagram and sequencing of the activities to take into consideration benefits from adjusting the sequencing to accelerate the completion of work. Fast tracking does include risk exposure associated with the re-sequencing. When schedule compression is needed, you may consider both options at the same time.

Look at Figure 8-15: Network Diagram Pre-Fast-Tracking to see that there are two paths.

The first path is A, B, D, E, F for a total duration of 13. The second path is A, C, D, E, F for a total duration of 12.

Path A,B,D,E,F is the critical path because it is the longer of the two paths.

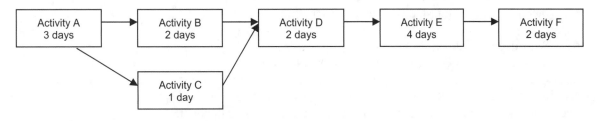

Figure 8-15: Network Diagram Pre-Fast-Tracking

If you need to compress the overall duration of the network diagram and want to use the fast tracking technique, you could re-sequence the diagram in Figure 8-16: Network Diagram Post-Fast-Tracking.

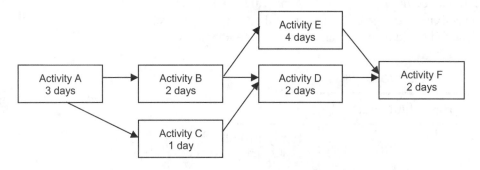

Figure 8-16: Network Diagram Post-Fast-Tracking

Path A,B,D,F has a total duration of 9. Path A,B,E,F has a total duration of 11 and path A, C, D, F has a total duration of 8.

Path A,B,E,F is the critical path because it is the longest of the three paths. Fast tracking has reduced the critical path from 13 (the original sequencing) to 11 (the revised sequencing).

Characteristics of both are listed in the following table.

Type of Compression Technique	Key Characteristics	Cost Characteristic	Quality Characteristic	Additional Characteristic
Crashing	**Putting more resources** on Critical Path activities	Usually increases cost	Minimal risk exposure (Compared to fast tracking)	Think of this as crashing a party! You have more people than originally planned.
Fast Tracking	**Doing activities in parallel** that are normally in sequence	Flexible, but increases cost from potential rework	Additional risk exposure because of possible rework	Can require additional communication to coordinate activities

Understand the Characteristics and benefits of "crashing" and "fast tracking."

8.5.9   Critical Chain Method
The critical chain method is a different approach for scheduling. It emphasizes resource flexibility and leveling over the course of the project. In this regard, it contrasts the more traditional approaches of Critical Path Method (CPM) and PERT, which emphasize task order and rigid scheduling.

Know the characteristics of the critical chain scheduling method.

8.5.10   Resource Leveling
As you create a schedule, you assign resources, and when you have your schedule complete, you usually notice a pattern of peaks and valleys, as depicted in Figure 8-17: Resource Allocation (Pre-Leveling). These peaks and valleys represent resources that can be applied for 12 hours one day but only 4 hours the next. Leveling is the process of adjusting these peaks and valleys to create a level usage of

PMP Exam Success Series: Certification Exam Manual
© 2007 Crosswind Project Management, Inc., www.crosswindpm.com

the resources, as depicted in Figure 8-18: Resource Allocation (Post-Leveling). Typically, when you apply resource leveling to your schedule, you sacrifice of the overall finish date, and it's common to see your schedule stretch out a little.

Resource leveling and schedule compression techniques are typically used together in several iterations to attain an optimal balance between delivery deadlines and resource utilization.

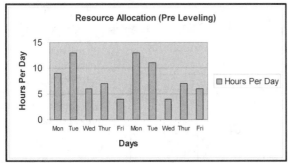

Figure 8-17: Resource Allocation (Pre-Leveling)

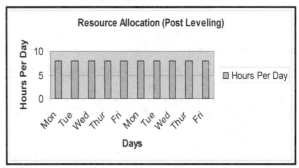

Figure 8-18: Resource Allocation (Post-Leveling)

8.5.11   Logic Bar Chart

A Logic Bar chart (sometimes called a Gantt chart) is the common chart used in project management. It has the table of information (usually activities, dates, resources, etc.) on the left, and on the right, horizontal bars showing when those activities are happening. **You use the Logic Bar chart to track the day-to-day details of the project.** The Logic Bar chart can also be called a Gantt chart. It could have (but not required) lines connecting the horizontal bars. Even though this chart shows sequencing, the ideal tool to view the sequences of activity is the network diagram, not the Logic Bar chart.

Know the characteristics of a Logic Bar chart.

Detailed Schedule with Logical (line) Relationships

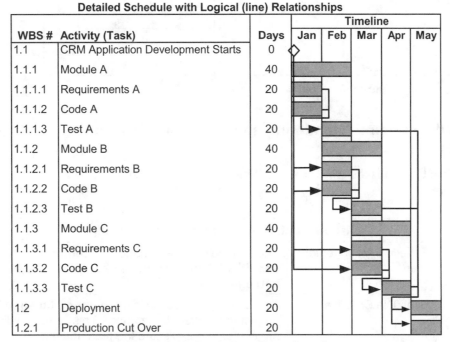

WBS #	Activity (Task)	Days	Jan	Feb	Mar	Apr	May
1.1	CRM Application Development Starts	0					
1.1.1	Module A	40					
1.1.1.1	Requirements A	20					
1.1.1.2	Code A	20					
1.1.1.3	Test A	20					
1.1.2	Module B	40					
1.1.2.1	Requirements B	20					
1.1.2.2	Code B	20					
1.1.2.3	Test B	20					
1.1.3	Module C	40					
1.1.3.1	Requirements C	20					
1.1.3.2	Code C	20					
1.1.3.3	Test C	20					
1.2	Deployment	20					
1.2.1	Production Cut Over	20					

Figure 8-19: Logic Bar Chart Sample

8.5.12   Milestone Schedule

The milestone schedule is **typically used in executive reporting**, and each milestone has a **zero(0) duration.** It lacks detail, generally listing only the main project milestones as diamonds instead of the Gantt bars. Like the Logic Bar chart, as defined by PMI, the milestone schedule does not require lines connecting the milestone diamonds either.

Executives usually don't want much detail so the milestone schedule fits their needs. Because project teams require more detail, they typically use Gantt charts.

Milestone Schedule

WBS #	Activity (Task)	Days	Jan	Feb	Mar	Apr	May
			Timeline				
1.1	CRM Application Development Starts	0	◇				
1.1.1	Module A	0		◇			
1.1.2	Module B	0			◇		
1.1.3	Module C	0				◇	
1.2	Deployment	0					◇
1.2.1	Production Cut Over	0					◇

Figure 8-20: Milestone Schedule Sample

8.5.13   Summary Schedule

The summary schedule shows an aggregate or rolled up view of the various activities at a summary level. It gives senior management, the project management team, and team members a picture of how long the summary level work packages are to take, and in what sequence they occur.

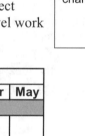

Summary Schedule

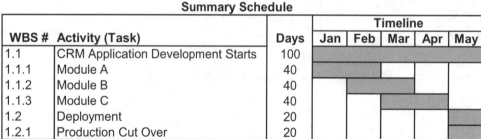

WBS #	Activity (Task)	Days	Jan	Feb	Mar	Apr	May
			Timeline				
1.1	CRM Application Development Starts	100					
1.1.1	Module A	40					
1.1.2	Module B	40					
1.1.3	Module C	40					
1.2	Deployment	20					
1.2.1	Production Cut Over	20					

Figure 8-21: Summary Schedule Sample

8.6   Schedule Control (Monitoring and Controlling Process Group)

Schedule Control is the process during which changes to the schedule are managed and controlled.

Schedule Control (Monitoring and Controlling)		
Key Inputs	Schedule Management Plan	The schedule management plan **communicates specifically how schedule changes are to be implemented**.
	Schedule Baseline	The Schedule Baseline is the **planned timeline** for the project to be executed around. This is the timeline the project team will execute the plan against.

Sidebar notes:

Know the characteristics of a milestone schedule.

A common misunderstanding about a milestone is the duration. This is something you should know for the exam. **A milestone has 0 (zero) duration.**

Know the characteristics of a summary schedule.

Know the Key Inputs, Tools & Techniques, and Outputs for Schedule Control.

PMP Exam Success Series: Certification Exam Manual
© 2007 Crosswind Project Management, Inc., www.crosswindpm.com

Key Inputs (cont.)	Performance Reports	Performance Reports communicate how accurate the plan is being worked and measure any variance.
	Approved Change Requests	Approved change requests are **changes that have been formally approved** by the official change control process on the project.
Key Tools & Techniques	Schedule Change Control System	The schedule change control system **addresses proposed schedule changes.**
	Progress Reporting	Progress reporting **shows what has been accomplished** in a specific time period on the project (but not the entire project).
	Performance Measurement Variance Analysis	Performance measurement and variance analysis **determine if any variance or required change exists**.
	Project Management Software	Project management software is **utilized to perform the schedule modification** (change). Examples include scheduling, cost, or estimating software. These can be helpful in organizing the pieces that make up the schedule and other pieces of the PMI processes.
Key Outputs	Schedule Baseline (Updates)	Schedule baseline updates are **done when approved change requests cause a modification of the schedule baseline.**
	Performance Measurement	Performance measurement is the **act of measuring what is happening on the schedule (earned value) and comparing it to what should be happening (planned value)** on the schedule.
	Requested Changes	Requested changes are **changes that have been requested but not yet formally approved** by the official change control process on the project.

Situational Question and Real World Application
Issues that can arise in Schedule Control could be multiple versions of a schedule, all different and all "official." Another issue could be old data being communicated to the team from an old or outdated schedule when the team should be working to new information. Any schedule that should be revised or updated could be an issue as well.

8.7   Time Formulas and Variables

Description	Formula	Variable (Component)	Example
Standard deviation is the measurement of variation within a distribution	(P-O)/6	Standard Deviation	(20-4)/6=2.67
The **variance** is a measure of how spread out a distribution is.	$((P-O)/6)^2$	Variance	$((20-4)/6)^2$=7.11
PERT represents an estimation technique used to calculate duration estimates.	PERT Duration= (P+O+(4*R))/6	PERT	(20+4+(4*14))/6= 13.33
Three point estimate	(P+O+R)/3	Three Point Estimate	(20+4+14)/3=12.67
Pessimistic estimate is a worse case estimate.	Provided on exam	P	P=10
Optimistic estimate is a best case estimate.	Provided on exam	O	O=4
Realistic (or most likely) estimate	Provided on exam	R (also could be M, "most likely")	R=6
Slack represents the amount of time (typically days) an activity can be delayed without causing impact.	Slack=LS-ES or LF-EF	Slack (Also called Float)	6-4=2 or 18-10=8
Forward pass formula	EF=ES+Duration-1 or provided on the exam	EF	6+2-1=7 or EF=10
Early Start is the earliest an activity can start	Provided on exam	ES	ES=4
Late Finish is the latest an activity can finish without causing impact	Provided on exam	LF	LF=18
Backward pass formula	LS=LF-Duration+1 or provided the exam	LS	10-5+1=6 or LS=6

PMP Exam Success Series: Certification Exam Manual
© 2007 Crosswind Project Management, Inc., www.crosswindpm.com

8.8   Time Terminology

Term	Description
Activity	A piece of the project that must be completed (performed); sometimes called a "task"; can be divided into smaller pieces; typically has an assigned resource, cost amount, and expected duration
Activity Definition	The identification of appropriate activities to complete the project deliverable
Activity Duration Estimating	The process of estimating the number of work periods (hours, days, weeks) to accomplish the activity
Activity List (Output/Input)	A detailed list of activities that project team members use to know what work on the project they are responsible for completing
Activity-on-Arrow (AOA)	A network diagramming method in which activities are shown on arrows and connected at nodes to show the sequence of activities
Activity-on-Node (AON)	A network diagramming method in which activities are shown on the boxes or circles of the network diagram and connected via arrows
Activity Resource Estimating	Determination of resources (people, material, equipment) needed for a project, including the determination of when (or how much of) the resources are needed
Activity Sequencing	The process of determining and documenting the logical relationships between activities on the project
Backward Pass	A network diagramming method that calculates the late start and late finish dates for each activity
Bar Chart (Tool)	A chart that shows a time relationship between the activities of the project; also commonly called a Gantt chart
Burst	The separation (or divergence) of activities on a network diagram from a central node
Crashing	A duration compression technique in which more people are added to critical path activities to shorten the duration of the critical path or other impacted areas of the schedule
Critical Chain Method (Technique)	A schedule technique used to evaluate the amount of float on the network paths; used to determine the minimum overall duration of the diagram
Critical Path	The series of activities that shows the overall duration of the project; can change as the project evolves
Critical Path Method (CPM) (Technique)	A network analysis method used to calculate total project duration
Dependency	A relationship between activities represented in the way activities are sequenced
Discretionary Dependency (Soft Logic)	A dependency in which the Project Manager (or other decision maker) can choose to allow it to be a dependency or not, depending upon the needs of the project (Ex: Buying a plane ticket before booking a hotel reservation)
Dummy Activities	A zero duration activity used in the arrow diagramming method (ADM) to show a logical relationship; represented graphically with an arrow having a dashed line
Duration	The overall amount of time on a project or activity
Early Finish Date (EF)	The earliest time an activity can finish based on the network logic
Early Start Date (ES)	The earliest time an activity can start based on the network logic
Effort	The amount of labor needed to complete an activity or work package; typically measured in hours, days, or weeks
Estimate (Output/Input)	A logical, educated prediction of some project component; typically includes a tolerance of accuracy
External Dependency	A dependency that lies outside the project team
Fast Tracking	A schedule compression technique in which the main focus is to find activities that can be done in parallel and to adjust the activity sequences to reflect this adjustment
Finish-to-Finish Dependency (FF)	A dependency used on project scheduling in which one activity cannot finish until the activity it is dependent upon finishes (Activity B cannot finish until Activity A finishes.)

Finish-to-Start Dependency (FS)	The default dependency type (with most project scheduling software) in which one activity cannot start until the one it is dependent upon finishes (Activity B cannot start until Activity A finishes.)
Float	See Slack.
Forward Pass	A network diagram technique that calculates the early start and early finish dates for each activity
Free Slack (Free Float)	The amount of time an activity can be delayed without causing slippage (delay) to the early start of any subsequent activities
Gantt Chart	The horizontal bar chart used in project management to show a time relationship between activities
Lag	A delay to a successor activity from the predecessor (Ex: Activity A finishes then has a three-day wait before Activity B can begin.)
Late Finish Date (LF)	The latest time an activity can be finished without delaying the project finish date
Late Start Date (LS)	The latest time an activity can start without delaying the project finish date
Lead	Acceleration to a successor from the predecessor (Ex: Activity A finishes. But with a three-day head start, Activity B can begin three days before Activity A finishes.)
Logical Relationship	A logical relationship between two or more components of a project schedule
Mandatory Dependency (Hard Logic)	A required dependency on a project; cannot be ignored (Ex: You must pour the foundation of a house before you can begin framing it.)
Master Schedule (Tool)	A high level schedule which displays summary information associated with activities, deliverables, milestones, and WBS components
Merge	A coming together (convergence) of activities on a network diagram
Milestone	A major achievement on a project; usually occurs after a series of activities leading up to its completion; has zero-days duration and could be related to a "deliverable"
Milestone Schedule (Tool)	A high level schedule which displays summary information associated with activities and milestones
Network Diagram	A schematic of logical relationships that make up the flow of activities on the project; always drawn from left to right
Network Logic	The connecting of activities on the network diagram to establish the structure of the network diagram
Network Path	A non-stop series of activities from the start to the finish of the network diagram
Path Divergence	A burst on the network diagram where the output of an activity goes to more than one activity
PERT Weighted Average	An estimating technique used to take the pessimistic, optimistic, and realistic (most likely) estimates to achieve a cumulative estimate (See formula section of this chapter.)
Precedence Diagramming Method (PDM)	A network diagramming process in which activities are represented in boxes
Project Network Diagram	A view of the logical relationship (sequencing) of project activities
Project Time Management	The processes associated with an attempt to complete the project on time
Resource Calendar	A calendar in the project management plan and schedule that shows working and non-working days
Rolling Wave Planning (Technique)	A progressive elaboration approach to managing a schedule where the initial phases are defined at a detailed level with the remaining work at a high level As the initial phases are done, the remaining phases are planned.
Schedule	The planned dates, sequencing, resources, and durations for activities and milestones on a project
Schedule Compression (Technique)	The process of shorting the project schedule without modifying the scope of the project (Ex: crashing and fast tracking)
Schedule Control	The process of managing and maintaining (controlling) changes to the schedule
Schedule Development	The process of using activity sequences, duration estimates, and resources to create the schedule

PMP Exam Success Series: Certification Exam Manual
© 2007 Crosswind Project Management, Inc., www.crosswindpm.com

Schedule Management Plan	Document that decomposes work packages, establishes the network diagram, determines required resources, determines activity durations, integrates activity components into a schedule, and deals with schedule changes and updates
Schedule Milestone	A major event in the project schedule; typically involves the start or completion of a major component of the project
Slack (Float)	The amount of time an activity can be delayed (slip) without causing a delay to the successor(s) activities, or the final finish date of the project
Start-to-Finish Dependency (SF)	A dependency used on project scheduling in which one activity cannot finish until the activity it is dependent on starts (Ex: Activity B cannot finish until Activity A starts)
Start-to-Start Dependency (SS)	A dependency used on project scheduling in which one activity cannot start until the activity it is dependent on starts (Activity B cannot start until Activity A starts.)
Sub-Network	A section of a network diagram; can be associated with a work package or some other type of logical decomposition
Successor	An activity that follows an activity logically connected to it
Summary Activity	An activity that sums up the detailed activities underneath it; typically used to evaluate work packages and facilitate executive reporting
Target Completion Date (TC)	A requested project completion date that can be a constraint for the project
Target Finish Date (TF)	The date that the project (or activity) is anticipated to be completed
Target Schedule	A preliminary schedule that can be used during initial stages of Planning; could differ from the baseline schedule at the conclusion of Planning
Target Start Date (TS)	The planned start date of the project or activity
Task	An activity to be completed on the project
Three Point Estimate (Technique)	An estimating technique that can be applied to schedule or budget; uses three estimates for each activity; uses an optimistic, pessimistic, and realistic (most likely) estimate
Total Float (TF)	The maximum amount of time an activity can slip without causing a delay to the project finish date
Total Slack (Total Float)	The amount of time an activity can slip (be delayed) from its early start date without delaying the overall finish date
Work Breakdown Structure (WBS)	An organized breakdown of the total work scope of the project, with each level of descent providing a greater level of detail and the deliverable being a key focus
Work Package	A component of work or a deliverable at the smallest level of the work breakdown structure
Work Performance Information (Output/Input)	Data associated with the completion of work on the project; can include deliverable status, actions associated with preventative and corrective measures, and change requests

8.9   Time Mind Map

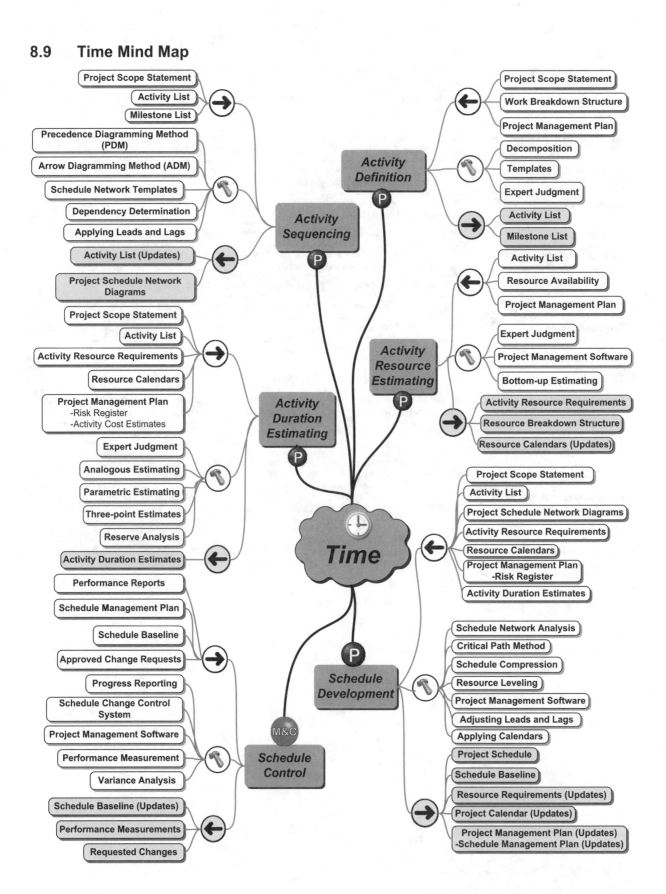

8.10   Time Exercises and Practice Tests

8.10.1   Time Network Diagramming Exercises
Answers are in section 8.11.1.

Exercise - Project A – Moving across the country
Activity A: Get bids on moving company
Activity B: Choose a moving company
Activity C: Go through belongings and decide what to keep and what to sell/give away (This will help ensure that you select a moving company capable of the scope of the job.)
Activity D: Prepare for and do a yard sale for unwanted items
Activity E: Give away unwanted items not sold in yard sale
Activity F: Inventory remaining items
Activity G: Pack remaining items
Activity H: Move

Activity	Preceding Activities	Duration in days
A	Start	9
B	A, C	3
C	Start	13
D	C	9
E	D	2
F	E	10
G	F	11
H	B, G	3

1.   Which path is the critical path and what is its duration?

2.   What is the slack/float for Activity B?

3.   Which path has the longest (most) slack?

4.   What is the slack of the path in question 3?

5.   If Activity B slips from three days to six days, what is the critical path?

6.   With the duration adjustment in question 5, what is the new slack of Activity B?

Exercise - Project B - Planning a Vacation

Activity A: Decide on vacation dates and location
Activity B: Buy airline tickets at least 21 days in advance of departure date
Activity C: Make hotel reservation
Activity D: Make car rental reservation
Activity E: Arrange for hold on mail delivery
Activity F: Arrange for hold on newspaper delivery
Activity G: Arrange for pets to be taken care of
Activity H: Pack for trip
Activity I: Depart

Activity	Preceding Activities	Duration in days
A	Start	8
B	A	4
C	A	10
D	B, C	2
E	D	2
F	D	2
G	D	3
H	E, F, G	2
I	H	1

1.   Which path is the critical path and what is its duration?

2.   What is the slack/slack for Activity F?

3.   What is the slack/slack for Activity B?

4.   If Activity E now takes four days instead of two days, has the critical path changed?

5.   Based on the information in question 4, what is the new critical path and what is its duration?

6.   Based on question number 4, what is the slack/float of the path with the longest (most) float?

7.   If the airline calls and says it has cancelled your flight but has scheduled you on another flight that leaves three days later, what is the project slack/float (based on the original values in the network diagram)?

Exercise - Project C – Planning for a Trade Show Event

Activity Start-A: Reserve booth location
Activity A-B: Develop displays for booth
Activity B-J: Prepare booth displays for shipping
Activity A-C: Develop marketing collateral for booth
Activity C-J: Prepare marketing collateral for shipping
Activity A-D: Develop mailer for customer mailing
Activity D-E: Mail mailer to customers
Activity A-F: Determine booth personnel required
Activity F-G: Confirm booth personnel availability
Activity G-H: Assign personnel to booth schedule
Activity H-I: Obtain company shirts for booth personnel
Activity I-J: Prepare shirts for shipping
Activity J-K: Ship booth displays, marketing collateral, and shirts to show
Activity K-End: Set up trade show booth and attend show

Activity	Duration in days	Activity	Duration in days
Start - A	2	G - H	1
A – B	15	H - I	5
A – C	15	I – J	2
A – D	5	C - J	2
D – E	3	B - J	3
E – J	Dummy	J – K	2
A – F	2	K - End	4
F – G	2		

1. What is the best network diagramming method to use to depict the logic of this project: Activity-on-arrow or Activity-on-node?

2. Which path is the critical path and what is its duration?

3. What is the slack/float of Activity B-J?

4. What is the slack/float of Activity G-H?

5. List all the activities that immediately precede Activity J-K.

6. If the duration of Activity C-J changes to 4, what is the impact on the project?

8.10.2   Time Quick Test

In this quiz, answer the question in a short essay of only a sentence or two or circle all correct answers for the question. Note that some questions may have more than one answer. Answers are in section 8.11.2.

1. Which of the following shows the sequencing of activities on a project?

    Gantt Chart   Network   AON   AOA   GERT
                       Diagram   Diagram   Diagram   Diagram

2. What is the process for eliminating the peaks and valleys of resource utilization and creating consistently level resource utilization?

3. Activity-on-node (AON) diagramming is also known as what?

    AOA (activity-on-arrow)
    PDM (precedence diagramming method)
    AOL (activity-on-line)
    ADM (arrow diagramming method)

4. What is the typical slack of a critical path?

5. What is the type of chart used to communicate high level schedule information to executives?

    Gantt   Milestone   Network   PERT   GERT

6. Which of the following processes puts more resources on the critical path?

    Crashing   Fast tracking   GERT   PERT

7. Which estimating method uses three estimates to create a single estimate?

    GERT   PERT   AON   Critical Path

8. Which diagramming technique uses a feedback loop?

    GERT   PERT   AON   Critical Path

9. What is the formula for standard deviation?

10. What is the act of placing a delay between activities on a network diagram?

PMP Exam Success Series: Certification Exam Manual
© 2007 Crosswind Project Management, Inc., www.crosswindpm.com

8.10.3　Time ITTO Matching Exercise

Match the correct ITTO term at the bottom of the page with the blanks to the right of the process. When a term is used multiple times, it is flagged by a parenthetical value indicating the number of times used. Also, match summary sentences with the process name that fits. Answers are in section 8.11.3.

	Inputs	Tools &Techniques	Outputs
Activity Definition	1) 2) 3)	1) 2) 3)	1) 2)
Summary:			
Activity Sequencing	1) 2) 3)	1) 2) 3) 4) 5)	1) 2)
Summary:			
Activity Resource Estimating	1) 2) 3)	1) 2) 3)	1) 2) 3)
Summary:			
Activity Duration Estimating	1) 2) 3) 4) 5) 6)	1) 2) 3) 4) 5)	1)
Summary:			
Schedule Development	1) 2) 3) 4) 5) 6) 7)	1) 2) 3) 4) 5) 6) 7)	1) 2) 3) 4) 5)
Summary:			
Schedule Control	1) 2) 3) 4)	1) 2) 3) 4) 5)	1) 2) 3)
Summary:			

Activities associated with updating and controlling the schedule

Creating the network diagram for the project

Creating activity lists to complete work packages

Creation of the project schedule

Determining how the long the activities on the project should take to complete

Determining what resources are needed for the project

Activity Duration Estimates (2)	Performance Measurements (2)	Resource Calendars (2)
Activity List (5)	Performance Reports	Resource Calendars (Updates)
Activity List (Updates)	Precedence Diagramming Method (PDM)	Resource Leveling
Adjusting Leads and Lags	Progress Reporting	Resource Requirements (Updates)
Activity Resource Requirements (3)	Project Calendar (Updates)	Schedule Baseline (2)

(continued on next page)

Analogous Estimating
Applying Calendars
Applying Leads and Lags (2)
Approved Change Requests
Arrow Diagramming Method (ADM)
Bottom-Up Estimating
Critical Path Method
Decomposition
Dependency Determination
Expert Judgment (3)
Milestone List (2)
Parametric Estimating

Project Mgt Plan (Activity Cost Estimates)
Project Mgt Plan (Risk Register) (2)
Project Management Plan (2)
Project Management Software (3)
Project Schedule
Project Schedule Network Diagrams (2)
Project Scope Statement (4)
Requested Changes
Reserve Analysis
Resource Availability
Resource Breakdown Structure

Schedule Baseline (Updates)
Schedule Change Control System
Schedule Compression
Schedule Management Plan
Schedule Management Plan (Updates)
Schedule Network Analysis
Schedule Network Templates
Templates
Three-point Estimates
Variance Analysis
Work Breakdown Structure

8.10.4   Time Terminology Matching Exercise

Match the correct term in the left column to the correct definition in the right column. See the exercise answer section of this chapter for the correct answer. Answers are in section 8.11.4.

Matching Exercise #1

	Term	Answer	Definition
1	Activity Definition		A. A relationship between activities represented in the way activities are sequenced
2	Activity Sequencing		B. Acceleration to a successor from the predecessor (Ex: Activity A finishes. But with a three-day head start, Activity B can begin three days before Activity A finishes.)
3	Bar Chart (Tool)		C. The process of managing and maintaining (controlling) changes to the schedule
4	Critical Path		D. The identification of appropriate activities to complete the project deliverable
5	Dependency		E. A preliminary schedule that can be used during initial stages of Planning; could differ from the baseline schedule at the conclusion of Planning
6	Duration		F. The series of activities that shows the overall duration of the project; can change as the project evolves
7	Early Finish Date (EF)		G. The maximum amount of time an activity can slip from the early start (ES) without causing a delay to the project finish date
8	Early Start Date (ES)		H. The earliest time an activity can start based on the network logic
9	External Dependency		I. The process of determining and documenting the logical relationships between activities on the project
10	Finish-to-Start Dependency (FS)		J. A coming together (convergence) of activities on a network diagram
11	Lag		K. The default dependency type (with most project scheduling software) in which one activity cannot start until the one it is dependent upon finishes (Ex: Activity B cannot start until Activity A finishes.)
12	Lead		L. The processes associated with an attempt to complete the project on time
13	Merge		M. A dependency that lies outside the project team
14	Network Diagram		N. A chart that shows a time relationship between the activities of the project; also commonly called a Gantt chart
15	Project Time Management		O. The overall amount of time on a project or activity
16	Schedule Control		P. A delay to a successor activity from the predecessor (Ex: Activity A finishes then has a three day wait before Activity B can begin.)
17	Slack		Q. The earliest time an activity can finish based on the network logic
18	Target Schedule		R. A schematic of logical relationships that make up the flow of activities on the project; always drawn from left to right
19	Total Float (TF)		S. The amount of time an activity can be delayed (slip) without causing a delay to the successor(s) activities, or the final finish date of the project
20	Work Breakdown Structure (WBS)		T. An organized breakdown of the total work scope of the project, with each level of descent providing a greater level of detail and the deliverable being a key focus

Matching Exercise #2

	Term	Answer	Definition
1	Activity		A. The planned dates, sequencing, resources, and durations for activities and milestones on a project
2	Activity List (Output/Input)		B. A zero duration activity used in the arrow diagramming method (ADM) to show a logical relationship represented graphically with an arrow having a dashed line
3	Crashing		C. The amount of time an activity can be delayed without causing slippage (delay) to the early start of any subsequent activities
4	Dummy Activities		D. A burst on the network diagram where the output of an activity goes to more than one activity
5	Effort		E. A required dependency on a project; cannot be ignored (Ex: You must pour the foundation of a house before you can begin framing it.)
6	Finish-to-Finish Dependency (FF)		F. A component of work or a deliverable at the smallest level of the work breakdown structure
7	Forward Pass		G. A dependency used on project scheduling in which one activity cannot finish until the activity it is dependent upon starts (Ex: Activity B cannot finish until Activity A starts)
8	Free Slack		H. The amount of labor needed to complete an activity or work package; typically measured in hours, days or weeks
9	Late Finish Date (LF)		I. A network diagram technique that calculates the early start and early finish dates for each activity
10	Mandatory Dependency (Hard Logic)		J. An activity that follows an activity logically connected to it
11	Network Logic		K. A calendar in the project management plan and schedule that shows working and non-working days
12	Path Divergence		L. The connecting of activities on the network diagram to establish the structure of the network diagram
13	Resource Calendars		M. The latest time an activity can be finished without delaying the project finish date
14	Schedule		N. A piece of the project that must be completed (performed); sometimes called a "task"; can be divided into smaller pieces; typically has an assigned resource, cost amount, and expected duration
15	Schedule Development		O. The planned start date of the project or activity
16	Start-to-Finish Dependency (SF)		P. A dependency used on project scheduling in which one activity cannot finish until the activity it is dependent on finishes (Activity B cannot finish until Activity A finishes)
17	Successor		Q. A detailed list of activities that project team members use to know what work on the project they are responsible for completing
18	Target Start Date (TS)		R. The process of using activity sequences, duration estimates, and resources to create the schedule
19	Task		S. A duration compression technique in which more people are added to critical path activities to shorten the duration of the critical path or other impacted areas of the schedule
20	Work Package		T. An activity to be completed on the project

PMP Exam Success Series: Certification Exam Manual
© 2007 Crosswind Project Management, Inc., www.crosswindpm.com

Matching Exercise #3

	Term	Answer	Definition
1	Activity Duration Estimating		A. A network diagramming process in which activities are represented in boxes
2	Activity-on-Arrow (AOA)		B. A network diagramming method that calculates the late start and late finish dates for each activity
3	Backward Pass		C. The date that the project (or activity) is anticipated to be completed
4	Critical Chain Method (Technique)		D. A dependency in which the Project Manager (or other decision maker) can choose to allow it to be a dependency or not, depending upon the needs of the project. (Ex: Buying a plane ticket before booking a hotel reservation)
5	Critical Path Method (CPM)		E. The process of estimating the number of work periods (hours, days, weeks) to accomplish the activity
6	Discretionary Dependency (Soft Logic)		F. A major event in the project schedule; typically involves the start or completion of a major component of the project
7	Estimate (Output/Input)		G. A logical relationship between two or more components of a project schedule
8	Fast Tracking		H. An estimating technique used to take the pessimistic, optimistic, and realistic (most likely) estimates to achieve a cumulative estimate
9	Gantt Chart		I. A schedule technique used to evaluate the amount of float on the network paths; used to determine the minimum overall duration of the diagram
10	Logical Relationship		J. A logical, educated prediction of some project component; typically includes a tolerance of accuracy
11	Milestone		K. An activity that sums up the detailed activities underneath it; typically used to evaluate work packages and facilitate executive reporting
12	PERT Weighted Average		L. The horizontal bar chart used in project management to show a time relationship between activities
13	Precedence Diagramming Method (PDM)		M. A progressive elaboration approach to managing a schedule where the initial phases are defined at a level with the remaining work at a high level As the initial phases are done, the remaining phases are planned.
14	Rolling Wave Planning (Technique)		N. A network diagramming method in which activities are shown on arrows and connected at nodes to show the sequence of activities
15	Schedule Compression (Technique)		O. The process of shorting the project schedule without modifying the scope of the project (Ex: crashing and fast tracking)
16	Schedule Milestone		P. A network analysis method used to calculate total project duration
17	Summary Activity		Q. A schedule compression technique in which the main focus is to find activities that can be done in parallel and to adjust the activity sequences to reflect that
18	Target Finish Date (TF)		R. A major achievement on a project; usually occurs after a series of activities leading up to its completion; has zero-days duration and could be related to a "deliverable"

Matching Exercise # 4

	Term	Answer	Definition
1	Activity-on-Node (AON)		A. Data associated with the completion of work on the project; can include deliverable status, actions associated with preventative and corrective measures, and change requests
2	Burst		B. A requested project completion date that can be a constraint for the project
3	Master Schedule (Tool)		C. A view of the logical relationship (sequencing) or project activity
4	Milestone Schedule		D. A high level schedule which displays summary information associated with activities, deliverables, milestones, and WBS components
5	Network Path		E. A network diagramming method in which activities are shown on the boxes or circles of the network diagram and connected via arrows
6	Project Network Diagram		F. The separation (or divergence) of activities on a network diagram from a central node
7	Start-to-Start Dependency (SS)		G. A non-stop series of activities from the start to the finish of the network diagram
8	Sub-network		H. A section of a network diagram; can be associated with a work package or some other type of logical decomposition
9	Target Completion Date (TC)		I. A high level schedule which displays summary information associated with activities and milestones
10	Total Slack		J. The amount of time an activity can slip (be delayed) from its early start date without delaying the overall finish date
11	Work Performance Information (Output/Input)		K. A dependency used on project scheduling in which one activity cannot start until the activity it is dependent on starts (Activity B cannot start until Activity A starts.)
12	Activity Resource Estimating		L. Determination of resources (people, material, equipment) needed for a project, including the determination of when (or how much of) the resources are needed

PMP Exam Success Series: Certification Exam Manual
© 2007 Crosswind Project Management, Inc., www.crosswindpm.com

8.10.5   Time Practice Test
Answers are in section 8.11.5.

1.   Calculate the variance for the following: Pessimistic=12, Optimistic=2, Realistic=5.

(A) 5
(B) 2.79
(C) 5.67
(D) Not enough information

2.   Crosswind Custom Homes is building a customer's dream house. However, rain has delayed the finish by two weeks. The Project Manager evaluates the schedule and determines that the electrical and plumbing work could occur at the same time instead of right after each other, as laid out in the schedule. This is an example of what?

(A) Mandatory dependencies
(B) Crashing
(C) Lag
(D) Fast tracking

3.   Which of the following is an example of a lag?

(A) The latest a new system can be ordered from the manufacturer without delaying the project
(B) The critical path
(C) A delay after the sheetrock (wall board) is done in a house to allow it to dry before continuing work in that area
(D) The earliest a new system can be ordered from the manufacturer

4.   Which of the following is a predecessor type of activity-on-arrow (AOA) diagrams?

(A) Start-to-start (SS)
(B) Finish-to-start (FS)
(C) Start-to-finish (SF)
(D) Finish-to-finish (FF)

5.   You are putting together the final schedule on your new project. The problem you are having is that you don't have a consistent usage of your resources. Some are working 12 hours a day, some 4 hours a day, and there are some days when they aren't scheduled to work at all on the schedule. Which of the following below fixes this problem?

(A) Resource leveling
(B) PERT analysis
(C) Fast tracking
(D) Crashing

6. Crosswind Custom Homes is building a customer's dream house. However, rain has delayed the finish by two weeks. The schedule shows that the next activity is to install the roof, then that is followed by the shingles. This is an example of what?

    (A) Mandatory dependencies
    (B) Lag
    (C) Discretionary dependencies
    (D) Crashing

7. Crosswind Custom Homes is building a customer's dream house. However, rain has delayed the finish by two weeks. The Project Manager is evaluating various ways to compress the schedule. The Project Manager suspects that the electrical and plumbing work could occur at the same time instead of right after each other as is laid out in the schedule. However, local zoning laws do not allow this concurrent work. This is an example of what?

    (A) Crashing
    (B) Mandatory dependencies
    (C) Discretionary dependencies
    (D) External dependencies

8. Calculate the standard deviation for the following: Pessimistic=12, Optimistic=2, Realistic=5.

    (A) 6
    (B) 1.67
    (C) 5.67
    (D) Not enough information

9. The Project Manager is creating an estimate for building a house. It is a house similar to what he builds quite often. He is using the rule of thumb of $85 per square foot to calculate the estimate. What type of estimate is this?

    (A) Parametric
    (B) Analogous
    (C) Gut feel
    (D) Bottom-up

10. The e-commerce project is six weeks behind schedule with five team members working on it. Three of these team members are working on the critical path-related items. What is the slack of the critical path?

    (A) Negative six weeks
    (B) 30
    (C) 0 (Zero)
    (D) Not enough information

11. The development team is building a new product for their company. This is a new product type at their company, and the market for the product is extremely unstable. According to the product manager, a key to success is the flexibility to adapt the product to the market changes that will occur during development. Which scheduling type best fits this need?

    (A) Rolling wave planning
    (B) Crashing
    (C) Fast tracking
    (D) Precedence diagramming

12. The e-commerce team is behind schedule on its project. The customer is considering killing the project if it cannot be brought back on track. The team is considering re-sequencing the critical path areas on the network diagram to shorten the length of the schedule. This is an example of what?

    (A) Crashing
    (B) Staff acquisition
    (C) Fast tracking
    (D) Re-planning

13. The development team is building a new product for its company. This is a new product type at the company, and the market for the product is extremely unstable. According to the product manager, a key to success is an extremely accurate estimate on the resource needs for the project, because the company is resource-constrained. Which type of duration estimating approach is the most accurate?

    (A) Bottom-up estimating
    (B) Parametric estimating
    (C) Fast tracking
    (D) Analogous estimating

14. You are the Project Manager on a defense project and are creating a network diagram. Activity A (3 days) and Activity B (6 days) can start immediately. Activity C (2 days) can start after Activity A is complete. Activity D (1 day) and Activity F (2 days) can start after Activity B is complete. Activity E (4 days) can start after Activity C and Activity D are complete. Activity G (5 days) can start after Activity D and Activity F are complete. When Activity E and Activity G are complete, the project is done. What is the critical path?

    (A) BDE
    (B) ACE
    (C) BFG
    (D) BDG

15. Using the original network diagram question, what is the slack of Activity D?

    (A) Two days
    (B) One day
    (C) Four days
    (D) Not enough information

16.   In the original network diagram question, if Activity D increases from one to three days, what is the critical path, and what is the length?

    (A) BDE, 13 days
    (B) ACE, 14 days
    (C) BFG, 13 days
    (D) BDG, 14 days

17.   Slack on a network diagram is also known as:

    (A) Lag
    (B) PERT
    (C) Float
    (D) GERT

18.   The defense project is progressing well. The Air Force Major who is the executive sponsor gets promoted and moves to a new base. His replacement is brought in from a new area and, upon arrival, asks to see where the project currently stands. Which of the following do you show him?

    (A) Network diagram
    (B) Work breakdown structure
    (C) Gantt chart
    (D) Milestone chart

19.   Crosswind Custom Homes is building a customer's dream house. However, the city inspector for building permits has been in training for the last two weeks and has no backup. This inspection delay causes a delay in the completion of the house. This is an example of what?

    (A) Mandatory dependencies
    (B) Lag
    (C) External dependencies
    (D) Crashing

20.   The construction project is underway after encountering some initial schedule delays associated with the weather. The team is working on the job site, and the city building inspector shows up and asks for their building permit for the next phase. The Project Manager discovers it wasn't applied for. The city inspector explains it will take a week to process the application after the application is submitted. This is an example of what?

    (A) A city employee not wanting to do his job
    (B) Discretionary dependency
    (C) External dependency
    (D) Mandatory dependency

PMP Exam Success Series: Certification Exam Manual
© 2007 Crosswind Project Management, Inc., www.crosswindpm.com

21.   The defense project is going well. There is a scope change and, as a result, a new team is brought in to assist the existing team in the new scope of the project. Upon arriving, the team asks to see where the project currently stands. What do you show them?

(A) Gantt chart
(B) Milestone chart
(C) Network diagram
(D) Work breakdown structure

22.   Which of the following best describes lag?

(A) Float
(B) The amount of time an activity can be delayed without delaying the project finish date
(C) Slack
(D) A delay inserted between activities

23.   The Project Manager is creating an estimate for a data warehouse. This is something he is quite experienced at. The client needs the estimate quickly. Which of the following types of estimates is he likely to provide?

(A) Analogous
(B) Gut feel
(C) Bottom-up
(D) Parametric

24.   The Project Manager is creating an estimate for building a company WAN (wide area network). It is something that is new to the Project Manager and his team. They decide to create a bottom-up estimate. All the following are advantages of this type of estimate except…

(A) It provides supporting detail of the estimate.
(B) It provides team buy-in when they help create it.
(C) It takes a great amount of time to create.
(D) There is a greater degree of accuracy because of the detail at which it was created.

25.   The e-commerce team is behind schedule on its project. The customer is considering killing the project if it cannot be brought back on track. The team is considering putting more resources on the critical path to accelerate the schedule. This is an example of what?

(A) Crashing
(B) Staff acquisition
(C) Fast tracking
(D) Re-planning

26. The project team is working together on detailed planning. They have had some issues coming to the same opinion on the planning. They are creating a network diagram. What will this show the team?

   (A) The sequencing of the activities on the project
   (B) The decomposition of the work of the project
   (C) The schedule
   (D) The duration estimate of the project

27. You and a fellow Project Manager are having a discussion about his project. He says the network diagram for it has two paths that have the maximum duration of 32 units on the diagram. He says he doesn't have a critical path because they are both the same length, and you can only have one critical path. Which of the following is a true statement?

   (A) You can have more than one critical path, but they are the longest paths on the project, and having more than one critical path increases your project risk.
   (B) The critical path is the shortest path on the project.
   (C) You can have more than one critical path, but they are the longest paths on the project, and having more than one critical path decreases your project risk.
   (D) You can have more than one critical path, but they are the shortest paths not the longest.

28. Float is calculated by which of the following?

   (A) Late finish-early finish (LF-EF)
   (B) Late start-early start (LS-ES)
   (C) Late finish-late start (LF-LS)
   (D) A and B

29. Calculate the PERT estimate for the following: Pessimistic=12, Optimistic=2, Realistic=5.

   (A) 5.67
   (B) 5
   (C) 6
   (D) Not enough information

30. A dummy is used in which of the following network diagram techniques?

   (A) Activity-on-arrow (AOA)
   (B) GERT
   (C) Activity-on-node (AON)
   (D) Gantt chart

8.11 Time Tests and Exercise Answers

8.11.1   Time Network Diagramming Exercises Answers

Exercise - Project A – Moving across the country - Answers

Activity A: Get bids on moving company

Activity B: Choose a moving company

Activity C: Go through belongings and decide what to keep and what to sell/give away (This will help ensure that you select a moving company capable of the scope of the job)

Activity D: Prepare for and do a yard sale for unwanted items

Activity E: Give away unwanted items not sold in yard sale

Activity F: Inventory remaining items

Activity G: Pack remaining items

Activity H: Move

Activity	Preceding Activities	Duration in days
A	Start	9
B	A, C	3
C	Start	13
D	C	9
E	D	2
F	E	10
G	F	11
H	B, G	3

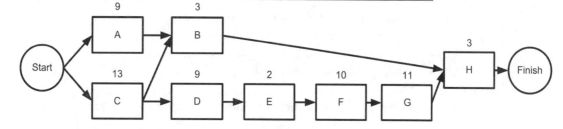

1.   Which path is the critical path and what is its duration?

The paths on the network diagram are as follows.
A+B+H   9+3+3=15
C+B+H   13+3+3=19
C+D+E+F+G+H   13+9+2+10+11+3=48

The critical path is the longest path; thus, C+D+E+F+G+H is the critical path, and the duration is 48.

2.   What is the slack/float for Activity B?

Calculate the slack for Activity B by taking the critical path length and subtracting the duration of the longest path that has Activity B in it. This path is C+B+H and the slack for Activity B is 48-19=29.

3. Which path has the longest (most) slack?

    The shortest path is subtracted from the critical path duration. That is 48-15=33 which is path A+B+H.

4. What is the slack of the path in question 3?

    The shortest path is subtracted from the critical path duration. That is 48-15=33.

5. If Activity B slips from three days to six days, what is the critical path?

    Increasing Activity B by three to six days doesn't change the critical path because there are more than three days of slack between every path with B on it. The critical path is still C+D+E+F+G+H for a total of 48.

6. With the duration adjustment in question 5, what is the new slack of Activity B?

    The new slack for Activity B is 26 days. Calculate it by taking the critical path (48 days) and subtracting from it the revised path of C+B+H (22 days), 48-22=26.

Exercise - Project B - Planning a Vacation - Answers

Activity A: Decide on vacation dates and location
Activity B: Buy airline tickets
Activity C: Make hotel reservation
Activity D: Make car rental reservation
Activity E: Arrange for hold on mail delivery
Activity F: Arrange for hold on newspaper delivery
Activity G: Arrange for pets to be taken care of
Activity H: Pack for trip
Activity I: Depart

Activity	Preceding Activities	Duration in days
A	Start	8
B	A	4
C	A	10
D	B, C	2
E	D	2
F	D	2
G	D	3
H	E, F, G	2
I	H	1

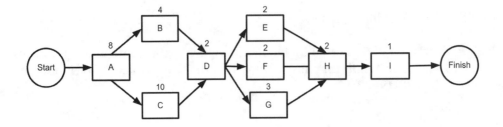

1.   Which path is the critical path and what is its duration?

        The paths on the network diagram are as follows.
        A+B+D+E+H+I = 8+4+2+2+2+1 = 19
        A+B+D+F+H+I = 8+4+2+2+2+1 = 19
        A+B+D+G+H+I = 8+4+2+3+2+1 = 20
        A+C+D+E+H+I = 8+10+2+2+2+1 = 25
        A+C+D+F+H+I = 8+10+2+2+2+1 = 25
        A+C+D+G+H+I = 8+10+2+3+2+1 = 26

        **The critical path is the longest path on the network diagram. That is path
        A+C+D+G+H+I with a total duration of 8+10+2+3+2+1 = 26.**

2.   What is the slack/float for Activity F?

        **To calculate this value, subtract the duration of the longest path with Activity F on it
        from the critical path. That is A+C+D+F+H+I which is 8+10+2+2+2+1 = 25. The total
        is 26 (critical path) - 25 (longest path with Activity F on it) = 1 day of slack.**

3.   What is the slack/float for Activity B?

        **To calculate this value, subtract the duration of the longest path with Activity B on it
        from the critical path. That is A+B+D+G+H+I which is 8+4+2+3+2+1 = 20. The total is
        26 (critical path) - 20 (longest path with Activity B on it) = 6 days of slack.**

4.   If Activity E now takes four days instead of two days, has the critical path changed?

        **Yes. It is now 27 days, where the previous critical path was 26 days. This is because
        Activity E previously had two days of slack and the longest path with Activity E on it
        previously was 25 days in length. If the duration of Activity E increases from two days
        to four days, it overtakes the duration of 26 as the new critical path with the duration of
        27 days.**

5.   Based on the information in question 4, what is the new critical path and what is its duration?

        **The new critical path is A+C+D+E+H+I with a duration calculated by adding
        8+10+2+4+2+1 to equal 27.**

6.   Based on question number 4, what is the slack/float of the path with the longest (most) slack?

        **The slack of the path with the longest slack is 8. Calculate this value by subtracting the
        shortest path from the critical path. The shortest path is A+B+D+F+H+I with duration
        of 8+4+2+2+2+1 = 19. 27 (new critical path)-19 (shortest path on the diagram) = 8.**

7.   If the airline calls and says it has cancelled your flight but has scheduled you on another flight
        that leaves three days later, what is the project slack/float?

        **The slack is -3. This value means that you were behind schedule three days because you
        arrived three days late. There can be negative slack on a network diagram.**

Exercise - Project C – Planning for a Trade Show Event - Answers

Activity Start-A: Reserve booth location
Activity A-B: Develop displays for booth
Activity B-J: Prepare booth displays for shipping
Activity A-C: Develop marketing collateral for booth
Activity C-J: Prepare marketing collateral for shipping
Activity A-D: Develop mailer for customer mailing
Activity D-E: Mail mailer to customers
Activity A-F: Determine booth personnel required
Activity F-G: Confirm booth personnel availability
Activity G-H: Assign personnel to booth schedule
Activity H-I: Obtain company shirts for booth personnel
Activity I-J: Prepare shirts for shipping
Activity J-K: Ship booth displays, marketing collateral, and shirts to show
Activity K-End: Set up trade show booth and attend show

Activity	Duration in days
Start - A	2
A – B	15
A – C	15
A – D	5
D – E	3
E – J	Dummy
A – F	2
F – G	2

Activity	Duration in days
G - H	1
H - I	5
I – J	2
C - J	2
B - J	3
J – K	2
K - End	4

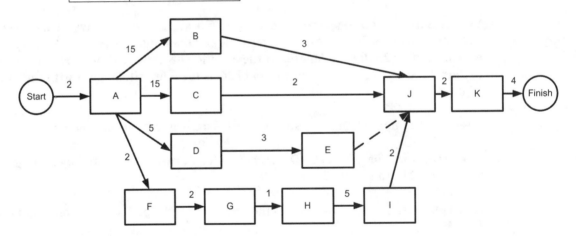

1.   What is the best network diagramming method to use to depict the logic of this project: Activity-on-arrow or activity-on-node?

This is an activity-on-arrow (AOA) diagram. The durations are actually on the arrow instead of on the blocks or squares. Such placement is representative of this type of diagram. Also, the dummy activity (dashed line) between Activity E and J is characteristic of this diagram.

PMP Exam Success Series: Certification Exam Manual
© 2007 Crosswind Project Management, Inc., www.crosswindpm.com

2.   Which path is the critical path and what is its duration?

The paths on the network diagram and their lengths are as follows.
Start-A, A-F,F-G,G-H,H-I,I-J,J-K,K-Finish = 2+2+2+1+5+2=2+4 = 20
Start-A, A-B,B-J, J-K, K-Finish = 2+15+3+2+4 = 26
Start-A, A-C, C-J, J-K, K-Finish = 2+15+2+2+4 = 25
Start-A, A-D, D-E, E-J, J-K, K-Finish = 2+5+3+2+4 = 16

The critical path is the longest path on the network diagram. That is path Start-A, A-B,B-J, J-K, K-Finish with the durations 2+15+3+2+4 for a total of 26 days for the critical path.

3.   What is the slack/float of Activity B-J?

The Activity B-J has 0 slack as it is on the critical path.

4.   What is the slack/float of Activity G-H?

The Activity G-H has slack of 6. Calculate this value by subtracting from the critical path duration (26) the length of the path with Activity G-H (20) on it. 26-20=6.

5.   List all the activities that immediately precede Activity J-K.

Activities, B-J, C-J, I-J are all activities that precede Activity J-K. E-J is a dummy. It is not an activity; therefore, it is not included in as a predecessor activity to Activity J-K.

6.   If the duration of Activity C-J changes to 4, what is the impact on the project?

This change creates a new critical path of Start-A, A-C, C-J, J-K, K-Finish. 2+15+4+2+4 for a new length of 27 days.

8.11.2   Time Quick Test Answers

1. Which of the following shows sequencing of activities on a project?

    Gantt   ⬭Network⬭   ⬭AON⬭   ⬭AOA⬭   ⬭GERT⬭
    Chart   ⬭Diagram⬭   ⬭Diagram⬭   ⬭Diagram⬭   ⬭Diagram⬭
    [section 8.2.2, section 8.2.3]

2. What is the process for eliminating the peaks and valleys of resource utilization and creating consistently level resource utilization?
    Resource leveling [section 8.5.10, section 11.6]

3. Activity-on-node (AON) diagramming is also known as what?

    AOA (activity-on-arrow)
    PDM (precedence diagramming method)
    AOL (activity-on-line)
    ADM (arrow diagramming method)
    [section 8.2.3]

4. What is the typical slack of a critical path?
    Zero (0) [section 8.5.1]

5. What is the type of chart used to communicate high level schedule information to executives?
    Gantt   ⬭Milestone⬭   Network   PERT   GERT
    [section 8.5.12, section 8.8]

6. Which of the following processes puts more resources on the critical path?
    ⬭Crashing⬭   Fast tracking   GERT   PERT
    [section 8.5.8, section 8.8]

7. Which estimating method uses three estimates to create a single estimate?
    GERT   ⬭**PERT**⬭   AON   Critical Path
    [section 8.3.2, section 8.7, section 8.8]

8. Which diagramming technique uses a feedback loop?
    ⬭GERT⬭   PERT   AON   Critical Path
    [section 8.2.3]

9. What is the formula for standard deviation?
    (P-O)/6 (P=Pessimistic, O=Optimistic) [section 8.7, section 10.8.9, section 10.11]

10. What is the act of placing a delay between activities on a network diagram?
    Lag [section 8.2.5, section 8.8]

8.11.3   Time ITTO Matching Exercise Answers

	Inputs	Tools &Techniques	Outputs
Activity Definition	1) Project Scope Statement 2) Work Breakdown Structure 3) Project Management Plan	1) Decomposition 2) Templates 3) Expert Judgment	1) Activity List 2) Milestone List
Summary:	Creating activity lists to complete work packages		
Activity Sequencing	1) Project Scope Statement 2) Activity List 3) Milestone List	1) Precedence Diagramming Method (PDM) 2) Arrow Diagramming Method (ADM) 3) Schedule Network Templates 4) Dependency Determination 5) Applying Leads and Lags	1) Project Schedule Network Diagrams 2) Activity List (Updates)
Summary:	Creating the network diagram for the project		
Activity Resource Estimating	1) Activity List 2) Resource Availability 3) Project Management Plan	1) Expert Judgment 2) Project Management Software 3) Bottom-Up Estimating	1) Activity Resource Requirements 2) Resource Breakdown Structure 3) Resource Calendars (Updates)
Summary:	Determining what resources are needed for the project		
Activity Duration Estimating	1) Project Scope Statement 2) Activity List 3) Activity Resource Requirements 4) Resource Calendars 5) Project Management Plan (Risk Register) 6) Project Management Plan (Activity Cost Estimates)	1) Expert Judgment 2) Analogous Estimating 3) Parametric Estimating 4) Three-Point Estimates 5) Reserve Analysis	1) Activity Duration Estimates
Summary:	Determining how long the activities on the project should take to complete		
Schedule Development	1) Project Scope Statement 2) Activity List 3) Activity Resource Requirements 4) Project Schedule Network Diagrams 5) Resource Calendars 6) Activity Duration Estimates 7) Project Management Plan (Risk Register)	1) Schedule Network Analysis 2) Critical Path Method 3) Schedule Compression 4) Resource Leveling 5) Project Management Software 6) Applying Calendars 7) Adjusting Leads and Lags	1) Project Schedule 2) Schedule Baseline 3) Resource Requirements (Updates) 4) Project Calendar (Updates) 5) Schedule Management Plan (Updates)
Summary:	Creation of the project schedule		
Schedule Control	1) Schedule Management Plan 2) Schedule Baseline 3) Performance Reports 4) Approved Change Requests	1) Progress Reporting 2) Schedule Change Control System 3) Performance Measurements 4) Project Management Software 5) Variance Analysis	1) Schedule Baseline (Updates) 2) Performance Measurements 3) Requested Changes
Summary:	Activities associated with updating and controlling the schedule		

8.11.4   Time Terminology Matching Exercise Answers

Matching Exercise #1 Answers

#	Term	Definition
1	Activity Definition	D. The identification of appropriate activities to complete the project deliverable
2	Activity Sequencing	I. The process of determining and documenting the logical relationships between activities on the project
3	Bar Chart (Tool)	N. A chart that shows a time relationship between the activities of the project; also commonly called a Gantt chart
4	Critical Path	F. The series of activities that shows the overall duration of the project; can change as the project evolves
5	Dependency	A. A relationship between activities represented in the way activities are sequenced
6	Duration	O. The overall amount of time on a project or activity
7	Early Finish Date (EF)	Q. The earliest time an activity can finish based on the network logic
8	Early Start Date (ES)	H. The earliest time an activity can start based on the network logic
9	External Dependency	M. A dependency that lies outside the project team
10	Finish-to-Start Dependency (FS)	K. The default dependency type (with most project scheduling software) in which one activity cannot start until the one it is dependent upon finishes (Activity B cannot start until Activity A finishes.)
11	Lag	P. A delay to a successor activity from the predecessor (Ex: Activity A finishes then has a three day wait before Activity B can begin.)
12	Lead	B. Acceleration to a successor from the predecessor (Ex: Activity A finishes. But with a three-day head start, Activity B can begin three days before Activity A finishes.)
13	Merge	J. A coming together (convergence) of activities on a network diagram
14	Network Diagram	R. A schematic of logical relationships that make up the flow of activities on the project; always drawn from left to right
15	Project Time Management	L. The processes associated with an attempt to complete the project on time
16	Schedule Control	C. The process of managing and maintaining (controlling) changes to the schedule
17	Slack	S. The amount of time an activity can be delayed (slip) without causing a delay to the successor(s) activities, or the final finish date of the project
18	Target Schedule	E. A preliminary schedule that can be used during initial stages of Planning; could differ from the baseline schedule at the conclusion of Planning
19	Total Float (TF)	G. The maximum amount of time an activity can slip from the early start (ES) without causing a delay to the project finish date
20	Work Breakdown Structure (WBS)	T. An organized breakdown of the total work scope of the project, with each level of descent providing a greater level of detail and the deliverable being a key focus

Matching Exercise #2 Answers

#	Term	Definition
1	Activity	N. A piece of the project that must be completed (performed); sometimes called a "task"; can be divided into activities; typically has an assigned resource, cost amount, and expected duration
2	Activity List (Output/Input)	Q. A detailed list of activities that project team members use to know what work on the project they are responsible for completing
3	Crashing	S. A duration compression technique in which more people are added to critical path activities to shorten the duration of the critical path or other impacted areas of the schedule
4	Dummy Activities	B. A zero duration activity used in the arrow diagramming method (ADM) to show a logical relationship represented graphically with an arrow having a dashed line

PMP Exam Success Series: Certification Exam Manual
© 2007 Crosswind Project Management, Inc., www.crosswindpm.com

5	Effort	H. The amount of labor needed to complete an activity or work package; typically measured in hours, days or weeks
6	Finish-to-Finish Dependency (FF)	P. A dependency used on project scheduling in which one activity cannot finish until the activity it is dependent upon finishes (Activity B cannot finish until Activity A finishes)
7	Forward Pass	I. A network diagram technique that calculates the early start and early finish dates for each activity
8	Free Slack	C. The amount of time an activity can be delayed without causing slippage (delay) to the early start of any subsequent activities
9	Late Finish Date (LF)	M. The latest time an activity can be finished without delaying the project finish date
10	Mandatory Dependency (Hard Logic)	E. A required dependency on a project; cannot be ignored (Ex: You must pour the foundation of a house before you can begin framing it.)
11	Network Logic	L. The connecting of activities on the network diagram to establish the structure of the network diagram
12	Path Divergence	D. A burst on the network diagram where the output of an activity goes to more than one activity
13	Resource Calendars	K. A calendar in the project management plan and schedule that shows working and non-working days
14	Schedule	A. The planned dates, sequencing, resources, and durations for activities and milestones on a project
15	Schedule Development	R. The process of using activity sequences, duration estimates, and resources to create the schedule
16	Start-to-Finish Dependency (SF)	G. A dependency used on project scheduling in which one activity cannot finish until the activity it is dependent on starts (Ex: Activity B cannot finish until Activity A starts)
17	Successor	J. An activity that follows an activity logically connected to it
18	Target Start Date (TS)	O. The planned start date of the project or activity
19	Task	T. An activity to be completed on the project
20	Work Package	F. A component of work or a deliverable at the smallest level of the work breakdown structure

Matching Exercise # 3 Answers

Term		Definition
1	Activity Duration Estimating	E. The process of estimating the number of work periods (hours, days, weeks) to accomplish the activity
2	Activity-on-Arrow (AOA)	N. A network diagramming method in which activities are shown on arrows and connected at nodes to show the sequence of activities
3	Backward Pass	B. A network diagramming method that calculates the late start and late finish dates for each activity
4	Critical Chain Method (Technique)	I. A schedule technique used to evaluate the amount of float on the network paths; used to determine the minimum overall duration of the diagram
5	Critical Path Method (CPM)	P. A network analysis method used to calculate total project duration
6	Discretionary Dependency (Soft Logic)	D. A dependency in which the Project Manager (or other decision maker) can choose to allow it to be a dependency or not, depending upon the needs of the project. (Ex: Buying a plane ticket before booking a hotel reservation)
7	Estimate (Output/Input)	J. A logical, educated prediction of some project component; typically includes a tolerance of accuracy
8	Fast Tracking	Q. A schedule compression technique in which the main focus is to find activities that can be done in parallel and to adjust the activity sequences to reflect that
9	Gantt Chart	L. The horizontal bar chart used in project management to show a time relationship between activities
10	Logical Relationship	G. A logical relationship between two or more components of a project schedule

11	Milestone	R. A major achievement on a project; usually occurs after a series of activities leading up to its completion; has zero-days duration and could be related to a "deliverable"
12	PERT Weighted Average	H. An estimating technique used to take the pessimistic, optimistic, and realistic (most likely) estimates to achieve a cumulative estimate
13	Precedence Diagramming Method (PDM)	A. A network diagramming process in which activities are represented in boxes
14	Rolling Wave Planning (Technique)	M. A progressive elaboration approach to managing a schedule where the initial phases are defined at a level with the remaining work at a high level As the initial phases are done, the remaining phases are planned.
15	Schedule Compression (Technique)	O. The process of shorting the project schedule without modifying the scope of the project (Ex: crashing and fast tracking)
16	Schedule Milestone	F. A major event in the project schedule; typically involves the start or completion of a major component of the project
17	Summary Activity	K. An activity that sums up the detailed activities underneath it; typically used to evaluate work packages and facilitate executive reporting
18	Target Finish Date (TF)	C. The date that the project (or activity) is anticipated to be completed

Matching Exercise #4 Answers

Term		Definition
1	Activity-on-Node (AON)	E. A network diagramming method in which activities are shown on the boxes or circles of the network diagram and connected via arrows
2	Burst	F. The separation (or divergence) of activities on a network diagram from a central node
3	Master Schedule (Tool)	D. A high level schedule which displays summary information associated with activities, deliverables, milestones, and WBS components
4.	Milestone Schedule	I. A high level schedule which displays summary information associated with activities and milestones
5	Network Path	G. A non-stop series of activities from the start to the finish of the network diagram
6	Project Network Diagram	C. A view of the logical relationship (sequencing) or project activity
7	Start-to-Start Dependency (SS)	K. A dependency used on project scheduling in which one activity cannot start until the activity it is dependent on starts (Activity B cannot start until Activity A starts.)
8	Sub-Network	H. A section of a network diagram; can be associated with a work package or some other type of logical decomposition
9	Target Completion Date (TC)	B. A requested project completion date that can be a constraint for the project
10	Total Slack	J. The amount of time an activity can slip (be delayed) from its early start date without delaying the overall finish date
11	Work Performance Information (Output/Input)	A. Data associated with the completion of work on the project; can include deliverable status, actions associated with preventative and corrective measures, and change requests
12	Activity Resource Estimating	L. Determination of resources (people, material, equipment) needed for a project, including the determination of when (or how much of) the resources are needed

PMP Exam Success Series: Certification Exam Manual
© 2007 Crosswind Project Management, Inc., www.crosswindpm.com

8.11.5   Time Practice Test Answers

1.   Calculate the variance for the following: Pessimistic=12, Optimistic=2, Realistic=5.

   Correct Answer: (B) 2.79
   Explanation: The formula for variance is Pessimistic-Optimistic divided by 6, squared. The answer is 2.79.
   [section 8.7]

2.   Crosswind Custom Homes is building a customer's dream house. However, rain has delayed the finish by two weeks. The Project Manager evaluates the schedule and determines that the electrical and plumbing work could occur at the same time instead of right after each other as laid out in the schedule. This is an example of what?

   Correct Answer: (D) Fast tracking
   Explanation: Fast tracking re-sequences activities on the network diagram to attain compression of the schedule. Crashing puts more resources on the critical path. Mandatory dependencies involve a required predecessor before something can begin. Lag is a delay between activities on the network diagram. [section 8.5.8, section 8.8]

3.   Which of the following is an example of a lag?

   Correct Answer: (C) A delay after the sheetrock (wall board) is done in a house to allow it to dry before continuing work in that area
   Explanation: A delay after the sheetrock is done to allow it to dry before continuing work in that area is an example of a lag. The delay is not part of either activity but happens between the activities. The other answers are noise. [section 8.2.5, section 8.8]

4.   Which of the following is a predecessor type of Activity-on-Arrow (AOA) diagrams?

   Correct Answer: (B) Finish-to-Start (FS)
   Explanation: Activity-on-arrow (AOA) diagramming uses the (FS) finish-to-start predecessor. The other answers work ONLY within the AON (activity-on-node) or PDM (precedence diagramming method). [section 8.2.3, section 8.2.4, section 8.8]

5.   You are putting together the final schedule on your new project. The problem you are having is that you don't have a consistent usage of your resources. Some are working 12 hours a day, some 4 hours a day, and there are some days when they aren't scheduled to work at all on the schedule. Which of the following below fixes this problem?

   Correct Answer: (A) Resource leveling
   Explanation: Resource leveling takes peaks and valleys and levels them off for a consistent utilization of resources. Fast tracking and crashing are schedule compression techniques; those techniques solve a different type of problem. "PERT analysis" is noise. [section 8.5.10]

6.   Crosswind Custom Homes is building a customer's dream house. However, rain has delayed the finish by two weeks. The schedule shows that the next activity is to install the roof, then that is followed by the shingles. This is an example of what?

   Correct Answer: (A) Mandatory dependencies
   Explanation: A mandatory dependency is required and internal to the organization. The external dependency is a dependency that is out of the control of the internal organization. Crashing and lag are noise. [section 8.2.1]

7. Crosswind Custom Homes is building a customer's dream house. However, rain has delayed the finish by two weeks. The Project Manager is evaluating various ways to compress the schedule. The Project Manager suspects that the electrical and plumbing work could occur at the same time instead of right after each other as laid out in the schedule. However, local zoning laws do not allow this concurrent work. This is an example of what?

    Correct Answer: (D) External dependencies
    Explanation: An external dependency is that which is at the determination of something outside of the control of the Project Manager and team. A mandatory dependency is required and internal to the organization. The other answers are noise. [section 8.2.1, section 8.8]

8. Calculate the standard deviation for the following: Pessimistic=12, Optimistic=2, Realistic=5.

    Correct Answer: (B) 1.67
    Explanation: The formula for standard deviation is Pessimistic-Optimistic divided by 6. The answer is 1.67. [section 8.7, section 10.8.9, section 10.11]

9. The Project Manager is creating an estimate for building a house. It is a house similar to what he builds quite often. He is using the rule of thumb of $85 per square foot to calculate the estimate. What type of estimate is this?

    Correct Answer: (A) Parametric
    Explanation: The parametric estimate uses a parameter of an amount per unit. In this case, $85 per square foot is the parameter. The analogous estimate is a top-down estimate. The bottom-up estimate is the detailed estimate created by the team. "Gut feel" is noise. [section 8.3.2]

10. The e-commerce project is six weeks behind schedule with five team members working on it. Three of these team members are working on the critical path-related items. What is the slack of the critical path?

    Correct Answer: (A) Negative six weeks
    Explanation: Technically, a critical path has a slack of zero. If the project is truly behind schedule, and the baseline date is still being used as the reference, the project could actually have negative slack on the critical path. In this case, the negative slack is six weeks. [section 8.5.3]

11. The development team is building a new product for their company. This is a new product type at their company, and the market for the product is extremely unstable. According to the product manager, a key to success is the flexibility to adapt the product to the market changes that will occur during development. Which scheduling type best fits this need?

    Correct Answer: (A) Rolling wave planning
    Explanation: In an environment where there is a great degree of flexibility or instability, it's good to use a rolling wave planning approach. This approach allows the team to plan out as much as reasonably possible, and as they execute that part of the plan, they continue to plan future work while they are learning more about it. Crashing puts more resources on critical path activities. Fast tracking re-sequences already defined activities to compress the overall duration of the schedule. Precedence diagramming is a network diagramming technique. [section 8.1, section 8.8]

12. The e-commerce team is behind schedule on its project. The customer is considering killing the project if it cannot be brought back on track. The team is considering re-sequencing the critical path areas on the network diagram to shorten the length of the schedule. This is an example of what?

Correct Answer: (C) Fast tracking
Explanation: Fast tracking is re-sequencing the critical path activities to achieve schedule compression. Crashing is the process of putting more resources on critical items. Staff acquisition doesn't fit here. "Re-planning" is noise. [section 8.5.8, section 8.8]

13. The development team is building a new product for its company. This is a new product type at the company, and the market for the product is extremely unstable. According to the product manager, a key to success is an extremely accurate estimate on the resource needs for the project, because the company is resource-constrained. Which type of duration estimating approach is the most accurate?

Correct Answer (A) Bottom-up estimating
Explanation: Bottom-up estimating is time-consuming because its input comes from the lowest level of the work details. It creates a very exhaustive, time-consuming, and accurate estimate from those details and rolls them up into a total overall estimate. Parametric estimating uses a parameter such as $5.00 a square yard for material. Fast tracking re-sequences already defined activities to compress the overall duration of the schedule. Analogous estimating creates a relatively quick, high level estimate. [section 8.3.2]

14. You are the Project Manager on a defense project and are creating a network diagram. Activity A (3 days) and Activity B (6 days) can start immediately. Activity C (2 days) can start after Activity A is complete. Activity D (1 day) and Activity F (2 days) can start after Activity B is complete. Activity E (4 days) can start after Activity C and Activity D are complete. Activity G (5 days) can start after Activity D and Activity F are complete. When Activity E and Activity G are complete, the project is done. What is the critical path?

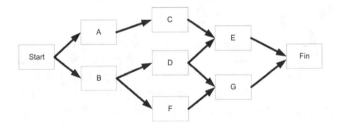

Correct Answer: (C) BFG
Explanation: The critical path is the longest path in the diagram. Of the four paths, BFG is the longest at 13 days. ACE is nine days long. BDE is 11 days. BDG is 12 days. [section 8.5.4]

15. Using the original network diagram question, what is the slack of Activity D?

Correct Answer: (B) One day
Explanation: The longest path with Activity D on it is path BDG with a duration of 12 days. The critical path of BFG is 13 days. Subtracting the length of BDG from the critical path (13-12) shows a difference of one day. This is the slack of Activity D. [section 8.5.6, section 8.7]

16.   In the original network diagram question, if Activity D increases from one to three days, what is the critical path, and what is the length?

Correct Answer: (D) BDG, 14 days

Explanation: By increasing Activity D from one day to three days the path BDG increases to fourteen days. This is the longest of the paths on the network diagram. [section 8.5.4]

17.   Slack on a network diagram is also known as...

Correct Answer: (C) Float

Explanation: Slack and float are interchangeable terminology. Lag is a delay between activities on a network diagram. GERT and PERT are noise. [section 8.5.2, section 8.8]

18.   The defense project is progressing well. The Air Force Major who is the executive sponsor gets promoted and moves to a new base. His replacement is brought in from a new area and, upon arrival, asks to see where the project currently stands. Which of the following do you show him?

Correct Answer: (D) Milestone chart

Explanation: The milestone chart is used for executive reporting. The Gantt chart shows the people doing the work where the project is working to the plan. The network diagram shows the sequencing of activities on the project. The work breakdown structure (WBS) shows the work that is in the project. [section 8.5.12]

19.   Crosswind Custom Homes is building a customer's dream house. However, the city inspector for building permits has been in training for the last two weeks and has no backup. This inspection delay causes a delay in the completion of the house. This is an example of what?

Correct Answer: (C) External dependencies

Explanation: The external dependency is a dependency that is outside the control of the internal organization. Mandatory dependency is required but internal to the organization. Crashing and lag are noise. [section 8.2.1, section 8.8]

20.   The construction project is underway after encountering some initial schedule delays associated with the weather. The team is working on the job site, and the city building inspector shows up and asks for their building permit for the next phase. The Project Manager discovers it wasn't applied for. The city inspector explains it will take a week to process the application after the application is submitted. This is an example of what?

Correct Answer: (C) External dependency

Explanation: The external dependency is a factor outside the organization's control. The building inspector fits this criterion. The mandatory dependency is required and internal to the project. The discretionary dependency is at the option of the Project Manager and team. The city employee answer is noise. [section 8.2.1, section 8.8]

21.   The defense project is going well. There is a scope change and, as a result, a new team is brought in to assist the existing team in the new scope of the project. Upon arriving, the team asks to see where the project currently stands. What do you show them?

Correct Answer: (A) Gantt chart

Explanation: The Gantt chart shows the people doing the work where the project is in relation to the plan. The milestone chart is used for executive reporting. The network diagram shows the sequencing of activities on the project. The work breakdown structure (WBS) shows the work that is in the project. [section 8.5.11]

22.   Which of the following best describes lag?

Correct Answer: (D) A delay inserted between activities
Explanation: Lag is a delay between activities on a network diagram. An example is allowing a two-day delay after texturing a wall before painting it. This delay allows the wall texture to dry, but the drying time isn't a part of either activity. The other answers are associated with slack. [section 8.2.5, section 8.8]

23.   The Project Manager is creating an estimate for a data warehouse. This is something he is quite experienced at. The client needs the estimate quickly. Which of the following types of estimates is he likely to provide?

Correct Answer: (A) Analogous
Explanation: The analogous estimate is also considered a top-down estimate. It can be quickly created because it is based on expert knowledge of an area from previous projects. Parametric is an estimating technique that uses parameters, such as so much time per unit. A bottom-up estimate is created by the team and can take time to create because of the details. "Gut feel" is noise. [section 8.3.2]

24.   The Project Manager is creating an estimate for building a company WAN (wide area network). It is something that is new to the Project Manager and his team. They decide to create a bottom-up estimate. All the following are advantages of this type of estimate except…

Correct Answer: (C) It takes a great amount of time to create
Explanation: All the answers are characteristic of the bottom-up estimate. Taking a great amount of time to create is not an advantage of the estimate. [section 8.3.2]

25.   The e-commerce team is behind schedule on its project. The customer is considering killing the project if it cannot be brought back on track. The team is considering putting more resources on the critical path to accelerate the schedule. This is an example of what?

Correct Answer: (A) Crashing
Explanation: Crashing is the process of putting more resources on the critical items. Fast tracking is re-sequencing critical path activities to achieve schedule compression. Staff acquisition doesn't fit here. "Re-planning" is noise. [section 8.5.8, section 8.8]

26.   The project team is working together on detailed planning. They have had some issues coming to the same opinion on the planning. They are creating a network diagram. What will this show the team?

Correct Answer: (A) The sequencing of the activities on the project
Explanation: The network diagram shows the sequencing of the activities on the project. The work breakdown structure (WBS) shows the decomposition of the work of the project. The duration estimate of the project comes from the schedule. [section 8.2.2, section 8.8]

27.   You and a fellow Project Manager are having a discussion about his project. He says the network diagram for it has two paths that have the maximum duration of 32 units on the diagram. He says he doesn't have a critical path because they are both the same length, and you can only have one critical path. Which of the following is a true statement?

Correct Answer: (A) You can have more than one critical path, but they are the longest paths on the project, and having more than one critical path increases your project risk.
Explanation: The critical path is the longest path on the project. If you have more than one path of identical length, you have multiple critical paths. The more of them you have, the riskier the project is. [section 8.5.3]

28.   Float is calculated by which of the following?

(A) Late finish-early finish (LF-EF)
(B) Late start-early start (LS-ES)

Correct Answer: (D) A and B
Explanation: Float is calculated by subtracting either the early finish (EF) from the late finish (LF), or the early start (ES) from the late start (LS). [section 8.7, 8.5.7]

29.   Calculate the PERT estimate for the following: Pessimistic=12, Optimistic=2, Realistic=5.

Correct Answer: (A) 5.67
Explanation: The PERT formula is (Pessimistic + Optimistic+ (4*Realistic)) divided by 6. The answer is 5.67. [section 8.3.2, section 8.7]

30.   A dummy is used in which of the following network diagram techniques?

Correct Answer: (A) Activity-on-arrow (AOA)
Explanation: The dummy is used in an activity-on-arrow (AOA) diagram. Activity-on-node (AON) doesn't use dummies. GERT and Gantt chart are noise. [section 8.2.3, section 8.8]

PMP Exam Success Series: Certification Exam Manual
© 2007 Crosswind Project Management, Inc., www.crosswindpm.com

Chapter 9

Cost

The Cost Knowledge Area typically intimidates many people going into it. One misperception is that you must be an accountant to become a PMP. This is not true. Although you must perform some basic calculations, you face nothing too extreme. In addition, much of what looks as though it might require calculation -- such as project selection techniques -- usually requires that you simply recognize which option makes the most financial sense. There are, however, some basic financial terms and concepts you should be familiar with. We have listed these at the front of the chapter, before we describe any processes that could potentially use them.

The earned value part of this chapter is not small compared to that in the *PMBOK Guide*. Along with providing various memorization tools in this chapter, we present the information in such a way that the material helps eliminate any confusion arising from other products that try to explain earned value. If you work through our memorization area, as well as the three exercises and the ten project earned value analysis exercises, you should have a solid understanding of the concepts and principles. As for algebra, a quick review can always help. The calculation rules for formulas are as follows:

Rule 1: First, perform any calculations inside parentheses.
Rule 2: Next, perform all multiplications and divisions, working from left to right.
Rule 3: Finally, perform all additions and subtractions, working from left to right.

In this chapter, we discuss the following:

Process Group	Process Name		Main Outputs
Planning	Cost **E**stimating	→	Activity Cost Estimates
			Cost Management Plan (Updates)
	Cost **B**udgeting	→	Cost Baseline
Monitoring and Controlling	Cost **C**ontrols	→	Performance Measurements
			Forecasted Completion

A memory tool for the process names is "**E**very**b**ody **C**ares."

☑   **Crosswind "Must Knows" For Cost**

	Key Inputs, Tools & Techniques, and Outputs for Cost Estimating
	Key Inputs, Tools & Techniques, and Outputs for Cost Budgeting
	Key Inputs, Tools & Techniques, and Outputs for Cost Control
	Cost range concept in this chapter
	Earned value management table in this chapter
	What standard depreciation and accelerated depreciation are
	Characteristics of actual cost (AC), earned value (EV), planned value (PV), and budget at completion (BAC)

	Characteristics and formulas for cost variance (CV), cost performance index (CPI), to complete performance index (TCPI), schedule variance (SV), schedule performance index (SPI), estimate at completion (EAC), estimate to complete (ETC), and variance at completion (VAC)
	How to recognize and differentiate the cost types: variable direct, variable indirect, fixed direct, and fixed indirect
	Understand and know how to calculate the benefit cost ratio (BCR)
	Principles of the payback period with project investment
	Principles of sunk cost
	Principles of life cycle costing
	Principles of opportunity cost
	What net present value (NPV), internal rate of return (IRR), Return on Investment (ROI), BCR, and other financial measurement methods represent and how they are used in project selection

Although helpful, this list is not all-inclusive for information needed from this area for the exam. It is only suggested material that, if understood and memorized, may increase your exam score.

9.1   Types of Cost

There are four types of cost on a project: direct, indirect, fixed, and variable. You may combine them, mixing direct or indirect with fixed or variable (such as fixed direct cost).

Business school teaches that costs we can forecast consistently each month are fixed costs, and those we can't are variable. THIS IS NOT THE CASE with project management. In project management, remember that a **fixed cost is something that we pay for once and can use many times; whereas, a variable cost is something that we have to pay per use.**

Some people get bogged down in details when studying this area because they look at when projects can incur cost and if the materials are used after the project. Look at the basics of the situation for what it is and don't necessarily read too much into it. Remember (for example), rent for a company is rent, an indirect cost; buying a computer for a project is a fixed direct cost. How they are calculated and when they hit the project in reality can differ from company to company.

Direct Cost	Direct cost is directly attributable to the project and **spent only on project work.** An example is: servers used for a software project.	Understand these types of cost well enough to recognize them on the exam.
Indirect Cost	Indirect cost is cost **needed for a project but not restricted to it;** it could be used by other projects as well. Such a cost could be rent or electricity for the building where work on the project is performed. It is likely that there are other groups or activities benefiting from such items, and your project pays its part as well.	Learn how to recognize and differentiate between the cost types variable direct, variable indirect, fixed direct and fixed indirect.
Fixed Cost	Fixed cost is cost that is **consistent on a project regardless of how many are used.** Creating a book cover for a large quantity of books is a good example. In this case, you pay once to have the cover created, regardless of the number of books you printed it on.	
Variable Cost	Variable cost is one that **fluctuates with what is produced.** The more of something you produce, the more of this type of cost you incur. An example is: the cost of printing each copy of a book. The more you print, the greater your cost.	

PMP Exam Success Series: Certification Exam Manual
© 2007 Crosswind Project Management, Inc., www.crosswindpm.com

9.2   Cost-Based Project Selection Techniques

There are many project selection techniques you can apply to help ensure that your organization makes prudent selection decisions. While the selection methods in this section are financial, to become a PMP does not require that you be an accountant or perform a multitude of calculations.

Project Selection Technique Name	Also Known As	Option to Select	Example
Return on Investment	ROI	The biggest number or percentage	$50,000 or 7%
Internal Rate of Return	IRR	The biggest percentage	15.50%
Net Present Value	NPV	The biggest number (Years are already factored in.)	$47,500
Benefit Cost Ratio	BCR	The biggest ratio	3.5:1
Opportunity Cost		The amounts that are not selected	You choose Project A ($7,000) over Project B ($5,000). The opportunity cost is $5,000 to select Project A.
Payback Period		The shortest duration	7 months

This table gives you shortcuts for memorization.

Technique	Discussion	
Return on Investment (ROI)	Return on investment is a general term. You may calculate it various ways. Typically, you choose the **biggest number** or **percentage** among the projects under consideration.	
Internal Rate of Return (IRR)	Often used in capital budgeting, interest rate makes the **net present value of all cash flow equal zero**. In the case of IRR and project selection, **select the larger number**.	Know what internal rate of return (IRR) represents and how it is used in project selection.
Net Present Value (NPV)	Net present value is used in capital budgeting, in which the present value of cash inflows is subtracted from the present value of cash outflows. NPV **compares the value of a dollar today versus the value of that same dollar in the future, after taking inflation and return into account.** Although it's unlikely the exam will ask you to calculate this value, you should know how to select a project using it. For example, with Project A having an NPV of $150,000 and six months or Project B having an NPV of $295,000 and a year, you select Project B because it has **the bigger number** AND the **years are already factored into the dollar amount**.	Know what net present value (NPV) represents and how it is used in project selection.

	Generally, this value focuses on income and expenses over time. If the expenses include capital acquisitions, capital **COULD** be included in NPV functionality.	
Benefit Cost Ratio (BCR)	Benefit cost ratio is a project selection and analysis technique that compares the **benefit** to the **cost** of the initiative. The format is 3.65:1, meaning that the benefits of the project outweigh the costs 3.65 to 1. Some exam questions could ask about profit in this area. That is noise. **The benefit, cost, and ratio between them are the main components.** For example, a project could have a BCR of less than 1 (0.75:1), meaning that it had a benefit of 75 cents for each dollar invested. Typically, you don't approve such projects unless there were some underlying factors such as Y2K issues. **Be prepared to calculate a BCR.** For example: $200,000 in revenue and $50,000 of cost have a BCR of 4:1. This ratio is attained by dividing revenue by cost and applying the quotient to 1.	Understand and know how to calculate the benefit cost ratio (BCR).
Opportunity Cost	**Opportunity cost is associated with taking another opportunity.** It is what you give up, or leave on the table to take the other opportunity. For example, if you take a $75,000 a year job over a $60,000 a year job, then the opportunity cost of taking the $75,000 job is $60,000.	Know the principles of opportunity cost.
Payback Period	Payback period is the **amount of time needed** to earn back the original investment on the project. PMI suggests that you select the project with the **shortest payback period.**	Know the principles of the payback period.

9.3   Future Value (FV)

Future value is the value of something such as cash or an investment at a specific point in the future. For example, if you had $1,000 now and could get 8% interest, what is the future value?

Don't expect to calculate this value. Focus on the concept of the time value of money such as: To produce the desired amount in the future, would a future amount at a certain interest rate require more or less money than that amount now? The exam could present something that looks like a calculation, so be sure all the formula components are there, if not "not enough information" is the best option. The formula is shown below with PV = present value, r = interest rate, n = number of periods, and FV = future value.

$$FV = PV * (1+r)^n \qquad \text{For example, } \$1,000 * (1+0.08)^3 = \$1,259.71$$

9.4   Present Value (PV)

Present value is the value of something today that you need to create a certain amount of investment in the future. Here's an example: if you wanted to have $2,500 in three years, what amount of money do you need today to produce this amount if the money was earning 8%?

The PMP Examination isn't the CPA exam so don't expect to calculate this value on the exam. Instead, recognize the concept, such as: Would you need more or less than a future amount now to have that amount in the future? You could also have something that looks like a calculation, but be sure all the components of the formula are there. If not, then "not enough information" is the best option. The formula is shown below with PV = present value, r = interest rate, N = number of periods, and FV = future value.

$$PV = \frac{FV}{(1+r)^n} \quad \text{For example,} \quad \frac{\$2{,}500}{(1+0.08)^3} = \$1{,}984.58$$

NOTE: PMI uses PV to represent Present Value and Planned Value. If you are measuring an investment, Present Value is used. If you are measuring the amount of work that should have been done at a point of time on the project (with Earned Value Management), Planned Value is used.

9.5   Expected Present Value (EPV)

Expected present value (EPV) is a present value analysis that takes into consideration the risk of the opportunity being considered. This calculation involves considering and weighting many potential outcomes. For example, a 40% chance of making $10,000 and a 60% chance of making $2,000 would create an expected cash flow of $5,200. Although there are various ways EPV could be calculated, a common way would be to multiply dollar amount by likelihood and add the outcomes similar to expected monetary value (in the Risk chapter).

9.6   Sunk Cost

Sunk cost is a cost that has already been spent on a project. **Do not consider sunk cost when making future project decisions.** Here's an example: If a project has a budget of $175,000 and has already spent $200,000, you would not consider the $200,000 when deciding whether to continue on the project or not.

Know the principles of sunk cost.

9.7   Depreciation

Depreciation is the process of devaluing a capital asset in the tax system. Capital assets are those that are purchased and depreciated over time. Examples of capital include office equipment, vehicles, and technology infrastructure. In using depreciation over a period of time (schedule), an asset's worth decreases until it has no value or a predefined value at the end of its depreciation schedule. Generally, calculating depreciation is complicated, involving tables, formulas, and more.

Although you will not be asked to do any complex calculations in this area on the exam, you need to know what standard depreciation and accelerated depreciation are, as well as how to calculate a basic depreciation situation.

Know what standard depreciation and accelerated depreciation are.

9.7.1   Standard Depreciation

Standard depreciation is performed with basic division. There are three things to know about something before you can depreciate it: They are:
- What is the start value or purchase price?
- What is the scrap value?
- What is the depreciation timeframe?

For example, a $5,000 video editing system has a five-year depreciation schedule with a scrap value of $0. $5,000/5 years means that the video editing system depreciates at $1,000 per year.

Another standard depreciation scenario could be a situation in which the scrap value is not equal to zero ($0), meaning you would not depreciate the full amount. For example, you purchased a copier for $10,000. Its worth is $2,000 after full depreciation over four years. The amount depreciated over the four years is the difference: $8,000, with yearly depreciation being $2,000.

9.7.2   Accelerated Depreciation

Accelerated depreciation is a little more complex and generally requires tables of data to calculate.

For the exam, you must know that there are two main types used. They are:

- Sum of the year's digits
- Double declining balance (DDB)

Accelerated depreciation does what its name implies; it **depreciates faster than standard depreciation.**

9.8   Life Cycle Costing

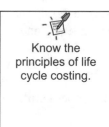

Know the principles of life cycle costing.

Life cycle costing (sometimes called TCO or Total Cost of Ownership) is the process of examining all costs associated with a project and its product once it goes into production. Without this focus, you could potentially create an environment that causes your company to incur additional cost associated with the product after it goes to production.

By taking production and the post project life into account, you can determine that your strategy to build the project might differ. Such an approach can result in an increase in project cost but a savings in operation cost, which saves the company money in the long run.

Here's an example: A vendor wants to charge your company $50,000 to create a prototype of something then charge $2,000 per item after that. The $50,000 might be higher than you prefer or had forecasted. You find another vendor that has a lower upfront cost but charges $4,000 per item. By selecting the vendor with the higher upfront cost, but lower unit cost, you can easily calculate that you would actually recognize a cost savings after the production of only 25 devices. There is even a greater cost savings when purchasing additional devices, as shown below.

	25 Devices	**30 Devices**
Vendor A	25*($2,000) + $50,000 = $100,000	30*($2,000) + $50,000 = $110,000
Vendor B	25*($4,000) = $100,000	30*($4,000) = $120,000

9.9   Earned Value Rules (Fixed Formula Progress Reporting)

Earned value rules (sometimes called **fixed formula progress reporting**) is a technique that creates a consistent status report for project activities. Instead of having the "gut feel" of a percent completion from each person on a project, this type of reporting is essentially binary. The project Planning process defines the split of the percentages (Ex: 25%/75%, or 50%/50%).

This process works as follows: When an activity starts, it receives the initial percentage (Ex: 25%). It receives the remaining percentage (Ex: 75%) only when the activity is complete, thereby reporting 100% complete to the activity. Then, as the summary activities are rolled up to create cumulative percentages, they are based on the (as an example) 0%, 25%, or 100% status of each activity.

This formula can be used for earned value management (EVM) or other less evolved means of capturing the schedule status. Typically, it is used on shorter duration activities or those generally **not exceeding two reporting periods**.

9.10   Weighted Milestone

The weighted milestone approach is utilized for activities or activities that typically are **longer than two reporting periods**. In this case, the work is divided into multiple milestones with a measurable output for each section of work.

9.11   Cost Estimating (Planning Process Group)

Know the Key Inputs, Tools & Techniques, and Outputs for Cost Estimating.

The Cost Estimating process is key because the accuracy of cost estimates directly impacts the likelihood that a project comes in on budget. In Cost Estimating, you focus on establishing the costs of either the work packages or the activities to help establish a total project cost.

There are a number of Cost Estimating methods you can use to establish the Activity Cost Estimates. They are as follows:

- Analogous (compared to a previous project)
- Parametric (parameters around which the estimate is built)
- Bottom-up (where individual items are estimated, then summed for a total cost)
- Computerized tools

Schedule, resources, and risk can influence which of these methods makes the most sense to use, depending on what is known about the project regarding scope.

Cost Estimating (Planning)		
Key Inputs	Project Scope Statement	The project scope statement helps **define the project**. Supporting detail provides the in-depth research and planning that the project scope statement rolls into.
	Work Breakdown Structure	Work breakdown structure (WBS) provides the **breakdown of the project and allows cost to be estimated** from it.
	Project Management Plan • Schedule Management Plan • Staffing Management Plan • Risk Register	The schedule management plan (from the project management plan) and the schedule component of it provide the **basis of the time involved with the various resources on the project to help create the cost estimates** for the project.
		The staffing management plan (from the project management plan) provides **staffing rates and other variables to help create project cost estimates**.
		The risk register (from the project management plan) is a piece of the project management plan that **contains information associated with what risks could occur** on a project, potential responses for those risks, their root causes, and risk categorization. It expands as risk management processes are further implemented.

Key Tools & Techniques	Analogous Estimating	Analogous estimating **requires expert judgment** and is created by an expert or group of experts, not just an executive pulling a number from the air. It is a **high level estimate**, not a detailed estimate. Quantitatively based duration estimates are used also, and can include program evaluation review techniques (PERT) estimation, as well as other math-based models.
	Determine Resource Cost Rates	Determine resource cost rates **establishes the cost of the resources** used on the project.
	Bottom-Up Estimating	Bottom-up estimating is used when the team and Project Manager **create an estimate from the activity (task) level and roll the estimates up to create a total project estimate**.
	Parametric Estimating	Parametric estimation is an estimating technique that **uses a quantitative approach based on the quantity of work and the productivity rate** per unit of work.
	Project Management Software	Project management software such as scheduling, cost, or estimating software can be **helpful in organizing all the pieces that make up the schedule and other pieces of the PMI processes**.
	Vendor Bid Analysis	If project work uses a **competitive bidding** process, the team may be involved in vendor bid analysis to **determine deliverable pricing or other contract requirements**.
	Cost of Quality	The cost of quality is factored in to **create the project cost estimates**. It includes the cost of conformance and non-conformance to quality.
	Reserve Analysis	Reserve analysis is used when a team wants to **plan for known unknowns (contingency reserves). It adds extra time or money to the estimates** from a work units or percentage estimate.
Key Outputs	Activity Cost Estimates	Activity cost estimates **provide the cost of the resources to complete the activities** of the project. These are typically measured in dollars, euros, or other forms of currency, although hours or days could be used as well.
	Requested Changes	Requested changes are **changes that have been requested but not yet formally approved** by the official change control process on the project.
	Cost Management Plan (Updates)	The cost management plan (which was created in the Develop Project Management Plan process) is **updated as more information is discovered regarding the cost baseline and the management approach for the project cost**. This plan can help define the precision level of the cost, units of measure (hours, dollars, etc.), how the organization's procedures are connected to each other (such as the WBS and control accounts), the control thresholds for managing variance, earned value rules, formats for reporting and process descriptions. The cost management plan that is established in the Develop Project Management Plan process helps define criteria associated with the planning, estimating, budgeting, and controlling of cost on the project.

Situational Question and Real World Application
If you fail to consider and complete, or if you totally ignore your cost estimates, your project could be terminated due to a funding shortfall. You could see your project terminated if subsequent cost analysis showed that it was operating at a loss or under an unacceptable profit margin. Also, your project could face delays because the company performing the work was unsure about the funding it needed to obtain all the resources necessary to carry out a project and complete it in a timely fashion.

9.11.1   Cost Management Plan

The cost management plan helps the Project Manager and team do the following:

- Establish the cost of activities and work packages on the project
- Establish the cost accounts and chart of accounts with the WBS and Schedule
- Establish policies associated with updating the budget and distribution of the budget through the work of the project
- Update actual costs and adjust the cost baseline
- Deal with cost changes

9.12   Cost Range

Cost range tolerance varies from company to company. A key principle in any environment is that the less that is known (earlier in the project), the wider the tolerance of the cost range should be compared to when more is known (later in the project), when the range is minimized.

The table that follows shows existing PMI standards in this area. To align with the new *PMBOK Guide*, you need to know that in **initiating a tolerance range for a rough order of magnitude (ROM) estimate could be -50% to +100%**, and as the project work gains momentum into **Executing, the tolerance could narrow to -10% to +15%.** Although the *PMBOK Guide* does not provide a term for this estimate, it could be considered a "**definitive** estimate" or "**control** estimate."

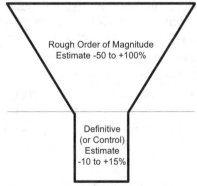

Figure 9-1: Cost Funnel

Use Figure 9-1: Cost Funnel to get a feel for how these two estimates come into the project. At the top of the funnel, the estimate has the widest tolerance with the rough order of magnitude estimate. The final definitive (or control) estimate has the least tolerance.

If a project had a $100,000 estimate (assuming it didn't change as it went through the estimating process), the rough order of magnitude tolerance is $50,000 to $200,000. The definitive (or control) estimate tolerance is $90,000 to $115,000.

The table that follows shows the range of estimates from previous *PMBOK Guide* that is good to be familiar with as well. The table shows the names and process areas in which they occur. A memory tool for the estimate names and process groups are "**O**h **B**oy **D**ave **I**t's **P**epperoni **P**izza."

Cost Range Table

Estimate Name	Process Group	Tolerance Range
Order of Magnitude	Initiating	-25% to +75%
Budget	Planning	-10% to +25%
Definitive	Planning	-5% to +10%

Understand the Cost Range Table.

Know the Key Inputs, Tools & Techniques, and Outputs for Cost Budgeting.

9.13 Cost Budgeting (Planning Process Group)

In Cost Budgeting, the primary activity is rolling up the cost estimates for the activities and work packages to create a total project budget amount that will serve as the cost baseline. At this point, you have a detailed estimate of what the project will cost, as well as its individual pieces. The cost baseline created at this point should include a time-based approach to help determine project cost needs as time passes. It establishes the basis for measuring, monitoring, and controlling project cost.

Cost Budgeting (Planning)		
Key Inputs	Project Scope Statement	The project scope statement **helps define the project**. Supporting detail provides the in-depth research and planning that the project scope statement rolls into.
	Work Breakdown Structure	Work breakdown structure (WBS) provides the **breakdown of the work** of the project to allow the application of cost elements to the work packages defined in the work breakdown structure (WBS).
	WBS Dictionary	The WBS dictionary is a result of the Create WBS process. It **compliments the WBS** by documenting the work packages, control accounts, listing the organizations responsible for completion of the work among other things.
	Activity Cost Estimates	Activity cost estimates provide the **cost of resources** to complete project activities.
	Project Schedule	Project schedule allows viewing of the **project timeline to show when cost is expected** to hit the project.
	Resource Calendars	Resource calendars **show the availability of the resources** that are being utilized on the project.
	Contract	If work is done for an outside party, a contract is needed **between buyer and seller**.
	Cost Management Plan	Cost management plan helps you determine **how to manage project cost**.

Key Tools & Techniques	Cost Aggregation	Cost aggregation is done to **roll up the project cost** starting with the activity level task to work packages and finally for a total project cost.
	Reserve Analysis	Reserve analysis is used when a team wants to **plan for known unknowns (contingency reserves). It adds extra time or money to the estimates** from a work unit or percentage estimate.
	Parametric Estimating	Parametric estimation is an estimating technique that **uses a quantitative approach based on the quantity of work and the productivity rate** per unit of work.
	Funding Limit Reconciliation	In funding limit reconciliation, **actual spending is balanced with the preset funding limits**, often defined by the customer.
Key Outputs	Cost Baseline	Cost baseline is the **cost estimate that the project planning team puts in place to work the details of the project to**. This value is the number (or numbers if it's broken down throughout the project) that the pieces of work are estimated to cost for a total project cost.
	Requested Changes	Requested changes are **changes that have been requested but not yet formally approved** by the official change control process on the project.
	Cost Management Plan (Updates)	The cost management plan (which was created in the Develop Project Management Plan process) is **updated as more information is discovered regarding the cost baseline and the management approach for the project cost**. This plan can help define the precision level of the cost, units of measure (hours, dollars, etc.), how the organization's procedures are connected to each other (such as the WBS and control accounts), the control thresholds for managing variance, earned value rules, formats for reporting and process descriptions. The cost management plan that is established in the Develop Project Management Plan process helps define criteria associated with the planning, estimating, budgeting, and controlling of cost on the project.

Situational Question and Real World Application
If you do not complete or you ignore Cost Budgeting, your project could encounter a multitude of problems. By failing to have estimates of what the individual activity or work should cost to complete, you could face cost overruns. As you attempt to clarify cost, your project could suffer delay because equipment or materials are not yet acquired for the project.

9.13.1   Chart of Accounts

A chart of accounts is a list of accounts used by the accounting and/or project management system of the company doing the project to establish and track budgets associated with work packages, projects, and other efforts that require defining a cost baseline and tracking actual cost against it. The Cost Budgeting process uses the chart of accounts to show where funds are allocated for the estimated work.

9.14 Cost Control (Monitoring and Controlling Process Group)

Know the Key Inputs, Tools & Techniques, and Outputs for Cost Control.

Cost Control focuses on how to control any project budget changes. Cost Control tools can include a cost change control system, earned value management (EVM) (see this chapter for details), and computerized tools. Cost Control can involve influencing and managing changes related to cost, managing cost levels compared to the baseline, analyzing and managing cost variance, documenting cost records, and communicating with stakeholders about cost issues.

Cost Control (Monitoring and Controlling)		
Key Inputs	Cost Baseline	Cost baseline provides the **overall cost standard** that the project is trying to achieve. It could be viewed as the budget.
	Performance Reports	Performance reports serve as the communication vehicle to show **how the project is performing** compared to what should be accomplished. The difference between the two is a variance.
	Work Performance Information	Work performance information provides a **status on what has been completed** (or not completed) on the project.
	Approved Change Requests	Approved change requests are **changes that have been formally approved** by the official change control process on the project.
Key Tools & Techniques	Cost Change Control System	Cost change control system is the system **used to evaluate change requests as they relate to cost** and to process the approval of those requests.
	Performance Measurement Analysis	Performance measurement analysis is the **act of measuring what is happening on the project and comparing it to what should be happening** on the project.
	Forecasting	Forecasting creates **estimates for future project performance** based on information presently available. This can include earned value technique measurements estimate at completion and estimate to complete.
	Project Performance Reviews	Project performance reviews **compare project cost performance (earned value) to what should be done (planned value)** on the project. This comparison could also be measured in work packages or milestones. The three main types of project performance reviews are variance analysis, trend analysis, and earned value technique.
	Project Management Software	Project management software includes **applications** such as scheduling software, spreadsheets, and enterprise reporting systems. They can be **used to track earned value data or what-if scenarios** when you are forecasting future activities.
Key Outputs	{Activity} Cost Estimates (Updates)	Cost estimates updates may be **needed if schedule activity cost estimates change**.
	Cost Baseline (Updates)	The cost baseline is **updated when there is a cost modification** that has been through a change approval process.

Key Outputs (cont.)	Performance Measurements	Performance measurements associated with earned value technique including cost performance index (CPI), schedule performance index (SPI), cost variance (CV), and schedule variance (SV) are **used with work packages to communicate project status**.
	Forecasted Completion	Forecasted completion is **communicated to the appropriate stakeholder via calculation of the estimate at completion (EAC) and estimate to complete (ETC)**.
	Requested Changes	Requested changes are **changes that have been requested but not yet formally approved** by the official change control process on the project.

Situational Question and Real World Application
Changes to the plan are inevitable on a project of any size. The lack of a Cost Control option could slow down project completion because time is spent trying to figure out what to do to eliminate any cost overruns or account for under runs.

9.14.1   Earned Value Management

Earned value management is a technique that integrates **scope, time,** and **cost** into a quantifiable reporting method for project status reporting of actual performance, compared to the baseline estimate. It communicates project status via key metrics, including performance indices, variance, and estimates associated with the completion of the project. It allows a Project Manager to see how the project is performing in relation to spending (cost) and activity completion (time). Some of the evolved changes in earned value for the new exam material involve cumulative measurements versus period(s) of time.

Regarding format, this new material may be confusing with regard to what to use where. A typical way to see a cumulative measurement is in a total time frame, such as "to date" or "through day 5" on the project. Non-cumulative measurements could be for a time period or periods such as a particular day or days.

Pay attention to the question though, because there is no guarantee that you will be asked for a cumulative measurement specifically. It could be implied, such as being given some data then asked: "What is the total earned value on the project?" or "What is the earned value on the project?" The key here is that because the question doesn't ask for the earned value over a specific period, it implies that it wants to know the total earned value, which is the cumulative earned value.

9.14.2   Earned Value Management Relationships

(See later in this chapter for descriptions of the acronyms below.) Let's evaluate how someone might have viewed project status before earned value management. For example, you were the Project Manager for a project that was 10 months long. Being five months into the project does not necessarily mean that you are at a halfway point. The question still is how much work do you have done (BCWP or EV) compared to what you should have done (BCWS or PV).

In another example, you had spent $5,000 on a $10,000 project. Does that mean you are halfway done with the project? Not necessarily because you don't know how much (or what the value of the) work (BCWP or EV) is actually completed to compare to what you paid (ACWP or AC) for the work.

The key that's missing in both of these situations is the earned value (EV or

BCWP). Just knowing how much you spent (ACWP or AC) and how much work you should have done (BCWS or PV) isn't enough to know where the project really stands thus, you need earned value management.

The description in the previous section is the "textbook" answer for earned value management. Now, let's apply Crosswind **Realistics®** to it. Earned value management deals with relationships between three pieces of data, then various relationships from there, depending on what questions need to be answered. The three pieces of data are described in Figure 9-2: Earned Value Analysis, but let's look at the interactions between the data as well. **See the table that follows this figure for descriptions of the acronyms in parenthesis.**

Would you agree that it's useful to know the difference between the amount of work (based on the budgeted value of the work) that is actually done (BCWP or EV) and the amount of work that should be done (BCWS or PV)? Yes, that relationship tells us the state of the schedule. It compares what we have done (BCWP or EV) to what we should have done (BCWS or PV). Later, we use this comparison to calculate the rate of progress on the schedule (SPI or schedule performance index) and difference of the amount of money (work) that we are ahead or behind schedule (SV or Schedule Variance).

Would you agree that it's useful to know the difference between the amount of work actually done (BCWP or EV) and the amount of money actually paid for the work to date (ACWP or AC)? Yes, that relationship tells us the state of the budget. This state is used to examine the spending efficiency (CPI or cost performance index) and the difference of the amount of money that we are over or under budget.

One key assumption that is very critical to success is establishing the cost baseline. If we can't say how much a particular activity or work package is worth by establishing the cost baseline, it is impossible to accurately perform earned value management because the earned value measurement cannot be accurately calculated.

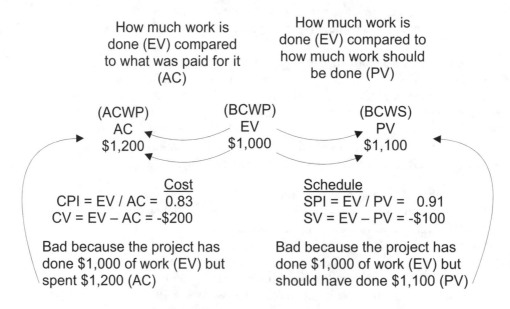

Figure 9-2: Earned Value Analysis

PMP Exam Success Series: Certification Exam Manual
© 2007 Crosswind Project Management, Inc., www.crosswindpm.com

9.14.3   Earned Value Management Data and S Curve

Data

Actual Cost (AC or ACWP)	What you have spent at a point in time or to date; **includes cost accrued ahead of schedule** This cost is the **sum of all costs to date** on the project. It is also known as **actual cost of work performed (ACWP)** from the 1996 *PMBOK Guide*.	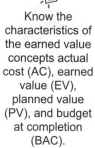 Know the characteristics of the earned value concepts actual cost (AC), earned value (EV), planned value (PV), and budget at completion (BAC).
Earned Value (EV or BCWP)	The value of the completed project work at a point in time or to date; what you have to show for the effort; **includes effort accomplished ahead of schedule** **This value is the percent complete of the activities (or project) multiplied by the planned value of the activities (or project)**, then the addition of the product of the various multiplications. It is also known as **budgeted cost of work performed (BCWP)** from the 1996 *PMBOK Guide*. **If you do not have percent complete detail for the individual activities** but for the project only, **multiply the percent complete of the project by the budget (BAC) of the project.** For example, a $10,000 project that is 40% complete has an earned value measurement of $4,000.	
Planned Value (PV or BCWS)	The value of the work you should have done (or spent) at a point in time or to date; **does not include any work started ahead of schedule** This value is the sum of the planned value of all activities (or relative percentage) through the point in time being measured. It is also known as **budgeted cost of work scheduled (BCWS)** from the 1996 *PMBOK Guide*. The planned value for an activity could also be considered the budget for the activity.	
Actual Cost of Work Scheduled (ACWS):	**WARNING:** This phrase doesn't apply to earned value. It is used as noise. If you see it on the test, do not select it because it is not a valid answer.	
Budget at Completion (BAC):	The total cost expected to be spent on the project. This value can be **calculated by adding all the planned values (PV) on the project**.	

S Curve

An S curve can be used to graphically display data related to earned value management (EVM). Figure 9-3: S Curve shows the interaction between the three main variables associated with EVM and how they interact over the life of the project. The point in time for measuring varies as a project evolves and can be used to show the state of the schedule, the budget, and project work already completed.

S Curve For Project Performance Measurement with Earned Value

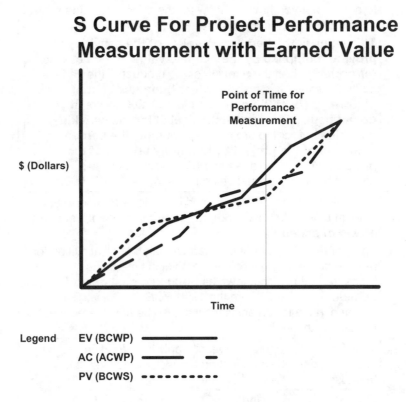

Figure 9-3: S Curve

Indices

Schedule Performance Index (SPI):	Measures progress at a percent of the rate originally planned. The formula is EV/PV. Be able to calculate EV or PV if given SPI and EV or PV.
Cost Performance Index (CPI):	Measures how many cents of return on each dollar spent based on a single point in time. The formula is EV/AC. Be able to calculate EV or AC if given CPI and EV or AC.
To Complete Performance Index (TCPI):	Represents the efficiency needed from the remaining resources to meet the cost goals of the project. The formula is (BAC-EV)/(BAC-AC) and can be demonstrated as follows: $$TCPI = \frac{\text{(Remaining Work)}}{\text{(Remaining Budget)}}$$ The graphic below shows similarities with the CPI (Cost Performance Index) formula. $$TCPI = \frac{(BAC - EV)}{(BAC - AC)}$$

Know the characteristics and formulas for cost variance (CV), cost performance index (CPI), to complete performance index (TCPI), schedule variance (SV), schedule performance index (SPI), estimate at completion (EAC), estimate to complete (ETC), and variance at completion (VAC).

Variances

Cost Variance (CV):	The difference in dollars between work completed (earned value) and what was spent to complete it (actual cost) The formula is EV-AC. Be able to calculate EV or AC if given CV and EV or AC.
Schedule Variance (SV):	The difference in dollars between work completed (earned value) and what should have been (planned value) The formula is EV-PV. Be able to calculate EV or PV if given SV and EV or PV.
Variance at Completion (VAC):	The difference (or variance) in dollars between the original or revised budget (BAC) and the anticipated completion cost based on the projected completion amount of the project (estimate at completion or EAC) The estimate at completion or EAC is discussed in more detail later in the chapter. The formula is BAC-EAC.

Earned Value Management Table

	Cost			Time		
	AC (ACWP)		EV (BCWP)		PV (BCWS)	
CPI	=	÷	⤶⤷	÷	=	SPI
CV $	=	−	⤶⤷	−	=	SV $

Memorize the earned value management table.

The earned value management table is ideal to memorize because it deals with the calculation of (cost or schedule) variances or performance indices. To read it, start with EV and follow the arrows. For example EV divided ($\div$) by PV equals SPI or EV minus AC equals CV.

Here are some keys to memorizing the earned value management table.

Performance Indices (CPI, SPI)	Variances (CV, SV)
Listed first (vertically)	Listed last (vertically)
Calculated by division	Calculated by subtraction
If less than one (<1), project is behind schedule or over budget	If negative, project is behind schedule or over budget
If greater than one (>1), project is ahead of schedule or under budget	If positive, project is ahead of schedule or under budget

NOTE: The AC (ACWP), EV (BCWP), and PV (BCWS) are listed alphabetically (horizontally).

9.14.4   Calculating the Basics of Earned Value Management (EVM)

Although the values for actual cost (AC), earned value (EV), and planned value (PV) are generally provided, you may have to calculate them. The details below describe how to calculate planned value (PV), actual cost (AC) and earned value (EV).

Planned Value (PV or BCWS)	Determine the date or "complete through" level. **Add the planned values of activities that should have happened as of the date or "complete through" level.** Do not add the planned value of activities that have started, that are ahead of schedule. Ex: Today is June 6th, and there are two activities that should not start until June 8th but have already started. If an activity should be partially complete at the point you are measuring, the percent (%) complete will have to be provided or assumed. Ex: A four-day activity is generally considered to be 50% done two days into the work.
Actual Cost (AC or ACWP)	**Add all "actual costs."** Regardless of status of activity (1% to 100%) even if it was started ahead of schedule Any and all costs related to the project
Earned Value (EV or BCWP)	1. List the planned value (PV) of all the following types of activities: • The activities that should have started and haven't started yet • The activities that should have started and have actually started • The activities that shouldn't have started and have (started ahead of schedule) 2. Determine the % complete of each activity listed in step 1. 3. Multiply planned value (PV) by the % complete for each activity, giving the earned value of an individual activity. 4. **Add all the earned value measurements** (calculated in step 3) from each activity to get the total earned value for the project or situation.

PMP Exam Success Series: Certification Exam Manual
© 2007 Crosswind Project Management, Inc., www.crosswindpm.com

Activity Name	Planned Day	Actual Cost($)	Earned Value($)†	% Complete	Planned Value($)
		(AC)	(EV)		(PV)
Activity A	Day 1	$300	$300	100%	$300
Activity B	Day 2	$200	$150	100%	$150
Activity C	Day 2	$150	$100	100%	$100
Activity D	Day 3	$225	$200	100%	$200
Activity E	Day 3	$100	$100	100%	$100
Activity F	Day 3	$300	$150	60%	$250
Activity G	Day 4	$140*	$130*	65%	$200
Activity H	Day 4	$100*	$80*	20%	$400
Activity I	Day 5	$0	$0	0%	$300
Activity J	Day 5	$0	$0	0%	$200

(The line between Activities F and G represents the measuring point for the analysis.)

† PV x % complete

* These activities started ahead of schedule, and the progress must be included.

We can use the example above to perform earned value analysis. The table shows that the project just completed day 3 with the horizontal line.

Budget at Completion	Calculate this figure by totaling the planned values for all the activities. The total budget at completion is $2,200.
Planned Value	To calculate planned value, add up the planned value for each activity through day 3. The total is $1,100 of planned value. This value represents the work that should be complete through day 3, meaning that you should have spent $1,100 through day 3. When looking at planned value in this case, even though some work is ahead of schedule, you should look only at the work that should have been done through day 3.
Actual Cost	Total what you have actually spent to date. This total includes **any and all costs**, even if the work was started ahead of schedule. That is actual cost, and it is $1,515.
Earned Value	Earned value is the planned value of each activity (**regardless if it should have started yet or not**) multiplied by the percentage complete (%). This value provides the earned value (EV) for each activity. The next step is to add the earned value (EV) of each activity for the total earned value (EV) for the project. This value represents the budgeted cost of work performed (BCWP) or earned value (EV), and it is $1,210.
Translation	Translation means that through day 3, you should have spent $1,100, and Activities A through F should be complete. You have spent $1,515 but have an earned value (the work to show for what you have spent) of only $1,210.

Using the earned value management table previously in this chapter, notice that the project has the following metrics:

CPI:	0.8	=	$1,210/$1,515	CV:	-$305	=	$1,210-$1,515
SPI:	1.1	=	$1,210/$1,100	SV:	$110	=	$1,210-$1,100

The CPI shows that the project is getting an 80-cent value for every dollar spent, with a CV that shows it is presently $305 over budget. The SPI shows that the project is progressing at 110% of that rate planned and has accomplished $110 more in work than was scheduled. The project is ahead of schedule but over budget.

9.14.5   Forecasts

Cost Forecast	Description	Formula
Estimate at Completion (EAC)	The estimate at completion (EAC) represents the current projected final cost based on the current spending efficiency (CPI). If you have a CPI greater than one (>1), the number will be less than the BAC, meaning that the project will likely finish under budget. If you have a CPI of less than one (<1), the number will be greater than the BAC, meaning that the project will finish over budget. If the CPI equals 1, the project will finish on budget. **EAC:** $2,750 (This is on pace to come in over the BAC of $2,200 in our example on the previous pages.)	BAC/CPI
Estimate to Complete (ETC)	The estimate to complete (ETC represents the amount needed to finish the project based on the current spending efficiency of the project.) This figure is the EAC without the actual cost to date. **ETC:** $1,235 (It is on pace to exceed the BAC amount when factoring in what has already been spent in our example in the previous pages.)	EAC-AC
Variance at Completion (VAC)	The variance at completion (VAC) is the difference between the budget at completion (BAC) and the estimate at completion (EAC). This difference tells how much over or under budget the project finished. Using the sample data above, we see the following values with EAC, ETC, and VAC. **VAC:** -$550 (This figure is the projected over budget amount, based on the current spending efficiency of the project in our example on the previous pages.)	BAC-EAC

The following Earned Value Forecast Table shows the three formulas above set up as a tic-tac-toe table. You can map out where the variables go in the table and see that EAC makes a diagonal line. Use this table as a quick reference for the PMI certification exam.

Earned Value Forecast Table

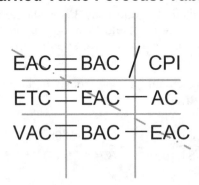

$$EAC = BAC / CPI$$
$$ETC = EAC - AC$$
$$VAC = BAC - EAC$$

PMP Exam Success Series: Certification Exam Manual
© 2007 Crosswind Project Management, Inc., www.crosswindpm.com

Consider the following as a scenario to express the EVM values on a project level:

Your project is to build a sunroom on a house in five (5) days. The cost is $2,000 per day. The project is currently 40% complete. It is now the end of day 3 and you have spent $5,000.	
AC (Sum of Actual Costs)	$5,000
EV (% Complete of Project)	$4,000
PV (Value of Scheduled Work)	$6,000
BAC (Total Budget)	$10,000
CPI (EV/AC)	0.8
CV (EV-AC)	-$1,000
SPI (EV/PV)	0.667
SV (EV-PV)	-$2,000
EAC (BAC/CPI)	$12,500
ETC (EAC-AC)	$7,500
VAC (BAC-EAC)	-$2,500
TCPI (Rem. Wk./Rem. $)	1.2

9.14.6   Cumulative Earned Value

Although the *PMBOK Guide Third Edition* describes the terms cumulative earned value, actual cost, and other associated variables, the PMI errata update for the *PMBOK Guide* has removed them. Because they may once again be incorporated into future *PMBOK Guide* text, exam material, or both, we have retained them as valid terms to consider.

9.15   Cost Formulas and Variables

Description	Formula	Variable (Component)	Example
Actual Cost (AC) represents the current amount actually spent on the project or during a particular time period.	The addition of actual expenses to date, or during a particular time period on the project	AC (ACWP)	AC = $5,000
Earned Value (EV) represents the current amount of work (product) completed during a particular time period, regardless of cost or time.	The percent complete of each activity multiplied by the planned value (PV) of the activity during a particular time period	EV (BCWP)	EV = $ 4,500 or EV = $4,500=$9,000 X 50% Complete
Planned Value (PV) represents the current amount that should have been spent on the project during a particular time period.	The addition of all work that should have been completed to date or during a particular time period on the project	PV (BCWS)	PV = $ 5,500

Description	Formula	Variable (Component)	Example
Budget at Completion (BAC) represents the total budget projected for the project. Also is the sum of all planned value (PV).	The total amount originally (or approved revision) expected to be spent on the project	BAC	BAC = $10,000
Cumulative Actual Cost (AC^C) represents the current amount actually spent on the project.	Total Actual Project Cost to Date	AC^C	AC^C = $5,000
Cumulative Earned Value (EV^C)	Total earned value cost to date	EV^C	EV^C = $4,500
Cost Performance Index (CPI) represents the current efficiency of spending on the project. Less than 1.0 is bad, greater than 1.0 is good, and 1.0 is on track.	CPI = EV/AC	CPI = cost performance index	CPI = 1.0 (on track 1 dollar spent, 1 dollar value) CPI = 0.8 (over budget 1 dollar spent, 0.80 cents value) CPI = 1.2 (under budget 1 dollar spent, 1.2 dollars value)
Cumulative Cost Performance Index (CPI^C) represents a potentially more accurate CPI (as described above) because it focuses on multiple reporting periods instead of just the more recent period.	$CPI^C = EV^C/AC^C$	CPI^C = Cumulative CPI	CPI^C = 1.0 (On track 1 dollar spent, one dollar value) CPI^C = 0.8 (Over budget 1 dollar spent, 0.80 cents value) CPI^C = 1.2 (Under budget 1 dollar spent, 1.2 dollars value)
Cost Variance (CV) represents the difference between what you have accomplished and what you have spent.	CV = EV-AC	CV = Cost Variance	CV = -$500 (spent more than allocated) CV = 0 (spent as planned) CV = $500 (spent less than allocated)
Schedule Performance Index (SPI) represents the current efficiency of progress on the project. Less than 1.0 is bad; greater than 1.0 is good; 1.0 is on track.	SPI = EV/PV	SPI = schedule performance index	SPI = 1.0 (On track and progressing as it should) SPI = 0.8 (Behind schedule, only progressing at 80% of planned) SPI = 1.2 (Ahead of schedule, progressing at 120% of planned)
Schedule Variance (SV) represents the difference between what you have accomplished and what it should have taken to do it.	SV = EV-PV	SV = schedule variance	SV = -$500 (took more time than allocated) SV = 0 (time as planned) SV = $500 (took less time than allocated)

PMP Exam Success Series: Certification Exam Manual
© 2007 Crosswind Project Management, Inc., www.crosswindpm.com

Description	Formula	Variable (Component)	Example
To Complete Performance Index (TCPI) represents the efficiency needed from the remaining resources to meet the cost goals of the project.	$TCPI = \dfrac{(BAC-EV)}{(BAC-AC)}$	TCPI = to complete performance index	TCPI = 1.25 = ($1,000-$500)/($1,000-$600) BAC = $1,000 EV = $500 AC = $600
Estimate at Completion (EAC) represents the current total project cost based on the current efficiency (CPI) of project spending.	$EAC = BAC/CPI$	EAC = estimate at completion	EAC = $50,000 EAC greater than BAC (over budget) EAC less than BAC (under budget)
Estimate to Complete (ETC) represents the current total project cost REMAINING to be spent, based on the current efficiency (CPI) of project spending.	$ETC = EAC-AC$	ETC = estimate to completion	ETC = $40,000
Variance at Completion (VAC) represents the difference between the BAC and EAC.	$VAC = BAC-EAC$	VAC = variance at completion	VAC = $32,500
Present Value (PV) shows the amount of money needed now at the interest rate (r) for a desired future outcome (FV) over a number of periods (n).	$PV = \dfrac{FV}{(1+r)^n}$	(PV) present value	PV = $207.81 if FV = $1,000, r = 8%, n = 10
Future Value (FV) Shows the amount of money in the future at the set interest rate (r) for an amount of money (PV) now over a number of periods (n).	$FV = PV* (1+r)^n$	(FV) future value	FV = $215.89 if PV = $100, r = 8%, n = 10
The **interest rate** of an investment in a project	Provided on the exam	r (interest rate)	r = 8% = 0.08
The **number of periods of time** (months, years, etc.) of investment in a project	Provided on the exam	n (number of periods)	n = 5 years

9.16   Cost Terminology

Term	Description
Actual Cost (AC)	Represents the total costs that have actually been accrued up to a particular point in time; also known as actual cost of work performed (ACWP)
Analogous Estimates (Technique)	Process of using a previous project of similar characteristic (size, cost, scope) to estimate a new project
Baseline	Estimate or plan that the project will try to achieve (cost, scope, time, etc.)
Bottom-Up Estimate	Detailed estimate that usually involves team input As the team builds the pieces of the estimate, they build the total estimate from the bottom up.
Budget	The total amount of money expected to be spent on a project based on the original cost estimates plus any approved changes
Budget at Completion (BAC)	Total project budget; amount of money planned to be spent by the time the project is complete; sum of all planned values
Budgetary Estimate	An estimate used to put money into a company's (or project's) budget
Chart of Accounts (Tool)	A structure used to monitor project cost that usually aligns with a company's accounting system
Code of Accounts (Tool)	A numbering system used in project management to identify pieces of the work breakdown structure
Contingency Reserves	Money included in an estimate that accounts for events which may be somewhat predicted (known unknowns)
Control Account (Tool)	A point where scope, time, budgeted cost, and actual cost come together to measure performance on a project The control account is used at multiple interface points on the project.
Cost Budgeting	Applying the overall cost estimates to the individual work elements to allow for a baseline cost measurement
Cost Control	The process of controlling changes to the budget
Cost Estimating	Estimating (educated consistent process) the cost of people and other resources to complete the project
Cost Management Plan	The document that explains how to handle cost estimations, budgeting, variances, and other cost-related items on the project
Cost Performance Index (CPI)	A ratio that shows the current efficiency of money being spent on the project; Formula: EV/AC A value of one means you are getting out what you put in (which is good); less than one is bad; greater than one is good.
Cost Variance (CV)	The difference between what has been built (EV) and what the cost was to build it (AC); Formula: EV-AC A value of zero (0) means the project is creating what it should for the cost as planned. A negative value means you are over budget; a positive value means you are under budget.
Definitive Estimate	A cost estimate that provides the accurate estimation of the project cost; the final estimate to be used on the project before implementation begins; Tolerance range: -10 to +15%
Direct Cost	Cost that is directly applicable to the project (Ex: test computer for software being created on the project, IC chips, or labor used on the project)
Earned Value (EV)	Represents the value of the work that has actually been accomplished or completed up to a particular point in time; the percent complete of each activity multiplied by the planned value; also known as budgeted cost of work performed (BCWP)
Earned Value Management (EVM)	Earned value management technique that factors in cost (AC) and time (PV) along with what has actually been accomplished (EV) to show the state of the project; produces a quantifiable status of the project instead of a "gut feel" estimate which can be inaccurate and inconsistent
Earned Value Technique (EVT) (Technique)	The technique associated with measuring the amount of completion of a work breakdown structure component, control account or project
Estimate at Completion (EAC)	Represents the projected total estimate, based on the current efficiency (CPI) with which you are spending money on the project; Formula: BAC/CPI

PMP Exam Success Series: Certification Exam Manual
© 2007 Crosswind Project Management, Inc., www.crosswindpm.com

Estimate to Complete (ETC)	Represents the projected total estimate remaining to be spent, based on the current efficiency (CPI) with which you are spending money on the project; Formula: EAC-AC
Indirect Cost	Cost that is not directly accrued on the project (Ex: electricity, taxes, rent)
Internal Rate of Return (IRR)	A project comparison value; represents the discounted rate that zeroes out the net present value (NPV)
Learning Curve Theory	A theory which states that the more of something that is produced, the lower the unit cost of it becomes due to an improvement in efficiency
Life Cycle Costing	Consideration of not just project cost, but total ownership (operations and support) cost of the item created by the project
Management Reserves	Money set aside to account for unpredictable items (unknown unknowns)
Net Present Value (NPV)	A value used in capital budgeting, in which the present value of cash inflow is subtracted from the present value of cash outflows; compares the value of a dollar today versus the value of that same dollar in the future, after taking inflation and return into account
Opportunity Cost	The cost associated with giving up one opportunity for another (Ex: Project A $50K, Project B $75K. If you select Project B, it has an opportunity cost of the total of Project A, which is $50K.)
Parametric Modeling	Application of a mathematical model used to estimate project components (time, cost, scope) by having other variables entered into the application
Planned Value (PV)	Represents the total costs that should have been spent up to a particular point in time; also known as budgeted cost of work scheduled (BCWS)
Profit	Money made after expenses have been subtracted from revenue
Profit Margin	Ratio between revenues and profit on a project, product, or initiative
Project Cost Management	Processes used to complete the project within the approved budget
Reserves	Money set aside in a budget used for items that are difficult to predict
Rough Order of Magnitude (ROM) Estimate	Very early cost estimate used to give a rough estimate of what the project will cost to complete: Tolerance range: -50% to +100%.
Schedule Performance Index (SPI)	Ratio of earned value and planned value that can be used to calculate how a project is progressing
Schedule Variance (SV)	The difference between what has been built (EV) and the time it should take to build it (PV); Formula: EV-PV A value of zero (0) means the project is creating what it should in the planned timeframe. A negative value means that it is taking longer than planned on the project to complete activities.
Sunk Cost	Money that has already been spent on a project; should not be considered when selecting or evaluating a project
Tangible Cost/Benefit	Easily measurable cost or benefit of a project; measured in dollars

9.17   Cost Mind Map

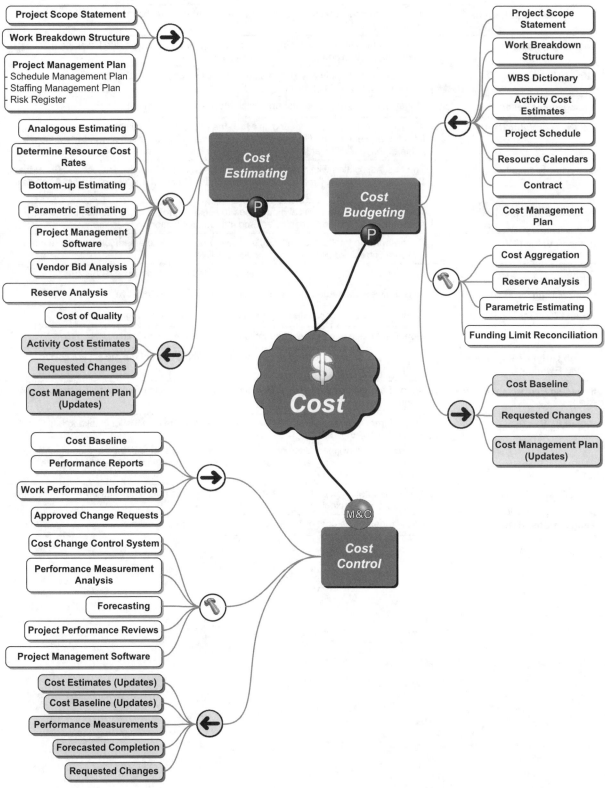

PMP Exam Success Series: Certification Exam Manual
© 2007 Crosswind Project Management, Inc., www.crosswindpm.com

9.18   Cost Tests and Exercises

9.18.1   Cost Quick Test

In this quiz, answer the question in a short essay of only a sentence or two or circle all correct answers for the question. Note that some questions may have more than one answer. Answers are in section 9.19.1.

1.   What shows how the project is progressing?

SPI (schedule performance index)   CPI (cost performance index)
CV (cost variance)   SV (schedule variance)

2.   What shows how the cost efficiency of the project is going?

SPI (schedule performance index)   CPI (cost performance index)
CV (cost variance)   SV (schedule variance)

3.   What shows the money remaining to be spent on the project?

VAC (variance at completion)   BAC (budget at completion)
ETC (estimate to completion)   EAC (estimate at completion)

4.   What shows the cost spent to date on the project?

AC (actual cost)   EV (earned value)
PV (planned value)   BAC (budget at completion)

5.   What is the name of the work accomplished to date on the project?

AC (actual cost)   EV (earned value)
PV (planned value)   BAC (budget at completion)

6.   What is the name of the original cost estimate for the project?

AC (actual cost)   EV (earned value)
PV (planned value)   BAC (budget at completion)

7.   Project A=$67,000 and Project B=$72,000. What is the opportunity cost of taking Project B?

8.   Project A has an NPV of $67,000 over three years and Project B has an NPV of $135,000 over six years. Which do you choose?

9.   What amount per year will a $15,000 item with a five-year shelf life depreciate at using straight depreciation (non-accelerated)?

10.   If you want a future amount of $10,000 in three years at 6.75% interest, do you need more or less than that amount now to get it in that time?

9.18.2 Cost ITTO Matching Exercise

Match the correct ITTO term at the bottom of the page with the blanks to the right of the process. When a term is used multiple times, it is flagged by a parenthetical value indicating the number of times used. Also, match summary sentences with the process name that fits. Answers are in section 9.19.2.

	Inputs	Tools &Techniques	Outputs
Cost Estimating	1) _____ 2) _____ 3) _____ 4) _____ 5) _____	1) _____ 2) _____ 3) _____ 4) _____ 5) _____ 6) _____ 7) _____ 8) _____	1) _____ 2) _____ 3) _____

Summary:

	Inputs	Tools &Techniques	Outputs
Cost Budgeting	1) _____ 2) _____ 3) _____ 4) _____ 5) _____ 6) _____ 7) _____ 8) _____	1) _____ 2) _____ 3) _____ 4) _____	1) _____ 2) _____ 3) _____

Summary:

	Inputs	Tools &Techniques	Outputs
Cost Control	1) _____ 2) _____ 3) _____ 4) _____	1) _____ 2) _____ 3) _____ 4) _____ 5) _____	1) _____ 2) _____ 3) _____ 4) _____ 5) _____

Summary:

Applying costs to individual activities   Determining overall project costs
Activities associated with monitoring and controlling project cost

Activity Cost Estimates (2)	Determine Resource Cost Rates	Project Schedule
Analogous Estimating	Forecasted Completion	Project Scope Statement (2)
Approved Change Requests	Forecasting	Requested Changes (3)
Bottom-Up Estimating	Funding Limit Reconciliation	Reserve Analysis (2)
Contract	Parametric Estimating (2)	Resource Calendars
Cost Aggregation	Performance Measurement Analysis	Vendor Bid Analysis
Cost Baseline (2)	Performance Measurements	WBS Dictionary
Cost Baseline (Updates)	Performance Reports	Work Breakdown Structure (2)
Cost Change Control System	Project Management Plan (Risk Register)	Work Performance Information
Cost Estimate (Updates)	Project Management Plan (Schedule Management Plan)	
Cost Management Plan	Project Management Plan (Staffing Management Plan)	
Cost of Quality	Project Management Software (2)	
Cost Mgt. Plan (Updates) (2)	Project Performance Reviews	

9.18.3   Project Selection Exercises
Complete the following table using project selection techniques from earlier in this chapter. Answers are in section 9.19.3.

Type of Measurement	Project A	Project B	Choice
IRR	14%	22%	
NPV	$10K over 12 months	$5K over 6 months	
Payback Period	4 months	12 months	
BCR	3.02:1	.68:1	
ROI	5%	12%	

9.18.4   Cost Type Exercises
Complete the following table by placing an X in the cells that describe the type of cost for the item. Select either direct or indirect **AND** fixed or variable for each. Example: direct AND variable. Answers are in section 9.19.4.

Item	Direct Cost	Indirect Cost	Fixed Cost	Variable Cost
Rent for the company building				
Parts to be used in the manufacturing process				
Setting up a book press to create 5000 books				
Cleaning supplies for the office				
Renting a suite for the post project party				
Training for each member of the team to use new software for the project				
Company-wide software licensing fees				

9.18.5　Earned Value Exercises

Complete the following table using the formulas associated with this chapter. Describe the status of each of the 10 projects below (behind or ahead of schedule, over budget, or under budget). Calculate anything with a dollar value to the nearest cent (Ex: $456.32) and anything else to three digits (Ex: 1.024). Recommendation: Use a basic calculator or your calculations could have rounding variance. Answers are in section 9.19.5.

#	AC	EV	PV	BAC	CPI	CV	SPI	SV	EAC	ETC
1	$500	$450	$525	$1,000						
2	$400	$395	$395	$500						
3	$1,000	$900	$1,000	$1,500						
4	$600	$590	$600	$800						
5	$800	$750	$750	$2,000						
6	$350	$325	$330	$2,000						
7	$500	$505	$550	$600						
8	$200	$175	$180	$350						
9	$450	$515	$520	$3,000						
10	$700	$650	$695	$950						

Describe the status of the above projects as behind or ahead of schedule, and over or under budget.

1.

2.

3.

4.

5.

6.

7.

8.

9.

10.

9.18.6   Situational Earned Value Exercises

Answers are in section 9.19.6.

Earned Value Exercise #1

You are managing a project to build a product. The project has seven activities, each with a finish-to-start relationship. Below is project baseline information indicating the planned schedule and budgeted cost of each activity. **Calculate anything with a dollar value to the nearest cent (Ex: $456.32) and anything else to three digits (Ex: 1.024).** Recommendation: Use a basic calculator or your calculations could have rounding variance. **Product Release 1.0 row is a summary activity reflecting the contents below it.**

Planned

Activity Name	% Complete	Baseline Duration	Baseline Start	Baseline Finish	Baseline Cost
Product Release 1.0	**0%**	**240 days**	**01/06/08**	**12/05/08**	**$295,000.00**
Requirements	0%	30 days	01/06/08	02/14/08	$30,000.00
Design	0%	60 days	02/17/08	05/09/08	$70,000.00
Proof of Concept	0%	30 days	05/12/08	06/20/08	$45,000.00
Build Product	0%	45 days	06/23/08	08/22/08	$60,000.00
Test Product	0%	45 days	08/25/08	10/24/08	$60,000.00
Deploy Product	0%	30 days	10/27/08	12/05/08	$30,000.00
Product Release Complete	0%	0 days	12/05/08	12/05/08	$0.00

The project is currently in the middle of the execution phase and the date is **June 20th**. The information in the chart below provides the schedule and cost information to-date.

Actual

Activity Name	% Complete	Actual Duration	Actual Start	Actual Finish	Actual Cost
Product Release 1.0	**47.63%**	**122 days**	**01/06/08**	**NA**	**$147,000.00**
Requirements	100%	35 days	01/06/08	02/21/08	$32,000.00
Design	100%	60 days	02/24/08	05/16/08	$70,000.00
Proof of Concept	90%	27 days	05/19/08	NA	$45,000.00
Build Product	0%	0 days	NA	NA	$0.00
Test Product	0%	0 days	NA	NA	$0.00
Deploy Product	0%	0 days	NA	NA	$0.00
Product Release Complete	0%	0 days	NA	NA	$0.00

Using the calculations from the data tables, provide a status report on the project by answering the following questions (Calculate to the nearest cent for dollars and three significant digits for everything else.):

1.   What measurement is used to determine whether the project is ahead of schedule, behind schedule, or on time, and how much is the amount?

2.   What measurement is used to determine the rate of the project's progress according to plan and what is its value?

3. Based on these schedule measurements, is the project on schedule, behind schedule, or on time?

4. At what percentage rate is the project progressing compared to its planned baseline rate of progression?

5. What measurement is used to determine whether the project is over budget, under budget, or if it is breaking even, and how much is the difference?

6. What measurement is used to determine the spending efficiency of the project, and what is its value?

7. Based on these measurements, is the project over budget, under budget, or breaking even?

8. Currently, the project is making how many cents for every dollar spent?

9. Based on the current status and performance of the project, how much do you estimate the project will cost at completion? On what measurement do you base this estimate?

10. How much money must be spent from this point forward to complete the project? What calculations have you made to support this figure?

11. Will the project be over budget, under budget, or right on target at completion? What information do you have to support this estimate?

PMP Exam Success Series: Certification Exam Manual
© 2007 Crosswind Project Management, Inc., www.crosswindpm.com

Earned Value Exercise #2

Because the project is both over budget and behind schedule, you must find a way to return the project results to baseline estimates. After reviewing all the options and their related risks, you determine that the best alternative is to fast track the project by allowing testing to begin early during the activity to build the product. This action imposes additional risk to the project but may also allow the project to complete as scheduled. **Calculate anything with a dollar value to the nearest cent (Ex: $456.32) and anything else to three digits (Ex: 1.024).** Recommendation: Use a basic calculator or your calculations could have rounding variance. **Product Release 1.0 row is a summary activity reflecting the contents below it.**

Planned

Activity Name	% Complete	Baseline Duration	Baseline Start	Baseline Finish	Baseline Cost
Product Release 1.0	**0%**	**240 days**	**01/06/08**	**12/05/08**	**$295,000.00**
Requirements	0%	30 days	01/06/08	02/14/08	$30,000.00
Design	0%	60 days	02/17/08	05/09/08	$70,000.00
Proof of Concept	0%	30 days	05/12/08	06/20/08	$45,000.00
Build Product	0%	45 days	06/23/08	08/22/08	$60,000.00
Test Product	0%	45 days	08/25/08	10/24/08	$60,000.00
Deploy Product	0%	30 days	10/27/08	12/05/08	$30,000.00
Product Release Complete	0%	0 days	12/05/08	12/05/08	$0.00

It is August 22nd. The product is being built and early testing has begun. Following is the current project schedule data and cost information. Using this information and the project baseline information above, determine the performance measurement values listed in the remainder of the exercise.

Actual

Activity Name	% Complete	Actual Duration	Actual Start	Actual Finish	Actual Cost
Product Release 1.0	**70%**	**164.72 days**	**01/06/08**	**NA**	**$217,000.00**
Requirements	100%	35 days	01/06/08	02/21/08	$32,000.00
Design	100%	60 days	02/24/08	05/16/08	$70,000.00
Proof of Concept	100%	30 days	05/19/08	06/27/08	$50,000.00
Build Product	80%	36 days	06/30/08	NA	$52,000.00
Test Product	22%	10 days	08/04/08	NA	$13,000.00
Deploy Product	0%	0 days	NA	NA	$0.00
Product Release Complete	0%	0 days	NA	NA	$0.00

Using the calculations from previous data, provide a status report on the project by answering the following questions:

1. Based on the measurements, is the project on schedule, behind schedule, or ahead of schedule? Indicate which measurement and its amount you are using to determine this status.

2. At what percentage rate is the project progressing compared to its planned baseline rate of progression?

3. Is the project over budget, under budget, or breaking even? How do you know?

4. Currently, the project is making how many cents for every dollar spent?

5. Based on the current status and performance of the project, how much do you estimate the project will cost at completion?

6. How much money must be spent from this point forward to complete the project?

7. Do you estimate the project will be over budget, under budget, or right on target at completion?

8. What is the variance between what the original budget was and the current budget estimate at completion?

PMP Exam Success Series: Certification Exam Manual
© 2007 Crosswind Project Management, Inc., www.crosswindpm.com

Earned Value Exercise #3

It is December 1st and the project is complete. Below is the project baseline information followed by the actual project information at the time of project completion. Based on the information reported below, determine the values of the performance measurements listed table that follows. **Calculate anything with a dollar value to the nearest cent (Ex: $456.32) and anything else to three digits (Ex: 1.024).** Recommendation: Use a basic calculator or your calculations could have rounding variance. **Product Release 1.0 row is a summary activity reflecting the contents below it.**

Planned

Activity Name	% Complete	Baseline Duration	Baseline Start	Baseline Finish	Baseline Cost
Product Release 1.0	**0%**	**240 days**	**01/06/08**	**12/05/08**	**$295,000.00**
Requirements	0%	30 days	01/06/08	02/14/08	$30,000.00
Design	0%	60 days	02/17/08	05/09/08	$70,000.00
Proof of Concept	0%	30 days	05/12/08	06/20/08	$45,000.00
Build Product	0%	45 days	06/23/08	08/22/08	$60,000.00
Test Product	0%	45 days	08/25/08	10/24/08	$60,000.00
Deploy Product	0%	30 days	10/27/08	12/05/08	$30,000.00
Product Release Complete	0%	0 days	12/05/08	12/05/08	$0.00

Actual

Activity Name	% Complete	Actual Duration	Actual Start	Actual Finish	Actual Cost
Product Release 1.0	**100%**	**236 days**	**01/06/08**	**12/01/08**	**$320,000.00**
Requirements	100%	35 days	01/06/08	02/21/08	$32,000.00
Design	100%	60 days	02/24/08	05/16/08	$70,000.00
Proof of Concept	100%	30 days	05/19/08	06/27/08	$50,000.00
Build Product	100%	55 days	06/30/08	09/12/08	$70,000.00
Test Product	100%	56 days	08/04/08	10/20/08	$68,000.00
Deploy Product	100%	30 days	10/21/08	12/01/08	$30,000.00
Product Release Complete	100%	0 days	12/01/08	12/01/08	$0.00

Using the calculations from above, provide the last status report on the project by answering the following questions:

1. Did the project complete early, late, or on time? Indicate the measurement and its value that you used to determine this status.

2. Did the project end up over budget, under budget, or breaking even?

3. By how much was the project over or under budget?

9.18.7   Cost Terminology Matching Exercise

Match the correct term in the left column to the correct definition in the right column. See the exercise answer section of this chapter for the correct answer. Answers are in section 9.19.7.

Matching Exercise #1

	Term	Answer	Definition
1	Actual Cost (AC)		A. Application of a mathematical model used to estimate project components (time, cost, scope) by having other variables entered into the application
2	Baseline		B. An estimate used to put money into a company's (or project's) budget
3	Bottom-Up Estimate		C. A cost estimate that provides the accurate estimation of the project cost; the final estimate to be used on the project before implementation begins; Tolerance range: -10 to +15%
4	Budget		D. Represents the projected total estimate, based on the current efficiency (CPI) with which you are spending money on the project; Formula: BAC/CPI
5	Budgetary Estimate		E. A numbering system used in project management to identify pieces of the work breakdown structure
6	Code of Accounts (Tool)		F. Money included in an estimate that accounts for events which may be somewhat predicted (known unknowns)
7	Contingency Reserves		G. Process used to complete the project within the approved budget
8	Control Account (Tool)		H. Detailed estimate that usually involves team input. As the team builds the pieces of the estimate, they build the total estimate from the bottom up.
9	Cost Estimating		I. Estimating (educated consistent process) the cost of people and other resources to complete the project
10	Definitive Estimate		J. Determination of resources (people, material, equipment) needed for a project, including the determination of when (or how much of) the resources are needed
11	Direct Cost		K. Represents the total costs that have actually been accrued up to a particular point in time; also known as actual cost of work performed (ACWP)
12	Estimate at Completion (EAC)		L. A point where scope, time, budgeted cost, and actual cost come together to measure performance on a project.
13	Indirect Cost		M. Money that has already been spent on a project; should not be considered when selecting or evaluating a project
14	Learning Curve Theory		N. The total amount of money expected to be spent on a project based on the original cost estimates plus any approved changes
15	Parametric Modeling		O. Ratio of earned value and planned value that can be used to calculate how a project is progressing
16	Project Cost Management		P. Cost that is directly applicable to the project (Ex: test computer for software being created on the project, IC chips, or labor used on the project)
17	Resource Planning		Q. Estimate or plan that the project will try to achieve (cost, scope, time, etc.)
18	Schedule Performance Index (SPI)		R. Cost that is not directly accrued on the project (Ex: electricity, taxes, rent)
19	Sunk Cost		S. A theory which states that the more of something that is produced, the lower the unit cost of it becomes due to an improvement in efficiency
20	Tangible Cost/Benefit		T. Easily measurable cost or benefit of a project; measured in dollars

Matching Exercise #2

	Term	Answer	Definition
1	Analogous Estimate (Technique)		A. The cost associated with giving up one opportunity for another (Ex: Project A $50K, Project B $75K. If you select Project B, it has an Opportunity Cost of the total of Project A, which is $50K.)
2	Budget at Completion (BAC)		B. A value used in capital budgeting, in which the present value of cash inflow is subtracted from the present value of cash outflows; compares the value of a dollar today versus the value of that same dollar in the future, after taking inflation and return into account
3	Chart of Accounts (Tool)		C. A ratio that shows the current efficiency of money being spent on the project; Formula: EV/AC A value of one means you are getting out what you put (which is good), less than one is bad; greater than one is good.
4	Cost Budgeting		D. Process of using a previous project of similar characteristic (size, cost, scope) to estimate a new project
5	Cost Control		E. A project comparison value; represents the discounted rate that zeroes out the net present value (NPV)
6	Cost Management Plan		F. A structure used to monitor project cost that usually aligns with a company's accounting system
7	Cost Performance Index (CPI)		G. The technique associated with measuring the amount of completion of a work breakdown structure component, control account or project
8	Cost Variance (CV)		H. Money made after expenses have been subtracted from revenue
9	Earned Value (EV)		I. Applying the overall cost estimates to the individual work elements to allow for a baseline cost measurement
10	Earned Value Technique (EVT) (Technique)		J. Consideration of not just project cost, but total ownership (operations and support) cost of the item created by the project
11	Internal Rate of Return (IRR)		K. The document that explains how to handle cost estimations, budgeting, variances, and other cost-related items on the project
12	Life Cycle Costing		L. Total project budget; amount of money planned to be spent by the time the project is complete; sum of all planned values
13	Net Present Value (NPV)		M. Represents the value of the work that has actually been accomplished or completed up to a particular point in time; the percent complete of each activity multiplied by the planned value; also known as budgeted cost of work performed (BCWP)
14	Opportunity Cost		N. Money set aside in a budget used for items that are difficult to predict
15	Planned Value		O. The process of controlling changes to the budget
16	Profit		P. The difference between what has been built (EV) and what the cost was to build it (AC); Formula: EV-AC A value of zero (0) means the project is creating what it should for the cost as planned. A negative value means you are over budget; a positive value means you are under budget.
17	Reserves		Q. Represents the total costs that should have been spent up to a particular point in time; also known as budgeted cost of work scheduled (BCWS)
18	Rough Order of Magnitude (ROM) Estimate		R. The difference between what has been built (EV) and the time it should take to build it (PV); Formula: EV-PV A value of zero (0) means the project is creating what it should in the planned timeframe. A negative value means that it is taking longer than planned on the project to complete activities.
19	Schedule Variance (SV)		S. Very early cost estimate used to give a rough estimate of what the project will cost to complete; Tolerance range: -50% to +100%.

9.18.8   Cost Practice Test
Answers are in section 9.19.8.

1.   Activity A is worth $200, is 100% complete, should have been done on day 1, and actually cost $200. Activity B is worth $75, is 90% complete, should have been done on day 2, and actually cost $120 so far. Activity C is worth $200, is 75% complete and should have been done on day 3, and has cost $175 so far. The total budget is $1,000. What is the planned value as of day 2?

      (A) $275.00
      (B) -$417.50
      (C) $495.00
      (D) -$275.00

2.   The project team is developing rules for reporting updates on the project. The majority of the activities are greater than two reporting periods long. Which format is best to use in this case?

      (A) Fixed formula progress reporting
      (B) Weighted milestone
      (C) Earned value
      (D) Forecast reporting

3.   Project A has an NPV of $165K over three years. Project B has an NPV of $330K over six years. Project C has an NPV of $170K over six years. Which of the following do you select?

      (A) Project A
      (B) Project B
      (C) Project C
      (D) Project A and C

4.   Activity A is worth $200, is 100% complete, and actually cost $200. Activity B is worth $75, is 90% complete, and actually cost $120 so far. Activity C is worth $200, is 75% complete, and has cost $175 so far. The total budget is $1,000. What is the cost performance index for the activities listed?

      (A) 0.84
      (B) 0.88
      (C) 1.16
      (D) 1.12

5.   Activity A is worth $200, is 100% complete, and actually cost $200. Activity B is worth $75, is 90% complete, and actually cost $120 so far. Activity C is worth $200, is 75% complete, and has cost $175 so far. The total budget is $1,000. What is the cost variance for the activities listed?

      (A) 0.84
      (B) 0.88
      (C) -$77.50
      (D) -$57.50

PMP Exam Success Series: Certification Exam Manual
© 2007 Crosswind Project Management, Inc., www.crosswindpm.com

6. Activity A is worth $200, is 100% complete, and actually cost $200. Activity B is worth $75, is 90% complete, and actually cost $120 so far. Activity C is worth $200, is 75% complete, and has cost $175 so far. The total budget is $1,000. What is the variance at completion for the activities listed?

    (A) -$186.24
    (B) $1,000
    (C) $690.63
    (D) $1,185.63

7. Company-wide software licensing fees are an example of what type of project cost?

    (A) Variable indirect
    (B) Variable
    (C) Fixed
    (D) Fixed direct

8. The project team is planning an upgrade to a client's Web site and infrastructure. During Planning, the team discovers the need for a data communications line to connect to the servers. What type of cost is this?

    (A) Direct
    (B) Indirect
    (C) Variable
    (D) Indirect fixed

9. The infrastructure project is behind schedule and over budget. So far, $3M has been spent on the project. The sponsor is considering if it should allow the project to continue. What should he consider the $3M that has been spent so far?

    (A) The amount for Phase 1
    (B) Sunk cost
    (C) The budgeted cost of work performed
    (D) Opportunity cost

10. The highway project is in the middle of Planning when the Project Manager presents a status reporting method to the team. The team members haven't heard of this method before. It's called earned value. To attain buy-in from the team, the Project Manager begins to explain what earned value status reporting can do for the project, explaining that it will measure which of the following?

    (A) Time and cost
    (B) Scope, time, and cost
    (C) Scope and cost
    (D) Scope and time

11. Activity A is worth $200, is 100% complete, and actually cost $200. Activity B is worth $75, is 90% complete, and actually cost $120 so far. Activity C is worth $200, is 75% complete, and has cost $175 so far. The total budget is $1,000. What is the estimate at completion for the activities listed?

    (A) $1,100.04
    (B) $690.63
    (C) $1,186.24
    (D) $1,000

12. Project A has an NPV of $275K over 2.5 years. Project B has an IRR of 3.2%. Project C has a BCR of 0.89:1. Project D has four people on it and is encountering scope creep. Which of the following projects stand the greatest chance of getting cancelled?

    (A) Project A
    (B) Project B
    (C) Project C
    (D) Project D

13. The BCR project comparison function utilizes what variable(s)?

    (A) Revenue and cost
    (B) Revenue and profit
    (C) Benefit and profit
    (D) Profit margin

14. The project Planning is progressing. The team has involved the accounting department to set up a system of codes that the accounting department will use to track work on the project. This is known as what?

    (A) Accounting codes
    (B) WBS numbering
    (C) Cost budgeting
    (D) Chart of accounts

15. The project management team has performed earned value analysis on its project and discovered that the project is behind schedule and over budget. The SPI is 0.82 and the CPI is 0.73. The team is trying to determine how efficient it needs to be with the remaining resources on the project to complete the project on budget. Which of the following is the team trying to calculate?

    (A) Cost variance
    (B) Cost performance index
    (C) Estimate to complete
    (D) To complete performance index

PMP Exam Success Series: Certification Exam Manual
© 2007 Crosswind Project Management, Inc., www.crosswindpm.com

16.   What is the range of a rough order of magnitude (ROM) estimate?

       (A) -10% to +5%
       (B) -5% to +10%
       (C) -50% to +100%
       (D) -300% to +75%

17.   The project is using a new server that cost $25,000. The Project Manager is told to set up
       depreciation for the server over a five-year schedule, with the server having a value of $0 at
       the end of five years. Standard depreciation will be used in the calculation. What is the
       amount per year the server will depreciate?

       (A) $5,000
       (B) $10,000
       (C) $2,500
       (D) Not enough information

18.   Activity A is worth $200, is 100% complete, and actually cost $200. Activity B is worth $75,
       is 90% complete, and actually cost $120 so far. Activity C is worth $200, is 75% complete,
       and has cost $175 so far. The total budget is $1,000. What is the estimate to complete for the
       activities listed?

       (A) $1,000
       (B) $1,100.04
       (C) $1,185.63
       (D) $691.24

19.   Which of the following shows the remaining amount to be spent on the project based on
       current spending efficiency?

       (A) Cost variance
       (B) Estimate to complete
       (C) Estimate at completion
       (D) Budget remaining

20.   Which of the following shows the rate at which the project is progressing compared to what
       was planned?

       (A) Schedule variance
       (B) Gantt chart
       (C) Variance report
       (D) Schedule performance index

21.   Which process applies budget amounts to the individual work packages or activities?

       (A) Cost Control
       (B) Cost Estimating
       (C) Cost Budgeting
       (D) Earned Value Management

22. The project team is planning an upgrade to a client's Web site and infrastructure. During Planning, the team members are confronted with the cost options for a data communications line to connect to the servers. They consider the cost of purchasing the communication line for the time they need to develop the project. After that, the customer takes over the purchase of the line. They are also considering a long-term commitment that the customer can make with the communication line provider, which provides a less costly solution over the use of the system. What type of analysis is the team considering?

    (A) Life cycle costing
    (B) Make-or-buy analysis
    (C) Fixed cost
    (D) Procurement planning

23. Activity A is worth $200, is 100% complete, and actually cost $200. Activity B is worth $75, is 90% complete, and actually cost $120 so far. Activity C is worth $200, is 75% complete, and has cost $175 so far. The total budget is $1,000. What is the total earned value for the activities listed?

    (A) $417.50
    (B) -$417.50
    (C) $495.00
    (D) $475.00

24. The project Planning is progressing. The team has involved a number of expert opinions in trying to get a total cost estimate for the overall project. This process is known as?

    (A) Cost Budgeting
    (B) Cost Control
    (C) Analogous Estimating
    (D) Cost Estimating

25. Which of the following is an example of fixed formula status reporting?

    (A) Getting status updates from the project team
    (B) PV multiplied by % complete
    (C) The Project Manager updating the status reports quantitatively
    (D) 30%/70% rule

26. The project is using some application and database servers in the development environment. The finance department explains that the servers will be depreciated using the double declining balance (DDB) format. This is an example of what?

    (A) Fixed cost
    (B) Fixed direct cost
    (C) Accelerated depreciation
    (D) Standard depreciation

PMP Exam Success Series: Certification Exam Manual
© 2007 Crosswind Project Management, Inc., www.crosswindpm.com

27.   The project team is developing rules for reporting updates on the project. The majority of their activities are less than two reporting periods long. Which format is best to use in this case?

(A) Fixed formula progress reporting
(B) Weighted milestone
(C) Earned value
(D) Forecast reporting

28.   You have $1,000 today and can earn 8%. In future years, how much money will this be worth?

(A) $1,175
(B) $883
(C) $1,202
(D) Not enough information

29.   Activity A is worth $200, is 100% complete, and actually cost $200. Activity B is worth $75, is 90% complete, and actually cost $120 so far. Activity C is worth $200, is 75% complete, and has cost $175 so far. The total budget is $1,000. What is the schedule variance for the activities listed?

(A) -$77.50
(B) -$57.50
(C) 0.84
(D) 0.88

30.   Which of the following metrics tells you if you are ahead of schedule?

(A) Schedule performance index (SPI)
(B) Cost performance Index (CPI)
(C) Cost variance (CV)
(D) Budget at completion (BAC)

9.19 Cost Tests and Exercise Answers

9.19.1 Cost Quick Test Answers

1. What shows how the project is progressing?
   SPI (schedule performance index) [section 9.14.2, section 9.14.3, section 9.15, section 9.16]

2. What shows how the cost efficiency of the project is going?
   CPI (cost performance index) [section 9.14.2, section 9.14.3, section 9.15, section 9.16]

3. What shows the money remaining to be spent on the project?
   ETC (estimate to completion) [section 9.14.5, section 9.15, section 9.16]

4. What shows the cost spent to date on the project?
   AC (actual cost) [section 9.14.2, section 9.14.3, section 9.14.4, section 9.15, section 9.16]

5. What is the name of the work accomplished to date on the project?
   EV (earned value) [section 9.14.2, section 9.14.3, section 9.14.4, section 9.15, section 9.16]

6. What is the name of the original Cost Estimate for the project?
   BAC (budget at completion) [section 9.14.3, section 9.14.4, section 9.15, section 9.16]

7. Project A=$67,000 and Project B=$72,000. What is the Opportunity Cost of taking Project B?
   The opportunity cost of selecting Project B is $67,000, or the cost of Project A.
   [section 9.2, section 9.16]

8. Project A has an NPV of $67,000 over three years and Project B has an NPV of $135,000 over six years. Which do you choose?
   Project B NPV of $135,000

9. What amount per year will a $15,000 item with a five-year shelf life depreciate at using straight depreciation (non-accelerated)?
   This is straight division with $15,000 divided by five years, for a value of $3,000 per year. [section 9.7, section 9.7.1]

10. If you want a future amount of $10,000 in three years at 6.75% interest, do you need more or less than that amount now to get it in that time?
    Per the future value (FV) function, you will need less than the $10,000 to have that amount in the future. [section 9.3, section 9.15]

PMP Exam Success Series: Certification Exam Manual
© 2007 Crosswind Project Management, Inc., www.crosswindpm.com

9.19.2 Cost ITTO Matching Exercise Answers

	Inputs	Tools &Techniques	Outputs
Cost Estimating	1) Project Scope Statement	1) Analogous Estimating	1) Activity Cost Estimates
	2) Work Breakdown Structure	2) Determine Resource Cost Rates	2) Requested Changes
	3) Project Management Plan (Schedule Mgt Plan)	3) Bottom-Up Estimating	3) Cost Management Plan (Updates)
	4) Project Management Plan (Staffing Mgt Plan)	4) Parametric Estimating	
	5) Project Management Plan (Risk Register)	5) Project Management Software	
		6) Vendor Bid Analysis	
		7) Cost of Quality	
		8) Reserve Analysis	
Summary:	Determining overall project cost		
Cost Budgeting	1) Project Scope Statement	1) Cost Aggregation	1) Cost Baseline
	2) Work Breakdown Structure	2) Reserve Analysis	2) Requested Changes
	3) WBS Dictionary	3) Parametric Estimating	3) Cost Management Plan (Updates)
	4) Activity Cost Estimates	4) Funding Limit Reconciliation	
	5) Project Schedule		
	6) Resource Calendars		
	7) Contract		
	8) Cost Management Plan		
Summary:	Applying costs to individual activities		
Cost Control	1) Cost Baseline	1) Cost Change Control System	1) Cost Estimate (Updates)
	2) Performance Reports	2) Performance Measurement Analysis	2) Cost Baseline (Updates)
	3) Work Performance Information	3) Forecasting	3) Performance Measurements
	4) Approved Change Requests	4) Project Performance Reviews	4) Forecasted Completion
		5) Project Management Software	5) Requested Changes
Summary:	Activities associated with monitoring and controlling project costs		

9.19.3   Project Selection Exercise Answers

Type of Measurement	Project A	Project B	Choice
IRR	14%	22%	22%
NPV	$10K over 12 months	$5K over 6 months	$10K over 12 months
Payback Period	4 months	12 months	4 months
BCR	3.02:1	.68:1	3.02:1
ROI	5%	12%	12%

9.19.4   Cost Type Exercise Answers

Item	Direct Cost	Indirect Cost	Fixed Cost	Variable Cost
Rent for the company building		X		X
Parts to be used in the manufacturing process	X			X
Setting up a book press to create 5000 books	X		X	
Cleaning supplies for the office		X		X
Renting a suite for the post project party	X			X
Training for each member of the team to use new software for the project	X			X
Company-wide software licensing fees		X		X

9.19.5   Earned Value Exercise Answers

#	AC	EV	PV	BAC	CPI	CV	SPI	SV	EAC	ETC
1	$500	$450	$525	$1,000	0.90	-$50.00	0.857	-$75.00	$1,111.11	$611.11
2	$400	$395	$395	$500	0.988	-$5	1.0	$0.00	$506.07	$106.07
3	$1,000	$900	$1,000	$1,500	0.90	-$100	0.90	-$100	$1,666.67	$666.67
4	$600	$590	$600	$800	0.983	-$10.00	0.983	-$10.00	$813.84	$213.84
5	$800	$750	$750	$2,000	0.938	-$50.00	1.00	$0.00	$2,132.20	$1,332.20
6	$350	$325	$330	$2,000	0.929	-$25.00	0.985	-$5.00	$2,152.85	$1,802.85
7	$500	$505	$550	$600	1.01	$5.00	0.918	-$45.00	$594.06	$94.06
8	$200	$175	$180	$350	0.875	-$25.00	0.972	-$5.00	$400.00	$200.00
9	$450	$515	$520	$3,000	1.14	$65.00	0.990	-$5.00	$2,631.58	$2,181.58
10	$700	$650	$695	$950	0.929	-$50.00	0.935	-$45.00	$1,022.60	$322.60

1. Over budget — Behind schedule
2. Slightly over budget — On schedule
3. Over budget — Behind schedule
4. Over budget — Behind schedule
5. Over budget — On schedule
6. Over budget — Slightly behind schedule
7. Slightly under budget — Behind schedule
8. Over budget — Behind schedule
9. Significantly under budget — Slightly behind schedule
10. Over budget — Behind schedule

9.19.6   Situational Earned Value Exercise Answers

Earned Value Exercise #1 Answers

You are managing a project to build a product. The project has seven activities, each with a finish-to-start relationship. Below is project baseline information indicating the planned schedule and budgeted cost of each activity. **Calculate anything with a dollar value to the nearest cent (Ex: $456.32) and anything else to three digits (Ex: 1.024).** Recommendation: Use a basic calculator or your calculations could have rounding variance. **Product Release 1.0 row is a summary activity reflecting the contents below it.**

Planned

Activity Name	% Complete	Baseline Duration	Baseline Start	Baseline Finish	Baseline Cost
Product Release 1.0	**0%**	**240 days**	**01/06/08**	**12/05/08**	**$295,000.00**
Requirements	0%	30 days	01/06/08	02/14/08	$30,000.00
Design	0%	60 days	02/17/08	05/09/08	$70,000.00
Proof of Concept	0%	30 days	05/12/08	06/20/08	$45,000.00
Build Product	0%	45 days	06/23/08	08/22/08	$60,000.00
Test Product	0%	45 days	08/25/08	10/24/08	$60,000.00
Deploy Product	0%	30 days	10/27/08	12/05/08	$30,000.00
Product Release Complete	0%	0 days	12/05/08	12/05/08	$0.00

The project is currently in the middle of the execution phase and the date is June 20th. The information in the chart below provides the schedule and cost information to-date.

Actual

Activity Name	% Complete	Actual Duration	Actual Start	Actual Finish	Actual Cost
Product Release 1.0	**47.63%**	**122 days**	**01/06/08**	**NA**	**$147,000.00**
Requirements	100%	35 days	01/06/08	02/21/08	$32,000.00
Design	100%	60 days	02/24/08	05/16/08	$70,000.00
Proof of Concept	90%	27 days	05/19/08	NA	$45,000.00
Build Product	0%	0 days	NA	NA	$0.00
Test Product	0%	0 days	NA	NA	$0.00
Deploy Product	0%	0 days	NA	NA	$0.00
Product Release Complete	0%	0 days	NA	NA	$0.00

Using the calculations from data tables, provide a status report on the project by answering the following questions (Calculate to the nearest cent for dollars and three significant digits for everything else.):

1.   What measurement is used to determine whether the project is ahead of schedule, behind schedule, or on time, and how much is the amount?

   SV – schedule variance

First, you must determine the value of the following:

AC = $147,000 (actual cost to-date)
PV = $145,000 (what was the planned value of the work to-date)
EV = $140,500 (what is the value of the work done to-date)
($30,000 + $70,000 + (90% of $45,000 = $40,500) = $140,500)

SV = EV – PV   SV = $140,500 – $145,000 = -$4,500

2. What measurement is used to determine the rate of the project's progress according to plan and what is its value?

SPI – schedule performance index
SPI = EV/PV   SPI = $140,500/$145,000 = 0.969

3. Based on these schedule measurements, is the project on schedule, behind schedule, or on time?

The project is behind schedule.

4. At what percentage rate is the project progressing compared to its planned baseline rate of progression?

The project is progressing at 96.9% of the rate of the original plan.

5. What measurement is used to determine whether the project is over budget, under budget, or if it is breaking even, and how much is the difference?

CV – cost variance
AC = $147,000 (actual cost to-date)
PV = $145,000 (what was the planned value of the work to-date)
EV = $140,500 (what is the value of the work done to-date)
($30,000 + $70,000 + (90% of $45,000 = $40,500) = $140,500)
CV = EV – AC   CV = $140,500 – $147,000 = -$6,500

6. What measurement is used to determine the spending efficiency of the project and what is its value?

CPI – cost performance index
CPI = EV/AC   CPI = $140,500/$147,000 = 0.956

7. Based on these measurements, is the project over budget, under budget, or breaking even?

The project is over budget.

8. Currently, the project is making how many cents for every dollar spent?

The project is making 96 cents on every dollar it spends.

9. Based on the current status and performance of the project, how much do you estimate the project will cost at completion? On what measurement do you base this estimate?

PMP Exam Success Series: Certification Exam Manual
© 2007 Crosswind Project Management, Inc., www.crosswindpm.com

The estimate at completion (EAC) is the value that tells what the project is expected to cost at the end, based on the project spending efficiency. This estimate is calculated in a variety of ways. Use BAC/CPI to calculate EAC. The BAC (budget at completion) is $295,000 and the CPI (cost performance index) is 0.956. This gives an EAC of $308,577.40.

10. How much money must be spent from this point forward to complete the project? What calculations have you made to support this figure?

This is the ETC (estimate to complete). Calculate it by subtracting AC (actual cost) from the EAC (estimate at completion). $308,577.40-$147,000 = $161,577.40

11. Will the project be over budget, under budget, or right on target at completion? What information do you have to support this estimate?

Based on the estimate at completion, the project will be over budget.

The budget at completion (BAC) is $295,000, the estimate at completion (EAC) $308,577.40.

The variance at completion (VAC) is BAC- EAC and in this project is $13,577.40 over budget.

Earned Value Exercise #2 Answers

Because the project is both over budget and behind schedule, you must find a way to return the project results to baseline estimates. After reviewing all the options and their related risks, you determine that the best alternative is to fast track the project by allowing testing to begin early during the activity to build the product. This action imposes additional risk to the project but may also allow the project to complete as scheduled. **Calculate anything with a dollar value to the nearest cent (Ex: $456.32) and anything else to three digits (Ex: 1.024).** Recommendation: Use a basic calculator or your calculations could have rounding variance. **Product Release 1.0 row is a summary activity reflecting the contents below it.**

Planned

Activity Name	% Complete	Baseline Duration	Baseline Start	Baseline Finish	Baseline Cost
Product Release 1.0	**0%**	**240 days**	**01/06/08**	**12/05/08**	**$295,000.00**
Requirements	0%	30 days	01/06/08	02/14/08	$30,000.00
Design	0%	60 days	02/17/08	05/09/08	$70,000.00
Proof of Concept	0%	30 days	05/12/08	06/20/08	$45,000.00
Build Product	0%	45 days	06/23/08	08/22/08	$60,000.00
Test Product	0%	45 days	08/25/08	10/24/08	$60,000.00
Deploy Product	0%	30 days	10/27/08	12/05/08	$30,000.00
Product Release Complete	0%	0 days	12/05/08	12/05/08	$0.00

It is August 22nd, the product is being built, and early testing has begun. Following is the current project schedule data, and cost information. Using this information and the project baseline information above, determine the performance measurement values listed in the remainder of the exercise.

Actual

Activity Name	% Complete	Actual Duration	Actual Start	Actual Finish	Actual Cost
Product Release 1.0	**70%**	**164.72 days**	**01/06/08**	**NA**	**$217,000.00**
Requirements	100%	35 days	01/06/08	02/21/08	$32,000.00
Design	100%	60 days	02/24/08	05/16/08	$70,000.00
Proof of Concept	100%	30 days	05/19/08	06/27/08	$50,000.00
Build Product	80%	36 days	06/30/08	NA	$52,000.00
Test Product	22%	10 days	08/04/08	NA	$13,000.00
Deploy Product	0%	0 days	NA	NA	$0.00
Product Release Complete	0%	0 days	NA	NA	$0.00

Using the calculations from previous data, provide a status report on the project by answering the following questions:

1. Based on the measurements, is the project on schedule, behind schedule, or ahead of schedule? Indicate which measurement and its amount you are using to determine this status.

   AC = $217,000 (actual cost to-date)
   PV = $205,000 (what was the planned value of the work to-date)
   EV = $206,200 (what is the value of the work done to-date)
   ($30,000 + $70,000 + $45,000 + (80% of $60,000 = $48,000) + (22% of $60,000 = $13,200) = $206,200)

   SV = EV – PV   **SV = $206,200 – $205,000 = $1,200**

   The project is on or slightly ahead of schedule.

2. At what percentage rate is the project progressing compared to its planned baseline rate of progression?

   SPI = EV / PV   **SPI = $206,200 / $205,000 = 1.006**

   The project is progressing at 100.6% of the rate originally planned.

3. Is the project over budget, under budget or breaking even? How do you know?

   CV = EV – AC   **CV = $206,200 – $217,000 = -$10,800**

   The project is over budget.

4. Currently, the project is making how many cents for every dollar spent?

   CPI = EV / AC   **CPI = $206,200 / $217,000 = 0.950**

   The project is making 95 cents on every dollar it spends.

5. Based on the current status and performance of the project, how much do you estimate the project will cost at completion?

PMP Exam Success Series: Certification Exam Manual
© 2007 Crosswind Project Management, Inc., www.crosswindpm.com

The estimate at completion (EAC) is the value shows what the project is expected to cost at the end based on the project spending efficiency. This is calculated a variety of ways. You use BAC/CPI to calculate EAC. The BAC (budget at completion) is $295,000 and the CPI (cost performance index) is 0.95. This gives an EAC of $310,526.31.

6. How much money must be spent from this point forward to complete the project?

$$ETC = EAC - AC \qquad ETC = \$310,526.31 - \$217,000 = \$93,526.31$$

7. Do you estimate the project will be over budget, under budget, or right on target at completion?

Over budget based on current EAC of $310,526.31

8. What is the variance between what the original budget was and the current budget estimate at completion?

$$VAC = BAC - EAC \qquad -\$15,526.31 = \$295,000.00 - \$310,526.31$$

Earned Value Exercise #3 Answers

It is December 1st and the project is complete. Below is the project baseline information followed by the actual project information at the time of project completion. Based on the information reported in the following table, determine the performance measurement values. **Calculate anything with a dollar value to the nearest cent (Ex: $456.32) and anything else to three digits (Ex: 1.024).**

Planned

Activity Name	% Complete	Baseline Duration	Baseline Start	Baseline Finish	Baseline Cost
Product Release 1.0	**0%**	**240 days**	**01/06/08**	**12/05/08**	**$295,000.00**
Requirements	0%	30 days	01/06/08	02/14/08	$30,000.00
Design	0%	60 days	02/17/08	05/09/08	$70,000.00
Proof of Concept	0%	30 days	05/12/08	06/20/08	$45,000.00
Build Product	0%	45 days	06/23/08	08/22/08	$60,000.00
Test Product	0%	45 days	08/25/08	10/24/08	$60,000.00
Deploy Product	0%	30 days	10/27/08	12/05/08	$30,000.00
Product Release Complete	0%	0 days	12/05/08	12/05/08	$0.00

Actual

Activity Name	% Complete	Actual Duration	Actual Start	Actual Finish	Actual Cost
Product Release 1.0	**100%**	**236 days**	**01/06/08**	**12/01/08**	**$320,000.00**
Requirements	100%	35 days	01/06/08	02/21/08	$32,000.00
Design	100%	60 days	02/24/08	05/16/08	$70,000.00
Proof of Concept	100%	30 days	05/19/08	06/27/08	$50,000.00
Build Product	100%	55 days	06/30/08	09/12/08	$70,000.00
Test Product	100%	56 days	08/04/08	10/20/08	$68,000.00
Deploy Product	100%	30 days	10/21/08	12/01/08	$30,000.00
Product Release Complete	100%	0 days	12/01/08	12/01/08	$0.00

Using the calculations from above, provide the last status report on the project by answering the following questions:

1. Did the project complete early, late, or on time? Indicate the measurement and its value that you used to determine this status.

    The project was completed ahead of schedule. (See actual finish vs. baseline finish.)

2. Did the project end up over budget, under budget or breaking even?

    Over budget

3. By how much was the project over or under budget?

    VAC = BAC – AC   **VAC = \$295,000 – \$320,000 = -\$25,000**

    Over budget by \$25,000

9.19.7 Cost Terminology Matching Exercise Answers
Match the correct term in the left column to the correct definition in the right column.

Matching Exercise #1 Answers

	Term	Definition
1	Actual Cost (AC)	K. Represents the total costs that have actually been accrued up to a particular point in time; also known as actual cost of work performed (ACWP)
2	Baseline	Q. Estimate or plan that the project will try to achieve (cost, scope, time, etc.)
3	Bottom-Up Estimate	H. Detailed estimate that usually involves team input As the team builds the pieces of the estimate, they build the total estimate from the bottom up.
4	Budget	N. The total amount of money expected to be spent on a project based on the original cost estimates plus any approved changes
5	Budgetary Estimate	B. An estimate used to put money into a company's (or project's) budget
6	Code of Accounts (Tool)	E. A numbering system used in project management to identify pieces of the work breakdown structure
7	Contingency Reserves	F. Money included in an estimate that accounts for events which may be somewhat predicted (known unknowns)
8	Control Account (Tool)	L. A point where scope, time, budgeted cost, and actual cost come together to measure performance on a project
9	Cost Estimating	I. Estimating (educated consistent process) the cost of people and other resources to complete the project
10	Definitive Estimate	C. A cost estimate that provides the accurate estimation of the project cost; the final estimate to be used on the project before implementation begins; Tolerance range: -10 to +15%
11	Direct Cost	P. Cost that is directly applicable to the project (Ex: Test computer for software being created on the project, IC chips, or labor used on the project)
12	Estimate at Completion (EAC)	D. Represents the projected total estimate, based on the current efficiency (CPI) with which you are spending money on the project; Formula: BAC/CPI
13	Indirect Cost	R. Cost that is not directly accrued on the project (Ex: electricity, taxes, rent)
14	Learning Curve Theory	S. A theory which states that the more of something that is produced, the lower the unit cost of it becomes due to an improvement in efficiency

15	Parametric Modeling	A. Application of a mathematical model used to estimate project components (time, cost, scope) by having other variables entered into the application
16	Project Cost Management	G. Process used to complete the project within the approved budget
17	Resource Planning	J. Determination of resources (people, material, equipment) needed for a project, including the determination of when (or how much of) the resources are needed
18	Schedule Performance Index (SPI)	O. Ratio of earned value and planned value that can be used to calculate how a project is progressing
19	Sunk Cost	M. Money that has already been spent on a project; should not be considered when selecting or evaluating a project
20	Tangible Cost/Benefit	T. Easily measurable cost or benefits of a project; measured in dollars

Matching Exercise #2 Answers

Term		Definition
1	Analogous Estimates (Technique)	D. Process of using a previous project of similar characteristic (size, cost, scope) to estimate a new project
2	Budget at Completion (BAC)	L. Total project budget; amount of money planned to be spent by the time the project is complete; sum of all planned values
3	Chart of Accounts (Tools)	F. A structure used to monitor project cost that usually aligns with a company's accounting system
4	Cost Budgeting	I. Applying the overall cost estimates to the individual work elements to allow for a baseline cost measurement
5	Cost Control	O. The process of controlling changes to the budget
6	Cost Management Plan	K. The document that explains how to handle cost estimations, budgeting, variances, and other cost-related items on the project
7	Cost Performance Index (CPI)	C. A ratio that shows the current efficiency of money being spent on the project; Formula: EV/AC A value of one means you are getting out what you put (which is good), less than one is bad; greater than one is good
8	Cost Variance (CV)	P. The difference between what has been built (EV) and what the cost was to build it (AC); Formula: EV-AC A value of zero (0) means the project is creating what it should for the cost as planned. A negative value means you are over budget; a positive value means you are under budget
9	Earned Value (EV)	M. Represents the value of the work that has actually been accomplished or completed up to a particular point in time; the percent complete of each activity multiplied by the planned value; also known as budgeted cost of work performed (BCWP)
10	Earned Value Technique (EVT) (Technique)	G. The technique associated with measuring the amount of completion of a work breakdown structure component, control account or project
11	Internal Rate of Return (IRR)	E. A project comparison value; represents the discounted rate that zeroes out the net present value (NPV)
12	Life Cycle Costing	J. Consideration of not just project cost, but total ownership (operations and support) cost of the item created by the project
13	Net Present Value (NPV)	B. A value used in capital budgeting, in which the present value of cash inflow is subtracted from the present value of cash outflows; compares the value of a dollar today versus the value of that same dollar in the future, after taking inflation and return into account
14	Opportunity Cost	A. The cost associated with giving up one opportunity for another (Ex: Project A $50K, Project B $75K. If you select Project B, it has an opportunity cost of the total of Project A, which is $50K.)
15	Planned Value	Q. Represents the total costs that should have been spent up to a particular point in time; also known as budgeted cost of work schedule (BCWS)
16	Profit	H. Money made after expenses have been subtracted from revenue
17	Reserves	N. Money set aside in a budget used for items that are difficult to predict

| 18 | Rough Order of Magnitude (ROM) Estimate | S. Very early cost estimate used to give a rough estimate of what the project will cost to complete; Tolerance range: -50% to +100%. |
| 19 | Schedule Variance (SV) | R. The difference between what has been built (EV) and the time it should take to build it (PV); Formula: EV-PV

A value of zero (0) means the project is creating what it should in the planned timeframe. A negative value means that it is taking longer than planned on the project to complete activities. |

9.19.8   Cost Practice Test Answers

1.   Activity A is worth $200, is 100% complete, should have been done on day 1, and actually cost $200. Activity B is worth $75, is 90% complete, should have been done on day 2, and actually cost $120 so far. Activity C is worth $200, is 75% complete and should have been done on day 3, and has cost $175 so far. The total budget is $1,000. What is the planned value as of day 2?

Correct Answer (A) $275.00
Explanation: The planned value as of day 2 is $275.00. Obtain this value by adding the planned value of Activity A and B, which should have been done as of day 2 on the project. [section 9.14.4, section 9.15, section 9.16]

2.   The project team is developing rules for reporting updates on the project. The majority of the activities are greater than two reporting periods long. Which format is best to use in this case?

Correct Answer (B) Weighted milestone
Explanation: The weighted milestone approach is ideal when an activity is over two reporting periods in length. Fixed formula uses a partial credit approach such as 50/50 and is ideal when an activity is short, such as less than two reporting periods long. Earned value shows the status of the scope, time, and cost of the project. Forecast reporting focuses on what is getting ready to be done on the project. [section 9.10]

3.   Project A has an NPV of $165K over three years. Project B has an NPV of $330K over six years. Project C has an NPV of $170K over six years. Which of the following do you select?

Correct Answer: (B) Project B
Explanation: Project B is the most attractive project because it has the highest dollar amount. The years listed with the NPV are noise because they are already factored into the dollar amount of the project. Project A and C are of less value than Project B. [section 9.2, section 9.16]

4.   Activity A is worth $200, is 100% complete, and actually cost $200. Activity B is worth $75, is 90% complete, and actually cost $120 so far. Activity C is worth $200, is 75% complete, and has cost $175 so far. The total budget is $1,000. What is the cost performance index for the activities listed?

Correct Answer: (A) 0.84
Explanation: To calculate this value, calculate earned value (EV) and actual cost (AC) first. Multiply the percent complete of each activity by its planned value (PV) to obtain the earned value (EV) for each activity. Sum the earned value of each activity to determine the total earned value. Sum the actual cost of each activity to determine the total actual cost. Divide the earned value of $417.50 by the actual cost of $495.00 to produce a CPI of 0.84. This value means that the project is getting $0.84 cents value for every dollar it is spending. [section 9.14.3, section 9.15, section 9.16]

5.   Activity A is worth $200, is 100% complete, and actually cost $200. Activity B is worth $75, is 90% complete, and actually cost $120 so far. Activity C is worth $200, is 75% complete,

and has cost $175 so far. The total budget is $1,000. What is the cost variance for the activities listed?

Correct Answer: (C) -$77.50
Explanation: To calculate this value, calculate earned value (EV) and actual cost (AC) first. Multiply the percent complete of each activity by its planned value (PV) to obtain the EV for each activity. Sum the earned value of each activity to determine the total earned value. Sum the actual cost of each activity to determine the total actual cost. Subtract the actual cost of $495.00 from the earned value of $417.50 to determine a CV of -$77.50. This value means that the project is $77.50 over budget. [section 9.14.3, section 9.15, section 9.16]

6.   Activity A is worth $200, is 100% complete, and actually cost $200. Activity B is worth $75, is 90% complete, and actually cost $120 so far. Activity C is worth $200, is 75% complete, and has cost $175 so far. The total budget is $1,000. What is the variance at completion for the activities listed?

Correct Answer: (A) -$186.24
Explanation: The variance at completion is the difference between the budget at completion and the estimate at completion. To calculate this value, subtract $1,186.24 (EAC) from $1,000 (BAC) for a difference of -$186.24. [section 9.14.3, section 9.15]

7.   Company-wide software licensing fees are an example of what type of project cost?

Correct Answer: (A) Variable indirect
Explanation: This type of cost typically increases for every user and is not likely associated with a project. Therefore, variable indirect is the best description. Variable is not the best answer. Fixed and fixed direct cost descriptions don't fit this type of cost. [section 9.1]

8.   The project team is planning an upgrade to a client's Web site and infrastructure. During Planning, the team members discover the need for a data communications line to connect to the servers. What type of cost is this?

Correct Answer: (A) Direct
Explanation: The data communication line is a direct cost. It is something purchased directly for the project. It is not an indirect or variable cost. [section 9.1, section 9.16]

9.   The infrastructure project is behind schedule and over budget. So far, $3M has been spent on the project. The sponsor is considering if it should allow the project to continue. What should he consider the $3M that has been spent so far?

Correct Answer: (B) Sunk cost
Explanation: Sunk cost is one that has already been spent on the project. It shouldn't be taken into consideration when determining whether to continue on the project. There is nothing in the situation about phasing the project. The budgeted cost of work performed is the earned value (EV). Opportunity cost doesn't apply here. [section 9.6, section 9.16]

10.   The highway project is in the middle of Planning when the Project Manager presents a status reporting method to the team. The team members haven't heard of this method before. It's called earned value. To attain buy-in from the team, the Project Manager begins to explain what earned value status reporting can do for the project, explaining that it will measure which of the following?

Correct Answer: (B) Scope, time, and cost

Explanation: Earned value deals with scope, time, and cost. Actual cost (AC) shows cost. Planned value (PV) shows time. Earned value (EV) shows scope. The formulas that work with these three variables show how the three are interacting together. [section 9.14.1, section 9.14.3, section 9.16]

11.   Activity A is worth $200, is 100% complete and actually cost $200. Activity B is worth $75, is 90% complete and actually cost $120 so far. Activity C is worth $200, is 75% complete, and has cost $175 so far. The total budget is $1,000. What is the estimate at completion for the activities listed?

Correct Answer: (C) $1,186.24

Explanation: To calculate this value, calculate the CPI first. To calculate the CPI, calculate earned value (EV) and actual cost (AC) first. To perform these calculations, multiply the percent complete of each activity by its planned value (PV) to obtain the EV for each activity. Sum the earned value of each activity to determine the total earned value. Sum the actual cost of each activity to determine the total actual cost. Divide the earned value of $417.50 by the actual cost of $495.00 to obtain a CPI of 0.843. Then, divide the BAC of $1,000 by the CPI to obtain an estimated at completion of $1,186.24. [section 9.14.5, section 9.15, section 9.16]

12.   Project A has an NPV of $275K over 2.5 years. Project B has an IRR of 3.2%. Project C has a BCR of 0.89:1. Project D has four people on it and is encountering scope creep. Which of the following projects stand the greatest chance of getting cancelled?

Correct Answer: (C) Project C

Explanation: Project C has a negative BCR in that it is creating less revenue than the cost. Project A and B have positive financials. Project D appears to have some issues, but we don't know enough about it to determine anything else. [section 9.2]

13.   The BCR project comparison function utilizes what variable(s)?

Correct Answer: (A) Revenue and cost

Explanation: The BCR is the benefit cost ratio. It considers the benefit (or revenue) and cost of an initiative. It doesn't factor in profit or profit margin. [section 9.2]

14.   The project Planning is progressing. The team has involved the accounting department to set up a system of codes that the accounting department will use to track work on the project. This is known as what?

Correct Answer: (D) Chart of accounts

Explanation: The chart of accounts sets up codes that will be used to track project cost. The other answers are noise. [section 9.13.1, section 9.16]

15.   The project management team has performed earned value analysis on its project and discovered that the project is behind schedule and over budget. The SPI is 0.82 and the CPI is 0.73. The team is trying to determine how efficient it needs to be with the remaining resources on the project to complete the project on budget. Which of the following is the team trying to calculate?

Correct Answer: (D) To complete performance index

Explanation: The to complete performance index or TCPI shows the efficiency needed of the remaining resources to come in on budget. Cost variance shows the difference between work done and what was paid for it. Cost performance index shows the ratio between the work done and what was paid for it. Estimate to complete shows the amount remaining to be spent based on the current spending efficiency (CPI). [section 9.14.3, section 9.15]

16. What is the range of a rough order of magnitude (ROM) estimate?

    Correct Answer: (C) -50% to +100%
    Explanation: The range of a rough order of magnitude (ROM) estimate is -50% to +100%. The other answers are noise. [section 9.12]

17. The project is using a new server that cost $25,000. The Project Manager is told to set up depreciation for the server over a five-year schedule, with the server having a value of $0 at the end of five years. Standard depreciation will be used in the calculation. What is the amount per year the server will depreciate?

    Correct Answer: (A) $5,000
    Explanation: To calculate this value, determine a few values first. What is the value of the asset at the end of the schedule? What is the amount of the asset to begin with? What is the number of years of the depreciation schedule? First, subtract the ending value of the asset from the beginning value of the asset ($25K-$0=$25K). The $25K is then divided by the years (5) of the depreciation schedule. This calculation results in $5K per year of depreciation. [section 9.7.1]

18. Activity A is worth $200, is 100% complete, and actually cost $200. Activity B is worth $75, is 90% complete, and actually cost $120 so far. Activity C is worth $200, is 75% complete, and has cost $175 so far. The total budget is $1,000. What is the estimate to complete for the activities listed?

    Correct Answer: (D) $691.24
    Explanation: To calculate this value, calculate the EAC first. To calculate the EAC, calculate the CPI first. To calculate the CPI, calculate earned value (EV) and actual cost (AC) first. Multiply the percent complete of each activity by its planned value (PV) to obtain the EV for each activity. Sum the earned value of each activity to determine the total earned value. Sum the actual cost of each activity to determine the total actual cost. Divide the earned value of $417.50 by the actual cost of $495.00 to obtain a CPI of 0.84. Divide the BAC of $1,000 by the CPI to obtain an estimated at completion of $1,186.24. To determine the estimate to complete, subtract the actual cost (AC) of $495.00 from the estimate at completion (EAC) of $1,186.24. The difference is $691.24. [section 9.14.5]

19. Which of the following shows the remaining amount to be spent on the project based on current spending efficiency?

    Correct Answer: (B) Estimate to complete
    Explanation: Estimate to complete shows the remaining amount to be spent on a project based on spending efficiency. This value is the difference between actual cost (AC) and estimate at completion. Estimate at completion is a forecast of total project cost, based on spending efficiency. Cost variance is the difference between the amount of work done and what was paid for it. "Budget remaining" is noise. [section 9.14.5, section 9.15, section 9.16]

20. Which of the following shows the rate at which the project is progressing compared to what was planned?

    Correct Answer: (D) Schedule performance index
    Explanation: The schedule performance index (SPI) shows the rate at which the schedule is progressing. The SPI is established by showing the ratio between work done, also known as earned value (EV) and work scheduled, also known as planned value (PV). The schedule variance (SV) is the difference between work done, also known as earned value (EV) and work scheduled, also known as planned value (PV). The Gantt chart shows the schedule of the project. A variance report shows the difference between two items being measured. [section 9.14.3, section 9.15, section 9.16]

21. Which process applies budget amounts to the individual work packages or activities?

Correct Answer: (C) Cost Budgeting
Explanation: Cost Budgeting applies costs to the individual work packages or activities. Cost Estimating obtains a high level cost estimate for the overall project. Cost Control manages the cost of the project. "Earned value management" is noise. [section 9.13, section 9.16]

22. The project team is planning an upgrade to a client's Web site and infrastructure. During Planning, the team members are confronted with the cost options for a data communications line to connect to the servers. They consider the cost of purchasing the communication line for the time they need to develop the project. After that, the customer takes over the purchase of the line. They are also considering a long-term commitment that the customer can make with the communication line provider, which provides a less costly solution over the use of the system. What type of analysis is the team considering?

Correct Answer: (A) Life cycle costing
Explanation: Life cycle costing looks at the long-term cost of something, instead of simply what it costs to create it. This can increase project cost but in the long run save the owner of the system money. The other answers are noise. [section 9.8, section 9.16]

23. Activity A is worth $200, is 100% complete, and actually cost $200. Activity B is worth $75, is 90% complete, and actually cost $120 so far. Activity C is worth $200, is 75% complete, and has cost $175 so far. The total budget is $1,000. What is the total earned value for the activities listed?

Correct Answer: (A) $417.50
Explanation: To calculate earned value (EV), multiply the percent complete of each activity by its planned value (PV); that provides the EV for each activity. The next step is to add the earned value for each activity to determine the total earned value for the project. This amount is $417.50. [section 9.14.4, section 9.15, section 9.16]

24. The project Planning is progressing. The team has involved a number of expert opinions in trying to get a total cost estimate for the overall project. This process is known as?

Correct Answer: (D) Cost Estimating
Explanation: Cost Estimating obtains a high level cost estimate for the overall project. Cost Budgeting applies costs to the individual work packages or activities. Cost Control manages the cost of the project. "Analogous estimating" is noise. [section 9.11, section 9.16]

25. Which of the following is an example of fixed formula status reporting?

Correct Answer: (D) 30%/70% rule
Explanation: The 30%/70% rule is an example of fixed formula progress reporting. It means that when the activity starts, it is given a 30% complete status and will not receive the remaining 70% until it is fully complete. PV x % Complete is the formula for earned value. The other answers are noise. [section 9.9]

26. The project is using some application and database servers in the development environment. The finance department explains that the servers will be depreciated using the double declining balance (DDB) format. This is an example of what?

Correct Answer: (C) Accelerated depreciation

Explanation: Double declining balance and sum of the digits are both examples of accelerated depreciation. DDB is not standard depreciation. The other answers are noise. [section 9.7.2]

27. The project team is developing rules for reporting updates on the project. The majority of their activities are less than two reporting periods long. Which format is best to use in this case?

Correct Answer: (A) Fixed formula progress reporting

Explanation: Fixed formula uses a partial credit approach such as 50/50 and is ideal when an activity is short, such as less than two reporting periods long. The weighted milestone approach is ideal when an activity is over two reporting periods in length. Earned value shows the status of the scope, time, and cost of the project. Forecast reporting focuses on what is getting ready to be done on the project. [section 9.9]

28. You have $1,000 today and can earn 8%. In future years, how much money will this be worth?

Correct Answer: (D) Not enough information

Explanation: To calculate future value (FV), you need to have a present value (PV), an interest rate, and the time period involved. Therefore, without a time period in the question there is not enough information to answer the question. [section 9.3, section 9.15]

29. Activity A is worth $200, is 100% complete, and actually cost $200. Activity B is worth $75, is 90% complete, and actually cost $120 so far. Activity C is worth $200, is 75% complete, and has cost $175 so far. The total budget is $1,000. What is the schedule variance for the activities listed?

Correct Answer: (B) -$57.50

Explanation: To calculate this value, calculate earned value (EV) and planned value (PV) first. Multiply the percent complete of each activity by its planned value (PV) to obtain the EV for each activity. Sum the earned value of each activity to determine the total earned value. Sum the planned value of each activity (to date) to determine the total planned value. Subtract the planned value of $475.00 from the earned value of $417.50 to obtain a SV of -$57.50. This value shows that the project is $57.50 behind schedule. [section 9.14.3, section 9.15, section 9.16]

30. Which of the following metrics tell you if you are ahead of schedule?

Correct Answer: (A) Schedule performance index (SPI)

Explanation: The schedule performance index tells you if you are ahead of, on, or behind schedule. An index less than 1.0 means you are having schedule problems. An index of 1.0 means you are doing exactly as planned on the schedule. An index greater than 1.0 means you are progressing faster than planned. The cost performance index shows the spending efficiency of the project. The budget at completion is the overall budget estimate for the project. The cost variance shows the amount that the project is over or under budget. [section 9.14.3, section 9.15, section 9.16]

Chapter 10

Quality

As a topic, Quality can have a variety of interpretations. If you have significant experience in quality, you might have to adjust your perspective as you prepare for the exam, due in part to process and terminology. For example, quality assurance and quality control are names often given to quality departments or personnel. In the PMI processes, they are different and have different functions relating to quality with regard to the PMP Examination. The goal of the quality processes is to align them with the International Organization for Standardization (ISO). They should align with concepts created by Deming, Juran, and Crosby, as well as TQM (Total Quality Management), Six Sigma, FMEA (Failure Mode and Effect Analysis), VOC (Voice of the Customer), Continuous Improvement, and COQ (Cost of Quality). Figure 10-1 shows the three quality processes.

A memory tool is **QPAC** (**Q**uality **P**lanning, **A**ssurance, **C**ontrol).

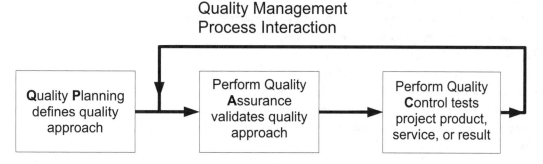

Figure 10-1: Quality Management Process Interaction

In this chapter, we discuss the following:

Process Group	Process Name		Main Outputs
Planning	Quality Planning	→	Quality Management Plan
			Quality Metrics
			Quality Improvement Plan
Executing	Perform Quality Assurance	→	Requested Changes
Monitoring and Controlling	Perform Quality Control	→	Quality Control Measurements
			Validated Deliverables

✓   **Crosswind "Must Knows" For Quality**

Key Inputs, Tools & Techniques, and Outputs for Quality Planning
Key Inputs, Tools & Techniques, and Outputs for Perform Quality Assurance
Key Inputs, Tools & Techniques, and Outputs for Perform Quality Control
The percentage of 1,2,3 and 6 Sigma
Difference between grade and quality, and how to apply them
Difference between precision and accuracy
Difference between prevention and inspection
Principles and components of a run (control) chart including the upper and lower control limits, upper and lower tolerance limits, and the mean
Characteristics of a scatter diagram
What specification limits, control limits and the mean represent
Definition of quality
What Total Quality Management is
What a Pareto diagram is and how to use it
Concept of prevention over inspection as it relates to quality
What gold plating means
Continuous improvement concepts
At what point the worker, the Project Manager, and senior management are all responsible for quality
Cost of conformance and nonconformance
Basics of probabilities and that the sum of all possible probabilities must equal 1.0 (100%)
What attributes and variables are as they relate to quality
Statistical independence and mutual exclusivity
What a Fishbone (a.k.a. Ishikawa, Cause/Effect) diagram is and in what situation it is used
Know the definition and application of Design of Experiments
Basics of Just-In-Time (JIT) inventory and that the amount of inventory needed is 0%
Principles of measuring a sample compared to the population
The Seven Run Rule

Although helpful, this list is not all-inclusive for information needed from this area for the exam. It is only suggested material that, if understood and memorized, may increase your exam score.

10.1   Definition of Quality

PMI defines quality **as the degree to which a set of inherent characteristics fulfill requirements**. It's key to understand that stated (or implied) needs are used to generate project requirements. Generating the requirements is typically accomplished via stakeholder management by using key (influential) stakeholder wants, needs, and expectations to generate those requirements during the processes associated with scoping out the project.

It's not a bad idea to be familiar with an older definition as well which is conformance to requirements and Fitness for Use.

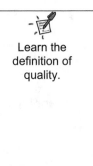

Learn the definition of quality.

10.2 Project Management and Quality Management

Project management and quality management should complement each other as they work together. Both focus on items such as customer satisfaction, management responsibility, continuous improvement, and prevention over inspection.

10.3 Total Quality Management (TQM)

Total Quality Management is a quality management philosophy conceived by **Dr. Deming.** In short, it focuses on a proactive attitude toward quality with a detail toward statistical analysis to document improvement. Dr. Deming felt that quality should be planned, not inspected when the work was complete. This view eliminates the end-of-process activity when people test functionality. Instead, it suggests that those who build the product must also test it as development progresses.

Know what Total Quality Management is.

W. Edwards Deming's 14 principles of management are generally seen as the founding basis for Total Quality Management. It's not a requirement to be familiar with these for the PMP Examination. If you are familiar with the basic principles of the points, you should be fine. These points include the following:

- Be proactive, not reactive.
- Utilize leadership and accountability.
- Measure and strive for constant improvement.

Testing while developing provides an immediate feedback loop. Process problems are more likely to be detected early on, instead of at the end. Continuous improvement of the process is a key foundation of his view on TQM.

10.4 Zero Defects

Zero Defects is a concept created by **Philip Crosby**. Its basic foundation is to **do something right initially, and you shouldn't have to repeat it.** As with most quality initiatives, if the money is spent upfront, the effort eliminates or minimizes the need for rework if defects occur.

10.5 Fitness for Use

The **Fitness for Use** concept was created by **Joseph Juran.** It implies that the **needs of the customers and stakeholders are defined and then attempted to satisfy.** The main goal is to satisfy the real need of the customers and stakeholders.

10.6 Continuous Improvement (Kaizen)

Continuous Improvement takes a **proactive stance to development, one that makes improvements throughout a process.** Corporate culture generally focuses on not accepting that things are as good as they can be, but instead seeks process improvement. Unless there is a major environment change, the bigger process improvements are likely to be at the beginning of an initiative with smaller improvements coming later.

Understand Continuous Improvement concepts.

One example is using automated shipping software instead of keying in data manually, thereby reducing the potential for error.

Understand what gold plating means.

10.7   Gold Plating

Gold plating is the practice of providing more than what the customer requested. Per PMI, this practice is unacceptable and professionally irresponsible. The Project Manager and team should provide only that which was approved. At Crosswind public courses, we are often asked why gold plating is bad. Some ask us: why is it wrong if customers receive something that increases the usage or value of what they are getting? The answer is straightforward and reflects all the process practices we have been discussing: you give your customers exactly what they ask for and what they approve in the project charter, no more or no less.

Here's an example of gold plating. You go to a car dealership, looking for a new car. The scope of what you want is an affordable basic 4-door car. You aren't interested in "add-ons" like rust proof undercoating or Scotchgard™ protection on the fabric. You explain to your salesperson what you want. You find a car you like and begin to discuss the price. Your salesperson explains in the pricing that car has the rust proof undercoating and the Scotchgard™ protection on the fabric, and that the two items cost $1,100 together. While you might perceive some value in these add-ons, they are not what you seek in the product you want.

Know the Key Inputs, Tools & Techniques, and Outputs for Quality Planning.

10.8   Quality Planning (Planning Process Group)

When you practice Quality Planning, you determine and design the project standards, policies, procedures, etc. You think through the rules that will define quality and establish rules to verify that the product will adhere to the quality needs of the project. This consideration means that not only was the project outcome built per requirements, but it was built to those requirements and will perform the overall functions that were planned when the project started.

Quality Planning (Planning)		
Key Inputs	Project Scope Statement	The project scope statement includes the product scope description and **provides a description of the scope** of the project.
	Project Management Plan	A project management plan (not a schedule!) **integrates plans representing the various Knowledge Areas** in the PMI approach to project management. Supporting detail is included to help validate the information in the project management plan.
Key Tools & Techniques	Cost-Benefit Analysis	Cost benefit analysis is a key tool used to analyze **how to minimize rework and maximize satisfaction and productivity**.
	Benchmarking	Benchmarking is a key tool for **comparing a product or service to other standards**.
	Cost of Quality (COQ)	Cost of quality (COQ) is the **cost associated with conformance to requirements and steps taken to eliminate non-conformance** to requirements.

Key Outputs	Quality Management Plan	The quality management plan **defines** what **standards** to work to, plus how to attain and test for those standards.
	Quality Metrics	Quality metrics define what something is and how the quality control process measures it. They provide the **standards that the work of the project will be specifically measured against**.
	Quality Checklist	A quality checklist is an output that **helps ensure that certain steps are taken or certain activities completed** with an overall process or project.
	Process Improvement Plan	The process improvement plan is part of the project management plan. It is **used for improving the project execution in the areas of non-value and waste**. It can include defining process boundaries, process configuration, and metrics, as well as targets for improved performance.
	Quality Baseline	Quality baseline is a key output that is the established **quality goal** for the project.

Situational Question and Real World Application
A typical problem in this area is a product whose scope falls short of or exceeds what is desired. It becomes evident that there is no real process to verify if something is acceptable or not, or why it is or isn't acceptable. There are no real quality "laws."

10.8.1   Quality Management Plan

The quality management plan helps the Project Manager and team do the following:

- Establish the definition of quality for the project and work of the project (Quality Baseline)
- Establish any checklists to ensure processes are followed
- Define any process steps
- Validate the quality processes are working
- Test the product of the project
- Format project/process data for communication to project stakeholders
- Deal with changes to the quality standards and processes on the project

10.8.2   Grade vs. Quality

Understand the difference between grade and quality. How the two compare and contrast can help you recognize a lot about the quality needs of the project.

Grade deals with the **characteristics of the product** whereas **quality** deals with the **stability or predictability of the product.** Examples of low grade could be a basic product without a lot of features such as an inexpensive nail gun. It provides basic functionality, but doesn't have a lot of extras, and is more likely used by a homeowner instead of a construction company. A high-grade product could be an automatic nail gun that can handle 10 kinds of nails, various levels of pressure, essentially meeting any type of nailing need.

Quality deals more with **how well something works.** How dependable is the lower grade or higher grade product? If it breaks, doesn't have good directions, or doesn't function as intended, it could be lacking quality.

Understand the differences between grade and quality and how to apply them.

10.8.3   Accuracy vs. Precision

Accuracy and precision are two components of quality that can often be confused. They are indeed different in nature.

Accuracy deals with the **alignment of a value with its target value.** For example, if you are testing a process and the target is 300 milliliters output, accuracy deals with how close the measurement is to the 300 milliliters target.

Precision deals with **consistency of the output**. If a test is acceptable or not, a consistent outcome is the goal when focusing on precision. For example, how many of the outputs are 300 milliliters from the accuracy example.

Understand the differences between precision and accuracy.

10.8.4   Prevention vs. Inspection

Prevention and inspection deal with different areas of the quality process.

Prevention deals with **eliminating defects and potential defects** from the process. This is the proactive approach to quality.

Inspection deals with **fixing errors or defects as they come up** in the process of creating the product or whatever is being tested or evaluated.

Understand the differences between prevention and inspection.

10.8.5   Cost of Quality

Think of the "cost of quality" as the cost of conforming or not conforming to a continuous improvement approach to quality. A company pays for quality one way or another. Conformance or nonconformance to quality is the key here.

Conformance to quality typically has a positive effect on the morale and corporate bottom line. Under this approach, a company pays for quality in a proactive way, typically up front in the Planning areas of a project. The company takes initiatives and makes training available for improved quality. It focuses on the activities for planning quality into the work instead of working the defects out, thereby resulting in lower inventory needed and reduced warranty support.

A nonconformance view to quality means the company pays for quality in a reactive way, on the back end of the project or rework. Nonconformance typically has a negative impact on the morale, customer perception, and the bottom line of a company. The cost of nonconformance typically comes from an organization that is reactive to issues, and waits for problems to come up. They end up paying for quality in areas such as excessive inventory, waste, and warranty support.

Cost of Conformance and Cost of Nonconformance

Cost Item	Conformance (Prevention)	Nonconformance (Inspection)
Proactive analysis of process improvement	X	
Company training relating to quality and continuous improvement	X	
Lower inventory needed	X	
Reduced warranty support	X	
Excessive inventory		X
Throwing away defective products		X
Warranty support		X
Reacting to problems after they happen		X

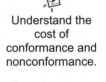

Understand the cost of conformance and nonconformance.

10.8.6   Design of Experiments

Design of Experiments (DOE) is a statistical process used to determine the factors that can influence variables associated with a process or product.

Know the definition and application of DOE.

10.8.7   Just-in-Time (JIT)

Just-in-Time (JIT) is an inventory management process that lets a company have little or no excess inventory in stock, other than what they need to build existing orders. Ideally, a company stocks **zero inventory**, with supplies arriving only when needed for the products being built. Remember, inventory costs money. Thus, an increase in quality that lets you use JIT can save your company money.

Know the basics of Just-in-Time (JIT) inventory and that the amount of inventory needed is 0%.

10.8.8   Normal Distribution

Normal distribution means that the project activity met with a typical outcome, nothing abnormal. Normal distribution is sometimes shown where the curve is tighter, or the "hill" is steeper. This depiction is still normal and merely means the data is much closer in the measurement. Other examples of distribution formats include beta and triangular distributions.

10.8.9   Sigma

Sigma is also known as standard deviation. The formula for standard deviation is (P-O)/6. P is Pessimistic; **O** is Optimistic. PMI does not require you to be a statistician to become a PMP, so let's apply a Crosswind concept called **"Realistics®."** Realistics applies a sensible way to use something such as Sigma. With Six Sigma, +/- is typically how things are measured. For example 68.26% is +/- 1 Sigma. PMI doesn't get this precise and simply would say it's 1 Sigma.

In the following diagram, **1 Sigma is 68.26%**. In the workplace, that is a quality standard. With 1 Sigma (68.26%), this is the minimum acceptable from your process. Building 100 widgets, with a 1 Sigma quality standard, you have success as long as 68.26% or more of whatever you build works. 31.74% (100%-68.26%) or less of what you build can be expected to fail, potentially leading to high cost of rework or scrap.

Memorize the percentages of 1, 2, 3, and 6 Sigma.

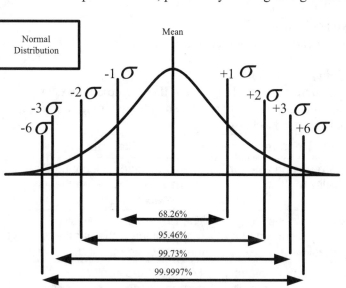

Figure 10-2: Normal Distribution Sample

By increasing the standard to **2 Sigma (95.46%)**, you increase the quantity of expected passing measurement or product to 95.46 units out of 100, or no more than 4.54 units fail. This decreases the cost of rework and waste, but you would likely have to spend on quality training and other proactive activities to achieve this standard.

The precision used to calculate these values can give you slightly different answers (e.g., 68.26%, 68.27%, 68.28% etc.). Be prepared to see slight variations of the percentages shown here, but knowing that the Sigma equals the shown percentage approximately (68.2X%, 95.X%, 99.7X%, 99.999X%) should suffice.

10.8.10   Probabilities

A probability is the likelihood that something will happen. It can be expressed in a percentage (1%, 75%, 100%) or in a more conventional number format (0.01, 0.75, 1.0). The decimal translates to a percentage. For the exam, it is key to understand that the sum of all probabilities equals 100% or 1.0.

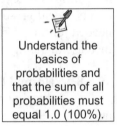
Understand the basics of probabilities and that the sum of all probabilities must equal 1.0 (100%).

10.8.11   6 Sigma

6 Sigma is a modern quality philosophy made popular by Motorola and other companies in the late 80s. It involves setting a very high standard of 6 Sigma for the products or processes that the company produces. In essence, this philosophy states that approximately **99.9997%** of everything a company creates or the processes it executes are error-free.

10.8.12   ISO 9000 (International Organization for Standardization)

The International Organization for Standardization (ISO) standard is associated with companies that wish to document their processes and adhere to those processes. While quality improvement is not always a given with this standard, the repeatability associated with it typically shows a positive benefit. A company can also use this as a requirement for its partners to ensure they have defined repeatable processes.

Generally ISO comes down to the following three steps:
- Document what you do
- Do what you document
- Document any variance (from the normal processes)

10.8.13   Quality Responsibility

Who is responsible for quality is something that will come up on the exam, because it's an easy way to pass the responsibility and let something slip if you aren't careful. The table details what you need to know.

Role	Level of Responsibility	Example
Team member or worker	They are responsible for the quality of their own work.	The electrician is accountable to ensure that work on the job is satisfactory.
Project Manager	They are responsible for the quality standards on the project.	The Project Manager is responsible for the quality on the networking project.
Senior/Executive Management	They are responsible for the quality standards at the company.	The CEO and senior management are responsible for quality at the company.

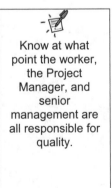
Know at what point the worker, the Project Manager, and senior management are all responsible for quality.

10.8.14   Quality Function Table

There are a number of functions used in the quality process and addressed on the exam. Use the table below as a memorization item to help you differentiate in what process you would potentially use the tools. Be sure to focus on when the item is used, not just created!

Quality Function	Quality Planning	Perform Quality Assurance	Perform Quality Control
Flowcharts	X	X	X
Fishbone/Ishikawa/Cause and Effect Diagram	X	X	X
Benchmarking	X	X	
Kaizen	X	X	
Inspection		X	X
Checklists	X	X	X
Control Charts		X	X
Pareto Diagram		X	X
Statistical Sampling		X	X

10.8.15   Checklists

Checklists are good tools you can use to ensure that everything which should be done in a process has been completed as planned. When you follow them, you can eliminate defects, thus improving quality. Think about it this way: if you were on a flight, do you want the pilot to complete the startup procedures without a checklist? Would you feel more comfortable if the pilot had 20 years experience? It seems that it might be less risky to have the pilot use the checklist.

Here is an example of a checklist you can use to prepare for the PMP Examination.

PMP Examination Review Checklist

- Verify experience is sufficient for exam qualification
- Evaluate training companies for exam review course and products
- Select a company for products or training (www.crosswindpm.com)
- Create study plan
- Execute study plan
- Apply for exam
- Receive approval from PMI for exam
- Schedule exam
- Final study review
- Take exam
- PASS TEST with PMP Exam Success Series!

10.8.16   Flowcharts

Flowcharting is a technique used in Quality Planning to map out the flow of a process or a technique. Flowcharting can help improve quality by increasing the stability and repeatability of a process.

The flowchart (sometimes called a process flow) is a good tool for defining what steps need to be completed and in what order to achieve a particular goal or output. Flowcharts can take a variety of formats. A common format follows.

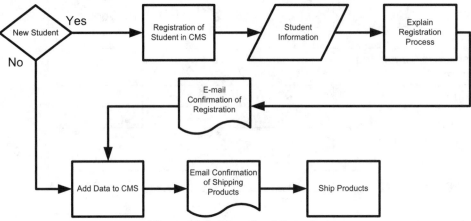

Figure 10-3: Flowchart Sample

10.8.17   Fishbone (a.k.a. Ishikawa, Cause/Effect) Diagram (Fish shape optional)

A Fishbone (cause/effect) diagram is a tool you can use initially in a project to **evaluate what could potentially cause defects** in a project or process. You can also use it after the project has started to **review symptoms to determine what the real problem is**. Some people view this similar to work decomposition except that it involves problems and symptoms instead of activities needing to be completed.

Understand what a Fishbone (cause/effect) diagram is and in what environment it is used.

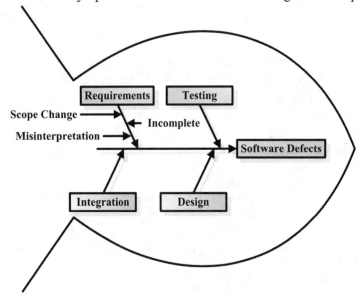

Figure 10-4: Fishbone Diagram

10.9   Perform Quality Assurance (Executing Process Group)

In Perform Quality Assurance, you verify or validate that the quality standards defined for the project will indeed meet the desired standards. This activity **validates the quality process, not the product.** It is not testing of everything that is created; it is a random sampling of items created to verify a desired level of acceptability. Generally, PMI expects the environment to have some type of quality assurance initiative in place for the situational questions.

Perform Quality Assurance (Executing)		
Key Inputs	Quality Management Plan	The quality management plan **defines** what **standards** to work to.
	Quality Metrics	Quality metrics define what something is and how the quality control process measures it. They **provide the standards that the work of the project will be specifically measured against**.
	Process Improvement Plan	The process improvement plan is part of the project management plan. It is **used for improving the project execution in the areas of non-value and waste**. It can include defining process boundaries, process configuration, and metrics, as well as targets for improved performance.
	Approved Change Requests	Approved change requests are **changes that are formally approved** by the project's official change control process.
	Quality Control Measurements	Quality control measurements are **inputs to the Perform Quality Assurance process** so the process can evaluate how well the quality control process is operating or if any modifications are needed.
	Implemented Change Requests	Implemented change requests are **approved changes that have been implemented** in the project.
Key Tools & Techniques	Quality Planning Tools and Techniques	Quality planning tools and techniques useful in this area are cause and effect **diagrams** and process **flowcharts**.
	Quality Audits	A quality audit is the process of reviewing quality activities that apply to lessons learned (about quality on the project) and can be applied to current and future projects. Quality audits **help verify process and output compliance**.
	Process Analysis	Process analysis uses the process improvement plan to determine **how to optimize project execution**. Root cause analysis is done to determine what is causing any problems and takes steps to eliminate similar problems in the future.
	Quality Control Tools and Techniques	To see other tools and techniques used in this process, see the Perform Quality Control Tools and Techniques.
Key Outputs	Requested Changes	Requested changes are **changes that have been requested but not yet formally approved** by the official change control process on the project.
	Recommended Corrective Actions	Recommended corrective actions are **modifications to the plan or work being completed** that modify output to attain a desired result that wasn't (typically) planned.

Situational Question and Real World Application
The output could be meeting functional standards but failing because specifications weren't accurate (too high or too low). There could also be a product being created that was not functional but met the specifications, even though the specifications were not accurate to define a functional product.

10.10 Perform Quality Control (Monitoring and Controlling Process Group)

Know the Key Inputs, Tools & Techniques, and Outputs for Perform Quality Control.

Perform Quality Control is the process area in which the product, or **the output of the process is measured against the specifications.** In Perform Quality Control, the items that "roll off the line" are measured against the approved standard. There are a number of tools/techniques and outputs that are key here, depending on the type of work being done in Perform Quality Control. Not all are useful in every situation, but they should be considered and used as needed.

Perform Quality Control (Monitoring and Controlling)		
Key Inputs	Quality Management Plan	Use the quality management plan and operational definitions for an accurate definition of **what to measure and what to do if things don't meet those standards**.
	Quality Metrics	Quality metrics define what something is and how the quality control process measures it. They **provide the standards that the work of the project will be specifically measured against**.
	Quality Checklists	Use quality checklists to **verify that the process is followed**.
	Work Performance Information	Work performance information provides a **status on what has been completed (or not completed)** on the project.
	Approved Change Requests	Approved change requests are **changes that have been formally approved** by the official change control process on the project.
	Deliverables	Deliverables represent the **completion of pieces of work** on the project that were defined in project planning.
Key Tools & Techniques	Cause and Effect Diagram	A cause and effect diagram (also known as Ishikawa and Fishbone) provides a tool that **helps in isolating any potential problems that relate to quality** on a project.
	Control Charts	Inspection and control charts **help measure and track output**. The control chart shows output over time so monitoring for variance and trends can be completed.
	Flowcharting	Flowcharting helps to **verify that the process is followed** accurately.
	Histogram	A histogram is a chart that uses vertical bars to **show the frequency of defects** on a sample or population being measured. It displays the percentage and number of defective cases while creating a curve with the cumulative percentage of defects.

PMP Exam Success Series: Certification Exam Manual
© 2007 Crosswind Project Management, Inc., www.crosswindpm.com

Key Tools & Techniques (cont.)	Pareto Chart	A Pareto chart **shows what areas are causing the most issues** and point to what needs it most on the project.
	Run Chart	A run chart **displays process output over time,** making it possible to perform trend analysis on the data being measured.
	Scatter Diagram	A scatter diagram is a diagram that **shows the relationship between two variables (on the X and Y axis)**. As the points create a diagonal line, the co-relation between two variables grows tighter.
	Statistical Sampling	Statistical sampling **tests an appropriate amount of output to detect defects**, but the quantity tested is not enough that the cost outweighs the benefit. It is often a key challenge in Quality Assurance (the previous Process Area).
	Inspection	Work inspection is the act of **verifying that the work was built as intended**.
Key Outputs	Quality Control Measurements	Quality control measurements are **measurements of the output of Perform Quality Control process**. They can be fed back into the Perform Quality Assurance process to **validate the efficiency and cost effectiveness of Perform Quality Control**.
	Validated Defect Repair	Validated defect repair is **performed on repaired items to ensure that they were satisfactorily repaired**.
	Recommended Corrective Actions	Recommended corrective actions are **modifications to the plan or work** being completed that typically modifies the output to achieve an unplanned desired result.
	Recommended Preventive Actions	Recommended preventive actions are **steps taken to proactively address a potential issue** on project.
	Requested Changes	Requested changes are **changes that have been requested but not yet formally approved** by the official change control process on the project.
	Validated Deliverables	Validated deliverables are the **outcome of acceptable quality control measurements**.

Situational Question and Real World Application
You may encounter problems if you ignore Quality Control or fail to implement it completely. Typically, what you see in a project lacking quality control is a situation in which people on the project follow an inconsistent process. Also common is excessive rework of the product being created, and potentially work coming back from customers to be repaired because things slip through the cracks when leaving the final stage of product verification.

10.10.1   Testing

Quality Control tests the process output. There are many items to consider when testing. Typically, you address these items in Quality Planning and apply them in Quality Control. We mention them here instead of in Quality Planning because you use them in this area. Focus on determining if testing will occur with the **population or a sample** and what the **sample criteria** will be. During testing, define the **attributes and variables** that are important. In addition, you must gain an understanding of **statistical independence and mutual exclusivity**.

Know the concept of prevention over inspection as it relates to quality.

10.10.2   Sample vs. Population

You need to determine **how much to test**. Testing **too much** can add **unneeded cost** to the project; testing **too little can hurt the level of quality**.

In **population testing, you test every item** created (Ex: every airplane built). The population is tested if the confidence level needed to be 100% such as with an election or with manufacturing medicine.

In sample testing, you determine how much of something must be tested to ensure that defects are caught. The sample testing process then tests that many of the items, for example, one of every five. You could adjust the sample later if Quality Assurance showed it was too lax (and not showing any failures) or too aggressive (catching many failures, leaving you to wonder how many were truly bad items slipping through).

In sample testing, there is a "confidence level." The more of something you test, the higher the confidence level. **Sample testing typically is done if you didn't need to test everything, or if testing everything is too costly or too destructive.**

Understand the principles of measuring a sample compared to measuring the entire population.

10.10.3   Variable

A variable is the characteristic that the Quality Control process is to measure. It is a **generic characteristic** or property, such as **capacity** or **height**.

10.10.4   Attribute

An attribute is the **specific measurement being recorded.** For example, **square feet, inches, or meters**. To remember the differences between a variable and an attribute, remember that an attribute is a unit of measurement. It's also good to know that you have to define the variable before you can define the attribute.

Know what attributes and variables are as they relate to quality.

10.10.5   Statistical Independence

Statistical independence is a state in which the **outcomes** of processes **are separate from one another**. For example, buying a lottery ticket last week doesn't increase your odds of winning the lottery this week.

10.10.6   Mutual Exclusivity

Under mutual exclusivity, **one choice does not include any other choices.** For example, shipping a product air overnight does not overlap with shipping the same product ground saver. They are separate options.

Understand statistical independence and mutual exclusivity.

10.10.7   Pareto Diagram

The Pareto diagram is **a cumulative histogram you can use to see where the key problems lie.** It is not uncommon to have only so much time to spend on issues or problems. If you must "choose your battles," this tool is a good radar screen to determine which battles to choose. With it, you can see what is causing the most frequency of problems plus a cumulative percentage of problems. Pareto diagrams do not necessarily dictate priority, unless that priority is by frequency of occurrence. **The general rule with a Pareto diagram is the 80/20 rule,** meaning that: as a general rule, 80% of the problems come from 20% of the issues. Therefore, if you can eliminate the issues, you can eliminate the problems.

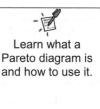

Learn what a Pareto diagram is and how to use it.

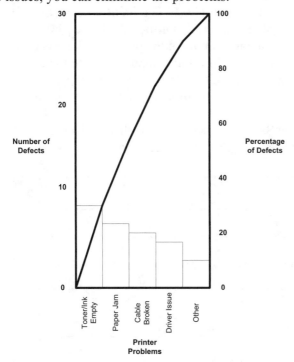

Figure 10-5: Pareto Diagram Sample

10.10.8   Scatter Diagram

The scatter diagram **shows a pattern between two variables associated with a process.** This helps see a correlation (or lack of) between variables, if it exists. The closer the output resembles a diagonal line, the more dependent the variables are. The less it resembles a diagonal line, the more independent the variables are.

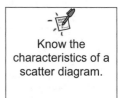

Know the characteristics of a scatter diagram.

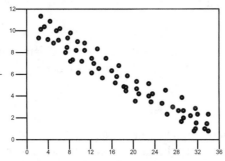

Figure 10-6: Scatter Diagram Sample

10.10.9   Run Chart

A run chart (sometimes called a control chart) gives you a picture of the **process output over time.** It could be used to track technical performance such as how well something works or schedule or cost performance such as how things were completed on time or budget, respectively. The primary difference between a run chart and a control chart is that the control chart has defined control and specification limits, whereas the run chart may not.

The **upper and lower control limits** represent the control points of the process. The process is under control if the data falls between the lower and upper control limits. This applies in all but one case (Seven Run Rule). **Typically, the upper control limit (UCL) and lower control limit (LCL) are set at +/- 3 Sigma.**

The upper and lower **tolerances** (sometimes called **upper (USL) and lower (LSL) specification limits)** represent the tolerance limits of the process. The process outcome is acceptable if the data falls between the lower and upper tolerance limits.

Think of a road. **The mean** is the middle of the road. The **control limits** are the stripes near the edge of the road, and the **tolerance limits** are the actual edges of the road.

Figure 10-7: Run Chart Diagram Sample shows a control chart and a number of different pieces of it. The mean represents the middle of the chart and the target measurement.

Learn what specification limits, control limits, and the mean represent.

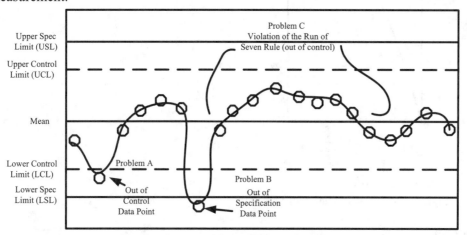

Figure 10-7: Run Chart Diagram Sample

Learn the principles and components of a run chart, including the upper and lower control limits, upper and lower specification limits, and the mean.

10.10.10   Heuristic

Heuristic is a rule of thumb and can apply to a variety of Knowledge Areas. It serves as a general rule to use when a rule specific to the situation might be too time-consuming or costly to generate for what is needed.

10.10.11   Run of Seven Rule

The Run of Seven Rule states that, if you have seven consecutive data points on either side of the mean, without crossing the other side (see above), the process is out of control and needs investigation.

Understand the Run of Seven Rule.

10.10.12   Assignable Cause

An assignable cause is a measurement on the control chart that must be researched before you can determine the reason for the failure (out of specification or out of control).

10.10.13 Special Causes vs. Common Causes

Special causes are sometimes called **unusual events**. They deal with activities or results that don't typically happen with a test process. **Common causes** are sometimes called **normal process variations** or **random causes.** They deal with variations that can happen within a process and with random events that can occur.

10.11 Quality Formulas and Variables

Description	Formula	Variable (Component)	Example
Standard Deviation shows how far the measurement is from the mean (average).	St Dev = (P-O)/6	P=Pessimistic Estimate O=Optimistic Estimate	(120-60)/6=10
Sigma (These values represent the pure math value, without factoring in process variance which can be up to 1.5 Sigma.)	N/A	**1 Sigma=68.26%** **2 Sigma=95.46%** **3 Sigma=99.73%** 4 Sigma=99.9937% 5 Sigma=99.999943% **6 Sigma=99.9999998% or 99.9997%** Memorize the Bold Values on 1,2,3, and 6!	1 Sigma=68.26% 2 Sigma=95.46% 3 Sigma=99.73% 4 Sigma=99.9937% 5 Sigma=99.999943% 6 Sigma=99.9999998% (This value is the pure math value. It could also be shown as 99.9997% which factors in the long-term dynamic mean variance or practical value.)
Upper Specification Limit is the maximum value used to determine if a process is within specification.	Data Provided	USL	USL=10
Upper Control Limit is the maximum value used to determine if a process is within control.	Data Provided	UCL	UCL=8
Lower Control Limit is the minimum value used to determine if a process is within control.	Data Provided	LCL	LCL=4
Lower Specification Limit is the minimum value used to determine if a process is within specification.	Data Provided	LSL	LSL=2
Mean is the average value of measurement.	Data Provided	Mean	Mean=6

10.12 Quality Terminology

Term	Description
Benchmarking	The comparison of a current product to industry standards or past standards to attain a measurement or baseline
Brainstorming	A data-generating technique which includes team members or subject matter experts for the purpose of solving project problems, identifying project risk, and planning-related activities
Conformance	Creation and delivery of a product that has met the specified requirements and conformance (or functionality) of use
Conformance to Requirement	The point where the project and product meet the standards of the written specifications defined at project inception (or modified through change control)
Control Chart	A graph of data that shows the measurement of a process over elapsed time
Control Limits	The area of measurement three standard deviations (or Sigma) from the mean on a control chart
Cost of Nonconformance	Cost associated with not meeting quality expectations of the project or product
Cost of Quality (COQ) (Technique)	Cost of conformance to requirements and non-conformance
Defect	A problem or error in the creation of the work of the project
Defect Repair	The process of correcting or improving an error in the creation of the project
Design of Experiments	A process that examines which variables have the greatest outcome on a process or product
Failure Mode and Effect Analysis (FMEA)	A process that analyzes every failure mode in every piece of a product The analysis is then reviewed for impact on every aspect of the system.
Features	The characteristics that the user desires built into a product
Fishbone Diagrams (Ishikawa Diagrams)	Diagrams that break down possible areas for failure in a process and allow analysis of impact for the area; sometimes considered an ideal tool for root cause analysis
Fitness for Use	A product that can be used as it was intended when designed
Flowcharts	Diagrams that display the connectivity of pieces of a system
Flowcharting (Technique)	A decomposition approach to breaking a system or process into block steps that can be repeated by following the diagram
Grade	A ranking to classify products that have different functions or features
Inspection (Technique)	Evaluating something created to ensure it meets the desired standards for use and conforms to requirements
Ishikawa Diagrams	(Fishbone Diagrams) Diagrams that break down possible areas for failure in a process and allow analysis of impact for the area; sometimes considered an ideal tool for root cause analysis
ISO 9000	Developed by the International Organization for Standardization (ISO) as a means to plan, control, and document processes, and overall improve quality
Kaizen	A technique that takes a proactive stance to process development, one that makes improvements throughout a process as time evolves
Mean	The average value in a measurement of a population
Normal Distribution	A bell-shaped curve that is in sync with the mean of the population
Parametric Estimating	An estimating technique that utilizes historical or industry data to create estimates based on parameters such as a per unit or size variable
Pareto Analysis	Identification of the few problems that have the most occurrence on a measurement in a system/project, etc.
Pareto Chart (Tool)	A histogram that allows prioritization of problem areas on a project, system, etc.
Performance	The level of success at which a product performs its intended use
Population	The entire group of similar criteria (Ex: All Americans, all owners of a particular product)

Prevention Cost	Cost of planning and executing a project within an acceptable range of error (or error free)
Procedure	A set of activities completed in a certain order to accomplish a desired objective
Process	A set of activities completed in a certain order to create a product, result, or service
Process Adjustments	Adjustments made to modify the output of a process to achieve a better degree of quality
Quality	The degree to which a set of inherent characteristics fulfill requirements
Quality Assurance	The periodic analysis of project performance to verify that the project will meet the applicable quality standards
Quality Audits	Reviews of quality activities that apply to lessons learned and can be applied to current and future projects
Quality Control	Observing project results to verify they meet the applicable quality standards while attempting to improve overall quality
Quality Management Plan I	Document that establishes the definition of quality, quality baseline, checklists; also defines and validates quality processes, tests the product, formats data for communication to project stakeholders, and deals with changes to quality standards and processes
Quality Planning	Identification of applicable quality standards and how to attain them on the project or product
Reliability	The likelihood of a product or service to function as planned
Rework	Actions used to modify/repair defective products to come within specification of the desired process outcome
Root Cause Analysis	A technique that is used to discover what is an underlying problem, defect, or variance with a system or product
Sample	A part of the population used for a measurement (instead of the entire population)
Seven Run Rule	A rule that states if seven consecutive data points are on one side of the mean (above or below) or increasing/decreasing, then the process is out of control and should be investigated
Sigma	A measurement of acceptability of a product or process
Special Cause	A non-random or intermittent variable in a system
Specification	A document (or piece of a document) that describes the requirements that something is to be created by or performed to, as well as verifiable when it has been created
Specification Limits	The area on the sides of a mean of a control chart that the customer has established as acceptable limits for testing; can be above or below but not between the control limits
Standard Deviation	The measurement of variation within a distribution
Statistical Sampling	Selecting a section of the population to use for a measurement (instead of the entire population)
Threshold	A value related to the project such as scope, time, cost, or quality that if crossed, activates some type of report, action, or procedure
Value Engineering (VE)	A technique which emphasizes executing the project and total cost of ownership over the product life cycle as efficiently and effectively as possible

10.13 Quality Mind Map

PMP Exam Success Series: Certification Exam Manual
© 2007 Crosswind Project Management, Inc., www.crosswindpm.com

10.14 Quality Tests and Exercises

10.14.1 Quality Quick Test

In this quiz, answer the question in a short essay of only a sentence or two or circle all correct answers for the question. Note that some questions may have more than one answer. Answers are in section 10.15.1.

1. What is the percentage of 3 Sigma?

2. Which tool lets you see the frequency of defects?

3. What shows output over time?

4. Quality audits are part of which process?

5. What is a higher value: the upper control limit (UCL) or upper specification limit (USL)?

6. Which tests more of something: a sample or population?

7. What is a heuristic?

8. A violation of the run of seven can occur in what process?

9. What is gold plating?

10. What is the definition of quality?

10.14.2 Quality ITTO Matching Exercise

Match the correct ITTO term at the bottom of the page with the blanks to the right of the process. When a term is used multiple times, it is flagged by a parenthetical value indicating the number of times used. Also, match summary sentences with the process name that fits. Answers are in section 10.15.2.

	Inputs	Tools &Techniques	Outputs
Quality Planning	1) _____ 2) _____	1) _____ 2) _____ 3) _____	1) _____ 2) _____ 3) _____ 4) _____ 5) _____

Summary: _____

	Inputs	Tools &Techniques	Outputs
Perform Quality Assurance	1) _____ 2) _____ 3) _____ 4) _____ 5) _____ 6) _____	1) _____ 2) _____ 3) _____ 4) _____	1) _____ 2) _____

Summary: _____

	Inputs	Tools &Techniques	Outputs
Perform Quality Control	1) _____ 2) _____ 3) _____ 4) _____ 5) _____ 6) _____	1) _____ 2) _____ 3) _____ 4) _____ 5) _____ 6) _____ 7) _____ 8) _____ 9) _____	1) _____ 2) _____ 3) _____ 4) _____ 5) _____ 6) _____

Summary: _____

Testing the work of the project
Validating the accuracy of the test procedures
Determining the quality standards of the project and how they will be attained

Approved Change Requests (2)	Process Analysis	Quality Metrics (3)
Benchmarking	Process Improvement Plan (2)	Quality Planning Tools and Techniques
Cause and Effect Diagram	Project Management Plan	
Control Charts	Project Scope Statement	Recommended Corrective Actions (2)
Cost of Quality (COQ)	Quality Audits	Recommended Preventive Actions
Cost-Benefit Analysis	Quality Baseline	Requested Changes (2)
Deliverables	Quality Checklists (2)	Run Chart
Flowcharting	Quality Control Measurements (2)	Scatter Diagram
Histogram	Quality Control Tools and Techniques	Statistical Sampling
Implemented Change Requests	Quality Management Plan (3)	Validated Defect Repair
Inspection		Validated Deliverables
Pareto Chart		Work Performance Information

10.14.3   Quality Terminology Matching Exercise

Match the correct term in the left column to the correct definition in the right column. See the exercise answer section of this chapter for the correct answer. Answers are in section 10.15.3.

Matching Exercise #1

	Term	Answer	Definition
1	Benchmarking		A. The level of success at which a product performs its intended use
2	Conformance to Requirement		B. The likelihood of a product or service to function as planned
3	Cost of Non-conformance		C. The process of correcting or improving an error in the creation of the project
4	Defect		D. A product that can be used as it was intended when designed
5	Defect Repair		E. Cost of planning and executing a project within an acceptable range of error (or error free)
6	Fitness for Use		F. The area on the sides of a mean of a control chart that the customer has established as acceptable limits for testing; can be above or below but not between the control limits
7	Flowcharts		G. Observing project results to verify they meet the applicable quality standards while attempting to improve overall quality
8	Grade		H. The point where the project and product meet the standards of the written specifications defined at project inception (or modified through change control)
9	Kaizen		I. A technique that takes a proactive stance to process development, one that makes improvements throughout a process as time evolves
10	Mean		J. A rule that states if seven consecutive data points are on one side of the mean (above or below) or increasing/decreasing, then the process is out of control and should be investigated
11	Performance		K. Cost associated with not meeting quality expectations of the project or product
12	Prevention Cost		L. Adjustments made to modify the output of a process to achieve a better degree of quality
13	Process Adjustments		M. A technique which emphasizes executing the project and total cost of ownership over the product life cycle as efficiently and effectively as possible
14	Quality		N. A problem or error in the creation of the work of the project
15	Quality Control		O. The comparison of a current product to industry standards or past standards to attain a measurement of baseline
16	Reliability		P. A non-random or intermittent variable in a system
17	Seven Run Rule		Q. A ranking to classify products that have different functions or features
18	Sigma		R. The degree to which a set of inherent characteristics fulfill requirements
19	Special Cause		S. Selecting a section of the population to use for a measurement (instead of the entire population)
20	Specification Limits		T. The average value in a measurement of a population
21	Statistical Sampling		U. A measurement of acceptability of a product or process
22	Value Engineering (VE)		V. Diagrams that display the connectivity of pieces of a system
23	ISO 9000		W. Identification of the few problems that have the most occurrence on a measurement in a system/project, etc.

24	Pareto Analysis		X. Identification of applicable quality standards and how to attain them on the project or product
25	Quality Planning		Y. Developed by the International Organization for Standardization (ISO) as a means to plan, control, and document processes, and overall improve quality

Matching Exercise #2

	Term	Answer	Definition
1	Brainstorming		A. An estimating technique that utilizes historical or industry data to create an estimate based on parameters such as a per unit or size variable
2	Control Limits		B. A histogram that allows prioritization of problem areas on a project, system, etc.
3	Failure Mode and Effect Analysis (FMEA)		C. A technique that is used to discover what is an underlying problem, defect, or variance with a system or product
4	Features		D. The area of measurement three standard deviations (or Sigma) from the mean on a control chart
5	Fishbone Diagrams		E. A value related to the project such as scope, time, cost, or quality that if crossed, activates some type of report, action, or procedure
6	Flowcharting (Technique)		F. A data-generating technique which includes team members or subject matter experts for the purpose of solving project problems, identifying project risk, and planning-related activities
7	Ishikawa Diagrams		G. Diagrams that break down possible areas for failure in a process and allow analysis of impact for the area; sometimes considered an ideal tool for root cause analysis
8	Normal Distribution		H. Diagrams that break down possible areas for failure in a process and allow analysis of impact for the area; sometimes considered an ideal tool for root cause analysis
9	Parametric Estimating		I. A set of activities completed in a certain order to accomplish a desired objective
10	Pareto Chart (Tool)		J. A process that analyzes every failure mode in every piece of a product The analysis is then reviewed for impact on every aspect of the system.
11	Population		K. The periodic analysis of project performance to verify that the project will meet the applicable quality standards
12	Procedure		L. A bell-shaped curve that is in sync with the mean of the population
13	Process		M. The characteristics that the user desires built into a product
14	Quality Assurance		N. A set of activities completed in a certain order to create a product, result, or service
15	Quality Audits		O. A decomposition approach to breaking a system or process into block steps that can be repeated by following the diagram
16	Rework		P. Actions used to modify/repair defective products to come within specification of the desired process outcome
17	Root Cause Analysis		Q. The entire group of similar criteria (Ex: All Americans, all owners of a particular product)
18	Sample		R. The measurement of variation within a distribution
19	Standard Deviation		S. A part of the population used for a measurement (instead of the entire population)
20	Threshold		T. Reviews of quality activities that apply to lessons learned and can be applied to current and future projects
21	Conformance		U. A graph of data that shows the measurement of a process over elapsed time
22	Control Chart		V. A process that examines which variables have the greatest outcomes on a process or product
23	Design of Experiments		W. Creation and delivery of a product that has met the specified requirements and conformance (or functionality) of use
24	Specification		X. A document (or piece of a document) that describes the requirements that something is to be created by or performed to, as well as verifiable when it has been created

10.14.4   Quality Practice Test
Answers are in section 10.15.4.

1.   The software developer is doing questionable work on his activities on the project. The Project Manager has spoken to him about it a few times to no resolution. Functional management has been made aware of this issue as well. Who is responsible for the quality of the work of the developer?

        (A) Senior management
        (B) Functional management
        (C) The developer
        (D) Project Manager

2.   The pilot for PM Airlines is flying from Dallas to Los Angeles. Adhering to the required pre-flight process, the pilot follows the procedures to ensure that he has properly selected and adjusted all the needed items to start up the plane for navigation. Which of the following did he likely use?

        (A) Process flowchart
        (B) Checklist
        (C) Cause and effect diagram
        (D) Company policy

3.   Ishikawa diagrams are also known as what?

        (A) Cause and effect diagram
        (B) Fishbone diagram
        (C) Pareto diagram
        (D) Cause/effect diagram AND Fishbone diagram

4.   You are defining the quality standards for the project. You have defined the variables to measure and determined what attributes are important to you. Which of the following is not an attribute?

        (A) Feet
        (B) Distance
        (C) Pounds
        (D) Kilometers

5.   You are the Project Manager on a project that will improve the manufacturing process at your company. Quality has been a big issue because there has been an excessive amount spent on inventory with a lot of waste in the building process and return of product after it has been sold. Presently, the company has a 1 Sigma quality standard with its manufacturing process. There is a general belief that there are process issues behind this problem. Which of the following options looks like the best way to help make the process more consistent?

        (A) Watching for violations of the Seven Run Rule
        (B) Making a greater use of checklists
        (C) Increasing the quality standard to a Sigma level greater than 1
        (D) Utilizing a Fishbone diagram

6. The project team is determining the accuracy of the work of the product. The project team members are utilizing a multiple pass approach. They discover that the process to measure the output isn't going to capture the data needed. What process will fix the problem?

    (A) Perform Quality Assurance
    (B) Perform Quality Control
    (C) Quality Planning
    (D) Quality Management

7. The project management team is analyzing defects and trying to isolate the cause of a problem on the project. They have isolated two variables via the data that is available. They suspect the problem is compounded by the impact of one variable on another. They want to see if there is a relationship between the two variables. Which of the following will help them verify this relationship?

    (A) Run chart
    (B) Pareto diagram
    (C) Control chart
    (D) Scatter diagram

8. The finance department is building a new call center for its new auto finance division. Given that this is its first venture utilizing a call center, there are a number of new processes that need to be created. Which of the following can help in documenting how to handle customers' various needs when they call the call center?

    (A) Checklist
    (B) Process flow
    (C) Control chart
    (D) Quality audit

9. The project is going through quality assurance. Which of the following is a key tool that will be utilized in this process?

    (A) Quality improvement
    (B) Quality audits
    (C) Quality testing
    (D) Quality management plan

10. You are doing Quality Planning on a project. The sponsor puts into the project charter that the quality standard wanted on the project is +/- 2 Sigma. This translates to what %?

    (A) 68.26%
    (B) 95.46%
    (C) 50%
    (D) 99.73%

11. The manufacturing process has been experiencing variance that is causing concern among the team. Some results have been above the specification limits, and some within the control tolerances. You want to learn more about the output of the process over the last month. Which item below shows you the most useful view of information?

   (A) Fishbone diagram
   (B) Pareto diagram
   (C) Checklist
   (D) Run chart

12. You are the Project Manager on a project that will improve the manufacturing process at your company. Quality has been a big issue because there has been an excessive amount spent on inventory with a lot of waste in the building process and return of product after it has been sold. Presently, the company has a 1 Sigma quality standard with its manufacturing process. There is talk of utilizing quality tools at the company to help minimize these problems. Which of the following options looks like the best example of a quality tool for problem isolation?

   (A) Utilizing a Fishbone diagram.
   (B) Watching for violations of the Seven Run Rule.
   (C) Increasing the quality to a Sigma level greater than 1.
   (D) Making a greater use of checklists.

13. The project is going through quality control. Which of the following is a key tool that will be utilized in this process?

   (A) Quality management plan
   (B) Inspection
   (C) Acceptance decisions
   (D) Rework

14. What does quality assurance involve?

   (A) Verifying that the quality plan will help achieve the desired results
   (B) Defining the quality rules as they relate to the project
   (C) Keeping the customer happy
   (D) Measuring the output of the project

15. The sum of all probabilities equals what?

   (A) 100
   (B) 1
   (C) 1 or 100%
   (D) 100%

16. The team is planning what quality standards are needed on the project. The team members are evaluating what could potentially cause problems in the process. Which of the following are they most likely to use to accomplish this goal?

    (A) Pareto diagram
    (B) Quality audit
    (C) Control chart
    (D) Fishbone diagram

17. What are seven consecutive data points on either side of the mean called?

    (A) Too tight of control limits
    (B) A violation of the Seven Run Rule
    (C) Too loose of specification limits
    (D) Acceptable measurements

18. The team is validating that the quality plan for the project will measure sufficiently the product of the project. What are the team members doing?

    (A) Quality control
    (B) Quality planning
    (C) Quality management
    (D) Quality audit

19. The company is implementing a quality improvement standard on its new projects, trying to improve the culture to make it conform to quality standards better. The company views the need to shift company mentality to a proactive approach to quality. Which of the following would it not expect to deal with in an environment that has a proactive approach to quality?

    (A) Increased warranty support
    (B) Greater quality standard
    (C) Less inventory needed
    (D) Decreased warranty support

20. The computer manufacturer is putting a policy in place to use Just-in-Time manufacturing. It feels this policy will help minimize excess inventory cost and improve efficiency. The amount of inventory needed for this type of process is what?

    (A) Minimal
    (B) 25%
    (C) Six Sigma
    (D) Zero

21. The project is going well. The problem is that, as the company starts to release the product of the project to market, the consumer isn't giving it much attention. This appears to be because the company has a bad perception in the marketplace for making products with too many defects. Who is ultimately responsible for the quality of what the project-based company makes?

     (A) Functional management
     (B) Project Manager
     (C) The developer
     (D) Senior management

22. The company is having issues with quality on its projects. Senior management has a mentality of dealing with problems after they arise instead of trying to eliminate them before they begin. Which of the following would the company not expect to deal with in an environment such as this?

     (A) Training for process improvement
     (B) Increased warranty support
     (C) More inventory needed
     (D) Dissatisfied customers

23. The company that won the procurement contract has begun development of the work of the project. Given that the company is trying to win more business with the customer, it is providing some extra reports and functionality with the product. Which of the following best describes this situation?

     (A) This is gold plating and it is a good thing to help them get more business.
     (B) This is gold plating and it is not a good practice.
     (C) This was an unsuccessful negotiation on the behalf of the company that won the contract.
     (D) This was a successful negotiation on the customer's behalf.

24. You are the Project Manager on a project that will improve the manufacturing process at your company. Quality has been a big issue because there has been an excessive amount spent on inventory with a lot of waste in the building process and return of product after it has been sold. Presently, the company has a 1 Sigma quality standard with its manufacturing process. There is talk of increasing the quality standard at the company to help minimize these problems. Which of the following looks like the best way to increase the quality standard?

     (A) Watching for violations of the Seven Run Rule
     (B) Making a greater use of checklists
     (C) Changing the quality to a Sigma level greater than 1
     (D) Utilizing a Fishbone diagram

25. All the following are advantages of testing a sample instead of a population except...

     (A) It is cheaper.
     (B) It is less destructive.
     (C) It is very thorough.
     (D) It is quicker.

26. The father of modern quality who preached Total Quality Management and continuous improvement was…

    (A) Deming
    (B) McGregor
    (C) Ansoff
    (D) Johnson

27. The company is in the testing phase of its project. It is tracking defects that come in from customers who are testing the project. Given the nature of a new project, a variety of defects are being discovered. Organizing and prioritizing the defects is becoming a challenge. What helps organize this better?

    (A) Pareto diagram
    (B) Flowchart
    (C) Ishikawa diagram
    (D) Fishbone diagram

28. What is the definition of quality?

    (A) Meeting the customers needs
    (B) Scope Verification
    (C) The degree to which a set of inherent characteristics fulfill requirements
    (D) Conformance to use and fitness of requirements

29. The control chart has an upper control limit of five and a lower control limit of two. What is the upper specification limit?

    (A) Seven
    (B) Greater than five
    (C) Between five and two
    (D) Less than two

30. You need something to help show quantity of defects, as well as the cumulative percentage they represent in a graphical format to help you prioritize where to spend time correcting issues. Which of the following do you use to provide this?

    (A) Pareto diagram
    (B) Ishikawa diagram
    (C) Fishbone diagram
    (D) Flowchart

10.15 Quality Tests and Exercise Answers

10.15.1   Quality Quick Test Answers

1. What is the percentage of 3 Sigma?
    99.73% is the percentage value for 3 Sigma. [section 10.8.9, section 10.11]

2. Which tool lets you see the frequency of defects?
    Pareto diagram [section 10.10.7, section 10.12]

3. What shows output over time?
    The run chart (sometimes called a control chart) [section 10.10.9, section 10.12]

4. Quality audits are part of which process?
    Perform Quality Assurance [section 10.9, section 10.13]

5. What is a higher value: the upper control limit (UCL) or upper specification limit (USL)?
    Upper specification limit (USL) [section 10.10.9, section 10.11]

6. Which tests more of something: a sample or population?
    Population [section 10.10.2, section 10.12]

7. What is a heuristic?
    A rule of thumb, for example 80% of the defects are caused by 20% of the problems.
    [section 10.10.10]

8. A violation of the run of seven can occur in what process?
    Perform Quality Control [section 10.10, section 10.12]

9. What is gold plating?
    Adding extra work to the project that is not in scope [section 10.7]

10. What is the definition of quality?
    The degree to which a set of inherent characteristics fulfill requirements [section 10.1, section 10.12]

10.15.2 Quality ITTO Matching Exercise Answers

	Inputs	Tools &Techniques	Outputs
Quality Planning	1) Project Scope Statement	1) Cost-Benefit Analysis	1) Quality Management Plan
	2) Project Management Plan	2) Benchmarking	2) Quality Metrics
		3) Cost of Quality (COQ)	3) Quality Checklists
			4) Process Improvement Plan
			5) Quality Baseline

Summary: Determining the quality standards of the project and how they will be attained

	Inputs	Tools &Techniques	Outputs
Perform Quality Assurance	1) Quality Management Plan	1) Quality Planning Tools and Techniques	1) Requested Changes
	2) Quality Metrics		2) Recommended Corrective Actions
	3) Approved Change Requests	2) Quality Audits	
	4) Process Improvement Plan	3) Process Analysis	
	5) Quality Control Measurements	4) Quality Control Tools and Techniques	
	6) Implemented Change Requests		

Summary: Validating the accuracy of the test procedures

	Inputs	Tools &Techniques	Outputs
Perform Quality Control	1) Quality Management Plan	1) Cause and Effect Diagram	1) Quality Control Measurements
	2) Quality Metrics	2) Control Charts	2) Validated Defect Repair
	3) Quality Checklists	3) Flowcharting	3) Recommended Correction Actions
	4) Work Performance Information	4) Histogram	4) Recommended Preventive Actions
	5) Approved Change Requests	5) Pareto Chart	5) Requested Changes
	6) Deliverables	6) Run Chart	6) Validated Deliverables
		7) Scatter Diagram	
		8) Statistical Sampling	
		9) Inspection	

Summary: Testing the work of the project

10.15.3 Quality Terminology Matching Exercise Answers

Matching Exercise #1 Answers

	Term		Definition
1	Benchmarking	O.	The comparison of a current product to industry standards or past standards to attain a measurement of Baseline
2	Conformance to Requirement	H.	The point where the project and product meet the standards of the written specifications defined at project inception (or modified through change control)
3	Cost of Non-conformance	K.	Cost associated with not meeting quality expectations of the project or product
4	Defect	N.	A problem or error in the creation of the work of the project
5	Defect Repair	C.	The process of correcting or improving an error in the creation of the project
6	Fitness for Use	D.	A product that can be used as it was intended when designed
7	Flowcharts	V.	Diagrams that display the connectivity of pieces of a system
8	Grade	Q.	A ranking to classify products that have different functions or features
9	Kaizen	I.	A technique that takes a proactive stance to process development, one that makes improvements throughout a process as time evolves
10	Mean	T.	The average value in a measurement of a population
11	Performance	A.	The level of success at which a product performs its intended use
12	Prevention Cost	E.	Cost of planning and executing a project within an acceptable range of error (or error free)
13	Process Adjustments	L.	Adjustments made to modify the output of a process to achieve a better degree of quality
14	Quality	R.	The degree to which a set of inherent characteristics fulfill requirements
15	Quality Control	G.	Observing project results to verify they meet the applicable quality standards while attempting to improve overall quality
16	Reliability	B.	The likelihood of a product or service to function as planned
17	Seven Run Rule	J.	A rule that states if seven consecutive data points are on one side of the mean (above or below) or increasing/decreasing, then the process is out of control and should be investigated
18	Sigma	U.	A measurement of acceptability of a product or process
19	Special Cause	P.	A non-random or intermittent variable in a system
20	Specification Limits	F.	The area on the sides of a mean of a control chart that the customer has established as acceptable limits for testing; can be above or below but not between the control limits
21	Statistical Sampling	S.	Selecting a section of the population to use for a measurement (instead of the entire population)
22	Value Engineering (VE)	M.	A technique which emphasizes executing the project and total cost of ownership over the product life cycle as efficiently and effectively as possible
23	ISO 9000	Y.	Developed by the International Organization for Standardization (ISO) as a means to plan, control, and document processes, and overall improve quality
24	Pareto Analysis	W.	Identification of the few problems that have the most occurrence on a measurement in a system/project, etc.
25	Quality Planning	X.	The identification of applicable quality standards and how to attain them on the project or product

PMP Exam Success Series: Certification Exam Manual

Matching Exercise #2 Answers

Term	Definition
1 **Brainstorming (Technique)**	F. A data-generating technique which includes team members or subject matter experts for the purpose of solving project problems, identifying project risk, and planning-related activities
2 **Control Limits**	D. The area of measurement three standard deviations (or Sigma) from the mean on a control chart
3 **Failure Mode and Effect Analysis (FMEA)**	J. A process that analyzes every failure mode in every piece of a product The analysis is then reviewed for impact on every aspect of the system
4 **Features**	M. The characteristics that the user desires built into a product
5 **Fishbone Diagrams**	G. Diagrams that break down possible areas for failure in a process and allow analysis of impact for the area; sometimes considered an ideal tool for root cause analysis
6 **Flowcharting (Technique)**	O. A decomposition approach to breaking a system or process into block steps that can be repeated by following the diagram
7 **Ishikawa Diagrams**	H. Diagrams that break down possible areas for failure in a process and allow analysis of impact for the area; sometimes considered an ideal tool for root cause analysis
8 **Normal Distribution**	L. A bell-shaped curve that is in sync with the mean of the population
9 **Parametric Estimating (Technique)**	A. An estimating technique that utilizes historical or industry data to create an estimate based on parameters such as a per unit or size variable
10 **Pareto Chart (Tool)**	B. A histogram that allows prioritization of problem areas on a project, system, etc.
11 **Population**	Q. The entire group of similar criteria (Ex: All Americans, all owners of a particular product)
12 **Procedure**	I. A set of activities completed in a certain order to accomplish a desired objective
13 **Process**	N. A set of activities completed in a certain order to create a product, result or service
14 **Quality Assurance**	K. The periodic analysis of project performance to verify that the project will meet the applicable quality standards
15 **Quality Audits**	T. Reviews of quality activities that apply to lessons learned and can be applied to current and future projects
16 **Rework**	P. Actions used to modify/repair defective products to come within specification of the desired process outcome
17 **Root Cause Analysis (Technique)**	C. A technique that is used to discover what is an underlying problem, defect, or variance with a system or product
18 **Sample**	S. A part of the population used for a measurement (instead of the entire population)
19 **Standard Deviation**	R. The measurement of variation within a distribution
20 **Threshold**	E. A value related to the project such as scope, time, cost, or quality that if crossed, activates some type of report, action, or procedure
21 **Conformance**	W. Creation and delivery of a product that has met the specified requirements and conformance (or functionality) of use
22 **Control Chart**	U. A graph of data that shows the measurement of a process over elapsed time
23 **Design of Experiments**	V. A process that examines which variables have the greatest outcomes on a process or product
24 **Specification**	X. A document (or piece of a document) that describes the requirements that something is to be created by or performed to, as well as verifiable when it has been created

10.15.4   Quality Practice Test Answers

1.   The software developer is doing questionable work on his activities on the project. The Project Manager has spoken to him about it a few times to no resolution. Functional management has been made aware of this issue as well. Who is responsible for the quality of the work of the developer?

     Correct Answer: (C) The developer
     Explanation: The developer is responsible for his own work. Senior management is responsible for the quality of the company. The Project Manager is responsible for the quality on the project. "Functional management" is noise. [section 10.8.13]

2.   The pilot for PM Airlines is flying from Dallas to Los Angeles. Adhering to the required pre-flight process, the pilot follows the procedures to ensure that he has properly selected and adjusted all the needed items to start up the plane for navigation. Which of the following did he likely use?

     Correct Answer: (B) Checklist
     Explanation: The checklist can help ensure that certain steps that need to be completed are done as planned. The process flowchart shows how activities flow. Cause and effect diagram is used for problem planning and solving. "Company policy" is noise. [section 10.8.15]

3.   Ishikawa diagram are also known as what?

     Correct Answer: (D) Cause/effect diagram AND Fishbone diagram
     Explanation: Ishikawa diagrams are known as both cause/effect diagrams AND Fishbone diagrams. Pareto deals with showing frequency of defects. [section 10.8.17, section 10.12]

4.   You are defining the quality standards for the project. You have defined the variables to measure and determined what attributes are important to you. Which of the following is not an attribute?

     Correct Answer: (B) Distance
     Explanation: Distance is a variable. It is something that you measure. The other answers are attributes. [section 10.10.3, section 10.10.4]

5.   You are the Project Manager on a project that will improve the manufacturing process at your company. Quality has been a big issue because there has been an excessive amount spent on inventory with a lot of waste in the building process and return of product after it has been sold. Presently, the company has a 1 Sigma quality standard with its manufacturing process. There is a general belief that there are process issues behind this problem. Which of the following options looks like the best way to help make the process more consistent?

     Correct Answer: (B) Making a greater use of checklists
     Explanation: When followed, checklists help the employee attain consistent process execution. Assuming the checklist is sufficient and that the employee follows it, the process should possess a greater degree of stability. Fishbone diagrams work with problem isolation. Increasing the quality level makes a process more consistent, but it takes tools to do that. The checklist is a good quick fix that can have standard long-term benefit, especially if the Sigma level is increased and higher quality expectations are put in place. [section 10.8.15]

6.   The project team is determining the accuracy of the work of the product. The team members are utilizing a multiple pass approach. They discover that the process to measure the output isn't going to capture the data needed. What process will fix the problem?

Correct Answer: (C) Quality Planning

Explanation: The Quality Planning process fixes the problem. Perform Quality Assurance and Perform Quality Control are involved in this situation, but the solution comes in Quality Planning. "Quality management" is noise. [section 10.8, section 10.12, section 10.13]

7.   The project management team is analyzing defects and trying to isolate the cause of a problem on the project. They have isolated two variables via the data that is available. They suspect the problem is compounded by the impact of one variable on another. They want to see if there is a relationship between the two variables. Which of the following will help them verify this relationship?

Correct Answer: (D) Scatter diagram

Explanation: The scatter diagram shows a relationship (or lack of a relationship) between two variables. The run chart (sometimes called a control chart) shows output over time. The Pareto diagram shows defect by quantity. [section 10.10.8]

8.   The finance department is building a new call center for its new auto finance division. Given that this is its first venture utilizing a call center, there are a number of new processes that need to be created. Which of the following can help in documenting how to handle customers' various needs when they call the call center?

Correct Answer: (B) Process flow

Explanation: The process flow helps define how company employees manage customers on the phone. A checklist helps to ensure that certain things are done. A control chart shows output over time. A quality audit ensures that the quality standards of the project will be met. [section 10.8.16]

9.   The project is going through quality assurance. Which of the following is a key tool that will be utilized in this process?

Correct Answer: (B) Quality audits

Explanation: The quality audit is used in Perform Quality Assurance to verify that Quality Planning meets the needs of the project. Quality improvement comes from quality control. Quality management plan is an output of Quality Planning. "Quality testing" is noise. [section 10.9, section 10.12, section 10.13]

10.   You are doing Quality Planning on a project. The sponsor puts into the project charter that the quality standard wanted on the project is +/- 2 Sigma. This translates to what %?

Correct Answer: (B) 95.46%

Explanation: The percentage for 1 Sigma is 68.26%, for 2 Sigma is 95.46%, and for 3 Sigma is 99.73%. "50%" is noise. [section 10.8.9, section 10.11]

11.   The manufacturing process has been experiencing variance that is causing concern among the team. Some results have been above the specification limits, and some within the control tolerances. You want to learn more about the output of the process over the last month. Which item below shows you the most useful view of information?

Correct Answer: (D) Run chart

Explanation: The run chart's main purpose is to show output over time. This provides an opportunity to catch any trends and variance with the process. Fishbone diagrams are used for problem isolation. The Pareto diagram shows defect by count. A checklist helps to ensure consistency in doing something. [section 10.10.9]

12.   You are the Project Manager on a project that will improve the manufacturing process at your company. Quality has been a big issue because there has been an excessive amount spent on inventory with a lot of waste in the building process and return of product after it has been sold. Presently, the company has a 1 Sigma quality standard with its manufacturing process. There is talk of utilizing quality tools at the company to help minimize these problems.

Which of the following options looks like the best example of a quality tool for problem isolation?

Correct Answer: (A) Utilizing a Fishbone diagram.
Explanation: The Fishbone diagram is a quality tool that can be used to look for the source or root cause of other symptoms you might be experiencing in an area. The Seven Run Rule can occur on a control chart when looking at output over time. Increasing the quality level is not a tool nor will it isolate a problem. A checklist could be used as a tool but won't help isolate problems. [section 10.8.17, section 10.12]

13.   The project is going through quality control. Which of the following is a key tool that will be utilized in this process?

Correct Answer: (B) Inspection
Explanation: Inspection is a key tool in quality control. It provides validation that the product was built as intended. A quality management plan establishes the standards and how to achieve them on the project. Rework comes when products are not built correctly. Acceptance decisions deal with defining what is and isn't acceptable. [section 10.10, section 10.8.4, section 10.12, section 10.13]

14.   What does quality assurance involve?

Correct Answer: (A) Verifying that the quality plan will help achieve the desired results
Explanation: Quality assurance ensures that the quality plan will achieve the desired results of the project. Defining the quality rules as they relate to the project is in Quality Planning. Measuring the output of the project is quality control. "Keeping the customer happy" is noise. [section 10.9, section 10.12, section 10.13]

15.   The sum of all probabilities equals what?

Correct Answer: (C) 1 or 100%
Explanation: The sum of all probabilities is equal to 1 or 100%. 100% is the maximum sum of all potential outcomes of a situation. [section 10.8.10]

16.   The team is planning what quality standards are needed on the project. The team members are evaluating what could potentially cause problems in the process. Which of the following are they most likely to use to accomplish this goal?

Correct Answer: (D) Fishbone diagram
Explanation: The Fishbone diagram can be used to look for problems that could show up on the project. The Pareto diagram shows the frequency of defects. The control chart shows output over time. A quality audit helps ensure that the project will meet the quality needs. [section 10.8.17, section 10.12]

17.   What are seven consecutive data points on either side of the mean called?

Correct Answer: (B) A violation of the Seven Run Rule
Explanation: The Seven Run Rule is a situation in which there are at least seven consecutive data points on one side of the mean, implying that the process could have some type of problem. The other answers are noise. [section 10.10.11, section 10.12]

18.   The team is validating that the quality plan for the project will measure sufficiently the product of the project. What are they doing?

Correct Answer: (D) Quality audit
Explanation: The quality audit helps ensure that the quality management plan will meet the quality needs of the project. Quality control deals with measuring the output of the project. Quality Planning deals with defining the quality rules of the project. "Quality management" is noise. [section 10.9, section 10.12, section 10.13]

19. The company is implementing a quality improvement standard on its new projects, trying to improve the culture to make it conform to quality standards better. The company views the need to shift company mentality to a proactive approach to quality. Which of the following would it not expect to deal with in an environment that has a proactive approach to quality?

Correct Answer: (A) Increased warranty support

Explanation: Typically, increased warranty support is not encountered in an environment that has a proactive approach to quality. The other answers are expected in an environment that proactively addresses quality. [section 10.8.5]

20. The computer manufacturer is putting a policy in place to use Just-in-Time manufacturing. It feels this will help minimize excess inventory cost and increase efficiency. The amount of inventory needed for this time of process is what?

Correct Answer: (D) Zero

Explanation: The amount of inventory needed for Just-in-Time (JIT) inventory is optimally zero days, implying that inventory arrives when it is needed. [section 10.8.7]

21. The project is going well. The problem is that, as the company starts to release the product of the project to market, the consumer isn't giving it much attention. This appears to be because the company has a bad perception in the marketplace for making products with too many defects. Who is ultimately responsible for the quality of what the project-based company makes?

Correct Answer: (D) Senior management

Explanation: Senior management is responsible for the quality of the company. The developer is responsible for his own work. The Project Manager is responsible for the quality on the project. "Functional management" is noise. [section 10.8.13]

22. The company is having issues with quality on its projects. Senior management has a mentality of dealing with problems after they arise instead of trying to eliminate them before they begin. Which of the following would the company not expect to deal with in an environment such as this?

Correct Answer: (A) Training for process improvement

Explanation: Training for process improvement is something that a company with a proactive approach to quality will do. The other answers deal with the reactive (nonconformance) environment described in the situation. [section 10.8.5]

23. The company that won the procurement contract has begun development of the work of the project. Given that the company is trying to win more business with the customer, it is providing some extra reports and functionality with the product. Which of the following best describes this situation?

Correct Answer: (B) This is gold plating and it is not a good practice.

Explanation: Gold plating is what is happening here. It is not good by any means because you should provide customers what they want and nothing more or less. Negotiations have nothing to do this situation. [section 10.7]

24. You are the Project Manager on a project that will improve the manufacturing process at your company. Quality has been a big issue because there has been an excessive amount spent on inventory with a lot of waste in the building process and return of product after it has been sold. Presently, the company has a 1 Sigma quality standard with its manufacturing process. There is talk of increasing the quality standard at the company to help minimize these problems. Which of the following looks like the best way to increase the quality standard?

Correct Answer: (C) Changing the quality to a Sigma level greater than 1

Explanation: This is a tricky question. Some of the answers will potentially improve quality, but you are being asked what will increase the quality standard. Increasing the quality standard from 1 Sigma to 2 (or greater) Sigma will increase the quality standard. [section 10.8.9]

25. All the following are advantages of testing a sample instead of a population except...

Correct Answer: (C) It is very thorough.

Explanation: It is very thorough is not always the case with testing a sample. Testing the population is thorough because it tests everything; whereas, sample testing tests only a portion of the population. [section 10.10.2, section 10.12]

26. The father of modern quality who preached Total Quality Management and continuous improvement was...

Correct Answer: (A) Deming

Explanation: Dr. Deming was the father of Total Quality Management (TQM). McGregor was associated with Theory X and Y. Ansoff is a strategic management methodologist. Johnson is the author of this book. [section 10.3]

27. The company is in the testing phase of its project. It is tracking defects that come in from customers who are testing the project. Given the nature of a new project, a variety of defects are being discovered. Organizing and prioritizing the defects is becoming a challenge. What helps organize this better?

Correct Answer: (A) Pareto diagram

Explanation: The Pareto diagram shows frequency of defects in a graphical format. The flowchart shows process flow. Fishbone and Ishikawa are the same. They show what problems could happen or might be happening. [section 10.10.7, section 10.12, section 10.13]

28. What is the definition of quality?

Correct Answer: (C) The degree to which a set of inherent characteristics fulfill requirements

Explanation: The PMI definition of quality is the degree to which a set of inherent characteristics fulfill requirements, implying that you build what the requirements say should be built, and that the product built will perform and function as defined and needed. [section 10.1, section 10.12]

29. The control chart has an upper control limit of five and a lower control limit of two. What is the upper specification limit?

Correct Answer: (B) Greater than five

Explanation: The upper specification limit (USL) is greater in value than the upper control limit (UCL); therefore, with an upper control limit of five, the upper specification limit is greater than five. [section 10.10.9, section 10.12]

30. You need something to help show quantity of defects, as well as the cumulative percentage they represent in a graphical format to help you prioritize where to spend time correcting issues. Which of the following do you use to provide this?

Correct Answer: (A) Pareto diagram

Explanation: The Pareto diagram shows frequency of defects in a graphical format. The flowchart shows process flow. Fishbone and Ishikawa are the same. They show what problems could happen or might be happening. [section 10.10.7, section 10.12, section 10.13]

Chapter 11

Human Resource

Human Resource is one of the easier Knowledge Areas to prepare for. If your background includes a business degree, you will likely see many similarities from college. It's not wise to take this area lightly though because there are a number of details that can trip you up if you aren't careful of the rules behind them. Remember, PMI's perspective on the exam is that the Project Manager has human resources responsibilities and authority.

Human Resource processes can be summed up as: "Plan 'em, Get 'em, Grow 'em, Run 'em."

In this chapter, we discuss the following:

Process Group	Process Name		Main Outputs
Planning	Human Resource Planning	→	Roles and Responsibilities
			Staffing Management Plan
			Project Organization Chart
Executing	Acquire Project Team	→	Project Staff Assignments
	Develop Project Team	→	Team Performance Assessment
Monitoring and Controlling	Manage Project Team	→	Requested Changes

☑ Crosswind "Must Knows" For Human Resource

☐	Key Inputs, Tools & Techniques, and Outputs for Human Resource Planning
☐	Key Inputs, Tools & Techniques, and Outputs for Acquire Project Team
☐	Key Inputs, Tools & Techniques, and Outputs for Develop Project Team
☐	Key Inputs, Tools & Techniques, and Outputs for Manage Project Team
☐	Roles of the Project Manager, project management team, sponsor, senior management, functional manager, stakeholder, team member and other roles defined in the framework chapter of this book as each relates to project management
☐	Characteristics and differences of power types of the Project Manager
☐	Characteristics and differences of conflict resolution techniques: confronting, compromising, withdrawal, smoothing, and forcing
☐	What each level of Maslow's Hierarchy of Needs is and what it overall represents
☐	Principles of a resource histogram and responsibility assignment matrix (RAM)
☐	Characteristics of an organizational breakdown structure
☐	Team development life cycle (form, storm, norm, perform)
☐	What perks and fringe benefits are, and the differences between them
☐	Halo Theory and Expectancy Theory
☐	Principles of McGregor's Theory X and Y for management and labor

Although helpful, this list is not all-inclusive for information needed from this area for the exam. It is only suggested material that, if understood and memorized, may increase your exam score.

11.1 Human Resource Planning (Planning Process Group)

In Human Resource Planning, you address the Planning needs of the project. This process determines what roles, what reporting structure, and what relationships the project needs, as well as the quantity of people on the project (which can change as the project evolves). Project team members can also be called project staff. Such planning could involve people external to the project or the company, as well as those on the project or at the company performing the work. It is not uncommon to discover after the WBS is established that more team members are needed. Depending upon the skill level of added team members, changes in staffing could impact the project in areas such as schedule, budget, and risk.

This Planning is typically done as early as possible in the project.

> Know the Key Inputs, Tools & Techniques, and Outputs for Human Resource Planning (Organizational Planning).

Human Resource Planning (Planning)		
Key Inputs	Project Management Plan • Activity Resource Requirements	A project management plan (not a schedule!) **integrates plans representing the various Knowledge Areas** in the PMI approach to project management. Supporting detail is also included to help validate the information in the project management plan. Supporting detail can occur in the form of enterprise environmental factors. Examples include organizational structure, technical approaches, interpersonal relationships, logistical issues, and political agendas. Applicable constraints should be addressed as well. These could include unions (collective bargaining agreements), economics, and organizational structure. Organizational process assets could also be created or reused (from previous projects). These assets could include templates and checklists useful in the Human Resource Planning processes.
		Activity resource requirements **provide the resources needed** for the project. They can include non-people resources such as infrastructure and conference rooms or personnel such as programmers and architects. They can also include quantity, start and finish dates, needed skill sets, and experience levels of the needed resources.
Key Tools & Techniques	Organization Charts and Position Descriptions	An organization chart (also known as an organizational breakdown structure (OBS) or a resource breakdown structure (RBS)) is used for a **graphical display of reporting relationships** on the project.
		Position descriptions **help team members understand their project responsibilities**.
	Organizational Theory	Organizational theory **helps establish how the organization or project should be structured**.

Key Outputs	Roles and Responsibilities	Key outputs include role and responsibilities which also **help personnel know exactly their positions on the project**, as well as what is expected of that position by those in charge of the project. Items to consider when determining roles and responsibilities include the role of the person and the authority needed to go with it, the responsibility needed with the role and the level of competency needed for the role, and what a potential candidate may possess.
	Project Organization Charts	A project organization chart (also known as an organizational breakdown structure, OBS) is used for a **graphical display of reporting relationships** on the project. It can have a number of different formats as described later in this section.
	Staffing Management Plan	A staffing management plan to **address how staffing needs will be filled and managed** on the project. This plan can include items associated with how to acquire staff for the project, desired timeframes, how to release team members, what training is required, safety and compliance, as well as any reward and recognition system.

Situational Question and Real World Application
If this area falls short on planning or implementation, problems are likely to occur where resources are not the ideal skill set, or if they were, they might start the job too early or late on the project.
The team members could also be somewhat confused regarding the person they report to and who could give them orders to complete the project.

11.1.1   Staffing Management Plan

The Staffing Management Plan helps the Project Manager and team do the following:

- Establish the staffing policies for the project
- Establish the organizational chart (OBS) for the project
- Define position descriptions for the project
- Get team members on the project
- Develop the group of people into a team
- Deal with team issues that arise

11.1.2   Responsibility Assignment Matrix (RAM) Charts

This tool lets the project team know who is involved in each area and what they are responsible for in that area. It can eliminate the "I didn't know" excuse and finger-pointing. It can be used at a high level of the WBS to identify the various pieces of work that each group is responsible for or at the detailed level of the WBS to cover individual responsibilities. In other pieces of the project management plan, there could be the need for a RAM chart. Examples include the risk owners in the risk register, quality plan for people associated with quality assurance and quality control, and finally the communication plan for the various communication requirements of the stakeholders. For the exam, you need to recognize the following table and know what the tool is used for.

Activity/Resource	Michael	Richard	Bev	Brett	Jessica
Planning	R	A	C	C	I
Design	I	R	A	I	C
Development	I	A	R	C	I
Testing	I	A	C	R	C
Closure	I	R	A	C	I

Legend:

Responsible=R, Accountable=A, Consult=C, Inform=I

11.1.3   Organization Charts

Organization charts can have a variety of formats depending upon their need. An organization chart, sometimes called an organizational breakdown structure (OBS), shows a reporting relationship between the resources in an organization. This structure is typically shown in company divisions, departments, and groups. Typically, it does not show details related to project organization and work.

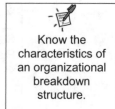

Know the characteristics of an organizational breakdown structure.

Organizational Breakdown Structure

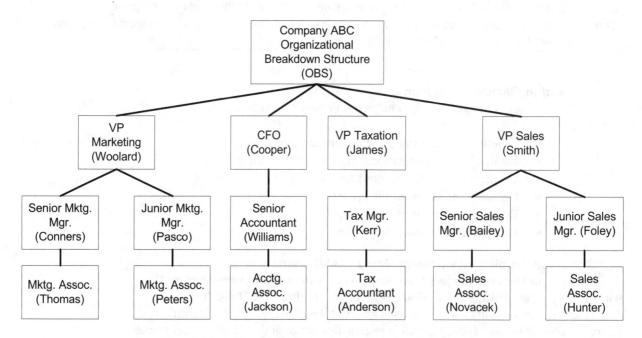

Figure 11-1: Organizational Breakdown Structure Sample

11.1.4   Motivational Theory

Motivational Theory involves strategies for motivating employees and creating a productive work environment. The following are some popular theories that you should be familiar with.

PMP Exam Success Series: Certification Exam Manual
© 2007 Crosswind Project Management, Inc., www.crosswindpm.com

Maslow's Hierarchy of Needs

Maslow's Hierarchy of Needs is a tool you can use to determine what can be used to motivate an employee. **The key is to find out where someone is in the triangle and use items from that area to motivate.**

For example, in the physiological area, the focus is on the basics of existence, such as shelter, food, survival. If someone on your team has a house, expensive car, and goes on extravagant vacations, you aren't going to motivate that person with something from the physiological area. Esteem or self-actualization represents forces likely to motivate. Things like the more expensive car, the promotion at work, or the extended vacation are the hot buttons for that person.

Know what each level of Maslow's Hierarchy of Needs is and what it represents overall.

Maslow's Hierarchy of Needs

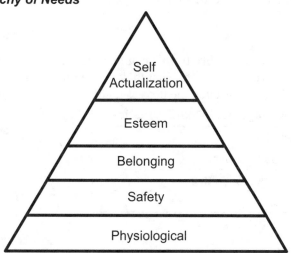

Figure 11-2: Maslow's Hierarchy of Needs

Physiological	Basics needed for survival, such as shelter and food
Safety	Items or elements that make us feel comfortable or protected
Belonging	Friends, finding love, existence, and association
Esteem	How we are perceived and feel about ourselves
Self Actualization (could be considered "Achievement")	Someone who performs a calling, someone with everything going right and feeling that life can't get much better

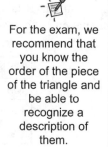

For the exam, we recommend that you know the order of the piece of the triangle and be able to recognize a description of them.

Herzberg's Motivational Theory

Herzberg had two main areas for workplace success. The first was **hygiene**, which focuses mainly on areas associated with the workplace. Factors such as a safe work environment, steady pay, and a stable job are examples of hygiene.

Motivating agents were his second area of focus, which deals with the non-financial characteristics of work. Examples can include the opportunity to improve and do more, education, and responsibility.

One basic assumption of Motivational Theory is that in most cases, **money does not create motivation.** Instead, endeavors like improving the workplace, showing appreciation toward the worker, and additional responsibility typically motivate workers more than simply throwing money at them.

McClelland's Achievement Theory

The **Achievement** Theory is **McClelland's** theory that revolves around **achievement, power, and affiliation**. The achievement focus is on being successful. The **power focus** is on influencing others, and the **affiliation focus** is on belonging. These three tie together as a group of people form a project team and work toward common goals.

McGregor's Theory X and Y

The X and Y theories can apply to management or labor. As you read the tables below, try to imagine a manager from Theory X and labor from Theory Y or the other way around. Is it a nightmare waiting to happen?

The tables that follow describe the characteristics of both types.

Know the principles of McGregor's Theory X and Y for management and labor.

McGregor's Theory X

Theory X is more an "old school" mentality from when factories produced the majority of the work. People went to work, were told what to do, and didn't want to have to evaluate what needed to be done, but wanted the boss to tell them.

Theory X Labor and Management Characteristics
Labor wants to be told what to do.
Management feels the need to supervise.
Labor is not necessarily motivated to work.
Labor does not want to work.

McGregor's Theory Y

Theory Y is a more "modern" perspective on labor and management. It is an environment in which management typically lets labor know what needs to be done and by when, and directs them toward it. This main difference stems from motivation. If labor can (and wants to) see the big picture of where work is going, management can set the expectation and lead instead of only manage.

Theory Y Labor and Management Characteristics
Labor can work with an end goal in mind.
Management can minimize supervision.
Labor is motivated to do what is necessary for work.
Labor wants to work and enjoys it.

11.1.5 Leadership and Management Styles with the Project Management Life Cycle

As the project goes further into the project management life cycle, the Project Manager's leadership and management approach evolves. **Earlier** in the project, the Project Manager has more of a **directing** approach. **As the project begins to evolve**, there is a shift toward a **coaching** approach. As the project maximizes momentum and experiences **a great deal of work accomplishment**, the style shifts to **facilitation** with **support** being the approach at **project closure**.

The table that follows summarizes the project stages and the concurring management approach to each.

Stage of Project	Management Approach
Early	Directing
Gains momentum	Coaching
Significant work complete	Facilitating
Closing	Supporting

11.1.6   Delegation

Delegation is a key tool a Project Manager can use to assign **work** (and the respective **authority** and **responsibility**) to team members for conducting activities on the project.

When used effectively, delegation is not simply giving team members the dirty work or telling them what to do. **Effective delegation involves** giving team members the **responsibility and authority to get the work** done on time. In return, the Project Manager expects accountability and reliability from the team member who has been assigned the work. This expectation should help team members accept the project work and become more involved.

Delegation involves communication. The **Project Manager assigns the work** with a **clear definition** of what **work is to be done**, the **expected results**, and how **progress is to be evaluated**. The team members assigned the work provide feedback as acceptance of the responsibility.

Effective project managers are sensitive to delegation and know what work they can delegate to subordinates and what work they need to perform themselves.

For Consideration to Delegate	Not to be Delegated
Technical activities	Evaluating or ranking team members
Cross-training-related work	Long term (strategic) planning
Routine activities	Monitoring extremely important activities
Enjoyable activities	Rewarding team members
Work that breaks the routine of some jobs	Determining policies
Work that others do better	Personnel selection

A **traditional role** of the Project Manager has been to focus on **planning, directing, organizing**, and other project activities of that nature. Given the **evolving project environment**, these activities should be considered for delegation where applicable with the **Project Manager focusing efforts** in areas such **as coaching, motivating, evolving team performance,** and **managing expectations** of the key stakeholders.

Effective delegation is not without obstacles. **Obstacles can come from** the **Project Manager, the team, or the organization**. There could be situations in which the Project Manager doesn't want to involve others for various reasons. Perhaps team members are unwilling to accept the delegated work or the organization fails to support the Project Manager in the delegation of (certain) work to others.

Delegation can also be used to show what others on the project are capable of doing, thereby preparing them for promotion or new positions in the organization.

11.1.7   Management Styles

There are a number of management styles that could appear on the exam. To a seasoned Project Manager, many are somewhat instinctive, but if you aren't familiar with their names, situational questions could cause you some problems. Remember, a Project Manager doesn't need to have just one of these styles. Style can vary as the situation dictates.

Autocratic	Autocratic managers have strong or unlimited power and authority.
Charismatic	Charismatic managers have an appealing persona that makes team members enjoy working with them.
Coach	The Coach brings out the best in the team, coaching members to their potential or where they need to be with regard to the project.
Director	The Director drives the direction of the team or team members to accomplish specific activities and goals.
Facilitator	The Facilitator helps keep things progressing, making them happen. This style is not super proactive nor does it have ownership.
Mediator	The Mediator tries to find a common goal when there is disagreement. This style is ideal when there are varying technical opinions or disagreement among resource managers.
Mentor	A Mentor is similar to Coach but focuses more on showing people how to improve, helping them take on new skills and roles.
Visionary	The Visionary sees what can be, where the company or team needs to go, focusing more on the big picture of the company, with others focusing on the day-to-day events.

11.1.8   Roles and Responsibilities

From PMI's view, it is key to understand the table detailing the various project management roles in the Framework chapter that describes roles and responsibilities as they relate to project management. The table in this chapter helps you understand who is ultimately responsible for what type of problem. **Typically, the situational questions reference a balanced matrix environment, unless otherwise stated.**

Understand the roles as each relates to project management.

There are various roles which can be constructive or destructive to the team.
Become familiar with the ones described.

Constructive Team Roles	
Initiators	A proactive role that takes initiatives on a project with contribution and ideas
Information Seeker	A role that works to enhance information and knowledge associated with the project
Information Giver	A role that shares information and thus helps enhance communication on the project
Encourager	A role that helps the project and team by focusing on what the project is creating, not the challenges of the project
Clarifier	A role that helps focus on making sure people on the project understand what the details of the project entail
Harmonizer	A role that helps evolve information and understanding on the project above the team members
Summarizer	A role that relates back to the overall picture of what the project is focusing on
Gate Keeper	In project management, a role that helps bring people into the project In business school, this term could be seen differently, including a role that keeps people out of something.

Destructive Team Roles	
Aggressor	A role with a negative attitude toward the project
Blocker	A role that interrupts information flow on the project
Withdrawer	A role that is non-participatory on the project regarding information and project issues
Recognition Seeker	A role that looks at the project first to see what they can get out of it
Topic Jumper	A role that doesn't stay focused on the primary topics of focus and conversation
Dominator	A role that consumes project communication and focus with their own views without considering others
Devil's Advocate	A role that contradicts popular views or opinions about the work of the project

11.1.9   Power

One of the keys to successful project management is the ability to use the power of the Project Manager to accomplish the challenges of the job. On the exam, you can expect to be quizzed on five different types of power, which is best, worst, and what type you have to earn on your own.

The table that follows displays the five types of power with examples.

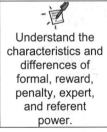

Understand the characteristics and differences of formal, reward, penalty, expert, and referent power.

Power	Description	Example
Formal	Formal power is **legitimate** power. It is the type of power that comes from senior management at a company authorizing you to be the Project Manager, and whatever authority comes with that.	As you saw at the kickoff meeting, the sponsor said that I am the Project Manager on this project and the team takes direction from me on matters related to the project.
Reward	A reward is usually the **best** form of power to use. With a reward, someone receives a benefit (reward) for doing something that is needed.	If you complete your work on the project ahead of schedule, we will send you to that training class you have been wanting to attend.
Penalty	A penalty is the **worst** form of power to use. With a penalty, people experience negative impact if they don't do what is desired.	If you don't complete the work as planned, I will make sure that you don't get your bonus like the other people will.
Expert	This form of power is one that Project Managers must **earn on their own**. With expert power, the Project Manager is perceived as an expert on the subject by those on the team or at the company.	We must listen to what he says regarding project management. He created the PMP Exam Success Series of products.
Referent	This type of power comes from an **attitude or "presence"** that a person has and the corresponding type of influence this person has on the team. It could also come from someone who **aligns** with other people **in a powerful position** at the company or on the team.	**Example #1:** I want to stay late and finish this before the morning like I promised the Project Manager. He has always been good to me and the rest of the team, and I don't want to let him down. **Example #2:** We must do what the Project Manager asks. She has lunch with our vice president every week, and they play golf together a lot. If we let her down, he will definitely hear about it.

Project Manager Power Types

Below are various power types you should understand.

Attitude Power	This type of power can involve using a middle person to negotiate for the Project Manager. This arrangement can minimize the "personal" effect or attitude that can arise when, during negotiations, the Project Manager **potentially takes some point or issue personally or more seriously than it should be taken.**
Commitment Power	This type of power uses **commitment via alliances and partnerships** on the project team to tackle challenges to the project as they arise. It has a potential connection with referent power.
Competition Power	This type of power **maximizes involvement** in the project or idea **in the form of competition** to help enhance the commitment of those involved to work toward a more successful outcome of the project or idea.
Investment Power	This type of power involves delaying key decision(s) so enough time passes that stakeholders or other such parties can make a **significant time investment in the project.** After this time investment is made, stakeholders and other such parties are typically more flexible in their negotiations with project management.

Knowledge of Needs Power	This type of power attempts to realize two things being negotiated: **What the other party says they are after, and what they are after that hasn't been made public.** Knowledge of these two items can help the Project Manager, with power focused on a solution instead of a moving target.
Moral or Ethical Power	This type of power **uses a moral or ethical perspective tied to one's values in the negotiation process.** Often times, this approach can be asking what is reasonable or fair in the negotiations process instead of an approach which could attempt to maximize opportunity.
Persistence Power	This type of power **sticks to the target of the negotiations or project.** In many cases, people simply give up after an initial rejection. Persistence involves holding on and working toward the target.
Persuasion Power	This type of power **discounts logic**, which technical people can often use to sell ideas instead of focusing on comparisons that relate to the experience of the negotiating parties, **creating evidence that can't be overlooked**, and showing how a solution will meet their needs.
Planning Power	This type of power uses **preparation** followed by **negotiation** to effectively plan the project.
Precedent Power	This type of power **uses something that has achieved desired results in the past** regardless if it was on the current project environment or elsewhere. It can include challenging ways things have always been done at a company to seeing a new way of doing things based on a precedent set elsewhere.
Professionalism Power	This type of power involves **being professional and practical when working with others.** It helps foster a win/win relationship with those that work with the project manager by allowing the project manager to look at the people and their needs.
Risk Power	This type of power **uses calculated risks in negotiations** to achieve project goals. Avoid getting attached to a position because it could limit you in negotiations. Also, to minimize surprises, know as much about the negotiation environment as possible.

11.2   Acquire Project Team (Executing Process Group)

Know the Key Inputs, Tools & Techniques, and Outputs for Acquire Project Team.

Project staffing needs are satisfied during Acquire Project Team. **The actual resources that will be working on the project are assigned to the project.** Factors to consider include cost, ability, experience, availability, and interest of resource(s). This is the "get 'em" part.

Acquire Project Team (Executing)		
Key Inputs	Roles and Responsibilities	Roles and responsibilities **help personnel know their positions** on the project, plus what those in charge expect of them.
	Project Organization Charts	A project organization chart (also known as an organizational breakdown structure, OBS) is used for a **graphical display of reporting project relationships**.
	Staffing Management Plan	The staffing management plan shows **what type of skill set is needed and can include location and timeframes**. Also included is general documentation associated with any plan to add staff to the project.

Key Tools & Techniques	Pre-Assignment	Pre-assignment occurs **when it is known in advance that certain people will be on the project team**.
	Negotiation	Techniques utilized can include resource negotiation, pre-assignment (or pre-allocation) to the project, and contact with any outside companies to help with the procurement needs of staff acquisition.
	Acquisition	Acquisition involves **getting people assigned to the project**. It could include hiring from outside, outsourcing, or transferring from within the company.
	Virtual Teams	Virtual teams are **comprised of people working in various locations**. They can work together virtually via technology for activity such as communication and information sharing. This collaboration can help bring expertise to the team, support multiple shifts, accommodate people with mobility issues, and allow projects to occur where travel expenses might have made the project otherwise impractical.
Key Outputs	Project Staff Assignments	When this process is complete, **staff assignments are established and dates set for staff to start** on the project.
	Resource Availability	Resource availability is determined to **ensure that the resources are available** as planned. Conflicts with availability can include different projects the resource could be assigned to, other work activities, vacation, and training.

Situational Question and Real World Application
If this area were not addressed adequately, the project could fail to meet its schedule by not having enough people assigned to it to complete the activities as needed, or just as bad -- the wrong people in terms of skill sets and experience levels. There could also be the situation in which a team directory (and similar organization communication) could be lacking, with people trying to do work but not aware of who their teammates are or what they do. This lack could cause difficulties in handing off work assignments from person to person.

11.2.1 Resource Histogram

A resource histogram is a tool you can use to see quantity of staffing over time. It can be set up to show hours by month, hours by week, total people on the project over time, or a particular skill set over time.

The following example shows total staffing hours by month.

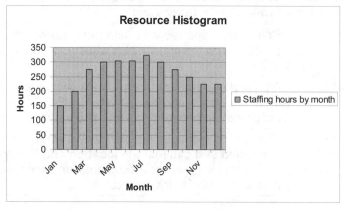

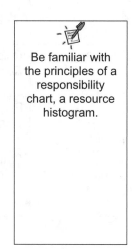

Be familiar with the principles of a responsibility chart, a resource histogram.

Figure 11-3: Resource Histogram Sample

PMP Exam Success Series: Certification Exam Manual
© 2007 Crosswind Project Management, Inc., www.crosswindpm.com

11.2.2   Benefits

From time to time, the exam can cover employee benefits as a motivational tool. There are two main types of benefits: fringe benefits and perks.

Fringe	These are the **types of benefits that everyone receives in the company (or project).** These are typically not a motivator because the person is already getting the benefit. Examples could be health insurance or paid holidays.
Perks	These are **special benefits offered for being on a certain project or doing a certain activity.** These are not available to everyone; thus, they can be useful for motivation. Examples could be going to a special training class or seminar.

Know what perks and fringe benefits are, and the differences between them.

11.2.3   Halo Theory

According to the Halo Theory, **people make good Project Managers simply because they are good in their fields, regardless of background training in project management.** The theory also implies that people who do not excel in their fields, they wouldn't be good at project management. This theory often becomes reality when someone is promoted to a Project Manager from a technical or hands-on position and **hasn't had the opportunity to receive any project management training.**

Know the Halo Theory.

11.2.4   Expectancy Theory

The Expectancy Theory states that **the employee works a great deal on the project and assumes that the reward will be relative to the amount of effort or perceived effort.** This assumption can usually be quite a disappointment for those believing they will be greatly rewarded when the project is done.

Know the Expectancy Theory.

11.3   Develop Project Team (Executing Process Group)

Develop Project Team or team-building continues throughout the project although the **majority of it occurs with the project in the Executing Process Group.** In some ways, organized activities and communication pull people together. In other ways, the unspoken communication that occurs as people work together forms the team bond.

The key to cohesion is the staff and the project management plan. Communication aligns the people of the project with the details of the project so they know what direction they are to work. Develop Project Team is driven by the Project Manager. Key areas of focus should be to increase trust and interactivity of the team, as well as the skill levels of the project team. This is the "grow 'em" part.

Know the Key Inputs, Tools & Techniques, and Outputs for Develop Project Team.

Develop Project Team (Executing)		
Key Inputs	Project Staff Assignments	Project **staff assignment is complete with the date set for staff to start** on the project.
	Staffing Management Plan	A staffing management plan comes into play **to address managing staff**.

Key Tools & Techniques	General Management Skills	Key tools include general management skills **to help you organize and run things**. They could include soft skills that help with interpersonal activities on the project.
	Training	Training is a key to team development as well. Training **focuses on developing of the individual**, which helps make the team stronger. There are a number of training formats that are quite effective. They can include online, computer-based, classroom, on-the-job, mentoring, coaching, and learning from other team members.
	Team-Building Activities	Team-building activities **help in team development**, which is more than just putting people together in a group. Activities could include group lunches or an evening away from work in a social environment. Reward and recognition are also helpful as motivational and appreciation tools for individual work efforts.
	Ground Rules	Ground rules help **set performance and other expectations** by the team members.
	Co-Location	With co-location, **team members are placed at the same location**. It generally helps facilitate team-building by having people working together.
	Recognition and Rewards	Recognition and rewards are part of the Human Resource Planning process that **helps reward good behavior** on the project. To help with cohesiveness, it's key to include rewards that all on the project can win, not just a certain person or a few.
Key Outputs	Team Performance Assessment	Team performance assessment **evaluates how the team performs as a unit, how individuals complete activities as needed, and how staff turnover is reduced**.

Situational Question and Real World Application
Ignoring this area may lead to a group of people on a project who are not a team, leading to the potential for disputes, tension, and issues that may delay work completion and even harm the project.

11.3.1   Form, Storm, Norm, Perform (Team Development Life Cycle)

Team development involves the convergence of a group of people into a performing organization. A common evolutional life cycle is characteristic with team development. The team development process includes form, storm, norm, perform, and is typical when a team is put in place.

Understand the team development life cycle (form, storm, norm, perform).

Form	Form refers to the creation of the team, when people on the team are put together per the project organizational Planning needs.
Storm	Storm refers to the chaos that occurs as people start to get accustomed to working together.
Norm	Norm refers to the point in time when team behavior starts to normalize and team members are accustomed to each other. The newness of the group of people has worn out.
Perform	Perform refers to the activity that transpires as the team works as a team instead of as a group of people. The group should be working at an optimal level in this phase.

PMP Exam Success Series: Certification Exam Manual
© 2007 Crosswind Project Management, Inc., www.crosswindpm.com

11.4   Manage Project Team (Monitoring and Controlling)

Know the Key Inputs, Tools & Techniques, and Outputs for Manage Project Team.

Manage Project Team is the process in which team performance is analyzed and feedback provided. It also involves coordination of project-related issues and optimization of project performance. This is the "run 'em" part.

Manage Project Team (Monitoring and Controlling)		
Key Inputs	Project Staff Assignment	Project staff assignment is **complete with the date set for staff to start** on the project.
	Roles and Responsibilities	Roles and responsibilities **help personnel know their positions** on the project, plus what those in charge expect of them.
	Project Organization Charts	A project organization chart (also known as an organizational breakdown structure, OBS) is used for a **graphical display of reporting project relationships**.
	Staffing Management Plan	The staffing management plan shows **what type of skill set is needed** and can include location and timeframes. Also included is general documentation associated with any plan to add staff to the project.
	Work Performance Information	Work performance information provides a **status on what has been completed (or not completed)** on the project.
	Performance Reports	Performance reports are key to **show current actual work complete** on the project.
Key Tools & Techniques	Observation and Conversation	Observation and conversation are **used to monitor work being accomplished by the team members**, plus their attitude or enjoyment level of work on the project.
	Project Performance Appraisals	Project performance appraisals can **evaluate team member performance**. They can be formal or informal and can be performed by supervisors, team members, or anyone else working with the team member under review. If an appraisal is conducted using feedback from more than a supervisor (such as anyone who works with the team member), it's sometimes called 360 degree feedback because the feedback comes from all around the team member.
	Conflict Management	Conflict management **helps raise productivity and enhance working relationships**. Common sources of conflict can be resource availability and scheduling priorities.
	Issue Logs	Issue logs are used to **track issues that arise** on the project. A log allows a **documentation trail for assignment and resolution**.
Key Outputs	Requested Changes	Requested changes related to staffing are common. These changes can be the **replacement of a resource, the reassignment of someone to a different area, or other staffing changes** needed. Such a change is then run through the Integrated Change Control process.

Situational Question and Real World Application
This is similar (regarding potential problems) to the Develop Project Team process in that if this area were ignored, there is a group of people on a project who are not a team, leading to the potential for arguments among them, tension, and issues that could delay work completion and even harm the project.

11.4.1   Sources of Conflict

Sources of conflict are an issue that is imperative in order to understand conflict. If Project Managers are aware of variables that can cause conflict, they can take a proactive approach to eliminating conflict before it occurs. They can also know that it is likely to come when the project addresses areas that simply can't be ignored, such as scheduling and resources. If conflict is managed correctly, there can be a greater output of the team and enhanced relationships among the team members.

Most people think that personality is the main reason for conflict. Studies have shown that this is rarely the case. **Traditionally, conflict occurs as Planning evolves.** Items such as scheduling priorities and resource utilization are the most likely sources of conflict. **Personality is typically the least source of conflict.** To minimize conflict, a Project Manager can utilize team ground rules, group norms, and project management practices.

Scheduling Priorities	Scarce Resources	Personal Workstyles	Technical Direction	Methodology Details	Cost	Personality

Greatest Source of Conflict   Least Source of Conflict

11.4.2   Conflict Resolution

Given the complexity of projects today, conflict is bound to happen. The days of eliminating conflict before it happens are gone. The process of resolving conflict is a key tool of the Project Manager.

Be familiar with the names of the various types of conflict resolution, as well as their characteristics.

Conflict Resolution Technique	Description	Example
Problem Solving (Confrontational)	Problem solving is an effort in which attempts are made to **work out the actual problem**. It is the **best** type of conflict resolution.	If you can't do what is needed with your current computer, get an upgrade that lets you accomplish what's needed for your job.
Compromise	Compromise is a negotiation attempt to get everyone involved **to give (concede) a little to find a common ground and resolution.** It is sometimes viewed as undesirable because when everyone gives something up, there is a potential that the solution will fail to meet anyone's needs.	If we can get labor to give in on benefits a little, and management to increase their raise increase a little, I think we can find agreement that both sides can live with.

PMBOK 3rd Edition - Formulas to know for the PMI Examination

- **Pert (3 times) Estimate:** Expected Activity time = $t_e = (O + 4m + P)/6$
- **Standard Deviation:** of an activity: $SD = \sigma = (P - O)/6$
- **Variance of an activity = $V = SD^2$**
- **Standard Deviation of a project = Square Root of Sum of Critical Path Variances**
- **Slack = LST – EST** (Latest Start Time – Earliest Start Time)
  = **LFT – EFT** (Latest Finish Time – Earliest Finish Time)
- **Crashing:** Slope = (Crash Cost – Normal Cost)/(Crash Time – Normal Time)
- **Progress Reporting:** 0/100; 50/50; 20/80
- **Cost Variance** = **CV** = EV-AC
- **Schedule Variance** = **SV** = EV-PV
- **Cost Performance Index** = **CPI** = EV/AC
- **Schedule Performance Index** = **SPI** = EV/PV
- **BAC** = Budget at Completion
- **ETC** = Estimate to Complete
- **EAC** = Estimate at Completion

Note: Alternate calculations for EAC and ETC depend upon variances to date:
1. "Atypical"; 2. "Typical" 3. Residual forecasts not reliable
   1. **EAC** = AC + (BAC-EV)   1. **ETC** = BAC - EV
   2. **EAC** = AC + (BAC-EV)/CPI   2. **ETC** = (BAC – EV)/CPI
   3. **EAC** = AC + ETC

- **VAC** = Variance at Completion = **BAC – EAC**
- **EAC "simplified" = BAC/CPI**
- **Present Value = FV/(1+r)ⁿ ; FV** = Future Value; **R** = Interest Rate; **n** = # of periods
- **BCR** = Benefit Cost Ratio
  BCR greater than 1 is good
  BCR less than 1 is bad
  BCR equal to 1 means costs equal benefits
- **Pay back** = period of time to recover investment through *cash flow*
- **Pareto:** 80% of problems come from 20% of the work

Quality:
- A normal distribution has the following standard deviations (sigma's):
- +/-1 sigma = 68.26%; +/-2 sigma = 95.46; +/-3 sigma = 99.73; +/- 6 sigma = 99.99
- **UCL / LCL** Upper Control Limit & Lower Control Limit on a control chart
- **Rule of 7:** 7 non-random points grouped on one side of the mean
- **Number of Communication paths** = n(n-1)/2
- **EMV** – Expected Monetary Value: **EMV** = Odds of occurrence x amount at stake
- **Point of Total Assumption (PTA)** The maximum amount that buyer will pay regardless of the amount cost exceeds the Ceiling Price (CP) on a Fixed Price Incentive Fee (FPIF contract that would also include a "sharing" provision for cost under or over runs. The Ceiling Price (CP) is usually a % of the Target Cost (TC); **SR = Share Ratio (buyer / seller); Target Price = Target Cost (TC) + Target Profit (TP)**

PTA = [(Ceiling Price – Target Price) / Buyer Share] + Target Cost

Forcing	Forcing is an action in which a **direct order** to resolve something is given. It is typically the **worst** type of conflict resolution.	You will stop using that software and switch to the authorized version or you will not be around here for long.
Smoothing	Smoothing is an attempt to **focus** on the **positive** and **distract** the attention from the **negative**.	Look at how well the requirements on the project went. We just have to apply that same view to this phase of the project as well.
Withdrawal	In withdrawal, the Project Manager **ignores the problem** and hopes it either fixes itself or disappears. Typically, withdrawal is not viewed by PMI as a conflict resolution technique because it's not a proactive approach to resolving conflict.	I know he is a pain to work with, and takes longer to do his work than we like, but maybe if we let him be, he will just quit and take a new job.

11.4.3   Reward and Recognition

A reward and recognition system is needed for team development and for optimizing performance. Such systems need to be defined, but they also need to be adaptable because different things motivate different people. A reward and recognition system could provide compensatory time for overtime hours worked or paying for a certification test or training. A successful reward and recognition system is possible when management follows through on its promises. Breaking your word to your team not only hurts the reward system, but your credibility as a Project Manager as well.

11.4.4   Problem Solving and Situational Questions

The exam uses situational questions to verify your understanding of who is responsible for solving various types of problems. Problem solving and situational questions are challenging areas given that, when studying for the exam begins, everyone has a different opinion of who is responsible for what.

11.5   Human Resource Formulas and Variables

No formulas for Human Resource

11.6   Human Resource Terminology

Term	Description
Aggressors	A role with a negative attitude toward the project
Attitude Power	A type of power that can involve using a middle person to negotiate for the Project Manager
Blockers	A role that interrupts information flow on the project
Clarifiers	A role that helps focus on making sure people on the project understand what the details of the project entail
Coercive/Penalty Power	A type of power that uses negative approaches including threatening and punishment to get people to do things they don't want to do
Commitment Power	A type of power that uses commitment via alliances and partnerships on the project team to tackle challenges to the project as they arise; has a potential connection with referent power
Competition Power	A type of power that maximizes involvement in the project or idea in the form of competition to help enhance the commitment of those involved to work toward a more successful outcome of the project or idea

Compromise	A conflict resolution technique in which a solution involves (typically) a little of what everyone is proposing for a solution
Confrontation	Directly dealing with a conflict via problem-solving techniques so that the parties can work through any disagreement
Devil's Advocate	A role that contradicts popular views or opinions about the work of the project
Dominators	A role that consumes project communication and focus with their own views without considering others
Empathetic Listening	Listening with the goal of understanding what the sender is trying to communicate
Encouragers	A role that helps the project and team by focusing on what the project is creating, not the challenges of the project
Expert Power	A capacity in which one uses personal knowledge and expert opinion to get others to do what is desired
Forcing	Applying an all or nothing (win/lose) to get the desired result
Gate Keepers	In project management, a role that helps bring people into the project In business school, this term could be viewed differently, including a role that keeps people out of something.
Harmonizers	A role that helps evolve information and understanding on the project above the team members
Hierarchy of Needs	A pyramid representation of Maslow's Theory that a person's motivation is based on needs (and where the person fits in this pyramid)
Information Givers	A role that shares information and thus helps enhance communication on the project
Information Seekers	A role that works to enhance information and knowledge associated with the project
Initiators	A proactive role that takes initiatives on a project with contribution and ideas
Investment Power	A type of power that involves delaying key decision(s) so enough time passes that stakeholders or other such parties can make a significant time investment in the project
Knowledge of Needs Power	A type of power that attempts to realize the two things that are negotiated for: what the other party says they are after, and what they are after that hasn't been made public
Legitimate Power	Getting people to do what you desire based on your authority
Mirroring	Matching behavior characteristics of another person or group
Moral or Ethical Power	A type of power that uses a moral or ethical perspective tied to one's values in the negotiation process
Organization Chart (Tool)	An organization chart that displays which group is responsible for each work item and can show reporting relationships as well; also known as an organizational breakdown structure
Organizational Breakdown Structure (OBS)	An organization chart that displays which group is responsible for each work item and can show reporting relationships as well
Organizational Planning	Determining, assigning, and documenting responsibilities, roles, and reporting relationships on a project
Over-Allocation	A situation in which a resource is applied to too many activities at the same time to accomplish them all within the acceptable timeframe
Persistence Power	Sticking to the target of the negotiations or project; involves holding on and working toward the target In many cases, people simply give up after an initial rejection.
Persuasion Power	Discounting logic, which technical people can often use to sell ideas instead of focusing on comparisons that relate to the experience of the negotiating parties, creating evidence that can't be overlooked, and showing how a solution will meet their needs
Planning Power	Using preparation followed by negotiation to effectively plan the project
Position Description (Tool)	A description of the roles and responsibilities of a team member
Power	The possible ability to influence behavior or performance of others
Precedent Power	A type of power that uses something which has achieved desired results in the past regardless if it was on the current project environment or elsewhere

PMP Exam Success Series: Certification Exam Manual
© 2007 Crosswind Project Management, Inc., www.crosswindpm.com

Professionalism Power	Being professional and practical when working with others; helps to foster a win/win relationship with those that work with the project manager by allowing the project manager to look at the people and their needs
Project Organization Chart (Output/Input)	An organization chart that displays which group is responsible for each work item and can show reporting relationships as well; also known as an organizational breakdown structure
Project Team	The group of people put together to plan and (or) execute the work of the project
Project Team Directory	A list of all project team members, their project roles, and their communication needs as they relate to the project
Rapport	Possessing comfort or a harmonious relationship with someone
Recognition Seekers	A role that looks at the project first to see what they can get out of it
Referent Power	Using personal charisma to attain desired results from others or using existing relationships to help get things done (who you know)
Resource	People, supplies, equipment, and other items used in the work of the project
Resource Breakdown Structure (RBS)	A structure that shows the decomposition of the resources being used on the project; can include personnel, divisions or departments, and job roles
Resource Histogram	A graph that displays the resources used over time on a project
Resource Leveling	The process of creating a consistent (even) workload for the resources on a project
Resource Loading	The process of applying resources to a schedule and its activities
Responsibility Assignment Matrix (RAM) (Tool)	A matrix that connects the work of the WBS to the personnel assigned to it in the OBS
Reward Power	A type of power that uses positive actions or consequences to attain desired results from other people
Risk Power	A type of power that uses calculated risks in negotiations to achieve project goals
Smoothing	A conflict resolution technique in which the focus is on areas of similarity and focus is taken off areas of difference
Staff Acquisition	The hiring and applying of the needed resources to the project
Staffing Management Plan	A document used to describe when resources will start and finish the project
Summarizers	A role that relates back to the overall picture of what the project is focusing on
Team Development	The creation of individual and team skills to maximize project output
Topic Jumpers	A role that doesn't stay focused on the primary topics of focus and conversation
Withdrawal	A conflict resolution technique in which you withdraw from the disagreement (or source of conflict)
Withdrawers	A role that is non-participatory on the project regarding information and project issues

11.7   Human Resource Mind Map

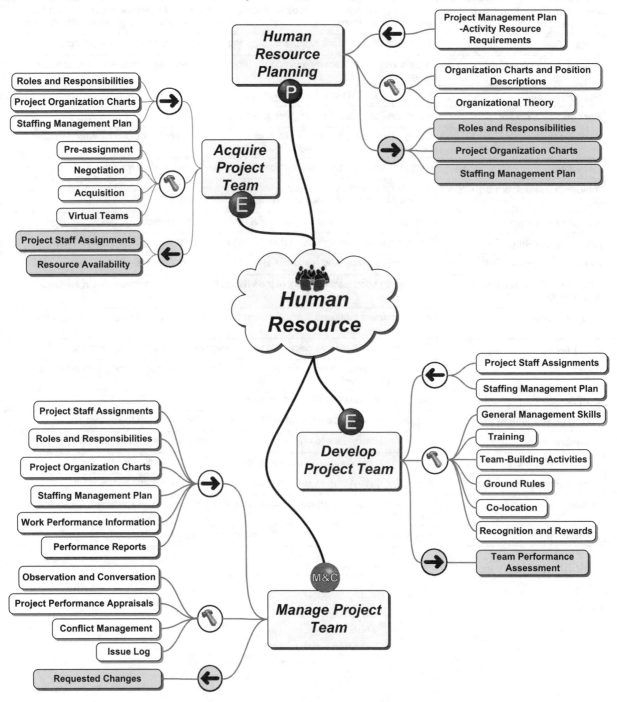

11.8   Human Resource Tests and Exercises

11.8.1   Human Resource Quick Test

In this quiz, answer the question in a short essay of only a sentence or two or circle all correct answers for the question. Note that some questions may have more than one answer. Answers are in section 11.9.1.

1.   What is the top level of Maslow's Hierarchy of Needs?

2.   What is the name of the document that defines the human resources needs for the project?

3.   When does the Develop Project Team process occur and what are the four stages of team development?

4.   What document shows reporting relationships in a company or on a project?

5.   What management theory focuses on employees who want to be self-managed and direct themselves?

6.   What document shows who is responsible for what on a project?

7.   What is the worst form of power for a Project Manager to use?

8.   What form of power do Project Managers earn themselves, instead of have assigned to them?

9.   What is the name of the theory which implies that a person good at technical skills would make a good Project Manager?

10.   What role on the project is typically responsible for paying for the project, or owning the product of the project when it is complete?

11.8.2   Human Resource ITTO Matching Exercise

Match the correct ITTO term at the bottom of the page with the blanks to the right of the process. When a term is used multiple times, it is flagged by a parenthetical value indicating the number of times used. Also, match summary sentences with the process name that fits. Answers are in section 11.9.2.

	Inputs	Tools & Techniques	Outputs
Human Resource Planning	1)	1) 2)	1) 2) 3)
Summary:			
Acquire Project Team	1) 2) 3)	1) 2) 3) 4)	1) 2)
Summary:			
Develop Project Team	1) 2)	1) 2) 3) 4) 5) 6)	1)
Summary:			
Manage Project Team	1) 2) 3) 4) 5) 6)	1) 2) 3) 4)	1)
Summary:			

Improving the performance of the team   Determining the staffing approach for the project
Build the project team   Monitoring team performance issues and changes

Acquisition	Organizational Theory	Requested Changes
Co-location	Performance Reports	Resource Availability
Conflict Management	Pre-Assignment	Roles and Responsibilities (3)
General Management Skills	Project Management Plan (Activity Resource Requirements)	Staffing Management Plan (4)
Ground Rules		Team Performance Assessment
Issue Log	Project Organization Charts (3)	Team-Building Activities
Negotiation	Project Performance Appraisals	Training
Observation and Conversation	Project Staff Assignments (3)	Virtual Teams
Organization Charts and Position Descriptions	Recognition and Rewards	Work Performance Information

PMP Exam Success Series: Certification Exam Manual
© 2007 Crosswind Project Management, Inc., www.crosswindpm.com

11.8.3   Human Resource Terminology Matching Exercise

Match the correct term in the left column to the correct definition in the right column. See the exercise answer section of this chapter for the correct answer. Answers are in section 11.9.3.

Matching Exercise #1

	Term	Answer	Definition
1	Coercive/Penalty Power		A. A list of all project team members, their project roles, and their communication needs as they relate to the project
2	Compromise		B. Listening with the goal of understanding what the sender is trying to communicate
3	Confrontation		C. A graph that displays the resources used over time on a project
4	Empathetic Listening		D. Getting people to do what you desire based on your authority
5	Forcing		E. A conflict resolution technique in which a solution involves (typically) a little of what everyone is proposing for a solution
6	Hierarchy of Needs		F. An organization chart that displays which group is responsible for each work item and can show reporting relationships as well
7	HR Planning		G. The process of applying resources to a schedule and its task
8	Legitimate Power		H. A conflict resolution technique in which you withdraw from the disagreement (or source of conflict)
9	Organization Chart (Tool)		I. The hiring and applying of the needed resources to the project
10	Organizational Breakdown Structure (OBS)		J. An organization chart that displays which group is responsible for each work item and can show reporting relationships as well; also known as an organizational breakdown structure
11	Position Description (Tool)		K. The use of negative approaches including threatening and punishment to get people to do things they don't want to do
12	Project Team Directory		L. Applying an all or nothing (win/lose) to get the desired result
13	Referent Power		M. Using personal charisma to attain desired results from others or using existing relationships to help get things done (who you know)
14	Resource		N. A description of the roles and responsibilities of a team member
15	Resource Histogram		O. Directly dealing with a conflict via problem-solving techniques so that the parties can work through any disagreement
16	Resource Loading		P. People, supplies, equipment, and other items used in the work of the project
17	Smoothing		Q. A pyramid representation of Maslow's Theory that a person's motivation is based on needs (and where the person fits in this pyramid)
18	Staff Acquisition		R. Determining, assigning, and documenting responsibilities, roles, and reporting relationships on a project
19	Team Development		S. The creation of individual and team skills to maximize project output
20	Withdrawal		T. A conflict resolution technique in which the focus is on areas of similarity and focus is taken off areas of difference

Matching Exercise #2

	Term	Answer	Definition
1	**Expert Power**		A. A matrix that connects the work of the WBS to the personnel assigned to it in the OBS
2	**Mirroring**		B. The possible ability to influence behavior or performance of others
3	**Power**		C. A structure that shows the decomposition of the resources being used on the project; can include personnel, divisions or departments, and job roles
4	**Project Organization Chart (Output/Input)**		D. Matching behavior characteristics of another person or group
5	**Project Team**		E. A capacity in which one uses personal knowledge and expert opinion to get others to do what is desired
6	**Rapport**		F. A document used to describe when resources will start and finish the project
7	**Resource Breakdown Structure (RBS)**		G. The process of creating a consistent (even) workload for the resources on a project
8	**Resource Leveling**		H. Using positive actions or consequences to attain desired results from other people
9	**Responsibility Assignment Matrix (RAM) (Tool)**		I. An organization chart that displays which group is responsible for each work item and can show reporting relationships as well; also known as organizational breakdown structure
10	**Reward Power**		J. Possessing comfort or a harmonious relationship with someone
11	**Staffing Management Plan**		K. The group of people put together to plan and (or) execute the work of the project

PMP Exam Success Series: Certification Exam Manual
© 2007 Crosswind Project Management, Inc., www.crosswindpm.com

11.8.4   Human Resource Practice Test

Answers are in section 11.9.4.

1.   Developing the project team is an important event directly related to project success. When does this occur in a project?

     (A) During execution
     (B) During planning
     (C) During off hours events
     (D) Throughout the project

2.   Which of the following is not a Human Resource process?

     (A) Team Motivation
     (B) Human Resource Planning
     (C) Acquire Project Team
     (D) Develop Project Team

3.   The Project Manager tells a team member on the project that she can attend some database training for a new technology. He further explains that this new skill will be used by the company in the future but not necessarily on the current project. He lets the team member know that he approved this training because of the good work the team member has done on the project. This is an example of what type of power?

     (A) Formal
     (B) Reward
     (C) Knowledge of Needs
     (D) Compromise

4.   What does a responsibility assignment matrix provide for the team?

     (A) Information about who is responsible for what work
     (B) Who does what work and when they are to do it
     (C) At what location the work is done
     (D) What sequence the resources are to perform the activities in

5.   The project is progressing well but has begun to experience resource conflicts with people who are working on critical path activities. What role typically helps resolve these resource issues?

     (A) Senior management
     (B) Functional management
     (C) Project management
     (D) Sponsor

6.   The Project Manager has created the staffing plan and is getting ready to start the project soon. Resumes are being reviewed, and some people have been interviewed. The lead candidate for the technical architecture position has been offered a position. What process is the Project Manager involved in?

(A) Hiring and interviewing
(B) Developing the project team
(C) Resource requirements
(D) Acquiring the project team

7.   The Project Manager has some issues on the team between two developers who disagree about how something should be done. What is the best method to resolve the conflict?

(A) Compromise
(B) Problem solving
(C) Withdrawal
(D) Reward

8.   The Project Manager has just received a patent for his design of a circuit for his most recent project. The current project is a product that complements the previous project's work. What type of power will the Project Manager utilize for the best results on the project?

(A) Formal
(B) Expert
(C) Referent
(D) Precedent

9.   Which of the following is not a level in Maslow's Hierarchy of Needs?

(A) Safety
(B) Psychiatric
(C) Esteem
(D) Belonging

10. The project charter has just been signed and the Project Manager assigned. What type of power does the Project Manager have as a result of this?

(A) Reward
(B) Formal
(C) Referent
(D) Persistence

11. The retail network upgrade project has a number of key stakeholders who have provided input to the direction of the project. Which of the following best describes a stakeholder?

(A) Someone who is impacted by the project
(B) Stockholders of the company
(C) Senior management
(D) Functional management

12.   What is the main expectation that can come from team development?

(A) Team-building activities
(B) Performance improvements
(C) The team becoming friends after the project is complete
(D) Smoothing

13.   What can a responsibility assignment matrix eliminate?

(A) Confusion on what order activities come in
(B) Confusion on who is responsible for doing what
(C) Confusion on how long the activities are
(D) Confusion on who is on the team

14.   The project has had some challenges. The Project Manager has been challenged with continually having to tell the team what to do. The team members also do not seem to trust management that much and often appear unmotivated. This is an example of what?

(A) Bad performance
(B) Theory X environment
(C) Forcing
(D) Theory Y environment

15.   The electrical engineer has recently been promoted from lead engineer to section manager. In this new position, he is responsible for managing projects and project resources. Over the five years he has been with the company, he was always ranked as one of the top engineers but has had no formal project management training. This is an example of what?

(A) Halo Theory
(B) Reward power
(C) Problem solving
(D) Equal opportunity employment

16.   The Project Manager is planning how many people he will need on the project. There is a lot of database creation and computer programming involved. This will very likely require more than one person with each skill set. He is reviewing the hours of each skill set that will be needed each week on the project. What will he likely use to visually represent this data?

(A) Resource histogram
(B) Responsibility assignment matrix (RAM)
(C) PERT chart
(D) Pareto diagram

17.   Which of the following is not likely a project resource for a technology project?

(A) Conference room near the team location
(B) Project Manager
(C) Functional Manager
(D) Computer programmer

18. What type of conflict resolution technique has the worst impact on the team?

    (A) Forcing
    (B) Formal
    (C) Penalty
    (D) Smoothing

19. The project has gone smoothly so far. The team members appear to be working with an end goal in mind and without a lot of supervision. They appear to be highly motivated and enjoying their work. This is an example of what?

    (A) Reward Theory
    (B) Theory Y environment
    (C) Motivation Theory
    (D) Theory X environment

20. The project is in a balanced matrix environment. There are significant challenges with the scope of the project. Project personnel have been complaining to the Project Manager about the environment. In this type of environment, who controls the resources?

    (A) Functional Manager
    (B) Project Manager
    (C) Project Coordinator
    (D) Senior management

21. The project is very challenging and has been very trying on a lot of people. Some key team members are considering leaving the project and returning to their old jobs at the company. Which of the following is a key motivator to keep them on the project?

    (A) Fringe benefits
    (B) Perks
    (C) Theory Y motivation strategy
    (D) Compromise

22. Human Resource Planning occurs during the planning of a project. Which of the following is not expected to be created during this process?

    (A) Role and responsibility assignments
    (B) Team development
    (C) Organizational chart
    (D) Staffing management plan

23. There is a technical disagreement between two important team members on the project. The Project Manager gets involved and tries to remind them of the good things that have happened on the project that they have been involved with. This is an example of what type of conflict resolution?

    (A) Smoothing
    (B) Compromise
    (C) Referent
    (D) Withdrawal

24.   An organizational breakdown structure (OBS) is also known as what?

(A) Staffing management plan
(B) Organizational chart
(C) Resource histogram
(D) Responsibility assignment matrix

25.   Which of the following is not an example of team development?

(A) Creating the WBS of the project
(B) Attending a sporting event as a group
(C) A team lunch
(D) Performance reviews

26.   The Project Manager is involved in an off-shore project utilizing a number of different resources. There have been several resource issues so far on the project. The Project Manager is evaluating what was used in establishing the management of the project team. All the following should be considered for managing the project team except…

(A) Project staff assignment
(B) Work performance information
(C) Project organization charts
(D) Ground rules

27.   The team is going through some resource over-utilization issues on the project. The database administrators are working excessive hours. The Project Manager has gone back to Planning to re-evaluate the situation. Which of the following can provide help in seeing how serious the issue is?

(A) Pareto diagram
(B) Control chart
(C) Staffing management plan
(D) Resource histogram

28.   The project coordinator is in charge of planning the semester classes at the university. They are trying to allocate various resource types to work together such as instructors, room, and audio/video equipment. Which of the following are they most likely to use to show this information?

(A) Organizational chart
(B) Resource breakdown structure
(C) Risk breakdown structure
(D) Responsibility assignment matrix

29. The senior Project Manager at the company is helping to look out for a less experienced
     Project Manager who is working on another project. They meet weekly to see how the less
     experienced person's project is performing, as well as discussing concepts that should help
     make the less experienced Project Manager more experienced. This is an example of what?

     (A) Forcing
     (B) Mentoring
     (C) An intern program
     (D) Motivational Theory

30. The Project Manager is in the process of planning the project. The company he works for has
     had issues with previous projects in which there has been confusion over who is accountable
     for completing various activities and processes associated with the projects. What document
     can he include in the project management plan that will help eliminate this problem?

     (A) Gantt chart
     (B) Staffing plan
     (C) Organization chart
     (D) Responsibility assignment matrix

11.9   Human Resource Tests and Exercise Answers

11.9.1   Human Resource Quick Test Answers

1.   What is the top level of Maslow's Hierarchy of Needs?
      Self actualization [section 11.1.4]

2.   What is the name of the document that defines the human resources needs for the project?
      Staffing management plan [section 11.1.1, section 11.6]

3.   When does the Develop Project Team process occur and what are the four stages of team development?
      Develop Project Team occurs in project Executing, although the team technically will be developing as a unit throughout the project. The four stages are form, storm, norm, perform. [section 11.3, section 11.3.1]

4.   What document shows reporting relationships in a company or on a project?
      Organizational chart, also known as an organizational breakdown structure [section 11.1.3, section 11.6]

5.   What management theory focuses on employees who want to be self-managed and direct themselves?
      Theory Y [section 11.1.4]

6.   What document shows who is responsible for what on a project?
      Responsibility assignment matrix (RAM) [section 11.1.2, section 11.6]

7.   What is the worst form of power for a Project Manager to use?
      Penalty [section 11.1.9]

8.   What form of power do Project Managers earn themselves, instead of have assigned to them?
      Expert [section 11.1.9]

9.   What is the name of the theory which implies that a person good at technical skills would make a good Project Manager?
      Halo Theory [section 11.2.3]

10.   What role on the project is typically responsible for paying for the project, or owning the product of the project when it is complete?
      The project sponsor [section 5.4.4]

11.9.2   Human Resource ITTO Matching Exercise Answers

	Inputs	Tools & Techniques	Outputs
Human Resource Planning	1) Project Management Plan (Activity Resource Requirements)	1) Organization Charts and Position Descriptions	1) Roles and Responsibilities
		2) Organizational Theory	2) Project Organization Charts
			3) Staffing Management Plan
Summary:	Determining the staffing approach for the project		
Acquire Project Team	1) Roles and Responsibilities	1) Pre-Assignment	1) Project Staff Assignments
	2) Project Organization Charts	2) Negotiation	2) Resource Availability
	3) Staffing Management Plan	3) Acquisition	
		4) Virtual Teams	
Summary:	Build the project team		
Develop Project Team	1) Project Staff Assignments	1) General Management Skills	1) Team Performance Assessment
	2) Staffing Management Plan	2) Training	
		3) Team-Building Activities	
		4) Ground Rules	
		5) Co-location	
		6) Recognition and Rewards	
Summary:	Improving the performance of the team		
Manage Project Team	1) Project Staff Assignments	1) Observation and Conversation	1) Requested Changes
	2) Roles and Responsibilities	2) Project Performance Appraisals	
	3) Project Organization Chart	3) Conflict Management	
	4) Staffing Management Plan	4) Issue Log	
	5) Work Performance Information		
	6) Performance Reports		
Summary:	Monitoring team performance issues and changes		

PMP Exam Success Series: Certification Exam Manual
© 2007 Crosswind Project Management, Inc., www.crosswindpm.com

11.9.3   Human Resource Terminology Matching Exercise Answers

Matching Exercise #1 Answers

	Term	Definition
1	Coercive/Penalty Power	K. The use of negative approaches including threatening and punishment to get people to do things they don't want to do
2	Compromise	E. A conflict resolution technique in which a solution involves (typically) a little of what everyone is proposing for a solution
3	Confrontation	O. Directly dealing with a conflict via problem-solving techniques so that the parties can work through any disagreement
4	Empathetic Listening	B. Listening with the goal of understanding what the sender is trying to communicate
5	Forcing	L. Applying an all or nothing (win/lose) to get the desired result
6	Hierarchy of Needs	Q. A pyramid representation of Maslow's Theory that a person's motivation is based on needs (and where the person fits in this pyramid)
7	HR Planning	R. Determining, assigning, and documenting responsibilities, roles, and reporting relationships on a project
8	Legitimate Power	D. Getting people to do what you desire based on your authority
9	Organization Chart (Tool)	J. An organization chart that displays which group is responsible for each work item and can show reporting relationships as well; also known as an organizational breakdown structure
10	Organizational Breakdown Structure (OBS)	F. An organization chart that displays which group is responsible for each work item and can show reporting relationships as well
11	Position Description (Tool)	N. A description of the roles and responsibilities of a team member
12	Project Team Directory	A. A list of all project team members, their project roles, and their communication needs as they relate to the project
13	Referent Power	M. Using personal charisma to attain desired results from others or using existing relationships to help get things done (who you know)
14	Resource	P. People, supplies, equipment, and other items used in the work of the project
15	Resource Histogram	C. A graph that displays the resources used over time on a project
16	Resource Loading	G. The process of applying resources to a schedule and its task
17	Smoothing	T. A conflict resolution technique in which the focus is on areas of similarity and focus is taken off areas of difference
18	Staff Acquisition	I. The hiring and applying of the needed resources to the project
19	Team Development	S. The creation of individual and team skills to maximize project output
20	Withdrawal	H. A conflict resolution technique in which you withdraw from the disagreement (or source of conflict)

Matching Exercise #2 Answers

	Term	Definition
1	Expert Power	E. A capacity in which one uses personal knowledge and expert opinion to get others to do what is desired
2	Mirroring	D. Matching behavior characteristics of another person or group
3	Power	B. The possible ability to influence behavior or performance of others
4	Project Organization Chart (Output/Input)	I. An organization chart that displays which group is responsible for each work item and can show reporting relationships as well; also known as organizational breakdown structure
5	Project Team	K. The group of people put together to plan and (or) execute the work of the project
6	Rapport	J. Possessing comfort or a harmonious relationship with someone

7	Resource Breakdown Structure (RBS)	C. A structure that shows the decomposition of the resources being used on the project; can include personnel, divisions or departments, and job roles
8	Resource Leveling	G. The process of creating a consistent (even) workload for the resources on a project
9	Responsibility Assignment Matrix (RAM) (Tool)	A. A matrix that connects the work of the WBS to the personnel assigned to it in the OBS
10	Reward Power	H. Using positive actions or consequences to attain desired results from other people
11	Staffing Management Plan	F. A document used to describe when resources will start and finish the project

11.9.4 Human Resource Practice Test Answers

1. Developing the project team is an important event directly related to project success. When does this occur in a project?

   Correct Answer: (A) During execution
   Explanation: Team-building occurs in execution of the project management plan. Planning creates the project management plan, the execution of which actually starts the team development. [section 11.3, section 11.7]

2. Which of the following is not a Human Resource process?

   Correct Answer: (A) Team Motivation
   Explanation: The four Human Resource processes are Human Resource Planning, Acquire Project Team, Develop Project Team, and Manage Project Team. [chapter 11]

3. The Project Manager tells a team member on the project that she can attend some database training for a new technology. He further explains that this new skill will be used by the company in the future but not necessarily on the current project. He lets the team member know that he approved this training because of the good work the team member has done on the project. This is an example of what type of power?

   Correct Answer: (B) Reward
   Explanation: The reward power comes from the Project Manager's ability to reward an employee for good work. Formal is the type of power that is derived from the project charter for the Project Manager. Compromise involves some concession from everyone to arrive at a solution. "Knowledge of Needs" is noise. [section 11.1.9, section 11.6]

4. What does a responsibility assignment matrix provide for the team?

   Correct Answer: (A) Information about who is responsible for what work
   Explanation: The responsibility assignment matrix shows who is responsible for what work on the project. The Gantt chart shows who does what work and when they are to do it. The network diagram provides the sequence that the resources are to perform the activities in. "At what location the work is done" is noise. [section 11.1.2, section 11.6]

5. The project is progressing well but has begun to experience resource conflicts with people who are working on critical path activities. What role typically helps resolve these resource issues?

   Correct Answer: (A) Senior management
   Explanation: Typically, most environments are between functional and projectized. That being the case, matrix environments typically have a Functional Manager controlling resources. This can lead to conflict between the Project Manager and Functional Managers. Senior management is usually the entity that resolves these conflicts. The sponsor traditionally gets involved when there is money. "Functional management" is noise. [section 5.4.4]

PMP Exam Success Series: Certification Exam Manual
© 2007 Crosswind Project Management, Inc., www.crosswindpm.com

6. The Project Manager has created the staffing plan and is getting ready to start the project soon. Resumes are being reviewed, and some people have been interviewed. The lead candidate for the technical architecture position has been offered a position. What process is the Project Manager involved in?

Correct Answer: (D) Acquiring the project team
Explanation: Acquiring the project team involves getting people on the project. Resource requirements have already been defined before the interviewing started. Developing the project team should happen after staff acquisition is complete. "Hiring and interviewing" is noise. [section 11.2]

7. The Project Manager has some issues on the team between two developers who disagree about how something should be done. What is the best method to resolve the conflict?

Correct Answer: (B) Problem solving
Explanation: Problem solving is the most proactive and lasting solution. Reward really doesn't fit here. Compromise could water down the solution. Withdrawing is professionally irresponsible. [section 11.4.2]

8. The Project Manager has just received a patent for his design of a circuit for his most recent project. The current project is a product that complements the previous project's work. What type of power will the Project Manager utilize for the best results on the project?

Correct Answer: (B) Expert
Explanation: Expert power implies that the person is bringing some type of specific knowledge to the area or project. Formal power comes from the charter. Referent power deals with whom you know in the organization. Precedent power is used on something that has worked previously. [section 11.1.9, section 11.6]

9. Which of the following is not a level in Maslow's Hierarchy of Needs?

Correct Answer: (B) Psychiatric
Explanation: The levels of Maslow's Hierarchy of Needs are Physiological, Safety, Belonging, Esteem, and Self Actualization. [section 11.1.4]

10. The project charter has just been signed and the Project Manager assigned. What type of power does the Project Manager have as a result of this?

Correct Answer: (B) Formal
Explanation: Once the project charter is signed, the Project Manager has formal authority. The level of authority is defined in the project charter. Reward provides incentives to people on the project. Referent involves whom you are connected to on the project or in the organization. The other answer is noise. [section 11.1.9]

11. The retail network upgrade project has a number of key stakeholders who have provided input to the direction of the project. Which of the following best describes a stakeholder?

Correct Answer: (A) Someone who is impacted by the project
Explanation: The stakeholder is someone who is impacted by the work of the project. That can include stockholders, senior management, and functional management. [section 5.4.4]

12. What is the main expectation that can come from team development?

Correct Answer: (B) Performance improvements
Explanation: Team development can be ongoing throughout a project. Generally speaking, it turns a group of people into a team, thereby giving rise to performance improvement. Team-building activities actually occur during team development. The other answers are noise. [section 11.3]

13. What can a responsibility assignment matrix eliminate?

Correct Answer: (B) Confusion on who is responsible for doing what
Explanation: The responsibility assignment matrix shows who is responsible for what areas on the project. The network diagram provides guidance on what order the activities occur. The organizational structure confirms who is on the team, and what the reporting structure is. The Gantt chart or schedule shows how long the activities are. [section 11.1.2, section 11.6]

14. The project has had some challenges. The Project Manager has been challenged with continually having to tell the team what to do. The team members also do not seem to trust management that much and often appear unmotivated. This is an example of what?

Correct Answer: (B) Theory X environment
Explanation: Typically in a Theory X environment, employees must be told what to do, have distrust for management, and lack motivation. Theory Y is the opposite. The other answers are noise. [section 11.1.4]

15. The electrical engineer has recently been promoted from lead engineer to section manager. In this new position, he is responsible for managing projects and project resources. Over the five years he has been with the company, he was always ranked as one of the top engineers but has had no formal project management training. This is an example of what?

Correct Answer: (A) Halo Theory
Explanation: The Halo Theory implies that because people are good at their current jobs, they would be good at project management regardless of their background or training. The other answers are noise. [section 11.2.3]

16. The Project Manager is planning how many people he will need on the project. There is a lot of database creation and computer programming involved. This will very likely require more than one person with each skill set. He is reviewing the hours of each skill set that will be needed each week on the project. What will he likely use to visually represent this data?

Correct Answer: (A) Resource histogram
Explanation: The resource histogram shows how certain resources are utilized over time. The responsibility assignment matrix shows who is responsible for what area of the project. The Pareto diagram shows defects in frequency of occurrence. "PERT chart" is noise. [section 11.2.1, section 11.6]

17. Which of the following is not likely a project resource for a technology project?

Correct Answer: (C) Functional Manager
Explanation: Resources can be anything that helps contribute to a project's success. No disrespect toward Functional Managers, but the other answers are clearly better examples of project resources that are used directly on a project. The Functional Manager might be involved in the project but usually only in controlling resources. [section 5.4.4]

18. What type of conflict resolution technique has the worst impact on the team?

Correct Answer: (A) Forcing
Explanation: Forcing people to do something they don't want to do has the worst long-term impact on the team. Smoothing is not as bad as forcing. Formal and penalty are types of power that the Project Manager has. [section 11.4.2, section 11.6]

19. The project has gone smoothly so far. The team members appear to be working with an end goal in mind and without a lot of supervision. They appear to be highly motivated and enjoying their work. This is an example of what?

Correct Answer: (B) Theory Y environment

Explanation: A Theory Y environment usually involves people who are motivated and can work with an end goal in mind, instead of being told what to do. They also do not require much supervision and tend to enjoy their work. A Theory X environment is usually the opposite type of environment. Motivation Theory and Reward Theory are noise. [section 11.1.4]

20. The project is in a balanced matrix environment. There are significant challenges with the scope of the project. Project personnel have been complaining to the Project Manager about the environment. In this type of environment, who controls the resources?

Correct Answer: (A) Functional Manager

Explanation: In a matrix environment, the Functional Manager traditionally controls the resources. The Project Manager has those resources available for project work as the Functional Manager sees necessary. Senior management helps resolve resource conflicts. "Project Coordinator" is noise. [section 5.6.2]

21. The project is very challenging and has been very trying on a lot of people. Some key team members are considering leaving the project and returning to their old jobs at the company. Which of the following is a key motivator to keep them on the project?

Correct Answer: (B) Perks

Explanation: Perks are benefits that are not available to everyone. These are items that might keep people on this project because the perks might not be available if they go to another area to work. Fringe benefits are benefits that everyone gets; therefore, they shouldn't be a motivator. Theory Y and compromise are noise. [section 11.2.2]

22. Human Resource Planning occurs during the Planning of a project. Which of the following is not expected to be created during this process?

Correct Answer: (B) Team development

Explanation: Team development must occur after the organizational planning because, until that point, there isn't even the basic definition of a team. [section 11.1]

23. There is a technical disagreement between two important team members on the project. The Project Manager gets involved and tries to remind them of the good things that have happened on the project that they have been involved with. This is an example of what type of conflict resolution?

Correct Answer: (A) Smoothing

Explanation: Smoothing tries to minimize the conflict on the project and remember things that have worked well. Compromise involves some concession from everyone to arrive at a solution. Referent is name-dropping or political alignment for power. Withdrawal is stepping away and ignoring the problem, which is professionally irresponsible. [section 11.4.2, section 11.6]

24. An organizational breakdown structure (OBS) is also known as what?

Correct Answer: (B) Organizational chart

Explanation: The organizational breakdown structure (OBS) is also known as an organizational chart. The staffing management plan defines the staffing rules as it relates to the project. The responsibility assignment matrix shows who is responsible for what on the project. The resource histogram shows what quantities of resources are utilized over time. [section 11.1.3, section 11.6]

25. Which of the following is not an example of team development?

Correct Answer: (D) Performance reviews

Explanation: A performance review is not a team-building event. Such a review is a Cost Control tool an employee and supervisor use to evaluate project performance. In team-building, a group of people on the project form a cohesive whole. [section 11.3, section 9.14]

26. The Project Manager is involved in an off-shore project utilizing a number of different resources. There have been several resource issues so far on the project. The Project Manager is evaluating what was used in establishing the management of the project team. All the following should be considered for managing the project team except...

Correct Answer: (D) Ground rules

Explanation: Ground rules are established in developing the project team. The other three items are inputs to managing the project team. Project staff assignment helps establish who is on the team. Work performance information provides details as to what work is being done and the project organization chart displays organization structure and reporting relationships. [section 11.4, section 11.3]

27. The team is going through some resource over-utilization issues on the project. The database administrators are working excessive hours. The Project Manager has gone back to Planning to re-evaluate the situation. Which of the following can provide help in seeing how serious the issue is?

Correct Answer: (D) Resource histogram

Explanation: The resource histogram displays how resources are utilized on the project. It can be displayed a number of ways, but the general view shows some criteria of resources on the project over a time scale. The Control chart shows output over time. The Pareto diagram shows frequency of defects. The staffing management plan addresses how to deal with staffing-related items on the project. [section 11.2.1, section 11.6]

28. The project coordinator is in charge of planning the semester classes at the university. They are trying to allocate various resource types to work together such as instructors, room, and audio/video equipment. Which of the following are they most likely to use to show this information?

Correct Answer: (B) Resource breakdown structure

Explanation: The resource breakdown structure shows resource utilization across the organization regardless of what division or group they report to. It works well for various resource types described above. The organizational chart shows who or what position reports to what person or position on the project. The risk breakdown structure shows a decomposition of the potential risks on the project. The responsibility assignment matrix shows who is responsible for what on the project. [section 11.6, section 8.3.1]

29. The senior Project Manager at the company is helping to look out for a less experienced Project Manager who is working on another project. They meet weekly to see how the less experienced person's project is performing, as well as discussing concepts that should help make the less experienced Project Manager more experienced. This is an example of what?

Correct Answer: (B) Mentoring

Explanation: Mentoring is an activity in which someone more experienced helps tutor someone not as experienced in the field of choice. An intern program doesn't exactly fit in this case. The other answers are noise. [section 11.1.7]

PMP Exam Success Series: Certification Exam Manual
© 2007 Crosswind Project Management, Inc., www.crosswindpm.com

30.   The Project Manager is in the process of planning the project. The company he works for has had issues with previous projects in which there has been confusion over who is accountable for completing various activities and processes associated with the projects. What document can he include in the project management plan that will help eliminate this problem?

Correct Answer: (D) Responsibility assignment matrix

Explanation: The responsibility assignment matrix shows who is responsible for what on the project. The Gantt chart shows when activities are done. The staffing plan addresses the staffing-related needs of the project. The organization chart shows how the organization is structured. [section 11.1.2, section 11.6]

Chapter 12

Communications

The Communications Knowledge Area is similar to the Human Resource Knowledge Area in that many of you are already familiar with a number of the terms. As it relates to project management, communication can include how to generate, collect, distribute, store, and retrieve the information on the project. The tables on communication types are "musts" to memorize, plus knowing who can solve what type of problem. Remember though, do not take this topic too lightly or it can surprise you when you least need it!

In this chapter, we discuss the following:

Process Group	Process Name		Main Outputs
Planning	Communications Planning	→	Communications Management Plan
Executing	Information Distribution	→	Requested Changes
Monitoring and Controlling	Performance Reporting	→	Performance Reports
			Forecasts
			Requested Changes
	Manage Stakeholders	→	Resolved Issues

✓ **Crosswind "Must Knows" For Communications**

Key Inputs, Tools & Techniques, and Outputs for Communication Planning
Key Inputs, Tools & Techniques, and Outputs for Information Distribution
Key Inputs, Tools & Techniques, and Outputs for Performance Reporting
Key Inputs, Tools & Techniques, and Outputs for Manage Stakeholders
What a communications management plan is and what it is used for
Concept of Information Distribution
How much Project Managers should want to control communication, and how much they are likely to control it (what % of their time is spent doing it)
Calculations for the total number of communication channels
Calculations for the total number of communication channels added or removed as team members are added or removed
Formal written, formal verbal, informal written and informal verbal communication types and how to recognize examples of them
How to use the communication channel formula to be able to calculate the number of communication channels or additional channels added on a project
Communication Model (sender, message, receiver)

Although helpful, this list is not all-inclusive for information needed from this area for the exam. It is only suggested material that, if understood and memorized, may increase your exam score.

12.1   Communication Skills

Communication skills differ from communication management in project management, but they are vital to successful project integration as the key pieces of the project come together per the project management plan. Components of communication skills can include the sender-receiver model (see later in this chapter), media format, writing styles, management and presentation techniques, encode, decode, message, medium, and noise.

12.2   Communication Types

The exam addresses four main types of communication, plus potentially a combination of the four. The types are:

- Formal
- Informal
- Written
- Verbal

Be familiar with the communication types and how to recognize examples of each.

In the public Crosswind courses, communication types occasionally cause some debate, so we recommend you try to understand the logic behind the classification, as well as what type of communication fits where.

Type	Description
Formal Written	The formal written type of communication should be used for the following: • legal communication • project documents • when distance or extreme complexity are involved The legal and project documents aspect lays the foundation for the intentions of all parties, where, if written communication wasn't involved, it could turn into he said/she said. Using this type of communication for distance or complexity helps ensure that the parties receive the exact intention. In the verbal area, there could be misinterpretation of the intent.
Formal Verbal	The formal verbal type of communication should be used in **official situations, presentations**, and other primarily **one-directional communication.** A meeting doesn't fit these criteria (because communication goes back and forth in a meeting). It is a presentation to see where the company plans to go or for a new product, with the main speaker doing the majority of presentation.
Informal Verbal	The informal verbal type of communication includes any communication that isn't formal, such as people talking together. This communication **does include meetings,** because meetings are bi-directional communication with the participants communicating among themselves.
Informal Written	The informal written type of communication includes **non-legal documents,** documentation that preceded any contracts, general documentation, and notes.

PMP Exam Success Series: Certification Exam Manual
© 2007 Crosswind Project Management, Inc., www.crosswindpm.com

Communications Scenario	Formal	Informal	Written	Verbal
Complex Technical Issue	X		X	
Meeting		X		X
Statement of Work (SOW)	X		X	
Hallway Communication		X		X
Corporate Presentation	X			X
Communicating with offshore Development Center	X		X	
Notes (Minutes) From a Meeting	X		X	
Email		X	X	

12.3   Communications Planning (Planning Process Group)

Know the Key Inputs, Tools & Techniques, and Outputs for Communications Planning.

In this area, the Project Manager **determines the communication needs of all the stakeholders.** Key criteria is what information they need, when it's needed, and in what format.

Communications Planning (Planning)		
Key Inputs	Project Scope Statement	The project scope statement **helps define the project**. Supporting detail provides the in-depth research and planning that the project scope statement rolls into.
	Project Management Plan • Constraints • Assumptions	Constraints, which are defined in the project management plan, **describe limitations** under which the project must operate. They can also relate to communication requirements and options. Examples are locations or technology.
		Assumptions, which are defined in the project management plan, are **suppositions related to Communications Planning** in this process.
Key Tools & Techniques	Communications Requirements Analysis	Communications requirements analysis **factors in the communication requirements to ensure they are properly addressed** in the communications management plan. This analysis can include organization charts, responsibility assignment matrixes (RAM), logistical needs, as well as internal and external information requirements.
	Communications Technology	Communications technology **distributes project information** per the requirements in the communications management plan. Variables that influence the use of the technology can be the importance of the information need, the use of the technology infrastructure, staffing levels, project length, and project team culture.

Key Outputs	Communications Management Plan	Communications management plan is the main document that **contains the communication needs and actions** for the project. This plan includes items such as how communication changes are to be addressed. It can also include format, detail, frequency, who is to send and receive the communications, and terminology to eliminate confusion. Also included could be rules for meetings and email.

Situational Question and Real World Application

Communications Planning is often ignored on most projects. It's not unusual to see communication breakdowns in which the right people aren't getting needed information or the wrong people are getting too much. Also, the timing of information can be an issue, if not addressed appropriately.

12.3.1   Communications Management Plan

The communications management plan defines the communication needs of the stakeholders, the communications format and frequency, and who delivers them. This communication can include reports, meeting schedules, change processes, and contact information for the team. It lets team members know the communication rules and the project expectations.

The plan helps the Project Manager and team do the following:

- Determine communication requirements for the project
- Establish and utilize communication infrastructure for distributing information on the project
- Report performance on the project to the appropriate stakeholders
- Deal with communication issues that arise

Know what a communications management plan is and what it is used for.

12.3.2   Communication Control

Controlling communication is vital to project management success. But controlling does not mean demanding that you be included in each and every bit of communication. It means that you are current on communication activity and that you are kept in the project communication loop as much as possible. What you may want to control and what you are likely to control are two different things.

You need to know how much Project Managers should want to control communication, and how much they can likely control it (what % of their time is spent on it). **Remember, approximately 90% of a Project Manager's job is communication.**

Be familiar with how much Project Managers handle control of communications.

12.3.3   Communication Channels Formula

Communications is a complex part of any project. The more people involved in a project, the greater the communication among them. The formula for this relationship is **N*(N-1)/2** with N being the number of people on the project. Don't forget to include the Project Manager as well.

Know the calculations for the total number of communication channels.

PMP Exam Success Series: Certification Exam Manual
© 2007 Crosswind Project Management, Inc., www.crosswindpm.com

Figure 12-1: Communication Channels shows how communication grows quickly as people are added to the project.

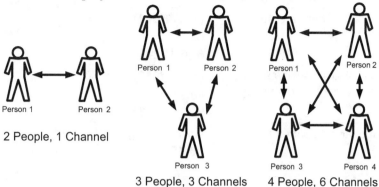

3 People, 3 Channels   4 People, 6 Channels

Figure 12-1: Communication Channels

Be prepared to calculate the number of communication channels on a project, as well as the number of channels added if team members are added or removed. **Also, be sensitive to questions in which you are the Project Manager with a team of a given number of people compared to a team of a given number of people. You must count yourself in the first situation.**

You must recognize if the PM is included in the situation…

> Know the calculations for the total number of communication channels added or removed as team members are added or removed

PM has a team of 6 (count 7 people)	The PM is described as "outside" the team, and the total count must be adjusted to include the PM in the communications channels.
Team has 6 people (count 6 people)	The PM is described as within the team. No adjustment to the total count is necessary.

Be able to calculate the following:

Number of channels total on project	Number of channels total on project when people are added	Number of channels added when people are added
Use the standard formula.	Use the standard formula for new total number of people.	Use the standard formulas for original number of people and for new total number of people then subtract the difference.
$N^{original} * (N^{original}-1)/2$	$N^{new} * (N^{new}-1)/2$	$(N^{new} * (N^{new}-1)/2)$ $- (N^{original} * (N^{original}-1)/2)$

Scenario: PM Already Counted	Standard Formula: $N*(N-1)/2$
With a team of 4, there are 6 channels	$4*(4-1)/2=6$
If 2 people are added to the team, there is now a team of 6 and a total of 15 channels.	$(4+2)*((4+2)-1)/2=15$ **Or** $6*(6-1)/2=15$
The total number of channels added is 9.	**New # - Original # = # added** **15-6=9**

Scenario: PM Counted "outside" the Team	Standard Formula: N*(N-1)/2
The PM has a team of 5. There are 15 channels.	(5+1)*((5+1)-1)/2=15 or 6*(6-1)/2=15
If 3 people are added, there are now 9 people (team plus PM) and a total of 36 channels.	(6+3)*((6+3)-1)/2=36 Or 9*(9-1)/2=36
The total number of channels added is 21.	New # - Original # = # added 36-15=21

12.4   Information Distribution (Executing Process Group)

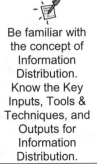

Be familiar with the concept of Information Distribution. Know the Key Inputs, Tools & Techniques, and Outputs for Information Distribution.

For Information Distribution, the main focus is **to deliver information to the project stakeholders.** Information about project work and activities is communicated as a result of the communication plan criteria and work results. These results are distributed to the various stakeholders in the frequency and the format as specified by the communications management plan.

Information Distribution (Executing)		
Key Inputs	Communications Management Plan	The communications management plan is the main document that **contains the communication needs and actions** for the project. This plan includes items such as how communication changes are to be addressed.
Key Tools & Techniques	Information Gathering and Retrieval Systems	Information gathering and retrieval systems are key tools because they **help create the distribution environment for the information** on the project. Information retrieval systems are systems that **allow team members access to key project information.** These systems can include filing systems, databases, project management software, and software that provides the opportunity to access schematics or other technical drawings.
	Information Distribution Methods	Information distribution methods include **any methods used to deliver project information to project personnel.** These methods can include meetings, documentation, network access, email, voicemail, and more.
	Lessons Learned Process	The lessons learned process **analyzes what worked well on the project and what didn't** so that historical information for future projects can benefit from this knowledge.
Key Outputs	Requested Changes	Requested changes are **changes that have been requested but not yet formally approved** by the official change control process on the project.

Situational Question and Real World Application
Coming up short in this area could result in the failure to capture appropriate data because the distribution was not adequately structured. Also, people could be receiving information in the wrong format or timeframe.

12.4.1 Communication Model

The basics of communication are covered in the Communication Model. The three main components are:

- Sender
- Message
- Receiver

> Be familiar with the Communication Model (sender, message, and receiver).

The medium is another component to consider because it is the medium that sets the format of the message. Communication can be impacted positively or negatively depending on the medium of the communication.

Given the global nature of projects and people on projects today, breaks in the model are not uncommon. The key responsibility of the sender is to correctly encode (communicate) the message to the receiver(s) so that they can (do what they are responsible for) correctly decode (understand) it.

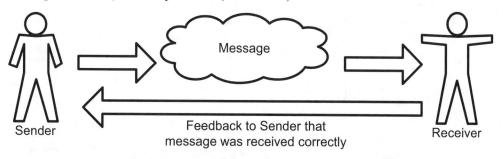

Figure 12-2: Sender/Receiver Interaction

12.4.2 Types of Communications Processes

There are a number of processes used in communications.

Active Listening	The receiver verifies with the sender that the message was interpreted correctly by asking for clarification or by providing feedback to the sender.
Effective Listening	The receiver observes visual and vocal clues, as well as asking for feedback from the sender.
Feedback	The sender receives feedback from the receiver, possibly by asking additional questions or using other methods to clarify the message.
Nonverbal	**Nonverbal exchange can be up to 55% of a communication.** Items in this category could include body and facial language. Think of times you knew something was wrong in a situation but no one mentioned it, something just felt weird (and it was).
Para-lingual	Voice characteristics come into play as the sender conveys the message.

12.4.3 Communication Blockers

Communication blockers are factors disrupting the message that the receiver is trying to interpret from the sender.

12.4.4 Meeting Rules

Meeting rules are commonly abused. As a result, our perception of how to handle meetings often comes from not doing it "right" because we never knew any better. Some basic rules for meetings are as follows:

- When a meeting is scheduled, an agenda should be created and distributed beforehand to give people a chance to review and prepare. This agenda should allocate a portion of time for each topic.
- All related documents should be distributed prior to the meeting.
- People should review the agenda and prepare for the meeting.
- In (or before) the meeting, a leader should be established to lead the meeting and follow the agenda. The leader (facilitator) doesn't always need to be the Project Manager.
- Anything added to the meeting outside of the agenda should be added at the end or to a future meeting.
- From an exam readiness perspective, if the project is a priority and a meeting has been scheduled, functional issues (generally speaking) do not delay the meeting with the team.

12.5 Performance Reporting (Monitoring and Controlling Process Group)

Know the Key Inputs, Tools & Techniques, and Outputs for Performance Reporting.

Performance Reporting is the area in which the output of the work results (performance) is reported. This reporting gives you the ability to see if the project is on track or not, and if not, how far off the baseline and how much needs to be adjusted to get the project back on track. In this area, performance-related information on the project is interpreted and analyzed, comparing what has been done (actuals) to what is forecast to be done on the project (baseline).

Performance Reporting (Monitoring and Controlling)		
Key Inputs	Work Performance Information	Work performance information **provides a status on what has been completed (or not completed)** on the project.
	Performance Measurements	Performance measurement **helps verify if a change is potentially needed**. It can alert you to the accuracy of the execution of the plan.
	Forecasted Completion	Forecasted completion is **communicated to the appropriate stakeholder via calculation of the estimate at completion (EAC) and estimate to complete (ETC).**
	Project Management Plan • Performance Measurement Baseline	The performance measurement baseline from the project management plan **establishes the plan for which the project execution is measured against**. This baseline can include scope, time, cost, quality, or technical performance.

PMP Exam Success Series: Certification Exam Manual
© 2007 Crosswind Project Management, Inc., www.crosswindpm.com

Key Tools & Techniques	Information Presentation Tools	Information presentation tools are **used to create presentations based on project data**. These tools can include word processing, spreadsheets, scheduling tools, graphics, and other applicable types of software.
	Performance Information Gathering and Compilation	Performance information gathering and compilation is **done by extracting information** from spreadsheets, filing systems, information storage systems and other areas where project information is available to create project forecasts, progress, status, and performance reports.
	Status Review Meetings	Status review meetings are used **to communicate project activity completion**. They can be conducted with the team or customer involved.
	Time Reporting Systems	Time reporting systems are used to **track time spent** on the project.
	Cost Reporting Systems	Cost reporting systems are used to **track cost spent** on the project.
Key Outputs	Performance Reports	Performance reports are key to **show the current actual work complete** on the project. These reports could include bar charts, tables, and histograms.
	Forecasts	Forecasts provide information about **what is expected to happen** on the project.
	Requested Changes	Requested changes **result from any variance or need to adjust the plan**.
	Recommended Corrective Actions	Recommended corrective actions are **modifications to the plan or work being completed** that will modify the output to achieve a desired result that wasn't (typically) planned.

Situational Question and Real World Application
Not knowing a project's health or completion is a key problem if this area were ignored. Not knowing if a change were required, or not knowing to recommend a required change could also be a problem.

12.5.1 Performance Reports

Reporting on a project can take a variety of formats; interpretations of the formats can vary. The following definitions should help clarify the subtle differences between the types.

Forecast Reports

Forecast reports provide information on what is expected to be happening on the project. Ex: What are we going to do? Forecast reporting associated with cost can include the following:

- Estimate at completion (EAC): The funds needed to totally finish the project based on current spending efficiency
- Estimate to complete (ETC): Additional funds needed as of this point in time to finish the project
- Variance at completion (VAC): The amount forecasted to be over/under budget based on budget at completion (BAC) versus estimate at completion (EAC)

For more information about the above, refer to the Cost chapter.

Progress Reports

Progress reports provide information on what has been done recently on the project. Ex: What have we done in the last week?

Status Reports

Status reports provide information on the present overall state of the project. Ex: What have we done total so far?

Team	Quarter 1	Quarter 2	Quarter 3	Quarter 4	Total
Team A	28	26	24	33	111
Team B	30	23	32	12	97

Progress Reports show what has happened since a previous measurement point

Status Reports show an overall state of progress such as the total score at any point in time

How work experience requires reports often conflicts with how PMI defines reports. To clarify progress and status, review the above example of a four-quarter game between two teams. A **progress report** shows how many points have been scored by period. A **status report** shows the overall score at any point in time. To apply these examples to a project, a **progress report shows what has been accomplished within a given time frame**. A **status report shows the overall state of the project**. **Remember: The Status Report is the sum of ALL Progress Reports.** For example, in a six-week project, with progress reporting weekly at the end of three weeks, the Status Report is the sum of information reported in Progress Reports for weeks 1, 2, and 3.

$$\begin{aligned} \textbf{Progress} &= \textbf{Points in time} \\ \textbf{Status} &= \textbf{Sum of all} \end{aligned}$$

Variance Reports

Variance reports show the difference between what was planned to happen and what actually happened. Ex: What is the difference between what we should have done AND have done?

Earned Value Reports

Earned value reports show the state of the schedule, budget, and scope of the project at various points in time.

12.6   Manage Stakeholders (Monitoring and Controlling Process Group)

Manage Stakeholders involves handling stakeholder communications to help ensure that their needs are met and that the project achieves its defined goals. A stakeholder's needs can evolve as the project progresses. For example, there are two projects, both halfway through execution. One has five key stakeholders, and the other has two key stakeholders. The complexity of the project with five stakeholders could be greater than the complexity of the project with only two because of varying and sometimes conflicting stakeholder needs.

Know the Key Inputs, Tools & Techniques, and Outputs for Manage Stakeholders.

Manage Stakeholders (Monitoring and Controlling)		
Key Inputs	Communications Management Plan	Communications management plan is the main document that **contains the communication needs and actions** for the project. This plan includes items such as how communication changes are to be addressed.
Key Tools & Techniques	Issue Logs	Issue logs are used to **track issues** that arise on the project. They provide a documentation trail for assignment and resolution.
Key Outputs	Resolved Issues	Resolved issues are **issues that have been satisfactorily addressed** and no longer require attention on the project.
	Approved Change Requests	Approved change requests are **changes that have been formally approved** by the official change control process on the project.
	Approved Corrective Actions	Approved corrective actions are **actions that have been through an approval process to remedy some issue or problem** on the project.

Situational Question and Real World Application
Problems in this area are likely to revolve around communication breakdowns with the stakeholders. For example, a failure to include a key stakeholder in project Scope Planning, status updates, or change requests and approvals can negatively impact the project.

12.7   Communications Formulas and Variables

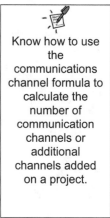

Know how to use the communications channel formula to calculate the number of communication channels or additional channels added on a project.

Description	Formula	Variable (Components)	Example
Communication Channels Formula This formula shows the number of communication channels on a project.	N*(N-1)/2=Number of Communication Channels	N=Number of people	6*(6-1)/2=15
N=the number of people on the project	Provided on the exam	N	22 people on a project

12.8   Communications Terminology

Term	Description
Communications Infrastructure	Tools and techniques used to create the foundation for information transfer on a project
Communications Management Plan	A document created to define the project communication needs
Communications Planning	Requirement gathering of the communication needs of the people on the project; what they will need and when, and in what format will they need it
Exception Report	A report that includes significant variations from the planned activities
Forecasts	Estimates related to future project performance that are based on historical information and current project knowledge
Information Distribution	Delivering needed project information to stakeholders in an appropriate timeframe
Kickoff Meeting	A meeting used to initiate the start of the project; typically attended by all the key stakeholders; can be done when Initiating or Planning is complete depending upon the organization
Performance Reporting (Output/Input)	The collection and interpretation of performance data; can include status, progress, and forecast reports
Progress Report	A report that states what has been accomplished in a specific amount of time on the project (but not the entire project)
Project Forecasting	A reporting method in which future performance is estimated based on past performance of the project
Status Report	A report that states the current shape or state of the project to date

PMP Exam Success Series: Certification Exam Manual
© 2007 Crosswind Project Management, Inc., www.crosswindpm.com

12.9   Communications Mind Map

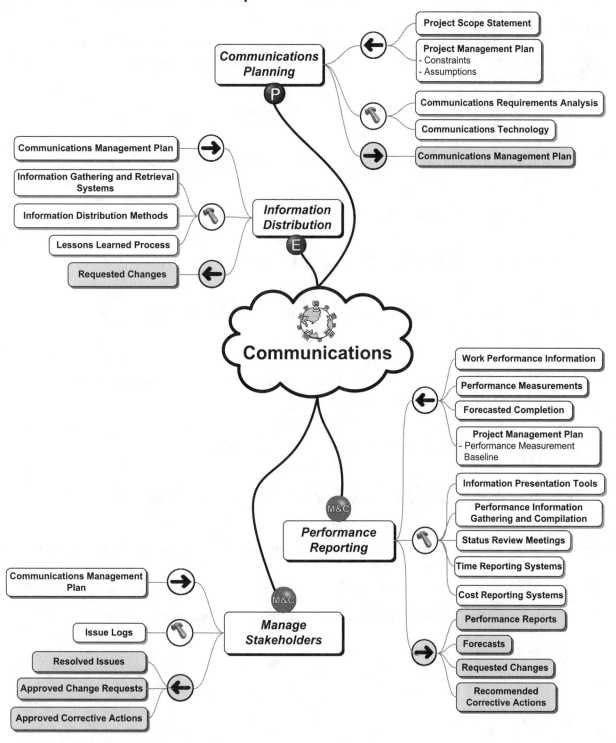

12.10 Communications Tests and Exercises

12.10.1   Communications Quick Test
In this quiz, answer the question in a short essay of only a sentence or two or circle all correct answers for the question. Note that some questions may have more than one answer. Answers are in section 12.11.1.

1.   What are the two roles in the Communication Model?

2.   What percentage of a Project Manager's job is spent communicating?

3.   What type of report focuses on what has been done recently on a project?

4.   What document is used to define the communication needs of the project?

5.   What is the number of communication channels if a Project Manager has a team of six people?

6.   How many fewer communication channels are there if the Project Manager loses two team members (from the previous question)?

7.   What does a variance report show?

8.   What are three things that the managing stakeholder process accomplishes?

9.   What type of communication is used to communicate highly technical information to a team spread out across two countries?

10.   What are the four main types of communication that can be used on a project?

12.10.2 Communications ITTO Matching Exercise

Match the correct ITTO term at the bottom of the page with the blanks to the right of the process. When a term is used multiple times, it is flagged by a parenthetical value indicating the number of times used. Also, match summary sentences with the process name that fits. Answers are in section 12.11.2.

	Inputs	Tools & Techniques	Outputs
Communications Planning	1) _____ 2) _____ 3) _____	1) _____ 2) _____	1) _____

Summary:

	Inputs	Tools & Techniques	Outputs
Information Distribution	1) _____	1) _____ 2) _____ 3) _____	1) _____

Summary:

	Inputs	Tools & Techniques	Outputs
Performance Reporting	1) _____ 2) _____ 3) _____ 4) _____	1) _____ 2) _____ 3) _____ 4) _____ 5) _____	1) _____ 2) _____ 3) _____ 4) _____

Summary:

	Inputs	Tools & Techniques	Outputs
Manage Stakeholders	1) _____	1) _____	1) _____ 2) _____ 3) _____

Summary:

Reporting information on the status of the project	Distributing project-related information to stakeholders
Managing communications to satisfy stakeholder needs	Determining the communications needs of the project

Approved Change Requests	Information Presentation Tools	Project Management Plan (Performance Measurement Baseline)
Approved Corrective Actions	Issue Logs	
Communications Management Plan (3)	Lessons Learned Process	
Communications Requirements Analysis	Performance Information Gathering and Compilation	Project Scope Statement
Communications Technology	Performance Measurements	Recommended Corrective Actions
Cost Reporting Systems	Performance Reports	Requested Changes (2)
Forecasts	Project Management Plan (Assumptions)	Resolved Issues
Forecasted Completion	Project Management Plan (Constraints)	Status Review Meetings
Information Distribution Methods		Time Reporting Systems
Information Gathering and Retrieval Systems		Work Performance Information

12.10.3   Communications Terminology Matching Exercise

Match the correct term in the left column to the correct definition in the right column.
Answers are in section 12.11.3.

Matching Exercise

	Term	Answer	Definition
1	Communications Infrastructure		A. A reporting method in which future performance is estimated based on past performance of the project
2	Communications Management Plan		B. Estimates related to future project performance that are based on historical information and current project knowledge
3	Communications Planning		C. Tools and techniques used to create the foundation for information transfer on a project
4	Exception Report		D. A report that states the current shape or state of the project to date
5	Forecasts		E. A meeting used to initiate the start of the project; typically attended by all the key stakeholders; can be done when Initiating or Planning is complete depending upon the organization
6	Information Distribution		F. A document created to define the project communication needs
7	Kickoff Meeting		G. A report that states what has been accomplished in a specific amount of time on the project (but not the entire project)
8	Performance Reporting (Output/Input)		H. A report that includes significant variations from the planned activities
9	Progress Report		I. The collection and interpretation of performance data; can include status, progress, and forecast reports
10	Project Forecasting		J. Delivering needed project information to stakeholders in an appropriate timeframe
11	Status Report		K. Requirement gathering of the communication needs of the people on the project; what they will need and when, and in what format will they need it

PMP Exam Success Series: Certification Exam Manual
© 2007 Crosswind Project Management, Inc., www.crosswindpm.com

12.10.4 Communications Practice Test

Answers are in section 12.11.4.

1.   Which of the following is an input to the communications management plan?

(A) Communications infrastructure
(B) Formal communication
(C) Stakeholder analysis
(D) Project scope statement

2.   Which of the following is not a good reason to cancel a meeting?

(A) The agenda wasn't published until right before the meeting.
(B) A key team member had to attend a different meeting.
(C) A Functional Manager wanted to meet with the Project Manager at the same time.
(D) The topic partially changed and the presentation material wasn't complete yet.

3.   Which of the following is not a component of the Communication Model?

(A) Sender
(B) Receiver
(C) Language
(D) Message

4.   What type of report shows what is expected to be completed in the next two weeks on the project?

(A) Earned value report
(B) Status report
(C) Forecast report
(D) Progress report

5.   What type of report shows what has been completed compared to what should have been completed on the project?

(A) Earned value report
(B) Status report
(C) Variance report
(D) Progress report

6.   In the Communication Model, the sender conveys which of the following to the receiver?

(A) Feedback
(B) Medium
(C) Noise
(D) Message

7. The Project Manager is communicating to the team the activities, their sequence, durations, and who is responsible for doing what work on the project. This document is known as what?

   (A) Schedule
   (B) Gantt chart
   (C) Work breakdown structure
   (D) Responsibility assignment matrix

8. The project is approximately 50% complete and in the middle of execution. The Project Manager is communicating with stakeholders regarding the status of the project. Which will he likely use to determine what to communicate to whom?

   (A) Information retrieval systems
   (B) Communications management plan
   (C) Formal communication
   (D) Verbal communication

9. All the following could be considered mediums for communication except…

   (A) Email
   (B) Staff meetings
   (C) Video conference
   (D) Message

10. Which of the following is the best form of communication for canceling a project?

    (A) Email
    (B) Verbal
    (C) Informal written
    (D) Formal written

11. Seven people report to the Project Manager. Three more people are added to the project. How many communication channels were added to the project?

    (A) 56 channels
    (B) 28 channels
    (C) 55 channels
    (D) 27 channels

12. What type of report shows what has been completed in the last week on the project?

    (A) Status report
    (B) Earned value report
    (C) Progress report
    (D) Variance report

PMP Exam Success Series: Certification Exam Manual
© 2007 Crosswind Project Management, Inc., www.crosswindpm.com

13.   All the following are examples of communication requirements on a project except…

(A) Project status meeting time and location
(B) The name of the HR manager for the company
(C) Steps to take regarding a project change request
(D) Names and contact information for the members of the project change control board

14.   Communication infrastructure is a very important component of project management. All the following are examples of communications infrastructure except…

(A) Conference rooms
(B) Spreadsheet applications
(C) Intranet site
(D) Email system

15.   In reporting performance on the project, the Project Manager needs which of the following?

(A) Status reports
(B) Work results
(C) Project archives
(D) Change request

16.   The Project Manager has weekly scheduled status meetings with the team. The meetings have been unorganized, chaotic, and lacking direction. Which of the following would improve the meetings?

(A) Determine who is in charge of the meeting.
(B) Send the team to communication training.
(C) Create and publish an agenda, and establish the leader of the meeting.
(D) Create and publish an agenda.

17.   You are the Project Manager on a defense project. You have been analyzing project data from the last reporting period. The main data you have been looking at is earned value, actual cost, and planned value. What type of report format are you viewing?

(A) Status report
(B) Progress report
(C) Variance report
(D) Performance report

18.   The Project Manager is planning the project. He is meeting with project stakeholders to determine their communication needs for the project. He is finding out what type of information they need, when it is needed, and in what format. What will he create as a result of this work?

(A) Team list
(B) Communications management plan
(C) Staffing plan
(D) Information distribution plan

19. The Project Manager spends a lot of time in meetings and talking with team members about the execution of the project. How much of a Project Manager's job is spent communicating?

    (A) 40 hours a week
    (B) Approximately 90%
    (C) 100%
    (D) 60+ hours a week

20. What type of report shows the schedule, cost, and scope performance on the project?

    (A) Earned value report
    (B) Status report
    (C) Variance report
    (D) Progress report

21. You are the Project Manager on a defense project. You have been analyzing project data from the last eight reporting periods. The main data you have been looking at is earned value, actual cost, and planned value. Which of the following represent this data graphically?

    (A) Bar chart
    (B) S curve
    (C) Pareto diagram
    (D) Scatter diagram

22. What type of report shows what has been completed to date on the project?

    (A) Earned value report
    (B) Status report
    (C) Variance report
    (D) Progress report

23. Which of the following is a good tool to stay current with stakeholder needs and problems?

    (A) Change control process
    (B) Issue log
    (C) Integrated change control
    (D) Project management plan

24. The Project Manager is involved in planning the communication needs for the project. What will he have completed when he is done with this part of Planning?

    (A) Communications management plan
    (B) Stakeholder analysis
    (C) Communication requirements
    (D) Information distribution system

25.   The statement of work on a project is viewed as what type of communication?

        (A) Formal
        (B) Formal written
        (C) Contract
        (D) Verbal

26.   The project has eight people on it. Two more are added. What is the total number of communication channels added to the project?

        (A) 45 channels
        (B) 17 channels
        (C) 28 channels
        (D) 10 channels

27.   You are the Project Manager for a software development project using an offshore development company. There have been a number of communication challenges with misinterpretation of requirements and failure to follow through with things that the Project Manager felt needed attention. What type of communication helps reduce these problems?

        (A) Formal written
        (B) Formal
        (C) Verbal
        (D) Informal verbal

28.   The Project Manager is working with the team to create a decomposition of the project work. The results of this effort will help determine resource needs, how long the project should take, and how much it should cost. What is the team creating?

        (A) Gantt chart
        (B) Schedule
        (C) Responsibility assignment matrix
        (D) Work breakdown structure

29.   In the Communication Model, who is responsible for ensuring that the receiver has received and understood the message correctly?

        (A) Project Manager
        (B) Both the sender and receiver
        (C) Sender
        (D) Receiver

30. The network infrastructure project is having problems with people not knowing about meetings and not involved in approval of project deliverables. The project is being audited for health. What document is likely show information that could fix this problem?

(A) Communications management plan
(B) Project management plan
(C) Performance reporting plan
(D) Information distribution system

PMP Exam Success Series: Certification Exam Manual
© 2007 Crosswind Project Management, Inc., www.crosswindpm.com

12.11 Communications Tests and Exercise Answers

12.11.1 Communications Quick Test Answers

1. What are the two roles in the Communication Model?
    Sender and Receiver [section 12.4.1]

2. What percentage of a Project Manager's job is spent communicating?
    90% or greater [section 12.3.2]

3. What type of report focuses on what has been done recently on a project?
    The progress report focuses on what has been done since the last reporting period.
    [section 12.5.1, section 12.8]

4. What document is used to define the communication needs of the project?
    The communications management plan [section 12.3.1, section 12.8, section 12.9]

5. What is the number of communication channels if a Project Manager has a team of six people?
    There are a total of seven people (1 Project Manager +6 people). The formula is N*(N-1)/2 or 7*6/2 or 42/2=21 communication channels. [section 12.3.3, section 12.7]

6. How many fewer communication channels are there if the Project Manager loses two team members (from the previous question)?
    The team now consists of five people (1 Project Manager +4 people). The formula is N*(N-1)/2 or 5*4/2 or 20/2=10 communication channels. Don't forget to subtract the original calculation of 10 channels from the 21 channels now. The correct answer to the problem is 11 channels. [section 12.3.3, section 12.7]

7. What does a variance report show?
    It shows the variance between the plan (baseline) and the actual results. [section 12.5.1]

8. What are three things that the managing stakeholder process accomplishes?
    Resolving issues, approving change requests, and approving corrective actions
    [section 12.6, section 12.9]

9. What type of communication is used to communicate highly technical information to a team spread out across two countries?
    Formal written [section 12.2]

10. What are the four main types of communication that can be used on a project?
    Formal, informal, written, and verbal, or formal written, informal written, formal verbal, informal verbal [section 12.2]

12.11.2   Communication ITTO Matching Exercise Answers

	Inputs	Tools & Techniques	Outputs
Communications Planning	1) Project Scope Statement 2) Project Management Plan (Constraints) 3) Project Management Plan (Assumptions)	1) Communications Requirement Analysis 2) Communications Technology	1) Communications Management Plan
Summary:	Determining the communication needs of the project		
Information Distribution	1) Communications Management Plan	1) Information Gathering and Retrieval Systems 2) Information Distribution Methods 3) Lessons Learned Process	1) Requested Changes
Summary:	Distributing project-related information to stakeholders		
Performance Reporting	1) Work Performance Information 2) Performance Measurements 3) Forecasted Completion 4) Project Management Plan (Performance Measurement Baseline)	1) Information Presentation Tools 2) Performance Information Gathering and Compilation 3) Status Review Meetings 4) Time Reporting Systems 5) Cost Reporting Systems	1) Performance Reports 2) Forecasts 3) Requested Changes 4) Recommended Corrective Actions
Summary:	Reporting information on the status of the project		
Manage Stakeholders	1) Communications Management Plan	1) Issues Logs	1) Resolved Issues 2) Approved Change Requests 3) Approved Corrective Actions
Summary:	Managing communications to satisfy stakeholder needs		

12.11.3   Communication Terminology Matching Exercise Answers

Matching Exercise Answers

	Term	Definition
1	**Communications Infrastructure**	C. Tools and techniques used to create the foundation for information transfer on a project
2	**Communications Management Plan**	F. A document created to define the project communication needs
3	**Communications Planning**	K. Requirement gathering of the communication needs of the people on the project; what they will need and when, and in what format will they need it
4	**Exception Report**	H. A report that includes significant variations from the planned activities
5	**Forecasts**	B. Estimates related to future project performance that are based on historical information and current project knowledge
6	**Information Distribution**	J. Delivering needed project information to stakeholders in an appropriate timeframe
7	**Kickoff Meeting**	E. A meeting used to initiate the start of the project; typically attended by all the key stakeholders; can be done when Initiating or Planning is complete depending upon the organization
8	**Performance Reporting (Output/Input)**	I. The collection and interpretation of performance data; can include status, progress, and forecast reports
9	**Progress Report**	G. A report that states what has been accomplished in a specific amount of time on the project (but not the entire project)

PMP Exam Success Series: Certification Exam Manual
© 2007 Crosswind Project Management, Inc., www.crosswindpm.com

10	Project Forecasting	A.	A reporting method in which future performance is estimated based on past performance of the project
11	Status Report	D.	A report that states the current shape or state of the project to date

12.11.4   Communication Practice Test Answers

1. Which of the following is an input to the communications management plan?

   Correct Answer: (D) Project scope statement
   Explanation: The project scope statement is an input to the communications management plan. The other answers are noise. [section 12.3, section 12.9]

2. Which of the following is not a good reason to cancel a meeting?

   Correct Answer: (C) A Functional Manager wanted to meet with the Project Manager at the same time.
   Explanation: The Functional Manager's decision to meet with the Project Manager at the same time as an existing team meeting is not a good reason to cancel a meeting. The Project Manager should offer to schedule a meeting for a different time with the Functional Manager because project-related work has a higher priority. [section 12.4.4]

3. Which of the following is not a component of the Communication Model?

   Correct Answer: (C) Language
   Explanation: The Communication Model includes the sender to deliver the message, the receiver to get the message, and the message as the information being exchanged. [section 12.4.1]

4. What type of report shows what is expected to be completed in the next two weeks on the project?

   Correct Answer: (C) Forecast report
   Explanation: The forecast report shows what is expected to happen on the project. The status report shows where the project is to date. The earned valued report shows earned value data. The progress report shows what has been completed since the last reporting period. [section 12.5.1]

5. What type of report shows what has been completed compared to what should have been completed on the project?

   Correct Answer: (C) Variance report
   Explanation: The variance report shows the difference between what is happening on the project and what should have happened. The status report shows what has been completed to date on the project. The earned value report focuses on earned value measurement. The progress report shows what has been done in a certain time period on the project. [section 12.5.1]

6. In the Communication Model, the sender conveys which of the following to the receiver?

   Correct Answer: (D) Message
   Explanation: In the Communication Model, the sender conveys the message to the receiver. The feedback is the communication from the receiver to the sender to either clarify the message or acknowledge understanding. The medium is the format used to deliver the message. Noise is anything that distorts the message. [section 12.4.1]

7. The Project Manager is communicating to the team the activities, their sequence, durations, and who is responsible for doing what work on the project. This document is known as what?

Correct Answer: (A) Schedule
Explanation: This is the schedule. It consists of the Gantt chart and work breakdown structure (WBS) among other items. The responsibility assignment matrix shows who is responsible for what areas on the project. [section 8.5]

8. The project is approximately 50% complete and in the middle of execution. The Project Manager is communicating with stakeholders regarding the status of the project. Which will he likely use to determine what to communicate to whom?

Correct Answer: (B) Communications management plan
Explanation: The communications management plan helps determine the stakeholders communication needs. The other answers are noise. [section 12.3.1, section 12.8, section 12.9]

9. All the following could be considered mediums for communication except...

Correct Answer: (D) Message
Explanation: The message is what is actually conveyed in the communication. The other answers are formats for conveying information. [section 12.4.1]

10. Which of the following is the best form of communication for canceling a project?

Correct Answer: (D) Formal written
Explanation: Formal written is the best form of communication to use for any official project documentation. Anything verbal or informal isn't sufficient for official documentation and doesn't integrate into the project archives. "Email" is noise. [section 12.2]

11. Seven people report to the Project Manager. Three more people are added to the project. How many communication channels were added to the project?

Correct Answer: (D) 27 channels
Explanation: The formula for communication channels is $N*(N-1)/2$. First, calculate the number of communication channels based on the existing team 7 AND the Project Manager=8). That is 28 communication channels. Next, calculate the number of communication channels with the new people added. This is 55 communication channels. Finally, subtract the difference (55-28=27). [section 12.3.3, section 12.7]

12. What type of report shows what has been completed in the last week on the project?

Correct Answer: (C) Progress report
Explanation: The progress report shows what has been done in a certain time period on the project. The status report shows what has been completed to date on the project. The earned value report focuses on earned value measurement. The variance report shows the difference between what is happening on the project, and what should have happened. [section 12.5.1, section 12.8]

13. All the following are examples of communication requirements on a project except...

Correct Answer: (B) The name of the HR manager for the company
Explanation: Project status meeting time and location, steps to take regarding a project change request, and contact information for the members of the CCB are all communication requirements on a project. The name of the HR manager is applicable only if that person was on the project, which isn't always a the case. [section 12.3.1]

14. Communication infrastructure is a very important component of project management. All the following are examples of communications infrastructure except...

Correct Answer: (B) Spreadsheet applications

Explanation: Spreadsheet applications are computer applications that are not necessarily part of a company's communications infrastructure. [section 12.8, section 12.2]

15. In reporting performance on the project, the Project Manager needs which of the following?

Correct Answer: (B) Work results

Explanation: Work results allow the Project Manager to report performance on the project. Status reports are generally an output of this area. Status reports can lead to change requests. Status reports typically end up in the project archives. [section 12.5, section 12.8]

16. The Project Manager has weekly scheduled status meetings with the team. The meetings have been unorganized, chaotic, and lacking direction. Which of the following would improve the meetings?

Correct Answer: (C) Create and publish an agenda, and establish the leader of the meeting.

Explanation: Creating and publishing an agenda and knowing who is in charge of a meeting are two ways to have a highly organized effective meeting. [section 12.4.4]

17. You are the Project Manager on a defense project. You have been analyzing project data from the last reporting period. The main data you have been looking at is earned value, actual cost, and planned value. What type of report format are you viewing?

Correct Answer: (B) Progress report

Explanation: The progress report shows what has been done recently. The status report shows where the project is to date. The variance report shows the difference between what should have happened and did happen. "Performance report" is noise. [section 12.5.1, section 12.8]

18. The Project Manager is planning the project. He is meeting with project stakeholders to determine their communication needs for the project. He is finding out what type of information they need, when it is needed, and in what format. What will he create as a result of this work?

Correct Answer: (B) Communications management plan

Explanation: The communications management plan helps define the communication needs of the project team members and stakeholders. The team list indicates who is on the team. The staffing plan helps define how to get people on the team. "Information distribution plan" is noise. [section 12.3.1, section 12.8, section 12.9]

19. The Project Manager spends a lot of time in meetings and talking with team members about the execution of the project. How much of a Project Manager's job is spent communicating?

Correct Answer: (B) Approximately 90%

Explanation: Approximately 90% of a Project Manager's time is spent communicating. This could be via email, meetings, listening, speaking, Web conference, etc. [section 12.3.2]

20. What type of report shows the schedule, cost, and scope performance on the project?

Correct Answer: (A) Earned value report

Explanation: The earned value report focuses on earned value measurements. The status report shows what has been completed to date on the project. The progress report shows what has been done in a certain time period on the project. The variance report shows the difference between what is happening on the project and what should have happened. [section 12.5.1]

21. You are the Project Manager on a defense project. You have been analyzing project data from the last eight reporting periods. The main data you have been looking at is earned value, actual cost, and planned value. Which of the following represent this data graphically?

     Correct Answer: (B) S curve
     Explanation: The S curve shows actual cost, earned value, and planned value data over time, so that variance can be observed rather easily. It show cumulative values for a period of time. The bar chart is also known as a control chart and shows output over time. This is typically a quality chart. The Pareto diagram shows defect by count. The scatter diagram displays (if applicable) a relationship between two variables. [section 9.14.3]

22. What type of report shows what has been completed to date on the project?

     Correct Answer: (B) Status report
     Explanation: The status report shows what has been completed to date on the project. The earned value report focuses on earned value measurement. The progress report shows what has been done in a certain time period on the project. The variance report shows the difference between what is happening on the project and what should have happened. [section 12.5.1, section 12.8]

23. Which of the following is a good tool to stay current with stakeholder needs and problems?

     Correct Answer: (B) Issue log
     Explanation: An issue log is a good tool to track the status of stakeholder needs and problems. The change control process and integrated change control are used to review and approve changes. The project management plan is the overall plan document for the project. [section 12.6, section 12.9]

24. The Project Manager is involved in planning the communication needs for the project. What will he have completed when he is done with this part of Planning?

     Correct Answer: (A) Communications management plan
     Explanation: The communications management plan defines the communication needs of the project. Stakeholder analysis is used to complete this plan by defining the communication requirements of the stakeholders. "Information distribution system" is noise. [section 12.3.1, section 12.8, section 12.9]

25. The statement of work on a project is viewed as what type of communication?

     Correct Answer: (B) Formal written
     Explanation: Any documentation associated with the contract or project management documentation is considered formal written. [section 12.2]

26. The project has eight people on it. Two more are added. What is the total number of communication channels added to the project?

     Correct Answer: (B) 17 Channels
     Explanation: To calculate this result, you need to calculate the number of communication channels with eight people. The formula is $N*(N-1)/2$. This means that with eight people, there are 28 channels of communication. Next, add the two additional people for a total of ten people and use the communication channel formula. This shows that there are 45 communication channels with ten people on the project. Subtract 28 from 45 for a difference, and the answer of 17 communication channels. [section 12.3.3, section 12.7]

27. You are the Project Manager for a software development project using an offshore development company. There have been a number of communication challenges with misinterpretation of requirements and failure to follow through with things that the Project Manager felt needed attention. What type of communication helps reduce these problems?

PMP Exam Success Series: Certification Exam Manual
© 2007 Crosswind Project Management, Inc., www.crosswindpm.com

Work Authorization Flow

Depicted using F-35 examples; Flow applies across LM Aero

Visit EV Navigator for the latest Version of this Map EV NAVIGATOR

RFP

Owner: *Customer*

Contract Statement of Work (CSOW)

1.0
2.0
3.0

The **CSOW** is provided by the Customer. It provides a high-level scope statement that must be decomposed by Lockheed Martin into further detail necessary for execution.

Owner: *Customer*

Contractual

The **IMP** establishes the plan to achieve major milestones on the contract. This includes Key Events (Es), Significant Accomplishments (SAs), Accomplishment Criteria (AC). May be contractually required; if not, an IMP Matrix is required.

The **WBS** is a structure that categorizes the work to be performed. It is common for the WBS to be the same for contracts under the same platform program.

Define the Scope

Work Authorization Memo (WAM)

The **WAM** is used by the Contracts organization to notify the PM that a contract has been signed and planning may begin.

Owner: *Contracts*
Tool: *ECS*

A Program Manager **may** use an **Initial WAD** to initiate planning. An e-mail can be considered an Initial WAD, if the PM includes the scope to be planned, the Period of Performance (POP), and budget authorization value for each CAM authorized to that work.

Initial WAD

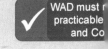
WAD must r
practicable
and Co

Owner: *PM*
Tool: *Various*

Ensure V
before any
in the co

Authorize the Scope, Budget, and POP

The **CAP Template** is used to time-phase cost types for all tasks. It is created in Excel and imported into CostView

Control Account Plan (CAP) Template

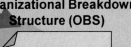

Owner: *CAM*
Tool: *Excel import to CostView*

Organizational Breakdown Structure (OBS)

JD Air System
JE Chief Engineer
JF Business Management
JG Global Production
JN Mission Systems
JS Sustainment
Z Suppliers

Owner: *LM's PM*

The PM
established
of Con

Integrated Master Schedule (IMS)

The **IMS** is used to represent all scope required to complete the contract. Supplemental Schedules such as BTP, SAP and Tooling are summarized in the IMS at a level required to accurately model the critical path.

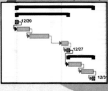
12/20
12/27
12/3

Owner: *CAM*
Tool: *Primavera*

The **OBS** defines <u>who</u> will perform the work. All organizations must be represented. Subcontractors must be listed in a separate OBS from LM.

Create the Control Account Plan and Establi

Integrated Master Plan (IMP)

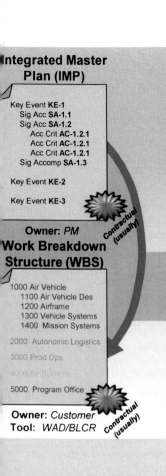

Key Event **KE-1**
  Sig Acc **SA-1.1**
  Sig Acc **SA-1.2**
    Acc Crit **AC-1.2.1**
    Acc Crit **AC-1.2.1**
    Acc Crit **AC-1.2.1**
  Sig Accomp **SA-1.3**

Key Event **KE-2**

Key Event **KE-3**

Owner: *PM*

Work Breakdown Structure (WBS)

1000 Air Vehicle
  1100 Air Vehicle Des
  1200 Airframe
  1300 Vehicle Systems
  1400 Mission Systems

2000 Autonomic Logistics

3000 Prod Ops

4000 Air Systems

5000 Program Office

Owner: *Customer*
Tool: *WAD/BLCR*

Contractual (usually)

The WBS Dictionary must include all CSOW work scope

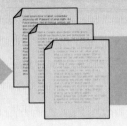

Proposal Basis of Estimates (BOEs)

*The **BOEs** included in the proposal include the initial plan for execution of the contract. These are prepared by the contractor before submitting the proposal and are then used to create the initial Control Account Plans.*

Owner: *PM (Proposal Mgr)*

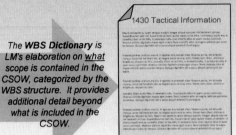

WBS Dictionary

1430 Tactical Information

*The **WBS Dictionary** is LM's elaboration on what scope is contained in the CSOW, categorized by the WBS structure. It provides additional detail beyond what is included in the CSOW.*

Owner: *CAM*

---

ference lowest evel of CSOW tract WBS

AD is dated harges appear trol account

Work Authorization Document (WAD)

*The **WAD** is the contract between the PM and the CAM. Initial WADs must be replaced with a WAD in the WAD/BLCR tool. The scope statement should expand on the description in the CSOW and the WBS Dictionary. The PM may incrementally increase the Scope, POP and Budget.*

Owner: *PM*
Tool: *WAD/BLCR*

Responsibility Assignment Matrix (RAM) Report

*The **RAM** identifies the contract's Control Account values at the intersection of who is doing what (the OBS and the WBS). One or more control accounts may be defined at the intersection, where the authorized budget is displayed. Each control account must have a single WBS and OBS reference.*

Control Account:
Intersection of OBS and WBS
Tool: *RAM Tool*

 WAD must match Control Account Budget on RAM

B must be within 60 days act Award

Program Management Baseline (PMB)

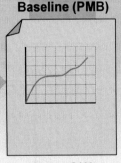

*The IMS, CAP and OBS are used to create the **Program Management Baseline (PMB)** across all Control Accounts.*

Owner: *CAM*

Internally-Directed Changes
restart process at WBS Dictionary update (skipping WAM)

Externally-Directed Changes
restart process from beginning

sh the Baseline

Correct Answer: (A) Formal written

Explanation: Formal written communication is good when communicating details or for long distance. Formal is a good answer but not as good as formal written. Both verbal answers expose the project to problems such as increasing the potential for misunderstanding. [section 12.2]

28.   The Project Manager is working with the team to create a decomposition of the project work. The results of this effort will help determine resource needs, how long the project should take, and how much it should cost. What is the team creating?

Correct Answer: (D) Work breakdown structure

Explanation: The team is creating the work breakdown structure (WBS), which shows the work of the project. The schedule shows sequencing and timelines plus the work of the project. The Gantt chart shows bars indicating when the activities happen. The responsibility assignment matrix shows who is responsible for what areas on the project. [section 7.3.1]

29.   In the Communication Model, who is responsible for ensuring that the receiver has received and understood the message correctly?

Correct Answer: (D) Receiver

Explanation: The receiver is responsible for actually interpreting (decoding) the message and providing feedback to the sender if additional clarification is required. The sender is responsible for encoding the message and delivering it. [section 12.4.1]

30.   The network infrastructure project is having problems with people not knowing about meetings and not involved in approval of project deliverables. The project is being audited for health. What document is likely to show information that could fix this problem?

Correct Answer: (A) Communications management plan

Explanation: The communications management plan should show what meetings are planned, who should be involved in the deliverables, signoff, and other communication needs of the project. This plan is in the project management plan. The other answers are noise. [section 12.3.1, section 12.8, section 12.9]

Chapter 13

Risk

Many Project Managers find Risk to be a challenge because the environment often doesn't allow them enough time to conduct an adequate amount of risk management. We can use this lack of experience to provide an opportunity to learn the processes the way that PMI prefers for the exam.

Think of risk management as being similar to time management, approaching it step by step. With time management (generally speaking), we get the activities, then the sequence, then the duration, and we have a schedule. We don't build it all at once. Approach risk management the same way. If you plan, identify, qualify, quantify, response plan, and monitor/control, you will follow the process as needed.

Remember that the majority of the risk processes happen in Planning; thus, the majority of the processes (other than Monitoring and Controlling) should generally happen before plan execution starts. When executing the project management plan, revisiting earlier processes is an acceptable practice as risks are discovered and as risk ranking possibly changes. A key overlying concept is consistency with a proactive approach to project risk.

Use Figure 13-1: Risk Processes Interaction as an overview to how the processes and pieces of risk work together.

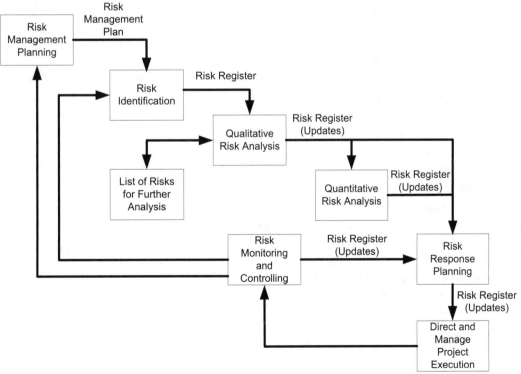

Figure 13-1: Risk Processes Interaction

In this chapter, we discuss the following:

Process Group	Process Name		Main Outputs
Planning	Risk Management Planning	→	Risk Management Plan
	Risk Identification	→	Risk Register
	Qualitative Risk Analysis	→	Risk Register (Updates)
	Quantitative Risk Analysis	→	
	Risk Response Planning	→	
Monitoring and Controlling	Risk Monitoring and Control	→	

☑	**Crosswind "Must Knows" For Risk**
	Key Inputs, Tools & Techniques, and Outputs for Risk Management Planning
	Key Inputs, Tools & Techniques, and Outputs for Risk Identification
	Key Inputs, Tools & Techniques, and Outputs for Qualitative Risk Analysis
	Key Inputs, Tools & Techniques, and Outputs for Quantitative Risk Analysis
	Key Inputs, Tools & Techniques, and Outputs for Risk Response Planning
	Key Inputs, Tools & Techniques, and Outputs for Risk Monitoring and Control
	Definition of a risk and that it can be a positive or negative event
	Definition of uncertainty
	Characteristics of a risk seeker, a risk-neutral person, and risk-averse person and how they relate to risk tolerance
	Concept and differences of pure risk and business risk
	Characteristics of a risk response plan including recognition of the strategies avoid, transfer, mitigate, exploit, share, enhance, accept risk and contingent responses
	What a risk register contains and its purpose
	Characteristics of management reserves (unknown unknowns) and contingency reserves (known unknowns)
	Impact and probabilities as they relate to risk management
	How to calculate expected monetary value (EMV) and make a project selection decision based on the outcome
	What Monte Carlo simulation does
	What a workaround is in relation to Risk Response Planning
	Benefits and risks of contracting
	Risk breakdown structure (RBS) and risk categorization such as internal, external, technology, organizational
	What risk owners are and what they are responsible for
	What residual and secondary risks are and how they are created
	What risk reviews and risk triggers are

Although helpful, this list is not all-inclusive for information needed from this area for the exam. It is only suggested material that, if understood and memorized, may increase your exam score.

PMP Exam Success Series: Certification Exam Manual
© 2007 Crosswind Project Management, Inc., www.crosswindpm.com

13.1 What is Risk?

Risk is an event with some degree of uncertainty. It may or may not occur. The objective of assessing risk is to offset any negative impact it may have and pursue any positive impact. A risk can have good or bad characteristics. An example of a negative risk is the reliance on a piece of software that is not available when needed or as planned, forcing the team to come up with an alternative.

A **positive risk** is an **opportunity**; a **negative risk** is a **threat**. An example of a positive risk event is accommodating the growth that results when the sales of a new product exceed expectations. A company will look at the negative risk associated with a project and consider it if the reward that can come seems to be in line with it.

Know the definition of a risk and that it can be a positive or negative event.

13.2 Risk Management Planning (Planning Process Group)

Risk Management Planning is the area in which the "rule book" -- as it relates to risk and risk management on the project -- is created. In Risk Management Planning, the Project Manager and the team proactively plan how to identify, rank, and address risk issues on the project.

The company's risk management policies help define what the team will do on the project regarding risk and risk management. If a policy details risk management, the company will likely conduct a great deal of risk management activity. If a policy does not detail risk management, the company probably does not value risk management and is unlikely to set aside time and resources for the Project Manager and team to deal with risk proactively.

Know the Key Inputs, Tools & Techniques, and Outputs for Risk Management Planning.

Risk Management Planning (Planning)		
Key Inputs	Project Scope Statement	The project scope statement **helps define the project**. Supporting detail provides the in-depth research and planning that the project scope statement rolls into.
	Project Management Plan	A project management plan (not a schedule!) **integrates plans representing the various Knowledge Areas** in the PMI approach to project management. Supporting detail is also included to help validate information in the project management plan.
Key Tools & Techniques	Planning Meetings and Analysis	Planning meetings and analysis **helps define risk management** on the project.
Key Outputs	Risk Management Plan	The risk management plan is the **rulebook for risk** as it relates to this project. This can include a methodology to manage risk for the project. Roles and responsibilities can be included to show who is responsible for what if a risk occurs. Budgeting and timing associated with risk are addressed. It could also include a risk breakdown structure (RBS) or risk categorization. Scoring, Interpretation, and Thresholds are covered so that risks are appropriately scored. How to report and how to track risks are also covered.

Situational Question and Real World Application

If this area is ignored, it is likely that the project will suffer from a reactive risk environment. When risk events do indeed happen, there is no predetermined response, no list of potential risks, or no process for addressing them.

13.2.1   Risk Management Plan

The Risk Management Plan helps the Project Manager and team do the following:

- Create the risk register or what specific version to use
- Identify risks (positive and negative) and triggers
- Define the probability and impact matrix and its thresholds
- Determine when and how to perform quantitative risk analysis, expected monetary value (EMV) and decision tree analysis
- Establish risk responses
- Establish risk owners and the responsibilities of each risk owner
- Plan how to monitor and respond to risks

The following risk breakdown structure and Risk Probabilities and Impact Rating Matrix are two examples of documents that can be created within the Risk Management Plan to help with effective risk management on the project. The risk breakdown structure is typically used in Risk Identification and the Probabilities and Impact Matrix is used in Qualitative Risk Analysis.

13.2.2   Risk Breakdown Structure (RBS)

You can use a risk breakdown structure (RBS) to help **break down the risks on a project**. If you look at risks and categorize them into a RBS, you can create a brainstorming type of environment that allows the team to come up with more ideas on risks. This approach is similar to decomposition of the work on a project to create a WBS, but in this case the team is creating the risk breakdown structure. Typical risk categories include project, company, client, technology, legal, and more.

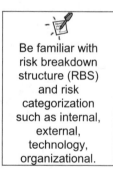

Be familiar with risk breakdown structure (RBS) and risk categorization such as internal, external, technology, organizational.

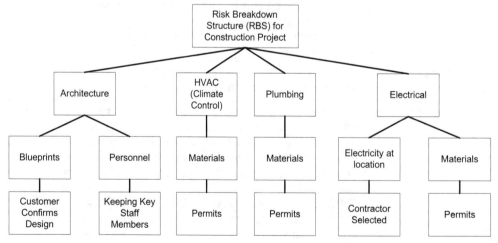

Figure 13-2: Risk Breakdown Structure Sample

13.2.3   Risk Probabilities and Impact Rating Matrix

The risk probabilities and impact rating matrix is part of the risk management plan that can be used to evaluate risks for their probability and impact. It is typically used in Qualitative Risk Analysis (later in this chapter). Its criteria are established by those associated with the project, including the sponsors, the Project Manager, or team members. The project objective row shows the probability range that something could happen. The next four rows show what defines a low, medium, or high impact to the scope, time, cost, or quality goal.

The threshold information in the table that follows is an example only. Specific thresholds are determined by the appropriate project party.

	Low Probability	**Medium Probability**	**High Probability**
Project Objective	0 to 0.33 (Probability)	0.34 to 0.66 (Probability)	0.67 to 1.00 (Probability)
Scope (Impact)	Minimal changes	Significant changes for functionality	Potentially useless product as built
Time (Impact)	5% or less delay	6% to 15% delay	16% or greater delay
Cost (Impact)	5% or less increase	6% to 15% increase	16% or greater increase
Quality (Impact)	Quality slippage minimal	Slippage requires sponsor signoff	Product is basically useless

13.2.4   Uncertainty

Uncertainty is a component of risk that deals with the amount of information known (or unknown) about the outcome. This could range from there being very little unknown about a possible outcome to not having a clue as to what can happen in the case of a risk event.

Know the definition of uncertainty.

13.2.5   Types of Risk

There are two types of risk -- pure risk and business risk.

Pure risk	Pure risk is a risk for which **insurance can be purchased,** thereby transferring the risk for financial benefit to the party accepting the risk.
Business risk	Business risk is **typically uninsurable**. It is what a business does when it opens its doors everyday for business. It's a risk inherent in the process of doing business. Think of it this way: when was the last time you could buy insurance for sales projections?

Be familiar with the concepts and differences of pure risk and business risk.

13.2.6   Risk and Contracting

There is a belief that if a company outsources a piece of work, the provider assumes the risk and the purchaser has no risk exposure. This is NOT THE CASE. When outsourcing, a **buyer can minimize risk exposure, but some risk remains. Plus, there is a new risk exposure.** An example of the new risk is the failure of the seller to provide the services as promised. See the Procurement chapter for more information about risk as it relates to the buyer, seller, and contracting.

Know the benefits and risk of contracting.

13.2.7   Risk Tolerance and Perspective

The risk tolerance for a person or organization can influence the project environment. There are three types of risk tolerance: Risk-Averse, Risk Seeker, and Risk-Neutral. Where a sponsor, Project Manager and the organization fall within these tolerances greatly impacts the project environment and tolerance for what can be done on the project. As you read the definitions below, try to imagine the sponsor of a project in one extreme type and the Project Manager in the other.

Type	Description
Risk-Averse	Risk-Averse is a mentality of **risk avoidance.** Selecting the low risk item or the sure thing is typical in this case.
Risk Seeker	Risk Seeker is a mentality of **looking for risk,** or worse case, not being afraid of it. This is typically the early adopter of new products, or the person or company that is willing to go for an all or nothing approach to an initiative.
Risk-Neutral	Risk-Neutral is a middle ground mentality toward risk. It can shift toward either seeker or averse, depending upon the situation but usually falls in the middle.

Know the characteristics of a risk seeker, a risk-neutral person, and risk-averse person and how they relate to risk tolerance.

13.3   Risk Identification (Planning Process Group)

In Risk Identification, the Project Manager, team, and any key stakeholders determine any risks that could occur on the project. These risks could be small impact risks with a low probability of happening to large impact risks with a high probability of happening. The team could also use a predefined list from previous projects as a starting point for the project. **When Risk Identification is complete, the team moves any risks to Qualitative Risk Analysis,** or determines that they don't need to devote time to developing a response strategy. If this is the case, the team will likely check on those types of risks throughout the project to ensure they haven't increased to the point that they require more attention.

Know the Key Inputs, Tools & Techniques, and Outputs for Risk Identification.

Risk Identification (Planning)		
Key Inputs	Project Scope Statement	The project scope statement **helps define the project.** Supporting detail provides the in-depth research and planning that the project scope statement rolls into.
	Risk Management Plan	The risk management plan is the **rulebook for risk** as it relates to this project. This plan can include a methodology to manage risk for the project. Roles and responsibilities can be included to show who is responsible for what if a risk occurs. Budgeting and timing associated with risk are addressed. Scoring, interpretation, and thresholds are covered so that risks are appropriately scored. How to report and track risks are covered as well.
	Project Management Plan	A project management plan (not a schedule!) **integrates plans representing the various Knowledge Areas** in the PMI approach to project management. Supporting detail is also included to help validate information in the project management plan.

Key Tools & Techniques	Documentation Reviews	Documentation reviews are done to **identify and evaluate potential risks and triggers**.
	Information Gathering Techniques	Documentation reviews and information gathering techniques are key for identifying potential risks. They can include brainstorming, the Delphi technique, interviewing, root cause identification, and SWOT (strengths, weaknesses, opportunities, and threats) analysis.
	Checklist Analysis	Checklist analysis is **useful for verification that things are done as planned**.
	Assumption Analysis	Assumptions analysis **assists in determining potential risk exposure**.
Key Outputs	Risk Register	The risk register is a piece of the project management plan that **contains information about what risks could occur** on a project, **potential responses** to those risks, **root causes** of the risks, and risk **categorization**. It expands as risk management processes are further implemented.

Situational Question and Real World Application
By failing to perform Risk Identification in project Planning, the Project Manager and team shift into a reactive mode regarding risk. When a risk event happens, they are forced to determine what needs to be done on the fly, instead of having the benefit of proactive planning.

13.3.1   Risk Register

The risk register is a part of the project management plan and is created during the risk planning processes. It evolves as the risk management processes and the project evolve, and it contains the following:

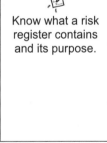

Know what a risk register contains and its purpose.

- Risks
- Triggers
- Probability (Likelihood) and Impact ($) from risk analysis
- Planned Responses
- Risk owners

13.3.2   Diagramming Techniques

Diagramming techniques may be used to help decompose or categorize risk. This activity could involve a number of techniques to learn an appropriate amount of information about the risk on the project. Examples could include cause and effect (Ishikawa) diagrams (see the Quality chapter), system or process flow charts (see the Quality chapter), and influence diagrams. Influence diagrams show graphical relationships associated with process timing and interactions.

13.3.3   Risk Triggers

Risk triggers are the characteristics which **indicate that a risk event is possible in the near future.** Typically, these triggers are identified when the risks are identified. As you monitor project progress and notice a trigger, you know that a risk event could occur soon.

Know what risk triggers and risk reviews are.

13.3.4   Risk Reviews

Risk reviews **assess the documented risks and the project for any new risks.** It helps ensure that the documented risks are still only risks, and that their ranking, characteristics, probabilities, and impacts haven't changed.

13.4   Qualitative Risk Analysis (Planning Process Group)

In Qualitative Risk Analysis, **risks are analyzed for probability and for their impact** if they were to occur. Helping to provide an overall risk ranking for the project, such analysis could come from evaluating a component (risk) of a project as high, medium, or low. You could also assign a number value to various parameters on the project, ending up with a total score.

Examples of parameters to evaluate are project length and number of people on the project. Historical information can help by providing past experience the team or company or both have had on similar projects. When you have finished analyzing all the risks on the project, depending upon the score of the project, you can determine into what range it fits (Ex: 0-5 low risk, 6-10 medium risk, 11-15 high risk), based upon the combined score of all the components being evaluated. See the example in section 13.4.1 of a risk probabilities impact rating matrix.

Know the Key Inputs, Tools & Techniques, and Outputs for Qualitative Risk Analysis.

Qualitative Risk Analysis (Planning)		
Key Inputs	Project Scope Statement	The project scope statement **helps define the project**. Supporting detail provides the in-depth research and planning that the project scope statement rolls into.
	Risk Management Plan	The risk management plan is the **rulebook for risk** as it relates to this project. It can include a methodology for handling risk on the project. Roles and responsibilities can be included to show who is responsible for what if a risk occurs. Budgeting and timing associated with risk are also addressed. Scoring, interpretation, and thresholds are covered so that risks are appropriately scored. How to report and track risks are covered as well.
	Risk Register	The risk register is a piece of the project management plan that **contains information associated with what risks could occur** on a project, **potential responses** for those risks, **root causes** of the risks, and risk **categorization**. It expands as risk management processes are further implemented.
Key Tools & Techniques	Risk Probability and Impact Assessment Probability and Impact Matrix	Risk probability and impact assessment **helps show what is likely to happen** on the project and the **possible effects** of a risk event by applying any assessment to a Probability and Impact Matrix. Project assumptions testing can help to define this area as "envisioning" what could potentially happen on the project.
	Risk Categorization	Risk categorization **helps to group sources of risk** and areas of project risk.
Key Outputs	Risk Register (Updates)	Risk register updates are **made as updates to the risk processes are completed**. In this case, while Qualitative Risk Analysis is executed, the risk register is updated, as appropriate. This updating could include modification of the project risks and their categorization, risks that require attention relatively soon or need more analysis performed, and any trends that may be showing up.

Situational Question and Real World Application
You will very likely encounter problems if you fail to implement this area satisfactorily. You won't be able to anticipate and address risk events. You won't know how big or small the risk events actually are. You won't know how much time and emphasis to place on them. You won't be able to gauge them to a low, medium, and high rating, so you can detect the risk potential of an event or project.

13.4.1   Probability and Impact Matrix

The probability and impact matrix that follows this paragraph can be used when an organization wants to evaluate the impact of a risk and the probability of its occurrence. The probability scale is on the left, and the impact is on the bottom. Where they intersect is the multiplication of the two. Depending upon the scoring, a risk could be viewed as low, medium, or high. For example, the table below shows any risk with a rating of 0.24 or less as low, 0.25 to 0.66 as medium, and 0.67 to 1.0 as high. Ideally, this is used if a company wanted to analyze the project risk by risk, instead of creating one overall risk value for the project. That said, a matrix such as this could be used to analyze each risk, then create an overall risk ranking for the project. One final key to remember is the data feeding this process needs to be unbiased and as accurate as possible or the outcome of the process could be skewed.

		Opportunities						Threats					
	0.90	0.045	0.090	0.225	0.450	0.675	0.810	0.810	0.675	0.450	0.225	0.090	0.045
	0.75	0.038	0.075	0.188	0.375	0.563	0.675	0.675	0.563	0.375	0.188	0.075	0.038
Probability	0.50	0.025	0.050	0.125	0.250	0.375	0.450	0.450	0.375	0.250	0.125	0.050	0.025
	0.25	0.013	0.025	0.063	0.125	0.188	0.225	0.225	0.188	0.125	0.063	0.025	0.013
	0.10	0.005	0.010	0.025	0.050	0.075	0.090	0.090	0.075	0.050	0.025	0.010	0.005
	0.05	0.003	0.005	0.013	0.025	0.038	0.045	0.045	0.038	0.025	0.013	0.005	0.003
	Impact>>	0.05	0.1	0.25	0.5	0.75	0.9	0.9	0.75	0.5	0.25	0.1	0.05

13.5   Quantitative Risk Analysis (Planning Process Group)

Know the Inputs, Tools & Techniques, and Outputs for Quantitative Risk Analysis.

Quantitative Risk Analysis evolves as a result of Risk Identification and Qualitative Risk Analysis. Quantitative Risk Analysis breaks down risks from a high, medium, and low ranking based on actual numerical values and probabilities of occurrence. **Risks that are higher in probability and impact are more likely to be evaluated via Quantitative Risk Analysis. Techniques used for Quantitative Risk Analysis can be decision tree analysis and Monte Carlo simulation.** These can help in getting realistic time and cost targets for the project in line with the documented risk.

The point is that risk can happen -- good or bad -- and it is imperative to know the impacts so you can maximize the good and minimize the bad, as they happen. Quantitative Risk Analysis provides the details necessary to recognize such impacts, whereas Qualitative Risk Analysis often may not.

It's a good idea to revisit Quantitative Risk Analysis after completing Risk Response Planning and Risk Monitoring and Control because this revisiting gives you an opportunity to see if project risk has been minimized to an acceptable level.

Quantitative Risk Analysis (Planning)		
Key Inputs	Project Scope Statement	The project scope statement **helps define the project**. Supporting detail provides the in-depth research and planning that the project scope statement rolls into.
	Risk Management Plan	The risk management plan is the **rulebook for risk** as it relates to this project. It can include a methodology for handling risk on the project. Roles and responsibilities can be included to show who is responsible for what if a risk occurs. Budgeting and timing associated with risk are addressed. Scoring, interpretation, and thresholds are covered so that risks are appropriately scored. How to report and track risks are covered as well.
	Risk Register	The risk register is a piece of the project management plan that **contains information associated with what risks could occur** on a project, **potential responses** for those risks, **root causes** of the risks, and risk **categorization**. It expands as risk management processes are further implemented.
	Project Schedule Management Plan	The project schedule management plan addresses **how the schedule is to be maintained** throughout the project.
	Project Cost Management Plan	Project cost management plan helps you **determine how to manage project cost**.
Key Tools & Techniques	Quantitative Risk Analysis and Modeling Techniques	Quantitative risk analysis and modeling techniques such as sensitivity analysis, expected monetary value (EMV), and decision tree analysis are **used to learn more about the characteristics of the risks** going through the Quantitative Risk Analysis process.
Key Outputs	Risk Register (Updates)	Risk register updates are **made as updates to the risk processes are completed**. In this case, while Quantitative Risk Analysis is executed, the risk register is updated, as appropriate. This updating could include updates to the probabilistic analysis of the project including the time and cost goals, any trends that are discovered, and a prioritized list of quantified risks.

Situational Question and Real World Application
When you encounter issues here, risk events – both good and bad – could be happening without your knowing the key thresholds for quantitative risk events. If you fail to address this area adequately, you will probably be aware of problems but lack the knowledge to maximize the good or minimize the bad impacts of the risks.

13.5.1   Probability

Probability is the likelihood that something will happen. In non-statistical language, it is: "What are the odds of this happening?" It is usually measured in percentages (0 to 100%) or real numbers (0.0 to 1.0). The **sum of all probabilities is equal to 100% or 1.0**. This basically means that you are looking at all possible outcomes (100%). Probability can also be measured in low, medium, and high or in some other non-numerical method if the numerical detail doesn't fit the situation.

Understand probability as it relates to risk management.

13.5.2   Impact

Impact is the consequence or amount at stake if something does happen. For example, if the government denies a request to approve a new drug for a specific disease, what is the impact to the company? Impact can be good or bad. Think back to the dot-com era when there was a commercial with a company launching its Web site, and the team members were all standing around watching the sales counter. After jumping into the thousands in the first few seconds, they look at each other, wondering what to do. That is good impact.

Understand impact as it relates to risk management.

13.5.3   Decision Trees and Expected Monetary Value (EMV)

Decision tree analysis is based on looking at the probability and impact of all potential decisions to determine the potential expected monetary value (EMV) of the opportunity as a whole.

This is accomplished by multiplying the probabilities and the impact straight across, then adding the sums of the multiplication for that project or opportunity.

A rule to consider is: The sum of all probabilities must equal 1.0 (or 100%). For example, 0.3 and 0.7 on Project A equal 1.0 or 100% of all possible outcomes.

Know how to calculate expected monetary value (EMV) and make a project selection decision based on the outcome.

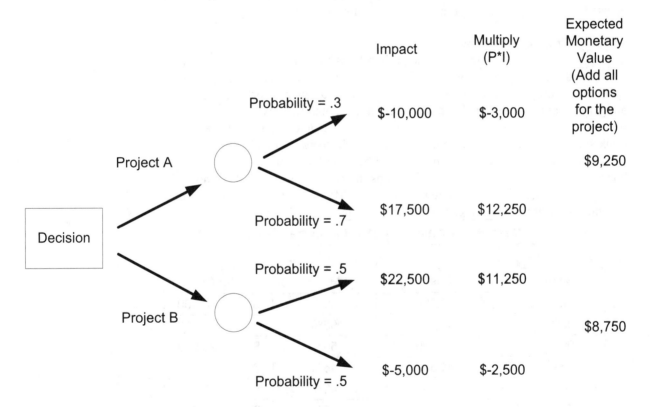

Figure 13-3: Decision Tree Sample

NOTE: If you are given only one percentage value, simply subtract that value from 100% to obtain the second percentage value. (Example: 70% is the provided value. Subtract it from 100% to obtain the value for other opportunities: 30%.)

In summary, if you are a company considering a project to do for revenue, you would choose Project A, which has the higher expected monetary value (EMV). If you are considering opportunities in which others will perform the work for you, you would choose Project B, which has the lower expected monetary value (EMV).

Based on Project A above, this exercise could also be shown in the following format.

Probability	Result
0.3	-$10,000
0.7	+$17,500

In the table above, verify that the sum of all probabilities equals 1.0 (100%). After that, multiply each row's probability and impact, then add all the products to calculate the EMV.

$$0.3 * -\$10,000 = -\$3,000$$
$$0.7 * \$17,500 = \$12,250$$

$$-\$3,000 + \$12,250 = \$9,250$$

13.5.4   Monte Carlo

Monte Carlo is a mock-up technique that uses software to simulate project characteristics to determine possible outcome. This simulation is typically done in the scheduling area to allow a reserve to be determined in schedule creation. It could be used in other areas of the project where it is also applicable.

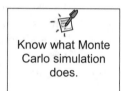

Know what Monte Carlo simulation does.

13.5.5   Probabilities Tables

The following tables show the probabilities associated with cost and time parameters for a project. Tables like this can be helpful. Instead of going with the "gut feel" of thinking; you can be a little ahead/behind schedule or a little over/under budget. If your boss asked about the project and wanted to know if you thought it was going to be completed for $41,000 or less, what would you say? Instead of "I think so," you can use a table from the Monte Carlo software to tell you that you have an 80% confidence level that the project will be completed for that cost. Confidence level typically increases as cost and durations increase because the likelihood of hitting those targets becomes more realistic. The Monte Carlo programs take into account many project variables to generate the data.

Quantitative Analysis For Total Budget Table					
Confidence			**Confidence**		
Level	**Total Cost**		**Level**	**Total Cost**	
100%	$	43,564	60%	$	30,000
95%	$	42,500	55%	$	27,500
90%	$	42,000	50%	$	25,000
85%	$	41,500	45%	$	22,500
80%	$	41,000	40%	$	20,000
75%	$	40,500	35%	$	17,500
70%	$	40,000	30%	$	15,000
65%	$	35,000	25%	$	14,500

Quantitative Analysis For Completion Date Table			
Confidence Level	**Date Complete**	**Confidence Level**	**Date Complete**
100%	12/15/2008	60%	8/15/2008
95%	12/1/2008	55%	8/1/2008
90%	11/15/2008	50%	7/15/2008
85%	11/1/2008	45%	7/1/2008
80%	10/15/2008	40%	6/15/2008
75%	10/1/2008	35%	6/1/2008
70%	9/15/2008	30%	5/15/2008
65%	9/1/2008	25%	5/1/2008

13.6   Risk Response Planning (Planning Process Group)

In Risk Response Planning, you determine responses for the potential risks that could occur. Responses could be anything from determining to do nothing to implementing a detailed risk response.

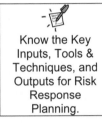

Know the Key Inputs, Tools & Techniques, and Outputs for Risk Response Planning.

Risk Response Planning (Planning)		
Key Inputs	Risk Management Plan	The risk management plan is the **rulebook for risk** as it relates to this project. It can include a methodology for handling risk on the project. Roles and responsibilities can be included to show who is responsible for what if a risk occurs. Budgeting and timing associated with risk are addressed. Scoring, interpretation, and thresholds are covered so that risks are appropriately scored. How to report and track risks are covered as well.
	Risk Register	The risk register is a piece of the project management plan that **contains information associated with what risks could occur** on a project, **potential responses** for those risks, **root causes** of the risks, and risk **categorization**. It expands as risk management processes are further implemented.
Key Tools & Techniques	Strategies for Negative Risk or Threats	Strategies for negative risks or threats are techniques that are **used to create risk responses for negative risks**. The main three types are **avoid** (sometimes known as avoidance), **transfer** (sometimes known as transference), and **mitigate** (sometimes known as mitigation). Avoiding risk is a process in which the risk is eliminated before it can happen. Transferring risk is typically done with outsourcing the work or purchasing insurance to compensate for the risk. Mitigation is trying to minimize the impact of the risk by utilizing various strategies that will minimize or eliminate the risk.

Key Tools & Techniques (cont.)	Strategies for Positive Risks or Opportunities	Strategies for positive risks or opportunities are techniques that are **used to maximize positive risks or opportunities**. The main three types are **exploit, share, and enhance**. Exploiting the risk is to take advantage of it and attempt to maximize the benefits of it. Sharing the risk is an action in which a third party who can help maximize the benefit gets involved. Enhancing attempts to increase the probability and/or impact of the risk.
	Strategy for Both Threats and Opportunities	Strategies for both threats and opportunities include acceptance and contingent response strategy. **Acceptance tolerates the risk** if it were to happen.
	Contingent Response Strategy	Contingent response strategy creates responses if certain events trigger the response.
Key Outputs	Risk Register (Updates)	Risk register updates are **made as updates to the risk processes are completed**. In this case, when risk responses are created, the risk register is updated, as appropriate. This updating can include updates to risks, owners and responsibilities, response strategies, risk symptoms, budget, and schedule-related items including contingency reserves.
	Project Management Plan (Updates)	The project management plan is **updated when risk responses have been added to the risk register**. This update potentially causes a ripple effect through the plan via Integrated Change Control.

Situational Question and Real World Application
Coming up short in this area could leave the Project Manager not knowing what to do when a risk event happens. The Project Manager could have a risk list and performed appropriate risk analysis, but with an incomplete risk response area, the project is still reactive with regard to risk.

Risk Management Known and Unknown Table			
Name	**Created For**	**Description**	**Example**
Contingency Reserves	Known Unknowns	For risk events that you know can happen on a project	Something costing more than planned, taking longer than planned, or scope creep
Management Reserves	Unknown Unknowns	For risk events you cannot forecast potentially happening on a project	Something you cannot envision happening on a project, such as a natural disaster or terrorist attack

Know the characteristics of management reserves (unknown unknowns) and contingency reserves (known unknowns).

13.6.1   Residual Risk

Residual risk is the **amount of risk remaining after a risk response (from the risk response plan) has been implemented.** For example, in a medical situation, residual risk is the risk that remains after attempting to cure someone.

13.6.2   Secondary Risk

Secondary risk is a jeopardy that **results from the implementation of a risk response.** In the medical example, it is side effects from a treatment.

Know what residual and secondary risks are and how they are created.

13.6.3   Workaround (From Risk Monitoring and Control)

Workaround is a contingency put into action when a risk response and any backup plans don't work. It is the reactive "wing it" response.

Know what a workaround is in relation to Risk Response Planning.

13.6.4   Risk Owner

The risk owner is the person responsible for a risk event if it happens and is similar to the person responsible for completing an activity. Risk owners know beforehand that they own particular risk events. They know that, if those events happen, they are responsible for implementing the response.

Know what risk owners are and what they are responsible for.

13.6.5   Risk Response Strategies

The following strategies are those recommended by PMI to use in planning risk responses. We recommend that you memorize each response type and be able to recognize it in a situation. A memory tool is **SEE** the **ATM**, as described in the following tables (share, exploit, enhance, avoid, transfer, mitigate).

Know the characteristics of a risk response plan including recognition of response strategies.

Risk Response Strategies for Positive Risks or Opportunities		
Risk Response Tool	**Description**	**Example**
Share	The share strategy **splits the responsibility** (and benefit) of the risk with a third party (or parties) to maximize an opportunity.	The technology company formed a partnership with a marketing company to launch a sales campaign to support the new product being developed.
Exploit	The exploit strategy takes steps to **ensure the success** and the risk of the event or project.	The new project had the best resources assigned to maximize the probability of success.
Enhance	The enhance strategy takes steps to **improve the size or capacity of the risk event** by determining the key components of the risk and maximizing those components.	When sales were exceeding projections, the company hired more sales people to ensure that as many customers as possible knew of their products.

Risk Response Strategies for Negative Risks or Threats		
Risk Response Tool	**Description**	**Example**
Avoid	Avoid involves modifying the plan so risk doesn't have to be dealt with. **To get rid of the problem.**	Selecting alternative potential vendors will keep you from running out of inventory.
Transfer	Transfer **reassigns risk** exposure **to another party.** In doing this, you do not necessarily eliminate all risk, but likely minimize some and create additional risk as well.	**Example #1:** Hiring an outside company to do something instead of doing it yourself **Example #2:** Buying insurance for something
Mitigate	Mitigate **minimizes the bad characteristics** of the risk.	Eliminating outside sources and doing work internally mitigates your risk if another company failed to meet the deliverables on your project.

Risk Response Strategies for Both Threats and Opportunities		
Risk Response Tool	**Description**	**Example**
Acceptance	Acceptance **tolerates the risk** and deals with it. It is a valid option if there are no other options available.	Determining that if a union goes on strike, the project will have to stop until the strike is settled.

Contingent Response Strategy		
Risk Response Tool	**Description**	**Example**
Contingent Response Strategy	This strategy is ideally created to be used if only certain conditions are present. It could be created if conditions change on the project or to accommodate for worst case situations.	The team developed a contingency plan to add staff to the project if the important development milestone was missed.

13.7 Risk Monitoring and Control (Monitoring and Controlling Process Group)

Know the Key Inputs, Tools & Techniques, and Outputs for Risk Monitoring and Control.

Risk Monitoring and Control is the area where the Project Manager and team focus on **observing the project activities for risk triggers and risks and implementing means to control them.** It can also include verifying if project assumptions are still applicable, if trends have occurred, and determination of contingency reserves for the schedule and budget.

PMP Exam Success Series: Certification Exam Manual
© 2007 Crosswind Project Management, Inc., www.crosswindpm.com

Risk Monitoring and Control (Monitoring and Controlling)		
Key Inputs	Risk Management Plan	The risk management plan is the **rulebook for risk** as it relates to this project. It can include a methodology for handling risk on the project. Roles and responsibilities can be included to show who is responsible for what if a risk occurs. Budgeting and timing associated with risk are addressed. Scoring, interpretation, and thresholds are covered so that risks are appropriately scored. How to report and track risks are covered as well.
	Risk Register	The risk register is a piece of the project management plan that **contains information associated with what risks could occur** on a project, **potential responses** for those risks, **root causes** of the risks, and risk **categorization**. It expands as risk management processes are further implemented.
	Approved Change Requests	Approved change requests are **changes that have been formally approved** by the official change control process on the project.
	Performance Reports	Performance reports are key to **show current actual work complete** on the project.
Key Tools & Techniques	Risk Reassessment	Risk reassessment should go on throughout the project to **reevaluate the probability and impact of the identified risks and monitor for any new risks**.
	Risk Audits	Risk audits are used for effectiveness because periodic project risk reviews can **help detect potential risk exposure**. Technical performance measurement helps verify if the project is performing compared to the planned standards.
	Reserve Analysis	Reserve analysis on a project **evaluates the amount of schedule or budget contingency reserve to the remaining risk** on the project.
Key Outputs	Risk Register (Updates)	Risk register updates are **made as updates to the risk processes are completed**. In this case, while Risk Monitoring and Control is ongoing, the risk register is updated, as appropriate. This updating can result in updating of risks, their probabilities and impact, prioritization and response planning. As the project is complete, the actual information associated with the risk management is recorded for use on future projects and throughout the organization.
	Requested Changes	Requested changes are **changes that have been requested but not yet formally approved** by the official change control process on the project.

Situational Question and Real World Application
Risk Monitoring and Control is a proactive approach. If this area were ignored or not completely supported, the main effect is a reactive environment where risk events occur as surprises. Because of the reactive environment, workarounds are commonplace when risk events happen. Also, there isn't a knowledge base of any risk information, thereby perpetuating the lack of a proactive environment.

13.8   Risk Formulas and Variables

Description	Formula	Variable (Components)	Example
The sum of all probabilities for outcome of an event must equal 1.0.	Total Probabilities = Sum of all probabilities	N/A	Outcome A = 0.5 Outcome B = 0.3 Outcome C = 0.2 Totals equal 1.0
EMV is expected monetary value. Here, the probability of the outcome is multiplied by the impact, then the products of the outcome are summed for a total EMV of the decision.	Probability X Impact (summed)	Probability = P Impact = I Expected Monetary Value = EMV	Outcome A = 0.5 X $100 Outcome B = 0.3 X $300 Outcome C = 0.2 X $300 Total probabilities equal 1.0 and EMV equals $200

13.9   Risk Terminology

Term	Description
Brainstorming	A process by which a group of people attempt to find a solution to a problem or generate ideas toward a goal spontaneously without judging others in the group
Buffer	Compensation in the planning for unknown items that could occur; typically schedule- or cost-related
Contingency Allowance	Compensation in the planning for unknown items that could occur; typically schedule- or cost-related; also commonly called buffer
Contingency Plans	Pre-established actions that the team executes if a known risk event occurs on the project
Contingency Reserves (Output/Input)	Reserves that can help mitigate schedule or cost issues (risk), in the case of changes with the scope or quality on the project
Decision Tree Analysis (Technique)	The product of multiplying the monetary value impact and probability of the risk event; helps an organization make decisions based on potential outcome and impact
Expected Monetary Value (EMV) (Analysis)	The product of multiplying the monetary value impact and probability of the risk event
Fallback Plans	A type of plan created for risks with a great impact on project goals, to be executed if attempts to minimize the risk are not successful
Monte Carlo Analysis	A technique used to simulate the outcome of a project many times to determine the range of possible outcomes and the probability of their occurrence
Preventive Action	Documented activities to execute, if needed, that should minimize (or eliminate) the impact of a negative risk on the project
Probability and Impact Matrix (Tool)	A tool used to determine where a risk fits on a project The typical rating is high, medium, or low for probability and impact.
Qualitative Risk Analysis	Analyzing risks and determining the priority of their effects on the project
Quantitative Risk Analysis	The process of measuring the probability and impact of the risks and estimating the impact on the project
Reserves	Compensation in the planning for unknown items that could occur; is typically schedule- or cost-related; also commonly called buffer
Residual Risk	Risk that remains after response strategies have been applied
Risk	The possibility of a negative (threat) or positive (opportunity) event
Risk Acceptance	Opting to accept the impact or consequences of a risk event
Risk-Averse	Possessing a low desire or tolerance for risk
Risk Avoidance	Eliminating a risk or threat, usually by eliminating the cause

PMP Exam Success Series: Certification Exam Manual
© 2007 Crosswind Project Management, Inc., www.crosswindpm.com

Risk Breakdown Structure (RBS) (Tool)	A decomposition of the risk categorization, and the risks within those categories that could occur on a project
Risk Category	A grouping of types of risk on a project (Ex: technology, organizational, customer, market)
Risk Database	A data repository that stores and manipulates information associated with the risk management processes
Risk Events	Events that may impact the project (either negative or positive)
Risk Factors	Numbers representing the risk of certain events, the likelihood of their happening, plus the impact on the project (if the event does happen)
Risk Identification	The process of determining which risks can impact a project and the documentation of their properties or characteristics
Risk Management Plan	A document that details and describes the plan for managing risk over the life of the project
Risk Mitigation	Minimizing the impact of a risk event by minimizing the likelihood (probability) of its occurrence
Risk Monitoring and Control	The process of monitoring known risks, reducing any risks, identifying any new risks, and monitoring risk reduction over the life of the project
Risk-Neutral	A middle ground between the risk taken and the benefit received
Risk Register (Output/Input)	The documented results of Risk Management Planning which can include the outputs of Qualitative Risk Analysis and Quantitative Risk Analysis, as well as Risk Response Planning
Risk Response Planning	The process of determining what risk responses will be used on risk events and who will be responsible for implementing the responses if the risks occur
Risk Seeking	Possessing a higher tolerance than most for risk
Risk Symptoms	Characteristics which indicate that a risk event is possibly starting to happen; could also be called risk triggers
Risk Tolerance	The level of satisfaction from a potential risk payoff
Risk Transference	Allocating the responsibility for and impact of the risk event to another party
Risk Utility	See Risk Tolerance.
Secondary Risks	Risks that result from the execution of a risk response
Sensitivity Analysis	A technique used in risk management that helps show which risks will likely have the most impact on the project
Strengths, Weaknesses, Opportunities, and Threats (SWOT) Analysis	A risk analysis technique which considers the strengths, weaknesses, opportunities, and threats of the project to facilitate a more knowledgeable risk management analysis
Threat	A negative risk to the project
Trigger	A signal that a risk event could occur or has occurred
Workaround (Technique)	A response to a risk that wasn't planned

13.10 Risk Mind Map

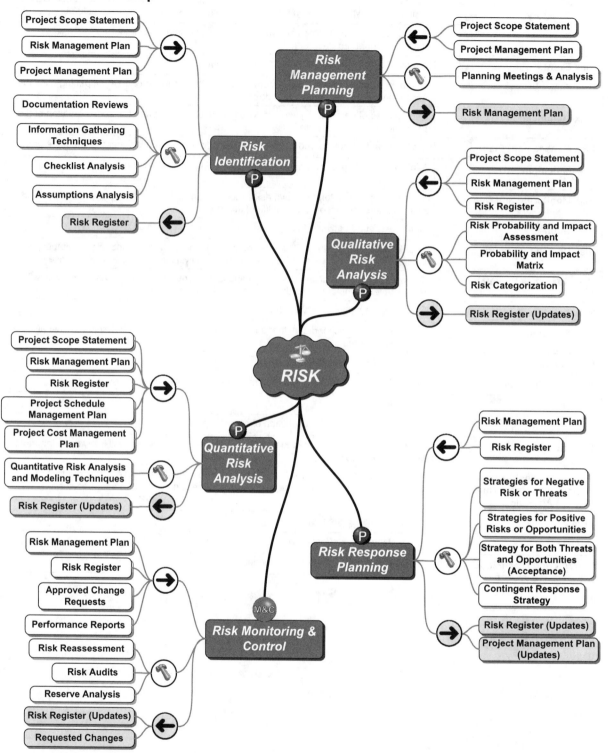

13.11 Risk Tests and Exercises

13.11.1   Risk Quick Test

In this quiz, answer the question in a short essay of only a sentence or two or circle all correct answers for the question. Note that some questions may have more than one answer. Answers are in section 13.12.1.

1.   What is the name for someone with a high tolerance for risk?

2.   Which happens first: a risk response or a workaround?

3.   Risk lists (part of the risk register) can be used from previous projects. True or False?

4.   What causes secondary risk?

5.   Expected monetary value (EMV) is created from decision trees. True or False?

6.   What are the responsibilities of a risk owner?

7.   What is the sum of all probabilities?

8.   What is a risk trigger?

9.   What are the two components that make up expected monetary value?

10. Needing more computers than planned on a project is an example of which of the following?

Known unknowns
Unknown unknowns

13.11.2   Risk ITTO Matching Exercise

Match the correct ITTO term at the bottom of the page with the blanks to the right of the process. When a term is used multiple times, it is flagged by a parenthetical value indicating the number of times used. Also, match summary sentences with the process name that fits. Answers are in section 13.12.2.

Inputs	Tools & Techniques	Outputs

Risk Management Planning
- Inputs: 1) ___ 2) ___
- Tools & Techniques: 1) ___
- Outputs: 1) ___

Summary: ___

Risk Identification
- Inputs: 1) ___ 2) ___ 3) ___
- Tools & Techniques: 1) ___ 2) ___ 3) ___ 4) ___
- Outputs: 1) ___

Summary: ___

Qualitative Risk Analysis
- Inputs: 1) ___ 2) ___ 3) ___
- Tools & Techniques: 1) ___ 2) ___ 3) ___
- Outputs: 1) ___

Summary: ___

Quantitative Risk Analysis
- Inputs: 1) ___ 2) ___ 3) ___ 4) ___ 5) ___
- Tools & Techniques: 1) ___
- Outputs: 1) ___

Summary: ___

Risk Response Planning
- Inputs: 1) ___ 2) ___
- Tools & Techniques: 1) ___ 2) ___ 3) ___ 4) ___
- Outputs: 1) ___ 2) ___

Summary: ___

Risk Monitoring and Control
- Inputs: 1) ___ 2) ___ 3) ___ 4) ___
- Tools & Techniques: 1) ___ 2) ___ 3) ___
- Outputs: 1) ___ 2) ___

Summary: ___

Prioritizing risks based on probability and impact
Creation of the risk approach to the project
Determining response to risk events

Watching for risk events and triggers to occur
Identifying risks and risk triggers
Numerical risk analysis of the project goals

Approved Change Requests	Project Management Plan (2)	Risk Management Plan (6)
Assumption Analysis	Project Management Plan (Updates)	Risk Probability and Impact Assessment
Checklist Analysis	Project Schedule Management Plan	Risk Reassessment
Contingent Response Strategy	Project Scope Statement (4)	Risk Register (5)
Documentation Reviews	Quantitative Risk Analysis and Modeling Techniques	Risk Register (Updates) (4)
Information Gathering Techniques	Requested Changes	Strategies for Positive Risks or Opportunities
Performance Reports	Reserve Analysis	Strategies for Negative Risk or Threats
Planning Meetings and Analysis	Risk Audits	Strategies for Both Threats and Opportunities
Probability and Impact Matrix	Risk Categorization	
Project Cost Management Plan		

13.11.3   Risk Terminology Matching Exercise

Match the correct term in the left column to the correct definition in the right column. See the exercise answer section of this chapter for the correct answer. Answers are in section 13.12.3.

Matching Exercise #1

	Term	Answer	Definition
1	Brainstorming		A. A technique used to simulate the outcome of a project many times, to determine the range of possible outcomes and the probability of their occurrence
2	Buffer		B. Minimizing the impact of a risk event by minimizing the likelihood (probability) of its occurrence
3	Contingency Reserves (Output/Input)		C. A risk analysis technique which considers the strengths, weaknesses, opportunities, and threats of the project to facilitate a more knowledgeable risk management analysis
4	Expected Monetary Value (EMV) (Analysis)		D. Compensation in the planning for unknown items that could occur; typically schedule- or cost-related
5	Monte Carlo Analysis		E. The process of measuring the probability and impact of the risks and estimating the impact on the project
6	Quantitative Risk Analysis		F. Events that may impact the project (either negative or positive)
7	Reserves		G. The level of satisfaction from a potential risk payoff (N can also be used)
8	Risk		H. Risks that result from the execution of a risk response
9	Risk-Averse		I. A process by which a group of people attempt to find a solution to a problem or generate ideas toward a goal spontaneously without judging others in the group
10	Risk Breakdown Structure (RBS) (Tool)		J. The possibility of a negative (threat) or positive (opportunity) event
11	Risk Events		K. A decomposition of the risk categorization, and the risks within those categories that could occur on a project
12	Risk Mitigation		L. The product of multiplying the monetary value and probability of the risk event
13	Risk-Neutral		M. Possessing a higher tolerance than most for risk
14	Risk Seeking		N. The level of satisfaction from a potential risk payoff (G can also be used)
15	Risk Symptoms		O. A response to a risk that wasn't planned
16	Risk Tolerance		P. A middle ground between the risk taken and the benefit received
17	Risk Utility		Q. Possessing a low desire or tolerance for risk
18	Secondary Risk		R. Reserves that can help mitigate schedule or cost issues (risk), in the case of changes with the scope or quality on the project
19	Strengths, Weaknesses, Opportunities, and Threats (SWOT) Analysis		S. Characteristics which indicate that a risk event is possibly starting to happen
20	Workaround (Technique)		T. Compensation in the planning for unknown items that could occur; typically schedule- or cost-related; also commonly called buffer

Matching Exercise #2

	Term	Answer	Definition
1	**Contingency Allowance**		A. A tool used to determine where a risk fits on a project The typical rating is high, medium, or low for probability and impact.
2	**Contingency Plans**		B. The process of determining which risks can impact a project and the documentation of their properties or characteristics
3	**Decision Tree Analysis (Technique)**		C. Compensation in the planning for unknown items that could occur; typically schedule- or cost-related
4	**Fallback Plans**		D. Characteristics which indicate that a risk event is possibly starting to happen (F can also be used)
5	**Preventive Actions**		E. The documented results of Risk Management Planning which can include the outputs of Qualitative Risk Analysis and Quantitative Risk Analysis, as well as Risk Response Planning
6	**Probability and Impact Matrix (Tool)**		F. A signal that a risk event could occur or has occurred (D can also be used)
7	**Qualitative Risk Analysis**		G. A grouping of types of risk on a project (Ex: technology, organizational, customer, market)
8	**Residual Risk**		H. A negative risk to the project
9	**Risk Avoidance**		I. A type of plan created for risks with a great impact on project goals, to be executed if attempts to minimize the risk are not successful
10	**Risk Category**		J. Pre-established actions that the team executes if a known risk event occurs on the project
11	**Risk Database**		K. Risk that remains after response strategies have been applied
12	**Risk Factors**		L. Eliminating a risk or threat, usually by eliminating the cause
13	**Risk Identification**		M. The product of multiplying the monetary value impact and probability of the risk event; helps an organization make decisions based on potential outcome and impact
14	**Risk Management Plan**		N. Numbers representing the risk of certain events, the likelihood of their happening, plus the impact on the project (if the event does happen)
15	**Risk Monitoring and Control**		O. Documented activities to execute if needed that should minimize (or eliminate) the impact of a negative risk on the project
16	**Risk Register (Output/Input)**		P. The process of monitoring known risks, reducing any risks, identifying any new risks, and monitoring risk reduction over the life of the project
17	**Risk Transference**		Q. A document that details and describes the plan for managing risk over the life of the project
18	**Risk Triggers**		R. A data repository that stores and manipulates information associated with the risk management processes
19	**Sensitivity Analysis**		S. Analyzing risks and determining the priority of their effects on the project
20	**Threat**		T. Allocating the responsibility for an impact of the risk event to another party
21	**Trigger**		U. A technique used in risk management that helps show which risks will likely have the most impact in the project

13.11.4   Risk Practice Test

Answers are in section 13.12.4.

1.   Calculate EMV from the following: 0.4 probability of $6,500, 0.3 probability of -$3,200, 0.2 probability of $2,000, 0.1 probability of $1,000.

(A) $10,500
(B) $2,700
(C) $2,140
(D) $2,500

2.   In defining a risk trigger, which of the following is most accurate?

(A) A trigger is an indicator that a risk event will occur.
(B) A trigger is the same as a risk.
(C) A trigger is an indicator that a risk event has occurred.
(D) A trigger is an indicator that a risk event could occur.

3.   The telecom project is scheduled to run until year's end. There is the possibility that the union collective bargaining agreement will not be renewed immediately upon its expiration next month. If this happens, senior management has decided to shift job responsibilities around with the non-union personnel so they could be involved in the union roles on the project, as well as their regular responsibilities. The goal is to minimize the schedule slippage on the project because union negotiation is not in their control. This is an example of what type of risk response?

(A) Avoid
(B) Transfer
(C) Mitigate
(D) Accept

4.   The CEO of your company is considering entering a market that is relatively untested. If your company enters the market successfully, the reward could be quite significant. If the entry fails, the company could go bankrupt. What is the CEO considered?

(A) Risk-averse
(B) Risk seeker
(C) Risk-neutral
(D) To be meeting stockholder expectations

5.   In defining risk, it is more accurate that risk can be which of the following?

(A) Negative events
(B) Positive events
(C) Either a negative or positive event
(D) Something that has already happened

6.   The telecom project is scheduled to run until year's end. There is the possibility that the union collective bargaining agreement will not be renewed immediately upon its expiration next month. If this happens, the Project Manager and senior management have decided to put the project on hold until the issue is resolved because union labor plays a key part in the project's success. This is an example of what type of risk response?

(A) Mitigate
(B) Transfer
(C) Accept
(D) Avoid

7.   The Project Manager and the team have just completed determining what will be done if risk events happen and who will be responsible for executing those actions. Which of the following best describes what they have just completed?

(A) Risk Identification
(B) Risk Response Planning
(C) Secondary Response Planning
(D) Qualitative Analysis

8.   Which of the following best describes risk reviews?

(A) Determining what risks are on the project
(B) Determining what the characteristics of the risks are on the project
(C) Determining the validity of the documented risks and looking for any new risks that could occur
(D) Determining who will implement a risk response plan

9.   The manufacturing company has added a new line for its electronic assembly business. This addition involves new technology to build printed circuit boards more quickly with fewer errors. The company anticipates that this improvement will let it make a greater type of product and boost output efficiency. Adding this line is an example of what?

(A) Business risk
(B) ISO 9000
(C) Conformance to quality
(D) Insurable risk

10. The reservation system has been working well. Today, the main database engine crashed, preventing the airline from creating reservations for its flights. The risk response didn't fix the problem. Which of the following steps does the airline perform first?

(A) Fix the problem
(B) Determine why the risk response plan failed
(C) Adjust the risk response plan
(D) Determine why the problem happened

11.   Qualitative Risk Analysis uses which of the following?

(A) A risk rating matrix
(B) Expected monetary value (EMV)
(C) Workarounds
(D) Risk triggers

12.   All the following can be created in Risk Response Planning except...

(A) Residual risks
(B) Secondary risk
(C) Updates to the risk register
(D) Risk management plan

13.   Quantitative Risk Analysis uses which of the following?

(A) A risk rating matrix
(B) Expected monetary value (EMV)
(C) Workarounds
(D) Risk triggers

14.   The team has implemented a risk response plan when a vendor was unable to fulfill a contract commitment. The response was to choose another vendor. Because of the short notice, the other vendor could not fulfill the need of the team. Which best describes what happened with the different vendor?

(A) Workaround
(B) Secondary risk
(C) Risk response plan
(D) Avoidance

15.   If a risk on the project has a high probability of occurring and a high impact if it does, it more than likely will go through what?

(A) Insurable risk
(B) Qualitative Risk Analysis
(C) Pure risk
(D) Quantitative Risk Analysis

16.   The construction company has been awarded a $20M contract to build a shopping community center. The company realizes that the land around this property will be valuable in the future as the work of the project is completed. They have chosen to buy this land and hold onto it until it can be developed or sold in the future after the value increases. This is an example of what type of risk response strategy?

(A) Exploit
(B) Share
(C) Mitigate
(D) Accept

17. Management reserves are created for what?

    (A) Known unknowns
    (B) Unknown unknowns
    (C) Contingency reserves
    (D) Risk management

18. The network project has been very challenging. The cost performance index is presently 0.95 and the schedule performance index is 0.91. Risk could have been managed better from the start of this project. Halfway through the execution of the project management plan, the Project Manager assigned one person to do nothing but monitor for risks and work with the people who implemented the risk response plans. What is a main goal to achieve from Risk Monitoring and Control?

    (A) Qualitative analysis
    (B) Corrective action
    (C) Overall risk ranking for the project
    (D) Quantitative analysis

19. The project management team has just completed the process of identifying risks on the project. They have broken the information into categories and displayed this information in a graphical format. What have they created?

    (A) Risk management plan
    (B) Risk breakdown structure
    (C) Risk register
    (D) Prioritized list of quantified risks

20. Contingency reserves are created for what?

    (A) Unknown unknowns
    (B) Known unknowns
    (C) Risk management
    (D) Management reserves

21. A manufacturing company has added a new line for its electronic assembly business. This addition involves new technology to build printed circuit boards more quickly with fewer errors. The company anticipates that this improvement will let it make a greater type of product and boost output efficiency. Because of the machine cost and the specific knowledge needed to repair it if it breaks, the company has purchased a service contract for the machine from the manufacturer. Purchasing the service contract is an example of what?

    (A) Business risk
    (B) Insurable risk
    (C) ISO 9000
    (D) Conformance to quality

PMP Exam Success Series: Certification Exam Manual
© 2007 Crosswind Project Management, Inc., www.crosswindpm.com

22. The construction company has been awarded a $20M contract to build a shopping community center. The company is relatively small, and this contract is bigger than anything it has been awarded to date. To ensure that it can effectively complete the contract and not jeopardize other work, it has chosen to partner with another company to do the work. This tactic is an example of what type of risk response strategy?

    (A) Exploit
    (B) Share
    (C) Mitigate
    (D) Accept

23. Your company is evaluating two projects for consideration. Project A has a 40% probability of $69,000 and a 60% probability of -$10,000. Project B has a 60% probability of $56,000 and a 40% probability of -$15,000. Which of the projects do you select based on the greatest expected monetary value?

    (A) Project A
    (B) Project B
    (C) Project A and B are of even value
    (D) The expected monetary value is not high enough on either to make a selection

24. The database project team members are planning the project. They are involved in Risk Response Planning, assigning risk owners. What is the risk owner responsible for?

    (A) Watching for additional risks on the project
    (B) Watching for risk triggers and telling the Project Manager if they happen
    (C) Letting the Project Manager know that the risk has happened
    (D) Implementing a risk response if the risk event occurs

25. The CEO of your company has decided to take a "wait and see" approach to a new direction the market appears to be headed in. He feels that waiting will minimize a great deal of the risk that could come with being first to market, in case the market adjustment isn't long lasting. What is the CEO considered?

    (A) Risk-neutral
    (B) To be meeting stockholder expectations
    (C) Risk-averse
    (D) Risk seeker

26. The telecom project is scheduled to run until year's end. There is the possibility that the union collective bargaining agreement will not be renewed immediately upon its expiration next month. If this happens, senior management has decided to outsource the work to a consulting company to deliver the work because they have no input to union negotiations and no assurance how long a strike could last. This is an example of what type of risk response?

    (A) Avoid
    (B) Transfer
    (C) Mitigate
    (D) Accept

27.   The project team is analyzing what could happen on the project, looking at things that could go wrong or better than expected. Where will this information ultimately be stored?

(A) Risk list
(B) Risk trigger
(C) Risk register
(D) Risk response

28.   The Project Manager and the team are in the process of Risk Identification on the project. They have learned recently that risk categorization will help organize risks better and potentially allow them to see risks that might have been missed otherwise. Which of the following is the best example of risk categories?

(A) Initiating, Planning, Executing, Monitoring and Controlling, Closing
(B) Scope, time, cost
(C) Quality, schedule, budget
(D) External, internal, technology, personnel

29.   The telecom project is scheduled to run until year's end. There is the possibility that the union collective bargaining agreement will not be renewed immediately upon its expiration next month. If this happens, senior management has decided to negotiate quickly for a resolution with the union because union labor plays a key part in the project's success, and the project finish date cannot slip. This is an example of what type of risk response?

(A) Mitigate
(B) Transfer
(C) Accept
(D) Avoid

30.   The Project Manager and team are planning the project. They are presently identifying things that could go differently than planned. They are also trying to identify warning signs which show that these events could be on the verge of occurring. What is the team doing?

(A) Risk analysis
(B) Risk identification
(C) Conformance to quality
(D) Problem solving

PMP Exam Success Series: Certification Exam Manual
© 2007 Crosswind Project Management, Inc., www.crosswindpm.com

13.12 Risk Tests and Exercise Answers

13.12.1 Risk Quick Test Answers

1. What is the name for someone with a high tolerance for risk?
   Risk seeker [section 13.2.7]

2. Which happens first: a risk response or a workaround?
   Risk response [section 13.6.3, section 13.9]

3. Risk lists (part of the risk register) can be used from previous projects. True or False?
   True [section 13.3.7, section 13.9]

4. What causes secondary risk?
   Implementing a risk response creates the secondary risk. For example, in the treatment for a medical condition, the secondary risk is a side effect. [section 13.6.2, section 13.9]

5. Expected monetary value (EMV) is created from decision trees. True or False?
   True [section 13.5.3, section 13.9]

6. What are the responsibilities of a risk owner?
   To implement a risk response plan when needed [section 13.6.4]

7. What is the sum of all probabilities?
   100% [section 13.5.1]

8. What is a risk trigger?
   A symptom that a risk event could soon be occurring [section 13.3.3, section 13.9]

9. What are the two components that make up expected monetary value?
   Probability multiplied by impact [section 13.5.3, section 13.8, section 13.9]

10. Needing more computers than planned on a project is an example of which of the following?
    Known unknowns [section 13.6]

13.12.2 Risk ITTO Matching Exercise Answers

	Inputs	Tools & Techniques	Outputs
Risk Management Planning	1) Project Scope Statement 2) Project Management Plan	1) Planning Meetings and Analysis	1) Risk Management Plan
Summary:	Creation of the risk approach to the project		
Risk Identification	1) Project Scope Statement 2) Risk Management Plan 3) Project Management Plan	1) Documentation Reviews 2) Information Gathering Techniques 3) Checklist Analysis 4) Assumptions Analysis	1) Risk Register
Summary:	Identifying risk and risk triggers		
Qualitative Risk Analysis	1) Project Scope Statement 2) Risk Management Plan 3) Risk Register	1) Risk Probability and Impact Assessment 2) Probability and Impact Matrix 3) Risk Categorization	1) Risk Register (Updates)
Summary:	Prioritizing risk analysis based on probability and impact		
Quantitative Risk Analysis	1) Project Scope Statement 2) Risk Management Plan 3) Risk Register 4) Project Schedule Management Plan 5) Project Cost Management Plan	1) Quantitative Risk Analysis and Modeling Techniques	1) Risk Register (Updates)
Summary:	Numerical risk analysis of the project goals		
Risk Response Planning	1) Risk Management Plan 2) Risk Register	1) Strategies for Negative Risk or Threats 2) Strategies for Positive Risks or Opportunities 3) Strategy for Both Threats and Opportunities 4) Contingent Response Strategy	1) Risk Register (Updates) 2) Project Management Plan (Updates)
Summary:	Determining response to risk events		
Risk Monitoring and Control	1) Risk Management Plan 2) Risk Register 3) Approved Change Requests 4) Performance Reports	1) Risk Reassessment 2) Risk Audits 3) Reserve Analysis	1) Risk Register (Updates) 2) Requested Changes
Summary:	Watching for risk events and triggers to occur		

PMP Exam Success Series: Certification Exam Manual
© 2007 Crosswind Project Management, Inc., www.crosswindpm.com

13.12.3   Risk Terminology Matching Exercise Answers

Matching Exercise #1 Answers

Term		Definition
1	**Brainstorming**	I. A process by which a group of people attempt to find a solution to a problem or generate ideas toward a goal spontaneously without judging others in the group
2	**Buffer**	D. Compensation in the planning for unknown items that could occur; typically schedule- or cost-related
3	**Contingency Reserves (Output/Input)**	R. Reserves that can help mitigate schedule or cost issues (risk), in the case of changes with the scope or quality on the project
4	**Expected Monetary Value (EMV) (Analysis)**	L. The product of multiplying the monetary value impact and probability of the risk event
5	**Monte Carlo Analysis**	A. A technique used to simulate the outcome of a project many times to determine the range of possible outcomes and the probability of their occurrence
6	**Quantitative Risk Analysis**	E. The process of measuring the probability and impact of the risks and estimating the impact on the project
7	**Reserves**	T. Compensation in the planning for unknown items that could occur; typically schedule- or cost-related; also commonly called buffer
8	**Risk**	J. The possibility of a negative (threat) or positive (opportunity) event (F can also be used)
9	**Risk-Averse**	Q. Possessing a low desire or tolerance for risk
10	**Risk Breakdown Structure (RBS) (Tool)**	K. A decomposition of the risk categorization, and the risks within those categories that could occur on a project
11	**Risk Events**	F. Events that may impact the project (either negative or positive) (J can also be used)
12	**Risk Mitigation**	B. Minimizing the impact of a risk event by minimizing the likelihood (probability) of its occurrence
13	**Risk-Neutral**	P. A middle ground between the risk taken and the benefit received
14	**Risk Seeking**	M. Possessing a higher tolerance than most for risk
15	**Risk Symptoms**	S. Characteristics which indicate that a risk event is possibly starting to happen
16	**Risk Tolerance**	G. The level of satisfaction from a potential risk payoff (N can also be used)
17	**Risk Utility**	N. The level of satisfaction from a potential risk payoff (G can also be used)
18	**Secondary Risk**	H. Risks that result from the execution of a risk response
19	**Strengths, Weaknesses, Opportunities, and Threats (SWOT) Analysis**	C. A risk analysis technique which considers the strengths, weaknesses, opportunities, and threats of the project to facilitate a more knowledgeable risk management analysis
20	**Workaround (Technique)**	O. A response to a risk that wasn't planned

Matching Exercise #2 Answers

Term		Definition
1	**Contingency Allowance**	C. Compensation in the planning for unknown items that could occur; typically schedule- or cost-related
2	**Contingency Plans**	J. Pre-established actions that the team executes if a known risk event occurs on the project
3	**Decision Tree Analysis (Technique)**	M. The product of multiplying the monetary value impact and probability of the risk event; helps an organization make decisions based on potential outcome and impact
4	**Fallback Plans**	I. A type of plan created for risks with a great impact on project goals, to be executed if attempts to minimize the risk are not successful
5	**Preventive Actions**	O. Documented activities to execute if needed that should minimize (or eliminate) the impact of a negative risk on the project

6	Probability and Impact Matrix (Tool)	A. A tool used to determine where a risk fits on a project. The typical rating is high, medium, or low for probability and impact
7	Qualitative Risk Analysis	S. Analyzing risks and determining the priority of their effects on the project
8	Residual Risk	K. Risk that remains after response strategies have been applied
9	Risk Avoidance	L. Eliminating a risk or threat, usually by eliminating the cause
10	Risk Category	G. A grouping of types of risk on a project (Ex: technology, organizational, customer, market)
11	Risk Database	R. A data repository that stores and manipulates information associated with the risk management processes
12	Risk Factors	N. Numbers representing the risk of certain events, the likelihood of their happening, plus the impact on the project (if the event does happen)
13	Risk Identification	B. The process of determining which risks can impact a project and the documentation of their properties or characteristics
14	Risk Management Plan	Q. A document that details and describes the plan for managing risk over the life of the project
15	Risk Monitoring and Control	P. The process of monitoring known risks, reducing any risks, identifying any new risks, and monitoring risk reduction over the life of the project
16	Risk Register (Output/Input)	E. The documented results of Risk Management Planning which can include the outputs of Qualitative Risk Analysis and Quantitative Risk Analysis, as well as Risk Response Planning
17	Risk Transference	T. Allocating the responsibility for an impact of the risk event to another party
18	Risk Triggers	D. Characteristics which indicate that a risk event is possibly starting to happen (F can also be used)
19	Sensitivity Analysis	U. A technique used in risk management that helps show which risks will likely have the most impact in the project
20	Threat	H. A negative risk to the project
21	Trigger	F. A signal that a risk event could occur or has occurred (D can also be used)

13.12.4   Risk Practice Test Answers

1.   Calculate EMV from the following: 0.4 probability of $6,500, 0.3 probability of -$3,200, 0.2 probability of $2,000, 0.1 probability of $1,000.

   Correct Answer: (C) $2,140
   Explanation: To calculate the expected monetary value (EMV), multiply each probability by its dollar amount and add the products of all multiplication. The result is a value of $2,140. [section 13.5.3, section 13.8, section 13.9]

2.   In defining a risk trigger, which of the following is most accurate?

   Correct Answer: (D) A trigger is an indicator that a risk event could occur.
   Explanation: A trigger is an occurrence which can imply that a risk event could happen. Just because a trigger occurs, don't automatically assume that a risk will happen. [section 13.3.3, section 13.9]

3.   The telecom project is scheduled to run until year's end. There is the possibility that the union collective bargaining agreement will not be renewed immediately upon its expiration next month. If this happens, senior management has decided to shift job responsibilities around with the non-union personnel so they could be involved in the union roles on the project, as well as their regular responsibilities. The goal is to minimize the schedule slippage on the project because union negotiation is not in their control. This is an example of what type of risk response?

Correct Answer: (C) Mitigate

Explanation: Risk mitigation attempts to minimize the bad risk or maximize the good risk. In this case, management is attempting to minimize the impact of a labor strike. Risk acceptance simply deals with the risk if it happens. Risk avoidance involves doing what can be done to eliminate the risk. Transference assigns or transfers the risk to some external party. [section 13.6.5]

4.   The CEO of your company is considering entering a market that is relatively untested. If your company enters the market successfully, the reward could be quite significant. If the entry fails, the company could go bankrupt. What is the CEO considered?

Correct Answer: (B) Risk seeker

Explanation: A risk seeker mentality is that of looking for the big reward and being prepared to pay significantly if it is missed. The risk-averse mentality is a very conservative approach to risk. A risk-neutral mentality is somewhere between that of a risk seeker and risk-averse mentality. The other answer is noise. [section 13.2.7]

5.   In defining risk, it is more accurate that risk can be which of the following?

Correct Answer: (C) Either a negative or positive event

Explanation: Risk can be of negative or positive consequence on a project. It is something that can happen but hasn't yet. Risk involves uncertainty with regard to what could happen, not what has happened. [section 13.1, section 13.9]

6.   The telecom project is scheduled to run until year's end. There is the possibility that the union collective bargaining agreement will not be renewed immediately upon its expiration next month. If this happens, the Project Manager and senior management have decided to put the project on hold until the issue is resolved because union labor plays a key part in the project's success. This is an example of what type of risk response?

Correct Answer: (C) Accept

Explanation: Risk acceptance simply deals with the risk if it happens. In this case, the project is put on hold as a means to deal with the union issue. Risk avoidance involves doing what can be done to eliminate the risk. Mitigation attempts to minimize the bad risk or maximize the good risk. Transference assigns or transfers the risk to someone else. [section 13.6.5]

7.   The Project Manager and the team have just completed determining what will be done if risk events happen and who will be responsible for executing those actions. Which of the following best describes what they have just completed?

Correct Answer: (B) Risk Response Planning

Explanation: Risk Response Planning documents who should do what if risk events occur. Risk Identification is the process of determining what risks and triggers could occur on the project. Qualitative analysis assigns probability and impact ratings to the risk. "Secondary response planning" is noise. [section 13.6]

8.   Which of the following best describes Risk Reviews?

Correct Answer: (C) Determining the validity of the documented risks and looking for any new risks that could occur

Explanation: Risk reviews verify that the risks are still valid and that no new risks have appeared on the project. The other answers come before or after risk reviews. [section 13.3.4]

9.   The manufacturing company has added a new line for its electronic assembly business. This addition involves new technology to build printed circuit boards more quickly with fewer errors. The company anticipates that this improvement will let it make a greater type of product and boost output efficiency. Adding this line is an example of what?

Correct Answer: (A) Business risk

Explanation: Business risk comes from simply operating the business. There is no guarantee that an idea will work as you hope. Pure risk is also known as insurable risk. Pure risk is a risk that you can buy insurance for. Conformance to quality is involved with quality management. ISO 9000 is a quality standard. [section 13.2.5]

10. The reservation system has been working well. Today, the main database engine crashed, preventing the airline from creating reservations for its flights. The risk response didn't fix the problem. Which of the following steps does the airline perform first?

Correct Answer: (A) Fix the problem

Explanation: This is a chicken or the egg question in that you more than likely will do all the answers, but what comes first? Fixing the problem, then determining why the risk response plan failed, and why the problem happened, then adjusting the risk response plan is the sequence for the other answers. [section 13.6.3, section 13.7]

11. Qualitative Risk Analysis uses which of the following?

Correct Answer: (A) A risk rating matrix

Explanation: Qualitative Risk Analysis uses a risk rating matrix to rank risks and create an overall risk rating for the project. Expected monetary value (EMV) is used in Quantitative Risk Analysis. Workarounds are what are done when risk events don't work. Risk triggers are indicators that a risk event could happen. [section 13.4, section 13.2.3]

12. All the following can be created in Risk Response Planning except...

Correct Answer: (D) Risk management plan

Explanation: The risk management plan is created in Risk Management Planning. Of the remaining answers, not all are created in Risk Response Planning but can be created if certain events happen. [section 13.6, section 13.2]

13. Quantitative Risk Analysis uses which of the following?

Correct Answer: (B) Expected monetary value (EMV)

Explanation: Expected monetary value (EMV) is used in Quantitative Risk Analysis. This can help in generating time and cost targets for the project. Qualitative Risk Analysis uses a risk rating matrix to rank risks and create an overall risk rating for the project. Workarounds are done when risk events don't work. Risk triggers are indicators that a risk event could happen. [section 13.5]

14. The team has implemented a risk response plan when a vendor was unable to fulfill a contract commitment. The response was to choose another vendor. Because of the short notice, the other vendor cannot fulfill the need of the team. Which best describes what happened with the different vendor?

Correct Answer: (B) Secondary risk

Explanation: Secondary risk is what happens when a risk event happens and creates new risk. The workaround is what is done when risk responses do not work as planned. The risk response plan defines what the risk responses will be if risk events occur. Avoidance is a risk response strategy. [section 13.6.2, section 13.9]

15. If a risk on the project has a high probability of occurring and a high impact if it does, it more than likely will go through what?

Correct Answer: (D) Quantitative Risk Analysis

Explanation: A risk undergoes Quantitative Risk Analysis if Qualitative Risk Analysis shows that the risk has a high probability of occurring and high impact if it does. Qualitative Risk Analysis helps determine the probability and impact of a risk; therefore, you must complete this analysis before you can evaluate the probability and impact of the risk. Insurable risk and pure risk don't fit the question here. [section 13.5]

16. The construction company has been awarded a $20M contract to build a shopping community center. The company realizes that the land around this property will be valuable in the future as the work of the project is completed. They have chosen to buy this land and hold onto it until it can be developed or sold in the future after the value increases. This is an example of what type of risk response strategy?

Correct Answer: (A) Exploit
Explanation: Exploiting the risk is to undertake activity that grows or expands the positive aspects of the risk. Sharing the risk is to work with someone else to maximize the risk. Mitigate attempts to minimize the bad or maximize the good impact of the risk. Accepting the risk is to tolerate whatever happened. [section 13.6.5]

17. Management reserves are created for what?

Correct Answer: (B) Unknown unknowns
Explanation: Management reserves are created for unknown unknowns. These are things that aren't expected to happen. Contingency reserves are created for known unknowns. These are things that we know will happen; we just don't know how much of it will happen. "Risk management" is noise. [section 13.6]

18. The network project has been very challenging. The cost performance index is presently 0.95 and the schedule performance index is 0.91. Risk could have been managed better from the start of this project. Halfway through the execution of the project management plan, the Project Manager assigned one person to do nothing but monitor for risks and work with the people who implemented the risk response plans. What is a main goal to achieve from Risk Monitoring and Control?

Correct Answer: (B) Corrective action
Explanation: Risk Monitoring and Control watches for risks and implements risk response plans if the risk occurs. Qualitative analysis and quantitative analysis occur before Risk Response Planning. The project's overall risk ranking comes from the qualitative and quantitative analyses. [section 5.4.1, section 13.7]

19. The project management team has just completed the process of identifying risks on the project. They have broken the information into categories and displayed this information in a graphical format. What have they created?

Correct Answer: (B) Risk breakdown structure
Explanation: The risk breakdown structure (RBS) is a graphical representation of the risk categorization and risks within those categories of the project. The risk management plan is the management approach to risk on the project. The risk register contains risk lists, analysis, responses, and risk owners for the project. Prioritized list of quantified risks comes in the risk register and involves risk ranking, not identification categorization. [section 13.2.2]

20. Contingency reserves are created for what?

Correct Answer: (B) Known unknowns
Explanation: Contingency reserves are created for known unknowns. These are things that we know will happen, we just don't know how much of it will happen. Management reserves are created for unknown unknowns. These are things that aren't expected to happen. "Risk management" is noise. [section 13.6]

21. A manufacturing company has added a new line for its electronic assembly business. This addition involves new technology to build printed circuit boards more quickly with fewer errors. The company anticipates that this improvement will let it make a greater type of product and boost output efficiency. Because of the machine cost and the specific knowledge needed to repair it if it breaks, the company has purchased a service contract for the machine from the manufacturer. Purchasing the service contract is an example of what?

Correct Answer: (B) Insurable risk
Explanation: Insurable risk is risk that you can buy insurance for, which in this case is an insurance policy that ensures what the company will have to pay if the machine breaks. Business Risk comes from simply operating the business. There is no guarantee that an idea will work as you hope. Conformance to quality is part of the definition of quality. ISO 9000 is a quality standard. [section 13.2.5]

22. The construction company has been awarded a $20M contract to build a shopping community center. The company is relatively small, and this contract is bigger than anything it has been awarded to date. To ensure that it can effectively complete the contract and not jeopardize other work, it has chosen to partner with another company to do the work. This tactic is an example of what type of risk response strategy?

Correct Answer: (B) Share
Explanation: Sharing the risk with another company is what is happening here. Exploiting the risk is to do things to grow or expand the positive aspects of the risk. Mitigate attempts to minimize the bad or maximize the good impact of the risk. Accepting the risk is to tolerate whatever happened. [section 13.6.5]

23. Your company is evaluating two projects for consideration. Project A has a 40% probability of $69,000 and a 60% probability of -$10,000. Project B has a 60% probability of $56,000 and a 40% probability of -$15,000. Which of the projects do you select based on the greatest expected monetary value?

Correct Answer: (B) Project B
Explanation: To calculate the expected monetary value (EMV), multiply the probabilities by their dollar amounts and add the products of the multiplication for each project. This results in a value of $21,600 for Project A and $27,600 for Project B. With the highest expected monetary value, Project B is the one to select. [section 13.5.3, section 13.8]

24. The database project team members are planning the project. They are involved in Risk Response Planning, assigning risk owners. What is the risk owner responsible for?

Correct Answer: (D) Implementing a risk response if the risk event occurs
Explanation: Risk owners are responsible for implementing the risk response assigned to them. Watching for additional risks on the project could fall under the responsibility of a risk owner, but isn't the main responsibility. Letting the Project Manager know that a risk event has happened isn't the main responsibility of the risk owner. Watching for risk triggers and telling the Project Manager if they happen isn't taking a proactive approach to risk or project management. [section 13.6.4]

25. The CEO of your company has decided to take a "wait and see" approach to a new direction the market appears to be headed in. He feels waiting will minimize a great deal of the risk that could come with being first to market, in case the market adjustment isn't long lasting. What is the CEO considered?

Correct Answer: (C) Risk-averse
Explanation: The risk-averse mentality is a very conservative approach to risk. A risk seeker mentality is that of looking for the big reward and being prepared to pay significantly if they miss it. A risk-neutral mentality is somewhere between that of a risk seeker and risk-averse mentality. The other answer is noise. [section 13.2.7, section 13.9]

26. The telecom project is scheduled to run until year's end. There is the possibility that the union collective bargaining agreement will not be renewed immediately upon its expiration next month. If this happens, senior management has decided to outsource the work to a consulting company to deliver the work because they have no input to union negotiations and no assurance how long a strike could last. This is an example of what type of risk response?

Correct Answer: (B) Transfer
Explanation: Risk transference assigns or transfers the risk to someone else. In this case, outsourcing the work is to transfer the risk associated with labor. Risk acceptance simply deals with the risk if it happens. Risk avoidance involves doing what can be done to eliminate the risk. Mitigation attempts to minimize the bad risk or maximize the good risk. [section 13.6.5]

27. The project team is analyzing what could happen on the project, looking at things that could go wrong or better than expected. Where will this information ultimately be stored?

Correct Answer: (C) Risk register
Explanation: The risk list and risk triggers are being created in this situation. The risk list and triggers end up in the risk register. Risk responses end up in the risk register after they are created in Risk Response Planning. [section 13.3.1]

28. The Project Manager and the team are in the process of Risk Identification on the project. They have learned recently that risk categorization will help organize risks better and potentially allow them to see risks that might have been missed otherwise. Which of the following is the best example of risk categories?

Correct Answer: (D) External, internal, technology, personnel
Explanation: Categorization of risk groups risks together by defining categories where they can fit. The correct answer fits this description. The other answers are noise because they relate to project management Process Groups or interpretations of the triple constraint. [section 13.3]

29. The telecom project is scheduled to run until year's end. There is the possibility that the union collective bargaining agreement will not be renewed immediately upon its expiration next month. If this happens, senior management has decided to negotiate quickly for a resolution with the union because union labor plays a key part in the project's success, and the project finish date cannot slip. This is an example of what type of risk response?

Correct Answer: (D) Avoid
Explanation: Risk avoidance involves doing what can be done to eliminate the risk. In this case, negotiating quickly for a resolution avoids the risk. Risk acceptance simply deals with the risk if it happens. Mitigation attempts to minimize the bad risk or maximize the good risk. Transference assigns or transfers the risk to someone else. [section 13.6.5]

30. The Project Manager and team are planning the project. They are presently identifying things that could go differently than planned. They are also trying to identify warning signs which show that these events could be on the verge of occurring. What is the team doing?

Correct Answer: (B) Risk identification
Explanation: Risk Identification is a process that should produce a list of risks and triggers. Risks are good or bad things that are un-forecasted. Triggers are indicators that a risk event could happen but is not imminent. The other answers are noise. [section 13.3]

Chapter 14

Procurement

Procurement can be frustrating even if you have experience in it. In procurement, you work with outside companies; mistakes can have legal consequences. Know the different contract types and procurement documents, and the differences between them. Understand processes and how they interconnect. Finally, note that, **unless stated otherwise, PMI and the exam reference procurement from a buyer's perspective.**

In this chapter, we discuss the following:

Process Group	Process Name		Main Outputs
Planning	Plan Purchases and Acquisitions	→	Procurement Management Plan
			Make-or-Buy Decisions
	Plan Contracting	→	Procurement Documents
			Evaluation Criteria
Executing	Request Seller Responses	→	Qualified Sellers List
			Proposals
	Select Sellers	→	Contract
			Contract Management Plan
Monitoring and Controlling	Contract Administration	→	Contract Documentation
			Requested Changes
Closing	Contract Closure	→	Closed Contracts

☑   **Crosswind "Must Knows" For Procurement**

	Key Inputs, Tools & Techniques, and Outputs for Plan Purchases and Acquisitions
	Key Inputs, Tools & Techniques, and Outputs for Plan Contracting
	Key Inputs, Tools & Techniques, and Outputs for Request Seller Responses
	Key Inputs, Tools & Techniques, and Outputs for Select Sellers
	Key Inputs, Tools & Techniques, and Outputs for Contract Administration
	Key Inputs, Tools & Techniques, and Outputs for Contract Closure
	How to recognize and calculate, as well as know the advantages and disadvantages of fixed-price (FP) also known as lump-sum, fixed-price-plus-incentive-fee (FPIF), fixed-price-economic-price-adjust (FPEPA), time & materials (T&M) contracts, cost-reimbursable (CR), cost-plus-fixed-fee (CPFF), cost-plus-incentive-fee (CPIF), and cost-plus-percentage of cost (CPPC)

	Incentive fees
	Various names for a buyer and seller
	What a contract is and the components that make a contract
	Difference between the Project Manager and Contract Administrator on a project in relation to the contract
	A request for proposal (RFP), request for information (RFI), invitation for bid (IFB), and a request for quote (RFQ) and know in which environment you would use them
	When you would use a non-competitive form of procurement
	Make-or-buy process and how to calculate it
	Different types of scope of work
	What a bidders conference is and what occurs at it
	What formal acceptance is and what can happen to the project once you have attained it
	Know the differences of terms and conditions, as well as special provisions
	Negotiating goals and options
	PMI's goal of negotiations is for both parties to win, not one party win and one lose
	Differences of centralized and decentralized contracting environments
	What a qualified sellers list is and how it's used

Although helpful, this list is not all-inclusive for information needed from this area for the exam. It is only suggested material that, if understood and memorized, may increase your exam score.

14.1   Plan Purchases and Acquisitions (Planning Process Group)

Know the Key Inputs, Tools & Techniques, and Outputs for Plan Purchases and Acquisitions.

In Plan Purchases and Acquisitions, a company analyzes its procurement or outsourcing needs. This planning could be for something which the company is already skilled in yet needs excess or surge capacity; it could be for a product, result, or service it is not skilled in but needs in order to attain a business goal. It's not uncommon for a company or group to involve people specialized in law, purchasing, or contracts at this point (or soon after) in the process.

Plan Purchases and Acquisitions (Planning)		
Key Inputs	Project Scope Statement	The project scope statement **helps define what it is that is being created or accomplished by the procurement initiative**.
	Work Breakdown Structure	The WBS provides a **decomposition of the project work** and can sometimes point out areas of the scope that were not sufficiently addressed in the project scope statement, thereby resulting in scope statement updates.
	Project Management Plan • Risk Register • Resource Requirements • Project Schedule • Activity Cost Estimates • Cost Baseline	The risk register (from the project management plan) is a piece of the project management plan that **contains information associated with what risks could occur** on a project, **potential responses** for those risks, **root causes** of the risks, and risk **categorization**. It expands as risk management processes are further implemented.
		Resource requirements (from the project management plan) **provide resource parameters that can be applied to what types of resources are needed and in what quantities**. They should describe what is needed, how much of it is needed, and what it should cost per unit.

Key Inputs (cont.)	Project Management Plan (cont.)	The project schedule (from the project management plan) **displays the time or schedule baseline** against which activity is measured.
		Activity cost estimates (from the project management plan) can be **used to create estimates for the resource needs** for the activities on the schedule.
		Cost baseline (from the project management plan) is the **cost estimate** that the project planning team has established for the project. This value is the number (or numbers if it's broken down throughout the project) that the pieces of work are estimated to cost.
Key Tools & Techniques	Make-or-Buy Analysis	Initially, the company must perform a make-or-buy analysis. This analysis should **show if it is more practical to create the product internally or outsource it**. While this analysis could factor in skill sets, experience, resource availability, and so on in real life, as it relates to the exam, the make-or-buy analysis is based on cost comparison between alternatives.
	Expert Judgment	Expert judgment can be invaluable in this area because experience can unearth factors not so obvious to the less experienced person. It can be more significant and accurate than the best modeling tools available.
	Contract Types	Contract type is a key tool, and a poorly selected contract type can doom a project in this area. No matter how well the project execution goes, if the contract is not a good fit, it can be a nightmare. Assuming that the decision is to buy (instead of make), contract type selection comes into the equation. This contract **could be a fixed-price contract (FP), cost-plus-fee (CPF), or time and materials (T&M)**, depending upon the nature of the work and knowledge available about it.
Key Outputs	Procurement Management Plan	When complete, there should be a procurement management plan. This plan **helps define how the procurement needs of the project will be addressed**. It could include contract type, evaluation criteria, procurement documentation to be used, contract administration, constraints and assumptions, scheduling and payments, qualifying sellers, and metrics.
	Contract Statement of Work	The contract statement of work (SOW) is also available at this time. It **helps define what needs to be created (or acquired** by the buyer), timeframes, cost parameters, and resources, as well as any other specific variables. This SOW can be created from the project scope statement and WBS.
	Make-or-Buy Decisions	Make-or-buy decisions come into consideration when a company is deciding if it should **outsource something or create it internally**. Issues like internal skills, resource capacity, and controlling the work or intellectual property can be deciding factors in this area.

Situational Question and Real World Application
When a company must perform Plan Purchases and Acquisitions, it can encounter issues such as not knowing if it should outsource or use internal resources, or determining the need for analysis when it is too late on the project. If Planning were short, there could be scope creep issues or gray areas relating to understanding the services to be provided that one party could exploit, negatively affecting the other.

14.1.1 Procurement Management Plan

The procurement management plan helps the Project Manager and team do the following:

- Determine make vs. buy for the various needs of the project
- Establish what procurement documents (RFP, RFI, RFQ) are needed for the project
- Create the procurement documents for the project
- Run bidders conferences
- Address single source and sole source procurement
- Select vendors to do work
- Establish contract(s) with vendors

14.1.2 Make-or-Buy Decisions

One of the basics of procurement is the make-or-buy decision. There are a number of considerations a company can use in making this decision. Some of the basic decision points are listed below.

Be familiar with the make-or-buy process and how to calculate it.

Make Decision Qualities	The buyer owns intellectual property associated with the work and considers doing the work internally in order to maintain control of the information.
	The buyer has excessive qualified capacity.
Buy Decision Qualities	The buyer doesn't possess the skills needed for the work.
	The buyer doesn't possess the capacity to do the work.

14.1.3 Rent or Buy Calculation

You may be quizzed on the calculation area of this topic. It is a straightforward calculation. The components are typically as follows:

- Purchase cost and daily maintenance with the purchase option
- Daily (or weekly, monthly) rental fee, which usually includes maintenance fees

Typically, you should be prepared to calculate the point where it makes sense to purchase, versus rent, or visa versa. Review the following example:

> You are the Project Manager for a housing developer. The development requires a skid loader to clean out the lots where the houses will be built. You can rent the skid loader for $100 per day (including maintenance) or you can purchase one for $5,000, with a $50 per day maintenance cost. What is the maximum time you would want to rent this tool before considering purchasing it?

To determine the best decision, first take the variables and make a formula. The options have rental at $100 per day or purchase at $5,000 with $50 per day maintenance. Translate this information into a formula as follows to solve for the variable X.

PMP Exam Success Series: Certification Exam Manual
© 2007 Crosswind Project Management, Inc., www.crosswindpm.com

The formula is ($ per day)x(number of days) = purchase price + (maintenance fee per day x number of days). An example is $100X=$5,000+$50X. Solve for X as the number of days.

Step 1. (-$50X)+$100X=$5,000 or $50X=$5,000 (Move all the pieces with the variable X to one side of the equation.)

Step 2. $5,000/$50=X (Divide to determine the value of X.)

Step 3. $5,000/$50=100

Step 4. X=100 (Here is the maximum number of days you would want to rent the tool before purchasing it.)

14.1.4   Contract

Know what a contract is and the components that make a contract.

A contract is a mutually binding legal agreement between buyer and seller. Other names for a contract could be a purchase order (PO), subcontract, or agreement. You should expect a few questions on this, so make sure that you know the components of a contract, plus when a contract is in place. A contract has five basic components. Without all these components, a contract does not exist.

The five components are as follows:

- Capacity (competency, of legal age, and individual legal entities)
- Consideration (the item to change possession from seller to buyer)
- Offer (a proposition to exchange something, for something)
- Legal purpose (the reason for the contract has to be for something legal)
- Acceptance (A buyer willing to accept the offer from the seller)

A memory tool for the contract is CCOLA—**C**apacity, **C**onsideration, **O**ffer, **L**egal, **A**cceptance.

Know how to recognize and calculate all contract types plus know their advantages and disadvantages.

14.1.5   Buyer and Seller Names

If the work of the project is not just for materials or products, the seller usually manages the project. This is the case for a greatly customized scope of work as well. In cases like this, the buyer becomes the customer. The seller's team is concerned with all the details of the project, not just procurement. That said, the seller's team has a greater degree of input to the overall project planning than if it were merely providing a product that had already been created.

The table below shows a number of terms that can be used to describe the buyer and seller. The seller's title could also change during the project duration. For example, a company could be a bidder, then a selected source, then a vendor.

Buyer	Seller
Client	Contractor
Customer	Subcontractor
Prime Contractor	Vendor
Contractor	Service Provider
Acquiring Organization	Supplier
Government Agency	
Service Requestor	
Purchaser	

Know the various names for a buyer and a seller.

14.1.6   Contract Type Selection

Contract type selection is a key to the PMP Examination. There are four main types of contracts represented in the following tables. Purchase order (PO), fixed-price (FP), time and materials (T&M), and cost-reimbursable (CR). Each of these contracts can involve variations including incentives, fees, and more. Selecting the wrong type of contract can spell doom for a project. **It is imperative that you understand the types of contracts, their differences, where they should (and should not) be applied, and the risk for buyer and seller.**

Contract	Risk for Buyer	Risk for Seller	Description	Example
Purchase Order (PO)	Neutral	Neutral	A **unilateral** agreement that requires approval by only one party because the other party has offered the product for the predefined price Typically, a PO is used for commodity items such as those that can be mass-produced. Some consultants have mentioned that the workplace typically gets a contract type signed off and then gets a purchase order. PMI doesn't view this as the case, seeing a PO as a separate contract type.	19" Computer monitors for $179.00 each
Fixed-price (FP) also known as Lump-Sum	Minimal	Significant	One of the most common contracts in business today, popular because a company can budget for a fixed price Because it **requires detail for the seller to estimate accurately,** an FP contract is typically used when there is a **detailed scope of work.** The downside for the seller is cost containment. For the seller, profit is everything after cost is covered.	Purchasing the implementation of a computer network at your company from an outside vendor for $2,000,000 after providing the seller a detailed scope of work
Fixed-Price-Incentive-Fee (FPIF)	Minimal	Significant	A contract type with the fixed-price component described above; **includes incentive fees** to motivate the seller to produce at a rate greater than the minimum required An FPIF is usually used to help accelerate a buyer's need, such as a market opportunity. It provides an opportunity for the seller to determine what is needed to make additional profit via the incentive fee.	A city buying services from a construction company to put in a new freeway for $4,000,000. For each week the seller finishes before a given date, it receives $65,000.
Fixed-Price Economic Price Adjustment (FPEPA)	Minimal	Significant	A fixed-price contract with the similar components listed above; associated with a multi-year contract **To compensate for economic changes from year to year,** the Economic Price Adjustment is factored in. The item determining the amount of	A city buys services from a construction company to build a new freeway for $4M over three years. At the start of each year, the amount varies relative to

PMP Exam Success Series: Certification Exam Manual
© 2007 Crosswind Project Management, Inc., www.crosswindpm.com

Contract	Risk for Buyer	Risk for Seller	Description	Example
			change from year to year is usually some national economic metric not directly tied to the buyer or the seller.	the national cost of living or some other negotiated standard.
Time and Materials (T&M)	Minimal	Minimal	Typically used **for smaller initiatives, staff supplementation,** or the initial piece of a project where the discovery occurs before the full details of the project are known; can also be used for materials on an initiative to complement the labor	Staff supplementation of a technical writer at $75 per hour, or having a bathroom added to your house at $50 per hour and the cost of materials
Cost-Plus-Fixed-Fee (CPFF)	Medium	Minimal	Typically used **when the buyer knows generally what is needed but lacks details** to know specifically what is needed to build it The CPFF covers the cost of the seller and includes a predefined fee for the work.	A buyer hires a vendor to produce a video training series but is not yet sure of all the detail needed, and agrees to pay the vendor for cost plus a $37,000 fee.
Cost-Plus-Incentive-Fee (CPIF)	Medium	Minimal	Typically used **when the buyer knows generally what is needed but lacks any details** to know specifically what is needed to build it Generally, the buyer has some sort of need which requires that something be created as soon as reasonably possible. The incentive fee gives the buyer an opportunity to motivate the seller to complete the project quicker, to higher quality standards, or other criteria.	A buyer hires a vendor to write a manual for publication and sale. Due to a market opportunity, the quicker to market, the higher the sales. The buyer agrees to pay cost plus an incentive fee of $7,500 for each week the project is done before the estimated completion date.
Cost-plus-percentage of Cost (CPPC) or Cost-Plus-Fee (CPF)	Significant	Minimal	**Covers the seller cost for building something for a buyer and pays a percentage of total costs as a fee** The more the seller spends, the higher the fees. Most companies will not enter into this type of contract because it can negatively impact the buyer if the seller is not ethical.	A buyer hires a company to install a computer network for 500 users and agrees to pay for the cost of the seller and 17% of all costs for a fee.

14.1.7   Share

A share is a contract component that divides any remaining money between the buyer and the seller. It is normally a negotiated split between the two parties. It is typically different from a traditional incentive fee in that an incentive fee pays compensation based on certain measurable performance metrics that have been established and agreed upon. You could be expected to calculate share on the exam.

Here's an example: The buyer and seller have contracted for the seller to provide a debit card add-on system in all 50 of the buyer's retail stores. The total price is to be $50,000. The need for implementation is great because the old systems are being leased and must be returned by a particular date. Both parties negotiate that if the project's actual cost is below the baseline (target) cost, the buyer and seller split the difference 60%/40%.

The project accrues an actual cost of $45,000 when complete. Calculate the share total amount and the share for the buyer and seller.

The project has a $5,000 share amount ($50,000-$45,000). Of that $5,000, 60% goes to the buyer and 40% to the seller. The buyer keeps $3,000 and the seller gets $2,000. With the actual cost of $45,000 and the share amount of $2,000, the seller makes $47,000 on the contract.

14.1.8   Point of Total Assumption

This calculation establishes **the point at which the seller is responsible for all cost overruns associated with a fixed-price incentive fee (FPIF) contract.** Contrary to what fixed-price may imply, a contract of this sort can be negotiated so that the buyer agrees to share in cost overruns or under-runs. The point of total assumption is reached when all cost overruns fall to the seller. This calculation is typically used in government or defense-type contracts.

Point of Total Assumption Variables and Calculation	
Purpose:	To calculate the maximum that a buyer pays in a fixed-price incentive-fee (FPIF) contract when taking into consideration the share ratio on cost overruns
Target Cost (TC)	The expected cost of the work in the contract (Ex: $1,000,000)
Target Profit (TP)	The expected profit of the work in the contract (Ex: $200,000)
Profit Rate at Target Cost	The profit margin of the target profit compared to the target cost (target profit/target cost) (Ex: 20%)
Target Price	The total of the target cost and target profit; should be the total target value of the contract work barring any overruns or under runs (Ex: $1,200,000)
Ceiling Price	A percentage of the target cost (TC) This value is the maximum total amount the work is expected to cost with any cost overruns being considered. (Ex: 140% of cost or $1,400,000)
Share Ratio (SR)	The ratio between the buyer and seller for any cost savings or overruns that impact the total contract amount and profit (Ex: 70/30)
Point of Total Assumption (PTA)	The total amount of money the buyer will pay regardless of cost overrun on the contract The formula is in the cell below. (Ex: $1,285,714.29)
Point of Total Assumption Formula	$$PTA = \left[\frac{\text{Ceiling Price} - \text{Target Price}}{\text{Buyer Share}} \right] + \text{Target Cost}$$ $$\$1,285,714.29 = \left[\frac{\$1,400,000 - \$1,200,000}{0.70} \right] + \$1,000,000$$ NOTE: The difference between ceiling price and target price is indeed divided by the buyer's share. This is not an error.

14.1.9   Scope of Work

Scope of work is typically the part of the contract that describes what the seller will do for the buyer. When the scope of work is done or complete, the main work of the project is done and Closing can begin. Because the level of detail and planning can vary among contracts, you can take several different approaches to develop the scope of work in the contract.

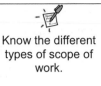

Know the different types of scope of work.

Scope of Work	Description	Example
Design	A scope of work type in which the buyer provides the seller with the **exact details of what is required** Design is typically used when buyers know exactly what they want and want no variance from specifications. It **typically** works with **fixed-price contracts.**	A company hires a vendor to build a prototype cabinet to house telecom equipment. The buyer provides the seller with specifications of what is to be built; it must hold a number of devices already created.
Functionality	A scope of work type in which the buyer details to the seller the **functionality needed in the new system or development** Functionality allows sellers to propose their own solutions as long as the end-results are achieved. **It typically works with cost-plus (CP) contracts.**	A company hires a vendor to implement a phone system. It provides the needed functionality requirements to the vendor, and as long as those are met, it allows the vendor the flexibility to build a solution as the vendor sees fit.

14.2   Plan Contracting (Planning Process Group)

In Plan Contracting, the company completes the solicitation needs for the project. After analysis and planning, the result is one or more procurement documents such as the request for proposal (RFP), request for information (RFI), or request for quote (RFQ).

Know the Key Inputs, Tools & Techniques, and Outputs for Plan Contracting.

	Plan Contracting (Planning)	
Key Inputs	Procurement Management Plan	The procurement management plan **helps define the procurement rules** for a project.
	Contract Statement of Work	The contract statement of work (SOW) **shows all the details of the work** needed.
	Project Management Plan • Risk Register • Activity Cost Estimates	The risk register (from the project management plan) is a piece of the project management plan that **contains information associated with what risks could occur** on a project, **potential responses** for those risks, **root causes** of the risks, and risk **categorization**. It expands as risk management processes are further implemented.
		Activity cost estimates (from the project management plan) can be **used to create estimates for the resource quantities** for the activities on the schedule.

Key Tools & Techniques	Standard Forms	Standard forms—predefined templates—**can save significant time** in the Planning.
	Expert Judgment	Expert judgment can help by providing expertise to smooth the Planning process.
Key Outputs	Procurement Documents	Procurement documents such as a request for proposal (RFP), request for information (RFI), request for quote (RFQ), tender notice, invitation for bid (IFB), invitation for negotiation, or contractor initial response are common outputs.
	Evaluation Criteria	Evaluation criteria **used to review and compare potential vendors** are common, as well as statement of work (SOW) updates. These criteria can include life cycle costs, technical capability and plans, project management methodology, financial capability, company size, references, and intellectual property ownership.

Situational Question and Real World Application
Coming up short in this area could result in either missing or incomplete procurement documents that could cause risk and scope issues on the project as it relates to the provided procurement services.

14.2.1   Procurement Documents

The documents associated with the procurement process lay the foundation for vendor relationships. They apply to the selected vendors and for those who are considering the work. An ideal procurement document answers the questions of the potential provider and allows them to make a well planned bid, which helps create a win/win relationship with the seller.

Be familiar with all types of procurement documents and know the environments in which to use them.

Type	Typical Purpose	Description	Example
Request for Quote (RFQ)	Typically used to solicit proposals for a small dollar amount or used for commodity type of products that do not require a great degree of customization	A document that requests a price for a standard item There is a general assumption that negotiation is not associated with this type of procurement document.	A request for prospective sellers wishing to provide pricing for customer-established server criteria: Quantity 50 XYZ Servers with 1Gig RAM, 200G hard drive to be purchased within 90 days of submittal
Request for Information (RFI)	Typically used to solicit information to learn more about a company that could provide service for a buyer	A document requesting information on a service provider's qualifications so a buyer can review them	A request from a state government to see if a consulting company has the appropriate experience in an area to bid for a project

Type	Typical Purpose	Description	Example
Request for Proposal (RFP) sometimes called Request for Tender (RFT)	Typically used to solicit proposals for bigger, higher priced, customized services or products Generally, the seller describes the detailed approach to the solution for the buyer, including previous experience in the area.	A document that requests an approach, price, and significant detail about how the seller proposes to do the requested work The general assumption is that negotiations occur based on scope, time, and cost of what the buyer requested and what the seller suggested.	A request for a proposal to prospective sellers for design, implementation, and training for a data warehouse to consolidate five different enterprise databases at fortune 500 company named Widgets, Inc.
Invitation for Bid (IFB) sometimes called Request for Bid (RFB)	Used for government sealed bidding processes with characteristics similar to those for a RFP (request for proposal)	A document that requests an approach, price, and significant detail about how the seller proposes to do the requested work The general assumption is that negotiations occur based on scope, time, and cost of what the buyer requested and what the seller suggested.	A request from a branch of the U.S. government for a proposal to sellers for the design, implementation and training of an enterprise reporting system The selection process is sealed bid and the contract is awarded on May 25, 2008.

14.3   Request Seller Responses (Executing Process Group)

Know the Key, Inputs, Tools & Techniques, and Outputs for Request Seller Responses.

In Request Seller Responses, a **buyer finds companies that can potentially provide the needed services for which the procurement is being done**. This search could be anything from a general search to focusing on a qualified sellers list.

Request Seller Responses (Executing)		
Key Inputs	Procurement Management Plan	The procurement management plan **helps define the procurement rules** for a project.
	Procurement Documents	Procurement documents such as a request for proposal (RFP), request for information (RFI), request for quote (RFQ), or invitation for bid (IFB) **provide service vendors information about the services requested of them.**
Key Tools & Techniques	Bidders Conferences	Bidders conferences **offer opportunities for prospective vendors to come together** and get clarification of what exactly the purchasing company is requesting.
	Develop Qualified Sellers List	Develop qualified sellers list is a tool **used to determine which vendors meet evaluation criteria** to be considered for work on the project.
Key Outputs	Qualified Sellers List	The qualified sellers list is a **list of vendors that have met the qualification criteria** to be considered for the work being solicited.
	Proposals	Proposals come from companies that seek to provide the service to the purchasing company.

Situational Question and Real World Application
Ignoring this area or only partially completing it could result in not having an adequate number of appropriate vendors available for consideration. This shortage could result in selecting an inadequate vendor or not the best vendor for the job because they weren't involved in the solicitation process.

14.3.1   Qualified Sellers List

The qualified sellers list is a **list that a buyer can use as a screening mechanism in the procurement process.** It allows a buyer to consider only sellers of services that have met some predefined qualifications. This list can save time by eliminating the preliminary screening process and allowing buyers to select from vendors that have already met the predefined qualifications.

Know what a qualified sellers list is and how it's used.

14.3.2   Bidders Conference

Bidders conferences are meetings during which companies considering bidding on a project can ask a buyer questions and get clarification on any potential issues before creation of a proposal. Such a conference can also include a formal presentation by the buyer.

The conference should let potential sellers ask questions and should make the questions and answers available to anyone considering bidding on the project. Buyer representatives need to be sure to make all questions and answers available to all potential sellers, as well as take all reasonable steps to ensure that potential sellers do not collude together on unfair pricing. This collusion could include Company A shooting high on a price to allow Company B to get the work for this project with the understanding that their roles will switch on the next project.

Know what a bidders conference is and what occurs at it.

14.3.3   Non-Competitive Form of Procurement

Typically, non-competitive procurement is done when there is **only one source for the products,** or the **buyer has an established relationship with the seller** and there are mechanisms in place to ensure that the buyer of the products or services attains a fair price. If a vendor is selected without competition, there is a chance for inappropriate selection and unreasonable pricing, so there should be a mechanism in place to assure that appropriate actions are taken in this area. The two main categories in this area are sole source and single source. These are defined in the following table.

Know when to use a non-competitive form of procurement.

Sole Source	**Single Source**
Sole source involves using a company that has no other competition for whatever you are acquiring from it. This company could be one that owns a patent or some other type of intellectual property associated with what you are purchasing.	Single source involves choosing a partner you prefer to work with or deciding not to look for competition. Whatever you are purchasing from the source might be available from others, but for whatever reason, you have decided not to look at others for the services. You might make this decision when you have a vendor you prefer, or when you might not have time to go through the full process to find others to do the work.

14.4 Select Sellers (Executing Process Group)

Know the Key Inputs, Tools & Techniques, and Outputs for Select Sellers.

In Select Sellers, the company attaining the services reviews proposals, possibly negotiates with more than one vendor, and determines the vendor(s) with whom it is going to sign a contract. Once that is determined, the company may send a letter of intent prior to negotiating and ultimately signing the contract.

Select Sellers (Executing)		
Key Inputs	Procurement Management Plan	The procurement management plan **helps define the procurement rules** for a project.
	Evaluation Criteria	Evaluation criteria help you **compare the proposals against any organizational policies that dictate source selection.** You may use any independent estimates to confirm proper source selection.
	Proposals	Proposals come **from companies that seek to provide the service** to the purchasing company.
	Qualified Sellers List	The qualified sellers list is a **list of vendors that have met the qualification criteria** to be considered for the work being solicited.
	Project Management Plan • Risk Register	The risk register (from the project management plan) **contains information associated with what risks could occur** on a project, **potential responses** for those risks, **root causes** of the risks, and risk **categorization**. It expands as risk management processes are further implemented.
Key Tools & Techniques	Weighting System	A weighting system **helps quantify the data provided by potential sellers.** It can help make evaluation more logical and eliminate emotional or personal bias. Typically, evaluation criteria are established and weights assigned to them. A seller's capability is then evaluated against the weights, and the weights are totaled.
	Independent Estimates	Independent estimates are **used to help validate what a project should cost.** These estimates could be created from within the company or by an outside source.
	Screening System	Screening systems are useful to **help you verify that you are considering properly qualified vendors.** You can use weighting systems to determine which vendors fit the requirements definition.
	Contract Negotiation	Contract negotiations **result in parameters that both parties can work with**, including terms and conditions for a contract.
	Expert Judgment	Expert judgment is of great value. It can be more significant and accurate than the best modeling tools.

Key Outputs	Selected Sellers	Selected sellers are **those that have passed the evaluation criteria and have been (or will be) awarded the work**. This selection could be based on cost, technical approach, references, or other predefined evaluation criteria.
	Contract	A contract is an **agreement** with the party providing the services.
	Contract Management Plan	The contract management plan (part of the project management plan) is **created for specific ways that a buyer needs to administer a contract**. Areas of focus can include performance, documentation, and delivery throughout the life of the contract.

Situational Question and Real World Application
Legal issues and scope understanding are the main problems here. When there is a misunderstanding regarding what is written in the contract and what is actually promised, the contract wins. There could be a situation in which the providing party was so eager to secure the contract that it quickly signed the contract without thinking through all the planning details to be sure that what it was asked to do will indeed meet the requirements. If such issues were not planned for, the providing company could see its profit disappear as it struggles to build a functional item (scope of the project).

14.4.1   Contract Management Plan

The Contract Management Plan helps the Project Manager and team do the following:

- Define the rules for archiving contract documentation (contract file)
- Establish payments for the work of the contract
- Address changes to the contract
- Validate that the work of the contract is complete
- Close the contract when work is complete

14.4.2   Incentive Fees

Incentive fees are those that a **buyer of services can use to get the seller aligned to a similar standard of productivity.** They are typically a premium that the buyer pays to the seller above the base price of the contract.

Know what incentive fees are.

14.4.3   Negotiations

Negotiations can take place in a number of project management areas. If you are outsourcing something to another company such as staff supplementation or a large project, negotiations occur to reach a deal between the parties. **One of the main keys that PMI has involving negotiation is that it is a win/win situation for both the buyer and seller.** Many people believe that one party must win and the other must lose in order to have successful negotiations. The better position is to accept a reasonable price for reasonable work.

You can use a number of negotiation strategies. Generally, these are items we see in everyday business. We recommend that you be able to recognize them in situational questions. Some common negotiation strategies follow.

Be familiar with the negotiating goals and options.

Know what the PMI's goal of negotiations is for both parties to win.

Competition	Using one seller (fictitious or real) against another to attain the best price or other terms the buyer desires
Deadline	Using a fictitious or real deadline to attempt to get a party to sign the contract
The Boss is Missing	Stating that another person who is key to approving something is not there, is busy, or is otherwise unable to be involved

14.4.4   Standard Terms and Conditions

Standard terms and conditions are typically common (non-negotiable) contract items. They can include negotiations but generally have a tight range of parameters from the company's legal department. This range could cover items such as payment options, intellectual property rights, and the ability to sub-contract.

14.4.5   Special Provisions

Special provisions are items typically **added to a contract to account for any standard terms and conditions that will not meet the needs of the work involved.** The buyer and seller negotiate these provisions, which complement any workable standard terms and conditions that have already been defined in the contract as acceptable.

> Know the differences of terms and conditions, as well as special provisions.

14.4.6   Contract Interpretation

Contract interpretation can keep you out of court or put you right in it. Generally, the contract administrator (see the next process) should understand what is defined in the contract, with the interpretation in line with general legal opinion. Some areas that you need to be sensitive to are as follows:

- The contract replaces anything that was agreed to before it was signed. If it is not in the contract, it's not a requirement.
- All the items of the contract should be completed, including reports, quality control, inspections, etc.
- It's better to spell out numbers than use the numerical characters only.
- Any agreement to modify the contract should be created and signed as an attachment to the contract (instead of just verbally agreed to).
- If any changes are made to the contract before it has been signed, the changes should be handwritten and initialed by all parties.
- Specific details associated with qualification criteria for the work should be defined at an appropriate level of detail. "System will work" falls short, as compared to "System will do requirements A through Z listed in the requirements of the scope of work."

14.5   Contract Administration (Monitoring and Controlling Process Group)

It is during Contract Administration that the contract administrator or other staff member **manages the contract** itself. This person verifies what is to be built or provided and measures it against the contract parameters (scope, time, and cost). The cost aspect of this process involves managing payments due the seller. In the case of larger projects with multiple vendors, **Contract Administration could include managing key interface points** with multiple vendors.

> Know the Key Inputs, Tools & Techniques, and Outputs for Contract Administration.

Contract Administration (Monitoring and Controlling)		
Key Inputs	Contract	The contract serves as a **baseline for the work being performed/provided by a seller** for a buyer.
	Contract Management Plan	The contract management plan (part of the project management plan) is **created to specify how a buyer needs to administer a contract**. Areas of focus can include performance, documentation, and delivery throughout the life of the contract.
	Performance Reports	Performance reports are key **to show current actual work complete** on the project.
	Approved Change Requests	Approved change requests are **changes that have been formally approved** by the official change control process on the project.
Key Tools & Techniques	Contract Change Control System	A contract change control system is used **to address and manage any needed and approved contract changes**.
	Inspections and Audits	Inspections and audits are performed as the contract is executed **to ensure the appropriate work and quality** of work is being completed per the terms of the contract.
	Performance Reporting	Performance reporting systems are used **to document and communicate project progress** and completion tracking.
	Payment System	Payment system is a tool used **to issue payments** to the sellers of products or services per the terms of the contract between the buyer and seller.
	Records Management System	A records management system is part of the project management information system (PMIS) and consists of automated tools and processes. It **ensures that appropriate contract-related records are created, communicated, and archived.**
Key Outputs	Contract Documentation	Contract documentation including the contract and attachments plus the procurement management plan, schedule, requirements, financial documentation, and warranty information are used **to help support the work that is to be done by the seller** for the buyer. This documentation can include organizational process assets updates such as correspondence between the buyer and seller, payment requests and a payment schedule, and seller performance evaluation documentation.
	Requested Changes	Requested changes are **changes that have been requested but not yet formally approved** by the official change control process on the project.

PMP Exam Success Series: Certification Exam Manual
© 2007 Crosswind Project Management, Inc., www.crosswindpm.com

Key Outputs (cont.)	Project Management Plan (Updates) • Procurement Management Plan • Contract Management Plan	The procurement management plan (from the project management plan) **helps define the procurement rules** for a project.
		The contract management plan (a part of the project management plan) is a plan **created for specific ways that a buyer needs to administer a contract**. Areas of focus can include performance, documentation, and delivery throughout the life of the contract. As change associated with the contract happens, the contract management plan can be updated as needed.

Situational Question and Real World Application
Communication and confusion are the main problems of procurement. A lack of communication on key issues between purchaser and seller is common. This lack of communication could be in areas such as invoicing, project or contract changes, and signoff of work packages being complete.

14.5.1 Contract Administrator

The contract administrator is the manager of the contract. The main responsibility is to protect the integrity and purpose of the contract. **Think of the contract as the law, and the contract administrator as the contract enforcement or police.**

Know the difference between the Project Manager and contract administrator on a project in relation to the contract.

14.5.2 Project Manager in the Contract Administration Area

In this area, the role of the Project Manager helps ensure successful execution of the contract. Project Managers typically work with the contract administrator to accomplish this successful execution as the scope, terms, and conditions of the contract are defined and as work results become complete. Remember that even though Project Managers are responsible for delivery of the project deliverables, they cannot change the contract. Only the contract administrator has that role.

14.5.3 Centralized and Decentralized Contracting

These environments have different positives and negatives for a contract administrator. The characteristics are similar to those of a PMO and being on a stand-alone project, or being the only Project Manager in a small company.

In a centralized environment, Contract Administrators support each other. They have career paths and likely have a great degree of shared expertise.

In a decentralized environment, the contract administrator is alone on a project without support of other contract administrators. The position is viewed more as a need instead of a career type position; the person likely works on only one project, or at least is the only contract administrator on the project.

Understand and know the differences of centralized and decentralized contracting environments.

14.6 Contract Closure (Closing Process Group)

In Contract Closure, **verification validates that contract terms and conditions have been met.** If they have, formal acceptance should be achieved, the contract file is completed, and the contract piece of the project is closed.

Know the Key Inputs, Tools & Techniques, and Outputs for Contract Closure.

Contract Closure (Closing)		
Key Inputs	Procurement Management Plan	The procurement management plan **helps define the procurement rules** for a project.
	Contract Management Plan	The contract management plan (a part of the project management plan) is created **to define how a buyer needs to administer a contract**. Areas of focus can include performance, documentation, and delivery throughout the life of the contract.
	Contract Documentation	Contract documentation is in place **to facilitate the comparison of contract-related work and products to the terms and conditions** of the contract.
Key Tools & Techniques	Procurement Audits	Procurement audits are **used to determine success and failure of the procurement process** for the project so those lessons can be applied to this project and others within the organization.
Key Outputs	Closed Contracts	Closed contracts are an **output when the work of the contract is complete**.
	Organizational Process Assets (Updates)	Organizational process asset **updates occur in the areas of the contract file, deliverables acceptance, and lessons learned documentation**. The contract file contains the contract and supporting documentation. Deliverables acceptance comes from the formal acceptance when customer (or sponsor) signs off on the work of the contract and potentially the project. Lessons learned documentation is valuable for helping future projects learn from the positives and negatives of this project or contract.

Situational Question and Real World Application
The biggest issue is likely an inability to gain formal acceptance of the project. This issue probably comes from confusion associated with elements verbally promised or overlooked, with subsequent changes needed to achieve Conformance to Requirements and Fitness for Use. If proper documentation techniques were not used, the contract file could be lacking.

14.6.1 Formal Acceptance

Formal acceptance is a key piece of the contract because it involves the buyer agreement that the work (or pieces of the work) is complete on the project. Upon completion of formal acceptance, the seller can begin the Contract Closure process of contract completion.

Know what formal acceptance is and what can happen to the project once you've attained it.

14.7   Procurement Formulas and Variables

Description	Formula	Variable (Component)	Example
The **expected cost** of the work in the contract for an FPIF contract	Sum of the costs of the work of the contract for the seller	(TC) Target Cost	TC = $1M
The **expected profit** of the work in the contract for an FPIF contract	Can be calculated in a variety of ways, depending on contract environment	(TP) Target Profit	TP = $200,000
The **profit margin** compared to the target cost for an FPIF contract	Typically established by industry and company	Profit Rate at Target Cost	20%
The **total of the Target Cost and Target Profit**; should be the total target value of the contract work barring any overruns or under-runs for an FPIF contract	Target Cost + Target Profit Target Price = TC + TP	Target Price	$1,200,000
A **percentage of the target cost (TC)** for an FPIF contract. This is the maximum total amount the buyer expects to pay for the work. Anything above this amount is covered by the seller.	Typically established by industry and company	Ceiling Price	140% of Cost or $1,400,000
The **ratio between the buyer and seller for any cost savings or overruns** that impact the total contract amount and profit for an FPIF contract or other applicable contract	Negotiated between buyer and seller	Share Ratio (SR)	70/30
The total **amount of money the buyer will pay** regardless of cost overrun on the contract for an FPIF contract	PTA=(Ceiling Price-Target Price)/Buyer Share + Target Cost $1,285,714.29= ($1,400,000-$1,200,000)/0.70+ $1,000,000	Point of Total Assumption (PTA)	$1,285,714.29
Calculation that determines the point at which it makes more sense **to make or buy** (rent) something needed for a project	($ per day)x(number of days) = purchase price + (maintenance fee per day x number of days)	Make-or-Buy Analysis	$100X=$5,000+$50X. Solve for X as the number of days

14.8   Procurement Terminology

Term	Description
Bill of Materials (BOM)	A formal document showing the hierarchy of components or pieces and their sub-components or sub-pieces that make up the product
Contract	A mutually binding agreement that requires the services provider to supply the specified services or goods and requires the buyer to pay for them per the terms of the document
Contract Administration	The process of managing the relationship between buyer and seller
Contract Closure	The process of completing the contract; includes settlement on any open items
Cost-Plus-Fixed-Fee (CPFF) Contract	A contract in which the supplier receives payment for allowable costs plus a fixed fee typically based on estimated cost
Cost-Plus-Incentive-Fee (CPIF) Contract	A contract in which the supplier receives payment for allowable costs, as well as a pre-negotiated fee and an incentive fee (if incentives are met)
Cost-Plus-Percentage of Cost (CPPC) Contract	A contract that reimburses the seller for cost, plus a negotiated percentage of the total costs
Cost-Reimbursable (CR) Contract	A contract in which a supplier is paid for direct and indirect cost actually incurred on the project
Firm-Fixed-Price (FFP) Contract	A contract in which the seller provides products or services based on a well defined scope of work for a set price
Fixed-Price-Incentive-Fee (FPIF) Contract	A contract in which the seller provides products or services based on a well defined scope of work for a set price; also includes a fee structure that provides more payment for achieving pre-defined performance objectives
Fixed-Price Contract	A contract that pays a seller a fixed price for a well defined or detailed product or service
Issue	A project item causing confusion or disagreement, or an unresolved item needing attention
Make-or-Buy Decision	An initial part of the procurement process in which a decision is made to either create the product by the company that needs it, or to outsource it and have another company create it
Plan Contracting	The creation of product requirements and documentation
Point of Total Assumption	The total amount of money the buyer will pay regardless of cost overrun on the contract
Procurement	The acquisition of goods or services from an outside source (vendor)
Procurement Documents (Output/Input)	Documents involved in the bidding and proposal activities; can include request for information (RFI), request for quote (RFQ), or request for proposal (RFP)
Procurement Management Plan	Document that determines make vs. buy decisions, establishes required procurement documents and creates them, defines how to run bidders conferences, addresses procurement sources, selects vendors, and establishes vendor contracts
Procurement Planning	The process of determining what to buy and the optimum method to make the purchase
Project Procurement Management	The process of attaining goods and services for a project from outside the organization
Request for Proposal (RFP)	A document that describes what the buyer wants from a potential supplier, as well as criteria for acceptability of the vendor
Request for Quote (RFQ)	A document used to get bids or quotes from possible suppliers, usually for commodity type items, with minimal customization
Retainage	A part of the payment per the terms of the contract that the buyer retains until the project is complete; used to ensure that the seller completes the work per terms of the contract
Seller	An individual or company that provides goods or services to a company or individual
Solicitation (Request Seller Responses)	The process of receiving proposals, quotes, bids, etc. for needed services or products
Source Selection (Select Sellers)	Deciding on a supplier to implement the needed solution
Statement of Work (SOW)	Typically, a piece of the contract that details the work to be done
Termination Clause	A clause in the contract that allows both the buyer and the seller to end the contract

PMP Exam Success Series: Certification Exam Manual
© 2007 Crosswind Project Management, Inc., www.crosswindpm.com

14.9   Procurement Mind Map

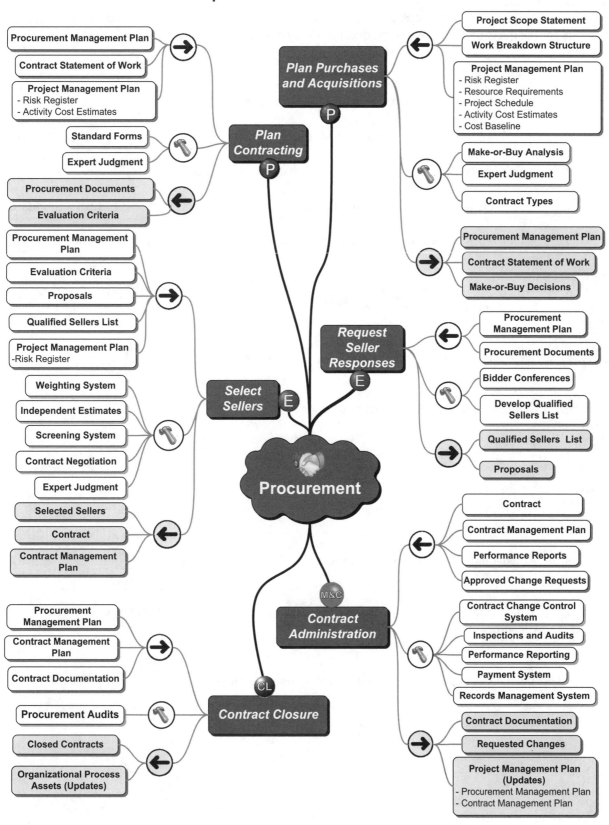

14.10 Procurement Tests and Exercises

14.10.1 Procurement Quick Test

In this quiz, answer the question in a short essay of only a sentence or two or circle all correct answers for the question. Note that some questions may have more than one answer. Answers are in section 14.11.1.

1. What type of contract is typically used for staff supplementation?

          Fixed-Price   Time and Materials   Cost-Plus   Purchase Order

2. A fixed-price contract typically requires what type of scope of work?

          General   Functional   Design   Industry Standard

3. Which type of scope of work is used when the performance specifications are known?

4. Which type of scope of work is used when the precise details of how the product of the project should be built are provided?

5. What type of contract has the most risk for the seller?

6. List three different procurement documents?

   1. _____
   2. _____
   3. _____

7. At what point in the procurement process is a make-or-buy decision made?

8. At what point in the procurement process is the contract managed?

9. Which comes first if it is done only once (each) on a project: Close Project or Contract Closure?

10. What are two disadvantages of using sole source or single source in the Select Sellers process?

PMP Exam Success Series: Certification Exam Manual
© 2007 Crosswind Project Management, Inc., www.crosswindpm.com

14.10.2   Procurement ITTO Matching Exercise

Match the correct ITTO term at the bottom of the page with the blanks to the right of the process. When a term is used multiple times, it is flagged by a parenthetical value indicating the number of times used. Also, match summary sentences with the process name that fits. Answers are in section 14.11.2.

	Inputs	Tools & Techniques	Outputs
Plan Purchases and Acquisitions	1) ___ 2) ___ 3) ___ 4) ___ 5) ___ 6) ___ 7) ___	1) ___ 2) ___ 3) ___	1) ___ 2) ___ 3) ___

Summary:

	Inputs	Tools & Techniques	Outputs
Plan Contracting	1) ___ 2) ___ 3) ___ 4) ___	1) ___ 2) ___	1) ___ 2) ___

Summary:

	Inputs	Tools & Techniques	Outputs
Request Seller Responses	1) ___ 2) ___	1) ___ 2) ___	1) ___ 2) ___

Summary:

	Inputs	Tools & Techniques	Outputs
Select Sellers	1) ___ 2) ___ 3) ___ 4) ___ 5) ___	1) ___ 2) ___ 3) ___ 4) ___ 5) ___	1) ___ 2) ___ 3) ___

Summary:

	Inputs	Tools & Techniques	Outputs
Contract Administration	1) ___ 2) ___ 3) ___ 4) ___	1) ___ 2) ___ 3) ___ 4) ___ 5) ___	1) ___ 2) ___ 3) ___ 4) ___

Summary:

	Inputs	Tools & Techniques	Outputs
Contract Closure	1) ___ 2) ___ 3) ___	1) ___	1) ___ 2) ___

Summary:

Deciding if services or products will be purchased or made
Managing the contract
Receiving proposals from potential sellers

Determining requirements and potential sellers
Determine who will provide the needed work
Closing the contract when needed

Approved Change Requests	Make-or-Buy Decisions	Project Management Plan (Project Schedule)
Bidders Conferences	Make-or-Buy Analysis	Project Management Plan (Resource Requirements)
Closed Contracts	Organizational Process Assets (Updates)	
Contract (2)	Payment System	Project Management Plan (Risk Register) (3)
Contract Change Control System	Performance Reporting	Project Scope Statement
Contract Documentation (2)	Performance Reports	Proposals (2)
Contract Management Plan (3)	Procurement Audits	Qualified Sellers List (2)
Contract Negotiation	Procurement Documents (2)	Records Management System
Contract Statement of Work (2)	Procurement Management Plan (5)	Requested Changes

(continued on next page)

Contract Types
Develop Qualified Sellers List
Evaluation Criteria (2)
Expert Judgment (3)
Independent Estimates
Inspections and Audits

PM Plan (Activity Cost Estimates) (2)
Project Management Plan (Updates)
    Contract Management Plan
Project Management Plan (Cost Baseline)
Project Management Plan (Updates)
    Procurement Management Plan

Screening System
Selected Sellers
Standard Forms
Weighting System
Work Breakdown Structure

14.10.3   Procurement Terminology Matching Exercise

Match the correct term in the left column to the correct definition in the right column. See the exercise answer section of this chapter for the correct answer. Answers are in section 14.11.3.

Matching Exercise #1

	Term	Answer	Definition
1	Bill of Materials (BOM)		A. An individual or company that provides goods or services to a company or individual
2	Contract		B. A contract in which a supplier is paid for direct and indirect cost actually incurred on the project
3	Contract Administration		C. The process of managing the relationship between buyer and seller
4	Cost-Plus-Fixed-Fee (CPFF) Contract		D. Documents involved in the bidding and proposal activities; can include request for information (RFI), request for quote (RFQ), or request for proposal (RFP) among others
5	Cost-Plus-Incentive-Fee (CPIF) Contract		E. A clause in the contract that allows both the buyer and seller to end the contract
6	Cost-Reimbursable (CR) Contract		F. A contract in which the seller provides products or services based on a well defined scope of work for a set price; also includes a fee structure that provides more payment for achieving predefined performance objectives
7	Fixed-Price-Incentive-Fee (FPIF) Contract		G. A document used to get bids or quotes form possible suppliers, usually for commodity type items, with minimal customization
8	Make-or-Buy Decision		H. A formal document showing the hierarchy of components or pieces and their sub-components or sub-pieces that make up the product
9	Procurement Documents (Output/Input)		I. A contract in which the supplier receives payment for allowable costs plus a fixed fee typically based on estimated cost
10	Project Procurement Management		J. A contract in which the supplier receives payment for allowable costs, as well as a pre-negotiated fee and an incentive fee (if incentives are met)
11	Request for Quote (RFQ)		K. An initial part of the procurement process in which a decision is made to either create the product by the company that needs it, or to outsource it and have another company create it
12	Request Seller Responses		L. Deciding on a supplier to implement the needed solution
13	Select Sellers		M. A mutually binding agreement that requires the services provider to supply the specified services or goods and requires the buyer to pay for them per the terms of the document
14	Seller		N. The process of receiving proposals, quotes, bids, etc. for needed services or products
15	Termination Clause		O. The process of attaining goods and services for a project from outside the organization

Matching Exercise #2

	Term	Answer	Definition
1	Contract Closure		A. A contract that pays a seller a fixed price for a well defined or detailed product or service
2	Cost-Plus-Percentage of Cost (CPPC) Contract		B. A contract that reimburses the seller for cost, plus a negotiated percentage of the total costs
3	Firm-Fixed-Price (FFP) Contract		C. Typically, a piece of the contract that details the work to be done
4	Fixed-Price/Lump-Sum Contract		D. The process of completing the contract; includes settlement on any open items
5	Issue		E. The acquisition of goods or services from an outside source (vendor)
6	Procurement		F. A document that describes what the buyer wants from a potential supplier, as well as criteria for acceptability of the vendor
7	Plan Purchases and Acquisitions		G. The process of determining what to buy and the optimum method to make the purchase
8	Request for Proposal (RFP)		H. A contract in which the seller provides products or services based on a well defined scope of work for a set price
9	Retainage		I. A project item causing confusion or disagreement, or an unresolved item needing attention
10	Plan Contracting		J. A part of the payment per the terms of the contract that the buyer retains until the project is complete; used to ensure that the seller completes the work per terms of the contract
11	Statement of Work (SOW)		K. The creation of product requirements and documentation

PMP Exam Success Series: Certification Exam Manual
© 2007 Crosswind Project Management, Inc., www.crosswindpm.com

14.10.4   Procurement Practice Test

Answers are in section 14.11.4.

1.   The project is using a company to provide the technicians for a national network upgrade project. Presently, the buyer is having issues with the seller accomplishing the work of the project according to the schedule in the contract. The buyer lets the seller know that it is in default for failure to execute per terms of the contract. The buyer also decides to stop payment for work already accomplished until the issue is resolved. What most accurately describes this situation?

(A) The buyer is right in stopping payment until the issue is resolved.
(B) The buyer is wrong in stopping payment until the issue is resolved.
(C) Both sides appear to be in default of the contract.
(D) The seller is wrong and needs to correct the situation.

2.   The contract is expected to cost $560K. Actual cost is $510K. There is a 50/50% share for any cost savings. What is the total value of the contract?

(A) $535K
(B) $510K
(C) $560K
(D) $610K

3.   You are the Project Manager working with the customer on a call center implementation. Your company is responsible for the call center infrastructure. The customer needs some modifications to the scope of the project due to some new functionality being available that wasn't available when the project started. This modification requires that the scope of work to the contract be modified. Who can modify the contract?

(A) The Project Manager for the buyer
(B) Contract administrator
(C) The Project Manager for the buyer and seller
(D) The Project Manager for the seller

4.   What type of contract exposes the seller to the most risk when entering into a contract?

(A) Fixed-price
(B) Cost-plus-percentage of cost
(C) Purchase order
(D) Time and materials

5.   Your company is involved in a new project in which the information and intellectual property associated with it are highly sensitive. Given this, which of the following makes the most sense when planning the project?

(A) Outsourcing and having the partner sign a non-disclosure agreement
(B) Having only the creators of the idea work on the project to control who knows about the intellectual property
(C) Outsourcing to an offshore development facility so your local competitors won't know your intellectual property details
(D) Making the product internally

6.   The project will be using a vendor to purchase network equipment for a national network upgrade project. The buyer of the equipment is providing the list of models and quantity of each piece of equipment that it wants to purchase. What type of document is being provided to the sellers?

(A) Request for information (RFI)
(B) Invitation for bid (IFB)
(C) Request for quote (RFQ)
(D) Request for proposal (RFP)

7.   You are purchasing 67 desktop computers, monitors, and a standard desktop software package for an upcoming project. What type of contract will you likely use?

(A) Purchase order
(B) Fixed-price
(C) Cost-plus-percentage of cost
(D) Net 30

8.   All the following are reasons for outsourcing work except...

(A) Your company doesn't possess the skills needed for the work.
(B) Your company doesn't have excessive capacity for the work.
(C) Your company isn't concerned about protecting the information associated with the work.
(D) Your company has excessive capacity for the work.

9.   Which of the following are examples of non-competitive forms of procurement?

(A) Qualified sellers list
(B) Single source
(C) Screening system
(D) Evaluation criteria

10. A city is buying services from a construction company to put in a new freeway for $4M over three years. At the start of each year, the amount fluctuates relative to the national cost of living. This is an example of what type of contract?

(A) Cost-plus
(B) Fixed-price-incentive-fee
(C) Fixed-price-economic-price-adjust
(D) Fixed-price

11. The project will be using a company to provide the technicians for a national network upgrade project. Presently, the team is negotiating a contract that will help select the vendor. In what process is the team involved?

    (A) Plan Purchases and Acquisitions
    (B) Plan Contracting
    (C) Request Seller Responses
    (D) Select Sellers

12. The project will be using a vendor to purchase a network solution for a national network upgrade project. The buyer of the solution is providing a list of requirements that the solution needs to be able to accomplish when the solution is complete. What type of scope of work is being provided to the sellers?

    (A) Functionality
    (B) Design
    (C) Analogous
    (D) Cost-plus

13. The project will be using a company to provide the technicians for a national network upgrade project. Presently, the team is in the middle of the execution of the contract. Both parties are communicating via status reports. The seller has submitted the first payment request. In what process is the team involved?

    (A) Plan Contracting
    (B) Request Seller Responses
    (C) Contract Administration
    (D) Select Sellers

14. Your company just completed a make-or-buy decision regarding a new area of development. The company has decided to buy the service. As a result of this decision, it is concerned about risk exposure in the contract type. Which type of contract would it prefer to use if it wants to control cost and minimize risk.

    (A) Purchase order
    (B) Unilateral order
    (C) Cost-plus-percentage of cost
    (D) Fixed-price

15. You are the Project Manager on a defense project. The buyer wants to get an idea on how much they will pay on cost overruns. With the following variables, calculate the point of total assumption: Expected Cost=$125,000; Expected Profit=$25,000; Target Price=$150,000; Buyer/Share Ratio=65/35%; Ceiling Price=$162,500; Maximum Overrun=130%.

    (A) $144,230.77
    (B) $137,019.23
    (C) $151,442.31
    (D) $129,807.69

16. The project will be using a company to provide the technicians for a national network upgrade project. The services buyer is providing to the prospective services sellers a greatly detailed description of what it wants the technicians to be able to do on the project. What type of scope of work is being provided to the sellers?

(A) Functionality
(B) Design
(C) Analogous
(D) Cost-plus

17. All the following items are needed to make a contract legal except...

(A) An offer
(B) Legal purpose
(C) Negotiation
(D) Consideration

18. The project will be using a company to provide the technicians for a national network upgrade project. The services buyer is providing to the prospective services sellers a greatly detailed description of what it wants the seller to be able to do on the project. What type of document is being provided to the sellers?

(A) Request for information (RFI)
(B) Request for proposals (RFP)
(C) Invitation for bid (IFB)
(D) Request for quote (RFQ)

19. You've hired a company to produce a video training series but aren't sure of the detail needed. You agree to pay the supplier for costs and a fee of $37K. What type of contract is this?

(A) Fixed-price
(B) Time and materials
(C) Cost-plus-fixed-fee
(D) Cost-plus

20. The project will be using a company to provide the technicians for a national network upgrade project. Presently, the team is negotiating a contract with potential vendors that will help select the vendor. They are negotiating criteria that will reward the technicians for getting done earlier than expected. This is a new type of approach the company is utilizing. What best described this type of criteria?

(A) Special provisions
(B) Standard terms
(C) Standard conditions
(D) Detailed negotiations

21. You are the Project Manager on a defense project. The buyer wants to get an idea on how much they will pay on cost overruns. With the following variables, calculate the point of total assumption: Expected Cost=$120,000; Expected Profit=$36,000; Target Price=$156,000; Buyer/Share Ratio=75/25%; Ceiling Price=$150,000; Maximum Overrun=125%.

    (A) $106,400.00
    (B) $112,000.00
    (C) $117,600.00
    (D) $100,800.00

22. You are the owner of a house painting company. You occasionally have the need for an automated paint sprayer. This tool sells for $1,250 and costs $20 a day to maintain. You can rent one for $150 a day with maintenance included. How many days would you need to use this tool before it makes sense to buy the tool instead of rent?

    (A) Twelve days
    (B) Six days
    (C) Ten days
    (D) Eight days

23. The project will be using a company to provide the technicians for a national network upgrade project. Presently, the team is determining the details needed for the documentation that will help select this vendor. This also includes evaluation criteria. In what process is the team involved?

    (A) Plan Purchases and Acquisitions
    (B) Plan Contracting
    (C) Request Seller Responses
    (D) Select Sellers

24. Why is a cost-plus-percentage of cost contract bad for the buyer?

    (A) It provides no reason for the seller to control cost.
    (B) It provides no reason for the buyer to control cost.
    (C) It requires the seller to audit all costs incurred.
    (D) It requires use of a more detailed request for proposal (RFP).

25. All the following are advantages of centralized contracting except...

    (A) Lack of career path for contract administrators
    (B) Career path for contract administrators
    (C) Contract administrators have teammates for contract-related support
    (D) Expertise in the contracting area

26. The project will be using a company to provide the technicians for a national network upgrade project. Presently, the team is meeting with potential vendors, showing them more details associated with the work of the project, as well as answering any questions they have about the work before their proposals are submitted. What is this called?

    (A) Request Seller Responses
    (B) Bidders Conference
    (C) Select Sellers
    (D) Request for Information

27. Your company is working with a staffing company for supplementing a technical writer for your newest project. The cost is $75 per hour. The technical writer will work on the project until it is complete, then the contract will end. What type of contract is this?

    (A) Cost-plus
    (B) Cost-plus-incentive-fee
    (C) Time and materials
    (D) Fixed-price

28. A single-phase medical software project is in the process of Closing. There are a number of processes coming together as things finish up. Which of the following is correct?

    (A) Contract Closure comes before Close Project.
    (B) Close Project happens only if the project is completed as planned.
    (C) Close Project and Contract Closure happen at the same time.
    (D) Close Project comes before Contract Closure.

29. You are the Project Manager on a defense project. The buyer wants to get an idea on how much they will pay on cost overruns. With the following variables, calculate the point of total assumption: Expected Cost=$150,000; Expected Profit=$37,500; Target Price=$187,500; Buyer/Share Ratio=60/40%; Ceiling Price=$225,000; Maximum Overrun=150%.

    (A) $201,875.00
    (B) $223,125.00
    (C) $212,500.00
    (D) $191,250.00

30. Which of the following best describes a unilateral contract?

    (A) The seller establishes a price, and the buyer simply has to purchase the item.
    (B) The buyer and seller establish contract parameters during a single negotiation session.
    (C) The buyer establishes a not-to-exceed price for the seller to accept or reject.
    (D) The seller establishes a not-to-exceed price for the buyer to accept or reject.

PMP Exam Success Series: Certification Exam Manual
© 2007 Crosswind Project Management, Inc., www.crosswindpm.com

14.11 Procurement Tests and Exercise Answers

14.11.1 Procurement Quick Test Answers

1. What type of contract is typically used for staff supplementation?

    Fixed-Price   (Time and Materials) Cost-Plus   Purchase Order
    [section 14.1.6]

2. A fixed-price contract typically requires what type of scope of work?

    General   Functional   (Design)   Industry Standard
    [section 14.1.6, section 14.1.9]

3. Which type of scope of work is used when the performance specifications are known?
    Functional [section 14.1.9]

4. Which type of scope of work is used when the precise details of how the product of the project should be built are provided?
    Design [section 14.1.9]

5. What type of contract has the most risk for the seller?
    Fixed-price [section 14.1.6]

6. List three different procurement documents?
    Request for proposal (RFP)/Request for tender (RFT)
    Request for information (RFI)
    Request for quote (RFQ)
    Invitation for bid (IFB)/Request for bid (RFB)
    Any of the above four are acceptable [section 14.2.1]

7. At what point in the procurement process is a make-or-buy decision made?
    Plan Purchases and Acquisitions [section 14.1, section 14.1.2]

8. At what point in the procurement process is the contract managed?
    Contract Administration [section 14.5]

9. Which comes first if they are only done once (each) on a project: Close Project or Contract Closure?
    Close Project [section 6.9, section 6.9.4, section 6.9.5]

10. What are two disadvantages of using sole source or single source in the Select Sellers process?
    Lack of a realistic controllable price
    Limited availability/supply
    [section 14.3.3]

14.11.2   Procurement ITTO Matching Exercise Answers

	Inputs	Tools & Techniques	Outputs
Plan Purchases and Acquisitions	1) Project Scope Statement	1) Make-or-Buy Analysis	1) Procurement Management Plan
	2) Work Breakdown Structure	2) Expert Judgment	2) Contract Statement of Work
	3) Project Management Plan (Risk Register)	3) Contract Types	3) Make-or-Buy Decisions
	4) Project Management Plan (Resource Requirements)		
	5) Project Management Plan (Project Schedule)		
	6) Project Management Plan (Activity Cost Estimates)		
	7) Project Management Plan (Cost Baseline)		
Summary:	Deciding if services or products will be purchased or made		
Plan Contracting	1) Procurement Management Plan	1) Standard Forms	1) Procurement Documents
	2) Contract Statement of Work	2) Expert Judgment	2) Evaluation Criteria
	3) Project Management Plan (Risk Register)		
	4) Project Management Plan (Activity Cost Estimates)		
Summary:	Determining requirements and potential sellers		
Request Seller Responses	1) Procurement Management Plan	1) Bidders Conferences	1) Qualified Sellers List
	2) Procurement Documents	2) Develop Qualified Sellers List	2) Proposals
Summary:	Receiving proposals from potential sellers		
Select Sellers	1) Procurement Management Plan	1) Weighting System	1) Selected Sellers
	2) Evaluation Criteria	2) Independent Estimates	2) Contract
	3) Proposals	3) Screening System	3) Contract Management Plan
	4) Qualified Sellers List	4) Contract Negotiation	
	5) Project Management Plan (Risk Register)	5) Expert Judgment	
Summary:	Determine who will provide the needed work		
Contract Administration	1) Contract	1) Contract Change Control System	1) Contract Documentation
	2) Contract Management Plan	2) Inspections and Audits	2) Requested Changes
	3) Performance Reports	3) Performance Reporting	3) Project Management Plan (Updates) Procurement Management Plan
	4) Approved Change Requests	4) Payment System	
		5) Records Management System	4) Project Management Plan (Updates) Contract Management Plan
Summary:	Managing the contract		
Contract Closure	1) Procurement Management Plan	1) Procurement Audits	1) Closed Contracts
	2) Contract Management Plan		2) Organizational Process Assets (Updates)
	3) Contract Documentation		
Summary:	Closing the contract when needed		

14.11.3   Procurement Terminology Matching Exercise Answers

Matching Exercise #1 Answers

	Term	Definition
1	Bill of Materials (BOM)	H. A formal document showing the hierarchy of components or pieces and their sub-components or sub-pieces that make up the product
2	Contract	M. A mutually binding agreement that requires the services provider to supply the specified services or goods and requires the buyer to pay for them per the terms of the document
3	Contract Administration	C. The process of managing the relationship between buyer and seller
4	Cost-Plus-Fixed-Fee (CPFF) Contract	I. A contract in which the supplier receives payment for allowable costs plus a fixed fee typically based on estimated cost
5	Cost-Plus-Incentive-Fee (CPIF)Contract	J. A contract in which the supplier receives payment for allowable costs, as well as a pre-negotiated fee and an incentive fee (if incentives are met)
6	Cost-Reimbursable (CR) Contract	B. A contract in which a supplier is paid for direct and indirect cost actually incurred on the project
7	Fixed-Price-Incentive-Fee (FPIF) Contract	F. A contract in which the seller provides products or services based on a well defined scope of work for a set price; also includes a fee structure that provides more payment for achieving predefined performance objectives
8	Make-or-Buy Decision	K. An initial part of the procurement process in which a decision is made to either create the product by the company that needs it, or to outsource it and have another company create it
9	Procurement Documents (Output/Input)	D. Documents involved in the bidding and proposal activities; can include request for information (RFI), request for quote (RFQ), or request for proposal (RFP) among others
10	Project Procurement Management	O. The process of attaining goods and services for a project from outside the organization
11	Request for Quote (RFQ)	G. A document used to get bids or quotes form possible suppliers, usually for commodity type items, with minimal customization
12	Request Seller Responses	N. The process of receiving proposals, quotes, bids, etc. for needed services or products
13	Select Sellers	L. Deciding on a supplier to implement the needed solution
14	Seller	A. An individual or company that provides goods or services to a company or individual
15	Termination Clause	E. A clause in the contract that allows both the buyer and seller to be able to end the contract

Matching Exercise #2 Answers

	Term	Definition
1	Contract Closure	D. The process of completing the contract; includes settlement on any open items
2	Cost-Plus-Percentage of Cost (CPPC) Contract	B. A contract that reimburses the seller for costs, plus a negotiated percentage of the total costs
3	Firm-Fixed-Price (FFP) Contract	A. A contract that pays a seller a fixed price for a well defined or detailed product or service (Answer H is also acceptable here)
4	Fixed-Price/Lump-Sum Contract	H. A contract in which the seller provides products or services based on a well defined scope of work for a set price (Answer A is also acceptable here)
5	Issue	I. A project item causing confusion or disagreement, or an unresolved item needing attention
6	Procurement	E. The acquisition of goods or services from an outside source (vendor)
7	Plan Purchases and Acquisitions	G. The process of determining what to buy and the optimum method to make the purchase

8	Request for Proposal (RFP)	F. A document that describes what the buyer wants from a potential supplier, as well as criteria for acceptability of the vendor
9	Retainage	J. A part of the payment per the terms of the contract that the buyer retains until the project is complete; used to ensure that the seller completes the work per terms of the contract
10	Plan Contracting	K. The creation of product requirements and documentation
11	Statement of Work (SOW)	C. Typically, a piece of the contract that details the work to be done

14.11.4   Procurement Practice Test Answers

1.   The project is using a company to provide the technicians for a national network upgrade project. Presently, the buyer is having issues with the seller accomplishing the work of the project according to the schedule in the contract. The buyer lets the seller know that it is in default for failure to execute per terms of the contract. The buyer also decides to stop payment for work already accomplished until the issue is resolved. What most accurately describes this situation?

Correct Answer: (C) Both sides appear to be in default of the contract.
Explanation: A seller who fails to perform as defined in the contract is in default of the contract. The buyer choosing to stop payment creates a default situation as well. Two wrongs do not make a right in this case. The buyer is not right in stopping payment just because the other side is in default. The other answers are both accurate, but they are not the best answer. [section 14.4.6]

2.   The contract is expected to cost $560K. Actual cost is $510K. There is a 50/50% share for any cost savings. What is the total value of the contract?

Correct Answer: (A) $535K
Explanation: This is a calculation question. The $560K is the expected value of the contract. Actual cost of the contract is $510K. This means that there is $50K saved. The 50/50% share means that $25K of the savings go to the seller. The actual cost of $510K and $25K saving share makes the total value of the contract worth $535K. [section 14.1.7]

3.   You are the Project Manager working with the customer on a call center implementation. Your company is responsible for the call center infrastructure. The customer needs some modifications to the scope of the project due to some new functionality being available that wasn't available when the project started. This modification requires that the scope of work to the contract be modified. Who can modify the contract?

Correct Answer: (B) Contract Administrator
Explanation: The Contract Administrator is the only person with the authority to change the contract. The Project Managers from the buyer and the seller will likely have input to the changes, but the Contract Administrator is the person making those changes to the contract. [section 14.5.1]

4.   What type of contract exposes the seller to the most risk when entering into a contract?

Correct Answer: (A) Fixed-price
Explanation: The fixed-price contract has the most risk for the seller because the contract limits the amount that the buyer will pay for the project. The seller must have a detailed understanding of exactly what is needed on the project so it can control cost. Cost-plus-percentage of cost provides the least risk to the seller. A purchase order provides the seller with no risk because the price for a commodity type item has been established. Time and materials contracts are typically used for smaller amounts of work and staff augmentation. [section 14.1.6]

PMP Exam Success Series: Certification Exam Manual
© 2007 Crosswind Project Management, Inc., www.crosswindpm.com

5.   Your company is involved in a new project in which the information and intellectual property associated with it are highly sensitive. Given this, which of the following makes the most sense when planning the project?

Correct Answer: (D) Making the product internally

Explanation: When intellectual property and proprietary information are involved, it makes sense for a company to keep the work internal. Having an outsourcing partner sign a non-disclosure agreement is not the best answer. The other answers are noise. [section 14.1.2]

6.   The project will be using a vendor to purchase network equipment for a national network upgrade project. The buyer of the equipment is providing the list of models and quantity of each piece of equipment that they want to purchase. What type of document is being provided to the sellers?

Correct Answer: (C) Request for quote (RFQ)

Explanation: A request for quotes (RFQ) obtains prices from a company for goods or services. A request for proposal (RFP) deals with a detailed, very specific approach to a customized solution. A request for information (RFI) deals with finding potential vendors for consideration for proposals or quotes. An invitation for bid (IFB) is similar to the RFP but is typically used in government contracting. [section 14.2.1]

7.   You are purchasing 67 desktop computers, monitors, and a standard desktop software package for an upcoming project. What type of contract will you likely use?

Correct Answer: (A) Purchase order

Explanation: The purchase order is a general purchase vehicle for commodity type purchases. Typically, it is for items that are standard, non-customized, and non-negotiable in price. Fixed-price is typically for a detailed, customized, negotiated solution. Cost-plus-percentage of cost is an outdated contract type, and not good for the buyer. "Net 30" is noise. [section 14.1.6]

8.   All the following are reasons for outsourcing work except…

Correct Answer: (D) Your company has excessive capacity for the work.

Explanation: Excessive capacity to do work is a good reason not to outsource the work. The other answers are good reasons to outsource the work. [section 14.1.2]

9.   Which of the following are examples of non-competitive forms of procurement?

Correct Answer: (B) Single source

Explanation: One type of non-competitive forms of procurement is single source, in which a single company is chosen even though others are available. The other form is sole source, in which there is only one source available. Generally, the provider possesses a patent or some other type of ownership associated with intellectual property. The other answers are noise. [section 14.3.3]

10.   A city is buying services from a construction company to put in a new freeway for $4M over three years. At the start of each year, the amount fluctuates relative to the national cost of living. This is an example of what type of contract?

Correct Answer: (C) Fixed-price-economic-price-adjust

Explanation: A fixed-price-economic-price-adjust contract deals with offering a contract that generally has a fixed price, but because of contract length, will adjust year-by-year as a neutral economic indicator moves upward or downward. The fixed-price contract has a seller doing work for a set price. The cost-plus contract pays a seller costs plus a negotiated fee. The fixed-price-incentive-fee pays a seller a fixed price plus an incentive fee for meeting performance goals. [section 14.1.6]

11. The project will be using a company to provide the technicians for a national network upgrade project. Presently, the team is negotiating a contract that will help select the vendor. In what process is the team involved?

Correct Answer: (D) Select Sellers
Explanation: Select Sellers involves choosing the company to do the work. Plan Purchases and Acquisitions involves a make-or-buy analysis to determine if the company will do the work itself or outsource it. Plan Contracting determines the approach to find a company who can do the work for you. Request Seller Responses handles the receipt and review of proposals from companies being considered for the work. [section 14.4]

12. The project will be using a vendor to purchase a network solution for a national network upgrade project. The buyer of the solution is providing a list of requirements that the solution needs to be able to accomplish when the solution is complete. What type of scope of work is being provided to the sellers?

Correct Answer: (A) Functionality
Explanation: The functionality scope of work shows the general functional specifications that the outcome of the project needs to have when complete. A design scope of work shows specifically what is to be created. Cost-plus and analogous are noise. [section 14.1.9]

13. The project will be using a company to provide the technicians for a national network upgrade project. Presently, the team is in the middle of the execution of the contract. Both parties are communicating via status reports. The seller has submitted the first payment request. In what process is the team involved?

Correct Answer: (C) Contract Administration
Explanation: Contract Administration manages the contract. Plan Contracting determines the approach to find a company who can do the work for you. Request Seller Responses handles the receipt and review of proposals from companies being considered for the work. Select Sellers involves choosing the company to do the work. [section 14.5]

14. Your company just completed a make-or-buy decision regarding a new area of development. The company has decided to buy the service. As a result of this decision, it is concerned about risk exposure in the contract type. Which type of contract would it prefer to use if it wants to control cost and minimize risk.

Correct Answer: (D) Fixed-price
Explanation: The fixed-price contract puts a maximum on cost and should provide the minimum risk exposure to the buyer because the maximum risk is absorbed by the seller. Cost-plus-percentage of cost has a great risk and no cost control for the buyer. Purchase orders are typically used to purchase commodity type items. "Unilateral order" is noise. [section 14.1.6]

15. You are the Project Manager on a defense project. The buyer wants to get an idea on how much they will pay on cost overruns. With the following variables, calculate the point of total assumption: Expected Cost=$125,000; Expected Profit=$25,000; Target Price=$150,000; Buyer/Share Ratio=65/35%; Ceiling Price=$162,500; Maximum Overrun=130%.

Correct Answer: (A) $144,230.77
Explanation: The formula for point of total assumption (PTA) is as follows:
((Ceiling Price-Target Price)/Buyer Share)+Target Cost.
$144,230.77 = ($162,500 - $150,000)/0.65 + $125,000
[section 14.1.8, section 14.7]

16.   The project will be using a company to provide the technicians for a national network upgrade project. The services buyer is providing to the prospective services sellers a greatly detailed description of what it wants the technicians to be able to do on the project. What type of scope of work is being provided to the sellers?

Correct Answer: (B) Design
Explanation: A design scope of work shows specifically what is to be created. The functionality scope of work shows the general functional specifications that the outcome of the project needs to have when complete. Cost-plus and analogous are noise. [section 14.1.9]

17.   All the following items are needed to make a contract legal except…

Correct Answer: (C) Negotiation
Explanation: Negotiation is not needed to make a contract legal. If the buyer and seller are in agreement on the offer and consideration, negotiation is not required. The other answers are all required to make a contract legal. [section 14.1.4]

18.   The project will be using a company to provide the technicians for a national network upgrade project. The services buyer is providing to the prospective services sellers a greatly detailed description of what it wants the seller to be able to do on the project. What type of document is being provided to the sellers?

Correct Answer: (B) Request for Proposals (RFP)
Explanation: A request for proposals (RFP) deals with a detailed, very specific approach to a customized solution. A request for information (RFI) deals with finding potential vendors for consideration for proposals or quotes. A request for quotes obtains prices from a company for goods or services. An invitation for bid (IFB) is similar to the RFP but typically used in government contracting. [section 14.2.1]

19.   You've hired a company to produce a video training series but aren't sure of the detail needed. You agree to pay the supplier for costs and a fee of $37K. What type of contract is this?

Correct Answer: (C) Cost-plus-fixed-fee
Explanation: The cost-plus-fixed-fee pays a seller costs plus a negotiated fixed fee. A time and materials (T&M) contract is typically used for smaller projects or staff augmentation. The fixed-price contract has a seller doing work for a set price. The cost-plus contract pays a seller costs plus a negotiated fee. [section 14.1.6]

20.   The project will be using a company to provide the technicians for a national network upgrade project. Presently, the team is negotiating a contract with potential vendors that will help select the vendor. They are negotiating criteria that will reward the technicians for getting done earlier than expected. This is a new type of approach the company is utilizing. What best described this type of criteria?

Correct Answer: (A) Special provisions
Explanation: Special provisions are extra items that are added to a contract after negotiations have occurred. Standard terms and conditions are typically part of a template the company will use in a contract. "Detailed negotiation" is noise. [section 14.4.5]

21.   You are the Project Manager on a defense project. The buyer wants to get an idea on how much they will pay on cost overruns. With the following variables, calculate the point of total assumption: Expected Cost=$120,000; Expected Profit=$36,000; Target Price=$156,000; Buyer/Share Ratio=75/25%; Ceiling Price=$150,000; Maximum Overrun=125%.

Correct Answer: (B) $112,000.00
Explanation: The formula for point of total assumption (PTA) is as follows:
((Ceiling Price-Target Price)/Buyer Share)+Target Cost.
$112,000.00 = ($150,000 - $156,000)/0.75 + $120,000
[section 14.1.8, section 14.7]

22. You are the owner of a house painting company. You occasionally have the need for an automated paint sprayer. This tool sells for $1,250 and costs $20 a day to maintain. You can rent one for $150 a day with maintenance included. How many days would you need to use this tool before it makes sense to buy the tool instead of rent?

Correct Answer: (C) Ten days
Explanation: To complete this question, solve for the number of days. The number of days is the variable D in the formula. $1,250+20D=$150D is the formula. First, move D to one side of the equation. Subtracting $20D from both sides gives $1,250=$130D. Next, divide both sides by 130, which isolates D. That equals 9.6 (rounded up), which means you would need to use the tool for ten full days before it makes sense to buy the tool. [section 14.1.2, section 14.7]

23. The project will be using a company to provide the technicians for a national network upgrade project. Presently, the team is determining the details needed for the documentation that will help select this vendor. This also includes evaluation criteria. In what process is the team involved?

Correct Answer: (B) Plan Contracting
Explanation: Plan Contracting determines the approach to find a company that can do the work. Select Sellers involves choosing the company to do the work. Plan Purchases and Acquisitions involves a make-or-buy analysis to determine if the company will do the work itself or outsource it. Request Seller Responses handles the receipt and review of proposals from companies being considered for the work. [section 14.2]

24. Why is a cost-plus-percentage of cost contract bad for the buyer?

Correct Answer: (A) It provides no reason for the seller to control cost.
Explanation: In a cost-plus-percentage of cost contract, the seller is paid a fee that is a percentage of the total cost. As a result of this characteristic of the contract, there is no incentive for the seller to control cost. The other answers are noise. [section 14.1.6]

25. All the following are advantages of centralized contracting except...

Correct Answer: (A) Lack of career path for contract administrators
Explanation: Centralized contracting provides a functional type of environment for the role, meaning that there is a career path for the person, instead of a lack of career path. The other answers fit the description of advantages for centralized contracting. [section 14.5.3, section 5.6.3]

26. The project will be using a company to provide the technicians for a national network upgrade project. Presently, the team is meeting with potential vendors, showing them more details associated with the work of the project, as well as answering any questions they have about the work before their proposals are submitted. What is this called?

Correct Answer: (B) Bidders Conference
Explanation: A bidders conference lets companies that are considering bidding on a project learn more about the project work and ask questions. The questions and answers are made available to all considering bidding for the work. Request Seller Responses is a process to find companies that can do the work. Request for information is a procurement document. Select Sellers involves making a decision on who will do the work on the project. [section 14.3.2]

27. Your company is working with a staffing company for supplementing a technical writer for your newest project. The cost is $75 per hour. The technical writer will work on the project until it is complete, then the contract will end. What type of contract is this?

    Correct Answer: (C) Time and materials
    Explanation: A time and materials contract is typically used for smaller projects or staff augmentation, such as this example. The fixed-price contract has a seller doing work for a set price. The cost-plus contract pays a seller costs plus a negotiated fee. The cost-plus-incentive-fee pays a seller costs plus an incentive fee for meeting performance goals. [section 14.1.6]

28. A single-phase medical software project is in the process of Closing. There are a number of processes coming together as things finish up. Which of the following is correct?

    Correct Answer: (D) Close Project comes before Contract Closure.
    Explanation: In a single-phase project, the phase (or project) is closed out before the Contract Closure process. If a project has multiple phases, they are closed out before Contract Closure (unless the contract was completed before that). Close Project happens regardless of how the project ends. [section 6.9.4]

29. You are the Project Manager on a defense project. The buyer wants to get an idea on how much they will pay on cost overruns. With the following variables, calculate the point of total assumption: Expected Cost=$150,000; Expected Profit=$37,500; Target Price=$187,500; Buyer/Share Ratio=60/40%; Ceiling Price=$225,000; Maximum Overrun=150%.

    Correct Answer: (C) $212,500.00
    Explanation: The formula for point of total assumption (PTA) is as follows:
    ((Ceiling Price-Target Price)/Buyer Share)+Target Cost.
    $212,500.00 = ($225,000 - $187,500)/0.6 + $150,000
    [section 14.1.8, section 14.7]

30. Which of the following best describes a unilateral contract?

    Correct Answer: (A) The seller establishes a price, and the buyer simply has to purchase the item.
    Explanation: In a unilateral contract, the seller establishes a price and the buyer has the option to purchase at that price. Thus, *uni* means one-sided on the negotiations. The other answers are noise. [section 14.1.6]

Chapter 15

Professional and Social Responsibility

Success at understanding this chapter does not come from using a calculator. Success comes from a solid foundation in values and ethics. As a person involved in project management, you must be willing and prepared to do what is proper and principled in every facet of your life, personally and professionally, whether at work or at home.

PMP Code of Professional Conduct and the Code of Ethics and Professional Conduct

As of the current printing of this book, PMI has evolved its *PMP Code of Professional Conduct* into a more comprehensive *Code of Ethics and Professional Conduct*. Although these new standards and guidelines are not yet reflected in the PMP Examination, we are introducing them now to prepare you for the impending cutover to the new guiding principles for project management professionals.

Until that time, the previous code remains essential to the current exam and can be summarized with its major points below. These valuable points are elaborated and described in constructive detail throughout this chapter.

I.   Responsibilities to the Profession
    a.   Compliance with all organizational rules and policies: You agree to provide accurate information to PMI regarding examination and requirements.
    b.   Candidate/Certificant Professional Practice: You agree to abide by all federal and local laws and regulations governing professional practice. You agree to act ethically and honestly when providing project management services.
    c.   Advancement of the Profession: You agree to respect the intellectual property of others, to act responsibly, and to support others in the profession and those who aspire to it.

II.   Responsibilities to Customers and the Public
    a.   Qualifications, experience, and performance of professional service: You agree to be accurate and truthful in all statements and reports with regard to your PM services. You agree to meet scope objectives and respect confidential information.
    b.   Conflict of interest situations and other prohibited professional conduct: You agree to ensure that a conflict of interest does not compromise the legitimate interests of the customer and does not influence your professional judgment.

III.   Administration of Code of Conduct: You agree to abide by the code and you acknowledge that a code violation could prompt PMI to revoke your PMP credentials.

☑	**Crosswind "Must Knows" For Professional and Social Responsibility**
	PMI Code of Ethics and Professional Conduct
	The need and benefit of helping team members gain more knowledge and experience
	How to behave responsibly and communicate accurate information to the appropriate party on a project even if the project is not going as planned

	The basics of problem solving (see Framework and Human Resource chapters)
	The importance of growing project management as a profession
	The importance of being flexible and professional with the team and stakeholders
	How to balance stakeholder interests (See Framework chapter)
	What a conflict of interest is and how to recognize it
	What to do if you note a company policy or government/law violation

Although helpful, this list is not all-inclusive for information needed from this area for the exam. It is only suggested material that, if understood and memorized, can increase your exam score.

15.1   Code of Ethics and Professional Conduct

PMI has developed the *Code of Ethics and Professional Conduct,* which explains what is expected of you as a Project Manager or other practitioner of project management. This document covers four values that a consensus of the global project management community deemed most significant and vital to the profession. These values are:

- Responsibility
- Respect
- Fairness
- Honesty

As of this printing, the document is located on the PMI Web site at http://www.pmi.org/prod/groups/public/documents/info/ap_pmicodeofethics.pdf. If PMI changes the link, search for "ethics" at www.pmi.org to find the document.

15.1.1   Applicability

This code applies to all PMI members and any non-member who holds a PMI certification, applies for certification, or volunteers for PMI. You must agree to abide by this code and uphold its values. You must establish ethical expectations for yourself and for others with the understanding that your conduct impacts the integrity and character of project management as a profession.

15.1.2   Growing Project Management as a Profession

One objective of the code is to build upon and evolve project management as a profession. It is important that we enlighten others about project management and its benefits, whether those others be within an entire industry or at your company.

There are, however, some who consider the PMP Examination the apex of their project management growth -- they have completed the exam and can cease the effort to mature as Project Managers. But it is imperative that Project Management Professionals pursue their own professional growth through Professional Development Units and continue their efforts to grow project management as a profession. Growing project management as a profession could include any of the following or more:

Understand the importance of growing project management as a profession.

- Writing papers on project management and related topics
- Explaining the value of project management to those who do not see or understand it
- Training people on project management
- Showing people how project management can help solve problems on projects at work
- Helping mentor others who want to learn more about project management

15.1.3   Helping Team Members Gain Experience and Knowledge

Understand the need and benefit of helping team members gain more knowledge and experience.

As a Project Manager, you are in a key position to influence the future of project team members. Depending on how you treat people, you could be the type of person who tries to help others grow to all that they can be, or you could keep them under control, letting them do what they always have, not giving them a chance to grow.

The first priority of the project is to accomplish the work of the project, per the defined goals. As that is being achieved, you can take into consideration the goals of those on the team, and you exercise professional and social responsibility by helping those people gain experience and knowledge based on the work and activities on the project. Doing so is not always an option because the project might not be able to allow it to happen. But when it is reasonable, you should make a conscious effort to help those on the team grow and develop with regard to experience and knowledge in the workplace, in their technical discipline, and if they are interested in project management as well.

15.2   Responsibility

Responsibility is a standard that addresses accountability, behavior, and reliability. You do what you say you will do. You accept only those assignments for which you are qualified. You honor the confidence placed in you and protect the interests of the company or other project stakeholders. If you make a mistake, you acknowledge the error, accept liability, and take action to resolve the issues and impacts.

15.2.1   Company Policy, Government, Law, or Standards

Know what to do if you note a company policy or government/law violation.

It is expected that employees of the company follow policies when such policies do not violate city, state, or federal law. A policy is not as strict as a law.

Reporting violations is a key aspect of professional and social responsibility. If something wrong is going on, you are obligated to report it. This reporting could be at the company, government, or legal level.

At the **company level**, reporting includes violations associated with **company policies**. For example, it may be against company policy to use the company shipping account for shipping personal merchandise. If you as the Project Manager discovered that this was happening, it is your responsibility to report it to the appropriate person at the company. There is **the assumption that the person** using the account for personal use **knew it was wrong or should have known better.**

At the **government level**, reporting includes **violations of city, county, state, or country laws.** Reporting at this level is more complicated than at the company level in that an action which is a violation at one level may be out of scope (jurisdiction) at another. This inconsistency rarely happens, but what can come into play here is jurisdiction. **Jurisdiction in non-legal speak means who presides over the enforcement of the violation.** Some examples are as follows:

If a music store were modifying its building by adding flooring and a new room without a required building permit, it is in violation of a city law.

If a business failed to pay state income tax for a state in which it does business, that business is in violation of a state tax law.

15.2.2   Respecting Intellectual Property, Professional Work, and Research

Much of the industry in which Project Managers work today deals with cutting edge information and ideas or, at a minimum, information that provides the company which owns it a competitive advantage. Respecting intellectual property, including copyrights, patents, and trademarked information is key for a PMP when practicing professional and social responsibility.

If you have signed a non-disclosure agreement (NDA) about certain information, you must follow it as it relates to that information and who can share in it. This NDA can include patented engineering and software, copyrighted publishing and writing, and trademarks associated with branding and names. Just because someone else copies it or violates the law doesn't mean you should.

15.2.3   Truthful and Accurate Reporting as it Relates to PMP Certification and the Certification Process

The experience, education, and training required for the PMP Certification exam are serious matters. It is unfortunate that some people don't take them as seriously as they should. When qualifying for the exam, you are expected to report accurate information in this area. If you know of someone who is not reporting accurate information, you should report the activity to PMI for corrective action.

Remember, advising people to stretch their qualifications is just as bad as stretching the qualifications yourself.

What do you do in the following situation? You become aware of someone who is expected to have each person in his PMO certified as a PMP. Someone working in the PMO as a Project Expeditor is only 21 years old and presently attending junior college. In other words, this person lacks a bachelor's degree. You learn that this person has just passed the PMP Examination. Besides wondering how this person qualified to take the test, what should you do? See the next topic.

15.2.4   Reporting of the PMI Code of Ethics and Professional Conduct

The PMI Code of Ethics and Professional Conduct describes the standards to which a project management practitioner is to be held, as well as acceptable and unacceptable behavior guidelines. If you know any intentional violation associated with the code of conduct, you are expected to alert PMI with their details. If the violation is accidental, you would likely bring it to the person's attention first, and if it were repeated (after being corrected originally), you would contact PMI.

Know and understand the PMI Code of Ethics and Professional Conduct.

15.2.5   Cooperating with PMI Regarding Information Associated with Ethics Violations

If PMI requests that you work with its staff providing information associated with a PMI Code of Ethics and Professional Conduct violation, you are expected to answer any and all questions they ask and supply all information you have that is associated with the potential violation.

15.3   Respect

Respect is a standard that revolves around a commitment to show esteem and consideration for yourself, for others, and for the resources entrusted to you.

You recognize others, their values, and their differences. You listen and learn to gain an understanding of various points of view and diverse perspectives. You hold yourself to high principles, conducting yourself professionally and dealing with conflict or disagreement in a positive direct approach. You negotiate in good faith and avoid taking advantage of others. You establish a positive and productive environment that fosters mutual cooperation to ultimately build trust, confidence, and performance excellence.

15.3.1   Cultural Sensitivity and Differences

Today, we work in a global environment and are exposed to a variety of cultures and lifestyles every day. Before these differences manifest themselves on a project, you have a responsibility as Project Manager to minimize culture shock and maximize the potential for the various cultures and lifestyles that make up the project. It is not uncommon to factor these into team-building events because this exposure can help educate those not familiar with the specifics of different cultures.

15.3.2   Professional Practice

As a PMP, you are expected to practice the art and skills of project management professionally as well as interact with others in a professional way. You are expected to show the professionalism similar to that of a CPA or doctor. PMP is not a position for the immature. Most PMPs are seasoned professionals.

15.3.3   Interpretation of the PMI Code of Ethics and Professional Conduct to Other PMPs and Candidates

Anything is open to interpretation. If you see someone stretching the rules associated with professional and social responsibility, it's your job to suggest that this person "review" what he or she is considering. For example: Someone was preparing to report that a project had a CPI of 1.18 when your company has never had a project hit a CPI of 1.0. You discover there is no way to realistically track earned value (a key component to the CPI). What would you think if you received that report and were told the status was accurate? This is an example of irresponsible reporting and for failing to let the person know he or she should review what is being reported as accurate in calculation.

15.4   Fairness

Fairness is a standard that governs how you make decisions without prejudice or favoritism and how you interact with others with equity and sincerity. You should set your own interests aside and open opportunities equally for all candidates and suggestions that advance the project toward its goal.

15.4.1   Sensitivity to Conflict of Interest or the Perception of Inappropriate Activities

According to PMI, it is unacceptable to be involved in a conflict of interest. It does nothing but hurt all parties involved. The perception of a conflict of interest can be just as damaging, even if no harm has been done (because no actual conflict existed). Companies usually have policies defining what constitutes a conflict of interest, and they expect their employees to follow them.

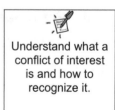

Understand what a conflict of interest is and how to recognize it.

If you are on a vendor selection committee and you just learned from your brother (whom you haven't had any contact with in 10 years) that he has accepted a new job as a sales executive at a company currently in the running for project selection by your company, what do you do? Has anything wrong happened? Does anyone suspect anything wrong could be happening?

Try this one…A vendor is implementing software at your company. The project is discovered to be running behind schedule. It is up to you to decide if this delay is acceptable. The company providing the services offers you a complimentary week-long trip to an industry trade show in Las Vegas. Is anything wrong? Do you accept this? What do they expect if you do?

In both cases, there are a number of ways you could look at these. There are also a number of ways that someone could see them differently from how you did. Does your brother's company have an unfair advantage? Should you remove yourself from the selection? What will others in your company think if they discover this relationship or if you stay on the committee after it is discovered?

What does the second situation sound like? The vendor is going to come in late, and as a result of your tolerance, offers you a free vacation? Regardless of intent, it doesn't look good.

The perception of a conflict of interest is just as bad as a conflict of interest itself. Remove yourself from a situation when your involvement could be perceived badly. Let people know up front about any potential conflict and let them make the decision on what to do.

15.5   Honesty

Honesty is a standard that encourages truthfulness in both communications and conduct. You must report information accurately and in a timely manner, without withholding any details that impact the outcome. When you commit to something, do so in good faith. You also need to nurture a safe environment that invites frank communication and open candor.

15.5.1   Maintain and Satisfy the Scope and Other Parameters of Work, Unless the Customer Requests Differently

It is the responsibility of the PMP to report accurate status on a project or work-related activities. If the project or work is going well or in bad shape, the reporting should be accurate and timely. If a project is in bad shape, you are professionally responsible when you report that status as soon as you know it. Some companies have a "Kill the messenger" mentality, in which the bearer of bad news feels the pressure when bad news is reported. Regardless of that, you are obligated to report timely, accurate, and honest status and facts about a project.

Know how to behave responsibly and communicate accurate information to the appropriate party on a project even if the project is not going as planned.

15.6   Formulas and Variables

No formulas or variables for professional and social responsibility

15.7   Professional and Social Responsibility Terminology

Term	Description
Company Policy	A standard established by a company
Confidentiality	The act of not providing certain confidential information to those who should not know about it
Conflict of Interest	A situation in which an individual or company engages in behavior that is inappropriate, but not necessarily illegal (it could be illegal)
Copyright	The process that protects the ownership rights of writing, songs, and other "creative" works; can include software, music, physical and electronic media.
Ethics	The standards we use to determine what is right and wrong; varies for everyone
Government	An organization that represents and manages an area The area can be a city, state, or country. In the United States, the federal government runs the country. Each state is responsible for operating the state. There can be city, state, or federal laws.
Inappropriate Compensation	Money or other items of value that are "earned" via improper activities
Intellectual Property	Ideas and concepts created by an individual or company, typically eligible for copyright or patent, thus providing ownership properties
Law	A standard created by a government (e.g., city, state, or country) that requires people and companies to follow it or the behavior is illegal
Non-Disclosure Agreement (NDA)	A document signed by the owner of intellectual property and those who view it when it is not generally exposed to the public, or if it is a new idea, before it is displayed to the public
Patent	A legal device which gives ownership of an idea or design to an individual or company that creates the idea or design
PMI Code of Ethics and Professional Conduct	A standard that PMI requires candidates to agree to before they take the PMP Examination
Professional and Social Responsibility	Ethics expected in Project Managers; includes balancing stakeholder interests and reporting violations

15.8   Professional and Social Responsibility Questions

15.8.1   Professional and Social Responsibility Terminology Matching Exercise
Match the correct term in the left column to the correct definition in the right column. See the exercise answer section of this chapter for the correct answer. Answers are in section 15.9.1.

Matching Exercise

	Term	Answer	Definition
1	Company Policy		A. Money or other items of value that are "earned" via improper activities
2	Confidentiality		B. The process that protects the ownership rights of writing, songs, and other "creative" works; can include software, music, physical and electronic media
3	Conflict of Interest		C. A standard created by a government (e.g., city, state, or country) that requires people and companies to follow it, or the behavior is illegal
4	Copyright		D. The act of not providing certain confidential information to those who should not know about it
5	Ethics		E. A legal device which gives ownership of an idea or design to an individual or company that creates the idea or design
6	Government		F. A standard established by a company
7	Inappropriate Compensation		G. A standard that PMI requires candidates to agree to before they take the PMP Examination
8	Intellectual Property		H. A document signed by the owner of intellectual property and those who view it when it is not generally exposed to the public, or if it is a new idea, before it is displayed to the public
9	Law		I. An organization that represents and manages an area The area can be a city, state, or country. In the United States, the federal government runs the country. Each state is responsible for operating the state. There can be city, state, or federal laws.
10	Non-Disclosure Agreement (NDA)		J. Ideas and concepts created by an individual or company, typically eligible for copyright or patent, thus providing ownership properties
11	Patent		K. The standards we use to determine what is right and wrong; varies for everyone
12	PMI Code of Ethics and Professional Conduct		L. A situation in which an individual or company engages in behavior that is inappropriate, but not necessarily illegal (it could be illegal)
13	Professional and Social Responsibility		M. Ethics expected in Project Managers; includes balancing stakeholder interests and reporting violations

15.8.2   Professional and Social Responsibility Questions

Answers are in section 15.9.2.

1.   You are a Project Manager involved in the procurement of $2,000,000 of infrastructure equipment. As negotiations begin between your company and the vendor, you are approached by the vendor's sales representative who offers you a trip to Jamaica if you can "help" the process along. What is your professional and social responsibility?

(A) Decline the trip until after the contract has been signed.
(B) The work you have put in on the project has been demanding, and you deserve the trip.
(C) Decline the trip and have it offered to your manager.
(D) Decline the trip because it is not in the best interest of the company.

2.   You learn that someone has been hired as a PMP in process. You ask him about this provision because you are not familiar with an "In-Process" specialization in the PMP Certification. The employer apparently assumed that this provision was a specialization in the certification when actually the person being hired was simply trying to indicate that he was studying for the exam. What would have best eliminated this confusion?

(A) The person being interviewed should have clarified the status to the employer when the confusion became apparent.
(B) The employer should have known more about the PMP Certification.
(C) The employer should have confirmed the certification on the PMI Web site.
(D) The employee should have kept quiet until he passed the test.

3.   A Project Manager is in the execution phase of a highly visible project and a major milestone is due in one week. The Project Manager has discovered that a vendor's deliverable for this milestone will be two weeks late. What should the Project Manager do?

(A) Do not report this problem in the status meeting.
(B) Meet with the team and brainstorm how to create a workaround for this problem.
(C) Halt all payments to the vendor until the deliverable is received.
(D) Report the status of the missed milestone.

4.   You have been contracted as a Project Manager to work on a project with highly confidential information for a company involved in defense work. The company has requested you do not divulge any information. What document will the company have you sign?

(A) Government secret clearance agreement
(B) Employment non-compete agreement
(C) Non-disclosure agreement
(D) Independent contract agreement

5.   A Functional Manager has come to you and reported that the work due today is going to be three weeks late. The manager has requested that you do not report this to senior management. What is your professional and social responsibility to the project?

(A) Report the status accurately and timely.
(B) Issue a status report that does not contain this information.
(C) Wait until you have some good news to report with the bad news.
(D) The manager has helped you so you won't report the slip, hoping it gets back on schedule.

6.   As a Project Manager, you have a professional and social responsibility to encourage the growth of project management at your company or industry. To help with this growth, you could…

(A) Train people on project management.
(B) Explain the value of project management to those that do not understand it.
(C) Show people how project management can help solve problems.
(D) All the answers

7.   Your project needs a video editing software program. The client has given you this project to test your ability to deliver. It doesn't pay that much, but if you do well, you will likely get more projects from the client worth a lot more money. Your budget on the project doesn't allow you the luxury of buying this software. What is the best way to acquire the software?

(A) Order a copy from the company or an authorized reseller.
(B) Get a copy from a friend and buy it for future projects if needed again.
(C) Use a demo copy.
(D) Download a copy from a file sharing system.

8.   A Project Manager has been working on quality process of a project at a major defense contractor. The Project Manager discovers that an employee has been reselling some repair material that he has declared as scrap material at a small profit. The item is very costly. What should the Project Manager do?

(A) Report this to the company.
(B) Report this to Homeland Security.
(C) Report this to General Accounting Office (GAO).
(D) Report the employee to the local authority.

9.   The data warehouse project is falling behind schedule. There has been confusion on the project between the team and the Project Manager. There has been major rework on the first two work packages. The combination of this confusion and rework will result in at least a two-month delay. In a meeting with the CEO, the Project Manager is asked how the project is going. The CEO says that she had been speaking to another Project Manager and heard that the project was going well. The Project Manager tells the CEO what?

(A) Confirms that the project is going well based on what the other Project Manager said
(B) That the update will be in the status report due at the end of the month
(C) Asks the CEO where she learned that about the project
(D) That there is a two-month delay because of some rework on the project

10. During a meeting you discover that a Project Manager has prepared a report which states that a project had a SPI of 1.2. You also learn that the way the Project Manager was calculating earned value was not correct and that the project is behind schedule. What is your professional and social responsibility toward this Project Manager?

    (A) Report the Project Manager to the sponsor.
    (B) Mentor the Project Manager on the correct way to calculate earned value.
    (C) Mentor the Project Manager on the correct way to calculate earned value and review with him what he is reporting.
    (D) Review with the Project Manager what he is reporting.

11. You are studying for your PMP Certification with a study group and a member of your study group says he has a copy of questions from a PMP Examination. You have been studying the PMI Code of Ethics and Professional Conduct. What is your primary responsibility as described by this document?

    (A) Continue to study with them because it has not been proven that these are exam questions.
    (B) Inform the group that you cannot study with them because these could be exam questions.
    (C) Inform PMI of this possible violation.
    (D) Continue to study with the group because your exam time is next week.

12. You are a Project Manager at a large telecommunications company. You have successfully completed the work on a large infrastructure network project. At the final team meeting, as part of professional and social responsibility, you should:

    (A) Reinforce to team members that, by being on the project, they gain knowledge and experience in project management.
    (B) Have a party celebrating the successful completion of the project.
    (C) Create letters of recommendation for team members for their personal files.
    (D) Thank members for their contribution.

13. You are a Project Manager involved in procuring $2,000,000 of infrastructure equipment. As negotiations begin between your company and the vendor, you realize that your brother works for this company but in a different department. What is your professional and social responsibility?

    (A) Because he works in a different department, you can remain on the project.
    (B) Remain on the project, but remove yourself from the negotiations.
    (C) Remove yourself from the project.
    (D) Remain on the project, but help another Project Manager negotiate the contract.

14. As part of professional and social responsibility, a Project Manager must balance the stakeholder's interests. A customer has requested a change in a project that is in the beginning stages of closure. What should the Project Manager tell the customer first?

    (A) Add the requested changes to the project.
    (B) Tell the customer "no" because the project is about to close.
    (C) Have senior management determine if it is necessary.
    (D) Ask for a product description and provide the customer time and cost estimates.

15.   When determining if a project needs to continue or be altered, what is the number one question that a Project Manager should ask about the project?

    (A) What does the project management plan say?
    (B) What does the project charter say?
    (C) Why is the project being done or what is the business need?
    (D) What does the statement of work say?

16.   You learn that a former boss of yours who is a PMP has committed to his boss that 100% of the PMO that he manages at their company will be certified. The only problem is that one of the people who passed the test is 22 years old and going to junior college. You know that this person has been working in this area for only two years at most. When asking about it, you are told that they were "creative" with the experience hours of the PMP application. What is the best thing to do?

    (A) Contact your former boss and let him know it's not appropriate.
    (B) Contact PMI to report the name(s) of the person(s), the name(s) of supervisor(s), and the company.
    (C) Tell your old boss to hire you back or you will turn him into PMI.
    (D) Ignore it because you don't work there anymore.

17.   Your project needs some Web site development software but the budget on the project doesn't include this software. You are having a drink after work with a friend from your dot-com career who has a lot of different types of software. He offers to make you a copy of this software that you need. What is the best way to acquire the software?

    (A) Take his copy and use it on your project.
    (B) Order a copy from the company or an authorized reseller.
    (C) Download a copy from a file sharing system.
    (D) Use a demo copy.

18.   The PMO is conducting a meeting and a fellow Project Manager is reporting that the project is on schedule and under budget. You discover from the project's team members that the project is behind schedule by four weeks and is over budget. What should you do?

    (A) Notify senior management.
    (B) Report the Project Manager to PMI.
    (C) Ask the PMO to investigate the project status.
    (D) Review with the Project Manager how this status was produced.

19.   As a Project Manager, your first priority is to accomplish the work of the project. After this work is achieved, you exercise professional and social responsibility by helping project team members gain experience and knowledge based on the work and activities on the project. What is the best answer for gaining this experience and knowledge?

    (A) Historical information
    (B) Lessons learned
    (C) Assumptions
    (D) Constraints

PMP Exam Success Series: Certification Exam Manual
© 2007 Crosswind Project Management, Inc., www.crosswindpm.com

20. A Project Manager is managing a project that has three development groups. One is in the U.S.; the other two are in Japan and Australia. Managing the project will be a challenge because of differences in time zones and cultures. What is the best thing the Project Manager can do to minimize the difference in culture between the groups?

    (A) Buy a book for each team member on the culture of the people of the U.S., Japan, and Australia.
    (B) Do team-building through video conferencing.
    (C) Do team-building while the members co-locate to one site during Planning phase.
    (D) Have the Project Manager study the cultures of each nation.

21. You are a Project Manager for a construction company managing the building of a restaurant. During installation of the electrical wiring, you cannot find a building permit. As the Project Manager, to whom do you report this violation?

    (A) The construction company
    (B) The local city authority
    (C) The local county authority
    (D) The state authority

22. As part of professional and social responsibility, a Project Manager must balance the stakeholder's interests. To ensure this success, the Project Manager will potentially address these areas except...

    (A) Communicate the impact and options associated with changes.
    (B) Decide which customer-requested changes will be implemented.
    (C) Do not tell customer "no."
    (D) Listen to wishes of the customer.

23. A Project Manager has been contacted by PMI to investigate a complaint against the company's most experienced senior Project Manager. The Project Manager reports this contact to the senior Project Manager. Which is the best answer?

    (A) The Project Manager must do what senior management has requested.
    (B) The Project Manager must protect his manager.
    (C) The Project Manager must take 5th amendment to protect his manager and the company.
    (D) The Project Manager must cooperate with PMI.

24. As a Project Manager, you have a professional and social responsibility to encourage the growth of project management at your company or industry. To help with this growth, you could do all the following except...

    (A) Mentor others who want to learn more about project management.
    (B) Create white papers on project management.
    (C) Provide senior management with information how outsourcing helps their companies.
    (D) Train people on project management.

25. A Project Manager has been contracted by a company to manage development of a software game. The Project Manager discovers that half the software developers are contractors and do not have legal software licenses. What should the Project Manager do in this case?

(A) Report this violation to the company's senior management.
(B) Report this violation to PMI.
(C) Call the software vendor.
(D) Fill out a Software Piracy Report.

26. A Project Manager is managing a project that has three development groups in the U.S., Japan, and Australia. This will be a challenge because of the time difference and cultures. Senior management and the sponsor realize that team-building is critical to help educate those who are not familiar with the different cultures. Who is responsible for this process?

(A) Sponsor
(B) Senior management
(C) Project Manager
(D) Stakeholders

27. Respecting intellectual property is an important part of professional and social responsibility. To protect its intellectual property, a company may have a Project Manager sign a non-disclosure agreement. What is a form of intellectual property?

(A) Patents
(B) Copyrights
(C) Trademarks
(D) All the answers

28. A Project Manager is managing a project that has three development groups. One is in the U.S.; the other two are in Japan and Australia. Managing the project will be a challenge because of differences in time zones and cultures. Senior management has given limited authority to the Project Manager to creating status reports and holding conference calls. The Functional Managers keep removing resources from the project. What is the best thing to do to resolve this problem?

(A) Acquire the necessary authority to correctly manage the project.
(B) Request weekly status reports instead of bi-weekly status reports.
(C) Escalate this problem to senior management.
(D) As the Project Manager, you do the best job you can.

29. You are a Project Manager and another Project Manager has come to you for help. The Project Manager realizes that he does not possess the skills to manage his project. What is the best answer to help solve this problem?

(A) Have the Project Manager tell his supervisor he does not have the appropriate skills.
(B) Mentor the Project Manager and help him develop the skills.
(C) Recommend a book with information that the Project Manager needs.
(D) Develop a new project scope statement.

30. You have been helping a senior Project Manager at your company to become a Project Management Professional, and you are aware that this manager has met the requirements by falsifying the number of project management training hours on the PMP application. As a Project Management Professional, what are you required to do?

    (A) Report this discrepancy to the area's PMI chapter.
    (B) Report this activity to senior management.
    (C) Report this activity to PMI for corrective action.
    (D) Ignore this situation because the manager is the senior Project Manager at your company.

15.9   Professional and Social Responsibility Tests and Exercise Answers

15.9.1   Professional and Social Responsibility Terminology Matching Exercise Answers

Matching Exercise Answers

	Term	Definition
1	Company Policy	F. A standard established by a company
2	Confidentiality	D. The act of not providing certain confidential information to those who should not know about it
3	Conflict of Interest	L. A situation in which an individual or company engages in behavior that is inappropriate, but not necessarily illegal (it could be illegal)
4	Copyright	B. The process that protects the ownership rights of writing, songs, and other "creative" works; can include software, music, physical and electronic media
5	Ethics	K. The standards we use to determine what is right and wrong; varies for everyone
6	Government	I. An organization that represents and manages an area The area can be a city, state, or country. In the United States, the federal government runs the country. Each state is responsible for operating the state. There can be city, state, or federal laws.
7	Inappropriate Compensation	A. Money or other items of value that are "earned" via improper activities
8	Intellectual Property	J. Ideas and concepts created by an individual or company, typically eligible for copyright or patent, thus providing ownership properties
9	Law	C. A standard created by a government (e.g., city, state, or country) that requires people and companies to follow it, or the behavior is illegal
10	Non-Disclosure Agreement (NDA)	H. A document signed by the owner of intellectual property and those who view it when it is not generally exposed to the public, or if it is a new idea, before it is displayed to the public
11	Patent	E. A legal device which gives ownership of an idea or design to an individual or company that creates the idea or design
12	PMI Code of Ethics and Professional Conduct	G. A standard that PMI requires candidates to agree to before they take the PMP Examination
13	Professional and Social Responsibility	M. Ethics expected in Project Managers; includes balancing stakeholder interests and reporting violations

15.9.2   Professional and Social Responsibility Questions Answers

1. You are a Project Manager involved in the procurement of $2,000,000 of infrastructure equipment. As negotiations begin between your company and the vendor, you are approached by the vendor's sales representative who offers you a trip to Jamaica if you can "help" the process along. What is your professional and social responsibility?

    Correct Answer: (D) Decline the trip because it is not in the best interest of the company.
    Explanation: According to professional and social responsibility, a Project Manager must refrain from offering or accepting inappropriate payments, gifts, or other forms of compensation. Both accepting the trip and declining the trip until after the contract has been signed break the PMI Code of Ethics and Professional Conduct. Declining the trip and having it offered to your manager creates a conflict of interest for your manager. [section 15.4.1]

2. You learn that someone has been hired as a PMP in process. You ask him about this provision because you are not familiar with an "In-Process" specialization in the PMP Certification. The employer apparently assumed that this provision was a specialization in the certification when actually the person being hired was simply trying to indicate that he was studying for the exam. What would have best eliminated this confusion?

    Correct Answer: (A) The person being interviewed should have clarified the status to the employer when the confusion became apparent.
    Explanation: Regardless of your status as a PMP, you should be professionally responsible and let someone know of any misinterpretation associated with your background or qualifications. The other answers are not correct because the responsibility falls on the person to report accurate information in a timely manner. [section 15.1.3]

3. A Project Manager is in the execution phase of a highly visible project and a major milestone is due in one week. The Project Manager has discovered that a vendor's deliverable for this milestone will be two weeks late. What should the Project Manager do?

    Correct Answer: (B) Meet with the team and brainstorm how to create a workaround for this problem
    Explanation: Meeting with the team and brainstorming how to create a workaround for this problem is the first step the Project Manager should try. Reporting the status of the missed milestone is the second option. Failure to report this problem in the status meeting violates professional and social responsibility on reporting accurate information. Halting all payments to the vendor puts your company in default of a signed contract. [section 15.1.3, section 13.6.3, section 13.7]

4. You have been contracted as a Project Manager to work on a project with highly confidential information for a company involved in defense work. The company has requested you do not divulge any information. What document will the company have you sign?

    Correct Answer: (C) Non-disclosure agreement
    Explanation: A non-disclosure agreement protects a company's intellectual property. Government secret clearance agreement, employment non-compete agreement, and independent contract agreement are noise. [section 15.2.2]

5. A Functional Manager has come to you and reported that the work due today is going to be three weeks late. The manager has requested that you do not report this to senior management. What is your professional and social responsibility to the project?

    Correct Answer: (A) Report the status accurately and timely.
    Explanation: As a Project Manager, you are required to report timely, accurate, and honest status and facts about a project. Failing to report the slip (while hoping it gets back on schedule), waiting until you have some good news

to report with the bad news, and issuing a status report that does not contain this information are failures to report honest facts about the project. [section 15.5.1]

6.   As a Project Manager, you have a professional and social responsibility to encourage the growth of project management at your company or industry. To help with this growth, you could do…

   (A) Train people on project management.
   (B) Explain the value of project management to those that do not understand it.
   (C) Show people how project management can help solve problems.

   Correct Answer: (D) All the answers
   Explanation: Training people to do better project management and showing them the value of project management and how it can solve their problems are processes that help cultivate project management as a profession. [section 15.1.2, section 15.1.3]

7.   Your project needs a video editing software program. The client has given you this project to test your ability to deliver. It doesn't pay that much, but if you do well, you will likely get more projects from the client worth a lot more money. Your budget on the project doesn't allow you the luxury of buying this software. What is the best way to acquire the software?

   Correct Answer: (A) Order a copy from the company or an authorized reseller.
   Explanation: The PMI Theory Pill in this area says that if you need more time and money to do the project, you get more time and money. Thus, if the software costs money, buy the software. Don't try to circumvent copyrights by using demos. Software that is created by someone else should be purchased and the license terms and conditions followed. Such terms and conditions often define how copies, demo copies, and file sharing systems are to be used with the software. [section 15.2.2]

8.   A Project Manager has been working on quality process of a project at a major defense contractor. The Project Manager discovers that an employee has been reselling some repair material that he has declared as scrap material at a small profit. The item is very costly. What should the Project Manager do?

   Correct Answer: (A) Report this to the company.
   Explanation: The company is responsible for resolving this issue, because the company has jurisdiction over materials. Reporting the employee to the local authority is the company's option. The answers on reporting to the General Accounting Office (GAO) and to Homeland Security are noise. [section 15.2.1]

9.   The data warehouse project is falling behind schedule. There has been confusion on the project between the team and the Project Manager. There has been major rework on the first two work packages. The combination of this confusion and rework will result in at least a two-month delay. In a meeting with the CEO, the Project Manager is asked how the project is going. The CEO says that she had been speaking to another Project Manager and heard that the project was going well. The Project Manager tells the CEO what?

   Correct Answer: (D) That there is a two-month delay because of some rework on the project
   Explanation: It is the responsibility of the Project Manager to communicate accurate status as it is known. This responsibility includes taking a proactive response to communicating status on a project regardless of good or bad status. Confirming what the other Project Manager said is irresponsible. Asking about where the information came from is dancing around the truth. Not reporting until the end of the month doesn't provide accurate status as it is known. [section 15.5.1]

10. During a meeting you discover that a Project Manager has prepared a report which states that a project had a SPI of 1.2. You also learn that the way the Project Manager was calculating earned value was not correct and that the project is behind schedule. What is your professional and social responsibility toward this Project Manager?

Correct Answer: (C) Mentor the Project Manager on the correct way to calculate earned value and review with him what he is reporting.

Explanation: Part of professional and social responsibility is to review the conduct of other PMPs and mentor them. Reviewing what is being reported helps you provide feedback that they are managing the project correctly and improving their skills. Reporting the Project Manager to the sponsor has no effect. [section 15.1.3]

11. You are studying for your PMP Certification with a study group and a member of your study group says he has a copy of questions from a PMP Examination. You have been studying the PMI Code of Ethics and Professional Conduct. What is your primary responsibility as described by this document?

Correct Answer: (C) Inform PMI of this possible violation.

Explanation: Your primary responsibility is to alert PMI of this possible ethics violation. Subsequent to that notification, you should remove yourself from the study group. Continuing to study with the group because it has not been proven that these are exam questions and continuing to study with the group because your exam time is next week could put you in violation. [section 15.2.4]

12. You are a Project Manager at a large telecommunications company. You have successfully completed the work on a large infrastructure network project. At the final team meeting, as part of professional and social responsibility, you should…

Correct Answer: (A) Reinforce to team members that, by being on the project, they gain knowledge and experience in project management.

Explanation: Helping team members gain knowledge and experience in project management is important for the advancement of the profession. Having a party to celebrate the successful completion of the project, thanking team members for their contribution, and creating letters of recommendation for team members for their personal files are team-building activities and rewards. [section 15.1.3]

13. You are a Project Manager involved in procuring $2,000,000 of infrastructure equipment. As negotiations begin between your company and the vendor, you realize that your brother works for this company but in a different department. What is your professional and social responsibility?

Correct Answer: (C) Remove yourself from the project.

Explanation: Remove yourself from the project. The PMI Code of Ethics and Professional Conduct specifies that you disclose any circumstance that could be construed as a conflict of interest or an appearance of impropriety. Remaining on the project because he works in a different department, remaining on the project but removing yourself from the negotiations, and remaining on the project but helping another Project Manager negotiate the contract all give the appearance of impropriety. [section 15.4.1]

14. As part of professional and social responsibility, a Project Manager must balance the stakeholder's interests. A customer has requested a change in a project that is in the beginning stages of closure. What should the Project Manager tell the customer first?

Correct Answer: (D) Ask for a product description and provide the customer time and cost estimates.

Explanation: Asking for a product description and providing the customer time and cost estimates force the customer to define what the change is. Adding a requested change to the project is a form of gold plating unless it is an approved change. As Project Manager, you do not tell the customer "no." It is the customer's decision to implement changes. Senior management should not approve changes requested by a customer. Changes must be approved by change control management. [section 15.5.1, section 5.5.1, section 12.6]

15. When determining if a project needs to continue or be altered, what is the number one question that a Project Manager should ask about the project?

Correct Answer: (C) Why is the project being done or what is the business need?
Explanation: Why is the project being done or the business need takes precedence over the project charter and the project management plan. "What does the statement of work say" is noise? [section 5.5.1]

16. You learn that a former boss of yours who is a PMP has committed to his boss that 100% of the PMO that he manages at their company will be certified. The only problem is that one of the people who passed the test is 22 years old and going to junior college. You know that this person has been working in this area for only two years at most. When asking about it, you are told that they were "creative" with the experience hours of the PMP application. What is the best thing to do?

Correct Answer: (B) Contact PMI to report the name(s) of the person(s), the name(s) of supervisor(s), and the company.
Explanation: As part of professional and social responsibility, you are responsible for reporting possible violations of the PMI Code of Ethics and Professional Conduct. Contacting your former boss and letting him know it's not appropriate, ignoring it because you don't work there anymore, and telling your old boss to hire you back or you will turn him into PMI do not abide with the PMI Code of Ethics and Professional Conduct. [section 15.2.4]

17. Your project needs some Web site development software but the budget on the project doesn't include this software. You are having a drink after work with a friend from your dot-com career who has a lot of different types of software. He offers to make you a copy of this software that you need. What is the best way to acquire the software?

Correct Answer: (B) Order a copy from the company or an authorized reseller.
Explanation: Software that is created by someone else should be purchased and the license terms and conditions followed. Such terms and conditions often define how copies, demo copies, and file sharing systems are to be used with the software. [section 15.2.1]

18. The PMO is conducting a meeting and a fellow Project Manager is reporting that the project is on schedule and under budget. You discovered from the project's team members that the project is behind schedule by four weeks and is over budget. What should you do?

Correct Answer: (D) Review with the Project Manager how this status was produced.
Explanation: As a Project Manager, you should review this information with the Project Manager regarding its accuracy. Asking the PMO to investigate the project status is the next step followed by notifying senior management. The final step is to report the Project Manager to PMI. [section 15.1.3]

19. As a Project Manager, your first priority is to accomplish the work of the project. After this work is achieved, you exercise professional and social responsibility by helping project team members gain experience and knowledge based on the work and activities on the project. What is the best answer for gaining this experience and knowledge?

Correct Answer: (B) Lessons learned
Explanation: Lessons learned allow team members to understand what successes and failures were encountered on the project, thereby helping the team grow and develop as it relates to experience and knowledge of future projects. Historical information is information from previous projects. Assumptions and constraints are noise. [section 15.1.3, section 6.9.3]

20. A Project Manager is managing a project that has three development groups. One is in the U.S.; the other two are in Japan and Australia. Managing the project will be a challenge because of differences in time zones and cultures. What is the best thing the Project Manager can do to minimize the difference in culture between the groups?

Correct Answer: (C) Do team-building while the members co-locate to one site during Planning phase.
Explanation: Team-building while the members co-locate to one site during Planning phase helps team members understand the different cultures of each country. Team-building through video conferencing give the team members the opportunity to put a face with a name. Buying a book on the culture of the people of the U.S., Japan, and Australia for each team member and having the Project Manager study the cultures of each nation would help, but would not be as effective as a meeting. [section 11.3, section 15.3.1]

21. You are a Project Manager for a construction company managing the building of a restaurant. During installation of the electrical wiring, you cannot find a building permit. As the Project Manager, to whom do you report this violation?

Correct Answer: (B) The local city authority
Explanation: Most city governments are responsible for issuing building permits. The local county and state authorities handle issues for different jurisdictions. The construction company has no jurisdiction over building permits. Responsibility for managing such permits falls to the project manager. [section 15.2.1]

22. As part of professional and social responsibility, a Project Manager must balance the stakeholder's interests. To ensure this success, the Project Manager will potentially address these areas except…

Correct Answer: (B) Decide which customer-requested changes will be implemented.
Explanation: The customer should determine what changes should be implemented. The Project Manager's job is to provide options to the customer. [section 5.5.1]

23. A Project Manager has been contacted by PMI to investigate a complaint against the company's most experienced senior Project Manager. The Project Manager reports this contact to the senior Project Manager. Which is the best answer?

Correct Answer: (D) The Project Manager must cooperate with PMI.
Explanation: The PMI Code of Ethics and Professional Conduct requires that a Project Manager cooperate with PMI during investigations. [section 15.2.5]

24. As a Project Manager, you have a professional and social responsibility to encourage the growth of project management at your company or industry. To help with this growth, you could do all the following except…

Correct Answer: (C) Provide senior management with information how outsourcing helps their companies.
Explanation: Providing senior management with information on how outsourcing helps their companies has nothing to do with professional and social responsibility. Training people on project management, mentoring others who want to learn more about project management, and creating white papers on project management are all elements of growing project management as a profession. [section 15.1.2]

25. A Project Manager has been contracted by a company to manage development of a software game. The Project Manager discovers that half the software developers are contractors and do not have legal software licenses. What should the Project Manager do in this case?

Correct Answer: (A) Report this violation to the company's senior management.
Explanation: It is senior management's responsibility to provide the correct number of software licenses for the contractors or enforce that they work with legal licenses as per terms of use for the software they need. Reporting to PMI, filling out a Software Piracy Report, and calling the software vendor are noise. [section 15.2.1]

26. A Project Manager is managing a project that has three development groups. One is in the U.S.; the other two are in Japan and Australia. Managing the project will be a challenge because of differences in time zones and cultures. Senior management and the sponsor realize that team-building is critical to help educate those who are not familiar with the different cultures. Who is responsible for this process?

Correct Answer: (C) Project Manager
Explanation: It is the Project Manager's responsibility to do team-building as part of the Human Resource process. Senior management, the sponsor, and stakeholders are noise. [section 11.3, section 15.3.1]

27. Respecting intellectual property is an important part of professional and social responsibility. To protect its intellectual property, a company may have a Project Manager sign a non-disclosure agreement. What is a form of intellectual property?

(A) Patents
(B) Copyrights
(C) Trademarks

Correct Answer: (D) All the answers
Explanation: Copyrights, patents, and trademarks are all forms of intellectual property. [section 15.2.2]

28. A Project Manager is managing a project that has three development groups. One is in the U.S.; the other two are in Japan and Australia. Managing the project will be a challenge because of differences in time zones and cultures. Senior management has given limited authority to the Project Manager to creating status reports and holding conference calls. The Functional Managers keep removing resources from the project. What is the best thing to do to resolve this problem?

Correct Answer: (A) Acquire the necessary authority to correctly manage the project
Explanation: Professional and social responsibility requires the Project Manager to acquire the authority to manage a project. Escalating this problem to senior management may help the resource issue but does not resolve who is in charge of the project, or if the level of authority is appropriate. Doing the best job you can will not help the project as it moves through the different project phases. Requesting weekly status reports instead of bi-weekly status reports will not help resolve the problem. [section 6.3.1]

29. You are a Project Manager and another Project Manager has come to you for help. The Project Manager realizes that he does not possess the skills to manage his project. What is the best answer to help solve this problem?

Correct Answer: (B) Mentor the Project Manager and help him develop the skills
Explanation: As part of advancement of the project management profession, you are responsible for mentoring others who want to learn more about project management. Recommending a book with information that the Project Manager needs would help, but it's not the best answer. "Develop a new project scope statement" is noise. Telling a supervisor he does not have the appropriate skills will not help the Project Manager. [section 15.1.3]

30. You have been helping a senior Project Manager at your company to become a Project Management Professional, and you are aware that this manager has not met the requirements

by falsifying the number of project management training hours on the PMP application. As a Project Management Professional, what are you required to do?

Correct Answer: (C) Report this activity to PMI for corrective action
Explanation: You are required to report possible violations of the PMI Code of Ethics and Professional Conduct. Ignoring this situation because the manager is the senior Project Manager at your company puts you in violation of the PMI Code of Ethics and Professional Conduct. Reporting this discrepancy to the area's PMI chapter and to senior management are not correct procedures in reporting this infraction. [section 15.1.3, section 15.2.4]

Table of Figures

Index

6

6 Sigma, 344

A

Accelerated depreciation, 282
Acceptance, 192, 462
Acceptance criteria, 192
Accuracy, 342
Acquire Project Team, 387
Active listening, 423
Activity, 241
Activity Definition, 216, 241
Activity Duration Estimating, 225, 241
Activity list, 241
Activity Resource Estimating, 223, 241
Activity Sequencing, 218, 241
Activity-on-arrow, 220, 221, 241
Activity-on-line, 220
Activity-on-node, 220, 221, 241
Actual cost, 291, 294, 295, 297, 300
Actual cost of work scheduled, 291
Actuals, 151
ACWS. *See* actual cost of work scheduled
ADM. *See* arrow diagramming method
Administrative closure, 156, 159
Algorithms, 147
All the answers questions, 19
Analogous estimate, 224, 283, 300
Analogy approach, 192
AOA. *See* activity-on-arrow
AOL. *See* activity-on-line
AON. *See* activity-on-node
Approved change request, 159
Approved changes, 155, 157
Archives, 159
Arrow diagramming method, 220
Assignable cause, 352
Assumptions, 150, 159
Attribute, 350
Authority, 123
Avoid, 462

B

BAC. *See* budget at completion
Backward pass, 241
Backward pass formula, 233, 240
Balanced matrix, 120
Bar chart, 241
Baseline, 151, 300
BCR. *See* benefit cost ratio
Belonging, 381
Benchmarking, 354
Benefit cost ratio, 147, 279, 280
Benefits, 389
Bidders conference, 498
Bill of materials, 190, 506
BOM. *See* bill of materials
Bottom-up approach, 192
Bottom-up estimate, 224, 283, 300
Brainstorming, 354, 464
Budget, 286, 300
Budget at completion, 291, 295, 298, 300
Budgetary estimate, 300
Buffer, 464
Burst, 241
Business risk, 451
Buy decision, 490

C

Calculation questions, 20
Cause/effect diagram, 346
Centralized contracting, 503
Change control, 159
Change control board, 155, 159
Change control system, 155, 159
Change request, 159
Charismatic, 384
Chart of accounts, 287, 300
Charter. *See* project charter
Checklists, 345
Chicken or the egg questions, 19
Close Project, 156
Closing Processes, 113, 123
Closing the project, 157

PMP Exam Success Series: Certification Exam Manual
© 2007 Crosswind Project Management Inc, www.crosswindpm.com

PMP Exam Success Series: Certification Exam Manual
© 2007 Crosswind Project Management Inc, www.crosswindpm.com

Linear programming, 147
Log, 159
Logic Bar chart. *See* Gantt chart
Logical relationship, 242
LS. *See* late start date
Lump-sum contract, 492

M

Make decision, 490
Make-or-buy decision, 490, 506
Manage Project Team, 391
Manage Stakeholders, 426
Management by objectives, 185
Management reserves, 301, 460
Management styles, 383
Mandatory dependency, 219, 242
Marking questions, 17
Maslow's Hierarchy of Needs, 381
Master schedule, 242
Matrix organization, 120
Matrix organization types, 120
Matrix organizational structure, 123
MBO. *See* management by objectives
McGregor's Theory X and Y, 382
Mean, 354
Mediator, 384
Mentor, 384
Merge, 242
Message, 423
Milestone, 192, 242
Milestone schedule, 238, 242
Milestone, weighted, 283
Mirroring, 394
Mitigate, 462
Monitor and Control Project Work, 152
Monitoring and Controlling, 113
Monitoring and Controlling Processes, 123
Monte Carlo, 224, 458, 464
Motivational Theory, 380
Mutual exclusivity, 350

N

NDA. *See* non-disclosure agreement
Negative float, 229
Negotiation, 500
Net present value, 147, 159, 279, 301

Network diagram, 219, 242
Network diagram analysis, 234
Network logic, 242
Network path, 242
Noise, 18
Non-competitive, 498
Non-disclosure agreement, 532, 535
None of the answers, 19
Non-linear programming, 147
Nonverbal, 423
Norm, 390
Normal distribution, 343, 354
NPV. *See* net present value

O

OBS. *See* organizational breakdown structure
Operations, 123
Operations management, 110
Opportunity cost, 147, 279, 280, 301
Optimistic estimate, 225, 240
Order of Magnitude, 286
Organization, 123
Organization chart, 380, 394
Organizational breakdown structure, 190, 380, 394
Organizational chart. *See* organizational breakdown structure
Organizational planning, 394
Organizational process assets, 123, 144
Organizational structures, 118
Over-allocation, 394

P

Para-lingual, 423
Parametric estimate, 224, 283, 354
Parametric modeling, 301
Pareto analysis, 354
Pareto diagram, 351, 354
Parkinson's Law, 226
Patents, 532, 535
Path divergence, 242
Payback period, 147, 159, 279, 280
PDM. *See* precedence diagramming method
Penalty power, 386
Perception of inappropriate activities, 533

Project slack, 229
Project team, 395
Project team directory, 395
Project Time Management, 242
Projectized organization, 121
Proposal, 497
Purchase order, 492
Pure risk, 451
PV. *See* planned value

Q

Qualified sellers list, 498
Qualitative Risk Analysis, 454, 464
Quality, 341, 355
Quality assurance, 355
Quality audit, 355
Quality control, 355
Quality management, 149
Quality management plan, 341, 355
Quality Planning, 355
Quantitative Risk Analysis, 455, 464
Question breakdown, 20
Question formats, 18
Question translation, 20

R

Rapport, 395
Rating matrix, 451
RBS, 450
Realistic estimate, 225, 240
Receiver, 423
Referent power, 386, 395
Regulation, 112, 124
Reliability, 355
Reporting of the PMI Code of Ethics and Professional Conduct, 532
Request for information, 495, 496
Request for proposal, 495, 497, 506
Request for quote, 495, 496, 506
Request Seller Responses, 497
Requested changes, 155
Requirement, 192
Reserves, 301, 464
Residual risk, 460, 464
Resource, 395

Resource breakdown structure, 190, 224, 395
Resource calendar, 242
Resource histogram, 388, 395
Resource leveling, 236, 395
Resource loading, 395
Responsibility assignment matrix, 379, 395
Retainage, 506
Return on investment, 147, 160, 279
Reward and recognition, 393
Reward power, 386, 395
Rework, 355
RFI. *See* request for information
RFP. *See* request for proposal
RFQ. *See* request for quote
Risk, 464
Risk acceptance, 464
Risk and contracting, 451
Risk avoidance, 464
Risk breakdown structure, 190, 450, 465
Risk category, 465
Risk database, 465
Risk events, 465
Risk factors, 465
Risk Identification, 452, 465
Risk list, 460
Risk management, 150
Risk management plan, 450, 465
Risk Management Planning, 449
Risk mitigation, 465
Risk Monitoring and Control, 462, 465
Risk owner, 461
Risk probabilities and impact rating matrix, 451
Risk register, 453, 465
Risk Response Planning, 459, 465
Risk response strategies, 461
Risk response strategies for both threats and opportunities, 462
Risk response strategies for negative risks or threats, 462
Risk response strategies for positive risks or opportunities, 461
Risk reviews, 453
Risk seeker, 452
Risk seeking, 465

PMP Exam Success Series: Certification Exam Manual
© 2007 Crosswind Project Management Inc, www.crosswindpm.com

Storm, 390

Strategic planning, 110, 160

Strengths, weaknesses, opportunities, and threats, 465

Strong matrix, 120

Sub-network, 243

Sub-phase, 124

Subproject, 124

Successor, 243

Sum of the year's digits, 282

Summary activity, 243

Summary schedule, 238

Sunk cost, 281, 301

SV. *See* schedule variance

System, 160

T

T&M. *See* time and materials contract

Tangible cost/benefit, 301

Target completion date, 243

Target cost, 494

Target finish date, 243

Target profit, 494

Target schedule, 243

Target start date, 243

Task, 243

TC. *See* target completion date

TCPI. *See* to complete performance index

Team development, 395

Team members, 531

Technical performance measurement, 160

Technique, 124

Template, 124

TF. *See* target finish date

The Boss is Missing, 501

Theory X. *See* McGregor's Theory of X and Y

Theory Y. *See* McGregor's Theory of X and Y

Threat, 465

Three point estimate, 240, 243

Threshold, 355

Tight matrix, 124

Time and materials contract, 493

Time management, 149

TMI. *See* too much information

To complete performance index, 293, 299

Too much information, 18

Tool, 160

Top-down approach, 193

Top-down estimate. *See* analogous estimate

Total Quality Management, 339

Total slack, 229, 243

Trademarks, 532

Transfer, 462

Trend analysis, 160

Trigger. *See* risk trigger

Triple constraint, 111

Truthful and accurate reporting, 532

TS. *See* target start date

Types of communications processes, 423

Types of cost, 278

U

Uncertainty, 451

User, 193

V

VAC. *See* variance at completion

Validation, 193

Value engineering, 355

Variable, 350

Variable cost, 278

Variance analysis, 124

Variance at completion, 293, 296, 299

Variance report, 426

VE. *See* value engineering

Verbal communication, 418

Verification, 193

Virtual team, 124

Visionary, 384

VOC. *See* voice of the customer

Voice of the customer, 124

W

War room, 124

WBS. *See* work breakdown structure

WBS dictionary, 189, 193

Weak matrix, 120

Weighted milestone, 283

Weighted scoring model, 160

Withdrawal, 393, 395

Work authorization, 160
Work authorization system, 152, 160
Work breakdown structure, 187, 193, 243
Work breakdown structure numbering, 189
Work package, 193, 243
Work performance information, 243
Work results, 113, 151, 424
Workaround, 461, 465

Written communication, 418
Wrong area, 18
Wrong point in time, 18

Z

Zero Defects, 339

Thank you for choosing this book. We hope your experience with it was as satisfying for you as it was for us to create.

-- Team Crosswind